Sylvia Porter's
NEW MONEY BOOK
for the 80's

Volume 2

SYLVIA PORTER'S
New Money Book
FOR THE 80'S

Volume 2

DOUBLEDAY & COMPANY, INC.
GARDEN CITY, NEW YORK

Copyright © 1975, 1979 by Sylvia Porter
All Rights Reserved
Printed in the United States of America

CONTENTS

11	Dress Well on Less	755
12	Jewelry and Beauty—Frosting on the Cake	779
13	How to Slash the Costs of Your Vacations in the 1980's	789
14	Sex . . . and . . . Money	815
15	Your Personal Banking Business	865
16	How to Borrow Cash and Use Credit	903
17	What Records Should You Keep?—and How?	981
18	How to Achieve Financial Independence and Personal Security in Your Older Years	987
19	Your Basic Guide to Wills, Estates, and Trusts	1065
20	Funeral Expenses—What to Do . . . How to Save . . . Where the Traps Are	1091
21	Your Guide to the Stock Markets	1101
22	Mutual Funds	1167
23	Your Guide to the Bond Markets—Obligations of the U. S. Treasury, Federal Agencies, Guaranteed or Partially Insured Mortgage Pools, States and Cities, U.S. Corporations—Short- and Long-Term	1193
24	Your Guide to United States Savings Bonds	1229

CONTENTS

25	Your Guide to the Exploding Commodity Markets—for Speculators and Hedgers	1245
26	Your Most Simple Guide to Buying Land	1267
27	Your Guide to Off-Beat and On-Target	1277
28	Know Your Rights!—and How to Use Them!	1323
29	How and Where to Get Help	1381
	EPILOGUE	1405
	INDEX	1415

11

DRESS WELL ON LESS

FINDING YOUR WAY AROUND THE CLOTHING "SUPERMARKET"	756
THE FUNDAMENTALS	756
SHOP FOR WHAT'S RIGHT FOR YOU	756
BUY CLOTHES THAT FIT YOU PROPERLY	757
STUDY CLOTHES LABELS	759
PLAN YOUR WARDROBE WITH MORE THAN ONE PURPOSE IN MIND	763
LOOK FOR GOOD WORKMANSHIP	763
AVOID IMPULSE BUYING	763
MAKE A CLOTHING BUDGET—AND STICK TO IT	763
TEN WAYS TO SLASH YOUR CLOTHING BUDGET	764
SIX RULES ON DRESSING FOR WORK AWAY FROM HOME	768
HOW TO BUY A SEWING MACHINE	769
BEWARE: SEWING MACHINE TRAPS	771
CUTTING YOUR CLOTHES CARE COSTS	772
TIME-TESTED TIPS	772
TWELVE WAYS TO REDUCE YOUR SHOE BILLS	774
THE ABCs OF BUYING FURS (or "How to Sound like a Fur Authority Without Really Being One")	776
ASK YOURSELF	776
A FEW FACTS	777
LANGUAGE OF FUR	777
FUR CARE	778
IF YOU FEEL YOU'VE BEEN GYPPED	778

Finding Your Way Around the Clothing "Supermarket"

Shopping for clothes in this era is somewhat like shopping in a supermarket. It's up to *you* to determine the various ingredients needed to create a wardrobe to your taste, and then to search the shelves and racks for sizes and styles to suit you, your way of life, and your budget. After you have reached a tentative decision, your best information will come from labels and your own ability to check and recognize quality. Salespeople (if you can find them) often are untrained and inexperienced, and far more concerned with closing a sale than with answering your questions or helping you to dress appropriately and attractively.

Clothes labels, as one skeptic put it, frequently look "like inventory lists in a chemical factory." Today, in addition to natural fibers—wool, cotton, linen, silk—there are hundreds upon hundreds of manufactured fibers and blends, more than three dozen mechanical and chemical fabric finishes, and thousands of construction and processing techniques, along with countless trade names.

On the minus side is the blunt fact that it's easy to be confused by continually changing technology. And, if you choose wrong, you probably won't be able to get your money back or even a replacement.

On the plus side are the far more important facts that:

There never has been a greater variety of clothing styles, fabrics, finishes, and desirable features available.

The price range is also the broadest ever.

Federal laws protecting you against mislabeling are the most varied and strictest in history.

And there's a wealth of information you can use to help you shop for and buy clothes for yourself and your family.

In the following pages, you'll find some of this "wealth" broken down into the most valuable nuggets that *you* can use to plan your—and your family's—wardrobe, and to shop for clothes to fill them.

The Fundamentals

SHOP FOR WHAT'S RIGHT FOR YOU

Your clothes speak for you before you've uttered a word: "I'm an individual." "I'm part of the crowd." "I'm someone to be reckoned with." "I'm creative." "I'm organized." "I'm up-to-the-minute." Or "I don't care how I look."

Most people want a wardrobe with enough versatility to make more than one statement, depending on the audience, activity, occasion, or maybe even a mood.

A good way to achieve this versatility is to establish one or two color themes and start with the most flattering basics you can find—perhaps separates to mix and match—and the best quality you can afford. These basics are simple, classic designs that stay in style and last several seasons and are *real* clothing bargains. To them, you can add the most alluring fashion craze or way-out accessories.

Since top-quality and durability aren't musts for items that will go out of style quickly, you don't have to spend a fortune to update or change the look of your basic wardrobe. Similarly, once-in-a-rare-while clothes, such as a special holiday skirt or shoes bought to go with just one outfit, can be selected more for effect than for wearing ability.

BUY CLOTHES THAT FIT YOU PROPERLY

This will add to the life of your wardrobe as well as to your comfort and good appearance.

Don't make the common error of buying sizes that are *too small* for you on the assumption that you're about to lose ten or fifteen pounds! If you can't get a really good fit, it's usually best to buy a size slightly *too large*. Generally it's easier to take in than to let out.

Use the following table, prepared by the Money Management Institute of Household Finance Corporation, Chicago, Illinois, as a guide to size ranges used by most clothing manufacturers for women's clothes. Note that, in addition to regular sizes, some types of clothing may be marked "tall," "medium" or "average," and "short" or "petite."

Size Classification	Size Range	Figure Type
Junior Petite	3–15	For figures 5'1" or shorter. The neckline and armholes are smaller and length from shoulder to waist and from waist to hemline is shorter than a Junior.
Junior	3–17	For figures 5'1½" to 5'5½" with a higher, smaller bust, narrower shoulders, and a shorter waistline than the Misses.
Misses Petite	8–18	For figures 4'11½" to 5'2" with a longer waist and a fuller bust than a Junior Petite. Smaller neckline and armholes than a Misses.

Size Classification	Size Range	Figure Type
Misses	6–22	For the well-proportioned figure 5'2½" to 5'6½". Hips moderately larger than bust and normal to low waist.
Misses Tall	10–22	For the well-proportioned figure over 5'7½".
Half Sizes	12½–26½	A mature Junior. Fuller throughout the bust, back, and shoulders, and shorter-waisted than the Junior.
Women's Sizes	34–52	The mature, more developed Misses figure. Fuller in the back and shoulders and longer-waisted than the Misses.

And use the following chart, published in *Your Clothing Dollar*,* as your guide to standard children's sizes, corresponding to body weight, height, and other measurements:

	Size	Weight	Height	Chest	Waist	Hip
Infants' and Babies'	(Months)					
	3	13	24	17		
	6	18	26½	18		
	12	22	29	19		
	18	26	31½	20		
	24	29	34	21		
	36	32	36½	22		
Toddlers'	(Years)					
	1	25	31	20	20	
	2	29	34	21	20½	
	3	34	37	22	21	
	4	38	40	23	21½	
Children's	2	29	34	21	20½	21½
	3	34	37	22	21	22½
	4	38	40	23	21½	23½
	5	44	43	25	22	24½
	6	49	46	25	22½	25½
	6X	54	48	25½	23	26½

* Household Finance Corporation, Copyright 1978.

Body measurements for the sizing of apparel for girls

Size	Weight	Height	Bust	Waist	Hip
7	60	50	26	23	27½
8	67	52	27	23½	28½
9	75	54	28	24	29½
10	83	56	29	24½	31
12	95	58½	30½	25½	33
14	107	61	32	26½	35

Body measurements for the sizing of apparel for boys

		Slim		Regular		Husky	
Size	Height	Chest	Waist	Chest	Waist	Chest	Waist
6	46	23½	20½	25	22½	26	24½
7	48	24½	21	25¾	23	26¾	25
8	50	25½	21½	26½	23½	27½	25½
9	52	26	22	27¼	24	28¼	26
10	54	26¾	22½	28	24½	29	26½
11	56	27½	23	28¾	25	30	27
12	58	28½	23½	29½	25½	31	27½
13	59½	29¼	24	30½	26	32	28
14	61	30	24½	31½	26½	33	29
15	62½	30¾	25	32¼	27	34	29½
16	64	31½	25½	33	27½	35	30
17	65	32¼	26	33¾	28	35¾	30½
18	66	33	26½	34½	28½	36½	31
19	67	33¾	27	35¼	29	37¼	31½
20	68	34½	27½	36	29½	38	32
21	69	35¼	28	36¾	30	38¾	32½
22	70	36	28½	37½	30½	39½	33
23	71	36¾	29	38¼	31	40¼	33½
24	72	37½	29½	39	31½	41	34

STUDY CLOTHES LABELS

Someday there may be one comprehensive label to tell you everything you want or need to know about an article of clothing. Until then, you must search at least a bit—but you will find vital information on many different tags, labels, and stickers.

The price tag usually will tell you the size, will give the retail price of the item (without local taxes), and may tell you the number of pieces included.

The size may be printed or stitched to clothing. Errors can occur, though, so it's wise (whenever possible) to try on each item before you buy it.

A manufacturer's and/or designer's label may be sewn almost anywhere on clothing, inside or out. This can be especially helpful if you've had either a good or bad experience in the past with other items carrying the same label.

A decade ago, a shopper had to have the equivalent of a special dictionary to translate the hundreds of trade names given to manufactured fibers into generic terms. Today, you're assisted by the United States Textile Fiber Products Identification Act. Under this law, all textile products must contain the following information on the label or tag:

• the *generic name* of the fibers (cotton, polyester, etc.), listed in order of predominance by weight;

• the *percentage* of each fiber weighing 5 per cent or more of the total;

• the *name* (or registered number) of the manufacturer or seller;

• the *country* from which an imported fiber comes.

In addition to the above, wool products, under the Wool Products Labeling Act, also must tell you what type of wool (virgin wool, reprocessed wool, reused wool) has been used, and the percentages.

Because care of clothing is important to its appearance and durability, the United States Federal Trade Commission has ruled that labels giving *care instructions* be permanently attached by manufacturers to most wearing apparel, and provided by fabric companies on labels that home sewers can stitch into seams of items they make.

These care instructions are to include the manufacturer's recommendations for cleaning or laundering, drying, and pressing or ironing (if needed), along with warnings against products and procedures that may cause damage, such as chlorine bleaches, excess heat, or the use of certain solvents.

Use your common sense when following these care instructions. But sometimes even a healthy dose of that won't help. Most manufacturers do not actually test each garment, and rely heavily on guidance from fabric makers. According to a spokesman for the International Fabricare Institute, a trade group representing launderers and dry cleaners, with research facilities in Silver Spring, Maryland, the method a label recommends "often actually damages the clothing."

For example, synthetics labeled "professionally dry-clean only" too often shrink. Laminates may stiffen and peel when cleaned by standard procedures used by most professional dry cleaners. Water spills, steam used in cleaning, and even perspiration may cause color bleeding. Clothes labeled "wash hot" wash well in home washing machines, but are damaged in the hotter wash cycle of commercial machines.

In contrast, some manufacturers are overly cautious about the information they put on their labels; a garment with "dry-clean only" on the tag may actually be machine-washable.

If your clothes are damaged after you've followed care instructions, return them with the sales receipt to the store. A reputable store should refund your money and return the item to the manufacturer. And clothes manufacturers, subject to FTC penalties for failing to comply with regulations, may label their garments more accurately if you besiege them with returns.

And, while reforming their care labels, you, a consumer, well might wonder why more manufacturers don't stencil information to clothing, or attach care labels to side seams, for most labels haphazardly sewn at the back of the collar can curl up and tickle the wearer to the point of annoyance after laundering or cleaning.

To supplement government-required labels, fiber producers, dyers, yarn and fabric makers, finishers, and clothing manufacturers will sometimes attach additional tags or stickers to clothing or packages, listing features and benefits, and offering more detailed care instructions.

Read this information carefully, too, to learn as much as you can about each article of clothing—fibers, yarn, fabric construction, dyes, finishes, care—and what each implies in durability, upkeep, cost, and appearance.

Fibers: These are the basis of yarn and largely determine a fabric's properties: warmth, wear, appearance, care, etc. They may be natural (cotton, silk, linen, wool—including hair, such as mohair, rabbit hair, or cashmere). They may be man-made (such as rayon, nylon, polyester, acrylic, etc.). Or they may be blends (combining natural and/or man-made fibers).

Yarns: Fiber strands are laid or twisted together to make yarns, from which fabrics are woven or knitted. Staple fibers are short and must be spun into long strands before being twisted into yarn. Cotton, linen, and wool are staple fibers. Filament fibers are continuous, and can be either laid or twisted together. Silk and man-made fibers are filament fibers, but they also can be cut short and handled like staple fibers. The strength, thickness, and texture of fibers, the number used, whether they're laid or twisted, and how tight the twist, are among factors that determine appearance, features, and wearability of a yarn.

Construction: The three basic types of fabric construction are woven (usually the closer the weave, the better the wear), knitted (loops provide a natural stretchability and wrinkle resistance), and non-woven (fibers are matted together with heat, pressure, and possibly chemicals). In addition, one of the three basic types of fabric may be used as a backing for another type (as in some bonded or laminated fabrics) or for a "plastic" (such as vinyl or polyurethane, which are used for man-made leathers).

Woven fabrics can be given the stretchability of a knit with fiber, yarn, or finish. Look for details on the label if you're buying a stretch fabric that's woven: comfort-stretch for every day, action-stretch for sports and exercise. A stretch fiber (spandex) or yarn construction (similar to a coil) may prove more satisfactory for your needs than a finish which may wash or dry-clean out.

Knits can be stabilized to the level of a woven fabric with a backing, lining, or by double-knitting. Many variations within each type of fabric construction create an almost infinite array of textures, designs, and weights from which clothing designers—and you—can select.

Color: Dyes can be added at almost any point in fabric production, from the moment when chemicals are mixed together to create man-made fibers until after fabric has been woven or knitted. Fiber- and yarn-dyed fabrics, generally considered stable, are easily recognized in checks and plaids, because colors are as clear on the underside of the fabric as on the surface. Vat-dyed yarns and fabrics are also considered stable. Fabrics printed only on the surface can be spotted quickly: although colors may be labeled "fast," prints may fade in time from abrasion.

There are many variables in dyes (some are absorbed by, others are bonded to yarn), and selection of the right dye for each fiber and quality control in the coloring process depend on the manufacturer. Check labels carefully for specific information, such as "sun- or perspiration-fast," "fade-resistant," or such warnings as "wash separately."

Finishes: A wide variety of temporary and durable finishes improve or add desirable features to fabrics, aiding appearance, comfort, ease of care, and protection from a wide range of possible problems. Most will boost the price of fabric and therefore of clothing, and some will require special care, but benefits can outweigh any added cost or attention. Among finishes available are those that:

• Alter appearance—adding or subtracting shine; brightening, drabbing, or fixing colors; improving drapability or softness; increasing crispness or body; reducing static; changing texture, etc.

• Increase comfort—providing a smooth "lining" for rough fabrics or thermal insulation; increasing moisture absorbency; repelling water; creating stretchability, etc.

• Simplify care—minimizing or eliminating wrinkles and ironing, such as wash and wear and permanent press (which also retains pleats and creases through both wear and laundering); increasing soil resistance; providing soil release, etc.

• Offer special protection—against spots, stains, shrinkage, moths, mildew, fading, etc. The United States Flammable Fabrics Act requires fabrics used in making children's sleepwear (up to size 14) to be flame-resistant. Pay special attention to labeling to learn whether the flame-resistant finish is temporary or durable, and carefully follow care instructions.

At home, save all information tags from new garments, mark them for identification, and file them in an indexed box kept near the laundry area, along with the sales receipt, extra buttons or darning yarn the manufacturer may have provided, and scraps of fabric left over (if alterations were made) for later patching.

Don't remove care labels that are sewn in.

Your best safeguard against clothing rip-offs is to buy from reputable retailers and clothing manufacturers, who will heed your complaints, and, if justified, will make refunds or exchanges. Having tags and the sales slip handy will make your case much stronger.

DRESS WELL ON LESS

PLAN YOUR WARDROBE WITH MORE THAN ONE PURPOSE IN MIND

For instance, in men's clothes, a top-notch buy is a raincoat with a detachable lining. Without lining, it can double as a topcoat in mild weather. With lining, it can get you through the coldest weather. Women's raincoats with detachable linings can be equally good buys.

Another bargain is a tweed suit with a coat which can double as a good-looking jacket to wear with slacks.

And either a man or a woman can buy a flannel suit with pants that can be worn with other jackets or jackets that can be worn with other pants.

LOOK FOR GOOD WORKMANSHIP

Consumers Union, the most prestigious consumer testing laboratory in the field, publishes in its monthly *Consumer Reports* and its annual "Buying Guide" issue excellent reports of controlled tests on standard clothing brands—from diapers to dinner jackets. You'll benefit from these reports on durability, color-fastness, appearance, laundering ease, quality of workmanship, etc., and learn exactly what to look for when you shop.

Specifically:

Seams should be smooth (no "puckering"), wide enough to let out if necessary, properly finished to prevent fraying.

Hems should be even, properly bound with tape, securely fastened, invisibly stitched, deep enough to permit lengthening.

Stitching should be even and close together.

Buttonholes should be sewn through on both sides of the cloth.

Linings—of the fabric and pockets—should be firm, closely woven, and made of a material which will not stretch or shrink.

Zippers, snaps, and decorative trim should be firmly attached and properly placed.

AVOID IMPULSE BUYING

If you need a spring raincoat, don't stop off at the section reserved for bathing suits and buy a bikini at top price. (And don't laugh, I've done this sort of thing plenty of times and I'll bet you have too!) The same goes for "bargains" which have no place at all in your wardrobe. They are not bargains to you if you don't need or really want the items.

And this applies equally to a variety of clothing accessories which you may find tempting in the store but which you didn't even dream of wanting until you spotted them.

MAKE A CLOTHING BUDGET—AND STICK TO IT

Clothes are among the most flexible of all your budget items, but as a general guide, below are a few national "averages" from the Bureau of Labor Statistics in Washington:

- On the average, out of each $1.00 a United States family spends on everything, about 9 cents goes for clothes and shoes. The share rises to more than 10½ cents when the cost of clothes upkeep is included.
- Our annual national clothes and shoes bill in the late 1970s ran about $370 for each man, woman, and child.
- Typically, clothing costs triple to quadruple between the ages of one and eighteen.
- On the average, women spend $3.00 out of every $5.00 of the family's clothing dollars. But these are merely averages and almost certainly they do not apply to you. Only you can set your own clothing budgets, priorities, and preferences. In your clothing budget:

Make room for luxuries as well as for necessities.

List all the items you must have and then the luxury items you'd like to have. Ask yourself what kind of clothing you need: for work at your job away from home; for sports and leisure-time activities; for social occasions. Just the listing will help you pinpoint the necessities you can appropriately buy at minimum prices and you then can apply whatever amounts you have saved to your luxury purchases.

Ten Ways to Slash Your Clothing Budget

You can truly slash your clothing costs—and be better-dressed than ever—by learning and following these ten specific guides:

(1) *Buy clothes off-season*—and achieve savings running to a sensational 30 to 50 per cent. March is the best time to buy ski outfits, for instance. January and August are good months to buy furs.

There are three major periods for storewide clearance sales: after Easter, after July 4, and after Christmas. These are excellent times to pick up clothes as well as a long list of other items—although you may run into shortages of styles, sizes, and colors if you don't shop as early as you possibly can in the sale (if possible, the day it begins).

List the clothing items of standard styles which you know you will need during the next six to twelve months. Study and use the clothing bargain calendar which follows.

Budget your cash and your credit so you have the funds to buy the items you need and want during the clothes-buying bargain seasons.

Your Calendar

Back-to-school clothes—August, October
Bathing suits—after Fourth of July in July and August
Children's clothing—July, September, November, December
Coats (women's, children's)—April, August, November, December
Costume and fine jewelry—January
Dresses—January, April, June, November

Furs—January, August
Handbags—January, May, July
Hats (children's)—July, December
Hats (men's)—January, July
Hosiery—March, October
Housecoats—April, May, June, October, November
Infants' wear—January, May, July
Lingerie—January, May, July
Millinery—February, April, July
Men's and boys' suits—April, November, December
Men's shirts—January, February, July
Piece goods—June, September, November
Shoes (boys' and girls')—January, March, July
Shoes (men's and women's)—January, July, November, December
Sportswear—January, February, May, July
Toiletries—January, July

Of course, bargains also turn up at odd times through the year because of special circumstances—a store going out of business or into business or moving, an anniversary celebration, an unusual holiday, etc. You can always use these opportunities to buy items you know you'll need later.

A warning is necessary at this point, though: watch out for those "going out of business" sales on clothes. They can be phonies—and you can spot one if the sale has been going on for months or even years.

(2) *Buy certain items in quantity*—and save 10 to 30 per cent.

If, say, you can buy one pair of stockings or panty hose or one pair of socks, a single run or hole can mean a total loss. But if you buy six pairs of the same type and color, you can match what is left and prolong the useful life of each item. (You can cut one leg out of a pair of panty hose when it runs, then one leg out of another pair, and wear both "good legs.") Buying in quantity is particularly practical if yours is a large family. Much clothing is sold on a "three for X dollars" basis.

(3) *Buy standard sizes.* If you're buying a man's sport shirt you will save by buying a small, medium, or large size. The price goes up when you buy shirts in more detailed neck and sleeve sizes. This principle holds for socks, gloves, and many other types of clothing—men's and women's.

(4) *Find and patronize a variety of clothing sellers.*

• Chain stores and catalog houses are particularly good for such staples as jeans, underwear, shirts, athletic socks, sneakers, boots, pajamas and nightgowns, scarves, belts, and work clothes. The larger ones commission major manufacturers to produce items to their specifications in sufficient volume to mean savings of from 10 to 20 per cent. When ordering by mail, be sure to include postage charges, which continue to swell.

• Check discount stores, including army-navy stores and co-ops, for special buys. Oversupplies, slightly irregular items, manufacturers' closeouts, and imported copies of popular American clothing are among the articles they may stock. Typically they are self-service, cash only (occasionally they accept a bank credit card), but savings range up to 25 per cent of the usual retail price.

• Factory outlets may offer excellent bargains. These no-frill, self-service, usually cash only clothing stores sometimes sell overruns of their own products, seconds, name-brand clothes made by others (with or without the manufacturer's label), or arrange to have garments made by contractors. Located in low-rent areas, most allow try-ons, but do not handle alterations, or, if they do, charge extra. Savings offered can go as high as 40 per cent.

• Thrift shops, clothing exchanges, and resale shops, sometimes operated for the benefit of a charitable organization, can be a bargain hunter's treasure troves. Next-to-new secondhand clothes and leftover clothing from retailers and manufacturers, frequently in least popular sizes, are offered at a fraction of the original price, and usually at much less than cost.

• High-fashion discount outlets, usually found only in or near large cities, are a delight if you have a champagne taste and a beer budget. Top designers, retailers, and manufacturers get rid of samples, display and fashion-show garments, overstocks and overruns at these stores. To supplement the "good" merchandise, outlets may also carry lesser "bargains," so you need an ability to separate the wheat from the chaff. And since the best merchandise is usually snapped up soon after it arrives, it may take several visits before you find what you want. Loehmann's (New York and several other cities) and Filene's Automatic Bargain Basement (Boston) are among the better-known stores of this type. Discounts can range from 10 to 50 per cent.

• Specialty stores and boutiques offer appealing value if your time is limited and you are willing to pay for preselection and personal attention. These stores offer a limited amount of clothing for a specific "type" of customer: tall men, large women, children, teenagers, devotees of certain designers, etc. Or they may offer a specific type of merchandise: handbags, lingerie, tennis fashions, etc. for a broader spectrum of people. Because these stores buy in limited quantities, most sales consist of end-of-season leftovers or slightly soiled or damaged clothing.

• Department stores in this era consist of a number of specialty shops and boutiques under one roof, and similar merchandise may be carried in more than one department at different prices, depending on what type of customer each department is trying to attract.

At certain times (see pages 56–58, 764–65), there are storewide sales; at others, individual departments hold their own sales. Some stores devote an entire department just to price-reduced merchandise year-round, supplementing marked-down clothing with special purchases and items brought in from branch stores.

Don't assume that a department store basement is the home of bargains; it may or it may not be.

Do assume that merchandise stocked and displayed near entrances, elevators, and escalators is geared to impulse buying.

Retailers measure their successes and failures in sales per square foot of floor space and constantly strive to to last year's figures by moving around departments, getting rid of merchandise that doesn't sell quickly, setting up new shops within the store, and creating excitement with promotions, fashion extravaganzas, bazaars, fairs, one-night-only sales for charge customers, and whatever else their imaginations can conjure. Merchandise bought for promotion purposes and quick sale may offer excellent buys *if* you need the item.

The clout of stores affiliated with large buying offices is considerable. Look, too, for "store brands."

Learn the various departments of your stores, but don't be surprised when they move or change.

(5) *Don't try to carry colors, sizes in your head.* If you've ever arrived home proudly with a new navy-blue belt for your old navy-blue dress to discover that the belt has a purplish cast and the dress a greenish one, or if you've confused sock and shoe sizes, you'll want to set up a little shopping file to carry with you. It can be as simple as an envelope taped to the last page in the address or appointment book you carry, as casual as a list tucked in your wallet, as elegant as a card case bought just for the purpose. The point is to keep your, and the family's, sizes together with snippets of fabric in a handy place. The bits of fabric can be carefully cut from seams or hems, but if there isn't a quarter inch to spare, you can match a spool of sewing thread to the color, and take along a few yards. With a shopping file for reference, you can buy more confidently at no-returns sales or when you spot something that looks just right.

(6) *Look without prejudice at clothing seconds.* As a general rule, the bigger the flaws in clothing seconds, the greater will be the price cut. The key point you must consider before buying seconds is whether the flaw is "basic" or simply on the surface. Will the blemish significantly reduce the item's usefulness, attractiveness, or durability? Can the defect be easily and inexpensively repaired? If the answers are favorable to the purchase, it could be an extraordinarily good one for you.

(7) *Steer away from frills, especially on utility items.* As an illustration, a sweater with a lavish belt or fur collar will be far more costly than the same sweater without the extras. The simple sweater also will be more useful, for the simpler it is the more occasions you'll be able to wear it (and the more you'll be able to dress it up or down on your own).

(8) *Match prices against utility.* For instance, if you have young children, the mortality rate on playclothes will be exceedingly high. Thus it's smart to get them at rock-bottom prices. You can extend this rule to a wide range of

clothing purchases for every member of your family, particularly in sports clothes. And, incidentally, remember this rule when you're shopping for your husband. Don't push him into the latest "peacock revolution"—wild frills, rainbow-colored shirts, newfangled shaped suits—if that's not where he's at.

(9) *Buy children's clothes by size, not age.* Buy according to your child's height and weight. Buy clothes which have room for growth as your child grows (i.e., deep hems and pants cuffs, adjustable straps on overalls and jumpers, elastic waistbands, raglan sleeves). Buy clothes which are durable and don't show wrinkles and dirt too readily. And don't impose your adult tastes on your child.

(10) *Use credit plans with caution.* You can easily overspend with easy charge plans. You also may miss sales opportunities in other stores because you're still paying off old bills to the store in which you have the revolving charge account. But if you have charge accounts at various stores you'll often get advance notice of special customer clearances—and you can use those clearances to get bargains.

Many department stores and clothing shops hold private "courtesy days" sales for charge-account customers a week or so before advertising them widely to the public. If you have charge accounts, you'll be on the stores' mailing lists and you'll have first pick of the sale items.

When you are fully aware of the advantages as well as the pitfalls of store credit plans you can use them for your own benefit. See Chapter 16, "How to Borrow Cash and Use Credit," for details on department store charge accounts.

SIX RULES ON DRESSING FOR WORK AWAY FROM HOME

Where you work and what you do determine how you'll dress on the job. These rules apply to both men and women:

(1) Unless you're in the fashion world, avoid imprisoning yourself in the latest styles, or even being in advance of any new clothing trend. Wait and see which trends "stick" before making a significant investment.

(2) Look around at what others wear at work, and take your cue from your boss rather than employees on your own level. How you dress won't determine your chances for promotions—but it can hinder your advancement.

(3) Test the wrinkle resistance of any garment you choose for a full day's wear at work by crinkling part of it in your hand at the store to see if it returns quickly to its original shape. If it doesn't, pass it up. This doesn't doom you solely to the purchase of polyester double knits; there are many marvelous fabrics that won't crush or muss, including a wide variety of wools, cotton blends, and silk and linen look-alikes.

(4) Be sure any garment you intend to wear all day long is comfortable.

Thus, when you try on clothes, sit down, raise your arms, and bend over—preferably in front of a mirror. Also consider temperature: heating and air conditioning that can't be adjusted make "layering" desirable. When it's cool, can you add a vest, sweater, or jacket? If it's steamy, can you peel down appropriately?

(5) Every job has its own special clothing limitations or requirements you must heed. For instance, in an office where ink, carbon paper, and dusty files are handled, white and light colors usually are impractical. Full skirts or pants, flowing scarves and ties, and loose sleeves are safety hazards near heavy machinery in a plant. A job that requires a lot of standing or walking means giving first consideration to shoes and hosiery. The business man or woman who must attend many black-tie banquets will want to budget evening wear as part of his or her working wardrobe. The traveler must consider the ease of packing and versatility for varying weather conditions.

(6) When in doubt, buy quality for greatest economy, and don't try to assemble an entire wardrobe in one shopping spree. It's far wiser to invest in one good and becoming suit or dress and add parts and accessories than to settle in a hurry for two or three outfits that are just so-so.

How to Buy a Sewing Machine

With roughly 45 million home sewing machines already in use and with hundreds of thousands being added in our homes each year, let's assume *you* are now in the market for a sewing machine—either a new one or one to replace your aging model. How should you shop? What type of machine should you buy?

Make up your mind how you will use your machine before you buy. If you'll be doing only utilitarian sewing, then you'll need only a basic, inexpensive machine, without many frills. If you love to create fancy things with a lot of embroidery, you may want a machine with all today's built-in features, which can cost hundreds of dollars.

Decide what you want your new machine to be able to do. Take a sewing course first if you do not know and rent a machine while you do it.

If you are a beginner, you might start with a basic portable machine that has straight, reverse, and zigzag stitching capabilities and which may be available for less than $100. These are neither heavy-duty machines nor do they have a long anticipated life-span. They are basic models, so try several before deciding which machine suits your needs. As an alternative, you might buy a secondhand or reconditioned machine from a dealer you are sure you can trust and learn on that one. (You may even decide to keep it indefinitely.)

Most sewing machine dealers will give basic operating instructions for your new machine even if it is a less expensive brand. Both the manufacturers and authorized dealers of the European machines are especially eager that you learn to take advantage of every feature on your new machine. One manufacturer even has a learn-by-doing instruction book. The new owner, under the supervision of the dealer, makes her own samples of each sewing technique and puts them in the instruction book for future reference. The fabric for the samples, also provided by the manufacturer, comes with the machine.

Stick to a well-known brand sold by a company which has an extensive network of sales and service dealerships throughout the country. If properly used and cared for, even a medium-priced sewing machine may last your lifetime.

Off brands, or "private labels," are a particular problem in the sewing machine business. If you buy an off brand in Los Angeles, and later move to New York, you probably will find that you are unable to locate a dealer who handles that brand; therefore, service and parts are for all practical purposes unattainable. A dealer in New York may handle exactly the same sewing machine you have but sell it under his own name. He is reluctant to accept your machine for service because he cannot tell from the outside whether he has the parts or can get them.

The two most wanted features in more sophisticated sewing machines are the zigzag and stretch stitches. There are zigzag attachments available for less expensive straight stitch machines: these attachments, though, move the fabric back and forth (as opposed to the built-in zigzag where the needle moves back and forth), they cannot handle all fabrics, and they are inconvenient and inefficient. The zigzag feature is invaluable for mending, sewing with elastic, making buttonholes, overcasting, and reinforcing what might otherwise have to be done by hand.

The least expensive zigzag machines usually come with manually insertable cams that allow you to do some decorative stitching. Higher in price are automatic machines, which contain pattern cams or built-in disks that can be "dialed," as well as additional cams that can be inserted. Highest of all in price are new electronic machines, which, instead of cams, contain solid-state circuitry which permits "push-button" stitch selection.

Don't be pushed into a decision beyond your needs and budget. Buy a machine with a zigzag or stretch stitch only *if you really intend to use them.* Start basic and trade up as your needs and skills increase.

A portable sewing machine will save you $30 or more over a cabinet model, assuming you have a permanent surface—possibly an old desk or kitchen table—so the machine always will be easily available. The salesman may tell you a cabinet is a must so that dust won't get into the machine. But the dust argument is nonsense, because if the portable doesn't come with a cover, all you need do to solve the dust problem is to whip up a simple dust cover as your first project—something like the covers used for office typewriters or your toaster. It's a lot less expensive than purchase of a bulky cabinet.

However, though a sewing machine cabinet does add to the original investment, it can save money in the long run.

First, by making the setup task easier, you well may sew more often—especially mending and maintenance sewing. Or you may use an available hour rather than wait for a full evening or day for sewing.

Second, a cabinet will add to your comfort—less eye strain tension, aggravation—and thus tend to produce better results.

Third, a cabinet is safer—less danger of dropping, knocking over—and thus protects your machine.

With either a portable or a cabinet model, be certain:

> It is a comfortable height for you to work on.
> You sit with center of your body in front of the needle.
> Leg room is adequate for you.
> Controller is comfortably positioned.
> Table leaf is well supported.
> Cutout holds machine level without wobbling.

Most sewing machine manufacturers suggest to their dealers a demonstration technique—and the better ones include the demonstrations of how the machines work on various commonly used fabrics. By all means, take advantage of the demonstrations; ask for them.

Be suspicious if your sewing machine dealer demonstrates a machine *only* on the very stiff cotton fabric that all dealers use. This fabric cannot show the shortcomings or the advantages of the various machines you may be considering. Remember that you will probably be sewing on many different fabrics, from soft nylon tricots (many dress fabrics are nylon tricot) to bulky wools, corduroys, or fake furs.

The most convincing sales demonstrations are those that show the performance of a machine on many different types of fabric, such as sweater knits, double knits, Lycra, nylon tricot, bulky wool or corduroy, leather, various stretch fabrics, and also problem fabrics. You may think you won't use all these, but how can you be certain now what fabric you will wish to sew on next year or the year after?

If your sewing machine dealer does not have any "real fabric" bring some of your own (bring some anyway!) and try the machine yourself.

Once you buy, use the machine. Your complaints will be handled more equitably early in your ownership than later. Don't grumble to yourself or your friends for a year before you tell the dealer of your dissatisfaction.

BEWARE: SEWING MACHINE TRAPS

Be particularly wary of the gypsters who operate on a grand scale in the area of sewing machines. A dealer, for example, may pass off inexpensive foreign-made machines as American-made by stenciling the names of well-known American machines on them, or by obliterating foreign-origin markings. Others may misrepresent old, well-known machines as being rebuilt by the manufacturer when actually they've only been given a once-over-lightly cleaning by some backroom mechanic. Some imply in their ads that a sewing machine is zigzag-equipped—but not, as you later discover, at the advertised price.

Some insist that their fabulous sewing machine offer is "good for today only"—to keep you from going out and comparing prices. Some give you (or send you) a discount in the form of a "check" for, say, $150—made payable to you but as yet unsigned. However, the price of the sewing machine well may have been jacked up so that it more than covers the discount. Or you may be a second-prize winner in a contest—entitling you to receive a sewing machine *only* if you buy an overpriced cabinet. Or you may be given the "opportunity" for a "free" sewing machine—and pay *"only"* $79.50 for a ten-year service contract. But the catch here is that most machines don't need much—if any—servicing within the first five years and you are still paying $79.50 for the machine, no matter what the disguise is.

Or it may be a "repossessed" sewing machine which has not actually been repossessed. Or the claim may be that the price charged is only the very low amount of the "unpaid balance"—which, by no coincidence, turns out to be just about what the machine is worth.

Beware these traps. And if you unluckily fall into any one, check your nearest consumer protection agency at once to find out your rights under federal and/or state law or regulation.

Cutting Your Clothes Care Costs

Buying (or making) clothes is only part of your investment in your wardrobe. Over the long run, an even larger chunk of your money may go to the cleaning, washing, storing, and repairing of many items in your wardrobe.

How do you keep *these* costs to a minimum—and at the same time make your clothes last as long and look as good as possible?

TIME-TESTED TIPS

To save money and keep your wardrobe looking better for a longer time, here are tried and trustworthy tips:

Wear washables (or old clothes) for dirty jobs—digging in the garden, preparing food, housecleaning, painting, washing the dog, repairing the car.

Protect good clothes—with smocks, aprons, overalls, napkins, bibs, or towels when near splashable or spillable items. Roll up sleeves before washing hands. Apply perfume, cologne, hair spray, and makeup before dressing. Always make sure deodorant or anti-perspirant is completely dry before putting on clothes. Consider the use of dress shields. Nail polish, remover, and lighter fluid can damage some fibers seriously, so handle them with special care.

Prepare when bad weather threatens or actually arrives by wearing a raincoat or cape and boots or shoe covers, carrying an umbrella. Roll up trouser legs (or tuck them into boots) before splashing through puddles or wading through snowdrifts; protect your handbag or briefcase by carrying either one in a plastic shopping bag.

Be careful about where you sit or lean to make sure your clothes aren't smeared with wet paint, grease, oil. Beware especially of chewing gum, bits of candy, or cigarette ashes on seats, of dust and dirt on revolving doors, turnstiles, and stairway railings.

Be sensibly cautious about what you put in your pockets—pens that might leak, heavy keys that may poke a hole through them, colored items (such as matchbooks and advertising flyers) that can rub off dye, candies or makeup that might melt. Don't overstuff pockets to a point that can tear seams, stretch clothes out of shape, and even wear fabric thin.

Look out for items that will snag or discolor clothes—a jangly bracelet or sharp ring that will catch in a knit; a dark bag or briefcase that can rub off against a light jacket, polished shoes that will smudge pants legs or skirt when legs are crossed, or even a bright handkerchief, scarf, or costume jewelry that may not be color-fast.

Check clothes immediately after removing them—for rips, spots, loose buttons or snaps, torn hems—and take care of problems as soon as possible. Mend small rips before they become large ones; tighten buttons before any fall off (which may mean replacing several buttons); spot-clean using the appropriate cleaner and technique for both the spot and the fiber of the garment. (If in doubt, check your dry cleaner.) Never press soiled or spotted clothing; heat may "set" stains and make them impossible to remove.

Launder or dry-clean soiled clothes as soon as possible. Cover clothes not worn frequently, or seasonal garments (be sure they're clean!) to prevent them from getting dusty, and brush clothes that are uncovered frequently. Once dirt has set in a fabric, it's hard to remove. Dirt also may attract moths and insects.

Hang up clothes at once after taking them off, using suitably shaped wood or plastic hangers (wire ones bend out of shape and can distort a shoulder line or may leave rust marks). Sweaters and other knit garments are best folded and placed on a shelf or in a drawer so that they won't stretch.

Leave damp clothes outside the closet until they're completely dry. Clothes hung in the closet should be separated so that air can flow around them and they don't crush each other. Zip zippers; button buttons. If sleeves are wrinkled, stuff them with tissue paper. Make sure collars, cuffs, pleats, and creases are straight.

Keep your clothes closet cool and dry; install a dehumidifier if you live in a high-humidity area.

Immediately clean or polish and place trees in shoes just worn. Shoes can then be stuffed with tissue paper and stored in shoe bags or boxes.

Hang a pomander ball in the closet to help keep air fresh and fragrant. This old-fashioned, long-lasting closet sachet is easy and inexpensive to make: stud a small firm orange with whole cloves until the rind is completely invisible. Mix together 1 teaspoon ground cinnamon and 1 tablespoon orrisroot powder in a paper bag, and drop in clove-studded orange; shake gently until orange is coated with the powder. Tie bag closed and put pomander in a dark, dry, cool place to "cure" for a week. Remove from bag and tie ribbon around it, using straight pins to hold ribbon if necessary. Hang on small nail or hook in back of closet. (Note: Several pomander balls can be made at the same time, and those not used immediately can be wrapped tightly in plastic film to preserve the fragrance. And they make nifty gifts!)

In home washing and drying of permanent-press fabrics and clothes with stain-resistant finishes, load your washer only to about 80 per cent capacity and remove the clothes from the dryer just as soon as they are dry.

Slash your dry-cleaning bills by using self-service dry-cleaning machines for the appropriate garments. These machines are especially valuable for children's winter jackets, woolen sweaters, and most of a long and varied list of items for which delicate hand pressing and steaming aren't necessary.

Follow clothes care labels when you iron. And remember that letting clothes simply steam awhile in the bathroom while you take a shower often will do the ironing for you.

Iron lightweight handkerchiefs and scarves (as well as fabric napkins and place mats) effectively by plastering them to a smooth wall, like the tile or glass around bathtub or shower, while they're sopping wet. Tape corners with strips of cellophane or masking tape to keep them from peeling off as they dry.

Also study the care labels on washing stretch fabrics. While most of these fabrics can be washed, the kind of fiber, the weave or knit, the color, and the finish may dictate the method and temperature to be used—and these will be indicated on the labels. (Be particularly careful with your stretch ski wear, which often can't even be washed, much less machine-dried.) Dry your stretch fabrics in a tumbler dryer, set at the correct temperature for the fabric. If you don't have a dryer, lay the garment flat and block it if necessary to ensure that, when dry, the garment comes back to the correct size. Never hang a garment to dry if it has lengthwise stretch. Never wear a damp stretch garment; it will lose its shape. Don't hang stretch garments for long periods even if dry. Store the garments flat in a drawer or on a shelf.

TWELVE WAYS TO REDUCE YOUR SHOE BILLS

Each year we buy an *average* of three to four pairs of shoes per person. Sneakers, slippers, galoshes, other footwear push the total to more than 1 billion pairs of shoes a year. Our annual footwear bill averaged more than $175 per family as the 1980s neared.

With the guides that follow, though, you can spectacularly reduce your shoe bills—and you'll also find you're enjoying your shoes far more.

(1) Obey the rules for a proper fit: make sure that your big toe doesn't reach the tip of the shoe when you're standing, that your little toe lies flat in the shoe, that the heel fits snugly, and that the sides don't yawn. (Poorly fitting shoes can impose the "hidden" extra cost of podiatrists' bills.)

(2) Don't buy shoes by size alone. A size 8 may fit perfectly in one style but not in another. Have each pair fitted.

(3) Shop for shoes in the middle of the day. Typically, the human foot swells 5 per cent with exercise and this swelling can obviously make a big difference in how a shoe fits.

(4) Economize on shoes you won't wear frequently, such as women's shoes dyed to match an outfit. Don't economize on work shoes or hiking shoes: the savings won't be savings if the shoes aren't comfortable or if they wear out quickly.

(5) Save money in men's shoes by buying those with composition soles and heels, usually no more expensive and actually more serviceable than leather.

(6) Choose simple, traditional styles. A simply styled shoe may cost one third less than its high style counterpart. And stick to darker colors, which look better for a longer time than lighter colors.

(7) Buy children's shoes at least a half size larger than is indicated by the measurement. But sturdy, well-fitting shoes are vital for children, so economize only on style. Use the following chart to guide you on how rapidly children's shoe sizes change as they grow up.

Rate of Change: Children's Shoes Sizes

Age of Child	Size Changes Every
1–6 years	1–2 months
6–10 years	2–3 months
10–12 years	3–4 months
12–15 years	4–5 months
15 years and older	6 months or more

(8) Don't misuse shoes by, say, wearing them out in the rain. Polish shoes regularly to protect them against dirt and bad weather. And note: few shoes can survive a washing machine.

(9) If your shoes become wet, stuff them with paper, dry them away from direct heat with a soft cloth, and rub them with a light film of mineral oil.

(10) Change your shoes at least once a day to give them a chance to

"rest" and dry out from foot moisture. If you do this, two pairs of shoes will outlast three which are not alternated during a day.

(11) When buying, look for: smooth, soft linings and smooth inside seams; stitching which is not too close to the edge of the shoe sole; flexible "uppers" and evenly trimmed edges; good material; reputable brands from a reputable retailer.

(12) Buy shoes for yourself and children during the seasonal sales—using both the winter and summer sales for maximum savings.

The ABCs of Buying Furs
(or "How to Sound like a Fur Authority Without Really Being One")

You know the type: she has just bought a raccoon coat and now she's the world's greatest authority on *all* furs, ready to advise friends, acquaintances, strangers, and *you* on what to look for and "where to get it wholesale."

Don't listen to her! It's impossible to compress years of fur-buying knowledge and experience into a few days, weeks, or even months, and "wholesale" usually means a reduced price on something not good enough for a store.

The best approach to buying furs is to ask yourself a few basic questions before you set out on your shopping trip, and then put yourself in the hands of a reliable furrier.

ASK YOURSELF

"Where and when do I plan to wear the fur?"

If your answer is "everywhere" and "anytime," you'll want something sturdy. This generally (though not always) means shorter- rather than longer-haired. However, longevity is crucially affected by the quality of the fur and how you treat it.

If you're looking for something in which to cuddle at football games, or can afford to shrug off practicality, that's a different matter entirely.

Be candid with the salesperson if you want the best advice.

"What kind of fur will look best on me?"

Forget the fable that you have to be skinny to wear fox, or over thirty to wear mink. Try-ons in front of a three-way mirror are full of pleasant surprises and the only reliable way to answer that question. It's wise to have at least a vague idea of color, so that the fur complements the rest of your wardrobe, but keep an open mind.

"How much can I afford?"

As the 1980s neared, you could get a marvelous curly-lamb jacket for under $300—or an opulent sable for $25,000 or even more. Determine a general price range, and then look for the best quality (and style for you) within that range. Better a superb muskrat than a poor mink!

A FEW FACTS

There are five hallmarks of a good fur:
(1) Bright luster
(2) Uniform color
(3) Density
(4) Silky texture
(5) Soft, pliable leather

When you're buying fur from a reliable furrier, there's no need to be concerned with whether the pelts are from a male or female animal, whether they come from an endangered species (they won't), or workmanship. Look at the general appearance of the fur and lining, but, most important, study the way *you* look wearing it. The selling price usually includes alterations, but it's sound to check the set of the shoulder seams and the weight of the coat, which usually can't be altered.

LANGUAGE OF FUR

A fur label always tells you the true name of the animal, the country of origin if outside the United States, and how the fur was processed If it's entirely or partially made of tails, paws, bellies, sides, flanks, or gills, the label also will tell you that.

(1) Basic fur terms include:

Pelt: The skin, including either or both underfur and guard hairs.

Underfur: The short thick hair next to the skin.

Guard hairs: Longer, stiffer, smoother hairs that protect an animal from rain and other elements.

Grotzen: The central back, long spinal region of a pelt.

(2) The words used in *processing* fur also are handy to know:

Let out: To retain the beauty of the pelt of a small animal, the skin is "let out" diagonally. This decreases the width and increases the length.

Let in: To make skins shorter and wider, pelts are cut into strips and joined with other matched skins.

Glazed: This process, applying a special fluid and steaming it into the fur under pressure, brings out the fur's clear, lustrous beauty. A fur may be reglazed from time to time.

Sheared: Fur is cut to even off or shorten underfur and guard hairs.

Plucked: Guard hairs are removed.

(3) *Coloring* terms are helpful too. Coloring may be used for uniformity; to bring out natural tints, tones, and shades; to add luster and highlights; to change color completely. They include:

Bleached: Natural color is lightened: light and white furs often are bleached to remove streaks or spots.

Tip-dyed: Only the ends of hairs are dyed.

Tipped: Leather side of a pelt has been dyed; this does not change the fur color, however.
Natural: Fur has not been colored in any way.
Mutation: A mutation occurs when the offspring differs radically from its parents. Fur ranchers breed mutations in foxes, minks, and nutria to produce exciting new colors. *Mutations are natural.*

FUR CARE

Furs should be worn! They thrive out of doors. They are for enjoyment, and shouldn't be buried in a closet.

Have furs professionally cleaned at least once a year, more often if they show soil or spots.

Put them in storage during the warm months.

Take them to your furrier the minute a repair is needed.

Do give fur "breathing space" in a closet (and don't cover it with a bag). Hang it on a padded hanger; if you've come in out of the rain or snow, let fur dry on the hanger (away from a radiator) before putting it in the closet.

Don't abuse fur with unnecessary friction, such as a shoulder bag strap. Don't comb or brush it (a good shaking is all it needs), and never pin flowers or jewelry to fur. Perfume, cleaning fluid, and hair spray can damage fur, so avoid using them near or on it.

IF YOU FEEL YOU'VE BEEN GYPPED

First discuss your misgivings with the furrier.

If still unhappy, write directly to the manufacturer, or, if you don't know the manufacturer's name, contact the Federal Trade Commission, Division of Furs and Textiles, Washington, D.C. 20580.

If you can provide the registration or identification number (which will appear on the bill of sale), both the manufacturer and the fur can be identified.

The FTC won't protect you from buying a poor fur, but will protect you from deceit about the identity of a fur.

12

JEWELRY AND BEAUTY —FROSTING ON THE CAKE

JEWELRY	780
NOT A NECESSITY—OR IS IT?	780
TEN TIPS FOR BUYING FINE JEWELRY	781
COSTUME JEWELRY	783
JEWELRY CARE	784
UNDERSTANDING TODAY'S WATCHES	784
A WATCH IS NOT ALWAYS FOREVER	784
THE HIGH PRICE TAG ON YOUTH AND BEAUTY	785
TEN WAYS TO LOWER IT	785

JEWELRY

NOT A NECESSITY—OR IS IT?

Jewelry is not a clothing necessity. Or is it?

In the late 1970s, Americans had adorned themselves with an estimated $6 billion worth of *fine* jewelry, more than half of it sparked with diamonds of varying sizes and quality. Fewer than 10 per cent of these diamonds and other stones were "investment" gems (see pages 1296–1302). Additional millions were being spent on *costume* jewelry.

Even when our long-ago ancestors dressed in leaves and skins, we know they wore jewelry: rings of bone, amber, ivory, and flint; necklaces and bracelets strung with choice shells, stones, and carvings; braided rushes and grasses.

Throughout recorded time, jewelry has played an important role in helping us proclaim our status—separating royalty from commoner, the married and engaged from the single, the rich from the poor, the old from the young.

Symbols for schools, colleges, fraternities, religions, political parties, peace, ecology, and women's rights in the forms of pendants, pins, and rings speak for us as loudly as words.

And individual pieces of jewelry have long been worn as "personal trademarks": the late author Fannie Hurst was never without her dramatic calla-lily pin; in the seventies, designer Pauline Trigère always wore a turtle in some form; and actress Arlene Francis' much-copied diamond-heart pendant necklace became almost as famous as she is.

For most of us, jewelry is a fashion accessory, worn to brighten ears, fingers, wrists, ankles, necks, or clothing. We would rather wear it than put it in a vault. If it's expensive, we expect to enjoy it for many years, perhaps pass it along to our children and grandchildren or even sell it in a pinch, for jewelry has long been a popular form of portable wealth. We don't want to lose it, have it fall apart, or go out of style. In brief, we want our money's worth!

JEWELRY AND BEAUTY—FROSTING ON THE CAKE

TEN TIPS FOR BUYING FINE JEWELRY

(1) Consider carefully whether the piece you're about to buy is a long-term "fashion investment" or a fad that might better be bought in costume jewelry. The fashion director for the nation's largest retailer of fine jewelry suggests this basic (and classic) wardrobe of fine jewelry, noting that it can be mixed or matched and that—as fashions change over the years—you can add pieces and supplement it with costume jewelry:

- 3 gold chains of different lengths, weights, and designs (one of which might be sparked with diamonds)
- 2 (or more) pendants, one of which could be jeweled and convertible to a pin
- 1 pearl necklace
- 1 pair of diamond stud earrings
- 1 pair of pearl earrings
- 1 pair of gold earrings, such as hoops
- 3 gold bangle (or gold chain) bracelets of different widths and designs
- 1 gold watch (a classic such as the "tank" watch)
- 1 "important" gold pin, possibly set with diamonds
- 1 jeweled pin
- 3 or 4 small pins (stickpins, scatter pins, bar pins) to wear singly or group together

For additions, the jewelry expert suggests:

- Neck ornaments—More chains, pendants; colored beads (such as jade, peridot, tourmaline, amber); and, if you're really flush, a diamond necklace.
- Earrings—Gold studs, drop earrings, as well as sapphire, ruby, and/or emerald studs. Stud "jackets," which slip around studs, make this type of earring especially versatile.
- Bracelets—More chains and/or bangles; a pearl bracelet; a circlet of diamonds; and a gold or gold-and-diamond evening watch.
- Rings—Another jeweled ring; more bands of different widths and designs.
- Pins—A large pin that separates into two smaller ones; additional scatter pins that can be clustered are useful accessories.

(2) Although platinum, silver, and other precious metals are used for fine-jewelry settings, gold is by far the most popular and practical because it is malleable, won't tarnish, and is available in a variety of colors. Always check the karat markings when buying gold:

An item marked 24K (24 karats*), or 999, is 100 per cent pure gold. However, pure gold is generally considered too soft for practical use in

---

* Stones are weighed in *carats;* the percentage of pure gold is expressed in *karats;* and both words are derived from "carob." Many centuries before the birth of Christ, precious gems and metals were measured on a scale balanced against carob seeds. Today a carat is approximately 200 milligrams.

jewelry, and since ancient times, gold has been alloyed (combined) with other metals. (See pages 1285–86.)

Each karat represents 1/24 part of pure gold: finest gold jewelry is usually 18K (eighteen parts pure gold and six parts of another metal). Most American-made gold jewelry is 14K (fourteen parts pure gold and ten parts other metal). By Federal Trade Commission regulation, no domestic jewelry can be stamped with percentages rather than karats.

The different colors of gold are determined by the other metal(s) with which pure gold is alloyed. Gold alloyed with copper has a warm reddish color; gold alloyed with nickel or palladium results in the white gold frequently used as a setting for diamonds.

In addition to its use in fine jewelry, gold is also used in costume jewelry. When the term *gold-filled* is used, it indicates that a layer of (at least 10K) gold has been mechanically bonded to a base metal. This layer must constitute at least 1/20 of the total weight of the finished metal piece. *Gold-plated* means that 10K or better gold has been electrolytically electroplated to base metal. Watch cases are frequently gold-filled or gold-plated.

(3) In addition to the intrinsic value of materials used in fine jewelry, other factors determine its cost: design, workmanship (including whether it's hand-wrought or machine-stamped), and the retail markup.

Check workmanship carefully to make sure that fine jewelry will hold up: make sure chain links are invisibly soldered closed; run your fingers over the piece to assure there are no rough edges to catch and snag clothing. Make sure fastenings not only close tightly, but that there are backups—safety chains, guards, and catches. Gems should be firmly set (never glued), and they must be rechecked from time to time. Earring posts or clips should be solidly attached; pearls and beads should be strung with knots between each one so that a break doesn't scatter them all to the winds; rings should be sized exactly to your fingers and heavy enough so that they don't bend when pressed.

(4) Many fine jewelry designs are copyrighted, and for these you usually pay a premium price. Successful copyrighted designs are, however, almost always adapted (but not always successfully!) by other manufacturers. If you wait a short while, you may be able to find a less expensive version of a piece of jewelry that you adore but can't afford when it's first introduced. Elsa Peretti's "Diamonds-by-the-Yard" design for Tiffany in the 1970s is an example of a successful copyrighted piece that was adapted successfully by others. (An exception is the copyrighted designs on which *any* manufacturer must pay a royalty, such as replicas of Snoopy, Little Orphan Annie, or Mickey Mouse.)

(5) The store with the fastest turnover in fine jewelry generally offers you the best "values," although it may not have the unique or valuable pieces you're seeking. Inventory for a jewelry store (or for the fine jewelry department of a larger store) is a sizable investment; the markup must cover

not only the usual cost of doing business, but also must give the retailer a fair return on the funds he has invested. Jewelry stores with many branches and jewelry departments in larger stores (many of which are operated by outside specialty chains) frequently are able to offer a considerable price edge, both because they save by buying in quantity and because they can ship slow-moving items to their other stores where they may sell more quickly.

(6) Beware of "bargain" jewelry stores. Whether you buy jewelry from a neighborhood shop, from a major jewelry chain, or from a department store, make sure of the store's reputation. Unless you are a jewelry expert yourself, and few of us are, you have to rely completely on the store for information on what you're buying.

(7) Get the facts in writing! Any reliable jewelry store or department will willingly describe the item you're buying in detail on the sales check. Ask for specifics: What is the karat of the gold? How many carats do the stones weigh? What are they and how many are there? If you're buying diamonds (other than tiny ones), be sure that color and clarity gradings are noted, and that the cut (round, pear, marquise, emerald, etc.) is described. If you plan to insure your jewelry, you'll need this information.

(8) If everything you admire is way beyond your capacity to buy, consider substitutes. Semi-precious stones and synthetic gems set in gold and combined with precious stones make excellent fashion investments. For the price of a small emerald ring, you can—for example—buy a sizable chrysoprase encircled with tiny diamonds. White sapphires are considerably less expensive than diamonds and, unless you're a purist, man-made sapphires, rubies, emeralds, and diamonds can't be detected from the real thing except under a jeweler's loupe!

(9) Buy slowly. If you can't afford a yard of diamonds, buy a chain with a single diamond—and then add more stones as you can afford them.

(10) Trade up. Some stores offer to give you full retail-price credit on selected jewelry pieces if you later trade them in for more expensive items. If a store tells you that it has this policy, and that what you've bought can be traded later, get the information *in writing* on the sales check—spelling out whether this applies only to the stones or also to the setting.

COSTUME JEWELRY

Jewelry made of any material other than precious metals and precious or semi-precious stones is generally considered "costume jewelry," although the prices for these items can far exceed prices for some "fine jewelry," and some costume jewelry may incorporate semi-precious stones as well as be set in silver.

Costume jewelry may imitate the real thing, be "frankly fake," or use totally different materials: plastic, wood, shell, clay, glass, fabric, enameled metal, papier-mâché, etc., for infinite variety and effects.

"Stones" are frequently set in gold-filled, gold- or silver-plated metal or silver. The intrinsic value of materials usually doesn't have as great an influence on price as design and workmanship.

If you see an inexpensive piece of costume jewelry that you do like, buy it! Just make sure that it won't harm your other clothing—that colors don't rub off or run, and that sharp edges won't snag or tear fabrics. Before you buy an expensive piece of costume jewelry, however, investigate the same workmanship details as you would for fine jewelry. In addition, look for even "coatings"—pearl, paint, enamel, etc.—to assure yourself they won't peel off easily. And consider materials in context with their use, remembering that rings and bracelets get harder wear than pins, necklaces, and earrings.

JEWELRY CARE

Whether you have a drawer full of jewelry or just a few pieces, and whether it's fine jewelry or costume jewelry, a compartmental jewelry box is a good investment—to guard chains from tangling, keep pairs of earrings together, and prevent knocks and scratches.

Take fine jewelry to a jeweler for occasional buffing, polishing, and professional cleaning, and to see that stones and fastenings are secure. Costume jewelry usually can be cleaned with a sponging of warm soapy water, after which it should be thoroughly dried.

Because of its value, keep your fine jewelry in a home (or bank) safe. Burglars are just as clever about finding hiding places as you are!

UNDERSTANDING TODAY'S WATCHES

Close to 70 million Americans buy or receive a watch each year, and if you are among them, the odds are three to one that it was purchased in December.

The watch may have been a $15 stocking-stuffer or a special $100,000 collector's item, a workhorse or an ornament, a one-and-only or an addition to a wardrobe of timepieces, but it probably cost in the neighborhood of $35.

Buying a watch continues to require more and more know-how.

A WATCH IS NOT ALWAYS FOREVER

Price is not the sole determining factor of a "good" watch. The same basic watch movement may come in a wide range of prices, depending on the case, dial, bracelet, and special features offered with it.

Like any item with moving parts, a watch needs special care.

Unless you have selected a pin-lever watch, which does not lend itself to service, a watch should be cleaned and serviced at least every two years, should be kept away from extreme temperatures, and generally should be treated with respect.

Except for installing a battery, don't try to fix it yourself if anything goes amiss, and never take a watch apart "just to look."

JEWELRY AND BEAUTY—FROSTING ON THE CAKE

Even if you buy one encased in precious metal and studded with gems, the finest watch in the world eventually will need repairs. Assuming you are not preserving it for its future value as an antique, there will come a time to consider replacing the inner workings rather than having it fixed, especially when parts are no longer available.

Check the guarantee carefully to see what is covered and for how long when you buy a watch, and keep the sales check with the warranty for future reference.

And just a few additional commonsense rules will help maintain it in top condition.

- Keep your watch away from powder, perfume, loose tobacco.
- Even though you have bought a water-resistant watch, don't risk wearing it in the swimming pool or shower. Why test it?
- If you have a mechanical hand-winding watch, wind it once a day, preferably after you get up, and wind it with thumb and forefinger after you have taken it off your wrist.
- Don't take even the smallest chance of overwinding. Play safe and stop winding the watch when you sense that the tension is close to the maximum.
- Don't expose your watch to overly vigorous treatment, even if it's supposedly shock-resistant.

The High Price Tag on Youth and Beauty

TEN WAYS TO LOWER IT

The beauty industry is considered recession-resistant by many security analysts.

The reason: given only a few dollars to spend on yourself, odds are you'll hand them over for a beauty product or service—lipstick or hairdo, shaving cream or haircut.

"If my hair's a mess, I feel downright dowdy—no matter what I'm wearing," moans the impeccably dressed, svelte vice-president of a major department store chain, who couldn't look dowdy if she tried.

Her statement echoes the feelings of American women (and men†), who were spending an estimated $7 billion a year on beauty services and products in the late 1970s, approximately $5 billion of that in beauty salons and barbershops, and unknown additional millions of dollars on beauty books and periodicals, exercise machines, scales, and other beauty-allied products.

If beautifying yourself takes a big bite out of *your* budget, here are ten ways to nibble away at the prices you pay:

(1) Do some of the work yourself. "The works" at your favorite beauty salon can make you feel, as well as look, like a million! Most salons won't

† A survey in the late 1970s by *Modern Salon*, a beauty-services trade publication, reveals that 76 per cent of the 153,000-plus beauty salons in the United States now cater to men as well as women, and that 54 per cent of these salons are doing 25 per cent or more of their business with men!

object, however, if you go for a cut and styling having just shampooed your own hair (a saving of from $1.00 to $5.00 or more, depending on the salon). And if you have one of the popular wash-and-wear styles, you can even forgo blow-drying or setting after a cut—an additional saving of from $3.00 to $15 or more!

(2) Watch for specials. Many department store beauty salons (others, too) have "specials" on slow days (generally during working hours, early in the week) and in certain months. January and February, for example, are traditionally "perm sale" months, and late summer–early fall "make-over packages" (hair styling, facial, makeup) are often real bargains to put you in a mood for clothes-shopping. Watch newspaper ads for these offers, or give your hairdresser a supply of addressed-to-you cards so he or she can drop you a line when a sale is in the offing.

Watch, too, for cosmetic and toiletry sales: during periods when product sales lag (after Christmas, for example), you'll find excellent buys.

(3) Be a guinea pig. Volunteer to be a "model" at a hairdressing (or barber) school. Putting your locks at the mercy of an unlicensed student who is practicing can be risky: however, instructors need models on whom to demonstrate various haircutting, perming, and coloring techniques, and you're usually assured first-rate work.

Similarly, advance hairdressing schools, attended by already licensed stylists who are taking brushup courses, offer great bargains: for a small service fee (sometimes without charge) you can get a new style by either an instructor or a professional hairdresser-student.

Check the Yellow Pages for beauty schools in your city. Also, if you hear that a big salon is about to open in your area, ask if the salon will need "models" for stylist training.

(4) Try before you buy. Salons and stores selling cosmetics often have "aestheticians" or "demonstrators" who will cheerfully (and without charge) turn you from ugly duckling to swan with the hope that you'll buy every product they use for the transformation. Since they usually work on commission, I'm not suggesting you get beautified for a big date without buying anything, but if you're in the market for a new eye shadow and lipstick anyway, why not plan to take advantage of their expertise; you can see how what you're buying will look, learn how to apply it—and have a professional makeup session at no cost.

Also, take advantage of samples and "trial sizes" of new products used as come-ons by many cosmetic and perfume manufacturers.

(5) Consider alternatives. Your great-grandmother probably softened her hands with pharmacy-mixed rosewater and glycerine, and shampooed her hair with liquid castile or green soap. These products are still available in many drugstores. You don't *need* expensive perfumed and prettily packaged creams, lotions, and potions to be beautiful.

Many dentists agree that brushing your teeth with a paste of bicarbonate of soda, salt, and water is as effective as most toothpastes. Mayonnaise (bottled or homemade) works as well as any hair conditioner on the market; unflavored gelatin dissolved in boiling water has few equals as a setting lotion.

For your skin, lanolin is a fine lubricant; witch hazel is a splendid astringent; and the lightly beaten white of an egg, smeared on your face until dry and then rinsed off, makes a time-revered "firming masque."

If your hair style requires frequent salon visits, consider an easier-to-care-for "do." Streaking, frosting, and highlighting let you have the fun of being a blonde without biweekly root touch-ups, and a gentle perm may make blow-drying or setting unnecessary.

(6) Check prices carefully. A department store may have two beauty salons: one offering head-to-toe pampering, the other (usually geared to a younger clientele) offering only the basics. The price difference can be substantial. Similarly, prices at a trimmer-snipper-type salon usually will be more modest than those at a full-fledged beauty department. If prices aren't clearly posted in the salon, don't be too embarrassed or intimidated to ask—and compare.

One trap into which many women (and men) fall is the "whatever you think best" syndrome. There you are, head full of suds, when the shampooer tells you casually that you're about to get a wonderful special bee's knees conditioning rinse.

Say "halt" until you find out what it does *and* what it will cost! The little extras at a salon can add up to a big ticket. If the bee's knees rinse is a must, perhaps you can buy it at the salon and use it at home; product cost is considerably less than 10 per cent of the price of a beauty salon service.

(7) Scout for store brands or name brands at discount. Absolutely convinced that a certain $25-a-jar night cream is totally responsible for her peaches-and-cream complexion (although she should be thanking her lucky genes!), one New York model made a discovery that cut her night-cream expenditures almost in half! She was near tears when her local drugstore temporarily ran out of the "miracle" wrinkle preventer and she proceeded to look for it elsewhere. Her first stop: a nearby discount store. Her night cream was nowhere in sight, and expecting to be told he'd never heard of it, she timidly asked a stock boy whether the store carried it. From inside a closed cabinet, he immediately pulled out a $25-size jar—marked $14.99!

The moral of this tale: shop for cut-rate prices on products you can't live without, and don't assume that everything is on display. Ask!

If you're not hooked on a particular brand, consider store brands. Large drug and department stores (many of which are parts of groups or chains) frequently carry the most popular cosmetic and toiletry products with their own brand-name labels—at considerable savings. These products may even be made by the same manufacturers who make name brands. Differences are usually slight: fragrance, color, and, of course, packaging.

(8) Buy in quantity. Twelve exercise classes for the cost of ten, a box of eight cakes of hand soap for the price of six sold separately, special beauty salon rates for groups of four or more—all add up to savings.

Find out if and how you can save by buying in quantity, including large sizes of items you use a great deal.

(9) Gift (or purchase) with purchase. Cosmetic manufacturers hate them; stores love them. You may—or may not—benefit from the highly competitive promotion gimmick of GWP (gift with purchase) or PWP (purchase with purchase). The way this works is that you buy an expensive brand-name product and receive (or can buy at cost or less), for example, a nifty travel bag filled with sample sizes of the manufacturer's other products. The manufacturer is delighted to have you sample the products and hopes you'll return to buy them in regular sizes; it's the extra that makes him wince. Each merchant wants you to buy that brand at his store, so insists that the manufacturer offer a (frequently exclusive) superbargain. If you were going to buy the expensive brand-name product anyway, and want—or can use the gift—you'll probably get a good buy. Otherwise, forget it.

(10) Avoid beauty charlatans. There are many around ready to take your money. Beauty products and services—even plastic surgery—won't work miracles. No known products can eliminate baldness, erase wrinkles, increase your bust six inches in a month, reduce your weight by twenty pounds in a week, or win you the love of your favorite movie star overnight.

Read ads, booklets, pamphlets, and packages carefully to make sure you aren't inferring performance promises that are merely implied.

Be wary of mail-order beauty bargains, club plans, and door-to-door salesmen and -women.

Beauty products taken internally—like special vitamins, protein supplements, diet pills—can be hazardous to your health, and should be used only with your doctor's approval. Others—such as scented feminine hygiene sprays, products "enriched with" vitamins, eggs, milk, etc., and skin bleaches—are considered by most legitimate beauty and health authorities to be simply a waste of money.

A week at a pleasant beauty spa can make you feel, even look better. But investigate the place carefully before you spend your money. Brochures can be deceiving, and you may find yourself living a Spartan existence in a remote area for the cost of a deluxe European vacation.

Common sense tells you that a facial will brighten your complexion by removing "dead" skin on the surface; cleverly applied cosmetics will create an illusion; a good haircut will give you a becoming, easy-care style; proper diet and exercise will improve your figure.

"Wishful thinking" sells beauty products and services, however.

Before you buy, determine whether a promise given *can* be kept.

Sometimes it can—but, unfortunately, often it can't.

Common sense can be your best guide. Let it be!

13

HOW TO SLASH THE COSTS OF YOUR VACATIONS IN THE 1980'S

DE-REGULATION OF AIR FARES	790
LIBERALIZED PUBLIC CHARTERS, TOO	791
ASK!	792
CAUTION ON MEDICATIONS FOR TRAVELERS	793
THE HANDICAPPED TRAVELER	793
TIME YOUR VACATION OFF-SEASON	795
SAVE BY GOING WHERE THE CROWDS ARE NOT	795
SAVE ON A PACKAGE PLAN	796
HOW TO SAVE ON SHOPPING UNDER UNITED STATES CUSTOMS LIMITATIONS	796
HOW TO SHOP FOR A VACATION TOUR	797
WHAT A TRAVEL AGENT CAN (AND CANNOT) DO FOR YOU	799
DO-IT-YOURSELF TRAVEL PLANNING	801
DO'S AND DON'TS FOR CUTTING YOUR HOTEL BILLS	803
WHOM AND HOW TO TIP	804
AND TIPPING ON WINTER CRUISES	806
SAVE BY HOSTELING	807
BUS PASSES AND BIKE TRAILS	807
MONEY-SAVING GUIDES FOR CAMPING TRIPS	809
TOURISM AND ENERGY SHORTAGES	811

De-regulation of Air Fares

With the opening of the 1980s, the traveling public and the airline industry are geared for the still utterly unforeseeable impact of the momentous action taken by the Civil Aeronautics Board when, in the late 1970s, it permitted United States airlines to cut fares by as much as 70 per cent without CAB approval. Even in an era of dramatic changes in commercial aviation, so drastic a move toward freedom from regulation by a federal agency made history.

It was only after intense and prolonged debate that the CAB finally adopted its amended policies. Under these policies now governing your air travel:

Ceiling fares on coach trips are set at the levels of September 1978.

Airlines have the discretion to cut their normal fares by as much as 50 per cent in all domestic markets.

On some of their flights (40 per cent of their seat miles a week), cuts of up to 70 per cent are permissible.

To remind you of how great are these changes, deep discounts had in the past generally been available to you only on capacity-controlled restrictive fares.

The policy for the 1980s has further ramifications to you as a traveler. It has abolished the prescription that first-class fares be set at a certain percentage above coach.

As a result airlines can set first-class fares at *any* level above coach fares. For some of you who travel first class the cost of flying your favorite airline actually could increase, therefore—despite the potential giant cuts. In addition, carriers may boost fares from 5 to 10 per cent on a large part of their route system, depending on the amount of competition on their system.

The CAB's action, which is only beginning to be felt by the traveling public, put pricing decisions and the consequences of those decisions back in the hands of the market place and the carrier management.

Previously, airlines had been forced to compete for passengers on the basis solely of schedules and amenities (the biggest steak).

Probably one of the greatest benefits to accrue to you, the air traveler, as a result of the Board's action is elimination of the bewildering array of air fares that always has defied public understanding.

While airlines still are fighting jammed telephone reservation lines as hundreds of thousands of air travelers seek answers to questions on the multitude of discount fares that have been built up over recent years, the CAB's action ultimately should wipe out the problem of complicated fares.

The industry is trying to work its way out of the maze of Discover America excursion fares, Unlimited Mileage fares, Freedom Excursion fares, Visit U.S.A. fares, Super Coach fares, Super Saver fares, etc., etc. They held out such airline lures as (if you can believe it!) round-trip travel at night except on weekends in seats purchased thirty days before departure if the return trip is made a week to forty-five days later!!

At one airline, the in joke was, "We have a new slogan: a fare a day on TWA."

At another major carrier, a horrified efficiency expert found nineteen fares between Los Angeles and Chicago alone!

The sweeping action of the Board in de-regulating plane fares must take a long time in producing overall results. However, you already are seeing the effect in the form of lower fares for long-haul markets and the elimination of many of those nightmarishly confusing discount fares in favor of generalized peak and off-peak pricing.

Liberalized Public Charters, Too

A second benefit now emerging in ever fuller measure for you, the traveling public of the 1980s, is the adoption of new liberalized charter regulations. These have replaced most current charter forms with a single form called "public charters."

Liberalized features of the new charter form include:

—No advance purchase requirement.
—No minimum stay requirement.
—No restrictions on discount pricing.
—No minimum size group.
—An end to open-ended round-trip charters.

The prohibition on open-ended round-trip charters is an important protection for the airline traveler.

Charters were responsible for nine out of ten complaints logged against agents and tour operators by the Office of the Consumer Advocate of the CAB in the late 1970s. Inherent in the problem was the infancy of the mass charter market, which really only began to take off in the middle of the decade. Horror stories spread about charter passengers sleeping at terminals overseas, about unexpected cancellations and defaults, about charters that took bookings and then never even got off the ground.

But now under the CAB rules, if you are a charter passenger, you may be able to cancel your reservation if:

• there is an alteration of departure or return date;

• the origin or destination city is changed;

• you are assigned a hotel other than the one named in the operator-participant contract;

• the price of your tour is hiked 10 per cent, whether all at once or in smaller chunks. No increases would be allowed after the tenth day before departure.

Should you be advised of a major change by the charter operator, you have seven days in which to cancel and you are entitled to receipt of a refund seven days after cancellation.

The bulk of all those confusing "alphabet soup" special regulation charter names no longer exist to befuddle you. Gone are such names as Advance Booking Charters (ABCs), Travel Group Charters (TGCs), Study Group Charters (SGCs), Inclusive Tour Charters (ITCs), and One-Stop-Inclusive Tour Operators (OTOs).

You can, though, still take affinity group and single-entity charters due to the specialized nature of the groups to which they appeal.

Ask!

If you are a traveler bound on a charter tour overseas, here is basic advice before you fly—*ask!*

—Ask who is the tour operator and what is his reputation.

—Ask what are the cancellation privileges and options available if the tour is canceled at the last minute.

—Ask if the tour operator is bonded or there is an escrow account—required by the CAB.

—Ask what penalties and refunds you can expect if you cancel your trip. Penalties can be substantial—up to 90 per cent of the tour price. Unless you cancel by a certain date, you may not be entitled to a refund.

—Ask at what kind of hotels you will stay. Don't misconstrue the European term for "first class" as being the best, for example. On the Continent this really describes establishments that are several grades below the top, which is "superior deluxe." You can check out your hotel in the *Official Hotel and Resort Guide*.

—Ask what the package includes.

—Ask what is extra. Transfers? Baggage handling at airports and hotels? Sight-seeing? Admissions? All meals?

If you run into problems on a tour that went wrong, you have recourse for complaints. Write the CAB, Office of the Consumer Advocate (1825 Connecticut Avenue N.W., Washington, D.C. 20428) or the American Society of Travel Agents (711 Fifth Avenue, New York, New York 10022).

You also can sue the operator in small-claims court or file a civil suit if the amount is large. In addition, you may find the office of your city or state consumer protection agency helpful as well as your state attorney general.

Caution on Medications for Travelers

All those who travel for a living—airline crews, entertainers, reporters such as myself—know that as a traveler you must be prepared for the worst.

Carried as standard for a traveling medicine chest: aspirin; vitamins, including B complex and C, the latter to compensate for body loss under stress; antibiotics; antacid; Lomotil or paregoric for symptomatic relief of that ancient malady—turista.

You also may want to include antihistamines, salt tablets, and possibly quinine.

Carry your medicines in duplicate—some on your person and some in your luggage. Carry a copy of any prescription you are required to take written in generic terms as well as the drug itself. Brand names of drugs may not be recognized in other countries.

Local health authorities will advise you on any immunizations you will need.

Consider a Medic Alert emblem if you have a special medical history with chronic conditions or allergies. Membership in the organization provides a twenty-four-hour phone number for physicians you can call for information or crucial assistance. The service is available for a $10 contribution to the non-profit, tax-deductible Medic Alert Foundation. Request an application form before mailing your contribution by writing the Foundation at Box 1009, Turlock, California 95380.

Before departure, also obtain a list of English-speaking doctors the world over in return for a contribution to the International Association for Medical Assistance to Travelers (IAMAT), 350 Fifth Avenue, New York, New York 10001.

In addition, Intermedic, 777 Third Avenue, New York, New York 10017, offers a *Directory of Participating Physicians* with fees that are fixed for the initial office visit or hotel call.

In many areas with socialized medicine (for example, Sweden and Great Britain), health care is free to the visitor.

You might arrange, too, for some form of trip cancellation insurance in the event you become ill before departure or on the trip.

And don't forget to pack that extra pair of eyeglasses.

The Handicapped Traveler

Millions of Americans have disabilities—temporary and permanent—that restrict their vacations. Advance planning can eliminate much of the trouble.

As the 1980s begin our government has adopted a more enlightened attitude about the problems of the handicapped in traveling. A new era is emerging for the disabled vacationer.

The United States Travel Service of the Department of Commerce reports that a growing awareness of the special needs of handicapped travelers has opened previously closed doors if you are in a wheelchair or have other physical disabilities.

Several government publications on travel facilities for the handicapped are available. These include *Travel Tips for the Handicapped*, *Access Travel*, and *Access Guide to the National Parks*. You may obtain the pamphlets from the Consumer Information Center, Pueblo, Colorado 81009 (free).

To aid you in your planning, here's what airlines, buses, and railroads offer you in services.

(1) *Airlines*—The Federal Aviation Administration mandates each airline to have a policy for the handicapped traveler approved by the FAA.

Make your reservations early.

Describe the nature of your disability. Many airlines provide attendants to assist in boarding and at the terminal.

When transporting your own wheelchair, be sure you have attached your name and address.

Arrive at the airport early. This will enable you to board ahead of others.

Safety regulations require that canes and crutches be stowed, so you will have to relinquish them while on board.

Advise the airline in advance if you plan to bring special equipment such as oxygen.

(2) *Buses*—Greyhound has a "Helping Hand" program and Trailways offers a "Good Samaritan" package—both to enable a handicapped person to travel with an attendant for the price of a single ticket.

You must provide a certificate from a physician noting that an attendant's services are required to qualify.

You can get more information by contacting the Director of Customer Relations at Greyhound Lines, Greyhound Tower, Phoenix, Arizona 85077; phone (602) 248-2920; or Continental Trailways, 1512 Commerce Street, Dallas, Texas 75201; phone (214) 655-7900.

(3) *Railroads*—Amtrak has put into service new cars with special facilities for the disabled.

Blind passengers, in company with an attendant, can get a 25 per cent discount on the regular one-way fare by presenting a certificate from the American Foundation for the Blind.

You can get detailed information about rail facilities for the handicapped by calling Amtrak's toll-free number, (800) 523-5720, and asking for the Special Movements Desk.

Time Your Vacation Off-season

If you take a trip to Rome during the Thanksgiving holidays, you well may save 20 per cent on a double room at one well-known luxury hotel as against the price you would pay during the packed, pushy, peak tourist summer days.

If you rent a car for an Irish holiday in October, you'll save even larger percentages as against the sum you would pay for the same car during the summer—and you'll enjoy additional savings on plane and boat fares, hotel rooms, meals, local transportation, entertainment.

If you take a three-week package tour of eight European countries starting in October, you well might pay $100 less than the same tour would cost you in June–August.

And if you are planning a week's skiing vacation this winter, you'll save 20 per cent or more on hotel accommodations just by waiting until late in the ski season, when the snow will be just as skiable, but the influx of skiers and après skiers will have slowed to a snowplow's pace.

Timing is at the very core of saving money on your vacation—either in the United States or abroad. What's more, since millions of you now have the privilege of taking your vacation whenever you wish during the year, this is a major money-saving weapon you can use at your discretion and to whatever extent you want.

You might even split your vacation into two holidays, taking advantage of bargain off-season rates at traditional summer resorts, then repeating your move and taking advantage of off-season rates at traditional winter resorts.

A key fact is that in many resort areas across the United States the weather is far more trustworthy in off-season than it is at the season's height. May and October are particularly glorious months in many foreign lands.

As a general rule, the expensive "high season" in the Caribbean runs from mid-December until mid-March. In Europe, it's more or less the reverse: the high season begins with June and runs to (or, in some cases and places, through) September. A short "shoulder season" with intermediate prices sits between the high and low seasons.

Save by Going Where the Crowds Are Not

But even if you must take your vacation during the peak weeks of summer, you can save by heading for the less-crowded areas and by avoiding the well-known paths.

Don't squeeze yourself into the popular national parks, or visit a jammed resort. Head for one of the less crowded western Canadian provinces, the wide-open spaces of Montana or Idaho, or a remote section of Upper Michigan. Or go to New York City while New Yorkers are off summer-vacationing themselves. Miami and the Florida Keys offer reduced summer rates (though increasing numbers of tourists are discovering the fact). The ski towns of Colorado don't have as many summer visitors as winter skiers, yet their year-round weather and accommodations are delightful.

You also will be extra smart in midsummer if you avoid day-by-day travel, and instead find a single resort or hotel which can accept your reservation for a week or two.

Save on a Package Plan

Another key way to save is by buying a vacation "package." Many hotels in resort areas advertise special rates for stays of a weekend or a week or more. Often these are part of a transportation package with the airline or railroad serving the resort. Travel agents can suggest literally hundreds of good, money-saving packages.

Of if you are buying a tour, consider a package, too, on unescorted standard-itinerary tours sold by tour operators. Included in the flat, low price will be your air ticket, hotel room, and certain sight-seeing expeditions. You pay only for meals and extras and you decide how you'll spend most of your time.

Ask your travel agent about the many other ways you can cut your vacation costs today. (See pages 463–71, 800–1.)

How to Save on Shopping Under United States Customs Limitations

If you plan to do your Christmas shopping at cut-rate duty-free shops, be warned: there are many limitations imposed by U. S. Customs.

Check the current maximum in exemptions at the time of your trip (based on fair retail value of each item in the country where acquired) which may be brought in free of duty subject to limitations on liquors and cigars.

There are strict rules on exemptions.

—The articles must be obtained for your personal or household use.

—The articles must be brought with you at the time you return to the United States and properly declared. If you purchase items and leave them for alterations or other reasons, their value cannot be applied to your exemption when shipped at a later date.

—You must stay abroad at least forty-eight hours. This time limitation does not apply if you are returning from Mexico or the U. S. Virgin Islands.

—You cannot use the exemptions within the preceding thirty-day period.

You may bring back one quart of liquor if you are twenty-one years old or older.

If you return directly from the U. S. Virgin Islands, American Samoa, or

Guam, you may receive a higher customs exemption based on fair retail value of the articles in the country where acquired.

If you cannot claim the exemptions because of the thirty-day or forty-eight-hour limitations, you can bring in duty-free articles acquired abroad for your personal or household use if the retail value is not over $10.

You can send bona fide gifts of not more than $10 in fair retail value where shipped to your friends and relations in the United States duty-free—provided the same person does not receive more than $10 in gift shipments in one day.

You pay no duty at all on original oil paintings, stamps, coins, books, or on antiques more than one hundred years old. Trademark restrictions curtail the number or amounts of certain items you may bring home—particularly watches, perfumes, clocks, and cameras.

If you buy an automobile abroad and want to bring it back with you, you'll have to pay duty, of course—although under most circumstances you and other members of your family may use all your individual exemptions to reduce the value of the car for duty purposes. The rate of duty on a passenger car in the late 1970s was 3 per cent of the "dutiable value," as determined by the customs inspector.

For more details on customs regulations, request the following pamphlets from the U. S. Customs, P. O. Box 7118, Washington, D.C. 20044:

U. S. Customs Trademark Information;
Know Before You Go;
Customs Hints for Returning U.S. Residents; and
Importing a Car

How to Shop for a Vacation Tour

In recent years scandal after scandal has erupted across the front pages of the nation about "bargain" vacation tours. If you were a victim, you found many real costs hidden in the small print; or your costs were vastly increased when omitted essentials were included; or your deluxe accommodations were marginal at best; or you, a single, discovered too late that you had been booked into a double room with a stranger. Or many, many times your departure was at an abysmally "off" off-hour.

But in strictly economic terms, the package tour *is* the least expensive way to take a vacation, particularly a vacation abroad, today.

Just what is a package tour? It is not, as you might think, always a highly organized, closely timetabled tour during which the tour members eat, tour, sight-see, practically sleep together, and are herded in and out of places and countries with stopwatch precision.

Some travelers, primarily older couples, single persons, and inexperienced travelers, may prefer the security of the traditional escorted group and require only that the relatively small group fly together to and from their destinations.

A tour package does have, though, a predetermined price, number of features, and period of time. Within those limits, you, the traveler, can do whatever you please when you please. The greatest advantage to the traveler is that the cost of the land tour arrangements and air fare in the package is far less than the costs the traveler would otherwise pay for each item separately.

But how do *you* avoid the traps? How do *you* shop for a tour?

Obviously, the prime rule—which I cannot repeat too often—is to deal only with an airline or tour operator or travel agent you have checked thoroughly and are confident is honest, reliable, and well established.

Obviously, it's no more than common sense to phone a couple of airlines, car rental firms, and the like to double-check whether the price of the tour you want really represents a saving over booking your vacation yourself or through a travel agent.

Now, use this check list to help you decide what you want from a vacation tour, to compare one tour against another, and to alert you to possible hidden costs.

Price: What's the total, including taxes and other extras, for the accommodations you want? If the tag says from "$198," will this minimum give you the comforts you need?

What's included: How many meals are provided each day? Fixed menu—or a la carte? Who pays tips for porters and tour guides? Who pays the hotel bills? For sight-seeing buses and guides? For theater tickets? For transfers between airports, train stations, and midtown? For transportation to your hotel? Is air fare included? If a rented car is part of the package, who pays for gas, a very costly item in most foreign lands? Typical *exclusions:* one or two meals a day, porters' tips, airport taxes, laundry and valet costs, taxi fares, snacks, excess baggage costs.

Accommodations: What type and class of hotel rooms are offered? Are the hotels named? Is there a clause permitting the tour operator to book you into substitute hotels for those named? Is the stated price for double occupancy? If you're traveling alone, is there a supplementary charge for a single room? Are such basic amenities as a bathroom included? Is the hotel's location convenient to where you're likely to be spending your time?

You'll save a lot of money by not bolting from the "package" to higher-cost hotel rooms. But if you prefer fancier surroundings, find out from the airline or tour operator the conditions and costs of trading up, if you so desire.

Terms: When do you have to pay for the tour? Is a deposit required and, if so, how much? What are the conditions for getting a refund if you cancel out or change your vacation plans? If you're paying on the installment plan, what annual interest rate is charged on the outstanding balance and how does this rate compare with the rate you might get on a loan from your bank or savings institution?

Your companions: How many other people will be along? Will they be interesting company for you—if you must be in close quarters (such as a bus) for long periods? Is there a theme for the tour to attract people with interests similar to yours?

Timing: How far in advance must you sign up? Choose a departure date and itinerary? Make a deposit? Pay in full?

Free time: How much will you have in each place you visit? Can you duck out for an afternoon or a day or two without being left behind, if you so wish? What's the likely pace of the tour? Will you be up to it? (As a general rule, if you travel more than nine or ten hours a day or more than 250 miles a day, you well might find your trip exhausting.) Will local guides shepherd you on certain legs of your trip and supplement your regular guide?

Find out these details *before* you sign up!

What a Travel Agent Can (and Cannot) Do for You

Let's say you are planning your first major vacation trip—either in the United States or abroad—and you have a general idea where you want to go and what you want to do. But you know absolutely nothing about costs, schedules, hotel accommodations. Just what could a travel agent do for you at what (if any) cost? How and where do you find a suitable travel agency?

A good travel agent should be well supplied with air and boat schedules; rates and costs for various types of travel; details on tours and group arrangements, schedules of festivals and other special events, hotel-motel room rates, cruise information.

A knowledgeable travel agent can:

• Guide you in applying for a passport and/or visa, alert you on immunizations you'll need for travel abroad, fill you in on customs rules and regulations.

• Sign you up for almost any kind of group tour (including tours the travel agency itself is putting together and selling).

• Make almost any kind of reservation or buy any kind of tickets for you —hotel, motel, plane, train, theater, ballet, bullfight, etc.—although many travel agencies do not sell bus and train tickets or short-haul air tickets or freighter accommodations.

• Sell you traveler's checks and counsel you on how to get the best deal when you change money abroad.

• Steer you to bargain vacation packages—including transportation, hotel rooms, car rentals, meals, etc., off-season deals, places which cater to and offer cut rates to families traveling with children.

• Tell you what are the "on" seasons, the "off" seasons, and the "shoulder" seasons in between—in various parts of the world.

- Advise on tipping customs, what kind of clothes to take, what kind of weather to expect, good restaurants.
- "Tailor-make" a trip or tour for you and your family—to fit *your* tastes, *your* interests, *your* budget. This type of trip is known in the travel trade as an Independent Inclusive Tour (IIT) and this category is further divided into the Domestic Independent Tour (DIT) and the Foreign Independent Tour (FIT).

How much do travel agents' services cost you, the traveler? How and by whom are these costs paid?

The bulk of travel agents' costs are paid by the airlines, steamship lines, railroads, hotels and resorts, tour operators, in the form of commissions. But you, the customer, well may be charged for such extras as:

> certain telegrams and long-distance telephone calls;
> reticketing;
> making reservations in certain foreign hotels;
> short-stay hotel reservations.

Many travel agents also charge you for arranging a special, fancy custom-designed trip abroad.

Okay, now that you know what travel agents do—and don't do—how do you find a good one?

Get recommendations from friends and others who have been customers of a travel agency with which you are considering doing business.

Try to find a travel agent who has himself (or herself) traveled in the area where *you* intend to go—and ask just how extensive the travel was.

Take time to *visit* the travel agency. How thorough and "personal" is the agent's interview with you to discover your travel needs and wants? What "extras" are offered—i.e., reading list on the countries you intend to visit?

Discuss your budget as well as your travel tastes frankly.

Ask if the agency is a member of the American Society of Travel Agents. (This is only a clue, since many reputable travel agencies are *not* members.)

Do not be misled by the size of a travel agency, for this is *not* necessarily an indication of the quality of its services. Good ones come both large and small.

Note whether the agent seems genuinely interested in steering you to travel bargains or whether he or she tries to push you into more expensive ways to "get there" than you can afford (remember, travel agents are paid commissions based on the cost of the accommodations). If the latter, go to another agency.

If you are booking a tour being sold by the travel agency, nail down details on deposits you'll be required to make, policies on refunds and cancellation fees. Each agency sets its own rules in this area and if the agency fails voluntarily to spell out the rules, *ask* what they are. You may lose 100 per cent of whatever amount you have paid toward a tour—if this is the written policy of the tour operator and/or travel agency selling the deal. The loss could include even air fares you've paid for overseas tours.

If a travel agency promises to make refunds for cancellations you have made for valid reasons, find out just what constitutes valid reasons.

If a "slight" penalty is to be imposed in the event you cancel, check just how slight is "slight."

If you ask a travel agent to draw up a special itinerary for you, find out in advance what the costs will be, whether you'll be required to make a deposit, and, if so, how much. The charge for a custom-planned trip can be as high as 25 to 50 per cent of the value of the package—if the planning involves a lot of the agent's time, thought, and expertise.

Consider purchasing some form of trip cancellation insurance. You will be partially or fully reimbursed—depending on your policy—if you have to cancel the trip. Shop around for cost and coverage; they vary. Some companies also will write baggage insurance in connection with trip cancellation insurance. You can get trip cancellation insurance through a travel agent although the agent may carry only one company's insurance, however.

If you have any suspicions about a travel agent with whom you're considering doing any substantial amount of business, check the agency's reputation with the local Better Business Bureau.

Do-It-Yourself Travel Planning

If you are booking on your own into one of the large hotels and hotel chains, use their toll-free telephone reservations number. You'll get an instant answer by phone or a letter at times by return mail to confirm your reservation.

If you are making your own airline reservations, ask any major airline to advise you on other airline schedules as well as on special rates offered by all airlines. Most will freely do so.

Call Amtrak for most U.S. rail travel. The toll-free number throughout the United States for reservations and information: (800) 523-5720. More than five thousand travel agents around the world also are authorized to sell Amtrak tickets. In Canada, contact Via Rail Canada, P.O. Box 8116, 1801 McGill College, Montreal, Quebec, Canada, H3C 3N3.

The two best-known domestic bus lines are Greyhound and Trailways. Both have offices located at Eighth Avenue and Forty-first Street, New York, New York 10014 (the New York Port Authority bus terminal).

Most of the key steamship lines have headquarters offices in New York City.

Look into the wide array of overseas travel information available from each major country's government travel office in New York (and, in some cases, in other cities as well).

Write the state Tourist Information Bureaus in the states you want to visit within our borders or the U. S. National Park Service, Department of the Interior, Eighteenth and C Streets, Washington, D.C. 20240.

Go to the nearest passport office for guidance on how to apply for a passport. In some cities and towns which have no passport office, this information is now available at the U.S. post office along with passport application forms; elsewhere, get the information and application forms from the clerk of a federal or state court or from your county clerk's office.

For details on international auto registration certificates and international driver's licenses, check the local affiliate of the American Automobile Association. And if you're a member of this organization, use its facilities to help plan your trip—including information on roads under construction and speed traps; maps; itinerary recommendation; regional guides to motels, restaurants (with ratings and tourist attractions).

Check your automobile insurance to be sure it covers you in all states you will visit. (Failure to take care of this would be very costly in the event of an accident.) If you will be traveling in Canada, ask your insurance company for a Canada Non-Resident Inter-Province Motor Vehicle Liability Insurance Card, required to prove your coverage to provincial officials. In Mexico, auto insurance laws are very strict. U.S. insurance is usually not valid for more than forty-eight hours after entry and you will need a more expensive Mexican policy for longer stays. *Be sure* to look into the car insurance problem *before* you leave home.

Study at least a couple of travel guides and books, which you can borrow from your library or buy at a bookstore. (Some have coupons which will buy you discounts for various tourist services.) Among the best ones:

Fielding's Travel Guide to Europe and many other Fielding guides (William Morrow).

Frommer's *Europe on $10 a Day* and other $10 and $15 a Day Guides (Simon & Schuster).

Fodor's *Europe* and other Fodor Guides (McKay).

Let's Go: Europe, a Student Guide (Harvard Student Agencies, Inc., distributed through E. P. Dutton & Co.).

The Mobil Travel Guides (Simon & Schuster).

Rand McNally Guidebooks: *Road Atlas, Travel Trailer Guide, Guidebook to Campgrounds, Campground and Trailering Guide, National Park Guide, Ski Guide.*

Woodall's *Parks and Campgrounds* (Woodall Publishing).

The Michelin Guides to France and other European countries and Michelin's *Green Guide to New York City* (Simon & Schuster).

A to Z Guides by Robert S. Kane (Doubleday).

Blue Guides (Rand McNally).

AAA Tour Book, one for each region of the United States; also *Eastern and*

Western AAA Campground Guide—all available to AAA members only.
The Official Student Travel Guide (International Student Travel Conference; 1560 Broadway, New York).
Whole World Handbook—A Student Guide to Work, Study, and Travel Abroad, 1980–81 Edition, 205 East 42nd Street, New York, New York 10017.
1001 Sources for Free Travel Information (Jens Jurgen, Kings Park, New York 11754).
PanAm's New Horizons World Guide and other PanAm guides to the United States, Canada, South America, European countries, Africa, Asia, the Middle East, and the Caribbean.

And finally the most important rule for all do-it-yourselfers: *plan ahead*, just as far ahead as you possibly can.

Do's and Don'ts for Cutting Your Hotel Bills

If you're a typical American today, your spending for hotel and/or motel bills will run into hundreds of dollars a year. So will your spending for food and drink away from home—on long weekends, holidays, vacations.

If you're typical, you'll also "waste" as much as $2.00 of every $10 you spend simply because you do not know the basic do's and don'ts for saving on your hotel and motel bills:

Do, when you make a room reservation, ask for a room by price category. (Most hotels have three categories: economy, standard, and luxury.) If you want the minimum rate, ask for it. Virtually all good hotels now provide radio, TV, phone, air conditioning—and if the hotel isn't full, many will give you better than minimum room accommodations even though you pay the lowest rate.

Don't underestimate the cost of room service. There usually is a room-service charge added to the bill the waiter gives you and the prices on the room-service menu usually are higher than prices for the same or similar items in the hotel coffee shop. Room service is a luxury which makes sense when you're on a special vacation, but it can add many dollars to your bills if you are a frequent traveler.

Do be careful about check-out time. If you want to stay an hour or two after check-out time, notify the manager or assistant manager directly, and unless your room is needed at once, he'll probably allow you to stay without charge. But if you stay as long as three hours after check-out time, the hotel may charge you $5.00 extra, and if you stay into the evening hours, you may be charged for a full extra day.

Don't, if you're traveling with your family, fail to inquire about the "family plan" that many hotels feature. It's ridiculous to pay for an extra room when—for no charge or for at most a nominal fee—the hotel will provide a folding bed which can be set up in your room. And this rule may apply to kids into their teens. Also, many hotels have special meal-ticket programs which will cut down on your family's dining bills.

Do take advantage of the toll-free electronic reservations system which most large chains provide. By doing so, you can save the expense of a phone call or of a wire ahead to hotels in other cities you are planning to visit.

Don't, if you are driving your own car, ignore the extent to which overnight parking fees can throw your budget out of line. Make sure the midtown hotel you choose offers free parking either on the premises or nearby. Even in New York City, major hotel chains park cars without charge. Frequently, however, a charge is made each time you take your car out of the garage.

Do find out in advance if the hotel at which you're planning to stay is on the regular route of an airport bus or limousine. If it isn't at one of the regular stops, you'll have the added expense of a taxi to get you to your destination.

Do take another look at famed old downtown hotels which you may bypass because you assume they're too expensive. To meet the competition of motor inns, airport and suburban hotels, many of these great establishments have cut their rates. You may be concentrating on saving a tip or two by staying in a motel, but as one great hotel man remarked, "I could never understand why anybody would want to spend $2.00 more for a room to save 25 cents on a tip."

Don't pay for the use of a hotel or motel swimming pool, sauna, gym, etc. (which may add $1.00 to $2.00 to daily room rates) if you don't intend to use the facilities.

And *do*, finally, try to plan your travels around the hotel package deals—off-season bargains, weekend plans, family specials—I've underlined in the preceding pages.

Whom and How to Tip

The old guideline for restaurants, resort hotels, taxis, etc.—tip 15 per cent of the bill—has been firmly upped to 15 to 20 per cent of the total if you want to be known as generous.

The old rule for *porters* carrying your luggage also has been upped from 25 cents a bag to a minimum of 50 cents, and frequently $1.00 is the minimum if you want to avoid scowls and recriminations from the porter.

The minimum tip for *taxi drivers* in big cities is 25 cents—which works out to 25 per cent of a $1.00 fare.

Of course, many travelers still tip well below these levels—and a surprising number of skinflints don't tip *anyone any* percentage at all. But tipping remains an economic institution in this land, and so:

The hotel doorman: Tip him 50 cents when you arrive, if he carries your baggage to the registration desk, $1.00 if you have three or more bags. Give him 25 cents each time he finds you a taxi—but give only a "thank you" if he merely waves forward a cab waiting in front of the hotel.

The bellhop: Tip him as you tipped the doorman, increasing your tips if your luggage is very heavy or cumbersome. Whenever he delivers anything give him 25 cents even if it is just a newspaper costing 10 cents. If he has paid for the item, of course, reimburse him.

The wine steward: Tip him 10 to 15 per cent of the cost of the wine, at the end of the meal.

Room service: Tip 50 cents each time an item is delivered. But tip $1.00 if the waiter brings ice and drink mixers and $1.50 to $2.00 if he brings a whole tray full of soda, glasses, ice, and other drinking equipment. When you have a meal sent to your room, tip as you would in a restaurant—15 to 20 per cent of the check.

Valet: Tip 50 cents per delivery. If you give the valet a rush order, though, or ask for extraordinary service—say a suit pressed and back within the hour—give him $1.00.

Chambermaid: You need not tip her if you spend only a night or two at a regular commercial hotel, but it's increasingly recommended that you leave her 50 cents a day if you stay longer. Leave the money in an envelope addressed "For the Chambermaid in Room ———" at the reception desk the last day of your stay and tell the housekeeping department you left it. Tip her $1.00 to $2.00 if you have a cocktail party in your room or suite, involving a big cleanup job for her. In a resort hotel, the standard minimum tip for the chambermaid is 50 cents per day for a single person, $1.00 per day for a couple, more for special service.

Travel abroad: Even if a substantial service charge has already been added to your hotel or restaurant bill, the trend today is toward adding another 10 per cent to the total rather than just leaving the small change. The trend also is toward personal distribution of the money to make sure the chambermaid, doorman, waiter, or others who have served you actually get the tips. And the trend too is for tipping above and beyond these percentages for any extra special services—for tips frequently are the sole source of income for service personnel in Europe and elsewhere abroad.

At a resort hotel—including those operating on the American plan (all meals included) or modified American plan (breakfast and dinner included) —a service charge of 15 per cent or more may be added to your total bill. If it isn't, tip your dining-room waiter 15 per cent of your restaurant bill. You'll probably find details on how much of your daily room rate is for your meals in the hotel directory in the dresser drawer of your room, but if not, ask the assistant manager or social director for pertinent facts. Tip bellboys 50 cents for each bag they carry and tip your chambermaid and pool boy 50 cents each per day per person, as you leave. Tip your resort's hairdresser 15 to 20 per cent.

Visiting friends: If there is a housekeeper or cook who helps make your stay more gracious and comfortable, you, as a visiting couple, might properly tip at least $1.00 to $2.00 a day as a "thank you."

P.S.: Perhaps as you grumble and struggle over whether to tip 10 per cent or 15 per cent or 20 per cent or whatever, you might remember that, by one definition, "TIPS" were originally intended as a means "To Insure Prompt Service." This reminder might help guide you to the right amount for the right persons.

AND TIPPING ON WINTER CRUISES

Let's say you are now making plans for your first winter vacation on a cruise ship. You've read all the brochures on what to wear, what to see, what to do. But one angle I'll wager you've missed is: whom to tip how much. Even if you already have been on every type of winter holiday, I'll bet you have made plenty of inadvertent tipping blunders.

Here, too, tipping expectations are being revised sharply upward in many instances from the old 10 to 15 per cent range to a new 15 to 20 per cent range—and employees who never were considered eligible for tips suddenly are turning up on the lists. Following, therefore, you will find up-to-date rules for cruise-ship tipping:

Tip your dining-room steward and your room steward or stewardess a minimum of $1.00 each per day per person. Thus, if you are a couple on a two-week cruise, tip a total of about $30. If your cruise lasts a week or less, tip at least $10 for each steward—at the end of the trip.

Tip the deck steward 50 cents a day or about $2.50 to $3.00 a week. Tip the headwaiter in the dining room a couple of dollars, plus $1.00 or $2.00 each time he performs some special service for you. Tip the bartender 15 to 20 per cent each time you are served a new drink. Tip the telephone operator $1.00 or $2.00 if she puts through complicated ship-to-shore calls for you.

On shore, tip tour guides 50 cents to 15 per cent of the cost of the tour if it's a half-day tour, $1.00 if it's a full-day tour. Tip the men who carry your luggage in U.S. ports at least 35 cents per bag—even if the dock is plastered with "no tipping" signs.

Don't tip the cruise's social director; or the person who leads calisthenics; or the purser or other ship's officers; or customs men in port. If you are in doubt, ask for guidelines from your travel agent, the cruise director, or the ship's purser. The excursion agent on board your ship can tell you if tipping is expected anywhere ashore.

Save by Hosteling

One of the very least expensive ways to "see the world" today is to use the world's extraordinary network of youth hostels. These are inexpensive dormitory-style accommodations providing shelter, bunks, or beds, and often some sort of kitchen facilities. Fees in the United States are typically $2.00 to $5.00 per day for lodging; abroad, fees are somewhat lower.

There are some 4,500 hostels today in 50 different countries, and the youth hosteling organizations offer a long list of special bargains to hostelers. You can go hosteling by foot, canoe, bike, public transportation, or car. You can go alone, or with friends, or with a group and trained leader.

Typical cost of a thirty-day American Youth Hostel tour within the United States in the late 1970s was in the $350 to $500 range and in the $1,250 to $1,500 range for tours abroad. Included were: transportation from a specified departure point; all costs of accommodations and food; insurance; leadership; and transportation back to the original departure point. *Not* included in this price were: equipment you must have (generally simple camping gear); spending money; cost of passports; bicycle shipping; transportation to or from trip starting point; AYH membership dues; and an emergency fund which must be deposited with the trip leader for unexpected expenses (unused amounts are returned).

Hostelers on a National Group Trip must be at least fourteen years old or must have completed tenth grade. For Hawaii, hostelers must be sixteen years old. For all trips, hostelers must be in good physical and mental health as certified by a physician. On International Trips campers must be at least sixteen years old or have previously completed a National Trip. There is no upper age limit, but most trips are intended for young travelers in good physical condition. A few, however, are for adults only.

Your passport to hostels throughout the world is a pass issued by AYH.

A junior pass in the late 1970s (for people under age eighteen) cost $5.00; a senior pass for older hostelers cost $11; a family membership covering children up to age eighteen cost $12. Only individual passes—junior and senior—can be used outside the United States.

For detailed information on trips and applications for passes, write American Youth Hostels, AYH National Campus, Delaplane, Virginia 22025.

Bus Passes and Bike Trails

Another way to cover a large territory on your vacation—at very low cost—is to go by bus. You can now get a special type of bus ticket, similar to the well-known Eurailpass, which will give you virtually unlimited bus travel in the United States and Canada for sixty days. Greyhound calls its version Ameripass and Continental Trailways calls its ticket Eaglepass, but both cost about $225 for thirty days and about $325 for sixty days. This worked out to $6.00 to $8.00 a day in the late 1970s—a clue to how great a bargain the passes really are.

Your only limitations in using either pass are: you may not take more than four round trips between any two points; neither pass is valid during the peak summer travel months.

More than 150,000 miles of routes in forty-eight states and Canada are yours to choose from, and Greyhound's pass also gives you a variety of discounts up to 20 per cent on hotels, car rentals, tours, and other services. Greyhound's pass may be used on the Trailways system where Greyhound does not provide service and vice versa. But it is most convenient to buy your pass from the line which serves your travel plans best.

An increasingly popular way to go camping—or just to sight-see at your vacation destination—is by bicycle. You can even combine it with bus travel. Bicycles are proliferating and it is becoming easier all the time to find places to combine this sport with camping. The Bureau of Outdoor Recreation, U. S. Department of Interior, estimates that there will be more than 200,000 miles of bike routes in the United States by the end of this decade. Ohio, for instance, has more than a half-dozen biking routes running through the most scenic areas of the state, and more are being laid out all the time. The average length of these routes is about 30 miles and all are marked by standard bikeway signs. (*Ohio Is Happening Along Bikeways,* from the Ohio Department of Development, Box 1011, Columbus, Ohio 43216, describes the trails.)

Or you can ride through Indiana's covered-bridge country on a bikeway running through Parke County. A longer trail is the towpath of the old Chesapeake and Ohio Canal from Georgetown, D.C., to Cumberland, Maryland—184 miles. Or you can ride 320 miles on the Wisconsin State Bikeway from the Mississippi River to Lake Michigan.

Many more trails are being planned for the future; most spurred locally, but some of them with financial help from the federal government. But you don't have to wait for official designation of trails. With a little help from cycling clubs and friends, plus some practice and experience on your own, you'll be able to choose the most enjoyable routes yourself from highway maps and government topographic maps.

Also, send for *The AYH North American Bike Atlas,* which describes sixty one-day trips throughout the United States and one hundred one-week to one-month trips throughout the United States and one hundred one-week to one-month trips in Canada, Mexico, and the Caribbean ($2.45; American Youth Hostels, Inc., AYH National Campus, Delaplane, Virginia 22025).

Try combining hostels, state and private campgrounds, perhaps a friendly farmer or two, and even on occasional motel. You'll surely find you can work out literally hundreds of real cycling adventures almost anywhere in the country—at astonishingly low cost. (The rules on how to *buy* a bicycle are in Chapter 7, "Getting to and from—by Wings, Wheels, and Water.")

Money-Saving Guides for Camping Trips

During most of the summer weeks each summer, tens of millions of you go off on camping trips and in the process spend more than $1 billion on travel trailers alone, plus hundreds of millions on camping equipment, plus millions more on getting to and from the camping grounds, on overnight fees, and on other expenses.

Until recently, camping in the United States meant stuffing a sleeping bag, some warm clothes, a few cooking utensils, and first-aid equipment into a rucksack, slinging it over your back, and heading for the hills. But today the typical camper travels in a fully equipped trailer or motor home, cooks on gas stoves instead of campfires, watches TV instead of beavers. Today's typical campsite provides creature comforts ranging from hot showers to hair dryers, clothes washers to canteens.

Obviously, camping has become a significant factor in the outdoor recreation industry and also a potentially whopping expense to the individual camper or camping family.

As one measure of camping's spectacular growth just in this decade, the Rand McNally *Campground and Trailer Park Guide* listed more than 20,000 campgrounds in the United States and Canada (with more than 600,000 individual campsites), up from 10,000 campgrounds listed in 1961. Rand McNally also counted thousands of camping areas specifically set up to accommodate travel trailers, with more than 400,000 separate sites for recreational vehicles.

If you're the back-to-nature type and really prefer to rough it, you and your family can go on a camping trip by foot or by canoe in any one of thousands of national and state parks for as little as $100 a week,* assuming you don't go too far from home and you already own basic equipment such as cooking utensils, sleeping bags, and backpacks. Even if you have to rent these basics, the total cost for a family of three or four needn't run over $200 a week. But if you prefer the "motel in the wilderness" type of camping, involving rented travel trailers, overnight fees at private campgrounds, electricity and gas bills, etc., costs can rise to $300 or more a week.

If you're considering taking your first camping expedition, your best bet is to avoid an outlay of hundreds of dollars to buy trailers, tents, etc. Rent them instead. Buy as little as possible until you find out whether or not you like the whole idea of camping and, if so, what style of camping you enjoy most.

If you decide to go the recreational vehicle route, you can choose from a

---

* All of these figures prevailed in the late 1970s.

wide range of travel trailers, campers, motor homes, etc.—at an even wider array of prices. (You will find the money-saving guides on buying recreational vehicles on pages 453–55.)

Another possibility is a U.S.- or foreign-made small camper which you can rent for about the price of renting a car at an airport. This type of camper will sleep four people and has the full range of kitchen equipment and other camping gear. The vehicles are available in many major U.S. cities and throughout Europe.

Here are more tips if you prefer to rough it:

The federal government offers a $10 Golden Eagle Passport card which will admit you and any passengers in your car to all areas of the national park system and give you the use of most facilities and services provided by the National Park Service during the year. (A free version, available to citizens more than sixty-two years old, also gives a 50 per cent discount on all special user fees on all federal lands—not just the national parks.)

Get your pass at any national park, at most national forests, or from any first- or second-class post office. Also write the U. S. Superintendent of Documents, Washington, D.C. 20402, for brochures entitled *Camping in the National Park System, Fishing in the National Park System,* and *Boating in the National Park System* (modest cost for each).

If you're inclined toward a really "wild" camping experience, full of educational information about the wild areas you visit and the ways to get there, it is hard to beat the package wilderness tours offered on a non-profit basis by several large conservation outdoor sport associations.

• If you are camping in a national park, choose your campsites carefully. Each year, more than 50 million people somehow squeeze themselves into fewer than 1 million campsites. In the process, many areas become overused, while some are underused. The name of the game, of course, is to find the latter.

• Be on the lookout for the creation of new national parks on the very edges of major cities. The current proposal of the Interior Department is to make 1 million park acres easily accessible near every city of 250,000 or more people.

• But even before these new areas are created, study the areas close to your home carefully. Often you'll find little gems of wilderness in the midst of urban areas, unfrequented by crowds whose urge to escape leads them to overlook their immediate neighborhood and to travel as far as possible. If you find one of these, restful camping may be yours for very little money and travel time.

• If your interest extends beyond camping to the more exacting sports—such as mountaineering, rock climbing, white-water canoeing, or scuba diving—you'll need special instructions as well as special gear. First-aid courses are also valuable if you plan to do much camping. You can get this training most economically from experienced friends or from local clubs, who usually share their knowledge willingly and without charge.

Nationally known groups, such as the Sierra Club or the Red Cross, are sound non-profit alternatives though they may charge for direct expenses. There are also dozens of commercial schools, whose reputations and costs are usually easy to check through knowledgeable devotees of the sport.

Tourism and Energy Shortages

Tourism is defined as travel 50 miles or more one way, in any form of transport, for any purpose other than commuting for work. It is a vital part of our country's life-style, employing 4 million people and accounting for $60 to $65 billion of spending each year (food, lodging, public transportation, fuel, auto operating costs, entertainment, sight-seeing). It is a labor-intensive, service industry, and in every state tourism is vital to our economic well-being (we take in each other's washing). In three states—Florida, Hawaii, and Nevada—tourism is the leading industry. In six others—California, Texas, Pennsylvania, Illinois, Michigan, Ohio—tourism brings in more than $1 billion annually. In seven other areas—Maine, Alaska, Arizona, Washington, D.C., the Virgin Islands, Puerto Rico, and Guam—the dependence on the travel dollar is extremely heavy.

Not only for your own physical and mental well-being, but also for your nation's welfare, the thing to do in this era of energy shortages is to plan your vacation so that, with the use of 75 per cent of the energy you consumed before the shortages emerged, you can enjoy 10 per cent of your life-style.

Here, therefore, are tips on travel designed specifically to help you conserve energy:

• Investigate with much more care than you formerly did fly/drive bus/drive, rail/drive, fly/sight-see packages. Be as flexible on dates and routing as you can and use public transportation where feasible.

• Fly/drive vacations now come in all types and sizes, involving rental cars and hotels. Nearly all the airlines have them. Check with a reputable travel agent for pertinent details.

• "Take me along" vacations are booming. For the very simple reason that it saves money, families are planning their vacations around convention and business trips.

• If you like national parks, you'll have no trouble getting to the park by bus these days as well as rail. And buses within the parks have been vastly improved too. There are two hundred park systems located within 100 miles of a metropolitan center—involving the use of a bus rather than a tankful of gas.

• Hotels and motels are offering minivacations and "escape weekends" to people within 100 miles at up to 50 per cent discounts. Most major attractions are within 100 miles of airports or rail terminals or can be reached by bus.

• When traveling by air, be much more flexible on dates, avoid Fridays and Sundays if possible. On routing, adjust your schedule if need be and don't insist on non-stop.

• Let your travel agent make one booking, and have a confirmed reservation. Avoid double booking—which means you are depriving someone else of a seat.

• Investigate Amtrak, especially for family travel and short-haul business travel. Railroads and motor coaches are the most economical users of fuel.

• Discover your own area close to home by motor coach. Travel in groups. Avoid congested areas by private auto. On these trips, you really waste gas because of traffic tie-ups and idling motors.

• Take buses to the airport, get there early, avoid gas-eating traffic jams, try not to meet friends at the airports.

• Forget haphazard touring. Do not plan an auto trip without a plan. Know where you want to go, when. Buy guides, know your wayside itinerary, make reservations.

• Now the universities are trying to lure us with vacation and travel opportunities on college campuses and surrounding areas. Mort's *Guide to Low-Cost Vacations and Lodgings on College Campuses* (Check prices in bookstores or from CMG Publications, Box 630, Princeton, New Jersey 08540) describes the great recreational and cultural facilities of 180 colleges in the United States and Canada which formerly have been enjoyed mostly by students but now are open to all of us at a fraction of commercial recreational, food, and lodging prices.

You need only make relatively easy adjustments. Try them, you'll even like them.

The Wilderness Society operates dozens of tours ranging from hiking, backpacking, and canoeing to horseback riding in wilderness areas throughout the United States. Emphasis is on getting to know the wilderness in a non-destructive way. (For information, write to the Wilderness Society, Western Regional Office, 4260 Evans Avenue, Denver, Colorado 80222.)

The American River Touring Association runs an extensive program of river touring in many distant parts of the world as well as in the United States. Prices in the late 1970s ranged from under $100 for weekend trips to up to $1,500 to $2,000 and more for international expeditions of from fifteen to twenty days.

The Sierra Club, the oldest and one of the largest (180,000 members) wilderness conservation clubs in the United States, sponsors hundreds of wilderness outings each year, including river trips (by raft or canoe), hiking/backpacking trips, and saddle trips. You may be continually moving or operate in a more leisurely fashion from a base camp. Many trips are specifically designed as family trips. You can write the Sierra Club for a publication describing the entire year's trips at 530 Bush Street, San Francisco, California 94108. Chapters also organize a regular schedule of local trips throughout the year at very low cost.

14

SEX ... AND ... MONEY

"Mingling Singles"	818
How Much Does It Cost to Get Married?	819
The Staggering Bridal Market	819
Figuring Out Wedding Costs	819
Get It in Writing!	821
twelve rules for buying engagement and wedding rings	821
stationery	822
photographs	823
flowers	824
music	824
wedding finery	825
transportation	825
catering—put it in writing!	825
What Happens if Plans Change?	826
The Honeymoon and Its Expenses	826
How to Save on Your Wedding and Honeymoon	827
Rules for Buying Wedding Gifts	827
After the Wedding Is Over	828
A Bride's Guide to Credit	828
The Low Cost of Not Having a Baby (or Having Fewer of Them)	830
the need for family planning	830
getting low-cost or free help in family planning	830
Contraception: Comparing the Options	831
methods available	831

CONTRACEPTION: COMPARING THE OPTIONS (CONTD)
- THE PILL — 832
- INTRAUTERINE DEVICE (IUD) — 833
- DIAPHRAGM (WITH CREAM, JELLY, OR FOAM) — 834
- FOAM, CREAM, OR JELLY ALONE — 835
- VAGINAL SUPPOSITORIES — 836
- RHYTHM METHOD — 837
- CONDOM — 838
- FEMALE STERILIZATION — 838
- MALE STERILIZATION — 839
- WITHDRAWAL (COITUS INTERRUPTUS) — 840
- DOUCHING — 840

COMPARATIVE COSTS OF CONTRACEPTIVE METHODS — 840
STERILIZATION — 841
BASIC FACTS ABOUT ABORTION — 842
HOW TO SHOP FOR—AND REDUCE THE COSTS OF—AN ABORTION — 843
INSURANCE COVERAGE: FOR ABORTIONS; FOR STERILIZATION — 845
TAX TIPS ON BIRTH CONTROL PILLS, ABORTIONS, STERILIZATION — 846
HOW MUCH DOES IT COST TO HAVE (OR ADOPT) A BABY? — 846
RUNDOWN ON COSTS OF HAVING A BABY — 846
TEN WAYS TO CUT THE HIGH COSTS OF MOTHERHOOD — 848
CHECK LIST FOR YOUR OWN BABY COSTS — 849
AND IF YOU ADOPT A CHILD? — 852
THE SOARING COSTS OF REARING A CHILD — 853
- WHERE THE MONEY GOES — 853
- WHAT THE MOTHER "LOSES": THE HIDDEN COSTS — 854

SO YOU WANT A DIVORCE . . . CAN YOU AFFORD ONE? — 855
- A "GROWTH INDUSTRY" — 855
- CAN YOU AFFORD A DIVORCE? — 855
- DOWNWARD TREND OF LEGAL FEES — 856
- ALIMONY AND CHILD SUPPORT — 856
- TAX CONSEQUENCES — 857
- ALIMONY FOR HUSBANDS — 857
- "HIDDEN" COSTS — 858
  - Family House — 858
  - Stocks, Bonds, and Other Assets — 858
  - Life Insurance Policies — 858
  - Medical Care — 858
  - College Expenses — 859

SEX ... AND ... MONEY

So You Want a Divorce ... Can You Afford One? (CONTD)
    MORE ON COSTS, TRAUMA, AND LAWYERS   859
    OTHER NEW TRENDS IN DIVORCE   860
        Grounds   860
        Ownership of Property   860
        Flexible Maintenance   861
        Custody   861
        Joint Custody   861
        Mingling Singles   861
        Grandparents' Visitation   861
    NO SUBSTITUTE FOR PLANNING IN ADVANCE   862
    TRACING ABSENTEE FATHERS   862

"Mingling Singles"

As the 1980s approached, close to 600,000 women in the under-twenty-five age bracket were living "alone" and loving it—more than double the number who were so living at the start of the decade. As for young men, the number of men under twenty-five living "alone" had nearly tripled from early 1970 to the late 1970s. And there were more than 4 million men and women in the under-thirty-five age group living "by themselves."

But were they living alone? Of course not! They were mostly "mingling singles"—young couples who had (temporarily, if not permanently) rejected the whole concept of a marriage with the attendant "nuisances" of ceremony and formality. Their substitute was a commitment without the legal ties so traditional in the United States and most other nations throughout the world.

Several states permit common-law marriage if both partners are free from other legal ties. Simply by the acknowledgement of married status over a period of time, common-law marriage is recognized in some states. In others, vows said in private are valid. And in still others, it is clearly illegal for members of the opposite sex to cohabit, even though today it's customary to wink at these laws.

A commitment is . . . a commitment, not to be taken lightly, even though to some it may appear to be rather a *noncommittal* arrangement!

In California, for example, where common-law marriage is not recognized, a precedent was set in the late 1970s: after a couple who had lived together openly for quite a while broke up, the woman sued (and won) her share of community property, as though they had been married.

If you are living with a member of the opposite sex to whom you are not married, *check now* with a lawyer to determine how you should establish your status clearly, especially when leases, insurances, wills, and other legal documents are concerned.

From a practical viewpoint, you also would be wise to keep accurate records of what's yours and what's his or hers, so that—should you decide to part—there need be no wrangling, and ownership of property is clearly defined. Until a lawyer tells you otherwise, beware of signing papers jointly (even Christmas cards), sharing major purchases, and letting people think of you officially as "Mr. and Mrs."

For "mingling singles" budgets see pages 43–46.

How Much Does It Cost to Get Married?

To the casual observer, weddings may appear to be definitely on the decline and young women may seem to be scorning legal ties and to be delighting in having illegitimate children. But well publicized as that image may be, it is just not the picture of the average young woman today. The fact is that no matter how casual (sloppy) you are in dressing, no matter how vehement and vocal you are about living according to your own ideals and goals rather than your parents' traditions, when it comes to your wedding, Miss America, you want a formal gown, attendants, and as elaborate a reception as your family can afford. Out of every five young brides, *Bride's* magazine reports, four choose a traditional, formal wedding. Out of every five, more than four brides still receive a diamond engagement ring.

The Staggering Bridal Market

Marriage itself is a powerful force in the U.S. economy, with more than 2 million marriages a year accounting for an estimated $12 billion-plus in annual retail sales and services.

If you are merely an average first-time bride and groom, with an average number of relatives and friends to be invited to your wedding, according to statistics gathered by *Modern Bride,* you will spend, roughly, $650 on wedding and engagement rings, $1,500 on a wedding reception (including $250 on a wedding dress), $1,250 for a honeymoon, trousseau, and luggage, and close to $3,500 on furnishing your first home. And that doesn't even take into consideration what others will spend on gifts for you, and such major expenditures as a new home, apartment, car, insurance.

Figuring Out Wedding Costs

Although cost is hardly the romantic part of a wedding, it's of bread-and-butter concern to the people who pay the bills after the bells have rung. Traditionally, the bride's family is responsible for both the wedding ceremony and the reception; the groom's family gives the rehearsal dinner; bridesmaids give a party for the bride, and ushers give a "bachelor party" for the groom. But today many weddings are limited to a ceremony and reception with the groom's family and even the bride and groom themselves sharing the cost of the reception.

How can you determine what *your* wedding will cost?

Obviously, prices vary widely—starting from the moment you agree to get married until you've settled down to married life—depending on where you live, what type of wedding you plan, and how many people you invite to share your happiness.

Among the expenses to consider are:

- *Engagement:* engagement ring*
  announcement party
  engagement portrait photograph

- *Wedding:* stationery (including invitations, announcements, thank-you notepaper, at-home cards, and special items such as cake boxes, matches, and cocktail napkins)

  flowers (for site of the ceremony, bridal attendants, mothers* and grandmothers,* ushers*; reception table arrangements, cake table, other areas where the reception will be held; bride's bouquet* and going-away corsage*; groom's boutonniere)

  photography (wedding portrait and candids, including cost of prints for parents, grandparents, attendants, friends, and relatives)

  music (for both the wedding and the reception)

  catering (including food, liquor, waiters, bartenders, wedding cake and "extras")

  bride's dress, headpiece, and veil

  attendants' dresses and headpieces

  groom's outfit*; ushers' outfits*

  rental fees (church, reception hall; canopies, awnings, carpets, and other equipment for both wedding ceremony and reception)

  special fees (clergy or ceremony official,* sexton, soloist, organist)—and, of course, the wedding license* and (in most states) blood tests

  wedding rings for the bride* and groom (if it's to be a double-ring ceremony)

  gifts for attendants (bride's and groom's*)

  transportation (limousines, rental cars, taxis, parking)

  hotel accommodations for attendants and out-of-town guests

* Asterisked items are traditionally paid for by the groom or his family.

Not included in this check list are the bride's present to the groom and vice versa, trousseau clothes, hairdresser's costs, taxis, tips, and the many other extras (such as rice-bag favors) that can quickly add as much as 25 per cent or more to the total cost.

Get It in Writing!

The first-time bride and groom compress a tremendous amount of planning, shopping, and buying into a few short, unusually busy months. In addition to planning the wedding, they are (or should be) thinking ahead to a honeymoon, furnishing a new home, and setting guidelines for their life together.

You can avoid many unpleasant moments by making all your wedding plans—clearly spelling out *all* arrangements—on paper and carefully reading every word before signing.

As you go down the check list, don't just guess at the prices or accept rough estimates. Don't assume that the experts with whom you're dealing have your best interests at heart. Weddings are big business, and once the word is out that you're getting married, you'll find people coming to you: musicians, photographers, caterers, insurance agents—whoever feels there's some money to be made.

Twelve Rules for Buying Engagement and Wedding Rings

Since you, the young husband-to-be, are, almost by definition, inexperienced in this field and since the occasion is in itself a temptation to splurge, you are likely to make costly errors. What rules are there to guide you?

(1) Do not spend more than three weeks' salary or 6 per cent of your annual income for the diamond ring.

Comparative-shop thoroughly for rings with your prospective mate—especially if diamonds are involved. Diamond prices skyrocketed in the 1970s under heavy speculative pressures, so set your price ranges in advance and between yourselves, agree on a maximum.

(2) Just because the tendency to overspend is so great on this occasion, protect yourself by telling the jeweler this agreed-upon price range as soon as you enter the store. If he is a reputable merchant, he will not try to talk you into buying in a higher price category.

(3) Try to buy your jewelry for cash, but if you must buy on credit, make sure you thoroughly understand all the terms: carrying charges, legal warranties, insurance coverage. And before you accept the financing deal offered by the jeweler, check on whether you can get more favorable terms at a local bank or credit union.

(4) Insure your jewelry. Diamonds, pearls, and rubies can and do fall from their mountings and they can be lost or stolen. And whether you're

buying with cash or on credit, find out the store's policy on guarantees and return of merchandise.

(5) Make sure you select a reputable and knowledgeable jewelry merchant. Ask your friends and relatives for guidance and check too with your local chamber of commerce or Better Business Bureau on a merchant's reputation.

(6) As soon as you enter a store, ask to speak with the expert in stones. At most stores, the manager or his assistant will be the expert.

(7) Learn the four basic characteristics of precious gems: color, clarity, cut, and weight—of which, despite common misconceptions, weight is the least important and color is the most important, followed by clarity and cut.

(8) Consider buying the stone and mounting separately. And if you're buying a truly gem-quality diamond, consult a gemologist, who will know more than just the basic C's of cut, clarity, color, and carat, and will be able to grade the stone.

(9) Seek quality merchandise guaranteed by established and reputable jewelers. A precious stone should (and in some cities must) carry a written guarantee from the merchant; insist on it.

(10) Take your expensive mounted stone back to the store periodically for inspection of the mounting and polishing.

(11) Steer clear of any merchant who offers ridiculous "bargains," and be on guard against fictitious savings claims, unreasonable discounts, and the "I'll let you have it for . . ." pitch.

(12) Walk away from any jeweler who directs you to a specific appraiser and choose your own. If what you've bought and what your appraiser tells you you've bought don't agree, return the stone or ring for a refund fast. Also, investigate trade-in arrangements. Despite the sentimentality of an engagement ring, many women trade in their rings some years later and some retailers guarantee the price, which is usually more than the value, on the trade.

STATIONERY

Etiquette books devote whole chapters to wedding invitations, RSVP cards, announcements, and how to word and address them. Choose the style of invitation that best suits you (and that includes handwritten notes). If the wedding ceremony or reception is off the beaten path, include a little road map.

Invitations generally should be ordered three months ahead, so that they are ready for mailing three or four weeks before the wedding. When you order them, get everything in writing:

• Delivery date of invitations (you can request envelopes in advance so that you can address them at your leisure);

• exact wording (and be sure you proofread carefully to make sure that

names are spelled correctly, the day of the week and date correspond, addresses are complete and accurate);
* style and color of engraving or printing (and which will be used; thermography—raised printing—is much less expensive than engraving);
* size, weight, and color of the paper for invitation, envelope, and any enclosures.

At the same time you order your invitations, order notepaper for thank-yous, and any printed wedding specialties you may wish to have—such as cake boxes and cocktail napkins or matches.

But don't be pressured into little gimmicks (swizzle sticks, balloons, garters). They're there to tempt you, but you must carefully weigh their cost against whether you really need or want them.

PHOTOGRAPHS

One or more of your relatives or close friends may have movie cameras and may want to take all the photographs for your wedding book. Thank them graciously and say no. If you're spending $2,000 or $3,000 on a once-in-a-lifetime party, it isn't unreasonable to spend $500 for a *professional* photographer, too.

Avoid referral photographers—either those who have called you when they heard you were getting married, or those suggested by the caterer, musicians, or florist (who are probably getting a cut).

Select an established photographer with a local studio, who will still be around five or more years from now should you decide to order an extra print. Visit the studio in person, examine the photographer's work (especially wedding party shots, family groups, and candids).

If you're having engagement and/or wedding portraits made, you may get a special package price, but make sure the photographer is good at both portrait work and candids. Again, once you've agreed on a price, get everything in writing, including:

* The name of the photographer who actually will hold the camera (no substitutes, please), with the exact times, dates, places he is to be.
* All terms of payment: minimum order (and what it includes), amount of deposit, whether there's a penalty for late return of proofs, when final payment is required (before or after you receive finished pictures).
* Cost (and size) of additional prints.
* Whether an album is included (it's usually less expensive for a photographer to supply the album than to buy one yourself, but make sure you have the privilege of "editing" the album, and see what it looks like before committing yourself).
* Specifics about the photographs: black and white or color prints; transparencies; slides; 8mm film; etc.

- Before the wedding and reception, be sure to outline pictures you want taken, together with the names of special guests that should be singled out for photographs.

FLOWERS

You clearly specified white lilacs, and you are crushed when you see gladiolas instead. Did you get a confirmation of your order in writing? Or did you leave the flowers to the caterer or church or hotel? If you really care (and most brides seem to), you'll want to specify exactly what flowers, leaves, and containers you want used, exactly how many arrangements are needed, how large they should be, where they are to be placed, what type of ribbon (if any) will adorn bouquets and corsages, and exactly where and when the flowers are to be delivered.

To keep flower costs in line, find out what blossoms are in season, and consider renting flowering plants to decorate church or reception room. In lieu of more traditional floral arrangements as table centerpieces at the reception, fresh fruit and fruit blossoms attractively arranged in baskets have their practical side; they can be carried home by family and guests for future enjoyment.

MUSIC

If you're being married in a church or temple, consult with the clergy member for suggestions, and possibly restrictions, about music. Traditional selections sometimes can be supplemented by a special arrangement that has personal meaning to the bride and groom. The clergy member can also suggest organists, soloists, cantors, and ensembles who have sung or played at other weddings. Plan the music carefully, and confirm in writing exactly who will provide music, the exact pieces to be included, and the cost. A fanfare of trumpets may seem a dandy idea, but if you're using musicians who are members of the local union, you may find you're paying them for a whole evening's worth of trumpeting even though the wedding lasts less than an hour.

At a reception, almost anything goes! Some hotels and banquet rooms do not permit outsiders, however. Before signing up your favorite group or band, check. Also consider whether instruments will have to be rented (piano movers can be very expensive), and whether the sound system is appropriate. If you have no preset ideas about who should play, the caterer can give you two or three suggestions, but hear them all before signing on the dotted line.

To economize a bit, don't rule out the use of records or tapes, but do hire a professional to provide the sound equipment and to play the recordings. Also, make the musical selections yourself.

When you receive confirmation about the music in writing (and insist on that), make sure that possible overtime charges are included in case exuberant parents want to continue the party on into the wee hours.

WEDDING FINERY

If yours is to be a formal wedding, order the men's clothing, bridesmaids' gowns, and your own dress well in advance. Keep a copy of all measurements you give the rental firm. Get a written pickup or delivery date on the receipt. Phone or visit the firm several days prior to the wedding to make sure your order is on schedule. If you have gowns custom-made, get written details of the fabric, color, trim, and a swatch of fabric.

It's preferable to deal with a firm you know, but if you can't, ask:

- How long has the firm been in business at the same location?
- What similar-sized wedding parties has it outfitted recently?
- What is the size of the dress shop staff?
- How many other weddings will it be serving the same week as yours? Insist on a delivery date that allows for corrections.
- Is all the work completed in-house?

And don't overlook accessories; you'll want to make sure that shoes, gloves, jewelry conform by reminding attendants in writing what to bring, or by providing them yourself. The groom traditionally supplies gloves and ascots or ties for the ushers and best man, too.

TRANSPORTATION

The logistics of getting bride, groom, families, attendants, and special guests from out of town to a ceremony, from the ceremony to the reception, and back home again (or off on a honeymoon) require special planning. So does parking near the church or temple and/or at the site of the reception. Chauffeur-driven limousines are the easiest, but most expensive, solution. Imaginative, but not necessarily practical, are double-decker buses or horse-drawn carriages. Even if you enlist family and friends, make sure that drivers know whom they're taking where—and when.

CATERING—PUT IT IN WRITING!

Finally, you must make arrangements for the reception (and possibly wedding) with a caterer or hotel or banquet hall.

Check the credentials of the caterer, and comparative-shop for prices.

Leave *nothing* to verbal agreements. When you are close to making a decision, tell your choice that, before you make final arrangements, you would like to visit a wedding the caterer is handling.

If you're holding the party at a private or community club, hotel, restaurant, or banquet club, ask whether there is a rental fee for the space—in addition to other costs.

Among points to consider:

• Date and hours—are they available? If there's another event scheduled immediately before or after yours, look elsewhere.
• Number of guests—is the size appropriate?
• Type of party—do you want a buffet meal, sit-down dinner, cocktails and hors d'oeuvres, punch and cake? Get prices for all.
• How many waiters will there be? bartenders? And what are their overtime rates if the reception lasts longer than expected?
• Determine the location of the receiving line, dance floor and bandstand, rest rooms, cloakroom, dressing rooms for bride, groom, and attendants, parking facilities.
• Specify brands of liquor and wine—and exactly when each will be served, and how much.
• Does the caterer provide entertainment or a master of ceremonies? Unless you know the act, you may want to hide under a table with embarrassment!
• Exactly what linens, silver, china, and glassware will be used? If you're shown elegant service pieces, make sure they are described—and specified—in the contract.
• From candles to cake knife, make certain that every last detail is mentioned, and priced.

What Happens if Plans Change?

If you become ill, or the wedding is postponed or canceled for any of a number of reasons, what then? When contracting for products and services, make sure that written agreements specify what you do (or don't) have to pay for if you don't take delivery, and by what date you must give notification before your commitment is uncancelable.

Changing your mind at the last minute can be very expensive!

The Honeymoon and Its Expenses

After the vows are said, the next major expense is the honeymoon, usually paid for by the husband.

There are so many variations on honeymoon expenses that to get an idea of costs I must invent a mythical couple. Okay, you're invented: you're an average groom and you're submitting typical questions.

Q. *How long is the average honeymoon trip?*
A. About nine days.

Q. *What is the average cost?*
A. It was about $720 in the late 1970s. Outside the United States (excluding Canada and Mexico) the average cost was well over $1,000. A survey of

Bride's readers indicates they travel an average of 1,980 miles on a honeymoon trip.

Q. *How do honeymooners in the States travel?*
A. Most couples go by car, about 30 per cent fly, the rest use rail or sea transportation.

Q. *What about a honeymoon abroad?*
A. In this case, you should have at least two or three weeks to make it worthwhile. If you get in on a special cut-rate deal, though, your transportation costs will be slashed. Your expenses in other countries are subject to enormous variation.

Q. *What about honeymoon costs in big cities?*
A. Again, the costs of honeymooning in such cities as New York, New Orleans, San Francisco, etc. vary immensely, but if you are a typical couple spending a week or so in one of these cities, you should expect to spend $500, $1,000, or more.

How to Save on Your Wedding and Honeymoon

How can you save money and still have the wedding and honeymoon you want? Here are six tips:

(1) Consider having a home wedding, an obvious major money-saving area. Make your reception simple. The completely open bar is giving way to a controlled serving of wine, champagne, or punch.

(2) Have a cocktail buffet instead of a sit-down dinner. It can be just as satisfying and will be much cheaper.

(3) Or consider the services of a "wedding palace"—a professional catering establishment which provides bells-to-bonbons wedding packages at various price levels.

(4) Choose a wedding dress that you can use for other occasions or even consider renting or borrowing a dress.

(5) Also select dresses for your attendants which they can use for other occasions, and the same goes for the costumes of the mothers.

(6) For your honeymoon, work with travel agents on package deals—and take advantage of bargain flights if you're going abroad. If you're renting a car, make it a compact. Plan ahead and, if feasible, make your reservations well in advance to take full advantage of any money-saving offers.

Rules for Buying Wedding Gifts

You need not spend nearly as much for wedding gifts as you think. Nor do you need to waste nearly as much time and effort as you do. Having learned over the years the value of expert guidance in this wedding minuet, I pass along to you my key hints on wedding gifts:

• Find out if and where the bride has registered for gifts and take advantage of the bridal registry to give her what she needs and wants. You can buy almost anything at a bridal registry now, for the concept has been broadened to include furniture, carpeting, and bedding as well as silver, china, and stemware.

• Decide at the start how much you want to spend and don't fall into the trap of spending too much in order to impress the bride's friends or to "repay" her family for a gift to your child. The gift-for-gift idea is costly, and in bad taste.

• Buy with an eye to the bride's life-style. What are her tastes, profession, plans? Will she live on a campus, in a city or suburb? In a private home or apartment? How does she dress?

• Stay away from "the most original gift in the world," for these are the gifts most often returned or exchanged.

• If you're a relative, resist overstressing your own tastes when the bride is registering her patterns and gift choices at her favorite store.

• If you're the bridegroom, be sure you, too, respect your bride's selections.

• Find out how sophisticated a cook the bride is. Be sure that the set of gourmet cookbooks or the case of rare wine you may offer is a respectful reflection of her interest (rather than yours) in the art of cooking and dining.

• When in doubt, buy quality silver; it probably will continue to rise substantially in value in coming years.

After the Wedding Is Over

You've set up your home and furnished it; your thank-you notes are written; you've talked to your insurance agents, notified the Social Security Administration of your marriage, (and name change), rewritten your wills, and changed the beneficiaries on company pension and profit-sharing plans.

In all likelihood, you'll continue to work (80 per cent of all brides work either full or part time, and 95 per cent will stay on the job at least for a while after the wedding).

Although you're not in the mood to contemplate such endings at this stage, the odds are almost 50-50 that your marriage will end in divorce. Whether or not it does, be prepared!

A Bride's Guide to Credit

You are about to establish credit standing as individuals as well as a husband-wife team. The following are twelve fundamental guides for women particularly:

(1) Open both checking and savings accounts at your bank in order to create financial identities. While these accounts in themselves do not build your credit history, they lead you to other lines of credit, such as bank credit cards, overdraft checking privileges, automobile loans, personal loans, mortgages, etc.

(2) Speed up your credit-building process, if you so desire, by taking out a small loan from your bank in your own name and then pay it back promptly. This transaction will be recorded in your favor, as an individual woman and wife, at the credit bureau.

(3) Buy some appliance or other product you want on the installment plan and open charge accounts at retail stores, again in your name, and here, too, be extra careful about your repayments. All this activity will establish your name at the bank and local credit bureau as a good credit risk.

(4) While you are building your credit rating, obey the basic limits on prudent borrowing. As one rule of thumb, the American Bankers Association suggests that not more than 10 to 15 per cent of your income should be used to repay loans—not counting your mortgage payments.

(5) As soon as you qualify, get a free credit card from your bank and use it as another loan device. When you use your card, you have at least thirty days before a payment comes due, and usually the period is even longer. During that time, you are using the bank's money, and if you pay your bank card bill in full each month, you won't pay any interest on this credit.

(6) Double-check to see whether your bank does indeed not charge you if you pay within the thirty-day limit, for some banks have started charging a monthly administrative fee even on accounts paid in full within the stated period. On the part of your bill not paid within the time limit, you will be charged 1½ per cent interest per month, or 18 per cent a year.

(7) Do use your credit cards to take advantage of unusual bargains. (Say, for instance, you grab a $350 air conditioner on sale at $300 and extend your credit card payments for three months. Even with the 1½ per cent per month interest on the balance, you still will realize 75 per cent of the savings you achieved by seizing the bargain while the price was right.)

(8) Take advantage, too, of overdraft checking—a credit tool that lets you write checks for more money than you have in the bank without fear that the check will bounce. The amount of overdrafts you'll be permitted to make will be based on the credit history you are now establishing, and the charge will be about 1 per cent a month or 12 per cent interest a year. (The average overdraft in the United States today is about $1,000.)

(9) As a working wife, your creditors must consider the combined income of both you and your husband when you apply for credit—and that goes even if your work is only part time. Be sure your banker does not discriminate against you because of your sex.

(10) Become fully informed about the federal laws now in effect which forbid lenders from forcing you to reapply for credit, or impose new condi-

tions when you get married. If you had a credit-worthy history before you were married, it is still valid now that you have become a wife and, quite probably, assumed your husband's last name. (See pages 1352–54 on your rights as a borrower.)

(11) If you want to keep your credit accounts separate from your husband's, just write your creditors, tell them your new name, and explain that you will continue to be as credit-worthy as before. The credit bureau and bank then will maintain independent histories of your credit standing.

(12) As a wife, use your own personal first name for credit account purposes—not your husband's first name. Credit under your husband's first name is merely an extension of his credit, and does nothing to establish your independent credit history for the future.

The Low Cost of Not Having a Baby
(or Having Fewer of Them)

THE NEED FOR FAMILY PLANNING

Family planning permits couples to say whether and when to have a baby. Some couples have religious or other reasons that may dispose them against certain methods of family planning; but most will endorse the principle that planning of some sort is desirable if children are to be properly cared for and families not strained to the breaking point.

GETTING LOW-COST OR FREE HELP IN FAMILY PLANNING

Where do you get family planning help?

• Your best source of clinic care is Planned Parenthood, which in the 1970s had 191 local affiliates operating more than 750 medically supervised clinics in forty-three states plus the District of Columbia. Fees vary around the country, and often are based on your income. However, *no one is ever turned away because of inability to pay.*

In San Francisco in the late 1970s fees ranged from $29 down to $10 for a year's services relating to contraception, including follow-up visits for any complications. A month's supply of pills cost $2.00 while other contraceptives cost much less than their usual retail price. In New York City, Planned Parenthood's fee for pregnancy detection was $15. Fees are adjustable and deferred payment may be worked out. The fees are never more than the patient can afford.

• For the location of the PP affiliate nearest you, check the white pages of your telephone directory or contact the organization's national headquarters at 810 Seventh Avenue, New York, New York 10019; telephone (212) 541-7800. The telephone directory's Yellow Pages sometimes show referral or service listings under "Birth Control." And your county medical society will usually be able to give you the names of private doctors offering birth control services in your area.

• If your income is limited, you should be able to get free or low-cost service from government-subsidized family planning clinics run by PP, county health departments, county hospitals, and neighborhood health centers. Medicaid recipients are eligible to receive free family planning services and supplies in most states.

• Some private hospitals also run family planning clinics, as do many community clinics and group practice plans. Inquire at facilities of this type or ask your regular physician for assistance.

Important note: An increasing number of private physicians and clinics (including Planned Parenthood) will provide birth control services, on a confidential basis, to minors upon their own request. Such physicians and clinics may offer treatment and services without charge. In some, however, parental consent is still required.

Finally, along with birth control services, many all-purpose outpatient clinics and health centers have been opening up and offering a whole spectrum of health services for women.

CONTRACEPTION: COMPARING THE OPTIONS

METHODS AVAILABLE

A full dozen methods of contraception are available today: some obtainable without a doctor's prescription or advice; others requiring a prescription and medical consultation and follow-up.

When choosing a method, the factors to consider are your personal preferences, psychological or religious attitudes, and individual medical history. But many of you looking for a suitable means of contraception know very little about the available methods—how they work, how effective they are, what side effects they may have, what health problems may be related to their use.

Here is basic information on the contraceptive methods most widely used today. It is beginning information only, to help you understand the choices. Discussion with your physician can help you make a selection.

It is essential that you realize no method of contraception is 100 per cent effective and that you must use the method correctly to make it as effective as possible. Other factors also contribute to failure: diaphragms that have been improperly fitted, intrauterine devices (IUDs) that can be expelled without the woman being aware of it, a foam or jelly that might be used too long before intercourse.

Effectiveness figures in the following are expressed in terms of pregnancies per 100 woman years, which means the number of women out of 100 who would become pregnant in one year when using the method. If no contraceptive method were used 60 to 80 women out of 100 would become pregnant.

A wide range of effectiveness is shown for some methods because people differ in how well they use them. For example, a method may be more effective when used by thirty-year-old college graduates but less effective when used by teenagers in high school.

THE PILL

Prescription Required

"The Pill" refers to any of the oral contraceptives. The most widely used contains two female hormones, estrogen and progestin, and is taken twenty-one days each month. Another (sometimes called the "mini pill") contains progestin only and is taken every day. You should be sure you receive from your druggist, doctor, or person who gives you the pills an FDA-required brochure that explains the use, benefits, and risks of the product in greater detail.

Effectiveness

Effectiveness depends on how correctly the method is used.

Of 100 women who use the combination estrogen and progestin pill for one year, fewer than 1 will become pregnant. Of 100 women who use the progestin only pill (minipill) for one year, 2 to 3 will become pregnant.

Advantages-Disadvantages

Advantages. The combination pill is the most effective of the popular methods for preventing pregnancy.

No inconvenient devices to bother with at time of intercourse.

Disadvantages. Must be taken regularly and exactly as instructed by the prescribing physician.

Side Effects

Side effects may include tender breasts, nausea or vomiting, gain or loss of weight, unexpected vaginal bleeding, higher levels of sugar and fat in the blood. Although it happens infrequently, use of the Pill can cause blood clots (in the lungs, brain, and heart). A clot that reaches the lungs or forms in the brain or heart can be fatal. Pill users have a greater risk of heart attack and stroke than non-users. This risk increases with age and is greater if the Pill user smokes.

Some Pill users tend to develop high blood pressure, but it usually is mild and may be reversed by discontinuing use. Pill users have a greater risk than non-users of having gallbladder disease requiring surgery. There is no evidence that taking the Pill increases the risk of cancer. Benign liver tumors occur very rarely in women on the Pill. Sometimes they rupture, causing fatal hemorrhage.

Health Factors to Consider

Women who smoke should not use the Pill because smoking increases the risk of heart attack or stroke. Other women who should not take the Pill are those who have had a heart attack, stroke, angina pectoris, blood clots, cancer of the breast or uterus, or scanty or irregular periods. A woman who believes she may be pregnant should not take the Pill because it increases the risk of defects in the fetus.

Health problems such as migraine headaches, mental depression, fibroids of the uterus, heart or kidney disease, asthma, high blood pressure, diabetes, or epilepsy may be made worse by use of the Pill.

Risks associated with the Pill increase with age, and as a woman enters her late thirties it is generally advisable to seek another method of contraception.

Long-term Effect on Ability to Have Children

There is no evidence that using the Pill will prevent a woman from becoming pregnant after she stops taking it, although there may be a delay before she is able to become pregnant. Women should wait a short time after stopping the Pill before becoming pregnant. During this time another method of contraception should be used. After childbirth the woman should consult her doctor before resuming use of the Pill. This is especially true for nursing mothers because the drugs in the Pill appear in the milk and the long-range effect on the infant is not known.

INTRAUTERINE DEVICE (IUD)

Prescription Required

The IUD is a small plastic or metal device that is placed in the uterus (womb) through the cervical canal (opening into the uterus). As long as the IUD stays in place pregnancy is prevented. Although how the IUD prevents pregnancy is not completely understood, IUDs seem to interfere in some manner with implantation of the fertilized egg in the wall of the uterus. There were five kinds of IUDs available at the start of the 1980s—Copper-7, Copper-T, Progestasert, Lippes Loop, and Saf-T-Coil. IUDs containing copper (Copper-7 and Copper-T) should be replaced every three years; those containing progesterone (Progestasert) should be replaced every year.

Effectiveness

Effectiveness depends on proper insertion by the physician and whether the IUD remains in place. Of 100 women who use an IUD for one year, 1 to 6 will become pregnant.

Advantages-Disadvantages

Advantages. Insertion by a physician, then no further care needed, except to see that the IUD remains in place (the user can check it herself but it should be checked once a year by her doctor).

Disadvantages. May cause pain or discomfort when inserted; afterward may cause cramps and a heavier menstrual flow. Some women will experience adverse effects that require removal of the IUD. The IUD can be expelled, sometimes without the woman being aware of it, leaving her unprotected.

Side Effects

Major complications, which are infrequent, include anemia, pregnancy outside the uterus, pelvic infection, perforation of the uterus or cervix, and septic abortion. A woman with heavy or irregular bleeding while using an IUD should consult her physician. Removal of the IUD may be necessary to prevent anemia.

Women susceptible to pelvic infection are more prone to infection when using an IUD.

Serious complications can occur if a woman becomes pregnant while using an IUD. Though rare, cases of blood poisoning, miscarriage, and even death have been reported. An IUD user who believes she may be pregnant should consult her doctor immediately. If pregnancy is confirmed, the IUD should be removed. Although it rarely happens, the IUD can pierce the wall of the uterus when it is being inserted. Surgery is required to remove it.

Health Factors to Consider

Before having an IUD inserted, a woman should tell her doctor if she has had any of the following: cancer or other abnormalities of the uterus or cervix; bleeding between periods or heavy menstrual flow; infection of the uterus, cervix, or pelvis (pus in fallopian tubes); prior IUD use; recent pregnancy, abortion, or miscarriage; uterine surgery; venereal disease; severe menstrual cramps; allergy to copper; anemia; fainting attacks; unexplained genital bleeding or vaginal discharge; suspicious or abnormal Pap smear.

Long-term Effect on Ability to Have Children

Pelvic infection in some IUD users may result in their future inability to have children.

DIAPHRAGM (WITH CREAM, JELLY, OR FOAM)

Prescription Required

A diaphragm is a shallow cup of thin rubber stretched over a flexible ring. A sperm-killing cream, jelly, or foam is put on both sides of the diaphragm, which you then place inside your vagina before intercourse. The device covers the opening of the uterus, thus preventing the sperm from entering the uterus.

Effectiveness

Effectiveness depends on how correctly the method is used. Of 100 women who use the diaphragm with a spermicidal product for one year, 2 to 20 will become pregnant.

Advantages-Disadvantages

Advantages. No routine schedule to be kept as with the Pill. The diaphragm with a spermicidal product is inserted by the user. Can be inserted up to two hours before intercourse.

No discomfort or cramping, as with the IUD. No effect on the chemical or physical processes of the body, as with the Pill or the IUD.

Disadvantages. Must be inserted before each intercourse and stay in place at least six hours afterwards.

Size and fit require yearly checkup, and should be checked if woman gains or loses more than 10 pounds. Should be refitted after childbirth or abortion.

Requires instruction on insertion technique. Some women find it difficult to insert and inconvenient to use.

Some women in whom the vagina is greatly relaxed, or in whom the uterus has "fallen," cannot use a diaphragm successfully.

Side Effects

No serious side effects.

Possible allergic reaction to the rubber or the spermicidal jelly. Condition easily corrected.

Health Factors to Consider

None.

Long-term Effect on Ability to Have Children

None.

FOAM, CREAM, OR JELLY ALONE

No Prescription Required

Several brands of vaginal foam, cream, or jelly can be used without a diaphragm. They form a chemical barrier at the opening of the uterus that prevents sperm from reaching an egg in the uterus; they also destroy sperm.

Effectiveness

Effectiveness depends on how correctly the method is used. Of 100 women who use aerosol foams alone for one year, 2 to 29 will become pregnant. Of 100 women who use jellies and creams alone for one year, 4 to 36 will become pregnant.

Advantages-Disadvantages

Advantages. Easy to obtain and use.
Disadvantages. Must be used one hour or less before intercourse. If douching is desired, must wait six to eight hours after intercourse.

Side Effects

No serious side effects. Burning or irritation of the vagina or penis may occur. Allergic reaction may be corrected by changing brands.

Health Factors to Consider

None.

Long-term Effect on Ability to Have Children

None.

VAGINAL SUPPOSITORIES

No Prescription Required

Vaginal suppositories are small waxy "tablets" that are placed at the opening of the uterus just before intercourse. Note: very few vaginal suppositories are intended for birth control. Ask before you buy.

Effectiveness

No figures available, considered fair to poor.

Advantages-Disadvantages

Advantages. No devices needed.
Disadvantages. Must be inserted fifteen minutes before intercourse. If placed earlier, they may become ineffective. If placed later (too close to intercourse) the suppository will not have time to melt and will be ineffective.

Side Effects

No adverse side effects.

Health Factors to Consider

None.

Long-term Effect on Ability to Have Children

None.

RHYTHM METHOD

The woman must refrain from sexual intercourse on days surrounding the predicted time of monthly ovulation or, for a higher degree of effectiveness, until a few days after the predicted time of ovulation. Ways to determine the approximate time of ovulation include a calendar method, a method based on body temperature, and a mucus method. Using the calendar method requires careful record-keeping of the time of the menstrual period, and calculation of the time in the month when the woman is fertile and must not have intercourse. To use the temperature method, you must use a special type of thermometer and keep an accurate daily record of your body temperature (body temperature rises after ovulation). To use the mucus method you, the woman, also must keep an accurate daily record of the type of vaginal secretions present. The temperature method or the mucus method used alone or concurrently with the calendar method are more effective than the calendar method alone.

Effectiveness

Effectiveness depends on how correctly the method is used. Of 100 women who use the temperature method for one year, 1 to 20 will become pregnant. Of 100 women who use the mucus method for one year, 1 to 25 will become pregnant. Of 100 women who use for one year the temperature or mucus method with intercourse only after ovulation, fewer than 1 to 7 will become pregnant.

Advantages-Disadvantages

Advantages. No drugs or devices needed.

Disadvantages. Requires careful record-keeping and estimation of the time each month when there can be no intercourse.

To use any of the three methods properly a physician's guidance may be needed, at least at the outset.

If menstrual cycles are irregular, it is especially difficult to use this method effectively.

Dissatisfaction because of extended time each month when sexual intercourse must be avoided.

Side Effects

No physical effects, but because the couple must refrain from having intercourse except on certain days of the month, using this method can create pressures on the couple's relationship.

Health Factors to Consider

None.

Long-term Effect on Ability to Have Children

None.

CONDOM

No Prescription Required

The condom is a thin sheath of rubber or processed lamb cecum that fits over the penis.

Effectiveness

Effectiveness depends on how correctly the method is used.

Of 100 women whose partner uses a condom for one year, 3 to 36 women will become pregnant.

Advantages-Disadvantages

Advantages. In addition to contraception, may afford some protection against venereal disease.

Easily available. Requires no "long-term" planning before intercourse.

Disadvantages. Some people feel the condom reduces pleasure in the sex act.

The male must interrupt foreplay and fit the condom in place before sexual entry into the woman.

The condom can slip or tear during use or spill during removal from the vagina.

Side Effects

No serious side effects. Occasionally an individual will be allergic to the rubber, causing burning, irritation, itching, rash, or swelling, but this can easily be treated. Switching to the natural skin condom may be a solution.

Health Factors to Consider

None.

Long-term Effect on Ability to Have Children

None.

FEMALE STERILIZATION

The primary method of sterilization for women is tubal sterilization, commonly referred to as "tying the tubes." A surgeon cuts, ties, or seals the fallopian tubes to prevent passage of eggs between the ovaries and the uterus. Several techniques are available. With one new technique, the operation can be performed in a hospital outpatient surgical clinic with either a local or general anesthetic. Using this method, the doctor makes a tiny incision in the abdomen or vagina and blocks the tubes by cutting, sealing with an electric current, or applying a small band or clip. Hysterectomy, a surgical procedure involving removal of all or part of the uterus, also prevents pregnancy, but is performed for other medical reasons and is not considered primarily a method of sterilization.

Effectiveness

Virtually 100 per cent.

Advantages-Disadvantages

Advantages. A one-time procedure—never any more bother with devices or preparations of any kind.

Disadvantages. Surgery is required. Although in some cases a sterilization procedure has been reversed through surgery, the procedure should be considered permanent.

Side Effects

As with any surgery, occasionally there are complications such as severe bleeding, infection, or injury to other organs which may require additional surgery to correct.

Health Factors to Consider

There is some risk associated with any surgical procedure, which varies with the general health of the patient.

Long-term Effect on Ability to Have Children

Procedure should be considered non-reversible. Once the surgery is performed successfully, the woman cannot become pregnant. There have been exceptions, but they are very uncommon.

MALE STERILIZATION

Sterilization of men involves severing the tubes through which the sperm travel to become part of the semen. The man continues to produce sperm but they are absorbed by the body rather than being released into the semen. This operation, called a vasectomy, takes about half an hour and may be performed in a doctor's office under local anesthetic. A vasectomy does not affect a man's physical ability to have intercourse.

Effectiveness

Virtually 100 per cent.

Advantages-Disadvantages

Advantages. A one-time procedure that does not require hospitalization and permits the man to resume normal activity almost immediately.

Disadvantages. Although in some cases a vasectomy may be reversed, it should be considered permanent.

The man is not sterile immediately after the operation—usually it takes a few months. Other means of contraception must be used during that time.

Side Effects

Complications occur in 2 to 4 per cent of cases, including infection, hematoma (trapped mass of clotted blood), granuloma (an inflammatory reaction to sperm that is absorbed by the body), and swelling and tenderness near the testes. Most such complications are minor and are treatable without surgery.

Studies by the National Institutes of Health show that vasectomy does not affect a man's sexual desire or ability.

Health Factors to Consider

None.

Long-term Effect on Ability to Have Children

Procedure is considered non-reversible. Once surgery is performed successfully, the man cannot father children. There have been exceptions, but they are very uncommon.

WITHDRAWAL (COITUS INTERRUPTUS)

This method of contraception requires withdrawal of the male organ (penis) from the vagina before the man ejaculates so the male sperm are not deposited at or near the birth canal. The failure rate with this method is high and it should not be considered effective for preventing pregnancy.

DOUCHING

Use of a vaginal douche immediately after sexual intercourse to wash out or inactivate sperm is completely ineffective for preventing pregnancy.

SOURCE: U. S. Department of Health, Education, and Welfare; Public Health Service, Food and Drug Administration, Office of Public Affairs, 5600 Fishers Lane, Rockville, Maryland 20857, HEW Publication No. (FDA) 78-3069.

COMPARATIVE COSTS OF CONTRACEPTIVE METHODS

The cost of preventing pregnancy can range from zero to more than $500, depending on the method you choose. Terminating a pregnancy also may cost you nothing, depending on your financial circumstances. However, using effective contraceptive methods is to be preferred to abortion for a variety of reasons—medical and personal as well as economic.

The method you choose to plan and space the birth of your children should depend largely on the factors already outlined. Still, you probably will wonder how the costs of the various methods compare, so here is a rundown.

The following chart summarizes the longer-range costs (1979) of each major type of birth control—annually and over a lifetime. Sexual activity one hundred times a year is assumed, over a period of thirty years during which fertility is an issue. It also is assumed that any checkups and follow-ups relating to using each method will not be counted as an "extra" cost. Gynecology exam costs not related to contraceptive use are not included in this table.

Method	First Year Cost	Lifetime Cost
Rhythm (calendar method)	No Cost	No Cost
Withdrawal	No Cost	No Cost
Condom*	$35 to $125	$1,050 to $3,750
Foam	$22.50 to $39.50	$675 to $1,185
Diaphragm†	$42 to $54.50	$804 to $879
IUD†	$40 to $100	$620 to $1,559
Pill†	$67 to $136	$2,210 to $4,080
Sterilization		Male: $50 to $250
		Female: $650 to $1,120

Sterilization

Sterilization, or permanent contraception, may well be the most costly method of birth control in terms of initial outlay. However, even a payment of $500 for the procedure could be less than the cost of the Pill taken over, say, a fifteen-year period. If your insurance covers sterilization, out-of-pocket costs to the patient may be only $100 or even less.

Sterilization also has the advantage of being virtually failproof. The failure rate for sterilization (male or female) is a minuscule .003 pregnancies for each 100 woman-years of use.

The male operation—the vasectomy—can be done in a doctor's office in only twenty minutes and costs about $250, although there are the usual variations above and below this. Fees at vasectomy clinics range from $150 down to zero, depending on the economic circumstances of the family involved. For the sake of the patient who may have some postoperative discomfort, doctors often schedule vasectomies on a Friday or Saturday so the patient is able to avoid missing time from work.

* Assumes 35 cents for plain latex; $1.25 for membrane (skin).
† Includes annual checkups after first year.

For a female, the most common surgical procedure, tubal ligation, as the 1980s neared, cost an average of $500, plus the charges for the one- to five-day hospital stay that this procedure usually entails. (The operation itself seldom takes more than twenty to thirty minutes. With today's charges for a semi-private room this could easily bring your total cost to between $650 and $1,120, not counting such "extras" as operating-room charges.)

To shave some of these costs and also for convenience, you may want to have the operation performed while you are in the hospital for the delivery of what you have decided will be your last child. Your recovery from the operation should take little time more than the usual recovery time from childbirth—perhaps an additional day or two.

In a few areas, female sterilization is now being done on an outpatient basis by a technique known as laparoscopy. With total time in the hospital reduced to less than twelve hours, costs are somewhat lower. Hospitals using this technique charge from $400 to $500 for the procedure, covering both the doctor's and hospital fees. Planned Parenthood's Laparoscopy Clinic in Syracuse charges $375—which includes the total package: surgeon's fee, operating room, initial fee, etc.

If you want further information or if you have trouble in getting a sterilization operation, contact the Association for Voluntary Sterilization, a nationwide organization, headquartered at 708 Third Avenue, New York, New York 10017; telephone (212) 986-3880. Or contact your local Planned Parenthood affiliate.

Basic Facts About Abortion

When contraceptive measures fail or are not used, abortion is the only means of stopping an unwanted pregnancy. At one time abortion was a risky, costly procedure that was usually done illegally. Today, however, costs and risks have plummeted and the number of legal instead of illegal abortions performed in the United States has been soaring at a spectacular rate.

The 1973 landmark U. S. Supreme Court decision, in effect, ruled that no state may restrict a woman from getting an abortion for any reason during her first trimester (twelve weeks) of pregnancy. The ruling also specified that states could intervene in the second trimester only to protect the health of the woman—through medical regulations covering the licensing of the facilities and persons involved. Although a number of state legislatures have contested this Supreme Court decision these challenges had not reversed the fundamental trend (as of the late 1970s) toward abortion on request—by unmarried and married women.

In the late 1970s an estimated 700,000 American women were undergoing legal abortions each year, compared to only about 6,000 in 1966, the year before Colorado became the first state to rewrite its restrictive law.

Costs, however, still remain a significant factor, although they are now generally far below what people were forced to pay in years past for an illegal abortion. They range across the nation from zero to $500, depending on the span of your pregnancy, your financial status, and, of course, the type of hospital, clinic, or office in which the abortion is done.

Here were typical charges in the late 1970s:

• At a New York state-licensed clinic or city hospital, an early abortion (done during the first twelve weeks of pregnancy, usually by vacuum aspiration or "suction") cost $140 to $175. This was generally also the top fee at similar facilities throughout the country.

• At a New York City voluntary (non-profit) hospital, the same procedure generally cost $200, while at private hospitals through private physicians, the fees began at $350 and varied greatly, depending on the individuals involved.

• Early second-trimester abortions (fourteenth to sixteenth week of pregnancy) at some hospitals and clinics are now being performed by "D&E" (dilation and evacuation), another vaginal method. Costs for this service may range as high as $300, according to the medical facility or anesthesia used. Late second-trimester abortions (sixteenth to twenty-fourth weeks) may be performed by saline injection, which induces labor. These are not only more risky but also cost more, since they may require a few days' hospitalization. You can count on paying at least double what you would have paid for an early abortion, with all-inclusive fees starting at a minimum of $350, but generally reaching totals significantly higher than this.

Since it may be difficult to get an abortion in some hospitals, communities, or states, you may have to add transportation and other travel expenses involved in getting to a place where you can have the operation.

How to Shop for—and Reduce the Costs of—an Abortion

• First, and above all, consult your family doctor or obstetrician or family planning clinic, and the sooner the better! *Avoid* profit-making abortion referral agencies which you may have seen advertised in your newspaper; you should *not* have to pay for a referral. Keep in mind that the cost and complexity of an abortion go up sharply after the twelfth week of pregnancy. Late abortions, it has been found, are three to four times more likely to result in complications than early abortions.

Keep in mind, too, that when you have missed one menstrual period you could be up to four weeks pregnant. If you've missed two periods, you may be as many as eight weeks pregnant. (Weeks are calculated from the last menstrual period, so actually at a missed period the week count is four.) Also, you should wait a full two weeks after a missed period to get an accurate reading of your possible pregnancy. Tests may show a false negative before this. If you have doubts about the reliability of your pregnancy test, repeat it to be sure the result is accurate.

If your doctor or clinic is unable or unwilling to arrange an abortion, call your local hospital and ask for a recommendation of a qualified physician or a specialist in obstetrics and gynecology ("OBG"). Also helpful may be your city or county public health department or medical society.

• Or you can look under "Birth Control" in the Yellow Pages of your telephone directory. In addition to local independent agencies such as women's groups or college counseling services, you also may find chapters or affiliates of such nationwide, non-profit organizations as Planned Parenthood, the Clergy Consultation Service, and Zero Population Growth (ZPG). The referrals and pregnancy counseling services of Planned Parenthood and the Clergy Consultation Service often are free.

• If none of these three organizations has an office near you, you can contact them at their central office or referral services:

Family Planning Information Service of Planned Parenthood, 380 Second Avenue, New York, New York 10010; telephone (212) 677-3040.

National Clergy Consultation Service, 55 Washington Square South, New York, New York 10012; telephone (212) 254-6230.

Zero Population Growth of New York, 52 Vanderbilt Avenue, New York, New York 10017; telephone (212) 697-3877.

These agencies, as well as others, also provide information on such alternatives to abortion as placing the child for adoption.

Quality is the most important factor in choosing the best abortion service. You may find you've been penny-wise and pound-foolish if you let cost considerations alone guide you in choosing. A phone call to any of the above organizations can help you make an informed decision, or you can call the National Organization for Women (NOW) in Chicago or its local office in your area.

Here are additional guides:

Whether you are dealing with a private doctor or with a clinic, make sure that you know what your *total* cost will be, including hospitalization (if necessary), medication, lab work, and checkup exam (usually two to three weeks after the abortion). Special medication, for example, may be necessary for Rh-negative patients. Not all doctors and clinics will volunteer this information. Then you may want to compare the range of charges elsewhere.

Agree on the payment terms before the operation, especially if you have to travel. In most cases, full payment is required in advance, particularly if you are a transient. Personal checks are generally not accepted. Some hospitals, however, take VISA or Master Charge.

If you are a woman in severe financial distress, ask an abortion-referral agency for suggestions of doctors and clinics who will perform abortions at reduced or no cost. Many states no longer pay for Medicaid abortions.

Insurance Coverage

FOR ABORTIONS

Abortion coverage is generally found within the maternity provisions of group health contracts. However, the coverage may be restricted. It can be spelled out in the contract itself. Single women may be covered. Daughters of insured workers may not be covered. A waiting period may be applied to married women and daughters who are covered. Usually conception must have taken place during the contract period. The size of the benefits may be very small, etc.

So far as Blue Cross and Blue Shield are concerned, in most local plans hospital and surgical expenses for abortion are covered. But there may be conflicts in coverage by Blue Cross (for hospital expenses) and Blue Shield (for surgical costs). For example, a Blue Shield plan may cover abortion while the Blue Cross plan in the same area does not.

In general, however, where a local Blue Cross plan offers obstetrical benefits, any abortions performed would be considered obstetrical benefits and covered according to the provisions of the specific contract. Where obstetrical benefits are restricted to family contracts, wives and single female dependents (usually those under nineteen years of age) would be covered.

Some Blue Cross plans now offer such coverage to all persons—including single women and dependent children—on all contracts. In fact, the Blue Cross Association has adopted a policy requiring its member plans to make abortion coverage available to all subscribers (including single women and female dependents) enrolled in *national* contracts—i.e., people belonging to large groups which include employees in more than one state.

Under this expanded benefit, new women enrollees who become pregnant no longer have to wait nine months before becoming eligible for coverage for a legal abortion. *But* it is *not* automatically included in national contracts—only to those specifically requesting it. Similar riders are available on a local basis, but again, only to those groups who want to include it as a benefit. Check your plan to see if and how your abortion is covered *before* you obtain one.

FOR STERILIZATION

Some Blue Cross policies also cover sterilization in a hospital for contraceptive reasons or for reasons of medical necessity—including vasectomy, tubal ligation, and the newer laparoscopy method. In a few areas, however, you are covered only after a specified waiting period.

Blue Shield may cover the cost of office vasectomies and in states where this is so, Blue Shield may pay from one third to one half of the fee for the procedure. Blue Shield covers sterilizations performed in a hospital, for either sex. Since there are wide variations in these and other health insurance contracts, you must check your *own coverage,* to be sure of the extent to which you are protected.

Medicaid—which covers eligible low-income families and individuals—pays for sterilization for medical reasons in all states with Medicaid plans (as of the late 1970s, Arizona had no Medicaid program).

But a fundamental point as the 1980s neared was that coverage for costs was "fragmented." In the words of a nationally acknowledged expert on the subject, Charlotte F. Muller, Associate Director, Center for Social Research, City University of New York, "group health insurance . . . has made an incomplete adaptation to legalization of abortion, and has done little to promote or underwrite contraception . . ."

Or putting it in blunter words, *you* still are mostly on your own.

Tax Tip on Birth Control Pills, Abortions, Sterilization

If you practice some form of birth control, virtually all your expenses now qualify as medical expenses that you can take as part of your itemized medical expense deduction. This includes: birth control pills you buy for your own personal use through a prescription provided by your physician and the costs of an operation for an abortion or sterilization, male or female, undertaken voluntarily, assuming the operation was legal under the applicable state law.

How Much Does It Cost to Have (or Adopt) a Baby?

All signs are now pointing toward substantial and continuing moderation in procreation. A first reason is that you are postponing your marriages—and, therefore, you are shortening your childbearing years. A second is that more women are now attending college for longer periods of time, and taking full-time jobs. And a third powerful force slowing our population growth rate is, I submit, the high cost of having babies and bringing them up.

Rundown on Costs of Having a Baby

It's not news to you that baby costs of every kind have been spiraling upward—primarily obstetricians' fees and hospital charges. In addition, we are going in for ever more expensive nursery supplies and other "baby equipment." So steep have been the increases that, according to the Health Insurance Institute, as the 1980s neared, the total cost of having a baby passed the $2,600 mark. That included only costs through the baby's first week at home.

Biggest expense of all is, of course, hospital care. In the late 1970s a single day in a short-term general hospital cost more than $145, and the average hospital stay in maternity cases is now about four days. Delivery room, nursery room charges, and other items count as "extras."

Next biggest cost is the layette for the baby—which easily can total more than $700. The layette includes a basic wardrobe for the baby plus a full range of nursery items, baby furniture, bathing equipment, etc.

Third biggest item is medical care—covering an obstetrician's services, usually offered as a complete package, through the delivery and hospital stay; plus a circumcision fee; plus the cost of a pediatrician's newborn baby care while the baby is in the hospital. Most obstetricians now charge about $400, but some charge $600, $800, or more.

Finally, the cost of a typical maternity wardrobe is calculated by the Health Insurance Institute at about $300.

The grand total adds up to well over $2,600 as the 1980s begin. And under certain circumstances the cost can run even higher. For example:

If you stay in a private room at a fashionable big-city hospital it easily might have cost more than $200 a day in the late 1970s, bringing this part of the cost to $800—far above the rate for a multiple-occupancy room.

If the birth is complicated, if the baby is born with special problems calling for surgery, extensive transfusion, or other special treatment, or if the birth involves caesarean section, the hospital part of the cost could skyrocket. Today about one in twenty babies is born by caesarean section, involving an average hospital stay of eight days, versus four for a normal delivery.

Hospital and physicians' services for a caesarean delivery tend to run about 50 per cent higher than the costs for a normal delivery. About one in twelve newborn babies must be temporarily confined in a glass "isolette"—involving extra charges. Rh blood factor complications at birth also can boost expenses.

If you have twins, this obviously will greatly increase your bills, although some department stores promise to give you a second set of everything if you have twins.

Or you may require expensive extra drugs, use of a fetal monitor, and medications somewhere along the line.

Or your hospital may slap on an extra fee of $150 or more for preparation of the delivery room and sharply increase its rates for nursery accommodations—in many cases to $75 or more per day.

Or if you have a boy you may find that in addition to a circumcision fee there frequently is a circumcision "setup" charge of $12 or so.

In the maternity clothes department, your costs will rise if your baby is born in winter (or early spring) and you need to buy heavy wool or knit clothes instead of lightweight ones. Or you well may decide you need more than two everyday dresses and more than one dress-up dress over the five-to-six-month period when you will need special maternity clothes.

And if you insist on elegant new christening clothes, you'll have no trouble spending $50 to $150 just for a dress.

Ten Ways to Cut the High Cost of Motherhood

But aren't there some circumstances under which the costs of having a baby might be greatly reduced?

Yes. For instance, a second or third child costs a lot less than the first baby—simply because you already have most of the baby and maternity clothes, nursery things, etc. on hand. If you live in a small town or in a rural area, the expenses are likely to be a lot lower than in a big city. Mothers who breast-feed their newborn babies don't have to invest in special formulas.

Here are ten specific ways in which you can cut the high costs of motherhood:

(1) Before you make an arrangement with a specific obstetrician, discuss fees fully and frankly. In your initial consultation ask about fees for prenatal examinations and care, delivery, probable costs of such common complications as breech birth and caesarean section. If you feel you simply cannot afford the fee scale, say so. If the physician isn't willing to reduce the fee, ask him to refer you to a less expensive colleague. It's a perfectly reasonable and legitimate request, so don't be shy.

(2) Go home as soon as sensibly possible after your baby is born, and alert your obstetrician to your desire to do this. You will be more comfortable at home, and the cost of hiring a practical nurse or home health aide at from $35 to $50 a day is far less than the cost of a hospital room. Although the American Hospital Association estimates that the average hospital stay for having a baby is about four days, some hospitals have shaved this to under three—and some new mothers pack up and go home after only a day or two in the hospital.

(3) Take advantage of all maternity benefits in your health insurance policies or prepaid health plan. A typical policy today contributes from $200 to $350 toward hospital and doctor bills—about half the total—and some policies also contain coverage for costly complications at birth.

(4) Check the coverage your employer (or your husband's employer) provides via group health insurance. If your company does provide group health insurance with a private insurer, chances are three out of four that maternity benefits are included. And the trend here is toward expanded maternity coverage.

(5) Carefully look into the health insurance provisions for your baby-to-

be as well as yourself. Does such coverage begin at birth? When the baby is discharged from the hospital? Or when? Whatever the provisions, notify the insurer as soon as your baby is born.

(6) Investigate midwife services or maternity clinics in your neighborhood, generally associated with large teaching hospitals. Although such clinics are often geared to the needs of low-income people or special obstetrical problems, many are open to all—and those alternatives almost invariably offer services at far lower costs than the typical hospital. For more information contact the National Association of Parents and Professionals for Safe Alternatives in Childbirth, Box 267, Marble Hill, Missouri 63764.

(7) In selecting a hospital, find out how room rates are levied. A few hospitals do not charge maternity patients arriving late at night for a full day, but instead charge for part of a day. And if you can, accept a semi-private room; it will be considerably less expensive than a private one.

(8) Eliminate the utterly unimportant, but expensive at-home frills: fancy toys, nursery lamps, bottle warmers, heated plates, bath tables. Let your affluent friends and/or grandparents-to-be come up with such expensive items as dress-up baby clothes.

(9) Check secondhand stores, discount houses, and nationally recognized charities for good, used nursery furniture and other baby equipment. Tell your friends and relatives what you really *need* as baby presents—and don't hesitate to accept what relatives and friends might be happy to pass along.

(10) Explore and compare the costs of signing up for a diaper service versus buying disposal diapers versus buying cloth ones and doing them in your own washing machine.

Check List for Your Own Baby Costs

You can spot other areas in which you could achieve significant savings simply by going over the following detailed check list of new-baby equipment, on which the $2,600 plus in costs is based.

	COST IN YOUR AREA
HOSPITAL AND MEDICAL CARE	
Four days' hospitalization	_____
Labor and delivery-room charge	_____
Nursery charges, four days	_____
Circumcision setup charge	_____
Obstetrician's fees	_____
Circumcision fee	_____
Pediatrician's newborn care	_____
TOTAL	_____

COST IN YOUR AREA

BABY'S WARDROBE
    4 to 6 shirts _____
    3 to 4 gowns _____
    1 to 2 sleeping bags _____
    3 to 4 stretch coveralls _____
    4 to 6 receiving blankets _____
    4 to 6 dozen diapers _____
        (if not using diaper service) _____
    Diaper pins _____
    Sweater or shawl _____
    4 waterproof panties _____
    Booties and bootie socks _____
    Bunting _____
    TOTAL _____

NURSERY ITEMS
    6 fitted crib sheets _____
    4 waterproof sheets _____
    5 waterproof pads _____
    3 crib blankets _____
    1 blanket sleeper _____
    Comforter or quilt _____
    1 mattress pad _____
    Bassinet or carrying blanket _____
    Crib _____
    Crib mattress _____
    Crib bumper _____
    Diaper pail _____
    Portable baby seat _____
    Wicker changer with drawers _____
    Nursery lamp _____
    Vaporizer _____
    Baby carriage _____
    TOTAL _____

FEEDING EQUIPMENT   COST IN YOUR AREA

    8 to 12 8-ounce nursers _____
    2 to 4 4-ounce nursers _____
    Extra nipples, caps _____
    Disposable nurser kit _____
    Sterilizer kit or separate formula utensils _____
    Bottle and nipple brush _____
    Hot plate _____
    Bottle warmer _____
    2 to 3 bibs _____
    TOTAL _____

BATH ITEMS

    Bath table or tub _____
    4 washcloths, 2 towels _____
    Lotion _____
    Baby oil _____
    Cream _____
    Powder _____
    Sterile cotton and swabs _____
    Baby shampoo _____
    Bathing cream or liquid _____
    Petroleum jelly _____
    TOTAL _____

MISCELLANEOUS

    Baby vitamins _____
    Sweater set _____
    30 disposable diapers _____
    Baby care book (Spock paperback) _____
    Diaper bag _____
    Brush and comb _____
    Diaper service
        (first week—70 diapers) _____
    Crib mobile _____
    Rectal thermometer _____
    Baby scissors _____
    Car bed or seat _____
    Birth announcements _____
    TOTAL _____

MATERNITY CLOTHES   COST IN YOUR AREA

- 3 dresses
- 2 skirts
- 4 tops
- 2 pants
- 2 slips
- 3 bras
- 1 girdle
- 4 panties

TOTAL

TOTALS

- Hospital and medical care
- Baby's wardrobe
- Nursery items
- Feeding equipment
- Bath items
- Miscellaneous
- Maternity clothes

GRAND TOTAL

Copy this table on a separate sheet of paper, study it, share it with your friends. Just having this detailed list will help you curb, cushion, and cut the costs.

One final note: *prepare* yourself for the expenses and make up your mind right now that, no matter how much you save on these items, your baby will cost more than you anticipate. So do your best to manage your expenses properly, and you'll come through with your financial banners flying.

AND IF YOU ADOPT A CHILD?

No rundown on the cost of a baby would be complete without at least a footnote on the costs of adopting a child. And adoption not only has become a widespread practice among childless and zero-population-growth-conscious couples, but is being done by increasing numbers of single American women as well.

The cost of baby clothes and equipment will depend on the age of your child. But the above itemized list will guide you on how much these might run if you adopt a babe in arms.

In most states, no charge is made for adoption if you adopt a child through an approved social welfare agency, or a private one that is state-recognized. Private adoption agencies, though, charge fees ranging from

$600 to $1,700 or charge on a sliding scale depending on family income. In relatively rare instances a licensed adoption agency may charge as much as 10 to 11 per cent of the husband's gross yearly income. Normally there is no need to hire a lawyer. However, some states *require* that you hire one. In this case, fees in the late 1970s ran between $80 and $400 and occasionally to as much as $800.

If you go the route of "black market" adoptions—usually arranged by lawyers outside normal channels and often without benefit of careful matching and screening of child and parents-to-be—you do so strictly at your own risk and probably at a very high cost in dollars and cents too.

Among your best sources of information on adoption are your local community welfare council, your state or local welfare department, reputable local adoption agencies, the U. S. Department of Health, Education, and Welfare's Office of Child Development.

A key source of information on adopting children from foreign countries is International Social Service, Inc., 345 East 46th Street, New York, New York 10017.

The best place to inquire about children with special problems who need adoptive homes is ARENA (Adoption Resource Exchange of North America), 67 Irving Place, New York, New York 10003.

The Soaring Costs of Rearing a Child

WHERE THE MONEY GOES

Of each child-rearing dollar being spent by a moderate-income north central city family of four, the United States Department of Agriculture calculated in an exhaustive study in the late 1970s:

> 26 cents goes for food
> 9 cents goes for clothes
> 32 cents goes for shelter
> 5 cents goes for medical care
> 1 cent goes for education
> 16 cents goes for transportation
> 11 cents goes for "all other"

Child-rearing costs vary widely from large family to small family, from city to country, from one part of the United States to another, from income level to income level—but in general:

• The yearly cost of rearing one child is approximately 15 to 17 per cent of family income.

• The costs of supporting an eighteen-year-old are 30 to 45 per cent higher than for a one-year-old.

- The costs of providing food and clothes for a growing child tend to rise at a much faster clip than other aspects of the child's support.

WHAT THE MOTHER "LOSES": THE HIDDEN COSTS

What's more, the enormous sums alone represent only the *direct* costs of rearing a child—food, clothes, schooling, etc. There also are such hidden costs as the lost earnings you, a homebound mother, accept by not taking a paying job outside the home.

The Commission on Population Growth and the American Future in 1969 counted a full $40,000 in these "lost-opportunity costs" for each mother assuming she stayed home until her youngest child reached age fourteen. These figures would be much, much higher today.

And these lost-opportunity costs skyrocket along with the educational level of the mother. The mother who remained at home until her youngest child reached age fourteen "lost" earnings totaling $58,904 if she had a high school diploma, $82,467 if she had a college degree, $103,023 if she had a postcollege education, the Commission found. (By now, these totals are grossly underestimated.)

Another fascinating point: the loss in income tends to be greatest in cases of premarital conception. (About one in three couples in the very low-income bracket experiences premarital pregnancy.) Reason: if she has the baby, the mother usually has less opportunity to complete her education or job training before the child-rearing process begins, or to work and build a nest egg during the early years of marriage. Also, the husband's education or training may have to be cut short to support his family.

According to one national study, among families in the under-$15,000-a-year bracket, those who experienced premarital pregnancy averaged approximately $800 a year less in income than those whose children were conceived after marriage.

On the opposite side, your costs of child rearing will surge even more if you send your children to private schools, Ivy League colleges, summer camps, or on summer expeditions to Europe. Or if you give your children automobiles when they reach sixteen or seventeen. Or if you must pay the high cost of orthodontia. Or even if you give your youngsters their own home encyclopedia.

Further, since the long-term trend of prices is ever upward in this century, this will be reflected in ever rising costs of rearing children. On top of this, the preferred living *standards* of children will keep climbing along with the standards of their parents—from their preferences for food to their choices of entertainment, transportation, personal care. What "everybody else" has today is a lot more and a lot better than what anybody else ever had before.

So You Want a Divorce . . . Can You Afford One?

A "GROWTH INDUSTRY"

At a cocktail party a while back, I overheard a conversation between a stockbroker and a divorce lawyer. The broker complimented the lawyer on being in a "growth industry." And even though the divorce rate in the United States appeared to be leveling off as the 1970s ended and actually may be heading for a decline in the 1980s, divorces have indeed been in a long-term upsurge. Just consider:

* Of every ten marriages in our country, four end in divorce, with teenage marriages *twice* as likely to be broken by divorce as marriages of men and women in their twenties.
* Of the 4.5 million Americans marrying in an average year during the 1970s, an estimated 1.8 million of them eventually go through the emotional and financial agony of a divorce.
* Even if the divorce rate levels off, about 1 million marriages in our nation will be breaking up every year, according to population experts, and 40 per cent of all children will live in a single-parent family at some time before they reach age eighteen.
* The reasons for a possible reversal in the long upswing in the divorce rate are by no means clear. It could be that since men and women are waiting longer to wed, today's marriages presumably will be more durable. Or it could be that many couples simply dispense with marriage altogether and live as "mingling singles," thus erasing any breakups from public records and making the marriage-divorce figures misleading. Or it could be that the experience of living together before marriage improves the odds on a successful marriage.

Whatever the qualifications about the future, the broker's remark was not only arresting but also quite perceptive.

CAN YOU AFFORD A DIVORCE?

No matter what your income bracket, when considering divorce, you *must* ask yourself bluntly, "Can I afford one?" The cost of an uncontested divorce entails legal fees which may be moderate—a separation agreement will increase the costs—and the costs zoom up from there, if the action is contested or if a legal fight develops. The cliché that "two can live (almost) as cheaply as one" becomes acutely pertinent if you are contemplating a divorce, for the simple reason that the same amount of money must cover all the costs of two households instead of one, unless the wife is or can become truly self-supporting. In most cases, both of you must be prepared to cut your former standards of living. In the sage words of one lawyer, "There is only one pie and no matter how it is sliced, the portions become smaller."

DOWNWARD TREND OF LEGAL FEES

Although the economic impact of your divorce will almost surely be drastic, there have been important recent developments in the area of attorneys' fees, which in contrast to the inflationary trend of most expenses, can (and should) substantially reduce the cost of obtaining a divorce:

(1) A Supreme Court decision in the late 1970s permits lawyers to advertise, and some do advertise "uncontested divorces" at extremely low fees. While a lawyer ideally should be chosen on the basis of personal recommendation rather than from an ad in the newspaper, the element of competition already has impelled many lawyers to charge more moderate fees.

(2) Some states allow inexpensive "do it yourself" divorce kits as an alternative to hiring a lawyer, and there never has been a specific prohibition against going to court without a lawyer.

(3) Local bar associations do not uniformly have your interest in mind, but several bar associations have established panels of qualified divorce lawyers under the umbrella of a "legal referral service" to help you, an average citizen, obtain legal assistance at a moderate cost. As the 1980s neared, over 250 such referral services were operating from coast to coast. One which had an excellent record was established by the Joint Committee of the Association of the Bar of the City of New York and the New York County Lawyers Association. The fee for a half-hour consultation was $15, an amount well below the cost of running a law office. Subsequent services, if needed after the initial consultation, were more realistically priced.

ALIMONY AND CHILD SUPPORT

Obviously, the major divorce expense is for alimony and child support. It is hazardous to generalize because no divorce is "typical" and guidelines vary in different parts of the country. A rule of thumb is that you, a husband without children, may be expected to pay between 20 and 25 per cent of your gross income as alimony. If your marriage is of short duration, though, and your wife has a good, well-paying job, she would be entitled to only nominal, if any, alimony.

If there are children involved, your alimony and child support package may go as high as 40 per cent of your gross income. In the past these amounts have been greater, but the flood of women into the work force and of jobs that provide steady incomes on which they can support themselves has reduced some ex-wives' need for large alimony payments.

In addition, some courts have become more sympathetic toward the sometimes crushing economic burden of alimony upon the husband.

Still another factor in the trend toward lower alimony and child support awards and settlements has been the realization that if the husband's obligations are too great, he often will default and even disappear.

Courts have a broad discretion, however, and will be guided by the facts of each particular case. Most divorces do end up in a negotiated settlement rather than in an award by the court. If the husband and wife are each represented by competent counsel, the separation agreement usually will be in line with what the lawyers expect a court would do.

The separation agreement generally is incorporated into the divorce decree and also may contain an "escalator clause" based on increases in the cost of living (consumer price) index or the husband's income. A key difference between a negotiated settlement and a court-imposed award is that the former usually cannot be changed. However, child support is subject to modifications by the court even if the separation agreement provides to the contrary. The theory is that children are "wards of the court" into whose best interests the court always can inquire, despite the existing contractual arrangements between you, their parents.

TAX CONSEQUENCES

An alternative to periodic alimony payments is a lump sum settlement. Lump sum payments, however, are *not* tax-deductible to the husband and taxable to the wife (the tax consequences of periodic alimony payments). The lump sum payment is not considered a gift. Therefore, if you, the husband, make the transfer in property other than cash, you, the husband, would be required to pay a capital gains tax on the difference between its cost and its fair market value. Also when considering a lump sum settlement, you must realize that if your former wife uses up the money and is likely to become a public charge, the courts in some states will award alimony to your former wife, regardless of the fact that she had traded periodic payments for a lump sum.

ALIMONY FOR HUSBANDS

Alimony traditionally has been viewed as payments from a husband to a wife, but as the 1980s neared, more than half of the states permitted a husband to receive alimony from you, his wife, if your financial circumstances warranted it. The remaining states will now be required to make similar provision for the husband because of a decision in the late 1970s by the United States Supreme Court.

In sum, the concept of alimony is changing from what once was an absolute right on the part of a wife to a pragmatic arrangement based upon personal economics.

While alimony is tax-deductible to the spouse who pays it, and child support is not, husbands in high tax brackets often arrange to pay an unallocated amount as "alimony" (instead of "alimony and child support") to wives who are in lower tax brackets. Thereby they obtain a major contribution by the government to their financial obligations. The Supreme Court has held that this is a perfectly legal loophole.

"HIDDEN" COSTS

In addition to legal fees, alimony, and child support, there are the so-called "hidden" costs of divorce. Who gets the family house? How are stocks, bonds, and other assets to be divided? What about life insurance? The high cost of medical care? The cost of a college education?

Family House

The family home often is a middle-class family's most valuable asset. Usually the wife gets possession until the last child moves out, at which time the house is sold and the proceeds are divided. However, if there are substantial assets other than the family home and the divorce is amicable, it is not unusual for the husband to deed the house to his wife. In either event, watch out for this pitfall:

Can the wife manage the increased expenses of maintaining the house out of her income, even when augmented by alimony and child support from her husband?

Stocks, Bonds, and Other Assets

If these assets are jointly owned they are usually divided equally by the husband and wife. Although assets acquired during a marriage once belonged to the person in whose name they were held, as the 1980s approached, three quarters of the states had statutes providing for a 50-50 split.

Even in the majority of states which have equitable distribution statutes, inherited money and money or other assets acquired before the marriage in general are excluded from divorce settlements.

Life Insurance Policies

Under the usual separation agreement, the husband's obligation to pay alimony and child support ceases upon his death. Therefore, in all situations in which there are insufficient capital assets to fund continuing support, life insurance becomes an absolute necessity, at least until the children become self-sufficient. Most states have lowered the age of majority to eighteen; many, though, still require child support payments until age twenty-one. The details of the insurance must be spelled out in the agreement, and it is imperative that there be a provision for annual disclosure and verification that the premiums are being paid and that there is no borrowing against the policy.

Medical Care

Because of the high costs of hospital and medical care, a separation agreement should provide for Blue Cross-Blue Shield and major-medical insurance for the benefit of the children. Often these items are fringe benefits of either spouse's employment as far as the children are concerned—but a divorced spouse will not be covered under the other spouse's group health insurance.

A separation agreement also may specify that expenses not covered by insurance—such as orthodontia, cosmetic surgery, and psychiatric treatment—will be undertaken or partially paid for by the husband.

College Expenses

A seasoned attorney representing you, a wife, undoubtedly will advise you to obtain a definite commitment in the separation agreement for your soon-to-be former husband to pay for as much of the college education of the children as possible, especially if it appears that your former husband intends to remarry and raise a new family. The attorney for you, the husband, on the other hand, usually will advise you to resist such an open-ended commitment especially in view of the ever increasing costs of a college education. The result is a matter for serious negotiations, based upon the circumstances of each case. The problem is compounded by the realization that a college education is roughly the equivalent of what a high school diploma once was. Thus, graduate or professional school is becoming the name of the game.

Yet it's an unusual separation agreement in which the husband undertakes such a significant additional commitment, especially if the children are still relatively young.

MORE ON COSTS, TRAUMA, AND LAWYERS

Despite the progress toward lower legal fees, they remain of great importance to the cost of divorce, especially if the divorce is contested or even if both parties agree to a divorce but cannot agree upon the terms of the financial settlement. If litigation is involved, attorneys' fees can run up to $15,000, depending in part upon (1) the duration and intensity of the controversy; (2) whether there is a custody fight; (3) your individual income brackets. You must face several difficult decisions in this area:

(1) If you can come to an agreement on your own without the intercession of lawyers, fees may be as low as $150, including disbursements, but not including a separation agreement. In simple situations, a separation agreement may not, in fact, be necessary.

(2) However, the tortuous question is: "When is a divorce and/or separation so simple that it requires no negotiations between lawyers?" By the nature of their responsibilities to their clients, lawyers cannot and should not represent both sides. The lawyer who does his (or her) job properly should be an advocate for you, the client. He is required to, and presumably will, negotiate on your behalf unimpaired by feelings of guilt, intimidation, or other blind spots which often will hamper you if you attempt to negotiate

your economic futures between yourselves without the aid of counsel. In this context, no divorce should be wholly uncontested.

(3) To avoid the expenses of hiring separate lawyers to negotiate as well as to perform the somewhat ministerial duties of obtaining an uncontested divorce, another option is to obtain the services of an intermediary with a background in psychological counseling. The problem here is that the disadvantages of the adversary system (principally the discomfort of confrontation and the substantial expense involved) may be outweighed by the therapist's imperfect attempts to serve two masters, or even worse, succumbing to the human temptation to play God.

(4) Even if you decide to proceed by the conventional route of each of you engaging separate lawyers, there is no reason to accede to open-ended charges of "whatever the traffic will bear." You should openly discuss fees with your lawyer at the start, and if they appear to you to be too high, you are free to consider other alternatives. Not everyone needs a "bomber" or should be required to pay a retainer of up to $10,000.

(5) You also might consider whether you should agree to a flat fee or an hourly rate. If you decide on the hourly rate, obtain an estimate of the anticipated number of hours your case will take. A lawyer's hourly charges vary, depending on experience, professional standing, and the section of the country in which he practices. Hourly charges can range from as little as $20 an hour to as high as $200 an hour. In large cities, most hourly rates will be within the $50-to-$100-an-hour range.

(6) And then—"who pays the legal fees?" In the past you, the husband, were customarily expected to pay all fees, including those of your wife's lawyer, except if your wife had her own independent assets or income, or if she was the spouse pressing for the divorce. In the late 1970s, though, the trend was toward a gainfully employed wife's paying her own attorney's fees. The prior practice, in fact, placed lawyers in the uncomfortable conflict-of-interest position of taking money from the adverse party.

OTHER NEW TRENDS IN DIVORCE

Grounds

The national trend has been toward no-fault divorce, thereby reducing the need for evidence on such harsh grounds as adultery, cruelty, or abandonment.

One result of the no-fault trend is practically to eliminate the need for "migratory divorce mills" where no-fault divorces could be obtained on the basis of an overnight stay in such places as Mexico, Haiti, and/or the Dominican Republic.

Ownership of Property

By the late 1970s about three quarters of the states had enacted some form of legislation providing for equitable distribution of property acquired during marriage, thereby reducing the advantage of the spouse in whose name the property happened to have been held.

Flexible Maintenance

Legislation providing for equitable distribution of property also changed the concept of alimony.

The characterization "maintenance" is used, whereby the courts have the discretion to relate the payments to a retraining period which would enable the dependent spouse to find remunerative employment.

Custody

More husbands are obtaining custody than ever before, but there is still a judicial bias in favor of the wife, especially when the children are young. The custody changes which ostensibly put fathers on an equal footing with mothers, unfortunately, have been used by many husbands as a weapon by which to intimidate their wives into accepting either inadequate financial support or the threat of a custody fight.

Joint Custody

Although this development has worked in special situations, many lawyers and psychologists view it principally as a compromise to salve wounded egos —creating more problems than it solves.

Mingling Singles

After the experience of divorce, more and more women with children are understandably reluctant to enter into a new legal entanglement. Instead they decide to establish a "family" relationship outside of marriage. However, alimony often ceases whenever this informal arrangement becomes known—and the ex-wife also becomes vulnerable to a custody fight by her ex-husband, who may be "aggrieved" over the effect her new life-style might have on the children. Nevertheless, courts still are reluctant to take a child away from the custodial parent unless the circumstances are extreme.

Living together as unmarried singles is indisputably on the rise. What happens when singles separate? Some courts say that a separated person may be entitled to what has become known as "palimony."

Grandparents' Visitation

Until recently, grandparents were victims without a remedy of bitter marital disputes after which the custodial parent (or, in the event of the death of a parent, the surviving parent) excluded the former in-laws from his or her new life, and barred them from visiting their grandchildren. Recognizing that such a situation is among the most heartbreaking results of a broken marriage, several states now give grandparents the right to apply to the court for reasonable visiting rights even over the objection of the custodial parent.

NO SUBSTITUTE FOR PLANNING IN ADVANCE

The economic and psychological costs of divorce can be, and all too often are, devastating. Recent trends in divorce costs and divorce arrangements plus sound advice may ease the situation somewhat.

But there is no substitute for *planning for economic survival in the event of divorce in advance of marriage.* This planning could range all the way from vocational education to (unromantic as it may seem) a premarriage contract along the lines of a partnership agreement.

TRACING ABSENTEE FATHERS

There soon will be no place to hide for husbands, ex-husbands, and/or fathers who skip out of supporting their families. Whether they flee from the nation's wealthiest areas or our worst slums, federal and state officials have geared up to track down fathers who leave their families and duck child-support payments.

That's bad news for these men. But it's good news for us, America's taxpayers, for it must lead to a sharp reduction in our welfare caseloads.

For years, welfare agencies and administrators have struggled with the costly problems of fathers who desert their families or who never marry the mothers. But in the late 1970s, under an amendment to the Social Security Act providing for the Child Support and Establishment of Paternity program, the government's authorized Parent Locator Service began assisting local welfare departments in tracking down absentee fathers. Through this, the cost to taxpayers of supporting children of errant fathers could be trimmed by as much as $1 billion a year.

An estimated 4.8 million American men had left their families and had failed to provide child support as the decade of the 1970s closed. We, the taxpayers, are burdened with a bill of many billions a year under the Aid to Families with Dependent Children program.

All mothers applying for welfare must, by law, name the father of the child except in cases involving rape, incest, and adoption or in certain situations that might endanger the child. Federal records from the IRS, Social Security, and the Defense Department are made available to local welfare departments to help locate the fathers.

The Parent Locator Service, as part of a computerized project, tracks down fathers who have disappeared. Requests coming into the Washington-based facility are reaching thousands a month. The PLS has located about 70 per cent of the fathers to date.

A return of $5.00 for every $1.00 invested in the program is projected in a study for the Health, Education, and Welfare Department. Even a $3.00 to $1.00 recovery rate would more than make the program worthwhile, the HEW study points out.

A recovery of $100 million a year is expected in New York, New Jersey,

Puerto Rico, and the Virgin Islands alone, for parents can no longer desert with impunity and assume that someone else will pay the cost of supporting their children.

Federal employees and military personnel, the latter previously free of garnishment of pay, are now subject to the law.

Title 4-D of the Social Security Act, as amended, provides for a central locator service and reimburses the states for enforcement actions they are mandated to take. This introduces a combination of new inducements and penalties.

The U. S. Treasury is bearing 75 per cent of the cost of finding deserting parents and fathers of children born out of wedlock. The states are obligated to help track down and recover support funds from such parents if they change residence to another state.

An early benefit is the increased co-operation of unwed mothers to establish paternity with the putative father accepting his obligation for child support without a paternity trial. And many fathers do have the capacity to pay but the states have not had the machinery or the perseverance to go after them, especially if they cross state lines.

If a state doesn't do what is required, it is assessed a 5 per cent penalty against the welfare fund (which can be hefty). New Jersey, for instance, gets 50 per cent of its welfare costs from the federal government.

The system may be used by families not on welfare. All families must be provided with the same services no matter what their incomes, if the families so request. In this category, HEW reimburses states for 75 per cent of the locator costs but allows the states to charge the families for an amount not to exceed the cost of the remainder of the services.

The law authorizes federal district courts to act. Regional offices of the HEW will be monitoring performances and programs, providing technical assistance and assessing penalties. And the return to us may be $5.00 for $1.00.

15

YOUR PERSONAL BANKING BUSINESS

Comparison Shopping Among Financial Institutions	867
What Each Financial Institution Is	869
Commercial Banks	870
Savings and Loan Associations	870
Mutual Savings Banks	871
Credit Unions	871
Your Checking Account	872
Regular Checking Accounts	873
Special Checking Accounts	874
New, Exciting Variations	874
Rules for Writing and Endorsing Checks	876
Key Questions About Writing Checks	878
Guarding Against Check Forgeries	879
How to Protect Yourself Against Cash-Machine Cons and Errors	880
New Protections for Electronic Banking Customers	882
How to Balance Your Checkbook	882
Your Savings Account	884
How Much Money Should You Keep in a Savings Account?	884
Key Forms of Savings Accounts	885
Which Type of Savings Account Is Best for You?	888
How Can You Force Yourself to Save—Gracefully?	889
What Is "Highest" Interest on Savings?	890
How Does a Savings Account Grow?	891

Computer Technology Changes Our Financial Habits	893
electronic funds transfer system—	
its meaning to you	894
How "Safe" Is Your Money?	896
Should You Rent a Safe Deposit Box?	899
Have You Forgotten Money You Own?	901

Comparison Shopping Among Financial Institutions

You easily may be befuddled by the array of financial institutions serving you today and the myriad of new services they offer. It isn't easy figuring out how to earn the most on your savings and where it's cheapest to open a checking account.

The once clear-cut functions of commercial banks and "thrift" institutions —credit unions, savings and loan associations, and mutual savings banks— have blurred. America's financial institutions have become increasingly similar in the services they offer and intensely competitive for your patronage.

For instance, many commercial banks, savings and loan associations, and credit unions offer what amount to interest-bearing checking accounts. At your commercial bank, this account may take the form of a prearranged transfer system, enabling you to have money moved automatically from your savings to your checking account when you pay your bills. At your S&L or credit union, you may accomplish the same objective with a negotiable order of withdrawal account (NOW) or a share draft account. No matter what it is called or how it is triggered—by telephone or writing a check—the important "plus" for you is that all your money is earning interest until you spend it.

But this very trend toward "sameness" makes many *differences* between the same *type*, as well as among different *classes*, of financial institutions. Major banks throughout the United States, for example, compute interest on savings accounts in more than fifty ways.

Checking account fees at different institutions can cost you little or nothing or as much as $80 a year.

Because costs and services can vary so widely and advertising tends to emphasize "free" gimmicks and "convenience" rather than conveying information that you can use to comparison shop, you need objective help to figure out the best deal for yourself.

Say you have just moved to a new town and you must have the services of a financial institution so you can get cash, pay bills, start a savings account, or arrange for a small loan. Where do you start? How do you weigh the virtues of bank "A" against those of bank "B" or against those of an S&L or credit union?

Or perhaps your present bank has just informed you that it's raising its checking account fees. Should you switch to another institution or merely take advantage of another type of program that your bank offers?

What's more, although you take for granted such traditional financial services as prepaid bank-by-mail envelopes, "free" checking, nearby branches, comprehensive statements, etc., banks and other institutions are cutting back on such routine amenities.

Why?

Because of higher costs coupled with your demand that deposits, including checking account funds, earn interest.

The rule of the game in the 1980s is that just about everyone and every service must pay its own way. While your bank or S&L still may offer "free" copying and notary services or travelers' checks, the chances are such extras will be tied to some requirement, such as maintaining a minimum balance in your savings or checking account.

Thus, it's silly and costly to channel your family's banking business to institution "A" simply because it offers you "free" money orders or "free" checking accounts. Don't allow such lures to mislead you.

Always keep shopping. View today's banks, S&Ls, and credit unions as little more than financial supermarkets. If the service or products in one becomes shoddy, don't hesitate to look elsewhere.

Compare which of the following institutions seem most important to you, then make up your mind:

Savings: Are a wide variety of savings plans offered? Are time deposit plans, savings certificates, other forms of savings programs available in addition to regular "passbook" accounts?

Interest: Is your institution's rate of interest on savings and checking accounts the maximum allowed? How frequently is interest compounded and credited on savings and checking? What kind of interest penalty will you have to pay if you withdraw money early from a time or savings account?

Availability: Are there any restrictions on withdrawals should you require your money in a hurry? Could your deposit be "frozen" without your being aware of it? What are the legal restrictions on withdrawals—if any?

Insurance: Are your deposits federally or state insured? With most deposits covered by the Federal Deposit Insurance Corporation (FDIC), the Federal Savings and Loan Insurance Corporation (FSLIC), or the National Credit Union Administration (NCUA), or state insurance corporations, they almost certainly are. But be sure.

Checking: Is the institution's rate of interest on checking, NOW, or share draft accounts competitive? What are the minimum balance requirements necessary in order to earn interest? How many free items, or checks, are you allowed to write each month? How much is the service charge? Does the institution offer a non-interest checking account? Can you get an automatic line of credit with checking?

Loans: How do the financial institutions compare on availability of credit —ease, lack of red tape, speed? And how do they compare on interest rates, other terms, range and availability of auto and similar loans? Does the institution run loan sales, offer interest rebates, provide preferential rates if you borrow against savings?

Mortgages: Are they easy to get? Are you charged a fee by the institution for originating a mortgage for you? Are mortgages available for co-operatives, condominiums, summer homes? Does the institution offer alternative mortgage plans—reverse annuity, variable interest, graduated payment plans, etc.? Is there a prepayment penalty if you pay off your loan early? Is interest paid on escrow accounts?

Trust Department: Has this department good junior as well as senior staff so that there will be continuity of trust services? Can you check the department's record on its investments to find out how it performed for other clients over a prolonged period?

Convenience: Does the financial institution have a branch or cash dispenser or twenty-four-hour automated teller near your home or office? Are late evening or weekend services provided? Are the teller lines long? Is there easy access to the institution's office? Is the service friendly and personal? How frequently do you receive statements, and do they include an accounting of all your loans, checks, savings, etc.?

Extra Services: Do you need or want these in light of the fact that all financial institutions are charging or beginning to charge you for the services you use? Interest-paying Christmas club? Help with your income tax forms? A travel service? Automatic bill-paying?

Continuity: If you do stay with the institution with which you've done business for a long time, will you receive preferential treatment—mortgage money when mortgages are tight, other special and valuable favors of this nature?

Electronic Services: Does the financial institution offer automatic transfer from savings to checking? Are automatic bill payer and payroll deposit and deduction services available? Does your institution provide check guarantee services through computer terminals located in stores in your area? Can you "talk" to the institution's computer to help with bill-paying or just to figure out where you stand financially?

What Each Financial Institution Is

All types of financial institutions today offer long-term mortgages, credit cards, savings instruments of varying maturity, checking accounts in one form or another. This movement toward uniformity, begun in the mid 1970s, continues but it is not yet complete. The following is a rundown of the major services provided by financial institutions as the 1980s approached.

COMMERCIAL BANKS

Also known as banks and trust companies and community banks.

Our country's roughly fifteen thousand commercial banks still remain our foremost financial "department stores," offering you almost every service and convenience a borrower or saver might seek.

At the corner commercial bank, you may get unsecured installment loans, saving instruments of varying denominations at varying rates of return and maturities; checking accounts; mortgage and home improvement loans; credit cards, debit cards, a whole new range of electronic banking system services; consumer loans for automobiles, appliances, and furniture, as well as student, personal, and farm loans; trust, investment, estate, and investment brokerage services.

Virtually all bank deposits are insured by the Federal Deposit Insurance Corporation (FDIC) in Washington.

While banks in general are at the top of the consumer credit and savings market, some are business-oriented; others concentrate on consumer borrowers.

As of the late seventies, banks are restricted by law to paying lower interest on savings accounts than other types of financial institutions.

This is changing.

SAVINGS AND LOAN ASSOCIATIONS

(Also known as building and loan associations, co-operative banks, savings associations, and homestead associations.)

If you are a typical customer of a savings and loan, you use the institution as a haven for your savings rather than a source of loans. S&Ls have five savers for each borrower because they have in the past been allowed by law to pay slightly more interest than banks. If you borrow, you usually seek a long-term mortgage loan from the S&L, which traditionally has played a key role in home financing.

But more and more, S&Ls are broadening their services to include: direct deposit of Social Security checks into a customer's account, Individual Retirement Accounts and Keogh Plans (see Chapter 18), passbook loans to customers with money on deposit; automatic account deductions for such bills as mortgage and insurance premium payments.

There are roughly five thousand S&Ls in the United States, classified as insured or uninsured, federally chartered or state chartered. Savings in federally chartered S&Ls are insured by the Federal Savings and Loan Insurance Corporation (FSLIC). Insurance for state-chartered institutions is optional, but most institutions provide savers with this protection. Privately insured associations may pay more interest on deposits than federally chartered S&Ls.

As the 1970s ended, state and federally chartered S&Ls in a number of states could offer what are essentially interest-bearing checking accounts, known as NOW or Negotiable Order of Withdrawal accounts. Associations in other parts of the country soon also will offer the interest-bearing checking accounts in some form.

MUTUAL SAVINGS BANKS

Since these were established in the early part of the nineteenth century, mutual savings banks have provided customers with some of the services of both commercial banks and of savings and loan associations. This holds true today.

In some of the seventeen states in which they operated as the 1980s opened, mutuals are virtual duplicates of commercial banks, offering you checking account services, bank credit cards, low-cost life insurance policies. The services are not uniform, however.

Like S&Ls, in the past the big attraction of mutual savings banks has been the slightly higher interest they were allowed to pay on savings. This higher rate vis-à-vis commercial banks applied to long-term certificate accounts, too. In exchange for the higher return on longer-term certificates, you, the saver, agreed to "freeze" your money in the institution for a specified period and, depending on the account, to make a minimum deposit. This differential well may be erased in the 1980s.

CREDIT UNIONS

Credit unions are non-profit savings and lending co-operatives made up of individuals with a common bond, such as place of employment, professional associates, area of residence, membership in a union, religious group, etc. Governed and run by members, credit unions have specialized in offering reasonably priced credit and often higher interest on savings than other financial institutions. They deal exclusively with households and individuals.

CU members are shareholders, not depositors, and they receive dividends on shares, not interest on deposits. Credit unions, at this date, are exempt from federal taxation. All federally chartered CUs are insured under the National Credit Union Administration. Many of the state-chartered institutions have the same federal insurance or state insurance.

While continuing to emphasize consumer loans and financial counseling, CUs recently have been granted new powers. Among them is the right to offer members longer-term mortgage loans, savings certificates, credit cards, and the equivalent of interest-bearing checking accounts, known as share draft accounts. Some CUs, too, have started to be involved in establishing such electronic banking services as automated teller machines and point-of-sale terminals.

Whether or not a particular credit union offers these or other services depends on the decisions made by each CU's directors, as well as rapidly changing state and federal regulations.

Your Checking Account

I remember, and I am sure you do as well, when a checking account was just that and nothing more. Your only option was to choose between a regular and a special account. But now the choices are so numerous they are almost mind-boggling.

The reasons lie first in the introduction of computer technology into the banking industry, making it possible for you to conduct much routine business with a plastic transaction card or turn bill-paying over to your financial institution almost entirely. Second, the increased competition among S&Ls, banks, and credit unions has broadened your options.

The purpose of a checking account or its equivalent NOW or share draft account is to give you a convenient and safe way to handle relatively large amounts of cash and to transfer money to other people. Of every four American families, three have at least one checking account, and more than 90 per cent of payments in this country are by check. (Still, about 25 per cent of households have no checking accounts and rely heavily on money orders.)

Despite all the talk about ours becoming a "checkless society," millions of you are reluctant to give up the accounts. You are familiar with checks; you rely on the proof they provide of to-whom-you-have-paid-how-much-and-when, and you like their stop-payment and "float" features. Thus, checks remain very much part of our financial transaction system.

To open a checking account, go to your bank or "thrift" institution's New Accounts Department, fill out a signature card, decide what type of account you want (or can afford) to open, and make your initial deposit. In some states, you must be at least eighteen or twenty-one years old to open an individual account. Otherwise, you may open a joint account with a parent or relative.

Before you investigate the different types of checking accounts or their equivalents available to you, figure out roughly how many checks you write each month. If you are average, you write fourteen to twenty-two. Consider your income, credit card use, and other factors that might affect the size of your deposits and your average and low monthly balance.

If you have had a checking account before, glance through your checking account statements of the past few years. When you have some idea of your check-writing habits and the size of your balance, calculate the interest you would earn on your balance if it were in a savings account. Estimate this figure according to the lowest rate paid by any savings institution in your area. A $500 minimum balance, for example, at 5 per cent interest, translates into a loss of about $25 in interest during one year.

It generally costs a financial institution between 10 and 30 cents to process a customer's check. To cover this and to make a profit, most institutions impose service charges and/or minimum balance requirements on you, a customer, and invest the money you leave in your accounts.

While computerized banking is supposed to cut an institution's check-processing costs by as much as 80 per cent, the systems are costly to put in place—one automatic teller can cost up to $50,000—and must be used heavily if savings are to be obtained. So usually (but not always), you'll have to pay some fee to maintain a checking account.

There are two main traditional types of checking accounts—regular accounts and special accounts.

REGULAR CHECKING ACCOUNTS

• In a regular checking account, you normally must keep a certain minimum balance—usually at least $100 and quite possibly $300 or more. Some banks state their requirement in terms of a person's "average" balance, while others look at the "low" balance. *The average balance* is more favorable to you, the customer.

As long as you maintain the required balance, many banks will permit you to write as many checks and make as many deposits as you please without paying any monthly service charge. However, if the amount in your regular checking account falls below the minimum, you may have to pay a monthly charge of $2.00 to $3.00 or more. Or the bank may levy a maintenance charge for your account each month, in addition to the required minimum balance. Still other banks will let you write a certain number of checks and make a certain number of deposits before any service charge is made.

Clearly, institutions which charge no maintenance or per item fees and have no minimum balance requirements are your best bargains.

Some banks which do not offer such low-cost checking to everyone, do make it available to older citizens, certain civil servants, persons on direct payroll deposit system, students, or other special groups.

Generally, a regular checking account is the best choice for you if you write a relatively large number of checks each month and can maintain the required minimum balance in your account.

The key point about any checking account that requires a minimum balance is that you are paying the bank a fee equal to at least the interest you could earn on the funds if they were kept in a savings account. For every $100 you keep in a checking account just to meet the bank's balance requirements, you give up at least $5 a year in interest.

Still, if you write more than four or five checks per month a regular checking account is usually the most economical type. If you choose it and it requires a minimum balance, try to maintain your deposit above the minimum to avert a monthly penalty charge.

As the 1970s ended, most commercial banks could transfer funds automatically from your savings accounts to cover a check or meet a minimum balance if you had requested and signed up for the service. This provided you with a protection against bounced checks (which generally cost you between $7.00 and $10) and not meeting a minimum balance requirement. The fee for this automatic service ranged between 25 cents and $1.00. The service also allowed you to collect interest on deposits longer.

To determine the cost of regular checking, multiply the monthly maintenance fee you are charged by 12. Add to it any charges for deposits and checks, plus 5 per cent of the minimum balance you are required to maintain. The result is the yearly cost of regular checking.

SPECIAL CHECKING ACCOUNTS

• With a special checking account (or "economy" account), you do not have to keep a minimum balance. However, you usually must pay a flat monthly service charge plus another 10-cent or 15-cent fee for each "item" processed. Some institutions count only checks as items, while others include both checks and deposits. Some even count each separate check listed on a single deposit slip as one "item."

To figure the annual cost of special checking, add up the number of checks you write each month. Multiply this figure by the cost the bank charges you per check. Add in the monthly maintenance charge and multiply the result by 12.

NEW, EXCITING VARIATIONS

Your other alternatives to traditional checking accounts include:

• *Bill-paying services:* Funds can be directly transferred from your savings accounts to cover such regular bills as mortgages or insurance premiums. Until then your deposit earns interest. You must give the institution initial authorization or telephone each time you wish a payment to be made or arrange each month to send the bills you wish paid.

• *Overdraft accounts,* also called automatic lines of credit: Some institutions simply will tack the "overdraft" feature to your regular checking account. Others will issue to you a special set of overdraft checks.

• *Electronic transfers:* Some institutions enable you to make deposits, withdrawals, move money from one type of account to another or make transfers directly from your account to a merchant's account through use of a computer terminal and a transaction card. For details, see pages 880–82.

• *Share drafts:* These are essentially interest-bearing checking accounts offered by credit unions. Interest is paid, however, generally on amounts deposited in your account by the tenth or twentieth of each month, provided they remain on deposit for the quarter. Credit unions usually do not charge their members any fees for this type of account. They keep their processing costs down by sending you statements quarterly, not monthly, and by not returning your canceled checks. Each share draft in your book of drafts is backed by copy paper, so you have a copy of every check as you write it.

• *NOW Accounts:* NOW or negotiable versions of withdrawal accounts are other "thrift" institutions' versions of interest-bearing checking accounts. It is likely the accounts will spread to other types of institutions early in this new decade and throughout the country.

NOWs could both hurt and help you, depending on several factors—for instance, your check-writing habits and how much money you keep in your account. If you are accustomed to writing many checks while holding low balances, you could end up paying more in service charges than you receive in interest. Say you have a NOW account with an average balance of $200; your bank pays 3 per cent interest, so your yearly interest payment is $6.00. If the bank charges $12 a year service fee, plus 11 cents per transaction, and you write fourteen checks a month, your total service charges would amount to $30.48 annually. Thus, the net cost to you of a 3 per cent NOW account would run $24.48.

In short, if institutions offering NOWs decide to charge you more for the services they provide, you could receive pennies in interest while spending dollars in service fees.

Of course, competition among different types, as well as the same class of institutions, for your household funds may hold service fees down. Institutions also may decide to cut back on services or they could raise the cost of borrowing money, so you, as a borrower, would subsidize savers.

When considering a NOW account, weigh (as you would with any checking account) your check-writing and deposit habits. Take note of any service fees the institution may charge and estimate whether these may exceed the interest you will earn. If they do not, then a NOW may be a sound choice, because in addition to its interest-earning feature a NOW enables you to avoid the costs involved in switching funds from savings to checking.

• *Telephone transfers:* Financial institutions may permit you to move money from your savings to your checking account merely by making a telephone call or transfer your funds automatically (once you have authorized them to do so). You, in effect, create your own interest-bearing checking account. Most of your funds earn interest until you need to pay a bill. There may be some time constraints, or fees may be charged for this service. An institution, for example, may require you to phone before noon if you want funds transferred that same day. Fees vary.

• *Money orders:* Traditionally money orders have been considered "the poor man's checking account," and completely secure. While the first part of this notion is generally correct, the latter is not, as large numbers of unfortunate Americans discovered when a big private money order company went bankrupt in the 1970s. Money orders, except for those issued by the U. S. Postal Service and insured banks, can be risky instruments. As a result, a few states now require or are working to require that all such payment instruments sold in their states be insured. No federal agency at the end of the 1970s regulated money orders nationwide. Until this occurs, one state superintendent of banks warns, "Money order purchasers are to a degree playing Russian roulette."

• *Money-market funds:* Some money-market funds, a category of mutual funds (see page 1174) which invest in highly liquid securities, allow you, a customer, to write checks on your accounts. Often there is no charge for this service but the amount of your check must be $500 or more. Unlike your treatment with regular checking accounts, you continue to earn interest until your check clears. Accounts are not insured, however, and, say, in the event of forgery, you may not have some of the legal rights that you have against a bank.

RULES FOR WRITING AND ENDORSING CHECKS

Millions of Americans do not know the basic rules for writing, endorsing, and depositing a check. Do not permit yourself to be among them—for you may be unwittingly courting the bank's refusal to honor your checks—or even inviting costly check-doctoring by a professional earning a living in this craft.

Heed these main do's and don'ts on writing checks:

Do date each check properly. A bank may refuse to accept a check which is dated ahead, or hold it until its date is reached. The bank's reasoning is that if the check were charged to your account before you expected it to be, it might cause other checks you wrote to bounce.

Don't leave any spaces between the dollar sign and the amount of the check you are writing, or between the amount you spell out in the middle line and the word "dollars" at the end of that line. Or, if you do leave such spaces, draw lines across them.

Do make sure each check is numbered properly—for your own bookkeeping purposes.

Don't alter the way you sign your checks (e.g., by adding your middle initial) once you have decided on a standard signature.

Do, if you are a married woman, sign checks with your own first name, plus your married name—"Mary Dowd," *not* "Mrs. Jack Dowd."

Don't use "Mr.," "Miss," or "Mrs." as part of your signature.

Do fill out the middle line ending with the word "dollars" in this format: "Five and 50/100," or "One hundred and fifty and no/100." If you write a check for less than $1.00, be sure to put a decimal point between the printed dollar sign and the amount of the check—followed by the word "cents." On the line where you write out the amount of the check, write, for example, "Only 95 cents," and cross out the word "dollars."

Don't use somebody else's check unless you punch a hole in at least one number of the special magnetic code which usually appears at the lower left-hand corner of the check-"reading" devices; if you don't actually cut out this account number, you risk having the check charged against your friend's account. (Technically, you can write a check on any surface from a paper bag to an eggshell, but banks shudder at this sort of eccentricity.)

For the identical reasons, don't lend anyone one of your checks. Because of the indelible symbols, your pre-imprinted check will be sorted according to its magnetic coding and charged to your account even if someone else, with no dishonest intentions at all, has crossed out your identifying number and name and written in his own.

Do endorse a check only on the back of the left-hand side (the perforated side, in one type of checkbook), *exactly* as your name appears on the front of the check. If this is not your usual signature, add the correct signature below your first endorsement. Of course, if your address is on the check too, you need not include this—or the "Miss," "Mrs.," or "Mr." which may also be included.

Don't ever underestimate the importance of your endorsement or forget that your endorsement on someone else's check means you would be willing to cover the check yourself should the bank for any reason refuse to honor it.

A blank endorsement—your signature only—means you transfer the ownership of the check to the person holding it at the time. This person may then cash it.

An endorsement in full—or special endorsement—means you sign a check over to someone else by writing on the back of a check "Pay to the order of" this person or organization.

A *restrictive endorsement* should be used on checks you wish to deposit by mail. You write "For deposit only" over your signature. Or, if you give someone a check which has been made out to you or cash, you write "Pay to the order of ———" and sign your name beneath this.

Do deposit all checks you receive as soon as you get them. Not only is it a big bookkeeping nuisance for the person who has issued the check if you keep it for a month or more, but many banks refuse to honor checks which are two or three months old—unless they are "reauthorized" to do so by the payer.

Don't write checks out to "cash" unless you yourself are cashing them at a bank, supermarket, or elsewhere. Such checks are negotiable by any bearer and leave you with no record of how the money was spent.

Do record on your check stub the key facts about every check you write. This includes the date, check number, payee, amount, and the purpose of the check if the "payee" notation doesn't make that evident. The best way to make sure you don't forget to record this information is to do so *before* you write the check itself.

And *don't* ever, ever give signed blank checks to anybody whom you do not trust completely; blank checks are as good as cash—unlimited amounts of it, for that matter. As a matter of fact, it's risky ever to sign a blank check!

KEY QUESTIONS ABOUT WRITING CHECKS

Now here are additional questions you almost surely would like to have answered—leading logically from the rules covered in the preceding pages.

Q. *When you deposit a check from another bank, how long should you wait for it to be cleared before you can safely draw checks against your deposit?*

A. If the other bank is in the same city, allow at least three days for the check to be collected. If the bank is out of town, allow five to fifteen days depending on its location. When it's important for you to know exactly when a check will actually be credited to your own account—so you won't risk having any of your own checks returned—ask one of your bank's officers about the particular check.

Q. *Is it legal to write a check in pencil?*

A. Yes. But it's obviously dangerous since anyone could erase the amount and substitute a larger one. Write all checks in ink.

Q. *May a check be dated on Saturday, Sunday, or a holiday?*

A. Yes. The folklore to the contrary is wrong. However, since some people who believe the folklore may refuse to accept the check, it's generally safer to date it on a previous day.

Q. *What happens when you make the mistake of writing one amount in words and another amount in figures?*

A. Some banks pay the amount which is spelled out, but many more return the check.

Q. *Should you ever erase or cross out anything on a check?*

A. No. Even if you initial the change, the bank often will not honor an altered check. And knowing this, you should never accept or cash an altered check yourself.

Q. *How long does a check remain valid?*

A. Technically, a check is good for six years. In actual practice, though, most banks consult with the payer before honoring a check which is more than six months old and many, I repeat, do this after only two or three months.

Q. *Will your bank give you a new check if you spoil one for which you've already paid?*

A. Yes.

Q. *How do you stop payment on a check?*

A. You can, for a fee of $4.00 to $9.00, stop payment on any check you have written simply by *telephoning* your bank's stop payment department and giving the details, including: the date, amount, name of payee, check number, and the reason for stopping the payment. Then immediately confirm the order in writing. The bank will issue a stop payment form which you must complete and which the bank will keep on file—to be sure your intention *not* to have the bank honor your check is properly carried out.

When you stop payment, be sure you notify the payee—the person or company or organization who was to have received the amount of money you specified on the check.

As a general rule, *don't* send a check in payment unless you are willing to have it honored. Stopping payment itself won't damage your credit rating but not paying your bill—unless it's in dispute—will.

GUARDING AGAINST CHECK FORGERIES

What would you do if you suddenly discovered your checkbook has been stolen and that a professional forger was using *your* name to write check after check against your account?

Do not dismiss the question, for check forgeries have been climbing at an alarming pace in recent years. As a simple precaution against becoming another victim, you should at least be aware of a few of the forger's favorite techniques.

Typically, the forger will find out when your bank mails out monthly statements and will loot your mailbox at that time. Armed with samples of your signature, a good idea of the amount of money you keep in your account, and the number of checks you usually write during the month, he will start raiding your account. You may not discover the damage until *his* canceled checks start coming home to you.

Or the forger may simply "raise" a carelessly written check of yours, by hiking the amount from "one" dollar to "one hundred" or "six" dollars to "sixty," or "twenty" to "seventy"—at the same time subtracting this amount from your account.

Here are a few key rules to protect yourself against check forgery:

• Guard your checks as if they were cash. I re-emphasize, in many ways, they're *better* than cash, since they can be written out for any amount.

• Notify your bank *immediately* if you lose even a single check, not to mention your entire checkbook. Note: Forgers frequently will steal checks from the *back* of your checkbook to postpone detection, so flip through your whole checkbook now and then as an added precaution.

• Notify the bank if you fail to receive your bank statement within a couple of days of the usual time.

• Reconcile your bank statement promptly each month and glance at each returned check for evidence of any tampering or forgery.

• Report any such evidence to the bank immediately. Banks normally are insured against such losses.

• Learn and obey the rules I've already given you for writing checks.

• Destroy all old checks if and when you change your name, address, account number—or become formally separated or divorced.

• Avoid the sweeping illegible "executive" signature—or a hand-printed signature. This is much easier to forge than a clear, freely written two-name signature with connected letters.

HOW TO PROTECT YOURSELF AGAINST CASH-MACHINE CONS AND ERRORS

Electronic banking devices—automated tellers, "money-matic" machines, "24-hour banking centers," cash dispensers, the like—are still relatively new. Even their developers have not grasped all of the problems which financial institutions and you, their customers, may encounter with them.

The machines are neither totally fail- nor fraud-proof.

In California a computer error put more than $30,000 into a savings account of a cafeteria worker. The man quickly withdrew the money and disappeared. As 1980 neared, he still was being sought on charges of grand theft.

• In Washington, D.C., a "money-matic" machine went on the blink one weekend and dispensed money to customers seeking withdrawals. The computer recorded the account numbers but not the amount of money each person withdrew. Some customers would or could not recall how much money they had withdrawn.

• In New York City during the introductory phase of some twenty-four-hour banking center terminals, some customers left their machines before they had shut down. On one occasion an observant con man noted a customer's identification code and, with the machine still running, he stole $1,000. The bank reimbursed the customer for his loss and has corrected the system so this type of electronic theft cannot happen again.

To avoid these and other types of electronic banking mishaps:

• Request a personal demonstration and explanation from a responsible bank official of how the computer device operates. This will eliminate any worry that you will operate the machine incorrectly and will make sure that the services the new technology provides will really be a convenience, not a headache. Most institutions accept liability for mechanical malfunctions and fraud if neither is due to your negligence.

• Do not write your personal identification number or code on your transaction card or anywhere else where it might be observed, stolen, or misplaced. This would be an example of negligence, so memorize your code or number. With some systems, if you forget your code or number, you must select a new one. Not even the financial institution keeps a record of it; it's totally confidential. Other systems, however, do keep track of such identification numbers or codes and will remind you of them if you supply proper identification.

- Do not lend your transaction card to anyone, and do not tell anyone your personal identification code or number.
- When using a computer terminal, be sure that the machine has turned itself off and that you have your card before you walk away.
- Depress all keys of the machine firmly and slowly to make certain your message gets across correctly. Most systems are designed to operate relatively slowly so even as a first-time user, you won't become confused and you will be able to keep up.
- Ask for and keep the receipts of the transactions that you have made. Study these receipts as soon as you get them to be certain that you didn't push the wrong buttons or the computer didn't make an error. Once you know your receipts are accurate, you have records against which you can compare your monthly statements and with which you can resolve any disputes.
- Make an entry into your checkbook after you have completed each transaction. Because you can make deposits, withdrawals, or transfers from savings to checking or vice versa so quickly, it is easy to forget to make the proper notations in your checkbook. But the entries are vitally important if you are to know how much money you have in your account.
- Avoid using cash dispensing machines located in low-traffic areas late at night or other odd hours. Although many computers have cameras strategically located nearby for your protection, don't make yourself an easy target for a crook who demands your card and code.
- Check your balance periodically on the computer to make sure that its record of your balance squares with your own. Make allowances, however, for any checks or deposits which may be outstanding. Not all systems are connected directly to the institution's main computer. Some terminals may record your transactions on magnetic tape or in other ways. This tape is periodically pulled from the machine and then fed into the institution's central recording facility. These machines do not automatically credit your deposits or withdrawals but act as a kind of overnight banking mailbox.
- Mainly because of this time lag, many systems limit the amount of money you can withdraw at any one time—say, $100 every three days. Some machines issue receipts which tell you when you can next make a withdrawal. If you need more money than this—for example, you will be traveling and know you'll need $300 every week for the next month or two—your bank often will upgrade your withdrawal limit on your request. The bank's willingness to do this will depend, of course, on your status as a customer, its policies, and the technology of its particular electronic system.
- Many computers have attached telephones which you can use to discuss problems with a "live" bank official or consumer representative. You don't have to wait until you get your monthly statement to discuss any discrepancies or problems.

NEW PROTECTIONS FOR ELECTRONIC BANKING CUSTOMERS

Under the Electronic Funds Transfer Act of 1978, consumers have some protection in the event their EFT transaction card is lost or stolen. But warning: you must notify the bank or other institution which issued you the card *at once*.

If you believe your card has been lost or stolen or if you think money is missing from your account, and you contact the bank within two business days after learning of the loss, you are liable for no more than $50.

If, however, someone uses your card without your permission you could lose as much as $500 if you fail to notify the institution within that time, and it can prove that it could have prevented the loss if you had informed it.

Also, if your monthly statement shows transfers that you did not make, and you don't notify the institution within sixty days after your regular statement was mailed to you, you may not get back any money you lost if the institution can show that if you had contacted it, it would have prevented the loss.

If you are traveling or hospitalized and cannot notify the institution of the unauthorized use of your card, these time periods may be extended.

The law also permits institutions to send you unsolicited EFT cards providing they can't be used until your identity is verified and the card is validated. You must also be told the following:

- how to dispose of the card if you don't want to use it.
- what your liability is in the event your card is lost or stolen and whom you should contact if that occurs.
- the type of electronic fund transfers that you can make and what you might be charged for such transactions.
- any limits on how often you may make transfers or how large they may be.
- whether you have the right to stop payment of a preauthorized transfer and, if so, how to go about it.
- whether or not you have the right to receive documentation of fund transfers.
- whether or not the institution has methods for resolving errors, what they are, and your rights under them.
- the circumstances under which a financial institution may disclose information about your account to such third parties as credit bureaus or government agencies.
- and finally whether or not the institution is liable to you for failing to make transfers that you have requested.

HOW TO BALANCE YOUR CHECKBOOK

As Chapter 2, "Budgets Are Back in Style," stressed, the monthly ritual of checkbook balancing should be assigned to whichever member of the family is the more deft at it and the more willing to do it *as soon as possible* after each bank statement comes in. An arbitrary decision that this chore should automatically go to the man in the family is downright foolish—if he has neither flair for nor an interest in it. Whoever gets the job can use this chart to guide you on the key steps to balancing a checkbook:

1. Your own checkbook balance	
2. Minus service charges appearing on your bank statement	
3. Your own new checkbook balance	
4. Balance in the bank's statement	
5. Plus recent deposits not yet recorded in bank statement	
6. Minus value of all outstanding checks — those not appearing on bank statement	
7. New bank statement balance	

This last total—item 7—should agree with item 3, your own "new checkbook balance." If it does not, go back and follow these steps:

(1) First compare the amount of each canceled check with the amount appearing in the bank statement. Make a notation after each check on the bank statement as you go.

(2) Now arrange the stack of checks in order of check numbers—which will permit you not only to recheck the amounts against those appearing in your own check records but also to tell immediately which ones are missing.

(3) Compare the amount of each check with the amount you have written on each appropriate stub—and check off each entry in your record as you go.

(4) Compare, and verify with a notation, all the deposits you have made and recorded with the deposits recorded on the bank statement.

(5) Add up, in the appropriate space provided on your bank statement, the amounts of all checks you have written which have not yet appeared on your statement and subtract this total from the balance appearing at the end of your bank statement. Make sure the amounts on the checks agree with the amounts recorded on your check register.

(6) Add to the statement balance the total amount of deposits you have made to your account which do not appear on the bank statement.

(7) Subtract any bank service charges appearing in your statement from

the balance which appears in your checkbook. Do this in your checkbook as well.

The revised totals for the bank statement and for your checkbook balance should agree to the penny.

But don't panic if they still don't agree. Here's what to do:

Recheck your original math in your checkbook. The bank's math is usually correct since it was probably done by a machine. However, errors of other sorts are entirely possible.

Recheck the balances you carried forward from page to page in your checkbook.

Double-check to be certain you have subtracted *all* outstanding checks from your bank statement balance—including those still missing from previous statements.

Double-check to be certain all the canceled checks which came with your statement are included in your checkbook record—and that you haven't forgotten to note *any non-checkbook checks* you may have written during the period of the statement.

If your accounts *still* don't balance, and you're completely stymied as to why, take the whole business to the bank and ask for help. You'll probably be given this help without charge—but don't delay. There is always the possibility, though remote, of sleight of hand with your bank balance—and the sooner any type of thievery is pinned down, the better your chance of avoiding financial losses. Most banks expect to be informed of a possible error within ten days.

Your Savings Account

HOW MUCH MONEY SHOULD YOU KEEP IN A SAVINGS ACCOUNT?

How much money should *you* keep in a savings account?

• The rule of thumb in Chapter 2, "Budgets Are Back in Style," is that your emergency fund should equal at least two months' income.

• Many of the major financial institutions of the country would call my total far too low, would recommend your reserve in the form of "liquid assets"—cash or its equivalent—should total three to six months' income.

• But the vital point which erases any apparent disagreement is that your own special financial circumstances must be the crucial factor deciding whether your emergency reserve can safely be as low as two months' income or should properly be equal to six months' earnings.

So how much should you keep in an emergency fund? For the answer, ask yourself these questions:

How many circumstances can you think of in which you might require really large sums of cash, literally at overnight notice?

What types of unexpected financial emergencies might conceivably befall you or your family? (A disabling accident, job layoff, big auto repair job.)

What share of the estimated costs of such emergencies would be covered by your other forms of financial protection such as major medical insurance, life insurance, other types of insurance, disability and survivor's benefits under Social Security, U.S. savings bonds you might have stashed away, stocks, mutual fund shares, bonds, other investments, benefits from your employer?

What emergency financial help could you realistically expect from parents, other relatives, or your employer?

Could you, the non-working wife, move into a paying job fairly readily—if need be?

If the family breadwinner should lose his or her job tomorrow due to a layoff, merger, or other development, how long would it probably be before he or she could find a comparable job in his or her field of training?

How big a financial nest egg in cash do you need to *feel* financially secure?

Are you preparing for big-ticket expenses and purchases in the months ahead—e.g., a down payment on a house, a new baby, a long-planned vacation, a big outlay to go into business for yourself?

The amount you really need as an emergency reserve will depend on your honest answers to these questions.

It well may be that *if* you're a young couple with no children and a modest income, the *maximum* you should keep is $1,000 to $1,500 in a regular savings account. And in some cases even less would be realistic if you have other safe financial reserves which you could readily tap.

For your emergency cash reserve—whatever its amount or wherever you deposit it—should be precisely what its name implies. It should be protection against unexpected financial emergencies. It should be no more nor less than that.

KEY FORMS OF SAVINGS ACCOUNTS

Within any single financial institution, you may choose between a variety of savings accounts, each one tailored to fit particular needs, each account with special advantages, and each with disadvantages. You must select the one which best fits your requirements.

In general, these will be offered to you:

Passbook Savings Accounts

Have complete flexibility. Your money is always instantly available. You may deposit or withdraw any amount at any time.

Interest you earn on this type of "liquid" savings will be the lowest among the major types of accounts. Commercial banks by law paid the lowest rates on passbook savings accounts in the mid-1970s—one of their key disadvantages.

"Liquidity" of this type of account is the highest, the best of all types of savings outside of your checking account or cash in your hand. Liquidity denotes the ease and speed with which you can convert your funds into cash, and the amount of interest you can earn on your savings tends to be lowest where the degree of liquidity is highest.

Interest is usually compounded annually, semi-annually, or quarterly, and in some cases daily.

These accounts are federally insured or state insured in almost all cases up to $40,000 for each account held in a different name (a joint account can be insured separately from the individual accounts of those sharing the joint account).

Funds in this type of account can be used as collateral for personal bank loans.

A tally of your savings balance may be kept in a passbook or reported periodically to you in computerized statements mailed by the financial institution holding your account. The passbook itself is being gradually phased out.

Time Deposit Open Accounts

Form of savings account in which you must leave your savings with the institution for a specified period of time in order to obtain the higher interest rate offered on these deposits. (Has many names. The trick name depends on the institution.) Note: you can usually withdraw the interest but not the principal.

Minimum initial deposits required, usually ranging from $500 to as much as $5,000.

While you can usually—but not always—add funds to this type of account or withdraw interest at any time, notice of thirty to ninety days is frequently required for withdrawal of the principal, with the actual interest you receive depending on how long you maintain your account.

Insurance features the same as for Passbook Savings Accounts.

Consumer Certificates of Deposit

• These are the certificates of deposit for individuals with savings of under $100,000. They are a medium for your most liquid funds—assuming you are confident you will not need to cash in your certificates before they mature.

• In the late 1970s, consumer CDs were available in denominations from $100 to as high as $5,000 to $10,000.

• Maturities ranged from ninety days to six years or more with the interest rate the highest paid on any savings account.

- Notice of withdrawal was required and a penalty imposed—in form of reduction of interest—in the event of prior withdrawal.
- Insurance features and all the rest identical with other forms of savings accounts.

On top of these basic forms of savings accounts, financial institutions are developing new savings programs or variations of older ones. As a banker remarked, "In my midwestern youth, our small-town bank had only two different devices to help me save. Today, that bank has nine variations and larger banks have still more." Just to indicate the scope, ponder these variations:

- *Monthly memo savings.* The bank lets you set a goal in total dollars, then it develops a savings plan to fit and determines what monthly deposits you need to make to meet the goal. Every month the bank sends a statement to the depositor reminding him that he "owes" the account a deposit of X dollars. The top of the statement can be detached and used as a deposit slip, with an attached prestamped envelope.
- *Assorted interest.* On many savings accounts, especially higher-interest time accounts, larger banks offer several options on payment of interest: interest can be credited to the time account, the regular savings account, the checking account, or mailed out on a quarterly basis.
- *Special savings withdrawal.* In one midwestern city, several banks have together installed a special-purpose computer system to provide instant savings withdrawal transactions for customers. Through an on-the-line system of ninety keyboard terminals, the teller keys in a savings account number and dollar amount any time a customer wants to make a withdrawal and gets a green, yellow, or red light response for Yes, Maybe, or No.
- *Quick deposits.* More and more banks have quick deposit boxes for savings so customers needn't stand in the teller line. There also has been great improvement in teller line traffic, drive-in and walk-up windows, express-lines, etc.
- *Safe deposit boxes.* Some banks give customers free use of safe deposit boxes if their savings accounts run a certain size. Other special promotions are widespread.
- *Insurance.* Based on the depositor's age and the size of his account, this program makes term insurance available at what amounts to a group policy rate or less.

The mutual savings banks in New York, Massachusetts, and Connecticut also sell low-cost life insurance over the counter. It is inexpensive insurance because it is sold directly to you—at the bank itself or by mail—and there are no salesmen's commissions to add to its price to you. Many savings banks now also sell shares in a no-load, no-redemption-fee mutual fund. (See Chapter 22 on investing in mutual funds, for details on no-load funds.)

Most credit unions provide life insurance without charge to you if you put your savings in the credit union.

Treasury Rate Certificates

At the end of the 1970s, many financial institutions were offering twenty-six-week saving certificates with interest rates pegged to those the U. S. Treasury was paying on its short-term securities.

The minimum deposit you, a saver, had to make to obtain such a "money market" certificate was $10,000.

If you went to a commercial bank or thrift institution, the amount of interest you could earn roughly equaled that paid on the previous week's U. S. Treasury Bills.

The short maturities on these new certificates demanded that the owners be on the constant alert to the due dates for rolling over the certificates into new paper, so you would not forfeit valuable interest by permitting an interruption in the payment schedules.

In addition, the interest that savers earned on the "money market" certificates was subject both to state and federal taxes, whereas that earned on U. S. Treasury securities was subject to federal taxes only.

WHICH TYPE OF SAVINGS ACCOUNT IS BEST FOR YOU?

You can decide which savings account is best suited for your personal needs and goals only when you know the variety of accounts available. In brief, you may choose among these major types:

(1) *An individual account.* This may be opened by only one person—adult or minor—and you are the sole owner, the only person who can draw on the account. You can open this type of account with a small deposit.

(2) *A joint account.* Two of you may open this type—usually a husband and wife. Either of you may deposit funds in the account and either of you may withdraw funds from the account. In the event that one of you dies, the balance will be payable to the survivor.

(3) *A voluntary trust account.* You may open this type in trust for your child or another person. You will control the account during your life—after which it will be payable to the person you name as beneficiary. You have the right to change the beneficiary of this account at any time.

(4) *A fiduciary account.* If you are appointed an administrator, executor of an estate, or a guardian of another person, you may open a fiduciary account for the funds entrusted to you.

(5) *An organization account.* If you belong to an organization which collects dues or fees and which therefore has funds to safeguard and if you are in charge of the funds, you can open an organization account. The organization might be a club, your church, your lodge, a mutual benefit society, or any other non-profit organization.

(6) *A school savings account.* Your child may open a regular school bank savings account with insignificant deposits—and as he or she learns how to

save and the virtues of saving, this tiny account may grow to become your child's regular savings account with a respectable deposit balance.

HOW CAN YOU FORCE YOURSELF TO SAVE—GRACEFULLY?

One way to save money is through a "loose money" system. Put aside at the end of each day all the change you have left in your pocket—or only all of your quarters, or even all your single dollar bills. Once every week, faithfully deposit your little hoard in a nearby bank or savings association. In just over eighteen months, the dollar-bill approach helped one family make the first payment on a piece of land in the exurbs for a weekend cabin.

Another way to build a nest egg is to save all windfall money—dividends, inheritances, bonuses, cash gifts, tax refunds. Put this money in your savings account the instant you get it. Don't even cash the check or do more than peer at the amount of cash in a gift envelope. Don't give the temptation to spend the windfall the slightest edge.

A third excellent way to save is to authorize your bank to deduct a specified percentage from your paycheck automatically when you deposit the paycheck in your checking account and to transfer this percentage to your savings account. Make it 10 per cent, if you can manage, or 5 per cent—but make the transfer automatic and regular. The automatic, regular feature is the secret, as stressed over and over in Chapter 2, "Budgets Are Back in Style."

Or maybe you will decide the best approach for you is an automatic deposit of X number of paychecks each year entirely in the savings account. For instance, you might decide to save every tenth weekly paycheck or the first check of every quarter of the year. Or if you're paid on a semi-monthly basis, you might decide you can manage to put away two or three full paychecks a year.

Or you might find a periodic "Nothing Week" is your best deal. During this week you would not spend any money on dinner out or stop at the bar on the way home from work or go out to the movies or go bowling—or whatever. You would eat inexpensive foods at home, read books, or look at TV—and add at least $25 to your nest egg.

Or surely you could save the money you formerly used for, say, cigarettes. I, for one, am saving more than $400 a year on this item alone since I quit.

And there are all sorts of tricks, of course. You might put, say, $50 in your savings account on every national holiday or family birthday. Or you might add an agreed-upon amount whenever you break a family rule. Or add that agreed-upon amount whenever you enjoy a particular pastime.

You can easily figure out your own approach, once you make up your mind to adopt one.

You'll save if you force yourself to by some method. Then you'll build your nest egg if you'll put the program on an automatic basis. You can't lose by trying this. You can only win.

WHAT IS "HIGHEST" INTEREST ON SAVINGS?

By law, banks and other financial institutions must state clearly in their advertisements the *true* annual interest rate they pay on savings—if they make any reference at all to interest in their ads—as well as any special conditions for getting the full interest rate.

But clear as this seems, it still leaves plenty of room for befuddlement. In fact, in this area of interest earned on savings, "highest" may not be highest at all—and the institution which advertises the top stated rate of interest on your funds may not actually be paying you the top total of dollars on your funds.

So much more than the stated rate of interest is involved. Far more revealing than the percentage which stands out in the ad may be what is not even included in the ad. How often is the interest promised you compounded —so that your interest earns interest? When does your deposit start to draw interest? Is there any penalty for frequent withdrawals or any bonus for no withdrawals for a specified period?

Banks compute interest in more than fifty ways and many don't readily disclose what method they use. You may think you are getting the best interest deal but you might be able to do significantly better at another institution a block away. You may think you are handling your savings sensibly, but you actually may be cutting your own return by the way you deposit and withdraw funds. Here are five questions you should be able to answer.

(1) What is the institution's policy on the compounding of interest? The more frequently interest is compounded the more interest your savings can earn. A rate of 6 per cent paid once a year is a straight 6 per cent—or $60 per $1,000 of savings. But a rate of 6 per cent paid to you every quarter is higher, because the interest credited to your account is added to your original amount every quarter and then the stated rate is paid on the bigger sum. A rate compounded every month comes out to still more and a rate compounded every day is most. The larger your savings and the longer you maintain your account, the more the factor of "compounding" matters.

(2) When does your savings account start to earn interest (or dividends)? Under a policy most favorable to you, the institution will pay interest on your account from the day of deposit to the day of withdrawal. Also, under a most favorable policy, the institution will pay interest on all funds you keep in your account during the interest period. Under a least favorable policy, the institution will pay interest only on the smallest balance you have in your account during the interest period.

(3) When is interest credited to your account? On the first of each

month? At the end of each quarter? At the end of June and December? Or just at the end of December? This is of major importance, for under the policies of many institutions, if you withdraw funds before the stated interest payment date, you will lose all the interest owed to you on these funds, for the interest period. When you withdraw funds, try to schedule the withdrawal immediately after the date for crediting interest.

(4) Is there any "grace period" during which you can withdraw funds around the interest payment date without being penalized by loss of interest? If so, how many days of grace are you allowed in which to withdraw funds and still be entitled to the interest the funds had earned? Also find out if there is a grace period after each interest payment date during which you can deposit funds and have them earn interest from the payment date. Pertinent too is whether the period of grace includes every calendar day or just business days. A period of grace which includes only business days will be longer than it appears offhand.

(5) What about penalties for frequent withdrawals? And what about payment of an interest bonus if you make no withdrawals for a specified period —say none for one year? Both penalties and bonuses are fairly commonplace.

Any reputable financial institution should automatically answer these questions (and others which may bother you). With the answers, you then may make an intelligent decision on where to keep your cash nest egg.

HOW DOES A SAVINGS ACCOUNT GROW?

Compound interest means that you are earning interest on the interest paid to you as well as interest on your own deposits.

Say you can deposit $5.00 to $50 a month. How will your savings grow at 5 per cent a year interest, compounded semi-annually? Here's how much:

HOW SAVINGS GROW	$5 MONTHLY	$10 MONTHLY	$15 MONTHLY	$20 MONTHLY	$25 MONTHLY	$50 MONTHLY
6 months	30.44	60.88	91.31	121.75	152.19	304.38
1 year	61.64	123.28	184.90	246.54	308.18	616.37
2 years	126.40	252.81	379.17	505.57	631.97	1,263.94
3 years	194.44	388.89	583.26	777.71	972.15	1,944.30
4 years	265.93	531.85	797.69	1,063.62	1,329.55	2,659.10
5 years	341.03	682.06	1,022.98	1,364.01	1,705.04	3,410.09
10 years	777.58	1,555.16	2,332.48	3,110.06	3,887.64	7,775.28
15 years	1,336.40	2,672.80	4,008.76	5,345.15	6,681.55	13,363.10
20 years	2,051.73	4,103.47	6,154.53	8,206.26	10,257.99	20,515.99

Or say you have $5,000 in cash to deposit in a savings account. How much will this sum grow at varying interest rates over the years, if compounded quarterly?

Here's that answer:

How a $5,000 Deposit Will Grow

INTEREST RATE	AFTER 1 YEAR	AFTER 3 YEARS	AFTER 5 YEARS	AFTER 10 YEARS
5.00%	$5,255	$5,804	$6,410	$8,218
5.25	5,268	5,847	6,490	8,423
5.50	5,281	5,890	6,570	8,634
5.75	5,294	5,934	6,652	8,849
6.00	5,307	5,978	6,734	9,070

Or say your objective is to save a specific sum—anywhere from $2,000 to $20,000. If you save X dollars a month, how many years will it take you—at Y interest compounded continuously—to achieve your goal?

The following compilation answers this one.

Start by setting your savings target in total dollars and years (the left-hand column). Follow across to one of the other columns and see how much you should save each month in order to reach your goal—at varying interest rates.

Or start with a rough idea of how much money you can put aside every month. Then look in the left-hand column to see what size nest egg you're aiming for.

Savings Time Table

If you want this amount:		Save this much each month at the interest rate of:	
		5%	5¼%
$ 2,000 in	1 year	$162.20	$161.53
	3 years	51.39	50.78
	5 years	29.28	28.70
$ 4,000 in	1 year	$324.40	$323.06
	3 years	102.78	101.56
	5 years	58.56	57.40
$ 6,000 in	1 year	$486.60	$484.59
	3 years	154.17	152.34
	5 years	87.84	86.10

YOUR PERSONAL BANKING BUSINESS

If you want this amount:		Save this much each month at the interest rate of: 5%	5¾%
$ 8,000 in	5 years	$117.12	$114.80
	10 years	51.28	49.21
	15 years	29.78	27.93
	20 years	19.36	17.72
$10,000 in	5 years	$146.40	$143.50
	10 years	64.10	61.51
	15 years	37.23	34.91
	20 years	24.20	22.15
$12,000 in	5 years	$175.68	$172.20
	10 years	76.92	73.82
	15 years	44.67	41.90
	20 years	29.04	26.58
$14,000 in	5 years	$204.96	$200.90
	10 years	89.74	86.12
	15 years	52.12	48.88
	20 years	33.88	31.01
$16,000 in	5 years	$234.24	$229.60
	10 years	102.56	98.42
	15 years	59.56	55.86
	20 years	38.72	35.44
$18,000 in	5 years	$263.52	$258.30
	10 years	115.38	110.72
	15 years	67.01	62.84
	20 years	43.56	39.87
$20,000 in	5 years	$292.80	$287.00
	10 years	128.20	123.03
	15 years	74.45	69.83
	20 years	48.40	44.30

NOTE: This table was prepared by the Continental Bank of Chicago. It is based on three assumptions: (1) Deposits monthly are made at the first of the month; (2) periodic deposits are monthly and are the same amount as the initial deposit; and (3) interest is compounded continuously.

Computer Technology Changes Our Financial Habits

The introduction of computer technology in the United States has dramatically changed the way you regard and conduct your financial affairs. As of the 1980s, in cities across the nation:

• You, a shopper, may pay for goods and services at retail stores by using a plastic card inserted in an electronic terminal. Your savings or checking accounts are charged electronically. You carry less cash.

• You, a bank customer, may deposit or withdraw cash at any time of day or night by using your cards in an unattended "robot" teller.

• You, an employee, may have your paychecks deposited directly into your checking or savings accounts. Your employer makes the deposits by delivering a magnetic tape to the depository institution.

• You, a family money manager, may pay monthly installments on your mortgage or loans or utility bills by preauthorized charges to your deposit accounts or by phoning your instructions to your bank, savings and loan, or credit union.

• Electronic banking or electronic funds transfer system (EFTS), as it is called, already is revolutionizing the way you manage your banking affairs. Many of your routine financial tasks—bill-paying, deposits, withdrawals, etc.—will be made easier. Banking could become more impersonal and automatic. You probably will conduct most everyday financial transactions without ever setting foot in the office of a financial institution.

ELECTRONIC FUNDS TRANSFER SYSTEM—IT'S MEANING TO YOU

The changes that EFTS has brought will mean greater convenience to you, the customer. What is not so obvious is the savings that the system is designed to offer the financial institutions themselves. The institutions could save a minimum of $10 billion a year by slashing check-processing costs and eliminating the need for additional branch offices.

Whether or not these savings will be passed along to you, the borrower or saver, is far from certain. You are likely to find depository institutions charging you for the individual services they perform—bill-paying, transfer of funds from savings to checking, etc. The day soon may come when U.S. financial institutions will make more of their money from service fees than from lending or investments.

Equally uncertain, as the 1980s unfold, is precisely what type of responsibility both you and your depository institution will be required to assume for the accuracy, safety, and confidentiality of any electronic transactions. (See pages 880–82.)

Despite these big unknowns, financial institutions will continue implementing EFTS and offering you an array of new services.

Below is a sample of these increasingly common offerings. When deciding whether or not you want to take advantage of them, be sure you know what they will cost, what the alternatives are, and who is liable for any errors or foul-ups—you or the institution.

(1) *Automatic bill-paying:* Many banks, savings and loan associations, and credit unions will automatically pay such routine monthly bills as utility charges, insurance premiums, or mortgage payments.

(2) *Automatic line of credit:* The line of credit is a preapproved, un-

secured amount of credit which essentially serves as overdraft protection on your checking account or as a means of financing purchases. The line of credit becomes available to you either through your regular checking account or a special checking account. If the credit is part of your regular checking account, you may write checks for more than your balance, up to the limit of the line of credit. The amount of credit forwarded to your account can be in standard denominations, such as $100. Once you have drawn on the credit, it is treated as a loan on which monthly payments must be made. There is usually no charge for the line of credit until you actually use it. If yours is a special checking account, the line of credit is the balance of the account. You receive a book of special checks to use against the predetermined maximum credit amount. Some of these accounts permit you to write the check for any amount. Others provide checks for specific amounts, say, $250 (as with travelers' checks). This service also may be available in conjunction with NOW (Negotiable Order of Withdrawal) accounts, essentially interest-bearing checking accounts, and credit union share draft accounts.

(3) *Automatic savings:* A financial institution will automatically transfer specified amounts of money at regular intervals from your checking to your regular or special savings account, just as it deducts payments for loans and bills. The institution also will invest these funds in United States Savings Bonds or designated mutual funds. If you have a trust account, you may have the dividends or interest from your investment automatically deposited into your savings account.

(4) *Telephone transfer:* Upon your request by phone, an institution will move funds from your savings to your checking account or vice versa if you ask for this service in advance. Some institutions may even move money from savings into checking automatically whenever there are not enough funds to cover a check.

(5) *Automatic payroll service:* Some institutions will perform a company's regular payroll services. The company and each employee have accounts at the institution. Once it records all employees and your salaries, it will deposit your earnings directly into your accounts, after making appropriate deductions for federal, state, and Social Security taxes. You, the employee, receive no paycheck but only a deposit slip indicating your salary, taxes withheld, net salary, and credits to your checking, savings accounts, or to your loan balance.

(6) *Direct deposit service:* This rests on the same principle as the automatic payroll system, but usually is done for paychecks, Social Security, and pension checks going to a number of individual accounts at various institutions.

(7) *The transaction card:* The transaction or debit, access or asset card is the foundation of EFTS. It looks like a plastic credit card but often is magnetically coded to your bank, S&L, or credit union accounts through a com-

puter system. The card permits you access to your accounts from a remote computer terminal. Some nationwide credit cards also are magnetically coded to permit access to your accounts. These cards frequently are used in conjunction with special identifying codes known as personal identification numbers (PINs).

(8) *Automatic teller machines (ATMs)*: ATMs are computer terminals which provide access only to the customer's accounts. You, the customer, operate these machines with push buttons like those found on a telephone and with the magnetically coded transaction card. By pushing the buttons, you can get cash from your checking or savings account, deposit money into your accounts, move funds from one account to another, or even make loan payments. ATMs most commonly are attached to the financial institution itself, but more are being located at remote locations of greater convenience to customers.

(9) *Check verification:* These cards, held by customers, are inserted into a computer terminal in a grocery or department store by the salesperson. The bank tells the merchant via the computer whether there are adequate funds in the customer's account to cover the check. The system is designed to protect stores against bad checks.

(10) *Point-of-sale terminal (POS)*: These terminals are found at stores. They permit you to pay for your purchases by immediately having money withdrawn from your account and transferred to the store's account. The debit card, which activates the POS, acts like an electronic check—one which neither bounces in the traditional way nor "floats" (the time—two to three or more days—it takes for a check to clear).

(11) *Push-button telephone banking:* Still experimental as the 1980s neared, this system involves attaching a small box, essentially a computer terminal, to your telephone. Your phone becomes an ATM, giving you access to your accounts at the push of the phone's buttons.

(12) *Travelers' checks via credit cards:* Under one American Express Company program, you may use your magnetically coded American Express card at ATM machines in airports around the country to obtain travelers' checks. The cost of these checks is automatically deducted from your checking account, not charged to your American Express account. Your bank must agree to participate.

How "Safe" Is Your Money?

It is almost impossible for most Americans to conceive of what it must have been like before the federal government insured bank and savings association deposits—to imagine the tragedy when an innocent family's lifetime savings disappeared in the crash of the trusted bank on the corner.

But ponder what it is like now:

In recent years, a fair number of banks failed—several of them frighteningly large institutions but *in no case did a depositor lose a single penny of his or her insured deposits.* The system has worked superbly well, there has been no worry—much less panic.

In recent years a fair number of savings and loan associations also failed —*but not one depositor in an institution federally insured lost one penny of his or her insured funds either.*

Today, 97 per cent of our banks are insured by the Federal Deposit Insurance Corporation in Washington. The insurance fund, contributed to by nearly fourteen thousand member banks throughout the nation, totals many billions of dollars. On top of this FDIC has authority to borrow as much as $3 billion additional from the U. S. Treasury.

As for us, 99 per cent of all bank depositors' savings and checking accounts are FDIC-insured, and as of the late 1970s most of the funds we had on deposit in insured banks were covered up to a $40,000 limit.

In a recent year, too, about 4,200 federal and state-chartered savings and loan associations—out of a total of roughly 5,400—were insured by the Federal Savings and Loan Insurance Corporation in Washington. The FSLIC's fund also totaled billions and covered more than 96 per cent of the savings in insured associations. The vast majority of associations not covered by the FSLIC are backed by state insurance funds.

In the late 1970s, all federally chartered credit unions were insured by the National Credit Union Administration—a total of approximately 13,000—and many of the 10,000-plus state-chartered credit unions were also federally insured. Other of the credit unions not protected by federal insurance have opted for other insurance alternatives and some states have mandatory laws for federal insurance.

It's not a perfect system for depositors, but it's coming close, and the performance record has been great.

Q. *What are the chances your bank might fail?*
A. Very slim indeed. In contrast to an average of 588 bank failures a year in the 1920s and an average of 2,277 in the 1930–33 period, bank failures averaged only five a year between the 1940s and 1970s among all banks, and only four a year for insured banks. The record has been similar for insured savings and loan associations.

Q. *Are only savings and checking accounts insured?*
A. No. These other types of deposits also are insured: Christmas savings and other open-account time deposits, uninvested trust funds, certified checks, cashier's checks, bank travelers' checks, and all other deposits "received by a bank in its usual course of business."

Q. *If you have both a checking and a savings account, is each insured up to $40,000?*

A. No. All deposits under you own name are added together and this total is insured up to $40,000.

Q. *What if you have, in addition to your own accounts, a joint account with your husband?*
A. Your joint account, with your husband or child, is insured separately for up to $40,000.

Q. *Are accounts kept at different banks insured separately?*
A. Yes. However, if you keep separate accounts at separate branches of your bank, all of these are considered as a single bank for the purposes of deposit insurance.

Q. *Are certificates of deposit covered?*
A. Yes. But they are not insured separately if they are held in the same bank at which you have other deposits in the same name.

Q. *My firm has some of its pension plans fund in an insured bank. Is my interest in the plan insured?*
A. Yes. Your interest in the plan is insured up to $40,000 regardless of any other accounts you may have at the same bank.

Q. *How and when would you be paid in the event your bank failed?*
A. You might be paid, probably within a week of the date your bank closed, by an FDIC check which you could then either cash or have deposited in your name in another insured bank. Or, more likely, your funds would be transferred to a new bank under new management, and become available to you within a few days. The payment period might be more prolonged in the case of a savings association failure, but the payment period of the FSLIC has generally been comparable to that of the FDIC.

Q. *Who pays for the insurance coverage on deposits?*
A. FDIC member banks, which are assessed approximately 1/30th of 1 per cent of their total deposits. Savings and loan associations pay higher assessments.

Here's a brief table to give you an idea of how much money you, a couple with one child, could keep in a single bank or savings and loan association, fully insured:

INDIVIDUAL ACCOUNTS
   Man: $ 40,000
   Wife: 40,000
   Child: 40,000

JOINT ACCOUNTS
   Man and wife: 40,000
   Man and child: 40,000
   Wife and child: 40,000

TESTAMENTARY REVOCABLE TRUST ACCOUNTS
Man (as trustee for wife):	$ 40,000
Man (as trustee for child):	40,000
Wife (as trustee for husband):	40,000
Wife (as trustee for child):	40,000

IRREVOCABLE TRUST ACCOUNTS
Man (as trustee for wife):	40,000
Man (as trustee for child):	40,000
Wife (as trustee for husband):	40,000
Wife (as trustee for child):	40,000
TOTAL:	$560,000

It's most unlikely anyone would keep this total in cash in a financial institution, but you can actually have *insured* savings of as much as $560,000 in one institution!

To get 100 per cent protection against the remote possibility of a bank failure, follow these two fundamental rules:

1. *Don't* keep more than the legal maximum in your individual accounts of all types in any one financial institution or its branches.

2. *Do* bank only with a federal- or state-insured institution. All insured institutions advertise this fact, so take the time to make sure your institution is properly insured.

But be reassured. Banking is among the more tightly regulated and closely scrutinized industries in the nation. And legal steps are continually being taken by federal and state regulatory agencies to make the system ever more failure-proof.

SHOULD YOU RENT A SAFE DEPOSIT BOX?

You almost surely own a collection of records and valuables which *should* be stored in a bank safe deposit box—particularly in this period of soaring numbers of home burglaries and in view of the fact that many types of documents are very difficult if not impossible to replace.

Today, it costs only $15 to $25 a year to rent the small (typically 2 or 3 by 5 by 22 inches) safe deposit box most people find adequate. In some areas the cost is less. And, assuming you use the box to store such income-producing property as stocks or bonds, the rental charge is deductible from your federal income tax.

To be specific, you *should* rent a safe deposit box and put into it your valuables, hard-to-replace or irreplaceable items, including:

Any stock or bond certificates or bank savings certificates which you do not keep at your bank or with your stockbroker.

Insurance policies—except life insurance policies, which should be kept in a more accessible place in the event of your death.

Property records, including mortgages, deeds, titles.

Personal documents such as birth certificates, marriage licenses, divorce papers, citizenship papers, adoption papers, diplomas, business contracts and agreements, important legal correspondence and income tax records, passports, military discharge papers, and trust agreements.

An inventory of all household items of any value, giving the cost and purchase date of each item as a reference in case of fire or theft. This inventory should include photographs of furs and jewelry and fine pieces of art and furniture; serial numbers of TV sets, stereo sets, etc.; details about valuable coin or stamp collections you keep at home; jewels, collections of stamps or coins, heirlooms which you seldom wear or use or refer to.

A copy of your will—but *not* the original, which should be filed at your lawyer's office, kept in the hands of an executor, or in some similar protected but accessible place. Frequently a bank safe deposit box is sealed by state law for a specified period after the box owner's death.

Should you, as a married couple, own a safe deposit box jointly? How do you arrange for someone besides yourself to get in the box if need be.

The advantages of joint ownership of a safe deposit box are strongly offset by the disadvantages. You may squabble—when it comes to removing the box's contents—over which of you owns what. Or if a lawsuit is brought against one of you, this would tie up the property of the other—if it's in a jointly owned safe deposit box. As for what happens when *one* of two renters dies, ask your lawyer what are your own specific state laws covering this aspect.

Instead of joint ownership, you might authorize the other (or a lawyer or trusted relative) to serve as his or her "agent" if necessary. The first spouse keeps the keys and, technically at least, owns the entire contents of the safe deposit box. If the second spouse has valuables or important records of her or his own, there is no reason why this partner shouldn't have a separate box.

Once you make the decision to rent a safe deposit box, here are further rules for you to follow:

Make a list of what is in your box and put the list in a safe place at home. Your list should include: an identification of each valuable in the box; serial numbers and dates of stock or bond certificates, insurance policies, etc.; written appraisals of jewelry; the date you put each item in the box; the date you remove any item; the date of your most recent inspection. Keep this inventory up to date.

Collect receipts or other papers which prove you own the items in the box and put them in a safe place outside the box. Then you will have the essential papers should the box ever be destroyed or burglarized (most unlikely but possible).

Check your homeowner's insurance coverage to find out if it covers the contents of your safe deposit box, and, if so, to what extent it insures you against loss. Also, check the agreement you sign or have signed with the institution from which you rent your box to find out if the agreement includes clauses which limit your protection. For instance, are you prohibited from putting cash or diamonds in the box?

Keep each other (husband and wife) informed about the location of your safe deposit box, the number of the box, the contents of the box, the place you keep the keys

Of course, the odds are overwhelmingly against any loss of the contents of your safe deposit box due to a robbery or some other catastrophe. This is obvious from the way boxes are built and the location of the vaults. And remember, *nobody* but you, the box holder (and any agent you may name), has keys which can open the box.

Have You Forgotten Money You Own?

In New York State alone in one year in the late 1970s, $123 million in "unclaimed or abandoned property"—most of it money forgotten by its owners (maybe you?)—was left in savings and checking accounts.

But this "unclaimed property" also included credit balances left with department stores, uncashed gift certificates, unclaimed payroll checks and dividends, uncashed airline tickets, travelers' checks, money orders, forgotten insurance benefits, utility company deposits and bonds, jewelry, coins, and cash left in long-abandoned safe deposit boxes.

In California, the total came to $15 million: in Illinois, to $11 million. Florida collected about $750,000 a year in unclaimed property; Wisconsin, close to $650,000; Alabama, about $1 million. Minnesota received almost $3 million in unclaimed property in fiscal 1978.

For many states, if not most, unclaimed property represents the largest source of revenue, next to taxes! In the late 1970s, about forty-five states had laws requiring banks, retail stores, and other businesses to turn over unclaimed property to the state after a certain number of years, usually seven but sometimes as long as twenty years. The state then holds the property in perpetuity for the owners. But since most owners or their heirs never claim their property, the individual state gets the funds.

Now, a drive is under way in many states to step up enforcement of unclaimed property laws.

The states deny that their more aggressive compliance and collection effort is a revenue-raising device. They insist it's an important service to you, the consumer.

But returning abandoned property to its owner (you?) isn't easy. Officials send notices to the owners' last known addresses and regularly publish ads in newspapers, listing owners' names. Businesses, banks, and insurance companies often do the same before they turn over the property to the state. But most owners of the unclaimed property never learn about it. The ads are too thick with names and Americans move so often to so many far-apart areas.

In Minnesota, late in the 1970s, the state treasurer traveled to different parts of his state two to four times a month, bringing with him a list of abandoned-property owners whose last known addresses were in that particular county. Local reporters frequently ended their stories or broadcasts with lists of a hundred or so names of people with unclaimed property worth $100 or more.

Up to 75 per cent of the individuals whose names were so displayed ultimately reclaimed their goods or money. The return rate from another list in a Minnesota TV magazine ran close to 50 per cent.

A legal but distasteful fringe development of this information campaign was the emergence of operators who scan the state's unclaimed property files (open to the public), copied down names, located the owners, then demanded a fee for reminding the owner that he or she owned an abandoned savings account or, say, payroll check. The operators can't be stopped but they are strongly opposed.

The biggest volume of unclaimed property, though, remains in the hands of the federal, not your state, government. No one knows precisely the value of the property—uncollected tax refunds, bonds, farm subsidy payments—but state officials want it turned over to their treasuries for eventual distribution to the proper owners.

Legislation was, in fact, being proposed to require such a federal-state transfer—or, at the very least, to require the U. S. Government to try to inform citizens it is holding their property.

Think hard. Can it be that I'm writing about you? I once saw in an abandoned property ad by a New York savings bank, the name of the bank's own president!

16

HOW TO BORROW CASH AND USE CREDIT

INTRODUCTION	906
THE SIZE OF THE CREDIT MARKET	907
IS ANYTHING WRONG WITH BORROWING?	907
THE RIGHT AND WRONG REASONS FOR BORROWING	908
THE RIGHT REASONS FOR BORROWING	908
THE WRONG REASONS FOR BORROWING	909
THE BASIC DO'S AND DON'TS OF CREDIT	911
HOW TO ESTABLISH A CREDIT RATING	913
WHAT IS THE DIFFERENCE BETWEEN CREDIT REPORTS AND INVESTIGATIVE REPORTS?	916
THE BASIC TYPES AND MATURITIES OF LOANS	917
THE SINGLE-PAYMENT LOAN	917
THE INSTALLMENT LOAN	917
THE SHORT-TERM LOAN	918
THE INTERMEDIATE-TERM LOAN	918
THE LONG-TERM LOAN	918
YOUR SOURCES OF LOANS IN CASH	918
THE "INSIDE" SOURCES	919
PARENTS OR OTHER RELATIVES	919
FRIENDS	920
ADVANCE AGAINST SALARY OR LOAN FROM EMPLOYER	921
THE "OUTSIDE" SOURCES	922
COMMERCIAL BANK	922
READY CREDIT (THE LOAN IN ADVANCE)	925

The "Outside" Sources (CONTD)

CREDIT UNION	926
SAVINGS BANK OR SAVINGS AND LOAN ASSOCIATION	928
LICENSED SMALL LOAN COMPANY	929
TUITION LOAN SPECIALISTS	930
LIFE INSURANCE COMPANY	932
YOUR STOCKBROKER	933
INDUSTRIAL LOAN COMPANY	934
ANOTHER MORTGAGE ON YOUR HOME	935
SECOND MORTGAGE COMPANY	935
YOUR OWN HOME MORTGAGE	936
THE ROLE OF INFLATION	937
RURAL FAMILY LOANS	938
PAWNBROKER	938
LOAN SHARK	939
Credit Cards	941
WHAT ARE THEY?	941
WHO ISSUES CREDIT CARDS?	941
HOW DO YOU GET A CREDIT CARD?	943
The Advantages and Disadvantages of Credit Cards	943
Cash Loans by Credit Card	944
Mail-order and Phone-order Credit Card Sales	945
How Do You Use Credit Cards?	946
Credit Cards—Convenience and Loans (Free and Otherwise)	946
Should You Use a Credit Card?	948
How to Protect Your Credit Card	948
Other Credit Sources for Goods and Services	950
SERVICE CREDIT	951
CHARGE ACCOUNTS	951
RETAIL INSTALLMENT CREDIT	951
Interest Rate Charges	952
HOW INTEREST AND REPAYMENTS "COMPOUND" THE PROBLEM	953
THE COMPLEX CALCULATIONS	954
INTEREST RATE AND PAYMENT DATA TABLE	955
SHOPPING FOR YOUR MONEY	956
OTHER QUESTIONS AND ANSWERS ABOUT INTEREST	957
How to Hold Down Your Borrowing Costs	959
The Great Pitfalls of Credit	961
"DEBT POOLING"	962
"SEWER SERVICE"	962

HOW TO BORROW CASH AND USE CREDIT   905

THE GREAT PITFALLS OF CREDIT (CONTD)
    "INCONVENIENT VENUE"   963
    "CONFESSION OF JUDGMENT"   963
    HARASSMENT   964
    REPOSSESSION   965
    "HOLDER IN DUE COURSE"   965
AND ALSO BEWARE THESE TRAPS!   967
HOW MUCH DEBT IS TOO MUCH DEBT?   967
    WHO RUNS UP TOO MUCH DEBT?   967
    WARNING SIGNS OF DEBT TROUBLE   968
    WHAT LIMITS SHOULD YOU SET?   969
    HOW TO MAINTAIN OR RESTORE A GOOD CREDIT RATING   970
WHAT IF YOU FIND YOU'RE OVER YOUR HEAD IN DEBT?   971
WHERE TO GO FOR HELP   972
HOW TO GO BANKRUPT   973
THE BAFFLEGAB OF BORROWING   974

Introduction

Should you borrow money *now*?

Of course you should—if you have sound (to you) reasons for doing so.

Is this the *right time* for you to borrow money?

Of course it is—if your reasons for borrowing are sound and your chances of repaying your debt within a tolerable period of time are good.

"Of course" always will be the answer to both these questions assuming your debt is for goods or services you feel you need or want, your loan is in line with your income, you have a plan for regular repayments.

There are two distinct sides to the possession of money: one is saving it, the other borrowing it. In our economy, both sides are crucially important to our financial health as a nation and as individuals. And both sides make vital contributions to our financial well-being as a nation and as individuals.

It is no exaggeration to say that almost uninterrupted buying on the installment plan or with a credit card has become a way of life in American homes to a point where a hefty percentage of the families we consider as representing the "ideal" in our nation are never out of debt and another hefty proportion seldom are.

That was, in fact, one of the most provocative findings that emerged from a survey I made a few years ago of the finalists in the "Mrs. America Pageant"—all outstanding women, bright, talented, good-looking, superb homemakers. What leaped first from their answers was how knowledgeable the women were, how acutely aware they were of money management, how devoted they were to budgeting, even "strict" down-to-the-penny keeping of the household accounts. And what leaped next from their answers and impressed me even more was the extent to which installment buying was an essential part of their family lives.

As one contestant put it to me: "We find that the best way to obtain major items is to maintain planned debt, purchasing one major item at a time for a cost which will fit into our budget and including interest as part of that cost." In the words of another, "We consider it worth the interest cost to use someone else's money and have earlier use of a product."

The Size of the Credit Market

Over the past thirty years the number of Americans owing installment debt has soared and so has the amount each one owes. The increases have been far greater than the population growth and much more than the rise in our take-home pay.

As of the late 1970s, more than one quarter of our disposable personal income, the money we have each month to spend, was being earmarked to repay installment debt. More than one out of every two U.S. families today owes some type of loan, in addition to the mortgage on their homes.

And it's all but certain that you have some installment debt if—
• you are between eighteen and thirty-five;
• you are married and the head of a family;
• you have children in their teens, or younger;
• your income is in the low to middle range of the medium-income brackets, roughly $10,000 to $30,000 a year in the late 1970s.

Is Anything Wrong with Borrowing?

I do not find the modern attitudes toward debt any cause for alarm. I see nothing wrong with paying money to use "someone else's money." I approve of "planned debt," which really is a kind of thrift. And, to an important degree, payments on an installment loan are merely replacing many old-time cash payments—like the money Americans used to dole out to the iceman or the cash we paid to the corner laundry.

In fact, I'll go beyond this and submit that the fundamental reason Americans have been borrowing so much today is precisely that they have had so much. This has intensified your desire to satisfy your aspirations rather than simply to finance your needs. And this in turn has led to unprecedented borrowing to achieve your aspirations at once.

Another factor is your increased financial security—through health insurance, Social Security, unemployment compensation, retirement pensions, employee savings and stock plans, ownership of stock and mutual funds, life insurance, etc.—and, very important, the income of the working wife. All these economic cushions are helping to make obsolete the traditional goal of protection against a "rainy day."

A third similarly subtle factor is the increased regularity of your income, which strengthens your capacity to take on responsibility for repaying installment debts. This development stems from the fundamental fact that our economy is now dominated by the service industries—and employment is much steadier in a service-oriented economy than in a predominantly industrial society.

Other factors include: the huge amounts of financial assets you as families are building up, primarily in your homes; the dramatic extension of credit to include unsophisticated as well as sophisticated borrowers, primarily through credit cards; the youthful hunger to acquire, instantly, all the things that other families have; and finally, the tendency of lenders to extend credit to borrowers at much younger ages than ever before.

And, of course, behind all the factors is the basic change that inflation has created in your attitudes toward being in debt and toward the goods and services that you appropriately may buy on time.

Perhaps as fundamental as any point is this: you, today's American, are far less interested than past generations in your legal total ownership of your toasters or automobiles or refrigerators. Instead, you are far more interested in the toasting services of that toaster, the transportation services of that automobile, the cooling service of that refrigerator. You are less and less impressed with owning things, more and more interested in the proper use of things. The growth of leasing and renting, not just of cars, but of a wide variety of other goods and services, is further testimony to this trait.

The Right and Wrong Reasons for Borrowing

Even in this era of high inflation, the cheapest way to buy any thing or non-thing is to buy it for cash. You always save money when you do this, for there are no extra charges added to your purchase price. As a buyer for cash, you can shop around for the best buy. Also, as a buyer for cash, you don't tie up future income, you are well aware of how many dollars you actually are spending, and you are not tempted to overbuy. The reason that retailers dangle the lure of "easy credit terms" before you is that the lure does work. It does encourage you to buy more. It does increase the retailer's sales.

But when you borrow to buy some things or non-things, you get the privilege of enjoying the purchase while you pay for it. You can start using at once something you need or want instead of being forced to wait until you can accumulate the savings to finance its purchase. Your buying on credit can teach you thrift. The discipline forced on you by your installment payments can spill over and encourage you to develop excellent saving habits. Many types of credit charge accounts are more convenient than cash or checks. Credit can be a crucial assist in a financial emergency.

To me, the advantages of buying on credit far outweigh the disadvantages of the cost of credit and the possible extravagance, provided, of course, that your reasons for credit-buying are sound and that you indulge in this type of purchasing with sensible moderation.

THE RIGHT REASONS FOR BORROWING

Regardless of whether you are equally convinced at this point, for the moment assume you agree that borrowing money—in the form of cash, or in the form of goods and services—is right for you if your reasons are right.

What might those reasons be?

(1) You are establishing a household or beginning to have a family. Either of these major events in life will take a lot of money—and it's in these, your early years, that you should learn how to use credit wisely and to the best advantage for yourself.

(2) You must make some major purchases. Few Americans can buy a car out of cash on hand and few can buy furniture or appliances that way either. These big-ticket items are traditionally bought with credit. As for a house, virtually all of us borrow to finance that key purchase of our lives. (See chapter on your home, pages 205–15.)

(3) You are faced with a genuine emergency and have not as yet had the opportunity to accumulate a sufficient emergency cash fund. Borrowing to meet emergencies is about as valid a reason as there can be.

(4) There are attractive seasonal sales or specials on which you can save money if you can use a charge account or a time-payment plan or get a low-cost loan from a financial institution. This assumes that the items on sale are ones you really want or need.

(5) You need money for college or other education expenses. This also is a top-notch reason for borrowing either by the student or by the parents. In fact, borrowing for college is the normal thing in America in this era. (See education chapter, pages 581–84 for details.)

(6) The price of an item you need in the future is heading sharply higher and it is ridiculous for you not to try to beat the price rise by borrowing the money to buy it now, and then repaying with cheaper dollars.

THE WRONG REASONS FOR BORROWING

(1) You haven't a reasonable prospect of repaying the loan, but you are going ahead anyway and borrowing because you need the money or want the goods or services. Or you are borrowing to the very hilt of your capacity to repay, which means that even a minor miscalculation on your part could force you to default.

(2) You are buying something impulsively and are primarily attached to the purchase, not because the product is of good quality and reasonably priced, but because the payment terms seem so easy and you are offered a long time to pay up. This is self-deception of the most dangerous kind from your personal financial point of view.

(3) You are charging purchases solely to boost your morale. Some individuals try to beat the blues with an extravagant shopping spree. Doing this on credit can bring an ever bigger attack of melancholy when the bills—with interest—finally come due.

(4) You are using credit to increase your status. Charging a purchase does allow you to pay for things while you're enjoying them. But credit alone can't raise your standard of living. Over the long run, if you "can't

afford" certain items on your present income, you can't afford to buy them on credit.

(5) You are overusing credit generally and failing to maintain an adequate cash reserve. People who do this also tend to live hand to mouth with their cash. They build up little or no savings fund to use during medical or other emergencies. So even if they are able to repay regular debts on schedule, any unexpected financial reversal can be their complete undoing.

(6) You are using credit against the expectation of future salary increases or windfall cash. When your income is on the rise, it's tempting to figure that your next raise is a cinch. But if you go ahead with major credit expenditures and then don't get the extra money, your budget can get very, very tight in a hurry.

(7) You are borrowing to gamble on some exceedingly risky venture—as distinct from borrowing to invest in a worthy enterprise you have thoroughly investigated. Borrowing to buy stocks or real estate or invest in a small business deal is entirely in order, particularly if you are young enough to recoup if you lose. But borrowing to gamble is begging for trouble—and the very fact that you have to borrow means that this is not extra money you can afford to lose.

(8) You are living so far beyond your income that you have to borrow to meet your current bills. On pages 967–70, analyzing how much debt is too much debt, you'll find several guidelines on the safe limits for borrowing. Suffice it to say here that when you must pile up debts just to manage your day-to-day living, you are headed for financial disaster.

(9) You are borrowing to buy something that will be used up or worn out long before you have made the final payment for it. This caution is exceedingly flexible, though, and you must use your common sense in applying it to yourself.

For instance, it might make sense to take out a twelve-month installment loan to pay for this year's vacation, for even though you would still be paying off the loan after the vacation is a memory, it could be worth it if you wouldn't have any vacation otherwise. But it would not make sense to take a two-year loan for this year's vacation, for in this case you would still be paying off this year's vacation when next year's vacation time rolls around.

Another illustration of this point (9) is borrowing to pay for college and education or special training courses. You well may be paying off a loan years after you've completed your education, but the value of your education will endure years and years after that. In this case, the value of your purchase is without time limit and cannot be measured by the yardstick which we use for material goods. But precisely the opposite is borrowing to pay for an exceedingly expensive gown. Buy this sort of gown for cash if you have it, and if this is your deep desire. But borrowing to buy it? That's financial stupidity.

Loans for such purposes—long-term installment debts for items which will be worn out or used before the loan is paid—are called "garbage debts." Remember the plaint of Willy Lohman, in Arthur Miller's *Death of a Salesman*. He wanted, just once, to be able to buy a new car which would not fall apart before his final payment was made.

The Basic Do's and Don'ts of Credit

No matter where you go for credit and no matter how many different types of loans you take out in the years to come, the basic do's and don'ts of credit will remain the same. Below you'll find them in the form of a simple check list to which you can refer again and again to make sure you are obeying these most fundamental of all credit rules.

Do always keep in mind that credit costs money. When you borrow you are, in essence, renting money—and just as you must pay when you rent an apartment or a car, so you must pay when you rent money. Anything you buy on credit will cost you more than the identical item bought for cash.

Do shop for credit as you shop for any other important purchase and buy your credit on the most advantageous terms to you. You can compare credit terms much more easily today than before the Truth in Lending law went into effect in 1969. Compare the price of any item bought for cash or bought on the installment plan. Find out whether it's cheaper for you to borrow from a bank or credit union and then buy the item you want for cash— or whether it's better for you to finance the purchase at the store or dealer's. (If you can meet the credit terms, it will *almost always* be cheaper, for example, to borrow from a bank or credit union than from the retailer, the dealer, or a small loan firm.)

Do check with care the maximum amount of credit you can soundly and safely carry. You can do it against the guidelines you'll find in this chapter, and you also can check your credit status with a responsible loan officer at your local bank, consumer finance office, credit union, other lending source. This officer is in the business of "selling" money—and nothing else—and he will want to make sure the person to whom he is selling the money is in a sound position to pay back.

Do ask lots of questions about the credit deal you are being offered, if you have any doubts at all. Insist on a written statement from the salesman showing you all charges plus the cash cost before you decide on buying.

Do ask yourself: would you buy the item for this amount of money in cash if you had the cash in your wallet or purse right now? Would you buy as expensive an item as the one you are considering if you had to put down the entire sum in cash now? In short, have you taken the proper time to make sure that this is a good purchase for you in view of the time it will take you to pay for it?

Do study your installment contract with utmost care and be sure you understand it before you sign it. When you sign, get a copy of the contract and keep it in a safe place.

Do keep receipts of your payments in a safe place.

Do pay off one major installment debt obligation before you take on another. Stagger your debts; time them; don't pile them one on top of another.

Do make sure that, in the installment deal you sign, all your monthly payments are roughly equal and make sure this applies particularly to your last payment. Avoid the danger that you'll be faced with a very big final installment ("balloon" payment). (See "The Great Pitfalls of Credit" later in this chapter.)

Do have the courage to say no to an installment deal if any of the above warning signals are flying—any of them.

And do continue saving regularly as you buy on credit. Even if you can save only a small amount each week, save it. For it's the regularity of savings and the discipline of the installment payments that will be the foundation of your own and your family's wealth.

Don't buy any item or service from any seller unless you have checked his reputation and have confidence he is a responsible retailer or dealer or whatever. Before you pledge to pay a specified part of your earnings for a protracted period, use your common sense and make sure you are dealing with a reputable businessman conducting a reputable business at a reputable place and that you can come back to him should your purchase turn out to be a lemon.

Don't buy anything you don't need or want—certainly not for credit. Learn how to handle high-pressure selling.

Don't carry several charge accounts that are seldom or never paid up. Revolving accounts make it very easy to maintain a permanent debt. But pay off each account periodically, for without this kind of self-discipline, revolving balances tend to grow ever larger (and more expensive) over periods of time.

Don't use your debts to establish your budgeting "system." Although some people would have no financial system at all if it weren't for their stack of bills, wise use of credit means month-by-month planning—not this sort of upside-down method.

Don't ever buy any thing or non-thing on credit without consulting your spouse or other person with whom you may be sharing financial responsibility and making sure that the two of you think the purchase is worthwhile. You must agree on any major purchase or you'll have great difficulty meeting the discipline of installment payments.

Don't be in any hurry to sign any installment contract or agreement.

Don't make the mistake of thinking you can get out of an installment debt simply by returning the merchandise you bought to the seller.

What you may have done when you bought the item is to sign two contracts: one for the actual appliance purchased and the second for the money to finance the purchase. This second loan contract will usually be sold immediately by the dealer to a finance company or bank, which then becomes what the lawyers call a "holder in due course." The bank or loan company has no ability to correct any defect in the item you have bought, and little interest in doing so either.

Under new legislation, you may have some protection in these situations, if the retailer from whom you bought the appliance also arranged for the loan for your purchase. But recognize that you are now dealing with third parties. You must go through the loan company to get the dealer to repair your TV set, dishwasher, or other appliance.

Don't rely on verbal warranties or pledges of the salesman, his boss, or even the owner. Get the promises in writing. But don't assume that because you *do* get it in writing, the promises will be honored. Under the Magnuson-Moss Warranty Act, there has been a vast improvement in disclosure of warranty terms to you, but little improvement has been made in compelling the companies who issue the warranties actually to fulfill them.

Don't buy any item on credit which does not have a value that will outlast the installment payments. This is an extension of the flexible wrong reason No. 9 for borrowing. The key word in this rule is "value."

Don't buy anything on credit of which you will tire before you finish the installment payments. You might really ponder this "don't" when buying your four-year-old an expensive and easily breakable toy game on a twelve-month payment plan.

Don't ever borrow money from a loan shark—even if you are desperate for the cash. In fact, the more desperate you are for the money, the more insane it is for you to commit yourself to pay back interest rates ranging to 1,000 per cent a year and more for the money. This way lies financial disaster.

Don't sign any loan contract that contains blank spaces that could be filled in to your disadvantage.

Don't co-sign a loan for anyone unless you have complete faith in that person's ability and willingness to repay the loan. For if the borrower whose note you co-sign defaults on the loan, you are responsible for paying off the entire indebtedness.

And, above all, *don't* borrow unless you will be able to *continue* to save regularly, too.

How to Establish a Credit Rating

A young army veteran, with a wife and two babies, was recently turned down for an FHA mortgage which he needed to buy a new home in eastern Texas. The reason: information at the local credit bureau showed him to be a bad credit risk. Astonished, the veteran visited the credit bureau and discovered that the reason for his credit troubles was that his former wife had run up a lot of unpaid bills just prior to their divorce. The veteran explained that under the separation agreement his estranged wife had signed a full year before she ran up the bills, she was legally responsible for all her debts, and his credit record had been wrongly damaged. His credit record was cleared and he got the mortgage he needed.

The ease with which Americans can open a charge account, get a new credit card, or take out a bank loan is directly dependent on the voluminous dossiers in the files of 2,500 credit bureaus throughout the United States and of large numbers of local merchants' associations on virtually every borrower. The bureaus freely exchange this information. They sell it to retailers, banks, other lenders, credit card companies, corporations, etc.—and a credit report almost surely will be obtained on you when you apply for a job or insurance or credit.

The consumer credit reporting industry processes from 125 to 150 million credit reports each year. Just one computerized credit reporting company says it maintains 30 million files, enters 4 million "pieces of information" on individuals each month, services 14,000 subscribers, and maintains on some individuals as many as 35 to 40 open accounts on which credit performance is reported.

Credit bureaus do not "rate" how good or bad a credit risk you are. They simply collect, from merchants with whom you have credit, public records, other sources of information on you which can be used in turn by banks, merchants, etc., to decide whether to grant you credit. The information ranges from your name, address, occupation, employer, and earnings to your former employment and earnings record, your marital history, your moving habits, your repayment patterns on previous loans, and records of any court proceedings against you.

The lenders then decide, on the basis of information provided by the credit bureau, whether or not you are a good credit risk. The guidelines vary from lender to lender, of course. A department store may be satisfied if you are in the habit of repaying charges within thirty to sixty days, while a bank may demand that, with very few exceptions, you repay bank loan installments on the due dates.

Or lenders may summarize their policies by telling you they are rating your application in terms of the "Three C's" of Credit. These Three C's are your:

Character: your personal characteristics, revealed through factual records, which indicate how you are likely to perform as a borrower. These would include your honesty, sense of responsibility, soundness of judgment, your trustworthiness.

Capacity: your financial ability to repay the loan. Your capacity would be judged on the basis of the job you hold, the amount of money you earn, the length of time you have held this or a previous job, your prospects in this or another job.

Capital: your assets which can serve as backing—collateral—for your loan. These assets would include your home, bank accounts, stocks and bonds, a car or cars, jewelry, valuable paintings, other tangible property.

These three qualities of Character, Capacity, and Capital form the foundation of any credit rating for you, as an individual or as a family.

To get even more specific, here are points that every lending officer will tick off when considering your application for a loan and your rating as a credit risk.

Your Employment Record: How long have you worked for the same company—although not necessarily in the same office or plant of the company? A prime consideration is the stability of your employment. It is up to you to prove your trustworthiness by showing you have not been a job-hopper who might once again leave for a job far away from your present one when, say, less than half your loan payments have been made.

Your Previous Loans: Have you ever paid off a loan before? The theory is that, if you have repaid a loan on time before this one, you will repay this loan, too. If you have defaulted on any previous loan, the danger is you'll default again. You'll almost certainly have a poor credit rating if you have any record of defaults or of repossession of items you have bought because you didn't maintain your payments or of suits for being delinquent in payments.

Your Home: Do you own your own home? Or have you lived in the apartment in which you now live for some time? If the answer is yes to either question, it's a sign that you probably are trustworthy.

Your Charge Accounts: Have you a record of paying your charge accounts regularly? If so, this will be a plus mark for you because it will indicate your sense of responsibility and your ability to repay.

Your Checking or Savings Accounts: Do you have either? If so, and particularly if they are at the bank to which you may be applying for a loan, this will be a great help.

Now here are six potential black marks on your credit rating:

(1) If you can't identify yourself. Surely you will have one or more of these: a driver's license, birth certificate, Social Security card, draft card, union card.

(2) If you have a "floating" address. This might be a furnished room in a rooming house or a transient hotel, a post office box number, a mail address in care of a friend. You might offset this, however, if previously you had lived in one place for a long time.

(3) If your employment is in an exceedingly unstable industry or profession and your own job is also basically volatile. If you're a ballet dancer . . . have a strictly seasonal job . . . are in a very restricted field . . .

(4) If, in some states, you are under twenty-one or eighteen and have no adult to co-sign for you. However, many stores do extend credit to teens

without a co-signer anyway, for as a group they have turned out to be good credit risks.

(5) If you apply for a loan at a bank or small loan company or other financial source far from your residence or if you have a record of dealing extensively with numerous small loan companies.

(6) If you are planning to go into the armed services before your loan is repaid. Under these circumstances, the lender almost surely will demand that a co-signer guarantee your loan repayment.

Under laws enacted in the late 1970s, it is much easier for a woman to get credit. In fact, lending institutions are now required to carry a wife's credit history under her own name, as well as that of her husband, if she requests it. (See pages 1352–54.)

But some lending organizations are engaging in other practices that can restrict credit. For example, banks—and some insurance companies—are turning down loans (and policies) simply because you have the wrong zip code, live in a particular neighborhood. And living *habits* are being used as criteria for establishing "character." If you are offending the "traditional" mores of society (using drugs, for example, keeping late, loud hours, or sharing your apartment with a member of the opposite sex), your life-style could be a factor in whether you are granted, or denied, a loan. (See pages 1347–55 on "Your Rights as a Borrower.")

What Is the Difference Between Credit Reports and Investigative Reports?

A regular credit report is compiled and maintained by a credit bureau for the purpose of helping consumers obtain credit. The credit bureaus do not make use of outside investigators, who are sometimes used in insurance reporting.

The information normally accumulated in your credit record consists of identity information, including your name, address, marital status, and Social Security number; present employment, which includes the position you hold, length of employment, and income; your personal history, such as date of birth, number of dependents, previous address, and previous employment information; credit history information including your credit experiences with credit granters; and public-record information which credit granters feel is important to know.

An investigative report consists of much more information—including data about a consumer's character, general reputation, personal characteristics, or mode of living. The information usually is obtained through personal interviews with the consumer's neighbors, friends, or associates or with others with whom the consumer is acquainted.

Credit bureaus do not normally compile this type of report, although an employment report made by a credit bureau will often contain some investigative information.

Both types of reports are subject to errors and one-sided presentations which can unfairly deny you credit and damage you in other ways. But you now have protection against such damages. (See pages 1355–62 on your rights.)

And because you have not been late in an installment payment or have not been turned down for a loan or credit application, don't assume your credit is excellent. If you have applied for a credit card and received no answer, for example, suspect that there is an unfavorable entry in your record. Or if you are turned down for a job, or not called back for a second interview, be equally suspicious.

Check your records, and correct any errors, *now,* before a financial emergency arises. And recheck every two or three years. Then, if you need money fast, you'll be more likely to get the loan quickly.

The Basic Types and Maturities of Loans

THE SINGLE-PAYMENT LOAN

This is precisely what its name implies: a loan you must repay in one lump sum. A single-payment loan may be a demand loan, meaning there will be no set time when you must repay but you will be obligated to pay back what you owe when the lender asks you to. Or the single-payment loan may be a time loan, meaning your loan will have a fixed maturity date and you'll have to pay back every penny on that prefixed maturity date.

Some single-payment loans call for the repayment of the amount borrowed in one lump sum, on demand or on a certain date, but also require that you pay interest on the amount borrowed periodically—monthly, quarterly, or annually.

A single-payment loan is usually made against collateral, meaning that you must put up certain valuable assets, such as your stocks, bonds, insurance policies, etc., to guarantee the loan repayment. The primary drawback of the single-payment loan is that you do not have periodic payments on it and thus you are not disciplined into reducing the loan month after month until it is all paid off. Instead you are faced with the entire repayment on a single date.

THE INSTALLMENT LOAN

This also is precisely what its name implies: a loan you must pay off in specified amounts at periodic intervals.

Usually you repay an installment loan in equal amounts every month over a period from twelve to sixty months. Usually, too, the interest cost is figured on the total amount of your loan.

In addition to these two basic types of loans, there are three major maturities on loans: short-term, intermediate, and long-term.

THE SHORT-TERM LOAN

This is the type of loan you use most frequently either to buy goods or to obtain cash or to finance everyday services.

For instance, you're using short-term credit when you buy a big-ticket appliance on the installment plan or with a credit card and promise to pay off within twelve to thirty-six, forty-eight, or even sixty months for autos. You are also using short-term credit when you get a cash loan—single-payment or installment payment—and promise to pay off within three years. Whether it's "cash" credit or "sales" credit, whether it's "installment" credit or "non-installment" credit, whether it's a "demand" loan or "time" loan, you're using short-term credit if you pledge to repay within a period ranging from as little as thirty days to five years.

THE INTERMEDIATE-TERM LOAN

This is the type of credit you use most often when you are financing major improvements or major repairs on your home. The maturity of this type of loan ranges from five to seven or even to ten or more for boats, home improvements, or household furnishings.

THE LONG-TERM LOAN

This type is implicit in its name. A familiar example is the real estate mortgage, extended over a period ranging from twenty to thirty and thirty-five years or even more—and repayable in regular installments at fixed intervals, usually monthly, during the life of the loan. Of course, you may get a long-term loan for other purposes but the mortgage is the best illustration of this category.

Your Sources of Loans in Cash

If you want to buy a new TV set, you don't just walk into the first TV store you pass and buy it. You look around, decide which model you prefer, then shop for the dealer who offers the set you want at the most favorable price to you.

Okay, you want to buy money.

Whatever the reasons—whatever goods or service you want to buy or whatever you want to build or finance—you need more money than you're earning each week or are able to commit for this single purpose. Whatever the amount—$500 or $2,500 or $5,000 or whatever—you are about to borrow (buy) money and pay the interest rate (price) asked by the lender (seller).

HOW TO BORROW CASH AND USE CREDIT

You live in a highly competitive economy, though, and the price of money in this competitive economy, like the price of everything else, will vary considerably. There are many sources for cash loans. Many compete for your patronage on the basis of price, convenience, service. Many also compete by specializing in specific types of loans. Many of them—such as your parents, other relatives, or friends—are simply "there." But never forget this key point: you easily can pay a price (interest rate) hundreds of dollars a year more than you need to pay by going to a lender who is not the best *for you*. You easily can cheat yourself disgracefully by not shopping for your money.

Let's approach this vital aspect of your financial life in the simplest way possible. To begin with, here are your sources of loans in cash.

The "Inside" Sources

Your sources of a loan fall into two broad, general categories: "inside" sources and "outside" sources. The inside sources are the people close to you, the ones who know you—your parents, other relatives, friends, your employer or even business associates.

The second category covers the outside sources—the broad spectrum of the financial community, ranging from traditional commercial banks to savings banks, savings and loan associations, small loan companies, credit card companies, employee credit unions, your life insurance company, your stock brokerage firm, pawnbrokers—and even loan sharks.

First, the "inside" sources.

PARENTS OR OTHER RELATIVES

Your parents or other relatives could be your best, easiest source of low-cost or no-cost loans. Assuming they have money available and are eager to help, your search for a cash loan may end right here.

Typical maximum you may borrow

That depends on your relatives' affluence, their attitudes toward lending you money, your needs, your relationships, etc. In short, obviously there is no "typical" maximum.

Typical annual interest rate

Yours could be a no-interest loan or you could insist on paying the same interest rate you would pay another lender (say, what you would pay the bank on the corner). I opt strongly for paying an interest rate and also for matching at least the minimum you might be charged by an outside source of credit. But this is your loan negotiation and again the obvious point is there is no "typical" charge.

Typical maximum maturity

There is no typical maximum maturity, and, just because most loans made by the parents would have no maturity date, the loan might drag on and on. This lack of a definite maturity can be both an advantage and a disadvantage.

Advantages

There is no legal pressure on you to meet regular monthly payments, even if you do have a moral, if not contractual, responsibility to try to pay back the loan as soon as you can.

Your parents may have a sympathetic understanding of the reasons you are borrowing and be eager to help you.

Disadvantages

The embarrassment of having to ask your parents or other relatives for financial help.

The very lack of pressure on you to repay may make you lazy about repaying and the debt could continue hanging over your head much longer than it need to or should.

The amounts you borrow may be too large or too small, because the personal relationships will affect your judgments on both sides.

FRIENDS

A loan from a close friend or a group of close friends with sufficient extra cash and interest in you to be your loan source is in the same general category as a loan from your parents or other relatives.

This applies even though your friends may be backing you in a venture they think is as exciting and promising as you do and even though there is a stated or implied pledge on your part to let them share liberally in any profits you make, for presumably you are also making the same explicit or implied pledge to share the profits with your own relatives. And if you aren't, you should.

Typical maximum you may borrow

None. See above.

Typical annual interest rate

Also none. But I repeat it's only common sense to insist on paying roughly the same interest rates you would pay the local bank.

Typical maximum maturity

None. However, again I suspect your friends will work out a maturity date of some sort—and if they don't, you work it out.

Advantages

In general, the same advantages that apply to a loan from parents or other relatives apply to loans from close friends. But I warn you: a loan from friends easily can corrode your friendship even if you pay it off promptly.

Disadvantages

The same disadvantages apply to these loans as to loans from relatives.

ADVANCE AGAINST SALARY OR LOAN FROM EMPLOYER

Most employers are reluctant to advance a salary paycheck or to make a personal loan. This generality, though, by no means applies to all employers, and in fact many corporations have special departments through which employees may borrow money with a minimum of red tape. Also your boss may be an acceptable loan source for you if yours is a close friendly relationship in a small office.

But an advance against your future salary—say your next two paychecks delivered right now—means you will face two empty pay periods some days hence.

Typical maximum you may borrow

This varies so widely from corporation to corporation and small business to small business that it would be a disservice to be specific. Also, in a small business, the maximum will depend on the business' profit picture, the employer's financial position, your relationship with the employer, your reasons for borrowing, and on and on.

Typical annual interest rate

Usually the same interest rate that you would be charged if you went to a bank for a loan. However, I know of no employer who charges interest on a salary advance. Other conditions of the salary advance are subject to private negotiation between the employer or the corporation personnel manager and the employee.

Typical maximum maturity

Usually six months to a year although, again, this maximum varies widely among both large and small businesses.

Advantages

The money is there.

Your employer may be a most sympathetic lender if he knows and approves the reasons you are borrowing.

The interest rate and repayment period will be among the best available from all sources.

An advance on your salary is simply borrowing in advance money due you in the future and involves no more than that.

Disadvantages

Borrowing money from your boss can hurt your relationship with him and place you in a sticky position.

This loan may permit him to ask and find out things about your personal financial life which you would prefer he not know.

If you take an advance on your salary, you may not be able to swing the payless pay periods and you may have to go to outside sources for cash after all.

The "Outside" Sources

During the 1970s, the inevitable trend toward elimination of our country's crazy-quilt pattern of money institutions grew ever more powerful—and with this trend will come benefits—and pitfalls—for all of us.

Traditional separations of functions are breaking down, "new traditions" are being established. As the 1980s began, commercial banks had begun to pay interest on checking accounts, while savings banks had also entered the checking account business with such devices as "negotiated orders of withdrawal," and both credit unions and savings and loan associations had broken down the barriers as well.

Employee credit unions are competing with commercial banks and savings banks. Even stock brokerage firms are offering what amounts to savings and checking accounts, in the form of "money funds," and these brokers are also actively soliciting their customers to take out loans against their stock portfolios. Credit card companies are offering loans, too.

While the financial community is in this state of flux, it becomes even more important for you to shop for your loan, for the best price and the best terms.

COMMERCIAL BANK

For most of you a commercial bank will be the most convenient loan source of all. For at this bank, which is probably a mere city block or two from where you live in town or only a couple miles away if you live in the suburbs, you may get the widest variety of loans including:

Personal loan

You may apply for a personal loan, repayable in one lump sum at its due date, or you may apply for an installment loan repayable in regular monthly installments over a period of twelve, eighteen, twenty-four, or thirty-six months.

Automobile loan

You may apply for an automobile loan to finance your new or used car. These loans usually are repayable in installments ranging from twelve to forty-two or even forty-eight to sixty months. Many automobile dealers as well as other merchants help the customer arrange for bank installment financing right in their showrooms.

Check loan

You may get money simply by writing a check, assuming you qualify. Your bank automatically enters the "loan" on your monthly statement of checking account transactions—when you write the special or overdraft check.

Mortgage and home improvement loan

You may get home improvement loans with intermediate maturities under which you can repair, remodel, expand, and generally improve your home. And you may get a long-term mortgage through which you may finance the purchase of your home in the first place.

Secured loan

You may get a loan quickly and comparatively inexpensively simply by putting up collateral to back your pledge to repay the loan. You can arrange to repay this loan in monthly installments. Your collateral may include your stocks or bonds or mutual fund shares or savings account passbook or the cash surrender value of your life insurance policy.

Student loan

Banks offer several types of student loans—some government subsidized, some not.

Credit card loan

You, the owner of a bank credit card, may use your card to buy goods at stores participating in the bank's credit card plan. The bank bills you monthly, and you, the borrower, pay interest on the unpaid balance you owe on your purchases.

Or you may use your bank credit card to borrow a limited amount of cash. (See special section below on credit cards and segment on "ready-credit" plans.)

Typical maximums you could borrow as 1980s opened

$10,000–$15,000 on a personal loan; $8,000–$10,000 on an auto loan.*
$75,000–$100,000 on a mortgage loan.*
$15,000–$20,000 on a home improvement loan.*
$2,500 a year on a federal-state guaranteed student loan.
$1,500–$2,000 on a check loan.
$1,500–$2,000 on a credit card plan.*

Up to the amount in your savings account on a passbook loan and up to a specified proportion of the estimated value of the collateral you put up to back a secured loan.

Typical annual interest rates were

So flexible and variable from year to year and loan to loan and area to area that no "typical" figure has meaning to you for long. However, here were typical rates as of the late 1970s:

Personal loan:	12–18%
Automobile loan:	
New car	10–14%
Used car	12–18%
Check (overdraft) loan:	10–16%
Mortgage loan:	8–12%
Home improvement loan:	10–15%
Passbook loan:	8–12%
Secured loan:	10–16%
Federal-guaranteed student loan:	8%
Credit card loan:	12–18%
Education loan:	9–12%

With inflation an acute problem during much of the 1970s, the interest rates listed above may vary considerably, up or down, depending on the state of the economy and where you live. However, they are a useful relative guide to commercial bank practices. The general rule is that unsecured loans cost more than secured loans, and the type of security affects the rate on secured loans.

Typical maximum maturities†

Three to five years on personal loans, auto loans, secured loans.
Five to ten years on home improvement loans.

* Although these are typical amounts in most cases, banks are not in any way limited to making loans in these amounts.
† Rates listed are typical, but actual maximums are set by each bank.

Up to thirty or thirty-five years on first mortgages and three to ten years on second mortgages.

Up to twenty-five to thirty years on refinancing mortgages.

By regulation, up to ten years after graduation on student loans.

Advantages

Simplicity: you fill out an application and a financial statement, have an interview with the loan officer, and quite likely your cash loan is approved within twenty-four hours.

Objectivity: you can get a loan whether or not you are a depositor at the bank and, although of course bank practices vary widely, generally you will qualify for a loan if your credit rating is okay and your income will enable you to handle the monthly payment.

Relatively inexpensive: rates on bank loans compare favorably with rates from most other loan sources and so do bank loan maturity terms.

No extra or hidden fees or charges; under the law, there must be full disclosure of terms.

Since co-makers are not usually required, you need not appeal to friends or business acquaintances to endorse your note.

When you have fulfilled the terms of the loan, as prescribed, you have established a valuable credit reference.

Disadvantages

The requirements—your personal financial standing, credit rating—are sometimes more rigid than other lenders may demand.

You will be penalized if you take out an installment loan and don't meet your monthly installments on schedule. The penalty is often a flat fee of 5 per cent, plus interest, for each delinquency. State laws generally prescribe allowable charges for delinquency.

READY CREDIT (THE LOAN IN ADVANCE)

How does this form of credit work? Who qualifies for it? When is it economical to use it and when not?

Ready credit is an automatic line of credit offered by your bank or credit card company. In some cases its reserve is an extension of your checking account. In others the reserve may be kept in a separate account involving special checks. Usually the reserve is between $500 and $2,500, but it may run up to $5,000 or more.

In either case, the overdraft check or special check you may write becomes a loan as soon as it reaches your bank. In either case also, the typical interest rate, including credit life insurance, is 1 per cent a month on the basis of the daily outstanding balance, which works out to a true annual interest rate of at least 12 per cent. Typically, no interest charge is made unless and until you actually use your special line of credit, and the interest charge stops when you repay the amount you have withdrawn from your reserve.

"Ready credit" is granted by a signed agreement to qualified customers, and the requirements for eligibility are generally stricter than those for ordinary bank loans because it is unsecured credit and, once granted, is available year after year to the responsible borrower. It may be canceled at any time by the bank, however.

As an illustration of the costs involved at 1 per cent a month interest (12 per cent a year annual rate) let's say you overdrew your checking account by $100. If you repaid the amount one month later, the cost to you would be $1.00. If you repaid the total after one week, the cost would be 23 cents. If you repaid it in one day, the cost would be 3 cents.

Under what circumstances is it to your advantage to use this type of credit and when is it a disadvantage? Here are the answers:

• If you spot a major bargain, an appliance selling at a big discount, for example, you probably would save by using the overdraft plan. Here, the amount of interest you would pay would be comfortably covered by your savings on the appliance, assuming you repaid the special loan within a few weeks or even a few months.

• If an emergency arises on a weekend, or when you are far from home, a reserve credit line may be the easiest and surest way to raise emergency funds.

• If you are a chronically bad bookkeeper, the interest on a reserve credit line might be less costly to you than a pile of service charges for department stores or for overdraft checks. It might also save you the tremendous embarrassment of bouncing checks.

• If you are self-employed or if your income goes into sharp but temporary dips, this credit may provide you with enough peace of mind to make it worth the interest you pay.

To save on interest expense, a fundamental guide is that your line of ready credit should be strictly for short-term purposes and your overdrafts should be repaid as quickly as possible. Thus, "ready credit" is not usually the right type for you when you're paying longer-term debts—financing a car, a planned home improvement, your college education. Banks offer other types of loans more appropriate for these purposes and generally at lower interest rates.

CREDIT UNION

A credit union may be the ideal answer to your borrowing problem if you have access to one and the union is efficiently managed.

Few, if any, regular lending agencies have the credit union's advantages of low operating costs, tax exemption, and often free office space, clerical and managerial help, too. Thus, naturally no other type of lender can afford to make loans at the low rates credit unions charge or can compete with the credit unions on service to borrowers.

Credit unions usually are formed by members of a closely knit group—such as employees of a business firm or members of a labor union, club, or lodge—and their purpose is implicit in their name. The union extends credit to its members when the members need the help.

There are now more than 22,500 credit unions operating in offices, churches, professional organizations, and communities across the country, chartered under federal or state laws. Moreover, if there isn't one around and you are part of a well-defined group, it is not too difficult to form one of your own. You can get help and precise rules for creating a credit union with either a federal or state charter by writing to CUNA, P. O. Box 431, Madison, Wisconsin 53701.

Credit unions specialize in small personal loans, particularly to a member faced with a sudden emergency. Credit unions also can make automobile, mortgage, and home improvement loans.

Recent changes in the obsolete Federal Credit Union Act of 1934 significantly broaden the type of loans that credit unions can make to their 30 to 35 million members, and the maximum loan amounts that credit unions can offer have been substantially raised.

Typical maximum you can borrow

The maximum a credit union member could borrow used to be $2,500 on your personal signature, but under the new legislation, there is no restriction. Individual credit unions, though, impose various maximums on the different types of loans they make.

Typical annual interest rates

Usually the lowest of any major category of lender, often ¼ per cent below the prevailing rate in your area for the type of loan you are seeking, and sometimes there is an even greater reduction.

Typical maximum maturities

These limits, too, have now been broadened, and maximum maturities on personal loans can go as high as twelve years, can range up to fifteen years on home improvement loans, and on mortgage loans can be as high as thirty years.

Advantages

The interest rates may substantially undercut rates charged by other lenders. A credit union is probably the cheapest borrowing source available to you.

You are dealing with fellow workers or friends or lodge members who have in common a special interest in the financial welfare of all credit union members.

Disadvantages

You must be a member to borrow. This means not all of us have the opportunity to borrow through one of these co-operatives.

You may hesitate to reveal your borrowing needs and financial problems to the committee of fellow workers who must approve your loan request.

SAVINGS BANK OR SAVINGS AND LOAN ASSOCIATION

Savings banks exist in only seventeen of our fifty states, mostly in the Northeast. Savings and loan associations exist in all states and number about 5,000; but in most they are given power to lend primarily for the purchase of home and for home improvements.

Both types of savings institutions specialize in mortgages and home improvement loans. (Savings and loan associations are authorized to make mobile home loans and educational loans, too.) Savings banks also frequently make personal loans.

Typical maximum you may borrow

Up to 100 per cent of your passbook savings total for passbook loans.
Up to $10,000 for personal loans.
Up to $100,000 for mortgages.
Up to $25,000 for home improvement loans.

Typical annual interest rates

Slightly less than a commercial bank for passbook loans and home improvement loans; about the same for other types of loans.

Typical maximum maturities

One year for passbook loans and up to three years for personal loans.
Up to twenty-five to forty years for mortgages.
Up to ten years for home improvement loans.

Advantages

Although you are borrowing your own money when you make a passbook loan, your net cost is far less than on any regular installment loan and you are disciplining yourself into maintaining your savings.

Savings institutions specialize in mortgage and home improvement financing. Their rates are competitive and their services superior.

Disadvantages

Really none.

LICENSED SMALL LOAN COMPANY

Over the years, leading small loan companies throughout the nation have spent countless tens of millions of dollars to advertise their willingness and readiness to extend financial aid to you, the little fellow. They have boasted that they exist to help solve your emergency problems and the littler you are the more welcome you are. Their very name—small loan company—inspires the trust of the would-be borrower. (Other well-known names are "consumer finance company" and "personal finance company." All have the same appeal.)

There is no doubt that these companies have filled and do fill an important place in our financial structure. You will note from the interest rate range below that the small loan companies charge a comparatively high rate of interest—but there are explanations. For one thing, they borrow part of their own capital from banks so they themselves are paying a high rate of interest to get the money to lend in turn to you. For another, small loan companies lend to individuals who do not have top credit ratings and who well might receive a flat no from a local bank. Inevitably, they have to write off a number of these risky loans or spend considerable money and time collecting the money due them.

Small loan companies specialize in personal and automobile loans and offer both single-payment and installment loans. As for security, the usual requirement of the small loan companies is nothing more than your promise to pay; i.e., your signature. Under certain conditions, they also ask additional security in the form of a chattel mortgage on your household furniture, to make sure that you will honor your debt.

If, though, you have a questionable credit rating and do not have a regular source of income, the small loan company may demand that a qualified friend co-sign for your loan. If you, the borrower, then fail to meet your payments, your co-signer will become responsible for the unpaid balance of your loan.

Typical maximum you may borrow

$500 to $1,500—with the actual limits (some are higher) depending on state law.

Typical annual interest rate

State laws generally prescribe interest rate ceilings but rates often are two to three times higher than bank interest charges.

Typical maximum maturities

One to three years.

Advantages

Frequently you can obtain a smaller loan from a small loan company than from a bank. You may even borrow just a few dollars if that is all you need.

The small loan companies are not as selective as banks. They can take greater risks just because they charge higher rates.

As the charge is based on the unpaid balance of your loan, you pay only for the credit you actually use.

Suits for collection are less frequent, the small loan company often preferring to tack extra interest onto the loan for delinquencies, since the rates are relatively high.

If you have a grievance against a small loan company, you may take it to the state banking department and get advice and help at no expense.

You also may take a gripe about a small loan company to the Consumer Affairs Center of the National Consumer Finance Association, 1000 Sixteenth Street, N.W., Washington, D.C. 20036. Telephone (202) 638-1340.

Disadvantages

The interest rates are much higher than those charged by full service commercial banks.

The maximum amount you can borrow is often less than you can get from banks and less than you need.

You may not be able to get the loan without a co-signer.

TUITION LOAN SPECIALISTS

Tuition loan companies are actually small loan institutions, some of which deal exclusively in loans to parents to pay tuitions for their children at private schools and colleges. They may be subsidiaries of national "small loan" firms, or they may be independent companies.

Usually, a school or college has arrangements with at least one tuition loan company, and when your child is accepted by the school, you are sent loan application forms to complete along with your registration contract.

The school and the loan company make it simple and easy for the parent to borrow the money—often too simple and easy. For tuition loans can be extremely costly, with the lending institution realizing as much as 32–40 per cent true annual interest on its money. When you consider that the tuition loan company has excellent security on its loan—the school will not "graduate" the student or supply his or her grades or transcripts of records—the true interest rates are extremely high.

Typically, you, as a parent, can borrow one to four years of tuition and repay the loan in one to seven years or even more in some cases. But you must realize that you usually will be paying interest on the full amount of the loan even though the tuition loan company may not forward the money to the school until much later. You will not, if you pay cash, have to forward the full year tuition all at once, but semester by semester. A bank loan, therefore, or even a credit card loan, or some "ready credit" arrangement with a bank or credit union is almost always significantly cheaper than the tuition loan company's interest rates.

Many of the better schools also have their own "tuition budget" plan, under which, for a nominal annual fee, you make monthly payments for ten to twelve months of the year, rather than two or three lump sum payments at the beginning of the semesters or trimesters.

This arrangement is the least expensive of any. When you and your child are "shopping" for schools, a key question should always be what, if any, type of tuition-payment plan they have. Since you will be paying $20,000 to $30,000 over a period of years, at charges in effect in the late 1970s, a tuition-budget plan could save you literally thousands of dollars in interest payments.

If you do decide to deal with a tuition loan company, though, you can expect that the advantages and disadvantages of a loan from a small loan company will apply.

Typical annual interest rates

Anywhere from 16 to 36 per cent true annual interest, based on the time the tuition loan company turns the money over to the school.

Typical maximum you can borrow

As much as 100 per cent of your youngster's tuition, room and board charges (costs of books and other school fees usually are not included).

Typical maximum maturities

Up to seven years for a loan covering the entire four-year tuition.

Advantages

Loan is usually relatively easy to obtain, and you need not worry about tuition payments. It's almost always a "mail-order" arrangement so you don't have to approach your local lending institutions.

Disadvantages

Interest rates are almost always higher than you could obtain elsewhere; tuition loan company usually has an arrangement with the school, so that if you default, your child may be embarrassed, perhaps even dropped from school for non-payment of the scheduled charges.

LIFE INSURANCE COMPANY

This may be your indisputably number one source for money. In fact, it is a source I suggest you check before you turn to any other. After a period of two or three years the premiums you have paid on a regular life insurance policy (not a term policy) become a prime cash asset. Your insurance company will then lend you your cash surrender value directly at a specified and relatively very low interest charge.

Typical maximum you may borrow

Generally up to 95 per cent of your life insurance policy's cash surrender value. And since every year the cash value of your policy increases, every year the total you may borrow increases, too.

Typical annual interest rates

This will depend on what your insurance contract states. For older persons, whose policies have been in effect many years, your interest rate may be as low as 5 per cent, but policies issued more recently may have provisions calling for loans at 8 per cent and higher. You must check this rate with far more care than ever before.

Typical maximum maturities

None.

Advantages

The loan is a cinch to get. You merely ask your company to send you the loan forms, fill them out, return them, and the cash is yours.

The interest charged is low by today's standards—a flat rate on the unpaid balance of your loan without any extras or hidden charges. Usually the company will collect the interest you owe at the time you pay your premiums: quarterly, semiannually, or annually.

You are not held to any specified time for repayment. This may be an advantage if you cannot take on the burden of regular payments right away.

Disadvantages

The amount of your loan decreases the face value of your life insurance policy—which means, of course, that you're temporarily undercutting the protection of your family.

The absence of a specified time for repayment might lull you into maintaining the loan indefinitely, thus continuing to pay interest indefinitely and decidedly increasing the overall cost of your loan.

YOUR STOCKBROKER

Another loan source is your own stockbroker, provided, of course, that you have stock, leave the certificates at the brokerage house "in street name," and have, or open, a "margin" account.

You can borrow up to a specified percentage of the current value of any stocks you own (usually 40–60 per cent), depending on the regulations in effect at the time. In this case you are arranging a single-payment loan and paying interest monthly or quarterly on the amount you have borrowed.

The interest rate is flexible, being ½ to 1½ per cent above what is called the broker's loan rate. This rate in turn is usually pegged slightly above the so-called prime rate, the rate at which bankers lend money to their largest and most credit-worthy corporate customers.

The traditional use of such "margin" loans is to enable stock market investors and traders to buy stock without paying the full market price, just the 40 to 60 per cent part-payment, with the rest being "financed" or "margined."

Recently, though, brokerage firms have been soliciting their margin customers to borrow money and take it in cash. It works this way: say you have 100 shares of five stocks, each stock worth $100 a share on a given day. Your portfolio is thus worth $50,000. If the margin percentage then was 50 per cent, you would be able to borrow $25,000. The interest rate would depend on your broker's policy and the current broker's loan rate.

The interest would be deducted from the funds in your brokerage account, or, if these funds were insufficient, you would be billed.

There are dangerous drawbacks in borrowing from your stockbroker, though. If the price of the stock declines, you could be required to advance substantial sums on short notice to "cover" your position. The same thing might happen if margin requirements were increased to a higher percentage. In addition interest costs may fluctuate widely, and recently rates have soared in short spans of time.

Typical maximum you may borrow

Varies from a normal 40 to 60 per cent of the value of your stock portfolio.

Typical annual interest rates

Fluctuating: range from ½ to 1½ per cent above the broker's loan rate, which in turn varies with the prime rate established by banks.

Typical maximum maturities

None, so long as your stock does not decline in value and the margin rates remain the same.

Advantages

Quick and easy, provided you have an adequate portfolio and have set up a margin account. A single call to your broker is enough to produce a check for the amount you want. Also, though interest rates vary, they are generally low, since the money is partially (40–60 per cent) secured. No amortization required.

Disadvantages

Many. Your interest rate can fluctuate widely. The margin requirements may be increased, forcing you to put up additional cash (in effect, pay back part of the loan) on extremely short notice. The market may drop rapidly, again producing margin calls for quick cash at short notice, just when economic conditions may be putting the squeeze on you from other directions, too. The fact that you do not have a regular schedule to amortize the loan may lead you to postpone repaying it.

INDUSTRIAL LOAN COMPANY

The "industrial" part of this source's name stems from the fact that the companies make loans mostly to industrial workers—not to the industrial corporations employing them.

Industrial loan companies fill a gap between the commercial bank and the small loan company. They make a wide variety of loans, ranging from a regular personal or auto loan to a second mortgage on your home.

Typical maximum you may borrow

Up to $10,000 on personal loans.
State laws prescribe limits on second mortgages.

Typical annual interest rates

Comparatively high compared to banks, but the companies may make loans at lower interest rates than small loan companies.

Typical maximum maturities

One to five years on personal or auto loans.
Ten years on second mortgages.

Advantages

They can make larger loans than small loan companies and might charge lower interest rates.

They will accept a wide variety of your possessions as collateral, ranging from your home to pieces of your furniture.

They might lend you money when you do not have a sufficient credit rating to get a loan from a bank.

Disadvantages

Interest rates are higher than charged by banks.

Industrial loan companies frequently insist on co-signers—which means you must ask your friends or business acquaintances to guarantee the repayment of your loan and this you may hate to do.

That interest rate of up to 18 per cent a year if you are not careful about paying.

The temptation to overuse this source of credit just because it's so easy.

ANOTHER MORTGAGE ON YOUR HOME

With the prices for houses climbing in recent years even faster than the inflation rate, an increasingly popular loan source is another mortgage on your house.

Assume you purchased your house twenty to thirty years ago, perhaps for $20,000 to $30,000. Today it may be worth $75,000 to $100,000. Furthermore, your original mortgage may be paid off or nearly so by now. You have, in effect, $70,000 to $90,000 "equity" in your home—some $60,000 to $75,000 of which you can again borrow against.

Depending on your circumstances, you can do one of two things: you can refinance your present mortgage, or you can take out a second mortgage. But, beware, both these courses of action have subtle but serious drawbacks. First, the second mortgage.

SECOND MORTGAGE COMPANY

These companies do precisely what their name implies: lend you money against your home on a second mortgage so you can meet your pressing obligations. On top of the first mortgage you are carrying to finance your original home purchase, you take out a second mortgage for a given period of time and then use the money raised from the second mortgage for purposes which may have nothing whatsoever to do with your home.

But this can be an exceedingly expensive source for money—and an unsound borrowing method, too. The interest stated on your mortgage may not seem high, but the extra charges can multiply the actual rate you are paying. At the same time, your second mortgage may run for years—meaning you'll be paying for the money long after you have forgotten the purpose for which you borrowed. And this, you will recall, breaks one of the cardinal rules for borrowing.

Typical maximum you may borrow

Up to $25,000 or 85 per cent of the equity you have in your home.

Typical annual interest rates

The legal maximum in the state plus "charges" which, I repeat, can build up to startlingly high percentages.

Typical maximum maturities

Three to ten years.

Advantages

Quick way to raise funds for just about any purpose.
Repayment can be strung out over a number of years.

Disadvantages

A second mortgage can add a financial burden undermining your entire investment in your house in bad times.

You take on a relatively long-term debt—three to ten years—to purchase a product or service that may have a much shorter life.

You could, without realizing it, commit yourself to paying an excessively steep rate for the money.

YOUR OWN HOME MORTGAGE

You may get a second mortgage on your home and raise substantial sums from other lenders besides a second mortgage company, of course. Or you may refinance your mortgage, take out a new mortgage with a new long-term life and new interest rate, to raise hefty sums. This you may do through the institution that gave you your first mortgage or through another bank, savings association, or an individual investor.

The trend toward borrowing on your own home to raise money for non-home purposes exploded in the 1960s and 1970s and the trend is apparently here to stay. What this represents, in effect, is the dramatic development of a twenty-to-thirty-year installment loan. The long-term mortgage is the vehicle through which money is raised for everything from college costs to pleasure boats.

Typical maximum amounts you may borrow

Depends on your deal.

Typical annual interest rates

The going rate for first mortgages.

Typical maximum maturities

From ten years up to original life—twenty, twenty-five, thirty years—of first mortgage, depending on age of the property.

Advantages and disadvantages

This trend toward using the home mortgage for purposes far removed from the original purchase of the home is so powerful that it demands more than a few short sentences stating the pros and cons. Thus read the following real-life illustration with care:

Mr. H.B.A. is a successful lawyer in his forties who bought a $50,000 house in a suburb near New York fourteen years ago with the help of a 6 per cent mortgage. H.B.A. now has one son in college, another entering this fall, and an extremely popular teenage daughter. In addition to tuition fees, he therefore has suddenly developed a wallet-emptying list of new "necessities": a car for the boys, a swimming pool, new terrace furniture, etc.

So H.B.A. recently refinanced his mortgage and raised $22,000 in new cash to be repaid over a twenty-year period. He has bought the car for his boys, he is decorating the terrace, and he is about to build the swimming pool. To him, this is an excellent deal—a way to borrow "instant cash" on the most painless repayment terms.

But right as the deal seems to H.B.A., it's wrong from a strictly dollars-and-cents viewpoint. For H.B.A. is breaking that fundamental rule of sound finance: he is "borrowing long to buy short." Years after his son's auto will have been junked, he'll be paying interest on the loan to purchase it. By committing himself to pay interest over a twenty-year period, he'll end up paying far more on this loan than he would have paid on a two-or-three-year loan at twice his borrowing rate.

That's H.B.A. Now let's take you as an illustration. Say you borrow $3,000 on a conventional installment loan, pay 9 per cent interest, agree to repay over a two-and-a-half-year period. Your true interest rate is almost double 9 per cent, or about 16.4 per cent. Your monthly repayment will be $122.50. Your total interest cost will come to $675 ($3,000 × .09 × 2.5 = $675).

Or say you borrow $3,000 by refinancing your mortgage over a twenty-year period. Your interest rate is a simple 6 per cent a year. Your monthly repayment will be only about $21.49. But over the twenty years the 240 monthly payments will total $5,158.30—an out-of-pocket interest cost to you of $2,158.30. In addition, you'll pay at least $250 for closing costs.

In the first case, your interest cost is $675. In the second, it's $2,408.30 —more than three and a half times as much.

(See the section in this chapter on knowing your true interest costs for a more complete discussion of interest charges.)

THE ROLE OF INFLATION

At this point, financial super-sophisticates among you might point out that over the past ten years the inflation rate in the United States (and in countries throughout the rest of the world the situation has been similar or worse) has been about 100 per cent or so. Stated another way, it means the dollar today is worth about half of what it was ten years ago!

If the same rate continues for the next ten years, the $3,000 will be worth about $1,500 and those $21.50 payments will be the equivalent of under $11. Assuming that your salary just keeps pace with inflation, your payments will be cut by more than 50 per cent long term.

But inflation does not take place all at once. Rather it erodes your dollar's value over the years. Furthermore, those closing costs are up front. If you don't have to pay them in a lump sum in advance, it will take you a year just to repay the loan fee.

Certainly, our inflation of recent years is largely responsible for our increasing tendencies to borrow and finance our purchases, rather than to pay cash. Both long-term and short-term borrowing have their places. But borrowing long to buy a short-term item never makes sense no matter what the inflation rate.

Now I can summarize the pros and cons, confident that you grasp the nuances. The easy appeal of refinancing a home mortgage to obtain cash for non-home equity purposes is undeniable but it glosses over the tremendous difference in interest costs. Like other financing methods that on the surface seem easiest and least expensive, this one turns out to be among the hardest and most costly.

RURAL FAMILY LOANS

If you are a farm family living in a rural area, you may be able to get a rural family farm or home loan at a comparatively low interest rate through a nearby production credit association. These are co-operative associations created to assist in providing credit for people living in rural regions—and you also may be able to get a loan to finance your farm or farm-related business or other enterprise.

You'll get details on these loans and your possible eligibility for them from the production credit association serving your area or from the Farm Credit Administration, 490 L'Enfant Plaza, N.W., Washington, D.C. 20578.

PAWNBROKER

The pawnbroker is not the worst of all loan sources but he's close to it. He certainly must be classed as a source of last resort for the desperate borrower. You'll not only pay an enormous annual interest rate on small loans; you'll also be able to borrow only a fraction of the auction value of the asset you pledge as collateral. And to get your funds, you'll have to turn over your property (which you may badly need) to the pawnbroker for the life of the loan.

Your loan usually will have a very short life and in many parts of the country you must redeem your collateral within thirty to sixty days or it becomes the property of the pawnbroker, who may then offer it for sale. A pawnbroker's terms underscore how limited are the options of the desperate borrower. The person least able to afford horrendous interest rates always is the one who pays them.

Typical maximum you may borrow

Up to 50 per cent (but possibly 60 per cent) of the auction value of the asset you pledge.

Typical annual interest rates

Three to four times higher than rates on personal loans charged by most major lending institutions.

Typical maximum maturities

180 days, possibly with the privilege of a 180-day extension.

Advantages

You have complete privacy, need not give any information about yourself or your financial circumstances. The pawnbroker doesn't care who you are so long as he's assured the asset you are pledging isn't stolen property.

You can borrow money at once against your possession and, if you need the cash in a matter of hours, this can be a crucial factor.

If you are in a very volatile profession—the theater, say—you can get periodic loans by pawning and redeeming the same asset over and over again.

Disadvantages

It's an excessively expensive way to borrow.

You do not have the use of your asset while the loan is outstanding—and you might need that asset to earn an income (a musical instrument, for instance, or a typewriter or special tools).

You can borrow only a small percentage of the value of your assets.

LOAN SHARK

Absolutely at the bottom of any list of loan sources is the loan shark—in every way an evil source, lending money to the desperate, innocent, and ignorant at sinfully high and openly illegal rates. He is a racketeer charging usurious rates for money and threatening punishment if the repayment is not on schedule.

A typical deal might be "7.50 for 5"—$7.50 for $5.00 borrowed until payday next week. That may seem only $2.50 in interest on your $5.00 loan, but it's actually 2,600 per cent a year, and that's a hellish rate by any yardstick. Moreover, the loan shark usually will try to keep you from repaying the entire sum you owe, for if part of your loan remains outstanding at all times, he can build up the interest you owe to ever higher totals. At the same time, he threatens you with punishment ranging from broken bones to death itself for failure to repay.

Yet the brutal fact is that the loan shark continues to thrive. Even though the Truth in Lending law forbids the collecting of debts by violent means, loan-sharking is a multibillion-dollar business dominated by organized crime. Even though there are many alternative sources for loans, these crooks can and do get away with charges running 1,000 per cent, 2,000 per cent, or more a year, and a conservative estimate is they are bilking the poor out of more than $350 million each year.

How do you spot a loan shark? Be suspicious if he:

does not show his state license prominently;

dates a loan prior to the time you get the money;

asks you to sign the papers before the figures are filled in;

requires more than one note for one loan;

refuses to give you a copy of the papers you signed or receipts for payments;

requires you to buy expensive insurance.

Get legal advice immediately if, when you attempt to repay part of a debt, the lender says you must repay the entire principal or none.

Appeal to local or state legal authorities at once if, when you admit to the lender that repayment is difficult, he sends you to someone else who seeks another fee in addition to the interest owed.

If a reputable lender's plan for repayment seems too difficult for you, turning to a disreputable lender will only intensify your problem.

Typical maximum amount you may borrow

None.

Typical annual interest rates

500 to 2,600 per cent.

Typical maximum maturities

None.

Advantages

None.

Disadvantages

Endless. The loan shark as a source for money is truly unspeakable.

Credit Cards

Bridging the area between loans for cash and credit for other goods and services (which in effect also are loans) is the credit card—the plastic foundation for our increasingly cashless society in this country.

First, the basics about a credit card.

WHAT ARE THEY?

What a credit card is: this is an identification card (usually plastic) permitting you, the holder, to charge a wide variety of goods and services simply on your signature. You agree to pay for all you charged either once a month or over an extended period. If you make only a partial payment on your account, your account is automatically treated as a loan and interest is charged.

If you have an airline card, you use it to charge air trips; an oil card, to charge gas and other purchases at a gas or service station; a travel and entertainment card, to charge travel and all sorts of hotel, restaurant, and entertainment bills the world over. This card is an automatic charge account at all the participating businesses in the plan to which you belong and may give you charge accounts at thousands of places.

If you have an all-purpose bank credit card, you also have automatic charge accounts at all the businesses participating in the bank's plan, which can include thousands of places all over the world.

The card issuer gets a record of what you have charged from the business at which you have charged a purchase of goods or services. The issuer then bills you, the holder of the card, once a month for the total of your charges. You write one check a month covering what you owe. If you don't pay off within twenty-five days on a bank credit card, your account also is automatically treated as a revolving account and finance fees are added on the unpaid balance.

You are expected to pay for charges on travel and entertainment cards upon receipt of a bill unless it is a major item which may be paid for in installments set up at time of purchase. If you haven't paid your debt within sixty days after receipt of your bill, you must pay a late charge and your card may be revoked.

WHO ISSUES CREDIT CARDS?

Credit cards issued by a variety of organizations ranging from local department stores to national retailing chains, from the telephone company to airlines, from car rental concerns to oil companies, from hotel/motel chains to local banks, from local restaurants to international travel companies—and, of course, from the giant firms specializing in credit cards alone.

In general, the credit cards fall into three broad categories: (1) single-purpose cards; (2) multipurpose travel, food, and entertainment cards; and (3) bank credit cards.

Single-purpose cards issued by all kinds of businesses—oil companies, motel chains, telephone companies, car-rental agencies, department stores, and the like. You pay nothing for them, and they allow you to charge merchandise or services, paying when billed. If you don't pay promptly, you will be charged interest, typically amounting to 1½ per cent a month. The aim of this kind of card is to encourage you to buy only from the company that issued the card to you. With most of these single-purpose cards you receive a receipt at the time you charge your purchase and a duplicate receipt when you receive your monthly bill. This helps you with your bookkeeping records since the separate receipts can be filed in their proper categories—by category of goods or services and chronologically.

With some cards, you get quantity discounts depending on the total amount of your purchases each year. This is an advantage to many business concerns who arrange for their employees to have these credit cards. Purchases by all employees then count toward the discount the company using the credit card receives. In addition, some firms (such as car rental concerns, for example) keep computer records of your preferences, and other data on you, to speed the completion of the transaction.

Some of these "single-purpose" cards, however, also enable you to charge services with related organizations. For instance, an oil company credit card will enable you to charge at a national hotel/motel chain (and vice versa). Others serve as identification to allow you to cash small-denomination checks when you are away from your hometown.

Food, travel, and entertainment or multipurpose cards, like Diners Club, Carte Blanche, and American Express. These are used mostly by businessmen and women, although anyone may apply. Holders of these cards pay a yearly fee—usually $20 to $30—to the issuer, and then can use the card in thousands of business places. Bars, restaurants, hotels, and expensive shops are this kind of card's best customers. Usually card holders are billed within thirty to sixty days and are expected to pay on receipt of the bill. No interest is charged if payment is prompt. But interest is added if your payment is delinquent by sixty to ninety days.

Frequently the so-called T&E (travel and entertainment) cards offer members additional services or opportunities, such as group life and health-and-accident insurance; free travel insurance if, for example, you charge your air or rail travel on their card; group discounts to businesses for high-volume usage.

These cards, too, provide individual receipts at the time the goods or services are charged and again with each monthly bill.

Bank credit cards, of which Visa (formerly BankAmericard) and Master Charge are the best known. All operate in much the same way. The bank issues you a card after checking your credit rating. There is no fee. You then may use the card in place of cash at any shop, restaurant, service station, or other business participating in the plan. The shop will turn the charge slips over to the bank, which will accumulate them until the end of the billing period. If you pay the bill within the time specified—usually twenty-five days from the date of billing—the use of the credit card is free. After that a service charge of 1 to 1½ per cent a month is levied against the balance.

The bank credit cards do not provide separate additional receipts each month, as do the single-purpose and T&E cards, so if you do not recognize a charge, you have to write to the bank credit card company.

HOW DO YOU GET A CREDIT CARD?

In the past, many organizations sent credit cards unsolicited in the mail. But now, since a person receiving such an unsolicited card is not responsible for charges made against it, this practice has stopped.

Still, credit cards today are widely—and often easily, perhaps too easily—available. You can obtain an application at virtually any commercial bank in the country—for either Visa or Master Charge. The T&E card applications are obtained from any merchant honoring the card. You simply complete the forms and mail them to the company, Diners Club, Carte Blanche, or American Express. The single-purpose cards are available from the companies that issue them, and their retail outlets carry application forms.

The Advantages and Disadvantages of Credit Cards

Use of credit cards has been growing at a fantastic rate as both the bank credit card companies and the travel and entertainment card firms vie for your business, as do the companies issuing single-purpose cards.

The modern credit card started in the 1950s and was, initially, issued primarily for use in restaurants. Quickly, though, its use spread to other areas, hotels, airlines, car rental firms.

Today, virtually every retail outlet in the country has some type of credit arrangement, often through a credit card. Doctors and dentists take Master Charge and Visa cards, as do some traffic courts.

The credit card has rapidly replaced other forms of short-term installment loans and credit. With these "plastic passports" to free spending, you can now use credit cards to pay for:

tooth extractions, tombstones, and taxi rides;

driving lessons, diamonds, and dog kennel fees;

ambulance service, apartment rent, and auto license fees;

music lessons, movie admissions, and marriage costs;

and savings bonds and scuba diving instructions, church tithes and college tuition, garbage removal and psychiatric care . . .

In the late 1970s, over 12,000 banks were participating in credit card plans and more than 75 million bank credit cards alone were in circulation. About 6 million travel-entertainment cards are in use. So it goes, for we are far into the era of plastic credit.

If you know how to handle your credit cards, they can be a tremendous convenience. They can help you keep detailed tax records for your travel and entertainment expenses. They can allow you to charge these costs anywhere in the world—without paying any interest. They can be a magnificent substitute for cash everywhere, a major benefit if you travel a lot. (And Americans lose more than $2 billion a year in cash, says the American Express Company.)

Or if you are among the millions who have all-purpose bank charge cards, you can greatly simplify your budgeting problems by paying for hundreds of dollars' worth of purchases of every kind with a single check at the end of the billing period. You can achieve substantial savings by buying an item on sale even if you're low on cash. You can order goods easily by mail or telephone—and also return merchandise with a minimum of trouble. And any arrangement that can give you the use of big amounts of cash for as long as twenty-five days without interest (from date of billing), as with bank charge cards, is advantageous to you.

Cash Loans by Credit Card

Credit cards, such as Master Charge and Visa, issued by banks throughout the country, are usually used to purchase goods and services on credit, but they also can be employed to secure cash loans.

There are a variety of plans under which you can obtain cash on your credit card. Some call for specific loan applications; others supply special checks you write to "trigger" loans. Still others automatically transfer money to your checking account any time you write an "overdraft" check—what used to be called a "rubber" check which would "bounce," or be returned for insufficient funds. Today, though, you are encouraged to do this, provided, of course, that you have arranged for the fund transfer ahead of time. Otherwise, your check will bounce as it has in the past.

You should be aware, though, that when you "buy" the use of money in this way, on your credit card, you don't get the twenty-to-twenty-five-day "grace" period as you do on the purchase of goods and services before interest starts. When you buy money this way, interest starts immediately.

In addition to the bank credit card loan plans, the so-called travel and entertainment cards, American Express, Diners Club, and Carte Blanche, also have introduced credit card loan plans.

Typical maximum you may borrow

$500 to $5,000 at any bank honoring the card.

Typical annual interest rates

Interest is not charged on any balance if paid within normal cycle from purchase date-billing date to repayment time—usually a span of twenty-five to thirty-five days from the date of billing.

Then interest accrues only on balances "rolled over" or unpaid after fee billing time allowance.

Annual rate of interest charged ranges from 12 to 18 per cent.

Typical maximum maturities

One to two years.

Advantages

It's quick, "easy," convenient credit.

You don't have to ask anyone directly for a loan; you just use your own previously established line of credit and get it.

At a few banks you even can get an instant $50 to $100 loan simply by slipping the bank's magnetically coded plastic card into a machine.

Disadvantages

See previous sections on the drawbacks of credit that is too easy to get. The very simplicity of this type of credit can induce impulse purchases, lure you into overbuying.

MAIL-ORDER AND PHONE-ORDER CREDIT CARD SALES

One significant side effect of the great growth of credit cards has been the increase in "mail-order" sale of appliances and other department and hardware store items via catalogs and promotional brochures. Your oil company credit card, for example, may be used to buy dinnerware or clothing or jewelry through the mail, on the installment plan. Furthermore, traditional "mail-order" firms—which once required a check or money order to accompany your "mail order," now accept your order via phone, often cross-country through a toll-free "800" line, creating, in effect, nationwide "phone-order" firms. These firms often are physically located in states that have low sales taxes, or none at all.

Furthermore, these firms are not required to collect sales tax on goods shipped out of their state. You, the receiver of the goods, are supposed to do that. But do you? As a result, mail- and phone-order firms, which do not have to maintain local outlets, either, frequently can sell for less.

Beware, though! Mail-order selling presents many pitfalls, and it is difficult to apply pressure to a firm that may be hundreds or thousands of miles from home.

How Do You Use Credit Cards?

Do you have at least three credit cards, most of them good only at a particular store or chain of stores?

Do you use at least one of these cards regularly?

Do you think of your card or cards primarily as a source of credit, and in only a secondary way as a convenience?

Do you write more checks than you used to, despite your use of the cards, too?

Do you have a basic, nagging fear that credit cards make it too easy for you to buy things you do not really want or cannot honestly afford?

Do you, as a result of this basic fear, tend to think of your cards as an evil—a necessary evil, but still an evil—and not as a good thing?

If you answered yes to every one of these probing questions, you are typical of today's credit user, according to one comprehensive study of the subject. Few Americans tend to think of credit cards as a good thing, whether they use them or not. Fully 75 per cent of all respondents said that credit cards made it too easy to buy things.

Now, check where you, a credit card owner, fit in the wide range of users analyzed.

• If you have a higher-than-average income and higher-than-average education, you're more likely to be a card user than those with lower incomes and educations. Income is the major determinant of credit card use.

• If you are a young family and have children, you are more likely to use cards than other groups and more likely to incur debt on your cards than other groups. Another determinant of credit card use is related to the age of the family head.

• If you live in the suburbs, it's probable that you are an active credit card user, while families living in central cities or rural areas are least likely to use such cards.

• If you use your cards to buy clothing more than any other category of goods, you're typical. On both bank and store credit cards, clothing is the most frequent type of purchase.

Credit Cards—Convenience and Loans (Free and Otherwise)

The big bank credit cards are making their greatest inroads in the area of retail installment credit.

Credit card users fall into two broad categories. One is those who use the card as a convenience, rather than carrying large amounts of cash or writing great numbers of checks each month. These users pay their credit card charges promptly within the twenty-to-twenty-five-day period required, and incur no interest charges. In effect, they have a free short-term loan.

The second broad category use the credit card's revolving installment loan features, virtually never completely paying off their obligations, incurring interest charges every month, and, in effect, budgeting their payments over a long-term period.

Several years ago one major bank attempted to impose a flat fee on what it called "free riders" who paid their bills promptly, avoiding interest charges. There was such an outraged reaction, however, that this proposal was shelved.

In fact, the prompt-payers were *not* "free-riders." The bank gets its money in two ways: through the purchaser who elects to pay for his acquisitions on the installment plan, paying interest; and, second, through the merchant, who pays a fee to the bank for acting as a sort of bookkeeper and collection agency.

These fees range up to 4 to 5 per cent a month on the charges processed. Although the bank does perform services for the merchant, the bank is, in effect, collecting "interest" of 48 to 60 per cent a year, from the merchant.

• If you're in any income group below the very top, you most likely use your card to obtain credit, and this is the most important use you make of the card. You see your card as another instrument for taking on installment debt and you treat your card debt like an installment loan—paying a little each month, generally the minimum allowable monthly payment.

• But if you're in the higher income group you use your card as a convenience—and whatever debt you incur on the card you attempt to pay off as quickly as you can, thus obtaining a free short-term loan along with the convenience you also gain.

According to a recent study, fully one third of you pay off your bank credit card charges, in full, within the "free" twenty-five-day period, thus avoiding the interest charges.

• And no matter what your special group, you write more checks than families who do not use cards.

What are some of the fundamental implications of all this? One prime implication is that, although all credit cards are substitutes for money or checks in transactions, they are not pushing us toward a "checkless society"—as was so widely forecast and is still so widely believed.

Another prime implication is that our consumer debt pattern is being changed by the addition of credit card debt to other types of consumer debt.

The use of credit card debt is most pronounced among higher-income families, who often have no other consumer debt and certainly could borrow at less than an 18 per cent annual rate. But these families aren't taking on long-term debt; they're using the cards as convenience and they pay off the debts quickly.

And a third implication is that most of you are using your eminent common sense in handling your credit cards—recognizing their dangers as well as their allure. Most Americans are indeed their own best money managers.

Should You Use a Credit Card?

As a general rule, you should—at any income level—if you have shown in the past that you can handle credit responsibly and that you will use your card as a convenient budgeting and record-keeping tool rather than a license to overspend.

As a general rule, though, you should not use cards if you're a habitual impulse buyer who frequently buys unnecessary things; if you're habitually late in meeting payments; if you've never managed to live comfortably within your income. And you should certainly shy away if, on top of all these characteristics, you do not have a steady income.

Here are the ways to use any credit card to your best advantage.

• Accept only those cards that you actually need and want and will use fairly regularly. For most of you in the middle-income bracket, one bank charge card and maybe a couple of oil company cards for gas are enough—although if you are in business you may find a travel-entertainment card helpful as well.

• Treat every purchase you are planning to charge as you would a cash purchase. Ask yourself: Do you really want and need the item? Can you really afford it? Can you repay the charge comfortably and on time?

• At the beginning of each month, decide on a maximum total of charges you'll be able to repay easily. Stick within that limit and repay the charges promptly to avoid any finance charges.

• Keep all your receipts until you receive your statement to check your spending and your totals against the statement for errors, which can easily occur (due, say, to no more than a clerk's bad handwriting).

How to Protect Your Credit Card

In just a matter of days in the 1970s:

• Three Long Island housewives went on a shopping spree, billed $16,000 worth of merchandise to stolen credit cards.

• A Pittsburgh gambler was arrested with $10,000 in his pocket—most of it refunds from airline tickets he had bought with other people's credit cards.

• A credit card thief posing as a health center operator ran up bills of more than $10,000 at gas stations by promising attendants health courses in his non-existent health center if they would make out phony bills against the credit card and give him cash.

These are not extreme examples, and the warning to you is implicit if you own a credit card or department store charge plate. Criminals have invaded the credit card field. Millions of cards are now being lost or stolen each year and are being used by thieves and other fraudulent operators to run up millions of dollars in unauthorized charges.

Fraudulent use of credit cards on sizable amounts is now a federal crime and the Truth in Lending law forbids the mailing of unsolicited credit cards.

The Truth in Lending law now also provides that a card holder is not liable for charges on a stolen or lost card if the issuer has failed to inform him that he is otherwise liable for up to $50 per card, or has failed to supply the holder with a self-addressed, prestamped notice to use if a card is lost or stolen. Your maximum liability in the case of unauthorized use of any credit card that has been stolen from you is $50 for each card. This maximum holds even if you fail to discover the loss for a considerable period of time and even if you fail to notify the issuer promptly. The law also provides that all cards must bear your signature, photograph, or similar means of identification.

But you also must take steps on your own to protect yourself. Here's what to do:

• As soon as you've finished reading this, go over every card you own. Make sure you have destroyed all you do not need. Cut unwanted cards in half and throw them away.

• Make a list of all credit cards you decide to keep with the names and addresses of the issuers and the account numbers. Keep this list in a safe place but not in your wallet.

• Sign each new card this minute. This will force anyone trying to use the card fraudulently to forge your signature on store bills, restaurant checks, etc.—no problem for the professional card-abuser, admittedly, but a definite deterrent to an amateur.

• Check your credit card collection every couple of weeks. If any card is missing, inform the issuer immediately—first by phone, then by letter or telegram in which you refer to your call. Some issuers now have twenty-four-hour answering services for just this purpose. Although there is a federal $50 limit on your liability, it applies to each card you own.

• Never lend your card to anyone else. This is a violation of your contract with the issuer.

• Make sure your card is returned to you each time you use it. Among the major suppliers of credit cards to fraudulent users are dishonest employees of legitimate establishments.

• Don't leave your credit card in the glove compartment of your car. This is one of the first places a professional credit card thief looks.

• Don't underestimate the value of your card because it's made of plastic. Consider it the equivalent of cash and at least as tempting to a thief as cash.

• Don't leave credit cards lying around in your office or hotel room any more than you would leave a stack of cash lying around. Instead, keep your cards securely in your wallet or purse.

In sum, either give up the advantages of owning credit cards and return to cash-check living or treat these cards with the respect that they—as the equivalent of cash in your wallet or purse—deserve.

OTHER CREDIT SOURCES FOR GOODS AND SERVICES

When you have a telephone in your apartment or house, make a number of phone calls, receive a bill, and pay the bill after you have made the calls, you probably have been using credit (unless, of course, you have a deposit with the telephone company, as often is required these days). Instead of a loan in the form of cash, you are getting credit in the form of the service provided to you by the telephone company. The same goes for an electric light bill or a gas bill or doctor bill or dentist bill.

You receive the service. The service is unmistakably, indisputably worth money. You do not, however, pay for the service, usually, until thirty days or more after you've taken advantage of the service. This is credit.

When you open a charge account at a local store, buy goods you want or need, use the goods, receive a bill the month after your purchase, and pay the bill usually at least thirty days later, you have been using credit, too. This time the credit is in the form of the goods provided to you by the store. This is credit just as much as a loan in cash is—with the vital distinction that the loan comes via goods given to you with the clear understanding that you will pay later under an agreed-upon schedule.

When you sign a charge account agreement, you have applied for credit. When you have filled in the lines of the application form asking about your income, outstanding debts, assets, family responsibilities, etc., you have in effect done the same thing you do when you fill out an application for a cash loan.

Similarly, when you sign a retail installment contract to buy an important product—TV set, furniture, kitchen appliances, a car—this too is a loan in the form of credit for the merchandise you are buying on time. The contract spells out the terms you, as buyer, and the merchant, as seller, agree upon. You, the buyer, do not own the goods until after you pay for them, and if you do not meet the terms of your contract, the seller may take back (repossess) the goods.

After you've signed an installment contract, you may receive instructions in the mail that you are to make your payments not to the merchant who sold you the TV set or auto or furniture, but instead to a bank or finance company. This means simply that the merchant has sold your contract or "paper" to the financial institution named in order to replenish his cash so he can continue offering installment contracts to other customers. That's all it means—just that you must make your payments to the financial institution that took over your contract.

HOW TO BORROW CASH AND USE CREDIT

Here are the types of credit you can get today in the form of goods and services and examples of these credit sources.

SERVICE CREDIT

Sources: utility companies; physicians; dentists; hospitals.

What it is: this is the free credit you use to get vital services such as utilities and professional help. You pay for the services only after you have taken advantage of them. Your debt is usually payable within thirty days after the service has been rendered.

Again, though, many physicians, dentists, hospitals, and clinics are switching to one or the other (or both) of the big national bank credit cards.

CHARGE ACCOUNTS

Sources: department stores; other types of retail stores.

What it is: an open (thirty-day) account is an account in which the store accepts your promise to pay for the goods you buy, usually within thirty days of your purchase.

A revolving account is one in which the store states a maximum amount of money you may owe the store at any one time. The limit is decided when you open the account and is based on your income and credit rating. You in turn agree to pay a stated amount on your balance every month and to pay interest on the unpaid balance you owe.

A budget account or flexible account is an account in which your monthly installment payments to the store are based on the size of your account balance and interest is charged on the unpaid amount. For instance, if your account balance is $100, you might be expected to make monthly installment payments of $25 each.

A coupon credit plan is an account in which you are given "credit coupons" which you may use in the store as cash while you pay for the coupons over, say, six months. This eliminates a monthly billing to you and the nuisance of detailed bookkeeping by the store.

Here, too, many retail outlets and even major department stores have either switched to a national bank credit card completely, or accept the bank credit cards if a customer does not have a charge account with that particular store.

RETAIL INSTALLMENT CREDIT

Sources: Department stores; appliance stores; furniture stores; automobile dealers; hardware stores; sales finance companies; door-to-door salesmen of big companies selling books, magazines, cosmetics, hardware items, etc.

What it is: this is the credit you use when you buy such big-ticket items as automobiles, vacuum cleaners, other household appliances, encyclopedias, the like. You usually make a down payment and then sign a contract to pay off within a period ranging from a few months to as much as five years in regular weekly or monthly amounts which you and the seller agree upon and which are stated in your contract. The retailer adds a finance charge to the cash price of the article, and you, the buyer, do not own what you have bought until you have completed your payments.

Sales finance companies specialize in auto loans but also finance such big items as boats, mobile homes, major home appliances.

INTEREST RATE CHARGES

The primary purpose of the 1969 Truth in Lending law, the landmark aid in consumer financial protection, is to help you understand just how much it costs you to borrow money either in the form of cash or in the form of goods and services.

That is why the law makes it mandatory for the lender or merchant to provide complete information to you. The theory is that, once you have this information and you know how much the credit costs, you will be in a position to judge whether or not it is worthwhile for you to borrow—and if you decide it is, you will be able to compare the costs at various sources.

Despite the law, though, most borrowers are still in an interest rate labyrinth. Even sophisticated borrowers admit they are still befuddled by the various ways interest charges are stated. As for most amateurs, they readily confess they are lost in the maze. Shockingly, a study made years after Truth in Lending became law disclosed that only two out of three borrowers knew what interest rate they were paying on their used-car loans. Even more shocking, one in seven didn't even know the rate of interest they were being charged on their home mortgages! This is something like buying a house without bothering to inquire about the price.

Thus, I think the easiest way to guide you through this labyrinth is to pretend the law doesn't compel disclosure and to take you through a series of fundamental questions and their answers.

Q. *What is the annual percentage rate?*

A. The annual percentage rate (APR) is the key yardstick by which you can measure and compare the costs of all types of credit. It is the basic interest rate you pay when you borrow—essentially a simple annual rate which relates the finance charge to the amount of credit you get and to the amount of time you have the money. With this information, you can compare financial terms offered by competing lenders, regardless of the terms of the loan or the amounts of credit offered or the difference in state laws.

When you know the annual percentage rate and the finance charge, you know the cost of borrowing money.

Q. *What is the finance charge?*

A. This is the total of all charges you are asked to pay to get credit.

HOW TO BORROW CASH AND USE CREDIT

Among the charges that must be included in the finance charge are interest, loan fees, finder's fee, service charge, points, investigation fees, premiums for life insurance if this is required, amount paid as a discount.

Some costs are not part of the finance charge, though: for instance, taxes, license fees, certain legal fees, some real estate closing costs, other costs you would pay if you were using cash instead of credit.

Q. *If I borrow $1,200 for twelve months at a dollar cost of $6.00 per $100, or $72 for the year, what rate of interest am I paying?*

A. That depends on your terms of repayment. If you repay the total amount of $1,200 plus $72 at the *end* of the year, your interest rate is a simple 6 per cent. But there are other ways of figuring interest, which raise the rate.

With a basic electronic calculator so inexpensive these days, you easily can determine true interest rates. In this case you simply divide your $72 interest by the $1,200 you borrowed. The answer is ".06," which represents the simple 6 per cent interest stated.

This is known as the "add-on" method of loan interest calculation.

HOW INTEREST AND REPAYMENT "COMPOUND" THE PROBLEM

Suppose, however, that you pay that same $72 up front, on the day you take out the loan. In effect, you do not get the full $1,200; you receive $1,200 *minus* the $72, or $1,128. In this case what is the true interest rate? It is 6.38 per cent—$72 divided by $1,128. This is known as the "discount" method, a misnomer.

Now, here are more complex, but still "do-able" examples, with an inexpensive calculator, reflecting the real world of "renting" money.

Again, let us assume you borrow $1,200. But you repay the money in twelve monthly installments of $106 each, a total of $72 interest. In this case, though, your interest rate is far more than 6 per cent—about 10.9 per cent in reality.

How is this figured? You don't have use of that full $1,200 for a complete year. You are steadily reducing the amount of the loan so that, in effect, you have the use of only little more than half the original amount over the full term of the loan.

The more expensive calculators will solve your "true interest" problems for you almost automatically; but you can do it yourself even with an inexpensive one.

First, multiply your monthly payments by the term of the loan, in this case, twelve months. You get $106 times 12, or $1,272. Your loan was $1,200, so, as before, your interest is $72. However, you are not paying $6.00 in interest each month. You must follow what is called "The Rule of 78s."

To understand this, remember that with a twelve-month loan, you have the use of the full amount of money—$1,200—for only *one* month, and you are paying back one-twelfth every month. So, you have the use of all of your money—*12*/12 of it—for only *1*/12 of the time. The next month you have the use of 11/12 of it (plus your first month's interest and less your first repayment) for 1/12 of the time; until the final month, when you have the use of about 1/12 of your money—$100, approximately—for 1/12 of the time.

You must add 12, plus 11, plus 10, and so on, down to 1. The sum is 78. Therefore, the full interest on a twelve-month loan is 78/78. In the first month you pay 12/78 of the interest; in the second, 11/78 of it, and so on down to the twelfth month, when you pay 1/78 of the interest.

THE COMPLEX CALCULATIONS

Using this Rule of 78s, note that 12/78 comes to 15.38 per cent of 78/78. (12 divided by 78.) Multiplying your $72 interest for the year by .1538 you get—roughly—$11.08 as the *first* month's interest.

If you wish to do the calculations for all twelve months, you simply repeat the process, using 11/78, 10/78, and so on, down to 1/78 in the final month. For example, in the second month you divide 11 by 78 to get 14.10 per cent of the $72, or $10.15. By the twelfth month, you have monthly interest of just 92.31 cents (1 divided by 78 equals 1.28 per cent, times $72 equals 92.31 cents).

Going back to your $1,200 loan for $72 interest per year:

In that first month that you've had use of the full $1,200, the interest has run your true debt to the lending institution up to $1,211.08. You then pay them $106. Therefore, in the second month you will be paying interest on $1,105.08 ($1,211.08−106=$1,105.08). Your second month's interest was $10.15. If you divide that $10.15 second month's interest by what you owe—the $1,105.08—you get the second month's interest *rate*, 11.02 per cent. The way you do this, incidentally, is to divide $10.15 by $1,105.08 to give you the *monthly* rate of 0.918 per cent. You then multiply this monthly rate by 12 to get the true *annual* rate, for the second month, of 11.02 per cent.

By the time the twelfth and final month of your loan comes around, the interest has dropped to 92.31 cents and the amount outstanding to roughly $105.08, for an interest rate then of 10.54 per cent. The average amount outstanding is about $661 and the average interest then becomes just under 10.9 per cent. The actual amounts will vary because the "Rule of 78" is not precise. Some months have thirty-one days, others thirty, etc.

But, from this, you can understand the principle, and get fairly precise answers.

The following tables show you your loan interest on both the "add-on" and "discount" methods of calculation, for one-year, two-year, three-year, and four-year loans.

Interest Rate and Payment Data Table

One-Year Loan

RATE PER $100 PER YEAR	ADD-ON INTEREST RATE % PER YEAR	YOU RECEIVE	PAYMENTS PER MONTH	TOTAL RE-PAYMENTS	DISCOUNT INTEREST RATE % PER YEAR	YOU RECEIVE	PAYMENTS PER MONTH	TOTAL RE-PAYMENTS
$ 4.00	7.3	$100.00	$8.67	$104.00	7.6	$96.00	$8.33	$100.00
4.50	8.2	100.00	8.71	104.50	8.6	95.50	8.33	100.00
5.00	9.1	100.00	8.75	105.00	9.6	95.00	8.33	100.00
5.50	10.0	100.00	8.79	105.50	10.6	94.50	8.33	100.00
6.00	10.9	100.00	8.83	106.00	11.6	94.00	8.33	100.00
6.50	11.8	100.00	8.88	106.50	12.6	93.50	8.33	100.00
7.00	12.7	100.00	8.92	107.00	13.6	93.00	8.33	100.00
7.50	13.6	100.00	8.96	107.50	14.6	92.50	8.33	100.00
8.00	14.5	100.00	9.00	108.00	15.7	92.00	8.33	100.00
9.00	16.2	100.00	9.08	109.00	17.8	91.00	8.33	100.00
10.00	18.0	100.00	9.17	110.00	19.9	90.00	8.33	100.00
11.00	19.7	100.00	9.25	111.00	22.1	89.00	8.33	100.00
12.00	21.5	100.00	9.33	112.00	24.3	88.00	8.33	100.00

Two-Year Loan

RATE	ADD-ON	YOU RECEIVE	PAYMENTS	TOTAL	DISCOUNT	YOU RECEIVE	PAYMENTS	TOTAL
4.00	7.5	100.00	4.50	108.00	8.0	92.00	4.16	100.00
4.50	8.4	100.00	4.54	109.00	9.1	91.00	4.16	100.00
5.00	9.3	100.00	4.58	110.00	10.2	90.00	4.16	100.00
5.50	10.2	100.00	4.63	111.00	11.3	89.00	4.16	100.00
6.00	11.2	100.00	4.67	112.00	12.4	88.00	4.16	100.00
6.50	12.0	100.00	4.71	113.00	13.6	87.00	4.16	100.00
7.00	12.9	100.00	4.75	114.00	14.7	86.00	4.16	100.00
7.50	13.8	100.00	4.79	115.00	16.0	85.00	4.16	100.00
8.00	14.6	100.00	4.83	116.00	17.2	84.00	4.16	100.00
8.50	15.6	100.00	4.88	117.00	18.4	83.00	4.16	100.00
9.00	16.5	100.00	4.92	118.00	19.7	82.00	4.16	100.00
9.50	17.3	100.00	4.96	119.00	20.9	81.00	4.16	100.00
10.00	18.2	100.00	5.00	120.00	22.2	80.00	4.16	100.00
11.00	19.8	100.00	5.08	121.00	24.9	78.00	4.16	100.00
12.00	21.6	100.00	5.17	122.00	27.7	76.00	4.16	100.00

Three-Year Loan

RATE	ADD-ON	YOU RECEIVE	PAYMENTS	TOTAL	DISCOUNT	YOU RECEIVE	PAYMENTS	TOTAL
4.00	7.5	100.00	3.11	112.00	8.4	88.00	2.78	100.00
4.50	8.4	100.00	3.15	113.50	9.7	86.50	2.78	100.00
5.00	9.2	100.00	3.19	115.00	10.9	85.00	2.78	100.00
5.50	10.3	100.00	3.24	116.50	12.2	83.50	2.78	100.00
6.00	11.1	100.00	3.28	118.00	13.4	82.00	2.78	100.00
6.50	12.0	100.00	3.32	119.50	14.7	80.50	2.78	100.00
7.00	12.8	100.00	3.36	121.00	16.1	79.00	2.78	100.00
7.50	13.6	100.00	3.40	122.50	17.4	77.50	2.78	100.00
8.00	14.5	100.00	3.44	124.00	18.8	76.00	2.78	100.00
8.50	15.4	100.00	3.49	125.50	20.3	74.50	2.78	100.00
9.00	16.3	100.00	3.53	127.00	21.8	73.00	2.78	100.00
10.00	18.1	100.00	3.61	130.00	24.9	70.00	2.78	100.00
11.00	19.5	100.00	3.69	133.00	28.2	67.00	2.78	100.00
12.00	21.2	100.00	3.78	136.00	31.8	64.00	2.78	100.00

Interest Rate and Payment Data Table (continued)

Four-Year Loan

Rate per $100 per Year	Add-on Interest Rate % per Year	You Receive	Payments per Month	Total Repayments	Discount Interest Rate % per Year	You Receive	Payments per Month	Total Repayments
$ 4.00	7.6	$100.00	$2.42	$116.00	8.7	$84.00	$2.08	$100.00
4.50	8.4	100.00	2.46	118.00	10.1	82.00	2.08	100.00
5.00	9.2	100.00	2.50	120.00	11.3	80.00	2.08	100.00
5.50	10.1	100.00	2.54	122.00	13.4	78.00	2.08	100.00
6.00	10.9	100.00	2.58	124.00	14.1	75.00	2.08	100.00
6.50	11.9	100.00	2.63	126.00	15.6	74.00	2.08	100.00
7.00	12.5	100.00	2.66	128.00	17.1	72.00	2.08	100.00
7.50	13.5	100.00	2.71	130.00	18.6	70.00	2.08	100.00
8.00	14.4	100.00	2.75	132.00	20.3	68.00	2.08	100.00
8.50	15.2	100.00	2.79	134.00	22.0	66.00	2.08	100.00
9.00	15.9	100.00	2.83	136.00	23.8	64.00	2.08	100.00
10.00	17.7	100.00	2.92	140.00	27.7	60.00	2.08	100.00
11.00	19.2	100.00	3.00	144.00	31.9	56.00	2.08	100.00
12.00	20.7	100.00	3.08	148.00	36.7	52.00	2.08	100.00

Monthly Payments Rounded to nearest cent, producing slight variations to total repayments.

SHOPPING FOR YOUR MONEY

What leaps out of these tables is that your actual dollar payments can vary considerably, depending on the length of your loan and how the interest is figured, in addition to *the actual amount you are borrowing.*

To illustrate how you can use these tables in typical buying situations—so that you can shop for your loan as well as your item purchased—say you wish to buy a $6,575 car. The total comes to 65.75 "hundreds."

You are quoted a rate of $7.50 per hundred per year "add-on" interest for a four-year loan. Checking the table, you see this is 13.5 per cent true annual interest and that you'll be repaying about $2.71 per month for every $100 borrowed. Your total monthly repayments for your 65.75 "hundreds," then, will come to $178.07—65.75 times your monthly per-hundred repayment. (It's *not* $179.18 because the tables are rounded; your actual monthly repayment is, in the case of a four-year loan, $2.7083333, etc., the $130 divided by the 48 monthly repayments. The rounding off of payments may *seem* insignificant, but the difference, even in the case of this four-year car loan, is worth noting and on a 30–40-year home mortgage on a $50,000–$75,000 home a ½ cent difference per hundred in monthly repayments could amount to thousands of dollars.)

In our example, though, the $178.07 monthly repayment on the car loan adds up to $8,547.50 in total repayments, so total interest paid is $1,972.50—those total repayments less the $6,575 car loan.

Now, however, let's say you continue your shopping for money. A second financial organization quoted you a rate of $7.50 per hundred per year *"discounted."* Checking the table, you see that your monthly repayments per hundred are much less, just $2.08 rather than $2.71. But you also see your true annual interest rate is far higher—18.6 per cent versus 13.5 per cent under the add-on method (both rounded).

Why? First, understand that you don't get that $6,575 if you borrow 65.75 "hundreds." You receive only $70 for every $100 you borrow; thus you have in your hands only $4,602.50. You are $1,972.50 short. Familiar figure? Yes. Your interest. It was taken out *in advance,* remember. "Discounted," to use the technical term. You really need 92.92857 of those "hundreds" ($6,575 divided by $70). Therefore, your monthly repayments are each $195.68, your total repayments are $9,392.86, and your total interest amounts to $2,817.86—a full $845 more under this "discount" method than you paid under the add-on formula.

From the tables you also can see the advantage of taking out loans for shorter terms. At the $7.50 per hundred add-on rate for three years, rather than four, your interest is just $1,479.38, though your monthly payments are $223.75. At two years, the interest is down to $986.25, although monthly payments are still higher, $315.05. For one year, interest is a mere $493.13, but monthly payments top $589.

OTHER QUESTIONS AND ANSWERS ABOUT INTEREST

Q. *Is a 6 per cent interest rate ever a simple 6 per cent annual rate (or 8 per cent or 9 per cent)?*

A. A 6 per cent annual rate is 6 per cent simple annual interest if you borrow the $100 for one year and repay it one year later with the $6.00 added on—or a total of $106 in a single payment.

A 6 per cent mortgage also is a true 6 per cent a year, for you are paying the 6 per cent on the declining balance of your mortgage, not on the original total.

Q. *What if I'm charged interest monthly on my unpaid balance?*

A. If you're charged monthly on the unpaid balance you owe, then:

¾% per month	is 9% simple annual rate
⅚	is 10
1	is 12
1¼	is 15
1½	is 18
2	is 24
2½	is 30
3½	is 42

Q. *How can I compare the dollar cost of different ways of charging interest?*

A. Take as an example a $500 loan to be repaid in twelve monthly installments. If the rates charged are:
* 1 per cent per month on the unpaid balance, the dollar cost will be $33.09.
* 6 per cent annual interest on the unpaid balance, the dollar cost will be $16.40.
* 6 per cent annual interest "add-on," with one lump-sum payment at the end the dollar cost will be $30.

If the payments are spread over eighteen months, each payment would be smaller, but the total dollar cost would of course be higher. For example, at 1 per cent per month on the unpaid balance, the cost over eighteen months would be $48.84 compared to $33.09 for twelve months.

Q. *Why does the percentage rate on an installment loan for twelve months sound so much higher than the dollar charge?*

A. Because the dollar charge is applied to the total amount of money you borrow, but on an installment loan you do not have the use of the money for the twelve months and this increases the percentage rate charged.

Q. *If I pay back a twelve-month installment loan in six months, will I get back half the interest added to my loan?*

A. No. You will get back less because in the first six months you've had the use of most of the loan funds, so it is only fair that you pay more of the interest in the first six months than in the last.

To illustrate go back to "The Rule of 78s." In the first month of your twelve-month loan, you have the use of 12/12 of the money. In the final month of your twelve-month loan, though, you have use of only 1/12 of the money.

Your rebate of interest on your installment loan will be figured on the basis of the "Rule of 78s" formula.

In the first month of your twelve-month loan, you pay off 12/78 of the interest; in the second, 11/78 of the interest; in the third, 10/78 of the interest, and so on to the last month, when you pay 1/78 of the interest.

Now, say you pay off your twelve-month loan at the end of the sixth month. You have already paid off 12/78, 11/78, 10/78, and on through 7/78. The total of 12+11+10+9+8+7=57. What's left is 21/78—or about 27 per cent of the interest initially added on to your loan. And that 27 per cent, not 50 per cent, is what your rebate would total.

It is a complicated formula and you need not puzzle over it. But in the case of the $500 one-year loan at 6 per cent with monthly repayments of $43.03, at the end of six months you would have repaid $258.18 of the total $516.40 you would have owed, with interest, by year's end. But you would get back only $4.43 of that $16.40 interest; you would owe $253.79 to pay off the loan early.

Q. *What about the charges on bank credit card and revolving credit accounts?*
A. Finance charges on these accounts are usually expressed as a percentage of the unpaid balance per month, as of the billing date. This is a simple monthly rate, which is then multiplied by 12 to give you the annual percentage rate, as listed above—e.g., ¾ per cent a month on the unpaid balance equals 9 per cent a year.

Q. *Why is the rate on credit card accounts higher than the rate on a simple installment loan?*
A. The main reason, say the banks, is that the amounts are smaller and the monthly processing expenses are high. Generally, the monthly processing on a regular installment loan involves only one operation—recording the monthly payment. With a credit card account, the bank or retailer, etc., must make a record of the charge every time the card is used, total the charges at the end of the billing period, compute the interest on any unpaid balance, make up a bill, mail it, and record your payment.

Q. *How are mortgage rates quoted?*
A. Mortgage rates have been traditionally described in terms of simple annual interest rates. However, if points, a finder's fee, or certain other charges are required, these now—under the Truth in Lending law—must be included in the finance charge. These "extras" make the true annual rate appear slightly larger than before the law went into effect.

Q. *Why are mortgage rates lower than rates on installment loans?*
A. The average cost to the lender per dollar loaned is lower for a mortgage loan because mortgage loans are substantially larger than most other types. Their sheer size helps to offset the monthly processing expenses, permitting the lender to pass the saving on to the borrower in the form of a lower interest rate.

Q. *What can I do when no credit charge is quoted at all?*
A. This is illegal. But, for illustration, let's say a sewing machine is offered to you at $100 and you can pay for the item in twelve monthly installments of $9.00 for a year. Multiplying the monthly payment by 12 will give you $108. You are therefore paying $8.00 or a 14.45 per cent true interest rate for the equivalent of an installment loan of $100.

How to Hold Down Your Borrowing Costs

How can you, an attractive credit risk, hold down your cost of borrowing? Throughout this section I have dropped in rules on this and you will find more hints for mortgages in the chapter on housing pages 205–15 and more rules for automobile loans in "Getting To and From" pages 362–65. But the guides below are the most fundamental of all and go across the board for all types of credit. Whatever repetition you note can only help underline their value to you.

(1) On any type of purchase on time, always keep in mind that the most expensive way to borrow money is to make a small down payment and to stretch out the life of the loan for the longest possible period.

(2) Thus, to save interest on any type of loan—from appliance to auto or mortgage—make the largest down payment you can manage and repay in the shortest period that's feasible for you. Unless you buy the pessimistic view that the United States will never be able to curb inflation, in which case the only way to protect yourself is to borrow as much as you can so you can pay back in dollars of dwindling value, you cannot dispute this rule's logic.

(3) Try to include a clause in any long-term loan contract giving you the privilege of prepayment of your loan at no penalty to you or at the lowest possible penalty. This will give you leeway to renegotiate your loan at more favorable rates when and as interest rate levels decline or to pay it off entirely. (Note, though: refinancing costs must be considered, and minimum loan charges are often set by policy and sometimes law.)

(4) On the other hand, don't pay off loans you might have outstanding at dramatically lower rates than now prevail. Just keep up your regular required payments and invest your extra cash so it earns more money for you than you're paying out on your old loans.

(5) Beware of ads for big-ticket items on "easy" repayment terms, and if the ads are befuddling despite Truth in Lending law requirements, use the formulas I've given you for determining how much you are paying on a true annual basis.

(6) Always keep in mind that any "instant cash" plan will be comparatively expensive to you. Whether it's a multipurpose credit card or an automatic line of credit at your bank, or any newer plan, the point is you'll almost surely end up paying more for this instant cash than you would for a traditional loan.

(7) In general, during periods of high interest rates, borrow only the exact amount you need. Borrowing more will mean paying peak interest rates for the extra cash. Borrowing too little will mean returning for another loan and paying extra processing costs.

(8) Offer the best security you can. A loan secured by top-notch collateral almost always may be obtained at a cheaper rate than a loan backed only by your signature. You lose nothing. You get back full possession of your asset when you pay off your debt.

(9) Before you borrow or buy on time, use whatever free credit you can get. For instance, use your regular twenty-five-to-thirty-day credit card grace period and thirty-day charge account as much as you can. If you buy at the start of the billing cycle, you won't be billed for about thirty days, and then

you have another thirty days to pay. If you have several credit cards, note when their billing cycles close and buy just before those dates. Often merchants are late in processing the paper work on your credit card purchases, giving you as much as fifty-five to sixty days free "credit" on what you buy.

(10) Before signing the papers on your next loan, check whether you are being charged for credit life and credit accident insurance. If such a charge has been made, think *three* times before accepting it. Such insurance is usually not obligatory, though many people think it is. For younger people especially, such insurance is highly overpriced, running to $700 or more on many auto or consolidation loans.

(11) In shopping around for bargain credit, don't overlook the occasional "money sales" or similar features offered by commercial banks. For regular bank customers who already have savings, checking accounts, and the bank's charge card, installment credit may be offered at ½ to 1 per cent less than the normal interest rates, if you let the bank deduct the monthly repayment directly from your checking account. A warning, though: some banks also have you sign a form that ties up your savings account, too. If your savings equal or exceed your loan, what you borrow is then, in effect, fully collateralized, and you should get a far more substantial reduction in your interest charges in such circumstances.

And if you have a number of small loans outstanding, ask your bank whether you would qualify for a "clean-up" type of loan at a lower rate. If so, by all means take advantage of the lower rate.

To dramatize it again, on that $6,575 car discussed previously, a difference of just 1/10 of 1 per cent of true annual interest would cost you almost $15–$17 on a four-year loan, a 1 per cent difference more than $150–$160 at typical rates.

The Great Pitfalls of Credit

Truth in Lending has not eliminated the credit tricksters and racketeers—and the likelihood is no law will ever wipe them out. As for us, it would be ridiculous to claim that even an excellent education on credit would be sufficient protection for the vast majority of Americans—particularly since eight out of ten Americans admit they are unable to find their way through what one observer once called the "wonderland of credit where percentages multiply and divide at will, where finance charges materialize on command and fees are collected on the way out."

Do you know how to read the fine print on a complicated installment sales contract? Do you even understand the bold-type statement of interest charges required under the Truth in Lending law? How, then, can you, the ordinary borrower, detect hidden interest charges, protect yourself against unsuspected loan costs? One very good way is by becoming aware of the great pitfalls of credit—and, by this awareness alone, learning how to avoid these yawning traps.

Many of the tactics listed are illegal; and new laws are regularly making others illegal, too. But this does not mean that the practices have stopped.

"DEBT POOLING"

No matter what your plight, avoid commercial debt poolers, who simply lump your debts together, collect one regular payment from you—then charge you as much as 35 per cent of your debts for this "service."

Debt pooling, or "prorating" or "debt adjusting" or "debt liquidating," for profit is now barred in a majority of our states and the District of Columbia. But it still thrives in many parts of the country, and you must be on guard.

Specifically, a "debt adjuster" may say to you: "If installment payments or past-due bills are troubling you, let us consolidate and arrange to pay all your bills, past due or not, with one low monthly payment you can afford." If you accept this offer, you will turn over part or all your income to a firm and your debts supposedly will be paid out of the income on a prorated basis. The basic difficulty with the arrangement is the fact that almost never is the plan carried to fruition. Either the creditors won't accept the plan or you, the debtor, find it impossible to live with the expected payments. Some "consolidators" simply pocket the money and never pay your creditors. As a consequence, the only thing you, the debtor, obtain is an expansion of your original debt because of the fee you must pay to the adjuster. The service charges are steep in debt consolidation and, typically, your whole first payment may be taken by the company for these charges—without a penny going to your creditors.

Debt adjusting or debt pooling has nothing to do with legitimate credit counseling services—nor should it be confused with legitimate bank or credit union debt consolidation loans. The debt adjuster merely takes the debtor's money with the understanding that he will make the payments to the creditors—after absorbing a substantial portion of the debtor's funds as payment for his services. He adds to the debtor's problems with excessive charges and makes no effort to offer financial counsel or budget guidance. In some cases, he leaves the debtor with far too little money to live on.

"SEWER SERVICE"

Let's say that you, a consumer committed to periodic payments on an installment loan, lose your job and subsequently default on a payment. Under the law, if a creditor wishes to sue you for payment, he is required to serve you a formal notice of the impending lawsuit.

But let's say you never receive the notice—quite likely if you are among the nation's millions of unsophisticated borrowers. If so, the next blow well may be a "default judgment" against you, the equivalent of a decision that you, the debtor, are at fault before you consult a lawyer and find out your rights, not to mention go to court.

"Sewer service" is the colloquial name for this technique, formally known as a default judgment, which is widely used by unscrupulous debt collectors to deprive the gullible low-income borrower of his or her legitimate rights. To summarize what happens: the summons or other legal document which the creditor is supposed to deliver to the debtor is simply chucked into any dead-end receptacle (thus, "sewer" service). Unless you manage to get the judgment set aside, you are automatically stamped as liable and may be legally bound to pay whatever the creditors say you owe and you may lose your right to defend yourself in court, no matter what the facts may be.

Sewer service is the least expensive way for an unprincipled creditor to force payment of a debt. It is used not only to collect payments on installment debts but also to deprive tenants of their rights to contest eviction by landlords.

This is a flagrant attack on your most basic rights. If it happens to you, complain immediately to a law enforcement agency and also to the court where the judgment was entered. Get a lawyer to move to set the judgment aside. If you can't afford a lawyer, tell the clerk of the court you want to make a motion to set aside a default judgment for lack of service and ask him for advice on how to file the necessary papers.

Don't take this lying down!

"INCONVENIENT VENUE"

"Inconvenient venue" is another technique designed to deprive debtors of their legal rights. Under this procedure, the creditor simply files suit against his victim from a branch, affiliate, or lending institution hundreds of miles away from the debtor's home. Again, the victim has no feasible means of defending himself against the suit.

"CONFESSION OF JUDGMENT"

Ranking with the most vicious of all ways in which debtors are being trapped is the "confession of judgment" clause appearing in so many installment sales contracts. In effect, this clause is a built-in confession of guilt should the borrower miss a single monthly payment unless, in many instances, he can come up with the entire amount he still owes. By signing the contract he has waived whatever legal rights he otherwise may have had in advance—and the creditor can move in to collect at once. Frequently, too, the first a debtor knows that such a judgment has been made against him is when he receives a notice that his property is being put up for a sheriff's sale within days.

Confession of judgment is legal in only a few states, but this technique is still being illegally used to some extent against consumers in many other states as well.

Of course, it is reasonable for lenders to insist that they be protected against default and, of course, there are explanations for each of these clauses. But this technique is an outrageous deprivation of the rights of the individual.

Even if you signed a confession of judgment, under recent Supreme Court decisions you may be able to have it set aside if you can show that you didn't understand the clause when you signed it and didn't have legal advice.

HARASSMENT

Harassment is the "normal" means, in countless cases, of collecting small debts and past-due installment payments. And you need not be a ghetto resident to come up against this: it can happen to you, whoever and wherever you are.

• A typical cornered debtor may first receive a flood of dunning notices from debt collection agencies with names that sound in some cases very like those of government agencies. The letters will threaten legal action and serious damage to the debtor's credit rating.

• In addition, the debtor may be subjected to repeated telephone calls at all hours of the day and night, not only at his home but also at his job.

• The caller may falsely represent himself as a lawyer, a policeman, a private detective. Or he may hint that he works for a government agency.

• He may call a debtor's neighbors, relatives, wife, even his children. He also may call the debtor's employer, a tactic that easily can lead to the debtor's losing his job.

Whatever the tricks, the harassment usually succeeds in frightening a debtor into "settling" his debt—even though the debt may have been imposed on him through fraudulent, illegal means and even though he may have a sound, legitimate, legal defense against the creditor who is harassing him.

As you might expect, laws have been passed to control this sort of viciousness. The Federal Trade Commission has proceeded against some unfair debt collection methods, and new investigations are being conducted to check on law violations. In Massachusetts debt collectors are licensed by the state, and a collector may lose his license if he calls you late at night, informs your employer that you owe money, or indicates on an envelope that you have not paid your bills. In New York City a regulation forbids creditors (or their lawyers or collection agencies) to "communicate or threaten to communicate with an alleged debtor's employer" without first obtaining a court judgment against the debtor. And the Federal Consumer Credit Protection Act makes it a federal crime for a creditor or his representative to use violence or threats of violence to collect debts.

But none of it is enough. Neither the new laws nor regulations are curbing, much less wiping out, the problems of debtor harassment.

REPOSSESSION

You buy a used car loaded with options for $3,600, including 18 per cent interest on your auto loan, fees, insurance; etc. You pledge to pay $130.15 a month including interest for three years.

After one year and over $1,560 in payments, you fail to meet a due date. A while later your car disappears from your driveway. A lending company which bought the note for your car from your used-car dealer has simply sent his "repo" man to your home. He has crossed the wires of your car to get it going and has driven off.

Repossession of automobiles, as well as of many other personal items, is a widespread and entirely legal practice used against the delinquent—particularly low-income—debtor in the United States today.‡ It also may be only the beginning, for the lender may then turn around and sell your repossessed car back to the original dealer for an amount to be credited to you. This resale price, if the participants are unprincipled, may be a rigged bargain sum of, say, $500 for your car. You are now sued for the remainder you still owe. You're also liable for extra charges.

You thus not only have no car but you also have a debt equal to more years of payments! And now the used-car dealer may in turn resell your repossessed car to another buyer for $1,500. Of course, cars are repossessed without such tactics—but a shocking number do involve deceit, fraud, and perjury, too.

Automobiles are only one category of consumer goods subject to repossession today. Another not untypical situation is repossession when the consumer buys a set of furniture on time, then defaults on a single payment. The seller or the holder of the installment loan contract may confiscate the entire set and then sue to collect the remainder of the debt, plus charges and fees. Many corrupt ghetto merchants, in fact, make a living selling goods over and over in this manner. Their profit depends on default in payment and a chance for resale—not on the original sale itself.

To crack down on these practices, laws are being urged at both federal and state levels which would permit creditors either to repossess their goods or to sue for payment of the debt—but not both. Meanwhile, the only protection you, the debtor, have is your own awareness of the pitfall.

"HOLDER IN DUE COURSE"

An elderly woman bought a hearing aid for her son, involving a fat down payment and an installment loan for the balance of her purchase. When the device failed to work, she took it back to the seller, who agreed to send it to

‡ However, the U. S. Supreme Court has ruled that certain repossession practices which have been widely used violate constitutional guarantees. The Court ruled that no item may be repossessed unless the buyer is notified that the matter is in court and given a chance —in formal hearings—to tell his side of the story.

the factory for repair. But when she returned again to pick up the hearing aid, she found that the seller had gone out of business—and had sold her installment loan contract to a local lender.

Incredibly, this woman remained under legal obligation to repay the loan plus stiff interest charges—despite the fact that her son still had no hearing aid.

This legal quirk—called the "holder in due course" doctrine—was once the most vicious of all consumer credit traps.

Under the holder in due course doctrine, an unscrupulous used-car dealer or other retailer would lure naïve consumers into buying a long list of products or services on time. He would then immediately sell the contract to a finance company. The product would turn out to be a lemon, or it would be badly damaged, or it needed servicing under the warranty, or it would not even be delivered. And the seller would flatly refuse to replace or repair the product. Nevertheless, the financial institution that owned your loan contract would sternly remind you that he was "in the business of financing, not repairing furniture or cars." If you refused to make payments as they came due, you could have been sued for the remainder of the loan, payable at once. Or, as an alternative, the finance company would repossess not only the item in question but also other personal goods.

Among the goods and services most frequently involved in holder in due course problems were: vacuum cleaners, furniture, carpeting, sewing machines, "lifetime" series of dancing or judo lessons or health spa visits, major appliances, home improvements.

In many cases the basic conditions under which the sale was made—for instance, the "referral" scheme, in which you were led to believe you'd get a product free if you referred a specified number of other customers to the seller—were fraudulent. But once your loan contract was turned over to a finance company, any rights you might have had to challenge the original terms of the deal also went out the window. Frequently, too, the finance company was far, far away.

Both the state and the federal governments have taken steps to outlaw the "holder in due course" practice. Under legislation passed in the 1970s, if the merchant who sells the goods or services also arranges for the installment loan, the finance company that bought your "paper" installment agreement from him cannot fall back on the holder in due course doctrine. It has been wiped off the books.

While federal and state governments are giving increasing attention to these credit abuses, your best defense is knowledge of what is and what is not legal. Every government service costs money, and the government itself is often startlingly inefficient, shockingly inadequate. It is one thing to have laws, quite another to have them enforced in an era of lethargy, and worse, on the part of many bureaucrats.

Fundamentally, it will be less expensive for you—in what you pay in interest charges and in what you pay in the way of taxes—to know what should and should not be done than to rely on some government agency to help you.

And Also Beware These Traps!

The add-on clause. Avoid the contract in which the seller keeps title to a whole list of items you are buying on credit until all payments have been completed (for instance, a fourteen-piece set of furniture). A single delinquent payment could permit the seller to repossess the entire set, even though you have paid all but a few dollars of the total. This gimmick also permits the installment seller to add purchase after purchase to your original installment contract. Then just one delinquent payment could permit the seller to repossess your whole collection of purchases.

The balloon contract, which provides for a final payment that is considerably larger than the previous monthly payments. If you are not aware of this and are not prepared to meet the final payment, your purchase may be repossessed before you can produce the money. Or you may be compelled to refinance at disastrously disadvantageous terms to you. Balloon payments are illegal in some states today because they are widely used to trick you into buying—at low initial monthly costs—things or services you cannot afford.

An acceleration clause. In this case, default in one single payment—or in some instances, the fact that you have lost your job—can make all other payments due at once. If you are unable to pay the total balance, your purchases could be carted away for resale and you still may not be absolved of all future liability.

Obscure provisions in your credit contract which stipulate you must buy extra items you may not want. These clauses are frequently buried in the contract so you don't realize they are there until after you have signed.

Exorbitant extra charges and "processing fees," adding substantially to your borrowing costs. A lender might list such charges separately to deceive you with seemingly very low loan rates.

Life insurance, or even disability insurance, is a gimmick widely used to inflate charges. Almost always the retailer who insists on such "protection for you" is getting a commission as an insurance agent. Furthermore, the rates for such insurance (essentially a decreasing face value term insurance contract) are exorbitant. If a merchant or bank insists on making insurance a part of the installment loan, take your business elsewhere.

How Much Debt Is Too Much Debt?

WHO RUNS UP TOO MUCH DEBT?

Who are the individuals and the families who get caught in an intolerable debt squeeze? Can we draw a fine but critical line between a healthy, bearable load of loans and an unhealthy, unbearable load?

The overextended credit individual is usually a faceless vexation in our society, according to a revealing study by a University of Wisconsin professor some years ago, who then drew this detailed portrait of the overextended credit family:

• The family is young, has more than the average number of children and an average income.

• The parents are easygoing, carefree, and impulsive, have "limited pleasure postponement mechanisms" and rubber wills when confronted with high-pressure salesmen.

• Although the husband, in most cases, is satisfied with his job, one in three wives is dissatisfied with her husband's pay.

• The family doesn't read anything, not even the daily newspaper. TV is the major communications medium in the family's life, and TV disproportionately influences the couple's buying decisions.

• The parents tend to blame their plight on vague, unavoidable "circumstances" or superficial backbreaking straws such as pregnancy, temporary loss of job, buying a car—and thus they feel their troubles are not really their fault.

• Neither husband nor wife assumes clear responsibility for managing the family's finances. Even among the couples who think they are sharing money management responsibilities, there is little indication of joint decision-making. As one husband remarked, "We don't quibble about it. If either one of us wants to buy, we buy!"

• The family moves from house to house more often than the average U.S. family.

Most consumer debts are adequately cushioned by our incomes and savings, our financial assets, and our earnings potentials. But there is a minority always in deep financial trouble—in the eighteen-to-twenty-four age bracket, and in the under $10,000 bracket, particularly.

Also increasingly prone to getting into (and staying in) deep financial trouble is the single-person household, especially those headed by women and by an individual who has been divorced, separated, or widowed.

The crucial difference between sound and unsound borrowing is whether or not you are carrying too much debt at any one time. Okay, then, how much debt is too much debt?

WARNING SIGNS OF DEBT TROUBLE

Deep and prolonged study has gone into this question—and there is considerable disagreement on the conclusions. However, the following are clear warning signals that you're moving dangerously close to the debt borderline and may be crossing it.

• You are continually lengthening the repayment periods on your installment purchases and putting down smaller and smaller initial payments. At the same time, your interest charge load is mounting just because you are sinking deeper and deeper into debt for longer periods.

- What you owe on your revolving charge accounts also is climbing steadily. You're never out of debt to the local stores at which you have revolving charge accounts.
- Before you have finished paying last month's bills this month's are piling in. You're always behind these days in your payments and you're now regularly receiving notices that you're delinquent. You might even get an occasional notice threatening repossession or legal action against you—something that has never happened to you before.
- Slowly but unquestionably, an ever-increasing share of your net income is going to pay your debts.
- You are so bedeviled by so many separate bills coming at you from so many sources each month that you turn to a lending institution or lending agency for a loan to "consolidate" and pay off all your debts and leave you with just this one big consolidation loan to meet. But you continue to buy on credit—thereby adding more new bills on top of your one big debt you must pay each month.
- You are taking cash advances on your credit card to pay such routine, regular monthly bills as utilities, rent, even food.

WHAT LIMITS SHOULD YOU SET?

Here are three different guidelines, drawn up by respected economists and money managers, of what your installment loan debt should be, exclusive of your home mortgage:
- Do not owe more than 20 per cent of your yearly after-tax income.
- Do not owe more than 10 per cent of the amount you could pay for out of your income within the next eighteen months.
- Do not owe more than one third of your discretionary income for the year—meaning the income you have left after you have paid for the basic needs of food, clothing, and shelter.

You can see that these guidelines give you a wide range of "acceptable" debt levels. But, in fact, any one of them may be too high, or too low, for you—depending on your income.

Obviously, a family in a high income bracket with relatively low expenses for basics such as shelter, food, and other essentials might easily be able to afford well over any one of those guidelines.

The "discretionary income" approach is the soundest. If you are in a relatively low take-home income bracket (or have extremely high expenses for "basics" such as home, tuition costs, and other fixed monthly charges) the formula permitting you to spend one third of this discretionary amount on installment payments could be too high.

The real test involves planning: figuring out what your actual expenses have been for *regular* outlays over the past several years (whether these outlays are for basics or not), since they reflect your *pattern* of spending.

You may, for example, have high commutation costs, an expensive hobby, or steep charges for medical or dental attention.

Furthermore, regardless of how much installment debt you decide you can *comfortably* incur, if you cannot also save a substantial portion of your income *every* month—at least 5 per cent of your take-home pay—then you should not be borrowing at all.

You should have an emergency fund in the bank, a life insurance program, and a regular savings plan to build a retirement income nest egg.

This is the ideal, of course. Fewer and fewer families are able to meet it. Nevertheless, these are fundamental economic facts.

Finally, in deciding how much debt your family can handle, ask yourself: how stable is your family breadwinner's job and income?

What is the chance of a layoff in his or her occupation and in your area? Is he or she eligible for unemployment compensation? How much? How long would this finance your needs? If both husband and wife work, your job security is obviously better than if there is only one wage earner in the family. How many protections does your family have against other disasters besides unemployment—insurance coverage for your home, health and life pension credits, savings and investments, equity in your home, etc.?

HOW TO MAINTAIN OR RESTORE A GOOD CREDIT RATING

How do you keep up a good credit record? Or restore one if it has gone bad? Here are the key rules:

• Avoid overloading yourself with installment debt. Note those guidelines on how much debt is too much debt for you and abide by them!

• Aim for and maintain a rainy-day fund in cash or its equivalent equal to two to three months' pay.

• Be truthful when you apply for credit and repay all your debts as agreed. But if you find you are unable to meet one or more payments on time, go to the creditors involved, explain your circumstances, and try to work out a more practical repayment schedule. The problem could be merely that payments on a loan or a purchase fall due on the twelfth of the month, though your paycheck doesn't arrive until the fifteenth.

In some cases, of course (too many), your credit rating can suffer because of an inadvertent human error. Wrong data is put in a computer. Your payment isn't credited properly. A bill goes astray in the mail. There is a dispute over a defective product, and the merchant elects to "write it off" rather than settling with you—but he enters into your record that you have not paid what you owed. (See pages 1355–62, "Your Rights to an Honest Credit Rating.")

Check *regularly* on your credit rating; and take action, immediately, if you are denied credit, or if your application for credit is simply not processed.

HOW TO BORROW CASH AND USE CREDIT

If you have legitimate payment problems, though, there are still actions you can take to avoid your credit rating being tarnished unduly.

What if You Find You're over Your Head in Debt?

Bill W. is an appliance serviceman, forty years old, married to Ann, who has a job at the post office. Together, they earn close to $23,000 a year, and because their two children are now teenagers, they recently bought a new home in a small midwest city on a $36,000 mortgage.

Bill and Ann are widely admired for their carefree way of living, and Bill's friends frequently ask for his sensitive, prudent financial advice, wishing that they, too, could afford a new home, two cars, at least two vacations a year.

But, unknown to their friends (and not fully realized by Bill and Ann either), their total monthly expenses now top $2,500, they owe a startling $32,283 to eighteen creditors, and they're going deeper into the red each month by $658.49.

In sum, this couple—so respected for its financial common sense—is flat broke.

"When I went shopping at Christmas for clothing and presents," said Ann, "I assumed the only way you could get them was with a plastic card. Cash was unheard-of."

"We really tried to make and stay within a mental budget, but it never seemed to work when it came time to pay the bills," added Bill. "In nine years, I can't recall more than two or three times that we seriously discussed our spending habits, let alone what we were saving. It all went unsaid somehow."

Who is this American who gets over his or her head in debt?—particularly at the Christmas holiday season?

It's *you*.

You may be a $50,000-plus executive working for one of America's top five hundred giant corporations. Or you may be a family receiving welfare.

Consumers coming to an office of the Consumer Credit Counseling Service of Greater New York for budgeting advice range across all income, age, and social classes.

In fact, you're merely typical of a consumer over your head in debt if this is your profile:

- head of a four-person household in your mid thirties;
- a gross annual income of around $13,600;
- debts averaging $7,600 to nine creditors;
- spending roughly $360 more per month than you earn.

At least one out of every twenty Americans is in serious financial trouble, well beyond the point at which you can hope to repay your staggering debts on your own.

Where to Go for Help

Even if you are over your head in debt, the statistics indicate that you can be saved from financial disaster.

It's estimated only about one in six families can*not* be helped by credit counselors, because their problems are psychological or legal or because they are "credit drunks" who simply are not willing to try to solve their problems. However, without counseling service, today's huge annual personal bankruptcy toll easily might be 50 per cent higher than it is.

The fact is, says the Family Service Association of America, "people do want help—desperately—but they don't know where to go, and until recently there hasn't been anywhere to go."

So what if you find you are over your head in debt?

• Start at your local bank: more and more banks are offering formal or informal debt counseling to overburdened customers.

• If your bank (or credit union or consumer finance company) can't or won't help, write to the National Foundation for Consumer Credit, 1819 H Street, N.W., Washington, D.C. 20006, for the address of one of the hundreds of existing Consumer Credit Counseling Services nearest to you. These non-profit organizations, backed by local banks, merchants, educators, and others, are set up to provide financial counseling to anyone, but offer special help to overextended families and individuals in an effort to find ways to get them out of trouble.

• Check the nearest Family Service Agency. Hundreds of Family Service Agencies across the nation either offer financial counseling or can refer you to some agency offering such counseling. If you don't know which agency offers such help in your area, write the Family Service Association of America, 44 East Twenty-third Street, New York, New York 10010.

• Other sources from which you may get some form of debt counseling include:

>   legal aid societies;
>
>   your labor union's community services counselors;
>
>   your employer's personnel department;
>
>   your church;
>
>   the Army and Navy also maintain debt counseling services to assist servicemen and their families.

• Do everything possible to avoid such extreme measures as repossession, litigation, or having your account turned over to a collection agency. However, if any of these is threatened, go to your credit granters first, explain what happened, and in many cases they will be willing to extend your payment schedule. Or they may refer you to a reliable local credit counseling service.

• Consider refinancing your loan to extend its term and reduce your monthly payments. This will, of course, increase the interest charges, but it may be a small price to pay to get through a critical financial period.

• On mortgage loans, try to arrange with your bank to make alternate payments, every other month, for six months, a year or more, or see if the bank will let you pay only the interest for a period of time. (Try, though, to avoid refinancing a mortgage at higher interest rates.)

If all else fails, however, you may want to consider "the ultimate solution," financially. Bankruptcy.

How to Go Bankrupt

Let's say all efforts and plans to bail you out have failed. The debt counseling service hasn't been able to come up with a plan your creditors will accept. No consolidation loan is available. The only option left seems to be bankruptcy.

If so, here are your final two "outs":

(1) "Chapter XIII." This method of debt reorganization is provided for under Chapter XIII of the Federal Bankruptcy Law. Under Chapter XIII, debtor, creditors, and a referee—all supervised by a federal judge—get together to work out a way for the debtor to pay his debts on an installment basis.

This is known as the wage earner plan, because it protects the wages and essential property of a debtor who wants to stay away from straight bankruptcy by repaying his or her debts from future earnings.

Whether rooted in puritanism, pride, or ego, the general attitude toward bankruptcy is negative and you well may find it difficult to live with. But there are other than social aspects to be considered. Your friends who co-signed your loans may turn into bitter enemies as they "pay off" for you; the cost of going into bankruptcy may reach $500 to $1,000 or more; bankruptcy almost invariably is the blackest possible mark on a credit rating.

Here's how the wage earner plan works.

Either you, the debtor, get a written extension of your debts, with more time to pay them off in full; or, less commonly, you arrange a "composition" in which you pay off only a certain percentage of the amount you owe each creditor.

One half of your creditors must approve your filing of the Chapter XIII petition, at which time all interest charges usually stop. Your wages, personal property, your home and furniture, secured loans, particularly mortgages on real estate, usually are not included in the plan for distribution of your assets to creditors.

In addition to legal fees, which a Chapter XIII petitioner must pay to the lawyer who files the petition, there are filing fees of about $15 to $25 and a trustee's fee of up to 5 per cent of the debts, plus expenses.

You, the debtor, make your required payments, spread over three years, to the trustee, who then pays your creditors—thus making the federal government, in effect, a collection agency. An employer may agree to deduct the payment from a debtor's salary and forward it to the trustee.

There is no uniformity of application of Chapter XIII, and top legal experts deplore the fact that it is not more widely used.

Important note: if you successfully complete this plan, it will be considered a "plus" on your credit rating.

(2) *Voluntary bankruptcy.* Finally, there is the voluntary petition for straight bankruptcy. To do this you must put together a list of all your assets and liabilities and pay a $50 filing fee. Ordinarily, the rest is routine. Except for clothing, tools, a selected list of household goods, and other items depending on the exemption laws of your state, all your assets will be collected by the court and liquidated—and the proceeds will then be distributed among your creditors. Once you, the debtor, have been discharged by the court, your financial slate is clean—except for the bankruptcy record, which, no matter what you are told, will dog your footsteps for years.

The Bafflegab of Borrowing

Many of the most crucially important terms to you in the sphere of credit already have been exhaustively explained in the immediately preceding pages. But many other words you'll hear or read have not yet been put into simple language. You'll come across them frequently enough, though, and they are of sufficient importance to demand that they be as clearly explained as possible.

ACCELERATION CLAUSE   See page 967.
ADD-ON CLAUSE   See page 967.
ADD-ON RATE   See pages 957–58.
ANNUAL PERCENTAGE RATE   See page 952.
ASSETS   Everything you own that has monetary worth.
BALANCE   The amount you own on an account or loan at any given time.
BALLOON CONTRACT   See page 967.
BORROWER   The person who borrows cash or who buys something on time.
CARRYING CHARGE   The charge you pay a store or any other lender for the privilege of having a period of time in which to pay for the goods or services you have already bought and which you may use in advance of payment.
CHARGE ACCOUNT   See page 951.
CHARGE OFF   To declare a loss and remove a loan from the assets of a lender because the loan cannot be collected from the dealer.
CHATTEL MORTGAGE   A legal document in which your personal property

(chattels) is put up as security for payment of your debt but generally is left in your hands so long as you keep up the payments as contracted.

CHECK CREDIT PLANS Consumer loan programs similar to credit lines businesses have under which the loans are approved in advance and funds are available when needed. The consumer who has been approved for check credit may borrow up to a stated amount at any time simply by writing a check. As the loan is repaid, the credit limit returns to the stated maximum. See page 923.

CLOSING DATE The day of the month on which credit accounts and monthly bills are calculated. Payments made after the closing date—or new charges or returns of merchandise—will not show on the bill you receive until the following month, when the next closing date will show subsequent payments, charges, and returns.

COLLATERAL Anything of value that you have against which you may borrow money—for example, equity in an automobile, real estate, stocks and bonds, savings account passbooks, the cash-surrender value of life insurance policies. If you fail to repay your loan, the lender can take possession of whatever you have put up as collateral. Note: not all loans must be secured by collateral.

CO-MAKER OR CO-SIGNER The other signer of a note when two people jointly guarantee to pay a loan. Parents often co-sign loans taken out by their minor children. Minors may not legally execute contracts.

CONDITIONAL SALES CONTRACT Form of installment contract under which you do not legally own the product—say a car—until you've made the final payment. And you must make your payments even if you are not satisfied with the purchase. You cannot cancel your obligation by just giving back the product (car). Term no longer in common use in many areas.

CONSOLIDATE To bring together several financial obligations under one agreement, contract, or note.

CONSUMER Any person who uses goods and/or services for personal, household, or family purposes.

CONSUMER CREDIT Credit offered or extended to a person primarily for personal or family purposes, for which a finance charge is imposed and which is repayable in installments. All consumer credit transactions divide into two types: (1) open-end credit, which includes revolving charge accounts and transactions through credit cards; and (2) installment credit, which is used by consumers to buy big-ticket items such as automobiles and appliances.

The one fact that consumer credit is used by individuals for personal and family needs distinguishes it from credit used for business, agricultural, or government purposes. Consumer credit usually refers to short-term and intermediate-term debt, thus excluding long-term home mortgage debt.

CONSUMER FINANCE COMPANIES State-licensed companies that make installment cash loans to consumers.

CONSUMER LOANS Loans to individuals or families, the proceeds to be used for personal consumption, as contrasted to loans for business or investment purposes.

CREDIT APPLICATION A form that you must fill out when you want to use consumer credit. It usually contains questions concerning your present and previous places of residence, work history, present earnings, other credit transactions, and loans outstanding.

CREDIT CARD See pages 941–50.

CREDIT CHARGE See Finance Charge.

CREDIT CONTRACT Usually a written agreement that says how, when, and how much you will pay.

CREDIT INVESTIGATION An inquiry undertaken by a prospective lender or creditor to verify information you give in your credit application or to investigate other aspects about you which the creditor considers relevant to your credit-worthiness.

CREDIT LIFE INSURANCE A type of term life insurance policy, required by some lenders, which pays off a loan in the event of the borrower's death.

CREDIT LINES (See Check Credit Plans): Preapproved loan privileges made available by banks to big businesses that qualify and maintain specified minimum checking account balances.

CREDITOR OR LENDER The person, store, company, bank, dealer, credit union, or other organization that lends money or sells things or services on time. Creditors are those to whom you owe money.

CREDIT RATE The ratio—expressed as a percentage—between credit charges and the average principal amount.

CREDIT RATING (also Credit Standing): An evaluation of your qualifications to receive credit based, in large measure, on your past record of meeting credit payments.

CREDIT RISK The chance of loss through non-payment of debt. One considered less than credit-worthy.

CREDIT SALE Any sale in which you are given time to pay for the goods you buy. There's usually an extra charge for the privilege of buying on time, and you usually pay for the goods in a series of installment payments which come due at regular intervals.

CREDIT SALE DISCLOSURE STATEMENT The form a dealer must fill out giving you the essential details of your financing costs when you buy any product or service on the installment plan. This is required under the Consumer Credit Protection (Truth in Lending) Act.

CREDIT-WORTHY Given a favorable credit rating and therefore entitled to use credit facilities.

DECLINING BALANCE The decreasing amount that you owe on a debt as you make your monthly payments.

DEFAULT Failure to pay a debt when due or to meet other terms of the contract.
DEFERRED PAYMENT Future payment or series of future payments on a contract entered into sometime before the payment or payments are made.
DELINQUENT A credit account that is past due and for which the debtor has made no satisfactory arrangement with the lender.
DISCOUNT (OR CASH CREDIT DISCOUNT) Deduction of finance charges from the total amount of your loan before you, the borrower, receive the balance in cash.
DISCOUNT RATE See page 953.
DOLLAR COST A way of stating the cost of credit. It is the difference between what you receive as a loan or in merchandise and what you must pay back.
DOWN PAYMENT Cash required at the outset of an installment sales credit transaction. Sometimes a used car, piece of furniture, or other durable goods will be accepted in place of part or all of the down payment.
DURABLE GOODS Usually big-ticket things that are useful to you, the consumer, over an extended period of time, such as automobiles, furniture, appliances.
FACE AMOUNT Total amount of your loan before deduction of finance charges.
FINANCE CHARGE See page 952.
FINANCIAL COUNSELING Expert advice on money and credit management.
FORFEIT Lose or let go—as giving up to a creditor some security when you, the borrower, have failed to meet a contractual obligation.
HIDDEN CLAUSE Any obscure provision in your credit contract that may stipulate requirements that may be against your interest—for instance, purchase of extra items you do not want.
HOLDER IN DUE COURSE See pages 965–67.
INSTALLMENT One of a series of payments to pay off a debt.
INSTALLMENT CASH CREDIT Cash loaned directly to an individual and repaid in periodic payments (usually monthly) within a specified period of time.
INSTALLMENT SALES CREDIT Credit through which an item of durable goods (a car, appliance) is bought and paid for in installment payments within a specified period of time.
INTERMEDIATE-TERM CREDIT Credit that is extended for a period ranging from three to ten years.
LOAN RATE The rate you are charged for borrowing money at a specific date for a specified period of time.
LENDING INSTITUTION A bank, loan company, or other organization that lends money and makes money by advancing funds to others.
LICENSED LENDER A lending organization authorized by license to conduct business in the state in which it is located.

LOAN SHARK See pages 939–40.
LONG-TERM CREDIT Credit that is extended for a period of ten years or more.
MARKET PLACE Any place where a transaction is made or prices are quoted on goods or service.
MATURED Fully paid up, fully carried out as to terms, completed as to time or as to contract.
MATURITY DATE (also Due Date): Date on which final payment on cash loan or installment purchase is due.
MORTGAGE A written pledge of valuable property to assure payment of a debt in case of default.
MORTGAGE CREDIT Money owed for those borrowing for the acquisition of land and/or buildings (frequently, homes) and which is paid back over an extended period of time.
NON-INSTALLMENT CREDIT A financial obligation that is repaid in a single lump sum.
NOTE A written, signed promise to pay which lists details of the repayment agreement: where, when, and in what size installments, etc. A note can be transferred to a third party.
OBLIGATION An amount of money one is morally or legally bound to pay.
OPEN-END CREDIT OR REVOLVING CREDIT See page 951.
OUTSTANDING The still unpaid part of a loan.
PAPER Nickname for a loan contract.
PERSONAL INSTALLMENT LOAN Money borrowed by an individual for personal needs which is repaid in regular monthly installments over a period of time.
PREPAYMENT PRIVILEGE The privilege, stated in loan contract, of repaying part or all of a loan in advance of date or dates stated in contract—with or without interest penalty for the prepayment.
PRINCIPAL The amount of money you borrow or the amount of credit you receive.
PROCEEDS The actual amount of money handed to a borrower—after deductions for interest charges, fees, etc.
PROMISSORY NOTE A paper you sign promising to repay the total sum you owe on specified terms.
REBATE Return of a portion of a payment. For instance, you receive a rebate when you pay off your debt in advance instead of in the monthly installments you agreed upon. It then costs you less to borrow your money, because you are paying off in a shorter period.
REFINANCE Revision of a payment timetable and, often, revision of the interest charges on the debt also.
REPOSSESSION The reclaiming or taking back of goods which you have purchased on an installment sales contract and for which you have fallen behind in your payments.

REVOLVING CHARGE ACCOUNT See page 951.

RIGHT OF RESCISSION Your right, guaranteed by the Consumer Credit Protection Act or various state statutes, to cancel a contract under certain circumstances (including cases in which you have put up an interest in your home as security) within three business days—without penalty and with full refund of any deposits you may have paid. The right to a "cooling-off period" is most frequently used in home improvements contracts, and the home improvement contractor must provide you with written notice of this right. It also applies, under a Federal Trade Commission rule, to sales made by door-to-door salespeople.

SHORT-TERM CREDIT Credit extended for a period up to three to five years.

SOLVENT Ability of the individual or group or organization to pay all of the debts owed. What the debtor owns is more than the total of the debts.

TERM The prescribed time you have in which to make installment or other payments, under your loan or credit contract.

TERMS Details and conditions of a loan (or other) contract: cash price, payment schedule, due date, etc.

THIRD-PARTY TRANSACTION A three-way transaction involving a buyer, a seller, and a source of consumer credit.

TITLE Legal ownership.

TOP CREDIT Ready credit. See Check Credit Plans.

TRADE IN Practice of trading in an old product for a new one. Trade-in allowance is the amount of money allowed for the article traded in as against the total purchase price of the article being bought.

TRUTH IN LENDING Popular name for the historic Consumer Credit Protection Act of 1969. The law applies to virtually all consumer borrowing transactions to individuals which involve amounts up to $25,000.

UNPAID BALANCE On a credit purchase, difference between purchase price and down payment or trade-in allowance. On cash loan, difference between total loan made and amount still owed (with charges included, of course).

UNSECURED LOAN Loan extended solely on basis of borrower's ability and pledge to repay.

WAGE ASSIGNMENT Clause in installment contract under which an employer may be requested to collect part of an employee's wages to pay off the employee's debt to the wage assignment holder.

WAGE EARNER PLAN See pages 973–74.

WAGE GARNISHMENT Classic legal procedure that creditors have used for generations to collect debts. Under "income execution" (its other name) a creditor gets a court order instructing the employer of the debtor to withhold a specified portion of his employee's wages until his debt is repaid.

17

WHAT RECORDS SHOULD YOU KEEP?
—AND HOW?

DISCARDING RECORDS AT HOME 982
DISCARDING UNNEEDED RECORDS AT YOUR BUSINESS 983
HOW TO KEEP YOUR OWN AND YOUR FAMILY'S HEALTH
  RECORDS 985

Are you among the millions of Americans—individuals and business owners—who are exaggerated savers of papers and records, receipts and canceled checks?

Do you know which of the many papers cluttering your home, or wasting valuable space in your office, are easily expendable and should be tossed out now?

Have you even a vague—much less clear and informed—knowledge of what records are needlessly overcrowding your filing cabinets or desk drawers and only confusing you?

No matter when you are reading this, it's an *excellent* time to update your filing system by getting rid of nonessentials. But while pamphlets and even books have been written to warn you what records to keep, little reliable guidance ever is given on what to discard.

As just one illustration, while you should keep checks and other receipts that may be needed for income tax purposes as proof of payment, it isn't at all important to keep all canceled checks. It's even silly.

In reviewing your own accumulation of records, don't overlook the fact that you often store more than one copy of the same record.

Overlooked, too, by many of you—individuals and businesses—is the need to transfer periodically records from your easily available files to inactive files in an out-of-the-way place.

Discarding Records at Home

• Concentrate your efforts on the most important documents that may be jamming your drawers. You can create a family filing system that is efficient and exceedingly helpful with little equipment and modest outlay. Once you have screened out the nonessentials, a filing box containing manila folders and costing only a few dollars plus a small safe deposit box, also available at little cost and tax deductible too, will provide all the file storage space your home will need.

• Dispose of your weekly and monthly salary statements after you have checked them against your annual W-2 wage forms.

• Lighten your files by using a canceled check that relates to an entry on your return as your record. Unless you fear that the nature of a medical expense is ambiguous, for example, your canceled check to your physician is adequate evidence that you have paid for a specific medical service. Look into your files. How many physicians' statements have you been needlessly accumulating in your files from years gone by? Pediatricians' bills? Orthondontists' statements? Other bills that are clearly identified by your checks?

Caution: Don't throw out bills from the drugstore. The IRS may request proof of deductible drugs vs. nondeductible items such as cosmetics, etc.

• As a rule of thumb, dispose of your personal tax records after six years. Federal tax statutes make your tax return vulnerable to challenge up to three years if yours are normal circumstances. The six-year period is considered the time frame for checking returns on which income has been understated by more than 25 per cent.

• If you income-average, discard returns over five years old. The IRS usually retains personal returns for six years and can supply copies at a moderate cost.

• After you have recorded the year's total dividend payments, discard these papers on receipt of the annual dividend tally supplied by the company. Be sure, though, to retain a record of capital-gain distribution dividends because they must be reported for tax purposes when the shares are sold.

• Discard checks paid out for maintenance costs on your house. The only real reason to keep records on such costs as papering and painting is if you plan to sell your house soon. But keep permanent improvement records that add to the value of your property, such as the addition of central air-conditioning.

• Periodically check your warranties and guarantees, and if they're out of date, discard them. Throw out health maintenance certificates that have expired. Old Blue Cross/Blue Shield cards that you have accumulated from different employers (or as you have changed internal medical programs) can be a jumble of befuddlement—particularly if you must search your files in a hurry for a current validation.

Discarding Unneeded Records at Your Business

When a small business, of which I was a half owner, was transferred to its faithful employees recently and I was forced to go through its records, I was actually embarrassed to discover what a paper clutter had been accumulated while it was in my hands. In the files I found canceled checks dating back more than twenty years, job applications that had been turned down more than a decade ago, correspondence that had absolutely no relevance to 1978. Equally shocking, I found several copies of one contract, and that contract so out-of-date it was an antique. I think I need confess no more.

If you're also a typical owner of a small business, it's more than likely that your clutter is almost as bad (it would be unusual for yours to be as awful) as mine. Thus, as guidelines:

• In your office, one central file is adequate to protect a contract permanently, and there is no sense for other departments to be retaining copies as well. It's even more ridiculous to retain all the copies after the contract has expired.

But do not downgrade the fact that there are close to a thousand federal and state regulations covering retention of records. These vary widely on tax, unemployment, and workmen's compensation.

So caution: Before disposing of your unwanted and needless records, it would be wise to check with your state tax commissioner's office to be sure you do not go too far on discarding.

• Discard audit reports after ten years; audit work papers after three years.

• Get rid of general correspondence after five years; and eliminate classified documents—inventories, reports, and receipts—after ten years.

• Dispose of contracts twenty years after settlement. Also throw out requests for services and requisitions for suppliers one year after the end of the fiscal year.

• Discard accident reports, injury claims, and settlement papers thirty years after settlement.

• Eliminate from your files applications, changes, and terminations after five years. As for attendance records, seven years is long enough to keep them while employee activity files become mere clutter two years after they have been superseded.

• Dispose of employee contracts six years after termination. Get rid of fidelity bonds three years after termination.

• Garnishments can be eliminated after five years; insurance records for employees are needless eleven years after termination; time cards go into the discard heap after three years; and union agreements (according to the Walsh-Healey Act) may be thrown out after three years.

• Throw out your building and maintenance records after ten years, unless there are special reasons to do otherwise.

• Dispose of bids and awards three years after termination; price lists, when obsolete; purchase orders and requisitions, three years after termination; and quotations, after one year.

• According to the Code of Federal Regulations, you can destroy after four years employee withholding records, excise exemption certificates, excise reports in manufacturing, and excise reports at the retail level.

If you are a compulsive saver of papers, records, canceled checks, etc.—the way so many individuals are compulsive savers of string—you might try to "cure" yourself by buying a simple loose-leaf notebook and using it as a working tool to make your record system work more efficiently and reduce your frustrations. You can change the individual pages as you revise any part of your files, add or subtract subjects.

This can work for you as owner or manager of a small business just as it can work for you as an individual or a family.

And if you find that, at the start, parting with your records is just too bold a move—or you're afraid you might discard a paper the IRS or the courts or some agency will request the very next week—then at least double-check the records to divide them into current and background. Then clean out your active files by keeping only the current records in them; and move your background records to inactive files in another storage place.

Get a copy of "Keeping Records, What to Discard," by sending a postcard to Consumer Information Center, Department 625E, Pueblo, Colorado 81009. It has some valuable hints and it's free.

How to Keep Your Own and Your Family's Health Records

If you have lived in one place and had the same physician all your life, you wouldn't have much need to keep your own health records. But if you're a typical American, you have moved your residence and changed your doctors or seen different specialists for specific health problems many times.

As a result, your health records almost surely have *not* kept up to you. And the only person who can maintain an accurate, complete medical history on yourself is you.

Here are the guides prepared for you by the Department of Health, Education and Welfare:

(1) Record any and all serious illnesses in your family background (heredity can play so vital a role in some diseases). Include the illness records of parents, brothers, and sisters on both sides of your family. List the histories of such diseases as cancer, diabetes, epilepsy, and heart conditions.

(2) If any of these relatives are deceased, record the causes and ages at the time of death. When discussing your own medical history, be sure you give this information to your new physician.

(3) Keep a regular record of fluctuations in your blood pressure and have your pressure checked every six to twelve months, so you'll be aware as soon as any significant changes occur.

(4) Record any and all injuries as well, for injuries from accidents may result in disabling conditions—or years later the injuries may be the basis of an illness, long since forgotten. Do not shrug off the potential for good in this injury record.

(5) Start your family's immunization program early in life, usually when a child is two to three months old. Keeping your immunization records up-to-date is an essential toward rearing a healthy family.

(6) Record the date of each immunization, so you will know when any

family member needs a "booster shot" to renew his or her protection. Immunization against preventable diseases is not always permanent, warns HEW. Several childhood vaccines often may be combined in a single shot—for instance, measles, rubella, and mumps. Or other immunizations may require initial series of injections over a span of weeks or months.

18

HOW TO ACHIEVE FINANCIAL INDEPENDENCE AND PERSONAL SECURITY IN YOUR OLDER YEARS

THE CULT OF YOUTH IS PASSING	990
ERA OF THE ELDERLY	990
PLANNING FOR YOUR RETIREMENT	991
YOU DON'T HAVE TO RETIRE AT SIXTY-FIVE!	992
"RETIREMENT SHOCK"	993
HOW MUCH WILL YOU NEED?	995
HELP FOR THE OVER-SIXTY-FIVE TAXPAYER	996
PRECAUTIONS IN CALCULATING YOUR NEEDS	997
FIGURING YOUR MONTHLY EXPENSES	998
HOW MUCH WILL YOU HAVE?	999
ESTIMATING YOUR RETIREMENT INCOME	999
PLANNING FOR YOUR PENSION	1000
WORKING TO QUALIFY	1001
THE SIZE OF YOUR PENSION	1002
YOUR SURVIVING SPOUSE	1003
YOUR PENSION RIGHTS	1004
HELP UNDERSTANDING PENSIONS	1005
SIMPLIFIED PENSION PLANS	1006
A SAFETY NET UNDER YOUR PENSION	1007
GETTING THE RETIREMENT INCOME YOU NEED	1008
DON'T MISS OUT ON KEOGH OR IRA PLAN	1009
HOW LONG WILL YOUR RETIREMENT CAPITAL LAST?	1010

WHAT YOU SHOULD KNOW ABOUT SOCIAL SECURITY—FOUNDATION OF YOUR RETIREMENT PROGRAM	1011
A BASIC PROBLEM	1011
LONGER-RANGE PROBLEM, TOO	1012
SOLUTIONS	1012
SOCIAL SECURITY AMENDMENTS HAVE PUT PROGRAM ON SOUND FOOTING	1013
BENEFITS WILL BE KEPT UP-TO-DATE WITH PRICES AND LEVEL OF LIVING	1013
PROJECTED BENEFITS FOR PERSONS RETIRING AT AGE SIXTY-FIVE	1015
HOW MUCH YOU WILL GET AS A RETIREE OR DEPENDENT	1015
OTHER SOCIAL SECURITY BENEFITS	1017
SUPPLEMENTAL SECURITY INCOME	1018
WHO IS ELIGIBLE FOR SOCIAL SECURITY?	1018
YOUR WORK CREDITS	1019
IF YOU WORK IN RETIREMENT	1020
THE "EDDIE CANTOR" RULE	1021
SOCIAL SECURITY AND WOMEN'S RIGHTS	1023
SOCIAL SECURITY'S INEQUITIES AFFECT US ALL	1025
BASIC REFORMS	1026
THE BAFFLEGAB OF SOCIAL SECURITY	1027
WHAT YOU SHOULD KNOW ABOUT LIFE INSURANCE	1028
DO YOU NEED LIFE INSURANCE?	1028
HOW TO FIGURE YOUR LIFE INSURANCE NEEDS	1030
HOW MUCH LIFE INSURANCE CAN YOU AFFORD?	1031
WHAT KIND OF LIFE INSURANCE FOR YOU?	1032
PRACTICAL EXAMPLES OF WHO NEEDS WHAT	1035
HOW TO FIND A "STRONG" INSURANCE COMPANY	1037
HOW TO SAVE ON YOUR INSURANCE	1037
HANDLING YOUR INSURANCE AT RETIREMENT	1039
IS YOUR LIFE INSURANCE UP-TO-DATE?	1039
HOW INFLATION HAS ERODED YOUR LIFE INSURANCE	1041
SHOULD YOU SWITCH INSURANCE POLICIES?	1042
WHAT ABOUT WIFE INSURANCE?	1043
AND WHAT ABOUT INSURANCE FOR CHILDREN?	1044
WHAT YOU SHOULD KNOW ABOUT ANNUITIES	1045
What They Are	1045
Pros and Cons of Annuities	1046
New Types of Annuities	1046
WHAT'S *your* RATE ON A LIFE INSURANCE LOAN?	1046

FINANCIAL INDEPENDENCE AND PERSONAL SECURITY   989

What You Should Know About Life Insurance (CONTD)
- BUYING LIFE INSURANCE BY MAIL — 1047
- PEOPLE FORGET — 1049
- LAPSED POLICY OR LAPSED MEMORY? — 1050

The Bafflegab of Life Insurance and Annuities — 1052
Veterans' Pensions — 1054
Veterans' Benefits — 1055
What Every Widow Should Know — 1056
- BASIC FACTS FOR WIDOWS — 1056
- HOW MUCH WOULD YOU GET? — 1057
  - Social Security — 1057
  - Civil Service and Railroad Workers' Benefits — 1058
  - Other Employee Benefits — 1059
  - Life Insurance — 1059

Beware: Gyps Aimed at the Elderly — 1059
- CAN YOU FIND THE FOUNTAIN OF YOUTH? — 1060
- WARNINGS ON BUYING A RETIREMENT HOMESITE — 1062

The Cult of Youth Is Passing

The cult of youth which has so dominated our society for so long is passing. As the decade of the 1980s rolls on, "family planning" will focus not on children and babies but on planning for our elderly population—how to accommodate them, support them, limit the numbers of dependent elderly, maximize the potential of the non-dependents.

This is just one of the probable consequences of the drastic declines in the U.S. birth rate. In the past decade, for instance our crude birth rate dropped to fewer than 15 per 1,000 population, lowest in U.S. history. Our fertility rate, at 2.0 children per family, is actually under the zero population growth level of 2.1 children.

What's more, the trend is continuing. Young couples more and more are reporting intentions to have smaller families or no children at all. Easier abortion laws, later marriages, increased numbers of divorces, the tendency for more women to remain single—all are factors in the startling change.

Era of the Elderly

The most obvious economic impact of ZPG will be on our marketing system for goods and services, for it will have to be geared to a stable rather than a soaring population. Other obvious economic implications are relief in pressures on our environment, a considerable easing of housing shortages, cutbacks in businesses catering to babies—ranging from obstetrics to diaper services, baby foods, and nursery schools. But far, far more fascinating are the implications for our elderly people. Among the specific forecasts of a major study by the Center for the Study of Democratic Institutions in Santa Barbara, California, coauthored by political scientist Harvey Wheeler and lawyer R. J. Carlson, are:

• A radical shift in emphasis from chronological age to "functional" age—not how old you are in years but how old you act and feel. Alongside this development will be not only tremendous new job opportunities for the elderly, but actually a new dependency on the elderly to perform a wide variety of public services. In the words of the authors: "The quality of public services will deteriorate if the talents of the elderly are not utilized."

- The formation of a new class of second-class citizens—the infirm "functionally elderly."
- New standards of beauty and morality which will be based on older rather than younger models (dizzying thought: wrinkles in fashion?).
- A complete overhaul of the present exclusive youth orientation of our educational system—with the big expansion in school enrollment in the future taking place in the thirty-and-over age bracket. In fact, says the report, a new educational boom will develop in high schools and at the post-high school level. "Colleges and universities will have to be redesigned with needs of the elderly uppermost in mind."
- "A new kind of revolutionary movement"—pressing for older Americans' rights in all spheres of life and led by the over-fifty because of their vast numbers and importance in our society.

These are just a few of the implications. I can think of dozens more: fundamental changes in both public and private pension systems, a growing gap between young workers paying even higher higher Social Security taxes and the elderly retired living on Social Security benefits, an enormous expansion in government medical care programs, a surge of population to warm-weather areas, and many more. So can you think of additional implications, I'm sure.

But the central point is that virtually everybody, including *you*, will be elderly one day. And then you will be forever glad that you planned now for your future financial and personal security.

Planning for Your Retirement

How can you protect yourself against an older age threatened by poverty? A large part of the answer lies in one four-letter word: *plan!*

If you are in your twenties or thirties, retirement may seem too far off to worry about. It's tough enough to cope with the problems of everyday living. You also may feel that any money worries you may now have will somehow disappear by the time you reach retirement age. Or you may simply put off even thinking about retirement for year after year until it finally is directly ahead of you.

But the cold fact is that retirement planning is as important to you, the younger worker, as it is to the worker now reaching retirement age. For one thing, the earlier you start planning, the less it will cost you to amass the capital and income you'll need in your retirement years. Consider, for example, the lower cost of life insurance when you are younger, or the greater flexibility you have in saving and investing your nest egg.

What's more, today's younger American will need more financial resources than a person who is retired today. You well may spend as many as twenty to twenty-five years in retirement, almost twice today's retirement span.

Even today, a man retiring at age sixty-five can look forward to a life expectancy of another thirteen and one half years, and his slightly younger wife can expect to live an average of nearly twenty more years. So the sooner you start, the better the chances you will have of laying the groundwork for the comfortable, independent life you'll want in your retirement years.

Just how do you start planning? Begin by asking yourself two questions:

"Do I want to retire at sixty-five or sooner?"

"How much income and reserves will I need to live comfortably at that age?"

Before you can answer these two questions, you'll have to ask yourself just what kind of retirement life you want to lead, just what your future needs and wants will be.

You Don't Have to Retire at Sixty-five

Landmark legislation went on our statute books in the late 1970s raising the legal mandatory retirement age for most of us in the U.S. work force from the long-standing, artificially established age of sixty-five to a just as artificial but more realistic age of seventy.

The new retirement age covers tens of millions of us in private enterprise and state-local government jobs (with two limited exemptions for top business executives and tenured college professors). Also, the federal government's retirement age of seventy for most civilian employees was abolished with restricted exceptions.

No longer are you forced to leave your job at age sixty-five, no matter how good your performance, your health, and how eager you are to stay on.

Nor are you required to stay on after the discarded retirement age of sixty-five, if you neither need nor want the job or pay.

The choice is where it belongs—up to you.

Even before this historic adjustment took place, the pluses and minuses were debated with seemingly endless anxiety. Opponents forecast that shock waves would roll over the entire business, industrial, and academic worlds; pension plans would have to be rewritten (or at least renegotiated); many giant firms tried to work out systems and tests under which workers with inferior, if not downright negative, records still could be compelled to retire at sixty-five; the extent to which the burden on the Social Security system would be eased is still being calculated and recalculated, etc., etc.

One key concern is how their own peers, who may be jealous, ambitious, or whatever, can define and then accurately measure incompetence among fellow executives, and particularly professors.

Another is how to judge whether an employee is deteriorating physically or mentally to the point where he or she is slated to become a drag on the company.

What is "deadwood" really? What is "competence" among top executives or professors who may be extremely unpopular but of undeniable value to their institutions?

How will younger workers respond when their promotions are delayed because those ahead of them in their categories are remaining on the job for longer periods?

What will be the impact on job opportunities for women and minorities, particularly, if the employment ranks are jammed?

Can workers truly keep performing at acceptable levels as they age?

An encouraging report, privately circulated by Prentice-Hall, suggested that "for many companies, keeping workers on the job until age seventy would pose very few problems."

Only three problems emerged as serious, the most serious being (1) the "delicate problem of dealing with reduced job performance among people who are only a few years away from retirement"; (2) increased costs due to absenteeism, benefits, etc.; and (3) "dealing with advancement for younger go-getters."

On the challenge of dissatisfied younger workers, possible solutions include: offering incentives or alluring bonuses to older workers to retire before age seventy; offering incentives to younger workers to stay with the company; revamping the company's compensation program to tie pay more closely to performance.

On the problem of jobs for women and minorities, few companies expect opportunities to shrink. Several corporations said, in fact, that they would make an extra effort to see that highly qualified minorities receive special advantages.

On the question of job performance, many employers said they would "tighten up" their policies to make sure employees in the older age groups are still working up to par.

A fascinating finding of Prentice-Hall was that while the mandatory retirement age is rising, the number of employees choosing to take early retirement also is increasing. Many of you would prefer to retire early if you can swing it financially.

No matter what your views as an individual, traditional discrimination on the basis of age alone is finally being eliminated from the law. Our society's attitude toward our elderly has been and is far more barbaric than the barbarians even dreamed of. I hail the step, although it is only one minor move forward. It has been so long in coming.

"Retirement Shock"

True tale: An Eastern machinery manufacturer found it increasingly difficult to recruit young, local residents. Even worse, a mounting number of younger employees were quitting. The company president was sufficiently concerned to call in an outside personnel consultant, who quickly discovered that retired employees were responsible. Despite liberal pension benefits, the retirees warned younger people in town not to work for the company if they wanted to avoid being treated as "just a name and address" after retiring.

True tale: A large utility filed a rate increase application with state authorities, anticipating that the required public hearing for approval would be routine. Unexpectedly, the application was opposed by an ad hoc committee of the utility's own retired employees, who felt they had been "discarded." The opposition resulted in considerable delay in the rate hike, in much unfavorable publicity, and led a chastened utility official to comment later, "A retired employee who is enjoying his retirement years is a living advertisement for his employer."

True tale: On a list of forty top stress producers, "retirement" ranks in a high ninth place—not far behind "death of a spouse"—a medical study a while ago disclosed. Not providing retirement counseling can be disastrous to the employee. And usually the company will be blamed for the trauma known as "retirement shock"—a stress-producing situation which recognizes no social or financial barriers.

Almost one third of our citizens over sixty-five live in poverty, yet many did not become poor until they became old. By itself, that flashes a red-hot signal of danger to all of us—and compounding it is the fact that there is a definite trend toward retirement at an earlier age than the traditional sixty-five. A recent study by West Coast corporate planners, in fact, predicts an average retirement age of fifty-five in two more decades—meaning that if current predictions on life expectancy hold and if you're an average worker now in your thirties, you can look forward to twenty-five years of retirement!

But "unexpected retirement or being unprepared for retirement can mean living without any framework," a retirement counselor pointed out at a seminar on "preparing employees for retirement" sponsored by the American Management Association. AMA is a non-profit educational organization which conducts worldwide management training programs for more than 100,000 business and government executives annually.

And the confrontation with retirement—which affects the top-level corporate executive as well as the assembly-line worker—the fear of idleness, loneliness, and deteriorating health, can affect an employee's job performance years before he or she actually retires.

Changes induced by retirement are more abrupt than those between other stages of life. And they occur when most people are least able in body and in mind to cope with change.

Putting it in simplest language, a company providing pre- and post-retirement counseling is simply using good business sense. Its retirement program will not only reduce the trauma of retirement stress but also will bring greater efficiency, higher employee morale, and, the AMA points out, "an added measure of valuable goodwill from the swelling ranks of retirees."

FINANCIAL INDEPENDENCE AND PERSONAL SECURITY

What might a thorough retirement program cover? At least these five points:

(1) Of course, finances—ranging from budgeting to investments, tax considerations, estate planning, and most particularly from the employee's viewpoint, crucial details on the company's pension plan.

(2) Health care, medical or geriatrics advice.

(3) Life-style adjustments, psychological factors, family relationships, housing arrangements such as selection of retirement location, climate considerations.

(4) Use of leisure time (hobbies, travel, educational opportunities, community services, second careers).

(5) And legal rights and responsibilities, ranging from sales of homes to writing wills to avoiding traps set by swindlers who concentrate on older people.

How Much Will You Need?

How will your total estimated income fit your actual financial needs during a retirement period which easily could stretch up to twenty years or more? The answer must rest to a large extent on your family's style of living, on the things and non-things you are accustomed to and would like to continue to have. But here are some guidelines for figuring your future retirement needs, so you can later calculate how big the gap is between your projected income and your actual future needs.

Some of your expenses will be higher.

For instance, your costs for medicine, both prescription and non-prescription, will average two and a half times higher than they do for younger Americans. With more leisure time, you may want to increase your spending on travel, dining out, entertainment, and hobbies.

On the other hand, many of the things that now figure in your budget will either cost less or cease to be at all important to you. By the time you retire the chances are that your home mortgage will have been paid off, or if you move to a smaller place, your overall housing expenses will be lower than they are now.

If you retire to a warm climate, your clothing needs also will be less, and your heating costs next to nothing.

When you reach age sixty-five, you will qualify for Medicare benefits, which could cut your costs for hospital and doctor bills. And these benefits are, of course, in addition to Social Security benefits.

By the time you retire, too, your life insurance policy may be paid up, or if it is not, you may find that you need less protection than you are carrying, which means a lower monthly premium cost or perhaps none.

The high cost of rearing and educating your children will be behind you.

And your food costs will be lower, simply because the calorie needs of older people are less than those of younger people.

You also will be eligible, in retirement, for important money-savings tax breaks. Under the tax laws of the late 1970s, you could claim, if you were sixty-five or older by the end of the tax year, an extra exemption plus a second exemption for your wife is she was sixty-five and filed a joint return with you.

If you are sixty-five or over or are retired, you could get a retirement income credit which could cut your tax directly.

If you are fifty-five or older before you sell at a profit a home in which you have lived for three of the previous five years, you are eligible for significant tax benefits on the gain.

If you are in this age category, you well may get significant breaks on your property taxes.

Above and beyond tax breaks on your federal income tax, most states offer some type of exemption, special deduction, or reduction for retirees. To find out the rules, check with your state tax department.

Finally, many of the expenses formerly associated with your job, ranging from eating in restaurants to commuting costs, will be sharply reduced.

The basic point remains, though: the actual dollar amount of your financial needs in retirement will depend on your expected standard of living—in housing, dining, clothes, transportation, vacationing, giving. It also will depend on the level of property and state income taxes in the area in which you decide to settle.

It also will be crucially affected—and in an adverse way to you—by the degree of inflation in our nation in coming years.

You cannot ignore this inflation factor if you are to avoid the financial panic of discovering too late how drastically you have underestimated your future needs.

Help for the Over-Sixty-five Taxpayer

Q. *Which U. S. Government agency provides nationwide toll-free telephone assistance, toll-free TV phones and teletypewriters for the deaf, free information booklets (many printed in extra-large type for the partially blind), runs overseas seminars, and offers free walk-in counseling services (some designed particularly for those who don't speak English) for the elderly, handicapped, and low-income citizens?*

A. The Internal Revenue Service.

Why? Because our tax laws are so complex and change so frequently that even if you are more informed than most taxpayers, you may not be aware of all the deductions, credits, and exemptions to which you are entitled.

FINANCIAL INDEPENDENCE AND PERSONAL SECURITY

To whom is this of extraordinary importance? The millions of you who are sixty-five or over, for when you reach sixty-five or retire you are suddenly faced with a myriad of new federal income tax provisions.

What's more, if you're retired, your taxes are no longer withheld by your employer. Your income comes largely from pensions, annuities, investments, business activities, etc. not subject to withholding. The laws governing these forms of income are among the most befuddling in the tax code and require you to fill out several additional schedules as well as the long form 1040.

In addition, Congress has passed many special tax relief provisions for the elderly—as a result of which about 18 million of the 24 million of Americans considered older citizens currently pay no federal income taxes at all. You can receive levels of income tax-free which are roughly double the tax-free income levels for those under sixty-five.

Of every four older Americans only about one actually pays income taxes. If you are relatively well-off, with your income averaging close to $20,000 a year, under current law, you too are entitled to special treatment.

As just one illustration, you are granted an extra personal exemption. And tax preferences for you cost the U. S. Treasury billions annually.

But while many of today's measures ease and new proposals would further reduce the tax burden of millions of you, they are of little value unless you know they exist and how to take advantage of them.

The IRS distributes publications to assist older taxpayers. *Tax Benefits for Older Americans* is the main information booklet. It is free and you can get a copy at IRS and Social Security offices. The brochure carries sample forms illustrating many of the tax situations which you, an older taxpayer, will face.

Precautions in Calculating Your Needs

Obviously, no matter what your style of living, you must be coldly realistic in estimating your own needs.

- You must aim to have an emergency savings fund always on hand to take care of utterly unforeseeable emergencies. (See Chapter 2, "Budgets Are Back in Style.")
- You must have extra health insurance to supplement Medicare.
- And you must have some kind of "inflation cushion." If inflation continues to chew away at the buying power of your retirement income at an annual rate of say, "only" 5 per cent, and you expect to retire twenty years from now, you will need *165 per cent* more than you need today. This means that what you can buy for $3,000 today would cost you $7,950 in twenty years. For what your $10,000 buys today, you would need $26,500 twenty years from now. (See pages 4–7 for calculations of future prices at *other* inflation rates.)

Figuring Your Monthly Expenses

Now, taking into account your own life-style and needs and allowing for inflation, figure your own monthly expenses now and after retirement on a work sheet that might look something like this:

Your Monthly Expenses

Item	Where Money Goes Now	After Retirement
Food—including meals away from home		
Clothing		
Laundry, cleaning		
Transportation		
Car expense (including operating expenses and depreciation)		
Auto insurance		
Train or bus, other routine travel		
Housing		
Rent or mortgage		
Homeowners' insurance		
Heat		
Gas and electric		
Telephone		
Repairs, maintenance		
Lawn and garden upkeep		
Property taxes		
Household help		
Furniture and furnishings		
Medical care (not covered by insurance)		
Medicare payments for doctor bills		
Other health insurance premiums		
Medicines		
Dental care		
Life insurance and annuity premiums		
Vacation and travel		
Education expenses		
Savings		
Newspapers, magazines, books		
Personal allowances (including grooming, haircuts)		

FINANCIAL INDEPENDENCE AND PERSONAL SECURITY

Item	Where Money Goes Now	After Retirement
Contributions and gifts	_____	_____
Entertainment (movies, theater, etc.)	_____	_____
Hobbies and sports, club dues	_____	_____
Miscellaneous	_____	_____
TOTAL MONTHLY EXPENSES	_____	_____
TOTAL ANNUAL EXPENSES	_____	_____

As a rule of thumb, many retired couples find that they can live comfortably on roughly two thirds of their preretirement after-tax incomes. You, though, may be able to—or have to—live on less. Or you may want to live on more.

To determine where you stand, the next step is to calculate what your retirement income is likely to be.

How Much Will You Have?

ESTIMATING YOUR RETIREMENT INCOME

Before estimating your retirement income, you have to estimate the age at which you will decide to—or think you will for some reason be ready to—retire.

What comes next will involve some arithmetic and paperwork, but this should not be difficult. The task is to make a list of all the sources from which you can anticipate retirement income.

• You can learn what you can expect in the way of Social Security benefits —most likely, the cornerstone of your retirement income program—in the section in this chapter called "What You Should Know About Social Security."

• Add to your expected Social Security benefits the amount of monthly income you can expect from your life insurance policies; annuities; and your company, union, or other pension program. These also are described in the sections that follow.

• Check such other key retirement income sources as cash savings, stocks, bonds, real estate. They are discussed in detail in various other chapters.

• Conservatively estimate the income you might get if you sold valuable assets you now own—art, stamp collections, your home, etc.—and reinvested the proceeds in various ways.

• Also very conservatively estimate what income you might get from a part-time job or business you are looking forward to having in retirement.

Just listing all these sources of income on the work sheet that follows will give you an idea of your expected total income. And that, along with what you have already estimated will be your future living needs, will give you a guide to how much more retirement income you should now be building to provide you with a comfortable standard of living later on.

Your Estimated Income

	MONTHLY	ANNUALLY
Social Security benefits (you and your spouse)	_____	_____
Private pension	_____	_____
Veteran's pension (if any)	_____	_____
Any other military, civil service, or railroad retirement benefits	_____	_____
Deferred profit sharing	_____	_____
Income from annuities	_____	_____
Income from investment of life insurance cash value	_____	_____
Dividends from investments	_____	_____
Interest from savings accounts	_____	_____
Interest from bonds	_____	_____
Capital gains from investments	_____	_____
Income from property (e.g., rent)	_____	_____
Payments on mortgages you hold	_____	_____
Investment of capital from home sale	_____	_____
Earnings from part-time job or self-employment	_____	_____
Income from a business	_____	_____
Other income from *any* source	_____	_____
TOTAL	_____	_____

PLANNING FOR YOUR PENSION

You are no more than normal if you shrink from the thought of growing old and shrink still further from the question of how you will be taken care of once you retire.

Most Americans simply assume that they will manage. They will get by, somehow they will be provided for. Why else have they been contributing to Social Security all these years? They assume, often unquestioningly, that the money taken out of their paychecks for a private pension plan will be returned to them at retirement.

The stark truth of the matter is that most of us can expect a dramatic drop in our incomes when we retire. Those without substantial savings, other assets, or family support well may face destitution.

Here are some of the reasons why:
- Less than half of the private work force is now covered by a private pension plan.
- Even among those who are covered, an estimated one third will never receive any payout from their pension plan. They won't work long or continuously enough to qualify. They may die before they collect. Or the plan might stop.
- But even if you should be lucky enough to receive a pension, the chances are it will not amount to much. In 1975, people sixty-five years old and over received private pensions that typically amounted to less than $200 a month. With Social Security payments to sixty-five-year-old workers retiring in 1979 averaging around $265 a month for individuals and $400 a month for couples, your prospects for a comfortable retirement aren't great.
- Your private pension benefits probably will not rise with the cost of living but will be fixed as of the date you retire and leave the plan. Increases in the benefits of retirees are generally not issues in collective bargaining, although employers sometimes voluntarily increase them.
- Not all pension plans are insured by the government insurance corporation, called the Pension Benefit Guarantee Corporation. Only plans under which you are promised a certain benefit (so-called "defined benefit" plans) are covered, and not all of them are covered. Plans financed by union dues are not covered. Neither are those with fewer than twenty-five employees set up by such professionals as doctors, lawyers, and performing artists.
- Even though your plan may be insured, not all of the benefits which you have been promised are covered by the government program.

By and large, pensions operate like insurance policies. Everyone pays in to protect themselves, but only a few ever draw benefits. The trouble with this model—trouble for you, the 40 million workers covered by private industry plans—is that while there is a chance you won't crack up the car or lose your house in a fire, you *will* get old, you *will* stop working, and you and your spouse will need a retirement income.

Take the time now, before you stare retirement in the face, to find out from your employer, plan administrator, or possibly your union the answers to these questions: How long do you have to work to qualify for a pension? If you leave the job for any reason and for any length of time, will you still get a pension? What size pension will you draw when you retire?

WORKING TO QUALIFY

You no longer must work a lifetime to earn the right to a pension—but by no means can you qualify for a pension overnight. On the contrary, first you must be covered by a plan; then if you are covered, you gain the right to a pension only after a substantial amount of time on the job. The requirements vary, and some plans are better, but most plans that promise workers a specific benefit require that they put in ten years with an employer contributing to the plan before they qualify for benefits.

Accumulating a decade of service with a single employer isn't easy today in view of the high mobility of the U.S. labor force. Labor Department figures in the early 1970s disclosed that only one out of four workers kept the same job continuously for ten years or more.

You should also know that if yours is a typical plan, there's a good chance that not all of your work for an employer will count toward the ten years you need to qualify for a pension. For example, your plan may not count early years on the job. Or if you were laid off or quit for a period, the years before your "break in service" won't count. Then too, if you start working under a plan when you are older, usually age sixty or above, none of your years may count.

To determine your chances of receiving a pension, find out if you are covered by your firm's plan. If so, how long do you have to work before qualifying to receive benefits? Will all your years of work count toward your pension? If you leave the job for any reason and for any length of time, how will your absence affect your chances of earning a right to a pension? Also find out what to do to collect your benefits if you leave your job before retirement age. What must you do before you retire to apply for your benefits? Try, if possible, to get the answers to these questions in writing from your plan administrator, boss, or possibly your union.

THE SIZE OF YOUR PENSION

What benefits does your plan promise you if you work until official retirement age? Quit? Get laid off or fired tomorrow? How is the amount of your benefit determined?

Most workers are covered by plans which pay benefits based on the number of years you are covered by the plan (which may not be the same as the number of years you have worked). These years are multiplied by a percentage of your salary during a particular year, or a percentage of your total average earnings, or a percentage of your earnings during the five years just before retirement to figure out your pension benefit.

Say you worked for ten years under a plan that provides benefits equal to 1 per cent of your final salary for each year of service that you had. If your final paycheck totaled $10,000 a year, your basic pension at age sixty-five would be about $83 a month or $1,000 a year.

But what if you retire early? Will you get any pension benefits and how much will they amount to? What if you are married and want your widow or widower to get a benefit? In both these situations your pension will be reduced. The reduction may be substantial. You should also check to see whether any benefits are paid if you are disabled.

One of the most important things you should find out is whether your plan

FINANCIAL INDEPENDENCE AND PERSONAL SECURITY 1003

is "integrated" with Social Security. Currently, firms with private plans may "integrate" or count part of your Social Security benefit when figuring out how much you will receive from your private plan.

Say your firm decides that your plan should provide an "integrated" benefit of 1½ per cent of your final average pay. You are an employee who has always earned the average wage, which in 1978 amounted to about $10,500 a year. If you worked for twenty years under this plan, your basic pension benefit would be about $3,000 a year.

If you retired in 1979 at age sixty-five and were single, your Social Security benefit could equal $5,000 a year. In figuring how much you'd receive in pension benefits, your firm might subtract 50 per cent (or more) of your Social Security benefit or $2,500 from $3,000. Thus, in this instance you'd retire with a yearly pension from your firm of only $500 or about $42 a month. If you had worked for fifteen years or less for the company, you'd get nothing from the plan. Your entire retirement income would come from your $5,000-a-year Social Security benefit.

In short, "integration" means lower-paid workers get less from their private pension plans than do higher-paid workers. The system is complicated and varies from plan to plan. Some are better for workers than others. If your plan is integrated, learn what this means in dollars and cents for you once you retire.

Ask how many employees in your company or division are slated to receive pensions. Ask what are the typical amounts which workers like you receive. Inquire if the plan has any provisions to hike postretirement benefits along with rises in the cost of living.

In addition, find out what size benefit—if any—you can reasonably expect to receive if your firm fails, changes owners or your plan terminates.

YOUR SURVIVING SPOUSE

Most of you working and covered by private pension plans believe that once you gain a right to a pension, it will automatically go to your widow, or widower, on your death. This is not the case. The pension system and the law do not consider an employee's pension joint property but view it as belonging to the employee alone.

When you retire, for instance, your pension will in most cases be automatically reduced so your surviving spouse can continue to get at least half of your benefits when you die. (You can sign a form stipulating that you don't want or cannot afford such a reduction. The size of any reduction depends on your age, your spouse's age and the details of your particular plan.)

Find out how much of a pension cut you must agree to accept if you elect this so-called "survivor's option." And if you die after you retire, how much will your surviving spouse receive? For how many years?

If you are still working and not ready to retire, yet you want to make sure your spouse gets some of your pension should you die, you can (under certain circumstances) opt early for a surviving spouse reduction. Find out how old you must be to take advantage of this chance to provide for your spouse. What if you were to die before this point or shortly after electing this option? Would your spouse receive anything, and if so what?

Since an employee's pension is viewed as his alone, there is little which gives a woman whose marriage breaks up any claim on her ex-husband's pension. However, in some states with community property laws, such as California, divorcées have been awarded a portion of future benefits.

Under Internal Revenue Service regulations, pension plans *may* require a spouse to have been married for one year on both the date her husband began to draw his reduced benefits and the date of his death. This rule, in effect, could make it impossible for a divorcée ever to collect a benefit even though her ex-husband opted for a reduction in his benefits in order to help provide for her.

Also, a divorced pensioner who wants to provide for his second wife could not do so, because they would not have been married when he began to collect his pension benefits.

Under the law, a retired worker whose spouse dies before him cannot reverse the reduction in his benefit and reclaim the full amount of his pension. Of course, some plans provide more than the law's minimum standards.

Find out what your plan provides for your spouse. Ask, too, about preretirement survivor's benefits, death or burial benefits or group term life insurance.

YOUR PENSION RIGHTS

Under the 1974 pension reform law, formally called the Employee Retirement Income Security Act (ERISA), all pension plan participants have these basic rights:

• To receive booklets giving you an explanation of your plan in "easy to understand" language. If you do not receive such a summary plan booklet, ask your plan administrator or employer for one. If you find that it is written in a way that is too complicated for you to understand, complain to the nearest office of the U. S. Department of Labor. Even if your plan seems simple enough, watch out for misleading language. "Eligibility" provisions, for instance, generally only tell you whether or not you are covered by a plan, not whether you are "eligible" to receive benefits. Too, the booklets often emphasize the terms and conditions under which you *will* receive a pension. They tend to downplay the circumstances under which you *won't* get a pension.

These booklets are *not* the final word on your plan. Many contain a disclaimer that says if there are any discrepancies between the language in the booklet and the plan's legal documents on file at the main plan office, you cannot rely on the booklet. The plan documents, not the booklet, prevail. Ask questions and insist on getting the answers in writing.

• To learn while you are working under the plan whether you are entitled to a pension. You have a right to learn how much you can expect to get and when. Make this request to your plan administrator. Make it in writing. You may obtain this information once a year.

• To be given a statement once you have earned the right to a pension and stopped working that tells you the amount you will receive. When you apply for your Social Security benefits (see pages 1013–15), you will get a copy of this statement that will tell you how much you can expect to get at normal retirement age, usually sixty-five. It will *not* indicate by how much that amount will be reduced if you retire before that point or if you are married. When you reach retirement age, it will still be up to you to go back to your company and apply for your pension.

• To be told where your pension money is being invested, how well and by whom. You will receive a summary of this information annually. But if you want to know more details about how your pension funds are being invested, you have to ask, in writing, for a copy of your plan's full Annual Report. If you believe that your plan's funds are being invested in risky or improper ways, contact the U. S. Labor Department. (See Chapter 29, "How and Where to Get Help.")

• To go to court, if you believe that you have been fired or discriminated against so the plan will not have to pay you your pension.

• To be told the reason why a plan has decided not to give you a pension. If you believe that your claim for a pension was unfairly denied, you should ask the plan to review its decision. If that fails, you may sue in state or federal court.

HELP UNDERSTANDING PENSIONS

Pensions, in general, and individual pension plans, in particular, are complicated. Even pension lawyers and actuaries whose business it is to be experts argue endlessly over the meanings of various clauses in the pension law and their own plans. Don't be discouraged or put off if your own investigation into how your plan operates takes time and study.

There are a number of books and pamphlets, besides your own plan's summary booklet, that can help you. Here are a few of them:

• *Pension Facts*. The Pension Rights Center, a non-profit public-interest group specializing in pension matters, publishes a series of clear, simple fact sheets. *Pension Facts #1* explains what the 1974 pension reform law does and does not do for workers. *Pension Facts #2* focuses on women, the group most disadvantaged by the private pension system. You can obtain these fact sheets for 25 cents each by sending a self-addressed stamped envelope for each copy to the Center, Room 1019, 1346 Connecticut Avenue N.W., Washington, D.C. 20036.

• *You and Your Pension.* This book by Ralph Nader and Kate Blackwell is a comprehensive description of how the private pension system works. Although it was written before the 1974 reform law was passed, it can give you good background material. It is available in bookstores (the publisher is Grossman, 1973) or for $1.00 from the Pension Rights Center.

• *What You Should Know About the Pension and Welfare Law* and *Often Asked Questions About the Employee Retirement Income Security Act of 1974* are two of several publications put out by the Labor Department. They are dry and rather technical but worth consulting. You can get them free through your local Labor Department office or by writing the Office of Procurement, Labor-Management Services Administration, U. S. Department of Labor, 200 Constitution Avenue N.W., Washington, D.C. 20216.

SIMPLIFIED PENSION PLANS

If your employer has no pension plan, partly because of the hassle and cost of administering one, you might suggest he (or she) investigate Simplified Pension Plans. The product of the Tax Reform Act of 1978, they are a great way to avoid ERISA paperwork.

Here's how the simplified plans work:

The employer makes contributions to an Individual Retirement Account in the employee's name. (See pages 1008–10 for more on IRAs.) The maximum contribution is 15 per cent of the employee's pay, up to $7,500 a year. This is a big jump up from the $1,500 a year maximum that an individual can contribute on behalf of himself to an IRA.

The employer can deduct the full amount of the IRA contribution from the firm's taxes as long as the pension plan qualifies as non-discriminatory. This means it must cover all employees twenty-five and over who have worked for the firm in any three of the past five years, including part-timers. The plan may not favor owners or top management; it must contribute the same percentage of everybody's pay.

The employee does not have to pay income tax on what his firm contributes. And when it amounts to less than $1,500, the employee can add the difference to his IRA account and take that figure as a deduction.

A big advantage for employees is that with these simplified plans you are fully vested at once, that is, qualify for benefits. In traditional plans, an employee who leaves before he vests forfeits his pension benefits. The sum the firm contributed on his behalf remains in the fund and is used to pay the pensions of those workers who stay. In this way, employees who leave reduce an employer's future contributions to the plan.

Despite this advantage, employees should be aware that there is a disadvantage to simplified plans. As with regular pension plans, it is possible for employers to contribute a higher percentage of pay for higher-salaried staff. They may do this by deducting Social Security taxes from the amount contributed to an IRA. (See discussion of "integration," pages 1002–3.)

The result might look like this:

	$10,000 Salary/Yr.	$60,000
Firm contributes 8 per cent of salary to IRA:	$800	$4,800
Minus: Social Security tax (1979)	613	1,404
Contribution	$187	$3,396
IRA contribution as per cent of pay	1.9%	5.8%

A SAFETY NET UNDER YOUR PENSION

Before the Pension Benefit Guaranty Corporation (PBGC) was established in 1974, it was just too bad for you, a worker covered by a private pension plan, if the benefits you were counting on for your retirement were wiped out because your plan went broke.

Today, the PBGC acts as a government safety net beneath the pension plan system. It protects covered workers in the same way the Federal Deposit Insurance Corporation protects bank depositors in the event their bank fails.

For the many workers whose plans have ended and especially for those whose plans did not have enough assets to cover their obligations, the guarantees the PBGC offers are vitally important.

You should realize, however, that the PBGC does not insure all types of private plans, only those called "defined benefit plans." Under these, an employer promises that once you retire, he will pay you certain fixed benefits based on the length of time you have worked.

Even with this type of plan, once the PBGC takes a plan over it is quite possible that your benefits will be reduced. The agency only protects what it terms "basic non-forfeitable benefits"—normal retirement annuities, certain early retirement benefits, disability benefits, and pensions for survivors. Generally severance pay, medical benefits, and life insurance are not included. There are limits, too, on the total non-forfeitable benefits that the PBGC can insure. If, for example, your plan folded in 1979 without sufficient assets, the maximum guaranteed benefits coming to you at age sixty-five would not exceed (1) your highest average salary for a consecutive five-year period or (2) $1,073 per month, whichever is less.

To find out if your plan is insured by the PBGC look at your summary plan description booklet that all plans are required to distribute. If yours is a plan paid for by union dues or if you are one of twenty-five or fewer employees covered by a plan set up by doctors, lawyers, architects, or similar professionals, it will not be insured. If you belong to a plan to which more than one employer contributes it is slated to become insured in July 1979, but this date may be pushed back.

Also, remember that if your plan stops before you have worked long enough to earn a right to a pension, your benefit will not be guaranteed. For more information about the PBGC's insurance program, write to its Office of Communications, 2020 K Street N.W., Washington, D.C. 20006, or call (202) 254-4817.

Getting the Retirement Income You Need

Whether the estimated retirement income you arrive at will be adequate will depend, of course, on your needs. If it is not adequate, several options are open to you.

One, obviously, is to do without certain things in your original retirement plan. Another is to beef up your income. Assuming you choose the second option, there are three stages in planning to get the retirement income you need.

(1) Accumulate as many resources as possible during your preretirement years. You can stint on some living expenses in this period in order to put more aside in savings accounts, mutual funds, growth stocks, high-grade bonds, or any of the other mediums analyzed in this book (see Contents).

(2) Use part of your current income and nest egg to buy an income for your retirement years. This income could come from life insurance, an annuity, or income-producing real estate.

(3) Plan on periodically withdrawing a portion of the capital in your nest egg during your retirement.

Also be alert to proposals in Congress that can help improve your retirement income situation—and make your views known.

Don't Miss Out on Keogh or IRA Plan

Q. *Why do so many millions of you fail to take advantage of superb tax shelter plans approved by the U. S. Government and specifically designed to help you accumulate money for your older years?*

Could it be that you simply don't know enough about the plans to establish them? Or that you don't know where to turn to get help? Or that it's just too much trouble to move on your own to benefit yourself?

Yet the facts are that the benefits you can derive from setting up one of the two types of tax-sheltered retirement plans created for you (Keogh or Individual Retirement Account) are both immediate and long-term; the earlier you arrange to participate the better off you and your family will be;

and despite any of your concern about complexities, the procedures really are easy.

More specifically:

• The most immediate benefit you will realize from establishing a tax shelter for your retirement is on the contribution you make to the plan. That money goes directly into the plan and is freed from current income taxes.

To show how significant this can be:

If you are only in the 19 per cent income tax bracket and can contribute $750, you will save $143. Putting it another way, you will be able to invest an additional $143 a year toward your retirement nest egg.

If you are in the 50 per cent tax bracket, and you can contribute $7,500, your tax savings jump to $3,750 each year.

Another extremely important benefit of these tax shelters is that the money you put aside under the shelter grows tax-free. You pay no taxes on the dividends, interest, or capital gains earned during the years your funds are under the shelter.

Again, merely to suggest the significance of this, if you are an individual in the 50 per cent bracket and you contribute $7,500 a year for thirty years to a tax-sheltered account compounding quarterly at 5 per cent (a cinch to arrange), you will have $362,834 more for your retirement years than you would have had if you hadn't bothered to create a tax shelter. Quite a difference, yes?

• How big the difference will be will vary according to the number of years you have a plan until your retirement, the amount of money you contribute each year, the return you are able to get on your investment, and the tax bracket you are in each year.

And as your income moves up and you shift into a higher tax bracket (even if inflation robs you of the increased buying power of your extra dollars), the benefits of your tax shelter grow.

If you are self-employed, whether full time or part time, you should consider a Keogh plan, under which, at the end of the 1970s, you could set aside each year $7,500 or 15 per cent of your self-employed income, whichever was less. Your contribution into a Keogh plan is tax-deductible. There are no estate taxes on a Keogh plan if it is paid to your beneficiary over two or more taxable years.

You can start to collect your Keogh funds at age fifty-nine and a half, or earlier if you are disabled and cannot continue to work. You must start withdrawals by seventy and a half years of age, even though contributions can continue as long as you have earned income. And the money in your plan is not attachable if you suffer personal bankruptcy.

If you are an employee not covered by a company, government, or union-sponsored plan, an Individual Retirement Account (IRA) is for you. With an IRA, you could at the end of the 1970s set aside 15 per cent or a maximum of $1,500 of your annual earnings—and if you use a marital IRA to provide IRA benefits to your non-working spouse, you could set aside up to $1,750 or 15 per cent of your income each year, divided equally between you and your spouse. The deadline for establishing a new IRA or for making contributions to an existing IRA as of the late 1970s was February 14. Other provisions are generally similar to Keogh.

For a good free *Guide to Retirement Planning,* outlining details on Keogh and IRA, write Lord, Abbott & Co., *Retirement,* P. O. Box 666, Wall Street Station, New York, New York 10005. Also excellent is *A Shopper's Guide to IRAs and Keogh Plans: Choosing a New Plan and Evaluating the One You Have,* available for $2.25 from N.R.O.C.A. Press, Box 12066, Dallas, Texas 75225.

How Long Will Your Retirement Capital Last?

How long will your nest egg last? That will depend on the rate of return it is earning and the amount you withdraw each year. Conceivably, your fund could last indefinitely, as the following chart indicates.

If you retire with a nest egg of $100,000, you can make it last for one decade, two, three, or even longer. Just how long will be determined by the rate of return on your capital and the amount you withdraw for living expenses each year. Suppose, for example, you need $9,000 a year and your fund is earning a 7 per cent return; then your money will last twenty-two years. If your return equals or exceeds your withdrawals your fund will last indefinitely, as indicated by the symbol ∞. (Always keep in mind that the dollars will buy less in the market place than they are buying as you read this.)

ANNUAL WITHDRAWAL	YEARS YOUR FUND WILL LAST AT THESE ANNUAL RATES OF RETURN*					
	5%	6%	7%	8%	9%	10%
$ 6,000	36	∞	∞	∞	∞	∞
7,000	25	33	∞	∞	∞	∞
8,000	20	23	30	∞	∞	∞
9,000	16	18	22	28	∞	∞
10,000	14	15	17	20	26	∞
11,000	12	13	14	16	19	25
12,000	11	11	12	14	15	18

*Copyright 1971 by Medical Economics Company, Oradell, N.J. 07649. Reprinted by permission.

Of course, if your nest egg amounts to just $50,000, you simply cut the annual withdrawal amounts in half and your money will last the same number of years shown in the chart.

What You Should Know About Social Security— Foundation of Your Retirement Program

A BASIC PROBLEM

Over decades of amendments, the Social Security law has become exceedingly complex, but the basic concept of Social Security remains simple. It is this: During your working years, you (employees, employers, and the self-employed) pay Social Security taxes—a percentage of earnings into trust funds. Then, in retirement, or in case of death or disability, payments are made from the funds to you, the worker and your dependents, or to your survivors.

The trust funds are not like a savings bank, with paid-in dollars held for you and returned on retirement with interest added. That kind of arrangement would require so huge a buildup of funds that the whole economy would be dislocated. And such a buildup isn't necessary in a government system that has continuity and can count on future generations of workers to contribute.

Instead, taxes are intended to bring in each year funds to pay benefits to those now on benefit rolls and to create just enough reserves to take care of contingencies. In effect, it's a pay-as-you-go system.

Collection of SS taxes began in January 1937, with the first monthly benefits paid in January 1940. From then until the mid-1970s—a span of almost forty years—the SS program was self-supporting. In almost every year until 1975, the system collected more than it paid out in benefits. The excess was invested in interest-bearing U.S. securities and the interest was added to the trust funds—separate funds maintained in the U. S. Treasury. Billions had been accumulated in the two cash benefit trust funds by the mid-1970s.

But starting in 1974, unemployment side by side with inflation wiped out huge totals. Part of the shrinkage in reserves was due to lost SS taxes that would otherwise have been collected had jobless and underemployed workers been getting paychecks. Part was due to galloping inflation; benefits to the millions on the rolls are automatically hiked to keep up with the cost of living and every 1 per cent increase in the inflation rate swells the annual benefit payout by hundreds of millions. In addition, all benefit payments in the future will be permanently higher because of past inflation and because the interest earnings lost by the trust funds due to shrunken reserves cannot be regained.

Had the jobless rate, instead of soaring, as it did, risen to no more than 5 per cent in that period, a Social Security Administration study shows, the cash benefits trusts funds would have grown by $25 billion between 1975 and 1981, instead of dwindling!

LONGER-RANGE PROBLEM, TOO

There was a longer-range financing problem, too, which would not even have hit until after the year 2000, assuming Congress did nothing to avert it. Congress did act, though, in its 1977 amendments. The two causes:

(1) A fluke in the benefit formula written into the law in 1972 which could have resulted in a large number of retirees in the twenty-first century receiving benefits higher than the top wages they had ever earned.

(2) The assumption that there will be a continued drop in U.S. birth and fertility rates.

In 1972, the law was amended to provide for automatic adjustment of benefits if and as prices rose moderately from year to year. (There was no anticipation of 1973-75's nightmare inflation!) The 1972 law additionally provides for the maximum taxable earnings under Social Security to rise as average wages rise from year to year.

But if you assume an indefinite continuation of a murderously steep rate of inflation, a strange situation would have resulted from the operation of these two provisions: benefits would run way ahead of wages and of the system's taxes from wages. This situation accounted for about half of the estimated long-range actuarial deficit of the system. (The 1977 amendments erased that problem.)

The other half of the projected deficit is based on that assumption about birth and fertility. If rates do continue dropping, there would, in the year 2010, be close to thirty Americans sixty-five and over for every 100 of working age. As the 1980s near, the proportion is 18.3 people 65 and over for every 100 of working age.

Predicting birth and fertility rates is risky—but even if these assumptions turn out to be accurate, there are offsetting factors. For instance, if the public cost of supporting the elderly went up, the cost of supporting and educating the young would be reduced. If fewer women were busy rearing children, more would be in the labor market and paying SS taxes. If fewer young people were entering the labor market, more elderly people could find jobs.

SOLUTIONS

Among the ways to provide additional financing for the Social Security programs are:

(1) Increase the SS tax rate and/or the SS taxable wage base substantially.

Under the law, the wage base goes up as average wages rise. Before 1979, only about 15 per cent of all workers had earnings above the wage base.

So, when and as the wage base is boosted, only higher earners and their employers are affected. If the tax rate is hiked, all workers—low as well as high income—are hit.

(2) General federal revenues can be drawn upon. Or provision can be made for other new sources of revenue—for instance, an earmarked tax on cigarettes or liquor, a value-added tax, or a surcharge on the income tax.

(3) Adding more workers to the SS rolls so more will be paying SS taxes is another way to increase revenues. However, nine out of every ten jobs already are covered by Social Security.

(4) As a last resort, benefits could be reduced, although no one ever has suggested reductions for those already on the benefit rolls. But there have been proposals for cutting back on some so-called fringe benefits and for lowering the "replacement rate" for workers retiring in the future. The "replacement rate" is the ratio of Social Security benefits to earnings just before retirement of the individual.

(5) And of course, there could be many combinations of all these elements.

SOCIAL SECURITY AMENDMENTS HAVE PUT PROGRAM ON SOUND FOOTING

Each of these options has its advantages and disadvantages, of course. Congress, in December of 1977, corrected the fluke in the benefit formula that had contributed in part to the long-range financing problem. In addition, it provided for the infusion of funds to meet the short-range deficit—financing that will be enough to pay all benefits as they fall due over the next fifty years at least.

The size of the payroll tax scheduled in the law has been spectacularly increased; further increases well may cause a nationwide rebellion—and are definitely "iffy," as a result.

In addition, the maximum amount of earnings to which the tax applies is now geared to go up much more than in previous law. This so-called "wage base" is scheduled to rise under the 1977 amendments to such a degree that it, too, may undergo major revision. These tax and wage base increases will have their strongest impact on employees at the middle-upper-income levels, increasing their Social Security tax contributions substantially. Employers who will be matching the employees' contributions are also affected. Public reaction to reports of these increases in the tax rates and wage base has been, I repeat, predictably strong. Overlooked has been the fact that those who would be paying more would be getting more.

BENEFITS WILL BE KEPT UP-TO-DATE WITH PRICES AND LEVEL OF LIVING

In the past, Social Security benefits had been based on a worker's average earnings over his working lifetime, counting in the years at the beginning of his career when his earnings were low and also disregarding any earnings in excess of the wage base that he might have had in any particular year.

But if you are working under Social Security today, you are not paying toward benefits of the level being paid today. Your benefits will be based on your lifetime wage *updated* to reflect the level of living at the time you retire, become disabled, or die. If, for example, you are in your forties and earning an average wage of around $10,000 a year, you will qualify for a Social Security benefit of around $15,000 when you retire at age sixty-five. Your wife (or husband) will get an additional $7,500 based on your record of earnings.

Workers who pay Social Security taxes on the maximum amount of earnings that counts toward Social Security can look forward to benefits of about $21,000 a year—over $30,000 for a couple. This compares to the $6,036 payable to a worker attaining age sixty-five in 1979 after earning the maximum, or the $6,624 maximum payable to a worker reaching age sixty-five and retiring in 1980. People under forty will get even higher benefits. Once on the benefit rolls, your benefits will be kept up-to-date with the cost of living.

You therefore can be sure that your Social Security retirement protection and also your disability and survivor's protection will rise as the cost of living and the standard of living go up.

The chart below shows the benefits payable upon retirement at age sixty-five to workers of low, average, and maximum earnings under Social Security. The benefits payable to workers who become disabled and to the dependents and survivors of workers are similarly improved.

If you are over fifty-six years of age, you can ask the Social Security Administration to check your Social Security record and give you an estimate of what your monthly benefits would be at age sixty-two and at age sixty-five. Just ask your nearest Social Security office for a copy of a preaddressed postcard—No. 7004. When you get it, fill it in and add the words "Benefit Estimate" at the top. Put a stamp on it and mail it. You will receive the estimates directly from Social Security Administration headquarters in about six weeks.

Social Security is much more than a retirement program.

It provides benefits for your dependents while you are on the benefit rolls as a retired or disabled worker, and if you die, it pays benefits to your survivors to help replace your earnings.

It also helps with hospital and medical expenses when you reach sixty-five or are disabled.

Most Americans, including young workers, just starting out, can expect to collect more in Social Security benefits than they paid in taxes.

Projected Benefits for Persons Retiring at Age 65

Calendar Year of Retirement	Earnings in Previous Year* LOW	AVERAGE	MAXIMUM	Annual Benefit Amount for Workers with Following Earnings LOW	AVERAGE	MAXIMUM
1979	$ 5,271	$10,572	$17,700	$3,142	$ 4,932	$ 6,165
1980	5,682	11,396	22,900	3,375	5,315	6,699
1981	6,085	12,205	25,900	3,635	5,740	7,257
1982	6,475	12,986	29,700	3,485	5,438	6,809
1983	6,863	13,766	31,800	3,607	5,643	7,257
1984	7,258	14,557	33,900	3,841	6,010	7,798
1985	7,675	15,394	36,000	4,099	6,409	8,390
1990	10,150	20,359	47,700	5,451	8,519	11,509
1995	13,424	26,925	63,000	7,198	11,243	15,605
2000	17,753	35,609	83,400	9,519	14,870	21,427

*Low earnings are defined as $4,600 in 1976. Average earnings are $9,266 in 1976. Maximum earnings are defined as the top wages subject to Social Security taxes in a particular year. In each case it is assumed that the worker has had an unbroken pattern of earnings at the relative level indicated. The following increases in wages were assumed: 1977, 5.99 per cent; 1978, 8.10 per cent; 1979, 7.80 per cent; 1980, 7.10 per cent; 1981, 6.40 per cent; 1982, 6.00 per cent; 1983 and later, 5.75 per cent.

HOW MUCH YOU WILL GET AS A RETIREE OR DEPENDENT

• If you retire at sixty-two, your benefit amount will be reduced by 20 per cent to take account of the extra three years during which you will be receiving payments. The closer you are to sixty-five when you take your benefits, the smaller the reduction. At age sixty-three, for example, you could collect 86⅔ of your full benefit, and at age sixty-four, 93⅓ per cent. On the other hand, if you defer your retirement until after age sixty-five, you get an increase in your benefit amount—3 per cent for each year between sixty-five and seventy-two. So, if you work on until age seventy, you will get a benefit at least 15 per cent higher than if you had retired at age sixty-five.

• When you become entitled to Social Security benefits, your wife can collect benefits equal to 50 per cent of yours if she is sixty-five, or somewhat lower benefits as early as age sixty-two. (If the wife, because of her own earnings, is entitled to an amount more than 50 per cent of her husband's benefit, she gets the bigger benefit.)

• Your wife also can collect that extra 50 per cent if she is younger, if she has in her care dependent children under eighteen (or over eighteen, but disabled before age twenty-two).

Each unmarried child under eighteen (or over eighteen, but disabled) or a full-time student eighteen to twenty-two also is eligible for a benefit equal to

50 per cent of your full benefit. The maximum amount of benefits payable to a family is limited, however. In 1978, the maximum payable to the family of a man retiring at sixty-five was $880.70.

• As of the late 1970s, a special minimum payment for certain low earnings retirees who had thirty years or more of Social Security coverage was $230 a month; with twenty-five years of coverage, the special minimum was $172.50 a month. It will rise as cost of living rises after 1979.

The 1977 amendments made several other improvements in Social Security of which you should be aware.

(1) A raise in benefits, effective 1979, for 130,000 remarried widows. The result: a mounting number of marriages between elderly couples who have been living as "mingling singles" because marriage would cut their combined SS benefits.

Widows on the SS benefit rolls who remarried after age sixty had their monthly payments increased to the rate that would have been payable to them if they had not remarried. A widow sixty or over gets SS benefits equal to 71.5 per cent to 100 per cent of her deceased husband's SS benefit amount. The closer she was to sixty-five at the time she first took her benefits, the higher the percentage. But a wife gets benefits equal to one half her husband's Social Security benefit amount if she is sixty-five or older and a reduced amount if she is sixty-two to sixty-five at the time.

Under the old law, when a woman who had been receiving benefits as a widow remarried, she became a wife and therefore eligible for the smaller percentage although she had perhaps been receiving 100 per cent of her deceased husband's benefit as a widow beneficiary.

About 130,000 remarried widows on the Social Security benefit rolls in 1977 are known to have had their benefits reduced upon their remarriage. Other elderly widows, it also was known, had decided to forgo a marriage ceremony to avoid a cut in their SS benefits.

For the first group—the remarried widows—benefits were hiked starting January 1979 to the rate that would have been payable if they had not remarried. For widows sixty or over who remarried in 1979 or later, there will be no slash in benefits.

(2) If you're a remarried widower, you also became eligible for the restoration of your benefit rates in January 1979. But since most of you get benefits based on your own higher earnings records, remarriage has been less likely to force a cut in your payments.

(3) Another change in the law makes it possible for women, divorced after at least 10 years of marriage, to qualify for benefits at retirement age —either as divorced wives, or if their former husband has died, as surviving divorced wives. Until 1979 if you were a woman divorced before your marriage had lasted a full twenty years, you lost all rights to benefits based on your former husband's SS earnings record.

If you are an eligible divorced wife, you can begin collecting benefits when

FINANCIAL INDEPENDENCE AND PERSONAL SECURITY

you are sixty-two. If you are an eligible surviving divorced wife, you can collect your benefits as early as age sixty.

If you are any divorced woman and you think you may be eligible for benefits under this provision, immediately contact your local Social Security office, so that you will not lose any of the benefits that are payable to you.

(4) Still another significant 1977 benefit improvement that is likely to be overlooked provides you with an added incentive to continue working past sixty-five. That was Congress' stated purpose.

Beginning in 1972, workers who delayed their retirement past age sixty-five earned a delayed retirement credit of 1 per cent per year (1/12 of 1 per cent per month). That credit was upped to 3 per cent a year for workers who reached sixty-five in January 1979 or later. The credits build up at the rate of ¼ of 1 per cent for each month that a worker between sixty-five and seventy-two does not collect Social Security benefits because he or she is still working.

The 1977 amendments also will give you, the surviving widow or widower, the benefit of any delayed retirement credits the worker has earned. Under previous law, the delayed retirement credits served to increase only the worker's own retirement benefit.

As Robert M. Ball, former commissioner of Social Security, noted: "The changes fit in with the need in the next century to have more people work past sixty-five and the need to have Social Security financing benefit from this additional employment of older people."

OTHER SOCIAL SECURITY BENEFITS

In addition to retirement benefits, monthly allowances will go to your survivors in the event of your death. You and certain members of your family also can collect important benefits if you become disabled. Or, if your income is very limited, you may qualify for benefits under the supplemental security income program. To illustrate the survivors' benefits:

• A widow who was first entitled to benefits at age sixty-five can receive a pension equal to the one her deceased husband would be collecting if he were still alive. If a widow begins drawing benefits exactly at age sixty, her allowance will be 71.5 per cent. If she is between sixty and sixty-five, her benefits will be between 71.5 per cent and 100 per cent depending upon how close she is to sixty-five. Widows may not start collecting benefits until they are sixty—unless they are disabled and aged fifty to fifty-nine, or have dependent children.

• A widow or widower under sixty-five caring for a young or disabled child can receive 75 per cent of the deceased spouse's primary benefit amount. Each dependent child, if unmarried, under eighteen (or eighteen to twenty-two if they are full-time students), or disabled before age twenty-two, also may receive 75 per cent of the deceased husband's full benefit, up to the current family maximum allowance.

• Benefits also may be paid to a surviving dependent parent or to a hus-

band aged sixty-two or over or a widower aged sixty or over, or a disabled dependent widow or widower aged fifty or over.
- If you yourself are disabled—that is, suffering from a condition, physical or mental, which is serious enough to prevent you from working for twelve months or more—you can collect a disability benefit while you are under age sixty-five. Your wife and each of your young, dependent, unmarried children also could collect amounts equal to 50 per cent of your benefit, subject to a family maximum.
- Rehabilitation costs and services are available to disabled workers in the form of paid job training, counseling and placement, physical therapy, and money to buy work tools and equipment.
- If you are blind as defined by the law, you can qualify for disability benefits without having to meet the requirement of substantial recent work. Under Social Security regulations, a worker considered "industrially blind"—that is, with the visual acuity of 20-200 or less in the better eye, with corrective lens—is considered totally blind. So is a person whose visual field is limited to 20°.

SUPPLEMENTAL SECURITY INCOME

The federal supplemental security income program (SSI) is designed for aged, blind, and disabled persons with very limited income and resources. It replaces the state-federal programs of Old Age Assistance, Aid to the Blind, and Aid to the Permanently and Totally Disabled. SSI is administered by the Social Security Administration but is financed from general revenues rather than from Social Security trust funds.

The program guarantees a standard, nationwide monthly income floor for eligible individuals. If your present income is below the levels set by the program and you are otherwise eligible you will get a monthly benefit raise to bring your total benefit up to at least these minimums. In some cases, this SSI payment is augmented by an extra state supplement. This extra sum is either paid separately by the state or included in the federal supplement check.

To qualify for SSI benefits, individual beneficiaries may have cash assets of up to $1,500 and, for couples, up to $2,250. You may own your home, household goods and other personal effects, and an automobile—as long as these are only of "reasonable value"—and still qualify. Your relatives' income and assets do *not* count as yours; your eligibility for SSI benefits is determined without regard for their assets. If, however, you are married to an ineligible spouse, his or her possessions *do* count as yours. If you think you —or a relative or friend—may be eligible, contact your nearest Social Security office.

WHO IS ELIGIBLE FOR SOCIAL SECURITY?

You qualify if you work or have worked a required length of time at any job which is covered by the Social Security law—and that now includes most jobs. You also may qualify if you're self-employed. Railroad workers are, in effect, jointly covered by Social Security and their own separate retirement system. Most federal civilian employees, those who are covered by the civil service retirement program or other staff retirement systems, are not covered by Social Security, although there is mounting discussion of merging their separate retirement systems with SS. Other occupations (such as farm labor, domestic employment, and state and local government employment) and some types of earnings (such as tips and wages in kind) may be affected by special provisions of the law.

If you're not sure you qualify, inquire at your local Social Security office.

YOUR WORK CREDITS

To qualify for benefits, you also must build up a certain number of work credits. You get credit for a "quarter of coverage"—for each $260 in 1979 in covered annual earnings—up to a total of four quarters in a year.

If you're self-employed, you need net earnings from self-employment of at least $400 in a year before you can get credit for any quarters. Military service during the World War II and postwar periods may give you additional wage credits for each month of active duty.

Note: If you served in the armed forces during 1957–67 or are a survivor of someone who did, and are now getting monthly Social Security benefit checks, contact your Social Security office. You may, under amendments passed in recent years, be eligible for a higher monthly benefit.

In order for your widow and children to be eligible for survivor benefits, you must have at least one and a half years of work credits within three years before your death, unless you already have worked long enough to be fully insured.

To be fully insured so that you and your family are entitled to retirement and all other benefits, you must, depending on your age, have anywhere from six to forty quarters or from one and a half to ten years of work credits, as indicated in the following tables:

FOR WORKERS BORN BEFORE 1929

If you were born before 1929, reach sixty-two, become disabled, or die in	You will need credit for this much work to be fully insured
1979	7
1981	7½
1983	8
1987	9
1991 or later	10

Workers born in 1929 or after will need forty quarters of coverage or ten full years of work in order to be fully insured for retirement benefits. The following chart shows how many years of credit they would need to be fully insured for the payment of all survivors' benefits.

For Workers Born after 1928

If you die when you are	You will be fully insured with credit for this much work
28 or younger	1½ years
30	2
32	2½
34	3
36	3½
38	4
40	4½
42	5
46	6
50	7
54	8
58	9
62 or older	10

Note: A person is fully insured if he has credit for a quarter year of work for each year after 1950 or after the year in which he reached age twenty-one and up to the year he reaches sixty-two, becomes disabled, or dies—whichever event occurs earlier.

To be eligible for disability benefits when you are thirty-one or older, you must be fully insured and must have credit for five years of work in the ten-year period ending with the time you become disabled. If you become disabled between the ages of twenty-four and thirty-one, you need credit for only one half the time between age twenty-one and the time you become unable to work. If disability starts before age twenty-four, you need credit for one and a half years of work in the three-year period before you become disabled.

You should know, too, that you do not automatically receive Social Security benefits as soon as you retire, become disabled, or a working member of your family dies or becomes disabled.

You must apply for these benefits at the nearest Social Security office.

IF YOU WORK IN RETIREMENT

Should there be any limit on how much you, an older person, can earn and still collect your Social Security benefits?

If so, how can a limit be set that will not penalize you if you work—and still be fair to other Social Security beneficiaries and to those of us who are working and paying Social Security taxes to finance the entire system?

These questions have been furiously debated since SS benefits first became payable. Back in 1940, under the so-called Retirement Test then in effect, an older person lost his entire SS benefit for any month in which his wages in work covered by SS amounted to one cent more than $14.99!

The law has been changed many times since, but the Retirement Test still remains—infuriating in its discriminations, inequities, and inconsistencies, unduly complicated by past attempts to improve and liberalize its provisions.

Why is there a Retirement Test?

Because, its defendants claim, the basic purpose of SS retirement benefits is not to pay benefits because you reach a specified age, but rather to replace the earnings you lose when old age cuts off or drastically reduces your earning power. The test was devised to measure whether that loss of earnings has occurred.

You do not have to stop work altogether to collect your benefits. If your earnings after you become eligible for benefits do not go over the "exempt amount" for the year, you get your full benefits for all twelve months.

The "exempt amount" rises each year as average earnings levels under SS go up.

The exempt amount for persons sixty-five or older was $4,500 as the 1970s closed and will rise by $500 steps each year until it reaches $6,000 in 1982 and will rise as the cost of living goes up after that. For retired workers who have taken their benefits before age sixty-five and for the dependents and survivors of workers who are under sixty-five, the exempt amount was set at $3,240 in the late 1970s and will rise over the years in tandem with the automatic cost-of-living adjustments in benefits.

Once you reach seventy-two, you get all your benefits no matter how much you earn. Without this provision (added to the law in the 1950s), those who work for good pay past age sixty-five might never receive any benefits despite their years of SS tax contributions. Beginning in 1982, you will be able to collect all your benefits as early as age seventy, no matter how much you earn.

If as an SS beneficiary under age seventy-two (or under seventy, beginning in 1982), you earn more than the exempt amount, you will lose $1.00 of benefits for every $2.00 by which your earnings for the year exceed the exempt amount.

THE "EDDIE CANTOR" RULE

When Eddie Cantor was invited to the TV spectacular celebrating his sixty-fifth birthday in January 1957, he never dreamed that he would be giving his name to a giant exception to the general rule that you forfeit benefits if your annual earnings exceed a specified total!

For this provision said that no matter how much you earn in a year, you would get your benefit check for any month in which you had wages that amount to no more than 1/12 of the exempt amount and you do not perform substantial services in self-employment.

Eddie Cantor received $2,000 for his appearance on the network broadcast in 1957, well over the exempt amount, which was $1,200 in that year. But since he did not plan to do any other work in 1957, he was eligible to collect his benefits for the remaining months of that year.

Approached by an enterprising U. S. Government public-information specialist, Cantor agreed to help publicize the then all but unknown exception—and also to remind Americans that Social Security benefits are an earned right, not welfare. He turned over his benefits to a favorite charity, a boys' camp at Surprise Lake, New York.

Millions of Americans became aware of the "Eddie Cantor" clause as a result of that 1957 publicity and a select group in each successive generation of retirees has taken advantage of it. But Congress did not design this exception to provide a bonanza for highly paid consultants, real estate salesmen, resort concession operators, technicians, and other specialists who upon reaching sixty-five can concentrate their work and earnings in one or two months and collect benefits for the balance of the year.

The exception was intended primarily for people who might retire in midyear or later, after earning substantial amounts, and would otherwise be unable to collect any SS benefits until the following year, even though they were completely retired. It also took note of the retiree who might be able to get an occasional job at good pay. For many years, an elite group of SS beneficiaries had been able to collect more benefits than contemporaries with the same or less earnings who were working year round.

No more!

Along with the drastic financing and other SS changes Congress enacted in 1977, it slapped a limit on the use of the Eddie Cantor clause. Now, you, an SS beneficiary, get the advantage of the exception only in your "initial year of retirement."

If you retire in the middle of the year, for example, and do not earn more than 1/12 the exempt amount during the remaining months of the year (and also do not perform substantial services in self-employment), you will be eligible for benefits for those months. It will not matter whether your earnings in the prior months of the year were way above the exempt amount.

But the next year will be a different story. You will have had your "initial year of retirement." If you have even one month in which you do not work after qualifying for retirement benefits, then you are considered to have had your "initial year of retirement."

Be careful, therefore, about setting your retirement date! Don't apply for benefits as soon as you are sixty-five if you plan to go on working. Try to plan for retirement early in the year. Also, you may want to wait to apply

FINANCIAL INDEPENDENCE AND PERSONAL SECURITY 1023

for your Medicare hospitalization insurance until you need it. An application for those hospital benefits, Part A of Medicare, is considered an application for retirement benefits and could kick off your initial year of retirement.

You can, though, apply for your medical insurance benefits under Part B of Medicare and start paying the premiums. That application will not start you on your initial year of retirement.

SOCIAL SECURITY AND WOMEN'S RIGHTS

In a unanimous decision in the mid-1970s, the Supreme Court declared a section of the Social Security law unconstitutional on the grounds that it discriminated against women workers—a ruling which primarily benefited men —and among men, mainly widowed fathers of young children.

The Court's decision represented a long overdue correction of an archaic assumption that "male workers' earnings are vital to the support of their families, while the earnings of female wage earners do not significantly contribute to their families' support." The "logical" extension of that now absurd assumption was that the surviving spouses of women workers who had paid their Social Security taxes were not entitled to the same protection as the surviving spouses of men workers who had paid their taxes.

With the rejection of that insulting premise—allowing widowers with young children to get the protection that widows with minor children have been getting—other Social Security provisions based on the same obsolete assumptions at last may also be on the way to oblivion.

Over the past forty years in which our Social Security system has been repeatedly modernized into a patchwork of amendments to the original law and court decisions, not one amendment has focused on the fundamental shifts that have occurred in U.S. family relationships and life-styles.

There has been no real challenge to the stereotypes which the framers of Social Security built into the law because those were the stereotypes in which they believed. There was the male family head—the breadwinner—and there was the housewife and, as a song of the period relates, "a boy for you, a girl for me." But even well before the law was enacted, these stereotypes were far from matching reality.

Women—and children—were employed in some of our earliest factories. The daughters of the poor were working in the mills of New England in the 1800s. Working wives and daughters were commonplace among immigrants to America. Women, black and white, labored on farms and plantations. In her book, *Enterprising Women,* Caroline Bird documents the enormous extent to which the wives of our Founding Fathers took over the running of their husbands' businesses and enhanced the family fortunes, while other women created products, provided services, filled a wide range of jobs outside the home to support themselves and educate their children.

Of course, giving the dependents of women workers the full rights enjoyed by the dependents of male workers is desirable and long, long overdue. But much more fundamental is the need to recognize that you—the American woman of the 1980s—do not fit neatly into either the category of lifelong housewife or lifelong earner.

An overwhelming 90 per cent of all women work outside the home for pay during at least some part of their lives. More than 45 per cent—almost half—of our paid work force today consist of women. A full 60 per cent of all women working for pay are married and are half of a working couple.

Since the 1940 census (following the enactment of Social Security legislation), the proportion of women in every age group in the work force has soared. Among women thirty-five to forty-four, it has doubled; among middle-aged women forty-five to sixty-four, it has jumped two and a half times; among women over sixty-five, the number working for pay has more than quadrupled.

The trend born in the 1930s became increasingly powerful after World War II, when women, who had been actively recruited to replace men called up for service and to meet defense industry requirements, wanted to continue working.

Other forces since then have added strength to the development, called "the single most outstanding phenomenon of our century" by labor market expert and Columbia University professor Eli Ginsberg. Among them: college attendance and women's desire for careers; the move toward later marriages; the steady decline in the birthrate since 1957; growing acceptance of childless marriages; rising divorce rates; greater longevity; the family's need or desire for two incomes, not just among the poor, but among families wanting to send their children to college or to maintain what has become known as a "middle class" life-style.

Yet, despite all the lip service paid to equality for women in the work force, disproportionate numbers are still in low-paying jobs. Nearly two thirds of full-time, year-round women workers in the earlier years of the 1970s earned less than $7,000 a year, while more than three quarters of full-time, year-round male workers earned more than $7,000. And male workers generally do not have their working careers—and their Social Security records—interrupted because of family responsibilities (having children).

A woman will work after she leaves school and until she drops out of the labor force to have children. She may return to work when the children are of school age, or earlier—or later. Or she may become divorced. (One of every three marriages now ends in divorce, and in 1975 the annual number of divorces in the United States passed the million mark.)

A housewife's services for her family (maid, cook, laundress, child rearer, etc.) are not considered "work" for Social Security purposes. An estimate, so conservative it was ridiculous, placed a value on her services at $19,000 a year in the late 1970s, however.

A woman's absences from the paid labor force mean that there will be blanks in her Social Security record. The effect is to reduce the average earnings that will be the basis for figuring any retired-worker benefits due her in the future.

Women will continue to receive lower Social Security retirement benefits than men, says a recent Social Security report. "Only if some proposal to 'fill in' the gaps in women's earnings records is adopted will this situation change."

Nor will any substantial percentage of women have much in the way of private pensions to supplement their Social Security benefits. They are less likely to be in jobs covered by private pensions. And if they are in these jobs, if they do work for a company with a pension plan, the irregularity of their employment or the fact that they work part time may mean they will never qualify.

The Social Security program cannot be held responsible for the traditionally low wages paid to women, nor for the irregularity of their employment because of their responsibilities as homemakers and mothers. That would stretch "guilt" beyond all logic.

But the system can be restructured to take those factors into account and to make it less blatantly unfair to women.

A new concept that points the way for the restructuring has been proposed that would assume work in the home has an economic value and also that marriage is an economic partnership.

Couples could elect to have a share of the family income credited to each of their Social Security records, just as they now have the option of filing a joint income tax return.

You, a lifelong housewife, would therefore be able to build up your own Social Security record while you, the woman in and out of the paid labor force, would have a steady record of earnings, instead of earnings "gaps." And you, a divorced woman, would have a record of earnings to take with you from a marriage that had not lasted for at least ten years.

Not only do women workers feel the inequities in our Social Security system's treatment of them but the husbands and widowers of women workers also often suffer from the fallout of these provisions.

SOCIAL SECURITY'S INEQUITIES AFFECT US ALL

Item: Millions of women who have worked long enough to qualify for benefits as retired workers have been found to be entitled to higher benefits as dependents—although a wife's benefit at age sixty-five is only one half the amount of the retired husband's benefit (less if the wife is between sixty-two and sixty-five at the time her husband retires). This is because a woman worker gets her own Social Security benefit, but if it is less than the amount that would be payable to her as a dependent wife, the difference is added to her benefit total.

In effect, she gets the higher of the two benefits—but no more than she would have received if she had never worked outside the home and had never paid a cent in Social Security taxes!

The injustice of this is so apparent on the surface that I would insult you if I indulged in further indignant explanation. Suffice it to say that this happens in so many cases because of (1) the low wages paid to women generally and (2) the irregularity of women's employment (it is commonplace for a woman to drop out of the labor force to have children, and not return for a period—the absences which leaves blanks in her Social Security record).

Item: A married couple with both partners working can end up with smaller retirement benefits than a couple with the same total earnings, but where the husband was the only worker. And if one of the working couple dies, the widowed husband or wife will get much lower benefits than the surviving partner in the case of the couple in which only one was a worker for pay.

Difficult as you may find that one to believe, the Social Security Administration's files are choked with cases documenting the unfair fallout of the discrimination against women workers.

Item: A woman who is widowed before age sixty receives mother's benefits if she has in her care children under eighteen or an older, disabled child. If there is no severely disabled child, her benefits will stop when the youngest child reaches eighteen—unless she is already age sixty by that time or is age fifty or over and very severely disabled.

With what seems to me almost incomprehensible lack of realism, the law assumes that a reasonably able-bodied, middle-aged woman with no work experience can just move right out into the vast, indifferent labor market and quickly find a job that will enable her to earn enough to support herself.

These are merely a sampling of actual situations which should shock you into full realization of the inequities in the treatment of women under Social Security. And they are not limited to any one group.

In one way or another, they affect us all—homemakers, divorcées, elderly wives and widows, high-earning professionals, low-paid domestics, the wives of laborers, and the wives of executives.

BASIC REFORMS

Congress ordered that a task force study the situation of women under Social Security. The group recommended some basic reforms. It suggested, for instance, that a way be devised for considering a couple's income jointly for Social Security purposes, just as the couple does in filing a joint tax return. Just about every woman would eventually wind up with a Social Security earnings record of her own on which to collect Social Security benefits, and so would every man. Under the proposal:

• Married persons who elected to file joint income tax returns would each year be given Social Security credit for 50 per cent of the couple's combined earnings in work covered by Social Security.

- The W-2 forms that couples attach to joint returns and the returns themselves would give all the information needed to apportion the earnings to their individual Social Security records.
- They would pay no additional Social Security taxes on these earnings.
- Homemakers would be given their own Social Security records and would be brought into the system in their own right—instead of being able to collect benefits only as dependents of their employed husbands. A divorced homemaker would have an SS record to take with her into her new life instead of losing her rights to wife's or widow's benefits as she does now if she had not been married ten years at the time of the divorce.
- Men would receive advantages, too, because with SS records of their own, couples would both build eligibility for disability benefits.
- There could be a transition period to guard against unanticipated adverse effects, special provisions for women widowed under age sixty, other clauses to protect a newly widowed middle-age homemaker who has few marketable skills and who could not be expected to enter the labor market immediately.

There are many other details in this proposal and the proposals might not provide complete equity for women who never marry. But it is at least a basic springboard Congress can use to explore the concept's feasibility and merits.

And through public debate, this idea can be developed and improved. Surely the time has come for equality for women under Social Security. And surely the obsolete stereotypes of the American women built into the system cannot be condoned much longer.

The Bafflegab of Social Security

DISABILITY INSURANCE BENEFIT Monthly benefit payable to a worker and his family if he has a severe physical or mental condition which prevents him from working and the condition is expected to last for at least twelve months. He also must have a certain required number of work credits.

LUMP-SUM DEATH BENEFIT A one-time benefit paid at the death of a worker covered under Social Security.

QUARTER OF COVERAGE See Work Credits.

RETIREMENT BENEFITS Monthly benefits payable to a man or woman at age sixty-two (reduced benefits) or age sixty-five (full benefits) who has stopped working or is substantially retired as measured by the Social Security Retirement Test.

RETIREMENT TEST Known also as the "annual earnings test" under the Social Security Act. This test is used to determine how much of a beneficiary's annual Social Security benefit will be paid. A beneficiary can earn up to the exempt amount in a calendar year and collect all of his Social Security benefits for that year.

SOCIAL SECURITY CONTRIBUTIONS (TAXES) Percentage of your earnings paid into the Social Security trust funds—matched by your employer.

SOCIAL SECURITY TRUST FUNDS The three funds into which Social Security contributions are paid: Old Age and Survivors Insurance Trust Fund, Disability Insurance Trust Fund, and Hospital Insurance Trust Fund. Social Security benefit costs are met out of these funds on a pay-as-you-go basis. The amounts kept in each fund are adjusted periodically by a special board of trustees.

SURVIVORS INSURANCE BENEFITS Monthly benefits are paid to your survivors in the event of your death if you have had the required number of work credits. There also is a one-time lump-sum death benefit.

WAGE BASE Amount of a worker's annual earnings which is taxed for Social Security.

WORK CREDITS Also known as "quarters of coverage." To get monthly Social Security benefits a person must have worked under Social Security for a certain period of time. An employee earns credit for one-quarter year of work if he is paid a certain amount—$260 in 1979 and rising in the future as average wages rise. For 1980, a self-employed person should have earned at least $1,160 before earning four quarters of coverage. The comparable figures were: $1,040 in 1979; and $1,000 in 1978.

What You Should Know About Life Insurance

DO YOU NEED LIFE INSURANCE?

Make no mistake about it: the main purpose of life insurance—*and nothing does it better*—is to create an "instant estate" for your family in the event of your death.

It's not difficult to argue that you don't need any life insurance if:

You have no children or other dependent relatives.

Your wife is working—or is perfectly capable of returning to work tomorrow, as she did before you were married.

You are collecting substantial monthly Social Security benefits and believe that the benefits that will be paid to your widow are adequate. (A man age forty without dependent children may be in the maximum Social Security bracket as far as income is concerned, but if he were to die that year his widow would not be eligible for any benefits until she reached the age of sixty-two.)

Your company promises to provide you with a good-sized pension when you retire, with adequate benefits for your survivor when you die.

You have fairly comfortable savings or other assets.

If you are such a person, you represent a distinct minority. And the fact remains that nine out of ten U.S. families and seven out of ten individuals in this country—both young and old—have life insurance today. The average insured American family in the mid-1970s had policies of one type or another giving the family at least $37,900 of protection—or the equivalent of two years of take-home pay.

With what else but life insurance could you—on a relatively modest salary and little chance to save—provide the sizable estate that would enable your survivors to maintain some semblance of their accustomed standard of living, perhaps even assure your children of college educations?

Or, after the children are grown, give your wife a lifetime income and help her pay off the mortgage on the family home?

Consider, too, these key advantages life insurance offers the survivors of the average policyholder:

• Unlike the returns from many other assets, death payments from life insurance, under almost all circumstances, are not subject to federal income taxes to the beneficiary.

• If you die, the processing of your estate may take months, even years before the proceeds can be distributed. The value of your life insurance, though, becomes available immediately to your beneficiaries upon your death.

• It does not cost you a cent, as it may in the case of a will, to change the beneficiary of your life insurance or to revise the terms under which the proceeds will be paid.

Life insurance has certain other attractive features—what insurance men call "living values"—although they should be regarded as secondary to the primary purpose of protection.

• One value, though not inherent in all types of insurance, is savings. There are more rewarding ways to save than via life insurance. But many families find that the only way they can be disciplined into saving any money at all is through regular forced payments of life insurance premiums.

• Increases in the cash value of your policy contributed from the insurance company's earnings are tax-free—so long as you keep your policy in force.

• No matter how bad your credit rating, you are guaranteed the right to use the cash value of your policy as collateral for a loan from your insurance company and you may repay at your convenience, whenever you wish. However, if you are purchasing a new policy which provides cash values *first,* investigate with care the loan interest provisions. Some companies are now building into policies an 8 per cent or higher loan interest charge. Others continue to issue policies with much lower interest charges. This may mean a great deal to you in the future if you need to borrow on your insurance.

• If you get in trouble with your creditors, they'll have a lot harder time laying hands on the cash value of your life insurance than, say, the money you have in securities or bank accounts. This is simply because creditors' rights under the law are considerably weaker vis-à-vis life insurance than toward most other types of investments.

• As an investment, life insurance has obvious drawbacks—but it does promise to yield a stated total of dollars, whereas stock investments involve fluctuating totals of dollars.

• And certain types of life insurance will pay you a guaranteed specified lump sum or a specified income for life when you are ready to retire.

You cannot, in sum, reasonably argue that there are *no* good reasons why you should buy and hold life insurance. Much more to the point is how you, as a young family, should shop for life insurance—or how you can make sure your existing coverage is all you think it is.

HOW TO FIGURE YOUR LIFE INSURANCE NEEDS

To reach a proper decision on just how much coverage you need for your wife and children, answer these key questions:

(1) How much income would your family need for living expenses if you were to die tomorrow?

Many experts say that a young family with children would need 60 to 75 per cent of its present after-tax income. If you have no children or your children are grown, your wife might be able to get by on as little as 40 per cent of what you earned.

Another pertinent question here: if the wife of the family breadwinner died, how much would it cost to hire others to perform her duties?

(2) What resources are there to produce this income?

Add up your total assets, including equity in your home or business, savings accounts, stocks, bonds, property, etc., and estimate how much income all this could produce.

(3) What would your family receive from Social Security?

To find out just what your family would receive on the basis of your earnings, fill out and mail the card available at Social Security offices to get a record of your income credits together with instructions on how to estimate your expected future annual benefits.

(4) How much pension income—including veteran's pension—can you expect when you retire, and would any of this income be available to your spouse if you were to die?

(5) Do you have a group life insurance policy?

If so, what amount of benefits will it produce? Will it continue past retirement from your job, and could you afford to convert it into an individual policy if you left your present employer?

(6) Will your wife have any income of her own?

Does she now work or could she get a job and at what salary? A wife who has not held a job for several years might have to invest a period of time in training before she could qualify for a well-paying job. While working she might have to deduct considerable amounts for child care expenses, commuting costs, restaurant lunches, etc.

(7) Is there a mortgage on your home?

If your family sold the home, the proceeds could be used for their other needs. Otherwise, your insurance should also provide enough to cover the mortgage in the event of your death.

(8) How much will your children need for their college education?

With college costs going up year after year to eye-popping levels, enough money must be set aside or otherwise made available to cover this expense. (See pages 581–612.)

(9) Do you have any large debts outstanding?

Include in your calculations any money you may owe on auto or personal loans, installment payments, etc. These, too, would have to be paid off after your death.

(10) What cash would be needed immediately?

Your family may need money for "final expenses"—medical bills, funeral costs, minor debts.

Now add up everything your family will need for living expenses, your mortgage, college costs, debt clearance, other expenses. From this total, subtract the money that will be coming in from Social Security and other pensions, salaries, savings, investments and other assets, as well as any outstanding life insurance. The difference is the amount of insurance needed to enable your survivors to reach that income level of 60 to 75 per cent after tax, or to provide adequately for their needs.

Family needs differ depending on age and number of children. A reputable life insurance agent also may be able to offer you helpful advice on the amount—and types—of life insurance you need. But one industry rule of thumb is that a family needs at least enough life insurance to cover four or five times its yearly income. More specifically, a family with an annual income of $20,000 needs a total of $80,000 to $100,000 of life insurance.

HOW MUCH LIFE INSURANCE CAN YOU AFFORD?

How much life insurance can you afford?

Even though you find a fairly satisfactory answer to the nagging question "How much life insurance do you need?", there are no hard answers to help you answer this second question, any more than there were any "tight" rules of thumb to lead you directly to the answers to the first.

You must start by asking and honestly analyzing what are your family's values in terms of financial security—as well as knowing what budget your family has.

If, for instance, your family is thinking of its future, it will try to cooperate to find the means to afford the protection you all want more than another family that thinks in terms only of its immediate or short-term needs.

After analyzing your family income and how you spend it, you will be on your way to determining what you can budget for life insurance. And always keep in mind: there are no rules of thumb and any salesperson who tells you otherwise is to be avoided.

If your family maintains a visibly high standard of living, you may find allocating 1 per cent of your gross earnings to insurance a financial hardship (if you won't give up anything).

If your family has a more sober life-style, you may find allocating 5 per cent or more a reasonable share, even if the life insurance protection does mean additional sacrifice.

It comes down to your values.

No honest reporter can give you guidelines or recommendations that can be an adequate substitute for your own and your own family's thinking about your protection now and in the future.

Only in the privacy of your own home and without outside pressures can you determine what your needs for life insurance are and how much your family is willing to spend to cover those needs.

WHAT KIND OF LIFE INSURANCE FOR YOU?

With hundreds of different life insurance policy types, combinations, and options available today, deciding just what kind of insurance may be best for you can be a confusing experience. Some policies are designed purely for protection; others stress savings; still others, retirement benefits; and many give you a combination of these features.

It will help if you think of life insurance as falling into one of five basic categories:

(1) *Term insurance*. This is the simplest, least costly type of coverage. As the name indicates, it gives you protection for a specific term or period of time. Naturally, the shorter the period of coverage and the younger you are, the lower the yearly premium.

Term policies pay off only if you die during the period covered by the policy. Like fire insurance, these policies generally have no cash or loan value. However, for young families with limited funds, they provide the best means of getting a maximum of protection. If you get *convertible term,* you have the option of swapping the policy for one of the higher-premium permanent protection plans without having to take another medical exam.

With *level term insurance,* the amount of insurance and your premium rate remain the same as long as your policy is in force or until it is renewed. This insurance is usually issued on a renewable basis for five or ten years, or on a non-renewable basis for longer periods or to age sixty, sixty-five, or seventy. At each renewal, the premium goes up to reflect the policyholder's increased age.

With *decreasing term insurance*—often used to cover such large debts as a mortgage—the amount of insurance declines a small amount from year to year until the policy finally expires.

(2) *Deposit term.* This type was developed by some companies to reward policyholders who maintain their insurance in force for a prolonged period.

Under a typical deposit term policy you are required to pay a deposit of $10 per $1,000 of insurance in addition to a low annual premium for the term coverage for ten years. The first-year deposit is returned, doubled, at the end of ten years. The doubled amount, guaranteed in the form of the tenth year cash value of the policy, represents a compounded interest return of 7.2 per cent. Under current tax rules—IRC Section 72 (e) (1) (B)—the interest on the return is tax-free to you. But should you let your policy lapse before the tenth policy year, some or all of the additional deposit is forfeited.

The blunt warning is, therefore:

This plan is neither intended nor recommended for individuals who do not feel reasonably certain that they can maintain coverage in force for the full ten years. It is, though, a plan of insurance uniquely designed to reward policyholders who maintain their policies in force for the required period.

The message is clear. *Do not buy* unless you believe you can meet this simple requirement. *Do investigate deposit term* at once if you are reasonably certain you'll hold your term policy for the full ten years. Your premium rates will be among the lowest on any form of term insurance. But before you buy deposit term and certainly before you replace any of your existing life insurance coverage with this policy, take these five steps:

(a) If you are advised to replace existing insurance with deposit term, obtain a written proposal of the suggested new program and send it to the companies which sold you the insurance you are being told to drop. Request the written opinions of the companies involved. Their answers well may be self-serving (which would be understandable) but their replies may help you focus on items that had not been clearly represented to you.

(b) Be sure you understand all the implications of a new contestable period in the event of your disability or death. This could be of crucial importance.

(c) Consider your investment-insurance goals. Do you wish to commit all your funds to equity programs for maximum yield or do you want to balance your investment program with reserve funds in a life insurance policy, even though the yield on this is low?

(d) If your answer is maximum yield, then double-check to be certain that the deposit term policy you buy does indeed give you a lower premium rate than regular term insurance.

(e) Obey the most basic rule of wise buying: compare costs before you buy! Just because you indicate confidence that you will hold your policy for a ten-year span, most companies issuing consumer-directed deposit term policies offer them at rates substantially lower than regular term insurance premiums. But some companies issue these policies at regular rates and pay very high commissions to their sales organizations on them. *Do not buy* deposit term unless you are sure you can meet the ten-year holding requirement. *Do weigh all its possible benefits* if you believe you will maintain the coverage.

(3) *Straight life (ordinary life or whole life)*. This type of policy is sometimes called a "bank account in an insurance policy," and costs considerably more than term because straight life must pay off, whereas a term policy may or may not pay off. The premium does not go up as you grow older, though, and you get permanent protection for your entire lifetime. In addition, your policy's cash value increases from year to year. By the time the policyholder reaches age sixty-five, the cash value usually amounts to more than half the face value of the policy. A key advantage of whole life insurance is that you, the owner of the policy, may borrow against its increasing cash value at any time, although you no longer can take very favorable low interest rates on life insurance loans for granted any more. In the late 1970s, most companies increased the loan interest provision to 8 per cent or more on new policies. Some companies still continue to issue policies with the low 5 or 6 per cent loan rate. Inquire about this loan provision when you are buying a new policy and thus avoid an unpleasant surprise in the future.

Moreover, a reasonably priced whole life policy is a useful device for those who require the mechanism of "forced savings."

You also have a number of other options with this particular type of policy. If you stop paying premiums, you can elect to continue to be covered in full for a specified period of time, or for a reduced amount of the policy's face value for the rest of your life. Or you can later cancel the policy and receive a cash settlement either in one lump sum or in the form of an income for a limited period of time, perhaps even for the rest of your life.

(4) *Limited-payment life*. In this variation of straight life, you pay premiums for only a specified number of years—usually ten, twenty, or thirty, or until you reach a certain age, such as sixty or sixty-five. Because of the limited premium-paying period, premiums are higher than for straight life policies. However, the higher premium builds up cash values correspondingly faster. Policies of this sort are favored by professional men, athletes, entertainers, and others whose earnings tend to be concentrated during a relatively short period.

(5) *Endowment*. This type of policy emphasizes savings and is designed for those who need not only protection for their dependents but, perhaps equally important, a specific sum of money—say, to provide funds for a child's college education or for a retirement income. Because of the emphasis on savings, cash value builds up most quickly in this type of policy. Consequently, it is also the most expensive.

There also are many variations and combinations of these basic types. A "family income" policy, for example, is a combination of permanent policy, usually straight life, and decreasing term insurance, and is a favorite of many couples with young children. With such a fifteen-year, $10,000 policy, the family will receive $10,000 plus $100 a month for ten years if the breadwinner dies five years after the policy is written. If the breadwinner outlives the fifteen-year family protection, the family still has a permanent policy for $10,000.

The "family plan" policy, which also combines straight life for the father with term insurance protection for the mother and children, simply covers the life of everybody in the family in varying amounts—all for one basic premium.

PRACTICAL EXAMPLES OF WHO NEEDS WHAT

For more guidance on how to pick the policies best suited to your needs consider these case histories:

Let's say you're twenty-five and just married. You started work a year ago after you finished college and your wife also is employed. Your income is $15,000 and your wife's income is $8,250 a year. You have a group life insurance policy through your employer which would pay your wife $15,000—one year's salary—in the event of your death. (You have no children yet, but plan to start a family soon.)

What type of individual life insurance should you have—if any? For what reasons?

Even though you are just starting out on limited resources, some life insurance experts say, you should invest in a straight life insurance policy with an option permitting you to buy additional insurance at later dates with no medical examination. This program would give you a means of continually increasing your insurance coverage as your family needs increase—and would at the same time provide a growing financial reserve in the form of increasing cash values. You may, if you need to, borrow against these cash values.

Or let's say you are a medical student, aged twenty-five, with a young wife, an infant child—and practically no income outside your summer earnings. The most practical type of insurance for you probably would be convertible term insurance covering the few years before you start to earn a big income, at which time you might convert to straight life, which covers you as long as you live and builds cash values as well.

Or let's say you are thirty, married and have two children, ages one and four. Your income is $30,500 a year. Your group insurance policy would pay a year's income, and you also have a straight life policy which you bought five years ago, prior to the birth of your first child.

Your primary need is for immediate insurance protection which would provide income for your wife in the event of your death while the children are dependent and would pay for your children's later education. You also should be creating some form of nestegg for emergencies.

To achieve these goals, consider buying a straight life policy with a twenty-year family income rider which would provide a monthly income to your widow from the date of your death to twenty years from the issue date. This income, when combined with your Social Security benefits (see pages 1056–58), would provide for most of the average income needs of a young widow with children.

Also, under this policy your wife would receive, in the event of your death, the face amount of the policy—plus your previous insurance coverage, which could fairly easily be translated into an additional monthly income supplement.

Or say you're the type who is simply incapable of saving to supplement your anticipated retirement income. A more expensive retirement income or endowment policy, with limited life insurance protection in the meantime, might be your best means of forced savings.

Or say you want to be sure your children can afford college should you, the breadwinner, die in the interim. A life policy on your life—not theirs—would be the best bet.

Or say you're a disciplined investor capable of building a hefty nestegg and protection for your family. You might find sufficient protection in a straight life policy or term insurance providing a death benefit just covering immediate cash needs and death taxes.

Or finally, say you have no dependents, you don't intend to marry, and you do have liquid assets more than adequate to cover death expenses, small debts, and probable death taxes. Then it's hard to justify any life insurance program for you at all.

If any rules can be formulated from all this, they would be:

• As a young family, your vital interest is in immediate protection—not in the amount of life insurance you might be able to carry in your older years or in building retirement income or whatever. So buy life insurance as early as you can, but of the kind that will give you the most protection, even if it is only temporary.

• If your funds are limited, buy term insurance.

• Buy term insurance that is renewable and convertible. Later on, when you can afford the larger premiums, you can explore the advantages, disadvantages, and ways of converting your term policy to permanent insurance.

• If you're in your middle years, you might be best off starting with straight life for at least your long-run needs. But don't go for this higher-priced policy if it means straining your budget and cutting down on your regular savings program.

Instead of paying a high premium for straight life, what about buying a term insurance policy for a fraction of that premium amount and investing the difference in some other form of savings? Calculate how much interest or other income you would have to earn on such an account to outperform a straight life "savings account."

FINANCIAL INDEPENDENCE AND PERSONAL SECURITY 1037

HOW TO FIND A "STRONG" INSURANCE COMPANY

• *Do not* assume all life insurance companies are financially sound! Instead, shop among the best 20 per cent of the companies available to you. That's not being too choosy at all.

• To find a financially strong company, consult *Best's Insurance Guide* or *Best's Insurance Reports*. Best's is the most authoritative insurance rating service available and you can find these publications in most public libraries.

Best's has five recommended ratings for life insurance companies:

      (1) A+ and A (Excellent)
      (2) B+ (Very Good)
      (3) B (Good)
      (4) C+ (Fairly Good)
      (5) C (Fair)

• If you buy a low-cost insurance policy from one of the top companies, you will not necessarily have to pay higher premiums. In fact, many of the low-cost companies are among the financially strongest and many of the high-cost companies are among the financially weakest.

• And of course, also take into account the services and professional advice the company offers you.

HOW TO SAVE ON YOUR INSURANCE

If you are paying higher than standard rates for your life insurance because of medical considerations, and if your health has improved since your policy was issued, call your insurance agent, tell him you want your policies reviewed, and then apply to your insurance company for a reduction or elimination of the extra-risk premiums. Even if your health hasn't improved, you might be able to get a lower risk rating.

This is just one way to save significant sums on your life insurance premiums. But there are other ways either to slash your overall insurance costs or to free funds to buy extra, needed coverage. Here are some of them:

• Find out whether any club, association, union, professional or fraternal organization to which either you or your spouse belongs offers any low-cost group life insurance plan. In some group term insurance plans you can save as much as 40 per cent over the cost of individual coverage. Most of these plans taper off coverage as you grow older, and the insurance may end at age sixty or sixty-five.

Another big advantage of group coverage is that medical exams are waived.

• Consider reducing or even dropping some or all of your present life insurance coverage—and thus also slashing your premiums—*if* your children have grown up and are self-supporting, *if* the beneficiary you originally designated for your policy has died or become financially independent, *if* you have built up a substantial outside nest egg, *if* you have no debts. But before you drop any life insurance, be sure you're not likely to need the coverage again, for if you're forced to rebuy a policy later, you'll pay a considerably higher premium and, should your health deteriorate, you may not be able to get any coverage at all. (See "Handling Your Insurance at Retirement," directly below.)

* *Shop* for whatever individual life insurance coverage you decide on—not only among local agents but also, in certain states, at savings banks, which generally offer over the counter lower-priced policies than insurance companies.
* Pay your premiums in as few installments as possible to avoid extra charges. A policy with a $150 annual premium might cost you $156 if you paid it in two semi-annual installments. If paid quarterly, it might cost you a total of $159, and monthly, $162 for the year, or $12 more than the one-time annual payment.
* If you have several policies, reduce the frequency of payment on all of them and make it easier for yourself by staggering your payments so that they aren't bunched near each other.
* If there is some special reason why you prefer to pay your premiums monthly, ask your agent about a cost-saving "preauthorized check" plan under which your bank automatically deducts the appropriate amount each month to the life insurance company from your regular checking account.
* If you are paying a higher-than-usual premium because of the nature of your occupation when you bought the policy, and have changed occupations, inform your insurance agent of this fact and request a reclassification.

Only recently, millions of Americans were regarded as virtually uninsurable—including wild animal trainers, steeplechase riders, car racers, deep-sea divers, test pilots, submariners, and mine police. But all of these today are insurable. Today, even armored car drivers and chemists in nitroglycerin plants are regarded as "standard risks." And premium rates for workers in almost all "dangerous" trades have sharply declined. Key reasons: improved job safety and successful trials by the insurance companies which offered coverage to workers in these occupations.

Admittedly, if you are a steeplechase rider, trapeze artist, or a Grand Prix race car driver, you'll have to pay a somewhat higher premium to get life insurance. Similarly, private avocations are taken into account in calculating insurance rates. "A sky diver who won't open his parachute until he reaches treetop level would be rated as a pretty bad risk," says one top industry spokesman. But the key point is that almost all workers are insurable and almost all at a reasonable cost.

* It may be cheaper for you to add to an existing policy than to buy a completely new one. A decreasing term or family income policy, for example, will cost less as a rider to your regular policy than if bought separately.
* If you are a World War II veteran and have a GI term insurance policy,

consider converting it to permanent government insurance, one of the best bargains ever offered veterans, even though the premium will be higher. Check with the nearest Veterans Administration office to see if the conversion is still possible in your case. (See Chapter 28, "Know Your Rights!—and How to Use Them," and Chapter 9, "Education After High School—and How to Finance It," for details on other veterans' rights and benefits.)

HANDLING YOUR INSURANCE AT RETIREMENT

When you reach retirement age—*and that's the latest date for doing this*—review and reevaluate all your life insurance policies in terms of your need for them and of your personal goals.

Do not be the least surprised to discover *you no longer need* your life insurance—for you no longer have a young family to protect. Your whole way of life has been drastically changed and straight life insurance simply doesn't fit into it.

When you took out your life insurance policies, you were forcing yourself to save out of your current income, but continuing to save after retirement is inconsistent with that concept. When you began your insurance program, you were intent on creating an instant estate for the benefit of your dependents in the event of your premature death. But when there's no need for protecting dependents this way, it's all wrong for any older person to deprive himself of a dollar to finance this protection.

You might cash in your policies and put the released funds to work earning more money for you—in a simple savings account or high-grade bonds or high-grade common or preferred stocks. Or you might put your insurance on a paid-up basis and relieve yourself of all further premium obligations.

Only if you are in the wealthier income brackets—in which life insurance could be an excellent way to pass on an estate or to provide cash for estate taxes—will you be told that it could be unwise to drop your policies. But this gets into a different area altogether.

IS YOUR LIFE INSURANCE UP-TO-DATE?

Now let's assume you already have adequate amounts of insurance—both group and individual.

As the preceding section on handling your insurance in retirement dramatized, it is vitally important for you to review your coverage at least every two or three years to make sure it is appropriate for your financial needs, geared to your rising or falling standard of living, realistic in terms of the number and ages of your children and properly tied into your other savings and investments.

Do both husband and wife know, for example, where all of your various family life insurance policies are now kept? The total value of all your life insurance protection—including veterans', fraternal organizations', group policies, credit life insurance, individual policies? The name and address of your insurance agent? Which members of the family are covered and for approximately how much? Are there children not covered? The amount and due date of premiums? Who are the beneficiaries of each policy? And the "secondary" or contingent beneficiaries—in the event both husband and wife are killed in a single accident? How benefits would be paid? The amount of cash values which have accumulated so far—against which loans could be made? If you've moved, does the insurance company have your new address?

Once you have the answers to these basic questions, explore these other important questions concerning your life insurance—and determine just where and just how big are the gaps in coverage:

What, if any, provision is there to cover the possibility that the family breadwinner might become disabled over a long period of time? Does your policy include a "waiver of premium" clause—a waiver of the obligation to pay further premiums in the event of total and permanent disability?

Does your policy contain a provision under which, if you for any reason fail to pay your premiums within the specified grace period (usually thirty-one days), the premium will automatically be paid by a loan against the cash value of the policy?

Does it also contain an "accidental death benefit" provision, often called "double indemnity," that doubles the amount payable if the insured dies accidentally? (Triple indemnity also is offered by some companies.)

Are your term policies renewable and convertible without your having to take another medical examination?

How much has the upsurge in the U.S. cost of living shrunk the actual buying power of your policies since you bought them? Have you made or can you make any provisions to offset this erosion? (See below.)

Do you meet the rule of thumb that you should have the equivalent of four to five years' pay in life insurance? You may need more of a cushion if you have several children, if you are loaded with debt, if your non-insurance financial protections are limited, and if you simply can't discipline yourself into saving. You may need less if your group coverage is extensive, if your wife is well trained for a job, if your debts are paid off, if your children have left the nest, if you have substantial savings and other investments.

How much income would all of your present life insurance policies provide when you retire—assuming you are using life insurance for this purpose at all? Add this income, figured on a monthly basis, to the amount you can expect from Social Security retirement benefits, from income on all your other savings and investments, and from your company pension.

If you own your business, is your life insurance adequate to keep it going should you die before you've trained a successor?

Is your designated beneficiary still the correct one—or should other dependents be added or substituted?

Should the wife be listed as the policyowner, even though it is written on the husband's life? If done validly, this could result in considerable savings in estate taxes. Get advice on this from your insurance agent, tax adviser, or lawyer.

Only when you have the answers to these questions will you know how much financial protection you and your family actually have. In this period of steep inflation, having these answers is absolutely vital to your financial security—now *and* later.

HOW INFLATION HAS ERODED YOUR LIFE INSURANCE

Q. *If you bought your life insurance policies to protect your family as recently as the late 1960s, are you aware of the degree to which the upsurge in the cost of living in the United States has shrunk your coverage just in the short span since?*
A. By a horrendous 70½ per cent! Just in one decade! And living costs are continuing to spiral upward—at intolerably high annual rates.

Q. *How long is it since you have put aside a quiet evening to discuss seriously with a trusted life insurance agent the adequacy of your life insurance in view of your pay hikes since the 1960s, your increasing obligations (children, a new home and mortgage, a job or business change of major importance, etc.) and the overall differences in your living style?*
A. If you're typical of most Americans, it has been years.

While the average insured family had $37,900 of life insurance as the 1980s neared, a new peak, and up a full $2,500 from 1976, it was equivalent to only twenty-four months of the average family's disposable income—or about two years of pay. To put against this, I repeat, the accepted rule of thumb is that an average family should have the equivalent of four to five years' pay in life insurance, savings, and other investments.

And you may need more of a cushion if you have several young children, if your non-insurance financial protection is limited, if you have only a modest amount in savings, and if you (typically) are carrying a heavy load of debts (in installment loans, other types of personal loans, a mortgage). You also may need less of a cushion than the rule of thumb suggests if your group coverage is extensive, if your wife also has a well-paying job or has easily marketable job skills should she need to go back to work, if your children are grown and on their own, if your debts are minor or paid off.

Q. *How much has the actual buying power of your life insurance policies been slashed since you bought them in 1967?*
A. The dollar which bought you 100 cents of goods and services in the market place in 1967 buys you only 50 cents worth of the same goods and services in the market place today.

If you consider the 1979 dollar as worth 100 cents today, and if you accept the "conservative" (but to me, intolerable) forecast of an inflation rate held to "only" 6 per cent a year, today's 100-cent dollar will be worth only 12½ cents in thirty-five years. If you are a young adult, that is when your insurance might be turning into an "instant estate" for your family.

Q. *How much income would all of your present life insurance coverage from all sources provide when you retire or when your family must get along without your contribution in earnings?*

How much does every asset on which your family can count for support add up to when you put together this life insurance income, figured on a monthly basis, plus what you can anticipate from Social Security benefits, from any company pension that seems safe, from income on your savings and other investments?

If you own your own business, is your life insurance protection adequate to keep the business going should you die before you have given a successor sufficient training?

Have you included all your dependents (or eliminated inappropriate ones) among your beneficiaries? Are your beneficiaries truly the ones you want to protect in 1988 as against 1968?

If you can answer satisfactorily all the questions in this report, your life insurance is up-to-date. If you cannot, get the answers now and put your instant estate in top-notch order.

SHOULD YOU SWITCH INSURANCE POLICIES?

If any insurance agent suggests you switch a policy you own—life or accident and health—for "a better one," the law in most states requires the agent to explain fully and clearly the differences between the policy the agent says you should cancel and the new one. If the agent doesn't make this "full disclosure" about the policies, he (or she) is breaking the law and could forfeit his license.

But even if the agent does tell you the differences there are many, many shadings to full disclosure—and you well may not understand what is being recommended. Even if you would be better off in some ways by switching, the disadvantages of changing might far outweigh the advantages the agent is stressing.

And even if you are persuaded by the arguments, heed this blunt warning: *in very few cases can changing insurance policies be advantageous to the policyholder*.

Unscrupulous insurance agents still do exist—although not on the scale of the past, when they thrived in the ghettos particularly. They still do sell to the poor and uninformed, then coax the ignorant policyholder into switching to other policies after only a couple of years—so that the buyer pays the front-end costs over and over again. There is still a real danger that you'll make a serious error in this area—if only because so many millions of you own so many more insurance policies and in such a wider variety than ever before.

FINANCIAL INDEPENDENCE AND PERSONAL SECURITY 1043

There are, of course, many reasons why you might change a life (or accident and health) policy. But the most likely reason is that an agent advises you that another policy from another insurance company is a better buy. Here, therefore, are basic guides to weigh if and when a switch is suggested:

(1) Realize that with any new policy you are paying the full front-end costs all over again—just as you did when you bought your original policy. Most agents' commissions and company administrative costs come out of your first-year premium. If you've had your policy for several years, you've already paid these costs once. Don't duplicate them without extraordinarily sound reasons.

(2) Also be fully aware of the importance of the contestability clause in most life insurance contracts—under which your insurance contract can't be broken because of statements you made on the application after the policy has been in force for a period, usually two years (except, of course, for a misstated age). With a new contract, you start a new two-year contestability period. The person who switches policies frequently not only pays the front-end costs over again but rarely gets out of the contestable period.

(3) Find out precisely what will be the premium payments for your new policy and compare them with what you are paying. If the benefits are similar, your premiums probably will be higher—merely because you are older than when you bought the first policy.

(4) Be wary about the waiting period involved when a new policy is issued. All too often people apply for a new policy and let the old one lapse before the new policy becomes effective. The tragedy here is that the person may die in the meantime, with no insurance at all in force.

(5) As your best protection, deal with an insurance agent who represents a reputable company. If you're thinking about changing policies, ask his advice. If you're not satisfied with what he recommends, ask the company. Throughout the entire process, do not forget that it is the agent's duty under the law to disclose clearly all the facts to you before you switch any policy.

If, after all this, you feel you've been unfairly treated by the company or its agents, you do have a recourse. You can lodge a complaint with your state insurance commissioner's office at the state capital.

WHAT ABOUT WIFE INSURANCE?

Assuming you are convinced that you, the breadwinner, must have some life insurance to protect your family against loss of your income, the next question is: should the life of your wife also be insured?

Do you, Mr. America, realize how great would be the added expenses to you should the lady of your house not be around to share, plan, cook, clean, mother, drive, take care?

And do you recognize what would be the financial impact of the loss if she also is a working mother who contributes substantially to the household's total income?

Today, three out of four wives are covered by life insurance and the proportion is growing steadily. As a guide on whether or not the wife in *your* household should have life insurance, the key functions of "wife insurance" are to:

(1) Cover final expenses in the event of her death. Expenses of final medical and hospital care, funeral costs, and all other incidentals can now total $5,000 or more—enough to wipe out most family nest eggs and even put the surviving mate quite deeply in debt. (See Chapter 20.)

(2) Help care for the young children, for a fair period at least, and perform the other tasks that go with running a home. The cost of a competent housekeeper, or even regular cleaning help, can run into hundreds of dollars a month.

(3) Help meet the increase in income taxes which results from the husband's loss of his wife's personal exemption and the joint-return privilege.

(4) Cover the loss of the wife's contribution to the family income, if it represents a vital part of the family budget.

(5) And a mother may want to leave an inheritance to her children.

What sort of policy would be best?

In most cases term or ordinary life should fill the bill.

Term if the ability to pay premiums is limited, and ordinary life if your budget can accommodate a somewhat higher premium. Remember, term insurance, while low in initial cost, will require higher premiums every year or every stated renewal period.

It also terminates at some age, usually sixty-five or seventy, so if you desire permanent insurance consider ordinary life.

The fundamental point is that the loss of a wife and mother is a financial blow to the family as real—although not as readily measurable—as the loss of the husband and breadwinner. Wife insurance is one way to safeguard the family against this loss.

AND WHAT ABOUT INSURANCE FOR CHILDREN?

On their grandson's fifth birthday recently, a smart couple we know bought him as a gift a $10,000 straight life insurance policy—with the pledge that they will pay the premiums until the boy reaches twenty-five and will arrange to have the policy paid up immediately should they die before that date.

Young Dick's parents were less than delighted. "If any life insurance is to be taken out," grumbled the disappointed father, "it should be on my life, not Dick's."

"I gave that boy the best present I could think of," said the equally disappointed grandfather, "and neither my daughter nor her husband understood it at all."

Actually, both grandfather and father were right and wrong. The first and top priority in life insurance must go to adequate coverage for the breadwinner. And since Dick's mother hasn't earned a penny since he was born and the family is having a tough struggle on one paycheck in today's inflation, our friends could have been a little less original in their gift to Dick. And if they were determined to give a life insurance policy, it should have been to their twenty-five-year-old son-in-law.

On the other hand, our friends are doing their daughter, son-in-law, and grandson a tremendous favor by buying that policy so early in Dick's life. Since millions of you will be directly or indirectly affected by this tale, here are the key reasons why.

* You can buy basic insurance coverage on a child's life at extremely low rates.
* One of the forms to investigate is called the "jumping juvenile policy."* This policy provides $1,000 of insurance, per unit, until age twenty-one and then increases to $5,000 without any additional premium. In addition the increases in cash value each year are substantial, and when your son, daughter, or grandchild assumes the premium-paying responsibility, he may find that each of his payments is exceeded by the growth in the cash value of the policy.
* Among other types of policies designed for children and some of the features you should investigate are:

Guaranteed Insurability Option. This would guarantee the child the right to buy additional life insurance equal to the original amount at ages twenty-five, twenty-eight, thirty-one, thirty-four, thirty-seven, and forty. Thus an original $10,000 policy could provide a total of $60,000 in additional insurance.

Payor Benefit. This provision will waive the premium until the child is twenty-one years of age if the payor dies or becomes disabled.

* And, of course, this life insurance is protection for the parents should their child die.

How you apply this tale is up to you entirely. But at least you should know what's available and what others are doing, so you can reach an intelligent, informed decision.

One basic caution, though: don't invest in this type of coverage—or even in wife insurance—unless and until the family breadwinner is adequately insured.

WHAT YOU SHOULD KNOW ABOUT ANNUITIES

What They Are

Annuities are sold by life insurance companies, but they should not be confused with life insurance. You buy life insurance primarily because, if you die, you want to have provided for those you leave behind. You buy an annuity primarily because you assume you will live and you want to have some sort of steady income to supplement what you'll get from Social Secu-

---

* Juvenile insurance also might be valuable in times of emergency or to help finance the child's education.

rity, and perhaps your company pension, savings, other investments during your retirement years.

An annuity is a contract or agreement under which an insurance company accepts a given sum of money from you and in return guarantees to pay you a regular (usually monthly) income for a stated period or, more typically, for as long as you live. The amounts of the payments are based on your life expectancy, according to the mortality tables and how much money you put in. Since women tend to live longer than men, they normally receive smaller monthly incomes from annuities than do men for the same dollar input, but over a longer period of time.

Pros and Cons of Annuities

An annuity program frees you from the responsibility of money management or investment decisions, guarantees you a fixed monthly payment, and assures you that you will never outlive your capital. But it must not be your entire retirement program in an era of inflation.

Although an annuity can generate a good monthly return, you may be able to do much, much better by investing at a young age in, say, real estate, stocks, or other mediums.

It's simply not that easy.

New Types of Annuities

Single Premium—Deferred Annuity: This type of annuity has become popular in recent years as a medium via which interest earned on the investment is tax-deferred until later years. In addition, the yield provided by insurance companies is frequently competitive with other money instruments such as savings accounts, certificates of deposit, and government notes. It is issued on a load or no load basis, meaning that either the sales charges are paid by the purchaser (load) or absorbed by the insurance company (no load). The usual contract guarantees only 3 to 4 per cent yield but provides for extra payments of interest in excess of the guarantee on an annual basis. The amount of such excess is set annually by the company's Board of Directors. Withdrawal of investment before a certain stipulated time usually calls for some loss of the accumulated dividends.

Flexible Premium—Deferred Annuity: Designed primarily for the Individual Retirement Account market (see pages 1008–10), this type of annuity requires annual payments which are tax-deductible if they meet the requirements of the Individual Retirement Act. The flexible feature permits you, the annuitant, to change or even skip annual payments. The yield on the accumulated funds will vary each year in accordance with the acts of the Board of Directors on payment of excess interest over guaranteed amounts.

WHAT'S YOUR RATE ON A LIFE INSURANCE LOAN?

Before you sign any contract to buy ordinary life insurance in the future, ask this crucial question and be certain you get an unqualified, clear, honest answer which you fully understand:

What interest rate will you be charged if you want to borrow against the cash value of your life insurance policy at any time you need or want to in coming years?

Will you be charged the cheap, bargain rates of 5 to 6 per cent with which you have long been familiar and probably take for granted?

Or will you be charged up to a hefty 8 per cent or more to borrow back your own money (the cash value of the premiums you have paid), which increasingly is becoming the norm?

The stable, low interest rate on life insurance policy loans has been one of the great selling points for ordinary life insurance over many years. It has been an advantage which observers such as myself have emphasized repeatedly to hard-pressed consumers, particularly during the mid-1970s era of double-digit interest rates on loans and hard-to-get credit.

It always has been cited by insurance policy salesmen.

There's no fooling around about this. In fact, the movement has reached the point where a mere handful of states still place a low statutory limit on life insurance policy loan interest.

The life insurance companies leading the drive have been among the nation's giants. They have argued that the low rates on policy loans deprive them of profits; charges to policyholders will be offset by "adjustments through dividends" paid to policyholders; many loans are taken out by borrowers not in economic need but seeking cheap money that they can reinvest elsewhere at higher interest rates.

But opposing the giants are life insurance companies which feel just as strongly that the boost to 8 per cent and above is an unjustifiable rip-off on policyholders, and that a retreat from the low borrowing rate concept would rob ordinary life insurance of a vital element. Say these executives: loans are generally taken because of need, not speculation; "debasing" this advantage of permanent life insurance will turn buyers to term insurance; what companies earn on their reserves is more than adequate to cover their loan rates; the policyholders are borrowing back their own cash, making this a 100 per cent guaranteed investment for the companies.

Be on guard! Do not take cheap policy loans for granted. Shop for loan rates. Recognize the differences can be of tremendous future importance to you. Insist that your insurance agent give you a straight answer on policy loan rates.

BUYING LIFE INSURANCE BY MAIL

If a life insurance sales agent has personally contacted you in the past year, you are in a minority of American households. A full two thirds of U.S. families have been utterly ignored—with the greatest decline in contacts concentrated among young, husband-wife families, traditionally the prime market for life insurance and the drop most apparent since the start of the 1970s.

The result? One is that buying of insurance by mail has been in a sharp upswing, for insurance companies that sell by mail have been saturating the market with print, broadcast, and mail ads. Another result is that premiums paid for insurance bought by mail have now punched through the $1 billion milestone.

Of course buying your insurance by mail has many advantages. Because the sales representations by their very nature are delivered entirely in writing, you can read and reread at your leisure in your own time, in your own home. You buy solely on the basis of what you see in writing, not on the persuasiveness of an agent's word. And while you must be extremely cautious about the responsibility of the insurance company with which you are dealing, and check with utmost vigilance, most insurance companies that sell by mail are licensed and are regulated by your state insurance department.

Insurance policies offered through mail, print, and broadcast media provide a wide range of life, accident and health, and casualty coverage. Hundreds of thousands of policies of these types are in force throughout the nation. Many of these policies are designed to supplement other insurance, providing the extra protection for expenses not covered by your existing insurance.

Q. *What generally should you look for?*
A. Ask yourself: Does this insurance fill your needs? Do you know what you are getting and not getting? Can you afford it?

Q. *What about buying accident and health insurance?*
A. You should understand what kinds of illness or injury are covered and what areas are specifically excluded from coverage.

Find out how many days of hospitalization the policy covers and if payments begin on the first day of hospitalization or if there's a waiting period. Usually, the longer the waiting period, the lower the premium (*but* the *average* hospital confinement is only seven days).

Check provisions under which your policy can be renewed. Many accident and health insurance policies are guaranteed renewable and cannot be canceled on an individual basis as long as premiums are paid on time. If there are provisions for increases in premiums or decreases in benefits at, say, age sixty-five, be sure you know them.

Find out about exclusions. Some policies may exclude payment for medical conditions that existed prior to the time you purchased your policy. Other exclusions might include confinement in a government hospital, mental or convalescent care.

Q. *How do you find out what policy is right for you?*
A. You must get some expert help here. A do-it-yourself life insurance program may be as bad as do-it-yourself medical care. Be sure the ad is explicit in describing the type of life insurance being offered ("term" or "whole" life).

FINANCIAL INDEPENDENCE AND PERSONAL SECURITY

Check whether your policy includes an option to buy additional life insurance in your later years without a physical exam, and note the specifically stated instances in which payment will not be made (such as death by suicide, acts of war, etc.).

Pay your insurance premiums annually (rather than quarterly or monthly), which will save you money.

Q. *How do you choose the right company for you?*
A. Ask your neighbors and friends about their experiences with individual companies on claims settlement, response to their communications, service to policyholders.

Ask your state insurance department if the company you are considering is licensed to sell in your state.

If you have any questions about a policy, ask the company to explain in writing or by phone to your satisfaction any aspect you don't fully understand.

PEOPLE FORGET

True tale: In the late 1970s a resident of Jersey City, New Jersey, borrowed—at 12.65 per cent interest—$1,500 from his local bank to finance some home improvements. He had forgotten that eight years ago he had elected to allow the dividends on his $30,000 ordinary life insurance policy to accumulate at interest—and his dividend account now contained $1,468.

Result: He was voluntarily forfeiting more than $100 a year in unnecessary bank interest charges. Reminded a month later during a routine visit from his insurance agent, he drew out the dividends, placed the money in the bank, and persuaded his banker to reissue the debt as a low-interest passbook loan.

True tale: A Denver resident, widowed for ten years, remarried at the age of sixty-seven, died five years later, and left his own widow nearly destitute. His life insurance had been made out to his wife. But he forgot that it had been made out to "my wife, Mary." His second wife's name was Hilda.

The $25,000 in proceeds passed to the estate of his first wife, who it developed, after making specific bequests to her husband and others had left the remainder of her estate to a favorite niece. The favorite niece received the $25,000.

People forget.

"And the thing that people most often forget," says the American Council of Life Insurance, "is that life insurance is a legal contract carrying all the force of law.

"The next thing they forget is that the passage of time can all too easily convert yesterday's wisdom into today's folly."

For many, many years, conventional wisdom has held that women, the major beneficiaries of life insurance, are incapable of managing their own financial affairs in widowhood. As a result, husbands often have elected to have the proceeds of their life insurance doled out to their widows in monthly installments.

Even during periods when the value of the dollar remains fairly stable, you, a policyholder, and you, the intended beneficiary, should examine this procedure with utmost care. But in eras of inflation, the consequences of deciding on the sufficiency of a fixed income can be doubly destructive.

A widow with, say, $50,000 of insurance could find herself strapped to an insurance income of $400 a month, with no way to reach the principal sum. Legally the money is hers. And just as legally the insurance company is bound by a contract which prevents her from drawing out any part of the principal in an emergency.

In response to anguished complaints of affected widows, many life insurers a while ago undertook lengthy and costly campaigns among policyholders who had elected the option, urging them to reconsider. Many policyholders did. Many who should have didn't.

There were an estimated 150 million policyholders in the United States in the late 1970s. If even 1 per cent of them have forgotten they have tied the hands of their beneficiaries this way, it means there are 1.5 million time bombs ticking away.

"It's really frightening," the Council emphasizes. "The income option can rescue people from paying unnecessary estate taxes. And if there are other assets a beneficiary can get at in an emergency, it's one way of being sure they can't outlive their incomes. But if it's used to insulate the widow from decisions about money, it's misused and can really hurt her."

If you doubt your beneficiary's ability to make sound decisions, leave a letter of instructions and suggestions. Or set up a life insurance trust. And certainly, insist that your wife learn the basics about handling money (while you're alive).

More shocking than the above are the instances of policyholders forgetting to tell their beneficiaries—or anybody else—that they have life insurance at all. Many forgotten term policies, for instance, would simply be carried in the records as having lapsed when, in fact, they had been in force and payable at the time of their owners' death—if a claim had been made.

The companies are ready to honor a valid claim years, even decades, after it was due. But if that claim isn't made, there's frequently no way of telling the difference between a lapsed policy and a lapsed memory.

LAPSED POLICY OR LAPSED MEMORY?

Each year millions of you buy life insurance policies for which you pay billions in premiums.

Among your reasons: As a man, because your wanted your home to be free and clear; or to be sure of ample funds for your children's education; or to be comfortable in later years. As a woman, to replace your value as a homemaker; or to replace the dollars you contribute to your home as a working wife; or if widowed or a separated head of household, to replace income vital to your children.

Yet, unless you act now—and that means today—many of those sound intentions may never be fulfilled. Why not?

The shocking answer is that an astounding number of you *never* make certain that the people for whom you are putting aside that money today will know about it in that distant tomorrow when you are not there to tell them.

Every year, millions of dollars in life insurance benefits that were meant for you go instead to the states as unclaimed personal property.

For thousands of you, that is money which could have been yours.

Life insurance companies, though, are obligated to turn this money over to the states after they have lost all hope of finding the rightful owners.

Before they do turn it over, the companies undertake exhaustive searches. One New York company, for example, has a ten-page itemized list of procedures for claims men to follow in tracking down the missing owners of "orphaned" funds. And life insurance files are loaded with successful searches.

But there also are those millions of dollars of failures they must ship each year to state treasuries—millions of dollars of promises unkept because you forgot to keep records.

Here's a sampling of letters received by the American Council of Life Insurance from individuals who believe they might be lost beneficiaries. The stories these letters tell could become the stories of your beneficiaries.

"My father was known to have carried a policy to protect my mother. She preceded my father in death and he had said only weeks before his own death that he was thinking of dropping this insurance. His effects were somewhat scattered and I was never able to determine what action was taken on this." A Kansas woman.

"When my husband died, I thought his insurance was $11,000 ($10,000 in my name and $1,000 in my son's). There were two policies missing, $2,000 each. I located the one which he had cashed, but cannot locate one for $2,000." A Pennsylvania widow.

"I'm writing in desperation. My husband always said I was protected, but would not discuss it." A Kentucky widow.

"In many of these cases, there never was a policy, or it lapsed, or was surrendered for cash. But not to know must be agonizing," says a Council spokesman. "And it's all so avoidable." His guides:

• Store your life insurance policies—including group insurance certificates—at home, preferably in a fireproof lockbox along with other key records (your will, instructions for heirs).

• In a separate letter, list the names of the companies with whom you are insured, the policy numbers, and the amounts. Leave this letter with your lawyer, store copies in your safe-deposit box and with a trusted relative.

- Inform your beneficiaries. Insist on this.
- Keep your records up-to-date. Note if you surrender a policy or let one lapse.
- Periodically re-examine your policies: your application, names of beneficiaries, settlement option, your action of dividends. If appropriate, make a change immediately and record it.
- Check out any policy you have dropped to be sure it has no value. Do not throw any away until you have checked the insurer.
- Notify your insurance companies when you move. The post office maintains records on new addresses for only about sixty days and since many insureds pay premiums annually or semi-annually, premium notices are returned frequently with the notation "not at address." The result: millions of insurance lapsed involuntarily each year.

One New York company maintains a staff that tries to locate such policyholders—but even after its staff calls the agent, employer, and family physician listed in the original application, the staff still cannot locate 50 per cent of the company's policyholders who move and do not notify the company of their new addresses.

The Bafflegab of Life Insurance and Annuities

ACCIDENTAL DEATH BENEFIT Extra benefit, often added to life insurance policies, which is paid in the event of death by accident. Often called "double indemnity," sometimes "triple indemnity."

ANNUITY Contract under which you pay the life insurance company a given sum of money and receive in return a regular (usually monthly) income for the remainder of your life. A *deferred annuity* provides for the income payments to begin at some future date—e.g., after a certain number of years or when you reach a certain age. A *variable annuity* is one in which payments may fluctuate, often reflecting stock price changes.

BENEFICIARY Person you name in your life insurance policy to receive the policy's proceeds in the event of your death. Also called "primary beneficiary."

BUSINESS LIFE (OR "KEY MAN") INSURANCE Life insurance bought by a corporation or partnership on the life of a key executive.

CASH SURRENDER VALUE Amount of money for which you can cash in your life insurance policy before it becomes payable by death or maturity.

CONTINGENT BENEFICIARY One or more additional persons you name in your policy to receive all or part of its proceeds in the event the primary beneficiary dies before you.

CREDIT LIFE INSURANCE Life insurance offered (and sometimes required) by lenders, providing for full payment of a home mortgage or other loan in the event the borrower dies.

DEPOSIT TERM Special type of term insurance. (See pages 1033–34.)

FINANCIAL INDEPENDENCE AND PERSONAL SECURITY

DIVIDEND Refund of part of premium on a participating policy not needed by the company. Since it actually represents the refund of an overpayment, it is not taxable.

ENDOWMENT INSURANCE Insurance in which the face value is payable at maturity to the policyholder if he is still living, or to his beneficiary if he dies before the policy matures.

FACE AMOUNT Amount, stated on the face of the policy, that will be paid on the death of the insured or at maturity of the contract.

FAMILY INCOME POLICY Policy which combines whole life insurance with decreasing term insurance and which pays your beneficiary a regular income for a specified period of time if you die before the end of that period. It also pays the full face amount of the policy at the death of the policyholder.

FAMILY POLICY Life insurance contract covering all members of your family. Generally, such a policy provides whole life insurance on the family breadwinner and limited amounts of term insurance on his wife and also on present and future children.

GRACE PERIOD Time span, usually thirty or thirty-one days after a premium is due, during which you may delay payment of your insurance premium without any penalty and without losing your coverage.

GROUP LIFE INSURANCE Low-priced life insurance usually issued to employees by employers, or to members by their unions or professional groups, without a medical examination.

INDUSTRIAL LIFE INSURANCE Insurance sold to individuals, usually in low-income brackets, in amounts of less than $1,000. Weekly or monthly premiums collected by an agent. Traditionally used to pay funeral expenses.

INSURED Person on whose life insurance policy is issued.

LEVEL PREMIUM INSURANCE A form of insurance in which the annual premium stays the same throughout the period over which premiums are payable.

LIMITED-PAYMENT LIFE INSURANCE Whole life insurance on which premiums are fully paid in a limited, specified number of years.

MATURITY Date when the face value of a policy becomes payable.

ORDINARY LIFE INSURANCE Individual life insurance, either or whole, which is sold in amounts of $1,000 or more. The proceeds can be in the form of a lump sum or as income or your policy can be converted to an annuity.

PAID-UP INSURANCE Insurance on which you have paid all required premiums. With reduced paid-up insurance, the plan for which you originally signed up remains in force, but the benefit amount is reduced, with no further premiums to pay.

PARTICIPATING INSURANCE Insurance on which the premium is somewhat higher than the actual cost of protection, but on which the company returns any amount it does not need in the form of policy dividends. Mostly sold by "mutual" life insurance companies. On *non-participating* life insurance, the premium you pay is calculated as closely as possible to the actual cost of the protection, and on this type of policy you receive no dividends. Sold by "stock" life insurance companies.

PERMANENT LIFE INSURANCE Any form of life insurance except term insurance. This type builds a cash value, which you can use as collateral to borrow from the insurance company, or which you may withdraw entirely by giving up the policy.

POLICY Printed document stating the terms of the contract with the life insurance company. This document should *not* be kept in your safety-deposit box, but rather in a safe place at home where your wife or other survivor can get at it quickly if and when she needs to.

POLICY LOAN Money you borrow from your life insurance company using as security the cash value of your policy.

PREMIUM Amount you pay periodically, usually once or twice or four times a year, or monthly (perhaps as a payroll deduction), for your life insurance coverage.

RENEWABLE TERM INSURANCE Temporary insurance which you may renew, for another limited period of time if you wish, when the original term of coverage runs out—even though you may have become "uninsurable" in the interim. However, your premium rates increase each time you renew your term insurance because you are older.

STRAIGHT LIFE (OR ORDINARY OR WHOLE LIFE) INSURANCE Insurance on which premiums are payable during your entire life.

TERM INSURANCE Relatively low-cost insurance which remains in force for a limited, specified period of time—usually five or ten years, or until you reach a certain age. Benefits are paid only if you die within this period of time. *Convertible* term insurance is guaranteed to be exchangeable for some other type of coverage, even if you, the policyholder, would not ordinarily be eligible for such coverage.

WHOLE LIFE (OR ORDINARY OR STRAIGHT) INSURANCE Insurance on which a lump-sum benefit is paid on your death. Also builds up a cash value based on premiums you have paid, and you may borrow against this amount at any time. Premiums are payable either during your entire life (straight life) or over limited number of years (limited-payment whole life insurance).

Veterans' Pensions

Another major category of retirement benefits is veterans' pensions. The conditions and amounts tend to change from year to year, as new legislation boosts and liberalizes these pensions. Pensions vary according to a veteran's income, the number of dependents he has, how severe his disability is, and his net worth.

But basically, VA pensions are reserved for veterans who are in considerable financial need, and so disabled that they are unable to pursue "substantially gainful employment." Veterans sixty-five and older are considered disabled for pension purposes.

Pension amounts are scaled according to need (as measured by the amount of other income available to the veteran). No pension benefits are payable if the veteran has sizable assets to draw on.

In the late 1970s, Congress made some major changes in the non-service-connected veterans' pension program, the first major amendments since 1959. Under a 1978 law, a single veteran was assured that his total income will be at least $3,500 a year; a married veteran can count on $4,651 per year with an additional $600 for each dependent child. Those veterans who need aid and attendance or are housebound get an additional allowance of $2,130 per year. Veterans of World War I and the Mexican Border War have another $800 added to their yearly rates—a belated acknowledgment that they never received the benefits of the GI Bill, such as educational assistance and home loan guarantees.

Under the new system, pension rates will be tied to the consumer price index and will be increased automatically as Social Security benefits are. Further, pensioners who receive Social Security benefits are protected from reductions in their VA pensions because of the cost-of-living increases in Social Security. In the past, it was possible for a veteran's Social Security benefit increase to be offset by reduction in his veterans' pension.

Veterans' Benefits

The Veterans Administration pays a dependency and indemnity compensation to widows of veterans who died while in service or from a service-connected disability, based on the husband's pay grade while he was in the service. In the late 1970s this ranged from $297 to $760 a month for a widow, with an additional $35 a month for each child under age eighteen.

If your husband died while on active duty (including training) or within 120 days after discharge and from a service-connected cause, there also is an award of a six months' death gratuity. This is a lump-sum payment of six times the veteran's monthly pay, but not more than $3,000 or less than $800, payable by his military service.

Under the law after the amendments of 1978, the surviving spouse of a veteran who died from non-service-connected causes could qualify for a Veterans Administration "death pension" in an amount sufficient to bring her (or his) income up to $2,379 per year; to $3,116 for a surviving spouse and one child; and with $600 added for each additional child. If the surviving spouse is so disabled that he or she is confined to the home, there is an extra allowance of $1,427 per year to cover needed aid and attendance.

These survivors' benefits, like veterans' pension benefits (see above), are to be increased to keep up with the cost of living.

There also is a burial expense grant of $300 for veterans whose death was not service-connected, and up to $1,100 if the death was service-connected. (See Chapter 20 "Funeral Expenses—What to Do . . . How to Save . . . Where the Traps Are," for more details on veterans' death benefits.)

If the funeral director does not alert the VA insurance division of your husband's death, contact the nearest VA center.

Unremarried widows of men who served in World War II, the Korean war, or the Vietnam war and who died in service or from service-connected disabilities also may qualify for GI home loans and educational benefits. (See page 211 for more on the GI home loan program, and also pages 594–95 on financing an education.)

In addition, widows are entitled, until they remarry, to special preference when applying for civil service positions. If the widow is the mother of a veteran who lost his life or became totally disabled, she also is entitled to special preference.

For answers to other questions you may have, or assistance you may need, write, phone, or visit your nearest VA regional office.

What Every Widow Should Know

BASIC FACTS FOR WIDOWS

The thirty-nine-year-old husband of a young friend was recently killed in an automobile accident, leaving his widow with two preschool children. The husband, a dentist, had life insurance policies which paid his widow $60,000; credit life insurance which completed mortgage payments on the family's home; automobile insurance which bought a new car to replace the wreck in which the husband was killed, as well as funeral expenses. His dental practice was put on the market at $25,000.

The young widow received Social Security benefits, amounting to about $1,100 per month. She was confident she could manage on $1,450 per month. Her cash reserve of $85,000 would, therefore, be able to earn the extra $350 per month she would need and would contribute toward the education of her children.

This is not a typical set of financial circumstances for the nation's 575,000 young widowed mothers. Few young husbands have this much protection (including a salable professional practice) for their families.

Yet if you, an American wife, are typically five years younger than your husband, the chances are three out of four that you will wind up as a widow. Because females have a seven-year greater life expectancy than males, even if you are the same age as your spouse, there is a two-out-of-three chance that you will outlive your husband. And if you happen to be five years older than your husband, you have a 50 per cent chance of becoming a widow.

For your protection, you should be aware of the ways to handle the ex-

FINANCIAL INDEPENDENCE AND PERSONAL SECURITY

penses that go with a final illness and funeral costs, and also with estates, wills, probates, and taxes. (See pages 1092–1100 on funeral expenses and how to control them, and pages 1067–90 on what you should know about wills, estates, and trusts.) Equally important, you should take steps now to find out what Social Security, life insurance, and other survivor benefits your family could automatically count on and how to go about getting them. It is never too early for a wife and husband to talk about the financial resources that would be available if the breadwinner were no longer around.

HOW MUCH WOULD YOU GET?

If you are typical, chances are it wouldn't be very much. So, to make sure that you overlook nothing, run down this list of possible sources of funds for you:

Social Security

There is a tremendous general ignorance of how Social Security protects women and young people in our country.

• The maximum family Social Security benefit being paid to young widows with two children in the late 1970s was $1,200 a month. This means that if your children are very young your family might receive an "inheritance" of benefits totaling as much as $200,000 during the entire period in which the benefits are payable.

• The full Social Security benefit is tax-free and continues to be paid until you remarry or until your children reach the age of eighteen unless a disabled child remains in your care, in which case your benefits may continue.

• If and when you remarry, your benefits ordinarily stop—but the children's benefits will continue to be paid and these benefits may amount to more than one half of the total.

• The total benefit begins to be reduced as each child reaches the age of eighteen (unless the child is disabled and has been before the age of twenty-two). After all children have reached this age, both widow's and children's benefits cease, unless there is a disabled child in the mother's care, in which case benefits for both may continue. However, if the children are full-time students the children's benefits continue until they reach the age of twenty-two.

• Social Security also pays a lump-sum death benefit of $255 to all widows covered by the system who were living in the same household with the worker at the time of his death.

• For other categories of benefits that may apply to you or the children, see earlier in this chapter or contact the nearest Social Security office.

• Caution: all Social Security benefits must be applied for—none is automatic. And delay in applying can cause the loss of some benefits. To save valuable time, contact the nearest Social Security office as soon as possible after the death of your husband. Take with you:

(1) A certified copy of the death certificate.

(2) Your husband's Social Security number.

(3) A record of his approximate earnings in the year previous to his death and his employer's name (the W-2 form that accompanies the U.S. income tax form should suffice).

(4) Your marriage certificate.

(5) Your Social Security numbers and those of your dependent children.

(6) Proof of your age and the ages of any dependent children under age twenty-three.

Civil Service and Railroad Workers' Benefits

You also may be eligible for a survivor annuity benefit under the civil service retirement system if you are a widow or widower of a person who completed at least eighteen months of civilian service and, at the time of death:

the deceased held a position covered by the retirement system;
or
had accepted a reduced annuity with survivor benefits to his or her spouse.

If you are a widow or disabled dependent widower of a person covered by the civil service retirement system, you must have been married to this person at least two years before his or her death or be the parent of a child born of the marriage.

As a general rule, the amount of your widow's or widower's annuity is based on the number of years your spouse worked and on the salary your spouse earned during this period. Your annuity ceases if you remarry before age sixty.

Any unmarried children of your deceased spouse who are under age eighteen (or under age twenty-two if they are full-time students) or who are incapable of supporting themselves because of a disability which began before age eighteen also are entitled to annuities.

If you are the widow or widower of a person who worked for the nation's railroads for fewer than ten years, the railroad retirement credits earned by your spouse will be transferred to and counted toward your survivors' benefits under the Social Security program.

If your spouse had more than ten years of railroad employment, his railroad retirement credits will be combined with his Social Security credits (if any) and counted toward survivors' benefits under either the Social Security program or the railroad retirement program, depending on whether he had a "current connection" with the railroad industry when he died.

For further details on railroad retirement benefits, contact your nearest Social Security office or your nearest Railroad Retirement office.

Other Employee Benefits

If your husband worked for a private company or had his own business, he probably had group life insurance and perhaps was covered by a profit-sharing or pension plan. Most likely your husband's employer will notify you about benefits to which you are entitled. If not, contact the employer.

Be sure to check out: any accrued vacation and sick pay; terminal pay allowances; unpaid commissions; service recognition awards; disability income; credit union balance; and anything else that also may be due your husband. At the same time, ask whether you and the children are still eligible for benefits under your husband's hospital, surgical, and disability coverage and, if so, for how long.

Life Insurance

Your husband's insurance agent or company will tell you what information you have to supply with your claim. If your husband did not already decide on whether you were to get a lump-sum settlement or monthly income payments and if you have no immediate need for all of the cash you would get in a lump-sum payment, you have a number of settlement options. Generally, your options fall into these categories:

You may leave all of the money with the company and draw interest on it, with a provision that gives you the right to withdraw as much as you want at any time.

Or you may arrange to receive fixed installments on set dates over your lifetime or over an agreed-on period of time. Your insurance agent can discuss the pros and cons of these possibilities with you.

Finally, make sure to apply for any Medicare benefits due your husband—hospital or doctor bills he may have incurred and paid directly before he died but for which he did not apply for Medicare reimbursement.

A useful forty-page guide for widows and those who may be called to help widows in their financial affairs—covering everything from contacting the funeral director to life insurance, estate taxes, and probate matters—is *What Does She Do Now?* put out by the Life Insurance Management Research Association. If your insurance agent cannot give you a copy, write the Association directly at 170 Sigourney Street, Hartford, Connecticut 06105.

BEWARE: GYPS AIMED AT THE ELDERLY

Would you believe that a special tablet could be "effective for the treatment of run-down and weak conditions . . . loss of enjoyment of life . . . inability to be the man or woman formerly possible" as well as make it easier for you to endure noisy children, coated tongue, and gas?

Would you lay out money to buy mail order "electronic pulsators," "special stimulants," "geriatric elixirs," or any other chemical or mechanical product advertised as capable of restoring "lost vigor," reviving sexual activity, or even rebuilding sex organs?

I hope you wouldn't. As the late Dr. Alfred Kinsey put it: "Good health, sufficient exercise and plenty of sleep still remain the most effective aphrodisiacs known to man."

But as an elderly American, you are now the major target of an endless variety of fountain-of-youth promoters in this country. You also are the target of an endless variety of other types of gypsters attempting to bilk you out of your limited retirement income.

For tips on how to recognize health quackery, see Chapter 8, on the high cost of good health.

Even if you are not yet retired, you probably have elderly friends or relatives. Surely you want to help them avoid the gyps which could seriously deplete their modest savings or slash their monthly benefit checks.

Here is a sampling of other widespread gyps and exaggerations aimed at our elderly population:

• In the dance studio racket, con men seduce lonely, elderly women into buying oversize packages of dancing lessons, payable in advance. In some cases, confused elderly widows agree to buy "lifetime memberships" in a dance studio, at a cost of thousands, even tens of thousands, of dollars.

• In the "vitamins forever" scheme, mail order houses of questionable reputation persuade the elderly to buy "subscriptions" to geriatric preparations but refuse to act on instructions to stop the cascade of pills.

• In another gyp, a phony "Social Security representative" offers to take over your benefit check and in return to prepare your taxes, pay your bills, etc. All too often, though, those offering such services take an unconscionable cut of cash for themselves—or even accept money for payment of income taxes but never file a return.

• In the sphere of often essential physical supports, hearing aids, eyeglasses, and dentures are advertised and sold through the mails to the elderly, without benefit of doctor's prescriptions or other data necessary for proper purchases. Or these vital aids are peddled by utterly unqualified, unlicensed promoters.

• In the world of finance, there always are the stock racketeers, who frequently are able to high-pressure older people into buying worthless securities just because the elderly are so pressed for money and eager to make an extra dollar.

CAN YOU FIND THE FOUNTAIN OF YOUTH?

One day fairly soon the intensive research now going on in the field of aging will make it possible for you to feel and look "young" into your oldest years. Imaginative experiments in the field of genetics are at last promising

FINANCIAL INDEPENDENCE AND PERSONAL SECURITY

exhilarating answers to some of the most depressing—and unaesthetic—problems of old age.

When that day comes, the cures for face wrinkles and crow's-feet in women, for baldness and other embarrassing failings in men, will cease to be "secrets" and "miracles." Then the cures will be promoted and sold on the basis of their own proven worth. There will be no reason for phony testimonials and faked photographs. Then the real cures will cost only a fraction of what the worthless or near worthless treatments cost today.

It will come. And I hope it will come in time to matter to me. In the meantime, though, I (along with American women from coast to coast) will spend an all-time high total of tens of millions of dollars for a fabulous array of cosmetic gadgets, creams, and secret "methods" to turn back the clock. Simultaneously, it's quite possible that you, along with American men from coast to coast, also will spend record amounts for cures, rejuvenators, and other gimmicks to "slow" the aging process.

And we will spend these fortunes despite this brutally cold observation recently by a respected dermatologist at the University of Southern California in Los Angeles:

"With time and exposure to light, the skin loses its tensile strength—like an old worn girdle. No amount of massage has ever been shown to restore an old girdle."

Here, therefore, are warnings and guidelines to help you not waste money in two important areas of aging today: face wrinkles and balding.

• None of the facial creams, hormone creams, or so-called rejuvenating creams being sold today has been proven capable of safely preventing or removing wrinkles. This is because wrinkles are the result of permanent changes in and under the skin.

• Facial massage can temporarily improve circulation of blood to the skin but it cannot remove wrinkles.

• Facial saunas also may temporarily improve skin appearance by promoting hydration. But so will applying hot towels or coating your face with oily cream.

• Exotic-sounding face cream ingredients may slow evaporation of water from the skin and thereby temporarily improve its appearance too—but they cannot remove wrinkles either.

• Chemosurgery—or face peeling—can, though, in a limited number of cases, bring about a real improvement in the appearance of aging skin. But the treatment can be exceedingly dangerous. Like plastic surgery (which can successfully remove wrinkles), it should be attempted only by qualified physicians—not unqualified "wrinkle farms."

• On balding, the key fact is that 95 per cent of male baldness is of the "male pattern baldness" type, for which there is no known massage or special preparation cure. However, at least one effective, if tedious and costly, treatment has emerged for this type of baldness: hair transplants performed by dermatologists specializing in this field. In the other 5 per cent of baldness cases (called alopecia areata) regrowth occurs by itself in almost all instances. The "before" and "after" pictures promoting baldness cures, incidentally, are often of this type of baldness.

WARNINGS ON BUYING A RETIREMENT HOMESITE

Thousands of Americans have been lured by newspaper and magazine ads to invest now in a retirement homesite in California, Florida, Texas, New Mexico, Arizona, Nevada. Thousands are being invited and flown to retirement home developments by the developers, put up in motels for a weekend, wined and dined, bused around the developed parts of the development, shown "then and now" movies of the area to prove how rapidly it is growing, and subjected to a grueling hard sell.

Thousands have been persuaded to pay anywhere from $2,000 to $5,000 for a fraction of an acre, very often on or at the edge of the desert, at enticingly low monthly terms. I have no argument with your paying $2,000 or $3,000 or whatever for a homesite in surroundings which are likely to enrich your later years. I will even salute the farsightedness of the land tycoons who bought up huge tracts of land fifteen or twenty years ago for $50 an acre and who now can sell it for $8,000 to $10,000 or more an acre. I will argue, though, with touting these tiny parcels as great "investments."

There are millions of land parcels on the market today, so scarcity certainly won't be a factor driving up prices in the foreseeable future. In many cases all of the "investment" value—and then some—is being reaped by the developers. Whenever credit gets tight, many real estate development operations are forced to a halt, and then it's anybody's guess when the promised improvements will be completed.

Moreover, because of high-pressure sales techniques, a lot of people buy land they can't really afford. Included in the price are the promoters' high costs of advertising, bringing buyers in for the weekend, etc.

If you—or a friend or relative—are in the market for a piece of ground on which to build a retirement home, here are important rules to follow:

(1) Ask the Better Business Bureau in the area in which you are considering buying for a report on the promoter. Also ask for material to help you determine whether the price being asked is fair in comparison with the deals others are offering.

(2) Be sure the land seller gives you a "property report," not unlike a stock prospectus. The Interstate Land Sales Full Disclosure Act of 1968 requires anyone who is selling or leasing fifty or more unimproved lots smaller than five acres in interstate commerce (e.g., through the mails or advertised in nationally circulated magazines or newspapers) to furnish each customer with a statement giving "all material facts" about the land, including (but not limited to) the following:

FINANCIAL INDEPENDENCE AND PERSONAL SECURITY

- Name and location of developer and development.
- Date of property report.
- The distance to nearby communities over paved or unpaved roads.
- Taxes and special assessments you must pay.
- Existence of liens on the land.
- Whether the payments you make will be placed in escrow until you get clear title to the land.
- Existing and planned utilities and services, and their costs.
- The number of homes occupied at the time of the statement.
- Details of any obstacles to building on the land.
- The type of title you will ultimately get.

The development must file a similar statement with the Office of Interstate Land Sales Registration, an agency of Housing and Urban Development in Washington which can help you get your money back if any part of the property report proves to be fiction.

You, the buyer, have a "cooling off" period after signing the contract to change your mind about buying. The law permits you to waive this right if you personally inspected the property, so read the contract carefully to be sure you do not do so unintentionally. If you discover the facts have been misrepresented, you may sue for damages in a federal court. HUD can halt sales of land if it finds a property statement misleading, and if the courts find a promoter guilty of fraud, the penalty can be stiff.

If a developer who is covered by this act fails to give you the legally required property report, be on guard.

(3) In addition to getting this property report, find out if the state in which you are considering buying can give you the property report it requires developers to file covering subdivisions or land sold by mail. California and Florida are two such states. A responsible developer will be willing to provide a report even if not required to by state or federal law.

(4) Find out how near or far the land is from roads, public transportation, churches, hospitals, refuse removal services, etc. If these are merely promised by the developer, make sure they are described in the sales contract.

(5) Before you sign any contract, have a lawyer or the local legal aid society go over it carefully.

(6) Inspect any retirement homesite personally—perhaps by combining this tour with a vacation—since you may spend ten, twenty, or thirty years of your life there.

(7) Most important, ask yourself these questions:

How do you envision your retirement home—surrounded by wide-open space and plenty of quiet and privacy, or in the middle of a busy community, surrounded by a lot of nearby neighbors?

How are you likely to spend your time? Hiking and fishing? Traveling frequently to other places? Attending theater, concerts, other cultural events?

How near do you want to be to old friends, children, and grandchildren in your retirement years?

A sunny climate, a big sky, and a patch of ground are not enough to make a happy retirement. (See Chapter 26, "Your Most Simple Guide to Buying Land.")

19

YOUR BASIC GUIDE TO WILLS, ESTATES, AND TRUSTS

Your Will	1067
Who Should Have a Will?	1067
Estate Taxes	1068
You Need Professional Help	1070
Assets Which Cannot Be Willed	1071
The Ingredients of Your Will	1072
Simultaneous Deaths	1074
Your Executor or Trustee	1075
Probate	1076
How About Do-It-Yourself Wills?	1076
Should a Wife Have a Will?	1077
Where Should You Keep Your Will?	1078
Check List for Your Personal Affairs	1078
How You Can Disinherit Members of Your Family	1080
Co-Ownership of Property	1081
Tenants In Common	1082
Joint Tenants	1082
Tenancy by the Entirety	1082
Community Property	1083
Joint Ownership by Husbands and Wives	1083
Joint Ownership Prior to 1977	1084
Estates and Trusts—Brief Answers to Fundamental Questions	1084
just what is an "estate tax"?	1084

ESTATES AND TRUSTS—BRIEF ANSWERS TO FUNDAMENTAL
   QUESTIONS (CONTD)
      CAN YOU GIVE AWAY PROPERTY PRIOR TO DEATH AND
         AVOID ESTATE TAXES?   1085
      WHEN WILL YOU GET YOUR INHERITANCE?   1085
      WHAT IS A TRUST?   1086
      WHAT CAN BE DONE WITH LIFE INSURANCE?   1087
THE BAFFLEGAB OF WILLS, ESTATES, AND TRUSTS   1087

Your Will

This chapter on wills is not intended to educate you in how to prepare your own will. Many of the general statements herein will vary in applicability from state to state. It is suggested that you consult a lawyer in your own state before drawing a will.

Who Should Have a Will?

To the threshold question of whether or not to have a will, the blunt answer is that next to your birth certificate and marriage license your will may be the most important document of your life. Yet an estimated seven out of ten in the United States die without leaving wills! About the only reason you should not have a will is if you are satisfied to die intestate (without a will) and have your estate divided and administered according to the state laws relating to intestacy. As an intestate:

• You would not have an executor chosen by you.

• The person who administers your estate would be determined by the law of your state. In many states your surviving spouse would have priority as an administrator over your children. That may be fine if your surviving spouse is the parent of your children. But suppose that your spouse is a step-parent who does not see eye to eye with your children by a former marriage. Even worse, suppose that in addition to your children by a former marriage you are also survived by children with your present spouse. These children would be favored by your spouse. Do you intend to treat your surviving children equally or do you want to perpetuate a family feud that will rage for years?

• And say you are survived by children, but not by a spouse. In most states the law says that each child has an equal right to administer your estate. That has divided an almost incredible number of families! The survivors draw up sides and fight bitterly and relentlessly to control the administration. This situation also applies when there is no surviving spouse or children but there are other family survivors entitled to administration.

• What happens if there is no one who is entitled by law to administration? The public administrator is then pressed into service. He is an absolute stranger to you and will administer your estate according to law but impersonally and with as much interest in your treasures as an indifferent salesman selling a pair of hideous shoes.

You are the master of your property and can dispose of it (with certain restrictions in the event of a surviving spouse or the amount that you can leave to charities) by will to anyone and in such amounts as you desire. You can reward those you love and eliminate the unfaithful. You can provide for friends or charities. However, if you die intestate, state law will decide the shares of your survivors. There can be no gifts to friends or charities, and if the law says that there are no surviving relatives close enough in kinship to inherit, the state will take all.

The tax consequences of dying without a will can be horrendous. For instance, your estate is entitled to a federal marital deduction on account of property left to a surviving spouse—which may require careful and expert estate planning.

Do you take full advantage of the marital deduction and increase your surviving spouse's potential taxable estate?

Do you provide income to your spouse for life, but with no option to dispose of the assets producing this income, and full tax? In this case the principal could go to your children without further taxes that might otherwise be required of your spouse's estate.

Do you sharpen a pencil and figure out your best options in dollars and cents? Not one of these options is available to you if you die intestate.

If you die survived by minor children and no spouse, do you want to designate their guardian? Or do you want your estate to pay for a bond for a court-appointed guardian or administrator and their attendant fees?

If you are the proprietor of a business, do you want it continued or liquidated? Are you concerned by the type of investment that your administrator will make according to law or do you want to leave some specific instructions? Do you have items of extreme sentimental value that you want to leave to particular friends or relatives and not sold to strangers? Can your family afford to have your assets tied up while the court appoints your administrator?

If none of the above matters is of any concern to you, then by all means die intestate.

Estate Taxes

Estate taxes combine both the certainties of death and taxes. The taxes are assessed by the federal *and* state governments on the value of property you leave behind—but the estate tax laws of states differ widely, and generally impose much smaller taxes than the federal estate tax laws. (The federal law also gives a certain amount of credit for estate taxes paid to states.)

In view of the great variation in state tax amounts, exemptions, and other

YOUR BASIC GUIDE TO WILLS, ESTATES, AND TRUSTS

circumstances, assume that such taxes exist and now concentrate on the federal tax aspects.

A fundamental warning on federal estate taxes. Forget any ideas you might have conceived prior to 1977! The Tax Reform Act of 1976 has made much traditional tax thinking obsolete.

The starting point for the present estate tax calculation is your "gross estate," which is simply the fair market value of all property you own. Against this you are allowed certain deductions for funeral expenses, debts, and administration expenses to arrive at your "adjusted gross estate." Beginning with January 1, 1977, a "marital deduction" is then allowed for the value of your property which passes to your surviving spouse to the extent of $250,000 or 50 per cent of your adjusted gross estate, whichever is greater. A further deduction is allowed for bequests to charities. The remaining amount of your gross estate less these deductions is your "taxable estate" upon which a tentative tax is calculated at rates progressing from 18 to 70 per cent.

Against this tentative tax the estate is allowed a "unified" credit of $38,000 for decedents dying in 1979; $42,500 for decedents dying in 1980; and $47,000 for decedents dying after 1980. Finally, a limited credit for state death taxes is allowed to arrive at the federal estate tax amount.

The following illustration of the estate tax calculation assumes that the decedent died after 1980 owning property worth $470,000 all of which is left by will to the spouse.

GROSS ESTATE	$470,000
Less: Debts, funeral, and administrative costs (estimated)	−40,000
ADJUSTED GROSS ESTATE:	430,000
Less: Marital deduction (50% of adjusted gross estate is $215,000 which is less than $250,000)	−250,000
TAXABLE ESTATE	$180,000
TENTATIVE TAX ON TAXABLE ESTATE	$ 48,400
Less: Unified credit—post 1980	−47,000
Less: State death tax credit	− 880
FEDERAL ESTATE TAX	$ 520*

* This amount will be somewhat larger if death occurred prior to January 1, 1981.

If the decedent in the above example has no surviving spouse, or children under twenty-one years of age, the federal estate tax would be $77,240, for the marital deduction would not be available. The following table shows approximate estate taxes for different-sized estates with and without the marital deduction for decedents dying after 1980 (earlier years' taxes are somewhat greater due to the escalating size of the unified credit):

SIZE OF ADJUSTED GROSS ESTATE	FULL MARITAL DEDUCTION	NO MARITAL DEDUCTION
$ 180,000	$ 0	$ 520
430,000	520	77,240
1,000,000	98,000	265,600

Once over the taxable threshold, estate taxes can be high indeed!

You Need Professional Help

If you do not now have a will or if your will was drawn prior to 1977 you need professional help, which means the help of a highly qualified lawyer. The law requires certain formalities in the execution of a will. If these formalities are ignored, even the most simple will may be void.

But say that you know the formalities. You have $350,000 of assets in your own name and your spouse has $350,000. You know that your spouse will take care of the children so you intend to leave $350,000 to your spouse and eliminate your children. You know that there is a marital deduction of the $250,000 and the unified tax credit will take care of the balance. So you spend 25 cents for a form at the local stationery store, and with your knowledge of the formalities you draw a legal will in favor of your surviving spouse.

No taxes! No legal fees! Everything is quite simple!

Right?

Wrong!

You have now increased your spouse's potential taxable estate from $350,000 to $700,000 and your spouse will not have any marital deduction available. With competent advice, you would have arranged a trust with income to your spouse for life and payment of the principal to the children upon death of your spouse. A tax savings of about $60,000 would have been the result.

Or suppose you have assets of $250,000 and your wife has assets of $100,000. You decide to take advantage of the full marital deduction of $250,000 and leave your wife everything. You have managed to die without owing the federal government one dollar in estate taxes. However, your wife now has a gross estate of $350,000 on which her estate taxes, less the unified credit (after 1980), will approximate $52,000.

This tax on the wife's estate could have been avoided if you had used your full unified tax credit and by creating a trust with income to your wife for life and with principal payable on her death to your children in the amount of $175,000 and bequeathed to her the sum of $75,000 for which you would get a marital deduction. Again you have managed to die without owing the federal government one dollar in estate taxes. Your wife still has the income from $350,000 but she has a taxable estate of only $175,000. Applying the unified credit to her tentative tax the net is a zero tax liability for her estate as well as for your estate. Your tax savings would have come to $52,000.

Even if your spouse owns little or no individual property, you still can achieve substantial tax savings with proper planning.

How much does your lawyer charge for drawing a will with its associated planning? That will depend to a great extent upon the lawyer's standing in his profession, whether your will is complicated or simple, and the place of execution. The lawyer's overhead in New York City, for instance, is a lot higher than in a small town in Idaho.

Talk to your lawyer about the fee. Compared to the need for a proper will, the cost is relatively low. A simple will probably runs between $50 and $150. A complicated will with trust provisions will cost more.

You can save time if you will prepare and take to your lawyer a valuation of your assets and liabilities. Your assets should include real estate, cash in banks, stocks and bonds, life insurance, interest in a business, antiques and works of art, motor vehicles, pension or profit-sharing benefits and other assets over which you have the power of disposition. You should make it clear whether your assets are owned alone or jointly. And you also should provide the names, addresses, and ages of your relatives and beneficiaries.

You can change your will as often as you desire. But you cannot do this by drawing lines through sentences or by adding new provisions.

A change can only be effected by a new will or a codicil. You can destroy your will and die intestate but the destruction must be intentional and you should leave evidence of such intent. How can anyone ask you after you die whether the destruction was intended?

Assets Which Cannot Be Willed

You may find it strange, but there are certain assets that you own which you cannot dispose of by will.

Your insurance policies are usually payable to named beneficiary. However, the proceeds of those policies are added to your gross estate for tax purposes unless you do not "own" the policies. You generally own an insurance policy when you can change the beneficiary designation. You probably have named your spouse or children as beneficiaries of your policies and will save money on executor's commissions because the proceeds do not pass by your will. Again it is time to sharpen your pencil. Is your estate liquid? Will a forced sale of your assets to pay taxes, funeral expenses, debts, and administration expenses result in a loss? If immediate cash is required, it may be necessary to have some of your insurance payable to your estate. Any excess funds not essential for the above purposes will go to the beneficiaries named in your will.

Jointly owned property passes outside the will. This most commonly occurs with bank accounts and real estate. A familiar example of joint ownership occurs when a husband and a wife own their home, and the survivor takes title upon the death of the other. Part or all of such property may be added to the gross estate for tax purposes but no executor's commissions are payable on joint properties as they pass outside the will. The taxation of joint property is too complicated for this short treatment of the subject; discuss this in detail with your lawyer.

If your pension benefits are continued in some form after your death, you probably have named a beneficiary. Again this is an asset that passes outside your will. Whether or not the pension benefits are taxable depends on many complex factors. Likewise, if you have purchased U.S. savings bonds you have named a beneficiary and cannot dispose of them by your will.

You cannot dispose of property which you expect to inherit but which you did not in fact receive before your death. However, if your benefactor already has died and you are entitled to the property after an event such as the death of a prior life tenant your interest is deemed "vested" and you may dispose of it by will.

The Ingredients of Your Will

What kind of instructions and information should your will contain? There are certain standard ingredients which turn up in most wills.

(1) Your will must have been written clearly enough to permit a court to determine your real intent. There is a story—perhaps apocryphal—of the man who left his favorite niece an annual income in his will for "as long as she remains above the ground." When she died, her husband simply installed her in a mausoleum above ground and collected the money for the rest of his life.

(2) The opening paragraph of your will should identify you, the "testator," by name, give your place of residence, and state that you are knowingly making your will. Generally included in this opening statement is a clause that makes it clear that you are revoking any previous wills or codicils (additions or "amendments" to your will) you may have made. When you make a will, it ordinarily remains valid unless and until you revoke it.

(3) Next you generally would write a statement that directs the prompt payment of your burial expenses and all your just debts, taxes, and costs of administration. These are the first claims against your estate. Unless you specify otherwise, all the assets in your estate are regarded as a single pool

of money from which these first-claim expenses are to be paid, and your executor must charge each beneficiary with a proportionate share of the taxes.

(4) Then comes the core of your will—the provision for the distribution of your assets. A typical division is one half to your wife and one half to your children. Typically, you list first all the specific and general bequests, including charitable gifts you want to make. You may, for instance, want to leave a relative or friend a particular heirloom or some other part of your personal property, say one hundred shares of stock. This is known as a specific legacy. A general legacy is a bequest that does not designate the particular fund out of which it is to be paid. An example would be leaving, say, $1,000 to a housekeeper or someone else who has been of particular service to you. As a rule, general and specific legacies must be paid before residual legacies. What remains in your estate after all specific gifts of money or property have been made under your will is called your "residual estate." This usually is given to your principal heir. You must be careful to limit your general and specific legacies because leaving too much in this fashion may not allow enough for your residual legatees—the real objects of your bounty. In establishing the size of specific legacies, also keep in mind that if you suffer financial reverses and neglect to change your will, your residuary estate may be smaller than you intended.

Other major parts of your will include:

• *The name of one or more executors of your estate*—who will manage and settle your estate according to your instructions.

• *Provisions for some type of trust for your wife, children, or others*—if you feel such protection is necessary to keep your estate from being frittered away by financially inexperienced or irresponsible heirs. Trusts also can save on taxes. Because trusts are subject to many laws governing their organization and administration, though, they should not be set up without legal help!

• *The name of a trustee, if your will provides for a trust,* to manage and invest your trust assets for its beneficiaries.

• *The name of a guardian for your minor children*—to take care of them and their property. If you are survived by a spouse who is the natural parent, your appointment will ordinarily be ineffective. You should consider an appointment if your spouse has predeceased you or if you are concerned about the possibility that both of you may die in the same accident. You also may provide that your appointive guardian does not have to file a bond which is otherwise required in some states, and save the costs of such a bond.

• Burial arrangements—to spare your bereaved family the effort and complications of haggling over burial costs and decisions as to what type of funeral you'll have (if any). The more specific you are in stating your funeral preferences, the less burdened will be your family with the cost of such lavish, utterly unnecessary trappings as coffins fitted with innerspring mattresses. Ponder—in advance—that a funeral director is in the most advantageous position of dealing with survivors who are under great emotional stress and he also is well aware that the estate of a deceased is responsible for paying burial costs even before it pays taxes.

• Specific instructions—to guide your executors and trustees according to your wishes. You may want them to retain certain investments, to carry on your business or to liquidate it. If you are silent, they will be governed by the powers and duties laid down by statute or recognized by the courts. Such rules may not allow your executor or trustee the flexibility in handling your property that you may wish.

• Witnesses—at the end of your will is a section containing your signature, the date of your signature, followed by an "attestation clause." This clause contains the signatures and addresses of your witnesses and a statement properly certifying that they saw you sign the will. The witnesses must sign in your presence and also in the presence of each other.

Most states require two witnesses, but some require three. Even if you live in a state which requires only two witnesses, it is better to have three anyway. This will make it easier to probate your will after your death in the event, say, that you own real estate in another state which requires three witnesses to a will. A beneficiary of your will should never be a witness.

In fact, if you do make the mistake of having a beneficiary as witness, it could result in this person being partially or *totally* disinherited!

A common procedure for getting a will witnessed is simply to call in any two people who happen to be around your house when you sign your will and ask them to serve as witnesses. This is not the best practice. Your executor may not be able to locate these witnesses when the time comes to offer your will for probate. If your lawyer presides at the execution of your will, he will provide witnesses from among his associates or staff who can be reasonably easy to locate when your will is probated.

SIMULTANEOUS DEATHS

One of the most difficult problems confronting the courts is to determine the order of death of two persons involved in a common disaster. Many people believe that survivorship where no other proof exists is based upon sex, age, physical condition, and strength of the parties. That was true under the old civil law but no longer applies in most jurisdictions and in those jurisdictions survivorship must be affirmatively proved. In those states there is no presumption of survivorship. Length of time of survivorship is unimportant; one breath by the survivor is all that need by proved. Think of a shipwreck or death by carbon monoxide in a closed garage and you can see the difficulty of proof.

Assume that you and your spouse each have $150,000 in each of your names. You have made mutual wills in favor of the other which both provide that if there is no surviving spouse, your children get everything regardless of which spouse is deemed to have lived even one breath longer than the other.

But how about the IRS? If the IRS agent can show that one spouse lived one second longer than the other spouse, the temporary survivor will have a $300,000 estate with no marital deduction available. Estate taxes will be payable.

The IRS would get nothing, however, if neither spouse was deemed to have survived the other. Both estates would be $150,000 and not taxable. If, instead of children in the above example, each spouse's will made his or her brother the alternate beneficiary, one side of the family would get $300,000 and the other side nothing depending on the exact sequence of death.

To deal with such contingencies, most states have adopted a statute known as the "Uniform Simultaneous Death Act" which provides that where the devolution of property depends upon priority of death and there is not sufficient evidence that the persons have died other than simultaneously, the property of each person shall (except as otherwise provided) be disposed of as it would have been if that person had survived.

Even the Uniform Simultaneous Death Act may not cover all aspects of this question. One simple well-drawn paragraph by your lawyer will take the guesswork out of survivorship.

Your Executor or Trustee

Whom should you choose as your fiduciaries?

This is a vitally important decision. You can select your surviving spouse or a close friend who might waive executor's commissions otherwise allowed by law.

But is he or she truly informed about taxes, filings, investments, gathering assets, appraisals, payment of debts, accounting, tax audits, and many other functions?

An unsophisticated executor will, it is hoped, know enough to work closely with the estate lawyer, but there still may be pitfalls. Saving commissions with an inexperienced executor may turn out to be your greatest extravagance. You have too much to lose if he or she lacks knowledge and experience.

If you have a simple estate such as a home, cash in the bank, insurance, and a few securities, there should be little problem. A member of the family or friend can probably manage, with the aid of your attorney, without trouble.

If your estate is complicated or if you are going to establish trusts, you will need a professional. Your lawyer and your bank are ready to serve in that capacity. You can add a family member or friend as co-executor or co-trustee if that will make you more content but this may increase the commissions, too. A trust beneficiary probably should not be named as a trustee unless there is a co-trustee.

Executor's and trustee's commissions are fixed by statute or determined by the courts and are based on the size or complexity of the estate or trust. If you have two fiduciaries, the fees usually are doubled and in some states if you have three or more fiduciaries they will split three commissions.

If you choose a bank as your fiduciary, talk to the bank's representative first. Many banks will not accept the appointment if the estate is too small. If they do accept a small estate, many banks require a guarantee of a minimum commission.

Probate

The submission of your will in the proper court with proof of due execution and its acceptance by the court is known as probate. Probate may be challenged by persons who would benefit if a prior will was probated or under the distribution rules of intestacy if your will was proved invalid. This procedure is known as a will contest. Once your will is probated your named fiduciaries have legal power to act.

How About Do-It-Yourself Wills?

A young friend who was flying around the tumultuous Middle East hastily wrote to her older sister as she departed: "If the Arabs blow up the plane, then I leave everything to be equally distributed between you two (her sister and her younger brother). This includes my checking and savings accounts, my share in our property, whatever stocks are in the Merrill Lynch account, etc. Love, Mary." Hers is a do-it-yourself "will" at its utmost in simplicity—and illegality. The probable outcome if Mary's plane did blow up: a large portion of her estate would be left to her husband (from whom she is separated but not divorced) and/or her father (who has no need whatsoever for Mary's financial assets).

You surely have seen simple do-it-yourself forms for filling out wills: they are advertised for a dollar or two. You've probably also heard of people who have handwritten their own wills and had these accepted by a court—even without having been witnessed.

But! Do it yourself at your own risk! If you make mistakes, they may be discovered when it's too late for anyone to fix them.

Responsible lawyers rarely use standard forms for a will. Objective sources also urge you to avoid them because the forms will channel your thinking in advance and, as a result, you may overlook vital aspects of your affairs.

Of course, laymen have written wills and there are some jurisdictions that will recognize a will in your own handwriting, with no witnesses. For soldiers or sailors in active service or mariners at sea, an oral will may be accepted if it is made within hearing of two witnesses. These wills, though, will be good only for a short time after discharge. And barring the most extreme circumstances, to handwrite or speak a will is most dangerous if only because whoever has to read the will eventually may not be able to decipher the writing, or the witnesses to an oral will may not remember accurately what was said.

You may be inclined to ridicule some of the legal formalities on which lawyers insist (for instance, fastening the pages with grommets so none can be detached or replaced, initialing each page and any correction, the ceremony with witnesses, etc.). But, says the Research Institute of America, consider the consequences of omitting some of these formalities:

• Where a handwritten will is allowed, no typewritten, printed, or stamped material can appear on the paper.

• A whole will can be voided by a page missing, replaced, or out of place.

• A change, addition, or deletion, not shown to have been made before you signed your will (as could be shown by initialing), may void a provision or the entire will.

• Any doubts about the witnesses having seen the testator or each other sign may be resolved by evidence that the same pen was used for the signatures.

• A will may become entirely void if any writing that disposes of property is placed after the signature. In any case, the added provision has no effect.

• You cannot void a will by writing "This will is void" at the end and signing your name. You must cancel with the same formality that you write the will—or destroy the documents entirely.

Should a Wife Have a Will?

Definitely! Even if the wife owns absolutely no property of her own, she probably will inherit a portion of her husband's at his death and must have a will of her own for the redistribution of that property.

Too many families figure that, since most wives outlive their husbands, they will have plenty of time to make a will after their husbands die. But many men beat the statistical probabilities and, if the non-working wife of one of these men dies without leaving a will, the laws of intestacy can work just as much to the disadvantage of the children as if the family breadwinner had died without a will.

Another reason a wife should have a will is that she can name the guardian and/or trustee who will care for minor children and/or family property if both parents die at the same time. And this, in turn, can avoid bitter custody battles among relatives that almost always hurt the children both emotionally and financially.

Many married women fail to make a will because they feel that their property is "just not worth" the trouble of drawing a will—despite the fact that their belongings may include valuable jewelry, furs, paintings, and heirlooms, as well as insurance policies, stocks, bonds, and real estate held in their names.

Let me make the point unmistakably clear:

Every married woman should view her own will as equal in importance to her husband's. Then, to make sure benefits end up where both the wife and husband want them to end, the wife should have their lawyer prepare a will for her that does not conflict with the provisions of her husband's will.

Where Should You Keep Your Will?

Your will should be kept where it can be found immediately and easily by your executor when it is needed; it should not be kept where it can be stolen, forgotten, mislaid, or lost.

You certainly do not want it in a place where a disgruntled distributee can lay hands on it and destroy it.

Usually it is not wise to keep your will in your own safe deposit box because, on death, this box may be sealed—and sealed even though you hold the box jointly with another person. In this case, your executor would have to go to the court for permission to open the safe deposit box to find your will—an unnecessary annoyance at a terribly trying time. This is not true in all states. In some states the bank is authorized to open a safe deposit box and remove the will.

Keep your will in your attorney's safe.

Or if your executor is a bank or trust company, give it to your executor for safekeeping.

Have a copy in a safe place in your home and let your key beneficiaries know where it is. In some states you may file your will with the probate court and it will be sealed until your death. Due to administrative considerations this really is not good practice unless there are special reasons for filing.

Check List for Your Personal Affairs

You already have read that you should give your lawyer a list of your assets and liabilities to guide him in your estate planning. In addition, prepare a personal affairs check list which will assist your executor and attorney in handling your estate and inform them about where it is at all times. On this check list:

• List the names, addresses, dates and places of birth of yourself, your wife or husband, your children, your father and mother, your brothers and sisters.

• Write on separate lines and in clear detail:

YOUR BASIC GUIDE TO WILLS, ESTATES, AND TRUSTS 1079

- Your Social Security number and where your card is located.
- The location of your birth certificate and, if you have one, veteran's discharge certificate.
- If you have more than one residence, the address of each residence, the time you spend in each, where you vote, and where you pay income taxes.
- The date and place of your marriage and where your marriage certificate can be found.
- If you have been married previously, your deceased or former wife's or husband's name.
- If you are divorced, the place of the divorce, whether it was contested, who brought the action, where your divorce papers are. This will help your lawyer determine whether your former spouse has any inheritance rights remaining. If separated by agreement or court action, all the details and the place where your separation agreement can be found.
- Where a copy of any prenuptial agreement into which you entered can be found.
- Whether any of your immediate relatives are handicapped or incompetent.
- Other family information, such as the state of health of its members, whether you have any adopted children, marital problems, family feuds; "difficult" family members, if any.
- The names and addresses of others you intend to make your beneficiaries.
- If you are the beneficiary under a trust or have created a trust, where your lawyer can obtain a copy of the document.
- If you have the right to exercise a power of appointment under someone's will or under a trust, also where this document can be found.

A statement of your approximate income and general standard of living for the past several years.

- The name and address of your accountant if you have one.
- The place where copies of your income and gift tax returns may be found and the name and address of the person who prepared them.
- Name and address of your employer.
- Details of any employment contract or stock purchase plan in which you are enrolled.
- Whether you are entitled to a pension, profit-sharing benefit, stock options, or any other employment benefits. Give the name of the person who handles your company's fringe benefits plus information on how the benefits are payable on your death.
- Any union or unions to which you belong and appropriate details.
- Life insurance policies owned by you on your life; policies owned by others on your life (stating who pays the premiums on them); and policies owned by you on the lives of others. Also list annuity policies owned by you. Include the name and address of each issuing company, name and address of

your insurance agent, policy numbers, principal amount of each policy, the beneficiaries, and whether there are any outstanding loans against any of the policies.
- An itemization of all your real estate. Give the location of each property, its approximate value, the price you paid for it, any mortgages on the property and whether you own the property by yourself or jointly with others. Give the location of deeds to any property you own.
- The location and total of stocks, bonds, and other securities you may own, the name and address of your broker or brokers.
- A complete rundown of all your other assets, the approximate value of each, its cost basis, and location of each. This would include bank accounts, any business ownership, as well as your more valuable personal effects, such as jewelry, furs, art objects, and the like. (Don't overlook details of debts due to you.)
- The location of your safe deposit box and the box key.
- A complete outline of your debts, including mortgages on your house or business, leases, and other obligations. Give the names and addresses of persons to whom you are indebted and the terms under which you are supposed to repay.
- The names and addresses of whomever you wish to name as your executors, trustees, and guardians.
- The name of your lawyer, his address, telephone number, and a list of your papers in his safekeeping.
- The name and address of any person to whom you have given power of attorney.
- The names of organizations—such as fraternal or trade societies—to which you belong. Make a special note here about any benefits which may be coming to your family from these organizations.
- If you have been in active military service, the branch and period of service and the date of your discharge.
- Funeral arrangements you prefer and any preparations you have made.
- In preparing your check list, consider once more:
- Have you married since you made your will? If so, call your lawyer, tell him so, and ask him what you should do about your will.
- If you have acquired a business interest, have you provided for its disposition at your death? No matter what the size of your interest, make a sound plan for its disposition. If your interest must be sold in a hurry to pay death taxes, it may be sacrificed—and your family may be badly hurt.

These questions are primarily designed to intrigue your interest. Your lawyer surely will bring up others.

How You Can Disinherit Members of Your Family

The idea of disinheriting your spouse or children may not even have crossed your mind. However, there are circumstances under which disinheriting a member of your family can be not only the most practical but also the most considerate thing you can do.

For instance, say one of your two children has become a huge financial success and is now worth many times the value of your estate. The other is disabled, unable to work, and badly needs all the financial protection you can offer. Your realistic decision here well might be to "cut out" the wealthy son and leave all to the dependent one.

You may be able to disinherit one or more children simply by specifically stating so in your will and giving your reasons for cutting them off. In many states an explanation is unnecessary, but advisable to show that this action was not due merely to oversight. You may avert a will contest by taking this precaution even if it is legally not required. In some states a child or his issue may under certain circumstances elect against an excessive charitable bequest.

In most states you may not completely disinherit your wife or husband unless such surviving spouse has abandoned you and such abandonment continues to date of death. Or there may be some other possible circumstances permitting disinheritance—all of which should be checked with your attorney.

Laws vary from state to state, but as a general rule a widow is entitled to one third or more of her husband's estate, and if he leaves her less than that in his will, the court may later grant it to her anyway.

Moreover, many states still recognize what is called the wife's right of dower. This means that she is legally entitled to the use of one third of her husband's real estate so long as she lives.

Some states give the husband a similar right to the real property of his deceased wife, known as the right of curtesy.

In states which have abolished the old dower rights, the wife may have the choice of going along with the provisions of her husband's will or renouncing the will and claiming the share of his estate that she would have received if he had died without a will. To illustrate: a man whose estate amounts to $120,000 at his death leaves his wife only $25,000 in his will. She could, in many states, choose to reject that sum and instead take one third of the estate, or $40,000—or possibly one half.

In still other states, however, a husband may satisfy the law by leaving his wife the minimum designated percentage of his estate in trust. She is then entitled to the income from this trust during her lifetime. When she dies, though, the principal passes to whomever the husband has named in his will.

Co-Ownership of Property

You may own property with another person in several different forms. Before buying property with another person find out from your lawyer which is the most advantageous.

Tenants in Common

This is the usual form of co-ownership. In most states, unless otherwise specified, it will be presumed that property in the names of two people creates a tenancy in common. In other words, a deed to John Doe and Richard Smith will be assumed by law to indicate a tenancy in common.

Tenants in common each own an undivided one-half interest in the whole property. Of course, if there are more than two owners, each owns a proportionately equal interest, unless they have agreed to some other formula. One party may own 75 per cent, but whatever his (or her) interest it is undivided. Each party may sell his share or dispose of his interest by will. The new owner will become a tenant in common with the other owners. Death of a tenant in common does not affect his property right from passing to whomever he chooses.

Joint Tenants

In this form of tenancy you also own an undivided interest in the whole property but upon the death of one joint tenant the entire property belongs to the surviving joint tenants (some states do not recognize this form of tenancy). Thus, you may have nothing that you can leave by will because your death could extinguish your interest in the property if you are the first to die. You have little that you can sell because you are basically selling a gamble that you will outlive the other joint tenants. This type of conveyance is sometimes employed by a parent who wants to keep property in the family line, thus: "to John, Harry, and Richard Roe, as joint tenants." The surviving Roe eventually will take all. Of course, all the joint tenants may get together and effectively convey good title to all the property during their lives.

Joint ownership is not only used for real estate, but also for bank accounts, U.S. savings bonds, etc. Talk to your lawyer about the legal effect of creating a joint tenancy. How much has each one contributed? Is there a present gift involved which requires the filing of a gift tax return? Will a gift tax return be required if the non-contributing tenant survives? If the non-contributing tenant withdraws funds from a joint bank account, is there a gift involved?

Tenancy by the Entirety

This is a form of joint tenancy which occurs only when real estate is jointly owned by a husband and wife, say "John Doe and Mary Doe, as tenants by the entirety." In many jurisdictions the owning of property by "John Doe and Mary Doe" where John and Mary are husband and wife creates a statutory presumption of joint ownership as opposed to tenancy in common if the parties were not husband and wife.

Community Property

Community property is another category of ownership, similar to jointly held property. The concept behind community property laws is that all property acquired by husband and wife after marriage is considered to be owned by them fifty-fifty—no matter whose name is on the deed or title to a given property. So far as the law in community property states is concerned, the family home is owned jointly by husband and wife.

Certain assets, known as "separate property," are excluded from community property. Examples: property which belonged to either spouse before marriage, or property acquired after marriage by gift or inheritance.

Community property is recognized in only a few states. If you live in such a state it is imperative to consult your lawyer on the law in your state.

Joint Ownership by Husbands and Wives

Q. *Should husbands and wives own property jointly and will they avoid the cost of probate by so doing?*

A. While there are advantages and disadvantages, the bad probably outweighs the good.

(1) You have $50,000 in your own name and decide to buy securities for that amount in both names. If under your state law your wife is able to terminate the joint ownership and claim half of the proceeds, you have made her a gift of $25,000 for which a gift tax is payable unless part of the marital deduction is used.

(2) Instead of buying stock you put the $50,000 in a joint bank account. There is no present gift because you can withdraw the $50,000 at any time. But suppose your wife gets to the bank first? Her withdrawal for her use is a gift at that time.

(3) You have reconsidered and decided to invest the $50,000 in U.S. savings bonds in both names. There is no gift because you may outlive your wife. But suppose she digs them out of your vault, surrenders them, and keeps the proceeds? You have just made a taxable gift.

(4) You use the $50,000 as a down payment on a $200,000 home and have a $150,000 mortgage. You may elect to treat half of the down payment and the yearly payments on the mortgage as a present gift by filing a gift tax return. If you do not make the election when the property is bought, the law will make the election for you when the property is sold and you divide the sales price with your wife.

In considering the tax consequences of your gifts to your wife, keep in mind that the first $3,000 of gifts in each year is excluded. In addition, since

1976 an unlimited marital deduction is allowed for the first $100,000 of lifetime gifts to the donor's spouse. The next $100,000 of lifetime gifts is fully taxable and does not qualify for the marital deduction. A 50 per cent deduction applies to lifetime gifts to the spouse in excess of $200,000. It is unnecessary to analyze gifts made prior to September 8, 1976, because those gifts can now be disregarded and do not count against the marital gifts made after January 1, 1977.

If you think that the IRS has become your generous "friend," rethink! For what the federal government gives with one policy, it takes away with another. Although you can make the gifts as indicated here, when it comes time to settle your estate, your executors will have to subtract from your marital deduction 50 per cent of the value of your lifetime transfers (not including your $3,000 per year exclusion) when the amount of lifetime gifts is $200,000 or less. This is because the first $100,000 is free of gift tax. The second $100,000 of gifts is completely taxable without a marital deduction and for gifts in excess of $200,000 you are paying a tax on only 50 per cent of the value and therefore are taking the marital deduction on the other portion.

Joint Ownership Prior to 1977

If you and your wife owned property by the entirety prior to December 31, 1976, and have done nothing about it, hurry to your lawyer. You may be missing a major tax strategy. Your ownership for estate tax purposes goes back to the pre-1977 era when the survivor must show proof of contribution to the purchase price or face the prospect of paying tax on the full value. The Tax Reform Act of 1976 permits you to re-establish the tenancy by a completed gift to your spouse and only one half is taxed to the survivor. In deciding whether or not to make this gift, weigh the ultimate tax consequences and whether the end result will be an advantage or disadvantage.

Estates and Trusts—Brief Answers to Fundamental Questions

Just What Is an "Estate Tax"?

Under federal law, an estate tax return must be filed for every estate with gross assets of more than $175,000 for the years after 1980 by your executor (or administrator) and any tax due on this return must be paid at the time it is filed.

This enhances the desirability of arranging your affairs in ways that will minimize the tax burden on your estate and beneficiaries.

Although the federal death tax is called an estate tax, a death levy imposed by the states may be called an inheritance tax, transfer tax, estate tax, or legacy tax. State death taxes vary so widely from state to state that there is no way to generalize on "typical" amounts—and they are imposed in every state except Nevada. The actual rate may depend, for instance, on the size of the estate or inheritance or the type of property involved or the closeness of the heir's blood relationship to the person who has died.

What's more, though some states allow roughly the same kind of exemptions and deductions that the federal government allows, they do not necessarily allow them in the same amounts. If a state exemption is lower, for example, you may have to pay a state tax even though you are not required to pay a federal tax. On top of this, both federal and state tax rates and regulations undergo frequent changes.

CAN YOU GIVE AWAY PROPERTY PRIOR TO DEATH AND AVOID ESTATE TAXES?

No. You will have to pay gift taxes which are assessed at rates equal to estate taxes under federal law. This is why estate taxes and gift taxes are said to be "unified."

But you may give away up to $3,000 per year to any person, and not pay taxes. If your spouse consents to having one half the gifts treated as made by him or her, your annual gifts may total $6,000 to each donee. Thus, a husband and wife with two children could give each of them $6,000 a year, or a total of $12,000 without gift tax consequences.

For other advantages of gifts made during your life, called "inter vivos gifts" by professionals, consult your attorney.

WHEN WILL YOU GET YOUR INHERITANCE?

As soon as the executor has been appointed by the court and has collected enough assets of the estate—such as cash in the bank—he can provide survivors with sufficient funds to meet immediate living expenses.

Certain other assets, such as proceeds from life insurance policies, also go to the beneficiaries almost immediately. If the estate is relatively small and thus not subject to taxation, and if there is no litigation or other complication, the proceeds often can be distributed within a year. But if it is a large estate, and if there are estate taxes to be paid, it may be several years before you can consider yourself "rich."

An executor may not distribute the proceeds of an estate until all the legal debts of the deceased have been paid. In most states, the way debts are uncovered is by giving notice to creditors and by requiring them to file their claims within a certain limited period of time. Notice is normally published in a local newspaper for the length of time required by statute; in most states the time limits for creditors to file claims against an estate range from six months to eighteen months after the decedent's death.

In some states a specific or general legacy is payable seven months after death and you may be entitled to interest if payment is delayed. You may not get it in seven months if the estate does not have enough liquid assets to pay funeral expenses, taxes, debts, and costs of administration. If you are a residuary legatee, you may have to wait until the estate is settled (two to three years) or until the death of life tenants if their interest precedes your enjoyment of the property.

Frequently, an estate's value is established for tax purposes as the value at the date of death. However, if the estate consists mainly of securities which have dwindled in value, the executor for estate tax purposes may want to take advantage of the optional valuation date, six months from the date of death. He cannot do this unless he maintains control of most of the estate's assets.

WHAT IS A TRUST?

A trust is an agreement under which the person who establishes the trust either by his will or by a legal agreement executed while he is alive gives property to a trustee to invest and manage for the advantage of the beneficiary. It is a highly flexible device that enables you to have a say in the use of your money after you have died as well as during your lifetime. Most trusts are established for the benefit of a surviving wife and children and most trusts remain in effect for some years. Trusts also can help save on taxes.

A typical provision is that only the income from the trust may go to one beneficiary, upon whose death the principal goes to another. Some trust agreements in addition contain an emergency clause which permits the trustee to invade the principal or part of it, if necessary, to provide for the education of a child or for other unforeseen needs such as major medical expenses.

Frequently a trust is used as a means of protecting beneficiaries against their own inexperience in managing financial assets. You may, for instance, want your wife to have the income from your property during her lifetime and your children to get the property later. Or, if you are a widower with children, you may want them to receive only the income from your property until they reach a given age (say thirty) and then to receive the principal outright.

Or a trust can be used to permit a desired standard of living for your family;

to educate a minor child;

to cover unexpected financial emergencies;

to provide a lifetime income for a wife or daughter or other relative;

to give a child his (or her) inheritance in installments;

to keep the child from squandering it all in a hurry and harmfully extravagant spree;

to provide for a favorite charity;

to achieve almost any type of personal or financial objective.

The organization, purpose, administration, duration, and eventual disposition of the principal of the trust are subject to many laws, and the laws governing your prospective trust depend on the state in which you live.

There are many different types of trusts—some fairly commonplace, others not so frequently established. You will find short definitions of the various types with which you might be concerned in the section "The Bafflegab of Wills, Estates, and Trusts" at the end of this chapter.

WHAT CAN BE DONE WITH LIFE INSURANCE?

If you own a considerable amount of life insurance you can create a life insurance trust and direct to whom and in what manner the proceeds from the policies are to be paid.

As an alternative, you can have the proceeds of your life insurance paid promptly upon your death simply by naming the beneficiary in the policy. This is most commonly done. And you or your beneficiaries may direct your insurance company to pay the proceeds in either a lump sum or a series of payments.

For instance, you can authorize the insurance company to make regular payments to your wife or children—including both the income and part of the principal—for a specific period of time.

A caution: should you direct that payments be made to your children and should you die while they are minors, a guardian may have to be appointed by the probate court to handle these proceeds. You can avoid this by a clause in your will authorizing your executor to receive the proceeds and handle them to the best advantage of the children.

Most life insurance proceeds must be included in computing the value of your gross estate for purposes of taxation, unless the policy was owned or controlled and paid for by the person whose life was insured.

But it is entirely possible for a man's life to be insured by his wife. Thus, if a wife takes out an insurance policy on her husband's life and has it registered in her name as owner, the policy will not have to be listed as an asset in the husband's estate and the wife will not have to share the proceeds with the tax collector.

The Bafflegab of Wills, Estates, and Trusts

ACCUMULATION TRUST Trust in which the yearly income on the capital in an estate is added to the principal for a designated period of time—e.g., usually during a young beneficiary's childhood.

ADMINISTRATOR (ADMINISTRATRIX) Individual or institution appointed by the court to handle the estate of a person who has not left a will which names an executor or executrix.

ATTESTATION CLAUSE Clause at the end of your will containing the signatures and addresses of the witnesses and a statement that they saw you sign the will.

BENEFICIARY Person entitled to receive funds or property from an estate, trust, or insurance policy.

BEQUEST (OR LEGACY) Gift of personal property via a will.

CHARITABLE TRUST Trust in which the grantor stipulates that a certain portion of the trust be used for charitable purposes. A charitable trust may last indefinitely. All other types of trusts must have cutoff dates.

CODICIL Addition, or "postscript," to a will, drawn up separately, but with all the formality of the will itself.

CO-EXECUTOR (-EXECUTRIX) Another equal executor appointed by will.

COMMUNITY PROPERTY The concept in some states of fifty-fifty property ownership of property acquired by a married couple during marriage.

CONVEY To give or sell property to someone else.

DEATH (OR ESTATE) TAXES Taxes levied on your estate by the federal and state governments, with the amounts varying according to the size of the estate.

DECEDENT Person who has died.

DEVISE Gift of real estate by will.

DOMICILE Legal home, where person votes, pays taxes, etc.

ESTATE All assets and liabilities left by a person at death.

EXECUTOR Individual and/or institution you name in your will to safeguard the assets of your estate while it is being probated, and to distribute it according to your wishes.

EXECUTOR'S FEE Fee paid to the person or institution handling your estate —with the amount (or percentage of the value of the estate) usually set by state law.

GUARDIAN Person appointed to look after a person or property—e.g., a minor, until he or she is old enough to manage his or her own affairs.

HOLOGRAPHIC WILL Handwritten will—recognized as legal only under certain circumstances and only in certain jurisdictions.

INTER VIVOS GIFT A gift while the donor is still alive to which the donor relinquishes all rights and control.

INTESTATE Dying without leaving a will.

ISSUE Children and direct descendants.

JOINT TENANCY (WITH RIGHT OF SURVIVORSHIP) Ownership by two or more people of a piece of property, title to which passes completely to the last survivor.

LEGACY (OR BEQUEST) Gift of property—especially money or other personal property—made under a will.

LIFE INSURANCE TRUST Type of trust in which the assets are the proceeds of life insurance policies.

LIFE TENANT MARITAL DEDUCTION Provision in our federal tax law designed to ameliorate the taxation of the same asset in two estates—at the

YOUR BASIC GUIDE TO WILLS, ESTATES, AND TRUSTS 1089

death of the wife as well as at the death of the husband. It permits a husband or wife leaving a part of his or her estate to the surviving spouse to take a deduction for such amount to the extent of $250,000 or 50 per cent of the adjusted gross estate, whichever is greater. Thus, such property will be effectively taxed only in the estate of the last to die.

MARITAL DEDUCTION TRUST (see "Life Tenant Marital Deduction" above) A trust which makes it possible to relieve from the burden of estate taxation, in the estate of the spouse first to die, certain property interests described as "deductible interest." These interests are not taxable as part of the estate of the first spouse, but rather as part of the estate of the surviving spouse. The surviving spouse receives all of the income from the trust; in some cases there is a right to invade the principal; and the surviving spouse must have the unqualified right to dispose of the principal of the trust in favor of himself or his estate. The residue of the estate may also be left to the surviving spouse in trust. This "residual trust" may provide for the payment of income to the survivor and contain provisions for invading the principal. It then will provide for the ultimate distribution of the principal. However, the principal of this residual trust is taxable to the estate of the creator of the trust, and not to that of the surviving spouse.

MUTUAL WILLS Common arrangement executed according to an agreement in which husband and wife leave everything to each other. Frequently a further provision is that, when the second spouse has died, the estate is shared by the children. A reciprocal will is one which contains reciprocal gifts for and among the makers.

OPTIONAL VALUATION DATE Date on which the size of your estate is computed for tax purposes can be either as of the date of your death or as of six months after your death—providing the assets are not disposed of in the interim—thus "optional" date. It provides a financial protection for the beneficiaries in the event of a sharp stock market slide, for if the value of the estate shrinks, the tax on it will be slashed too.

POWER OF APPOINTMENT Equivalent of absolute ownership of part or all of a trust, since the person having this power may name the ultimate recipients of the assets of the trust.

PRENUPTIAL AGREEMENT Agreement made prior to marriage—often one in which both spouses forfeit any interest in the other's estate.

PRESUMPTION OF SURVIVORSHIP Clause in your will establishing a way to decide the order of death if both spouses die simultaneously.

PROBATE COSTS Costs of administering an estate.

PROBATE COURT Court in which estate settlements are made; in some states, estates are handled by a circuit court, orphans court, or surrogate's court.

PROBATING A WILL Processing a will through a court in order to establish its validity.

RESIDUARY CLAUSE Usually the key clause in your will since it covers the bulk of your "residuary estate"—typically, "all the rest, residue, and remainder" of the estate—after special, individual bequests of money and/or property have been covered.

REVOCABLE LIVING TRUST Trust in which the income from the trust is paid to a beneficiary during his or her lifetime, and to his heirs or to some other person after he dies. This type of trust may be amended or revoked at any time during the grantor's lifetime. An irrevocable living trust cannot be revoked or amended without the consent of all beneficiaries involved.

RIGHT OF CURTESY Husband's life interest in the property of his deceased wife.

RIGHT OF DOWER Wife's life interest in the estate of her deceased husband.

SPENDTHRIFT TRUST Trust in which only the income but not the principal may be touched by the beneficiary—no matter how urgent the demands or needs of the beneficiary.

TENANCY IN COMMON Title held jointly by two people, usually unmarried, to a given piece of property—i.e., real estate—although each person keeps control over his individual share of the property. Either may sell or will his interest in the property independently of the other.

TENANCY BY THE ENTIRETY Ownership by both the husband and wife in their home and/or other real estate.

TESTAMENTARY TRUST Trust established by a will to take effect after that person dies.

TESTATOR Person making a will.

TOTTEN TRUST Way, often used by grandparents, to leave money to their grandchildren. The donor opens a bank account in the name of one person "in trust for" the grandchild or other beneficiary but retains control over the trust during his or her lifetime. The proceeds are part of the taxable estate.

TRUST Property or money set aside for a certain person or persons to be managed by a trustee for the best advantage of the beneficiary.

TRUST DEPARTMENT Department of a financial institution which is staffed with specialists in the administration of estates and in handling trust funds.

TRUSTEE Individual or institution designated to oversee the handling and distribution of a trust fund.

WILL Legal document—usually in writing and properly witnessed—which describes how a person wants his or her property to be distributed after death.

20

FUNERAL EXPENSES
WHAT TO DO ... HOW TO SAVE ...
WHERE THE TRAPS ARE

Would You Know What to Do?	1092
CARE AND DISPOSITION OF THE BODY	1092
OPTIONAL PROCEDURES FOR DISPOSITION OF THE BODY	1093
ADDITIONAL POINTS	1094
MEETING THE SOCIAL AND EMOTIONAL NEEDS OF SURVIVORS	1094
Death Education	1095
FUNDAMENTAL GUIDES	1095
Preplanning Saves Money and Minimizes Misery	1096
ABOUT BURIAL LAWS	1097
Funeral Benefits—Social Security, Veterans, and Other	1098
If You Are a Dependent Widow	1099
Beware: Death Traps	1099

Would You Know What to Do?

Would you know what to do if suddenly confronted with a death in the family?

Are you aware that in the United States just the average cost of an ordinary funeral with the usual trimmings has now crossed the $2,000 milestone? "Death" has become a multibillion dollar industry, commonly involving distasteful ostentation and wasteful expenses. Each year countless thousands of families are plunged desperately and unnecessarily into debt because of these costs alone. Yet with intelligent planning the expenses connected with death need be only a small fraction of the $2,000 figure.

There are two immediate and closely related problems with which to cope at time of death:

CARE AND DISPOSITION OF THE BODY

You have several choices.

The least expensive is to donate the body to a medical school. Many educated, public-minded Americans do this. Sometimes a funeral service is held beforehand; sometimes the body is taken immediately to the medical school and a memorial service is held afterward. In that case there may be no funeral expenses at all. In most areas the medical schools pay the entire transportation costs.

Your next choice is cremation. This too can be carried out either following a funeral service or immediately after death, with a memorial service held later if desired. In the latter case no embalming or cosmetic work is required and a simple fiberboard container or a stretcher can be used, thus greatly reducing expense. You need not buy an urn for the ashes if you don't want to, and the crematory will provide a simple container without charge. (As stated previously, ashes may be sent by ordinary parcel post or the container may be carried in a suitcase.) The ashes may be scattered wherever you wish, with or without a ceremony. This may be done any time, even years later. Cremation is a clean, orderly way of returning the body to the elements and is steadily gaining acceptance.

Caution: While the actual cremation costs only around $100, funeral directors sometimes sell the family extra goods and services which can run up the bill into the thousand-dollar range, even without a funeral service.

If your family or your friends wish to build a box and take the body to the crematory themselves in their own conveyance you can do so in most states, but you first must take the death certificate to the county health officer and get a transportation permit. If a time lapse of more than a few hours is involved, or if the body is to be transported for a considerable distance, you can have the body embalmed by a funeral director or, less expensive, you can place a supply of dry ice in the box. (Embalming is mandatory if a common carrier, such as an airline, is to be used.) You must make sure in advance that the crematory will accept a body from a person who is not a funeral director. Some crematories are unwilling to do this, for fear of offending the funeral directors. Other crematories are quite willing.

Your last and most expensive choice is earth burial. As with other alternatives this can be carried out immediately after death, with a memorial service afterward, or can be done following a funeral service. Immediate burial is, of course, less costly.

OPTIONAL PROCEDURES FOR DISPOSITION OF THE BODY

These are shown below in ascending order of cost. The sequence may vary a bit with different localities and circumstances.

METHOD	COST
Bequeathal to medical school. Immediate removal of body, with memorial service to be held afterwards if desired.	Usually no cost.
Cremation. Immediate removal of body followed by memorial service if desired.	Small cost, if properly planned.
Bequeathal to medical school after a funeral service.	Usually more expensive. Depends on type of service.
Burial. Immediate removal of body followed by memorial service if desired.	May be either less or more than the above.
Cremation, after a funeral service.	Comparable to the above two methods.
Burial after a funeral service.	Most expensive of all.

(For concise, straightforward information on funeral costs and other vital facts on how to cope with the financial and emotional problems associated with death, order a copy of "A Manual of Death Education and Simple Burial" by Ernest Morgan. Cost: $2.00, plus 50 cents for postage, Celo Press, Burnsville, North Carolina 28714. It also includes directories of memorial societies, medical schools, eye banks and other tissue banks.)

ADDITIONAL POINTS

If you opt for bequeathal but plan to have a funeral service first, be sure the funeral director contacts the medical school to find out exactly what kind of embalming the school wants. Ordinary embalming usually is not acceptable.

If the body is to go immediately to the medical school, the school usually will make arrangements with the funeral director and instruct him.

If you wish the ashes returned from the medical school after the body has been used, be sure to let the school officers in charge know in writing.

If you choose cremation without a funeral service, ask that a simple fiberboard container, or the equivalent, be used instead of an expensive casket. Specify that no embalming is to be done, and no cosmetic work. The same applies to immediate burial. If possible, use a cemetery that does not require a vault or liner; these are costly.

If ashes are to be scattered, they should be pulverized first. The "ashes" consist of soft bone fragments which can be placed in a large bowl and pulverized with the handle of a hammer.

MEETING THE SOCIAL AND EMOTIONAL NEEDS OF SURVIVORS

The way these needs are met has an important impact both on the expenses involved at time of death and on the social and emotional well-being of the survivors.

All human cultures, and some animal cultures as well, have death ceremonies of one kind or another. Funeral directors point out, and correctly, that these ceremonies help meet the social and emotional needs of the survivors. It is important to remember, however, that the amount of money spent on death ceremonies bears little relation to the effectiveness of these ceremonies in meeting human needs. For example, a thoughtful memorial service held in a church, private home, or other meeting place at little or no expense can sometimes actually be more helpful than a costly funeral service.

There are two basic forms of death ceremony:

A funeral service is, by definition, a service held in the presence of the body. Because of the necessary time lapse between the hour of death and the meeting, it is generally necessary to embalm the body. It is common practice in our country to use a funeral parlor for the ceremony, though the funeral director can, if desired, bring the body to a church or other meeting place. Some funeral services are conducted with the casket closed, others with it open to permit viewing of the body. For purposes of viewing, the face of the person who has died is carefully prepared to appear lifelike. Whether the viewing of a lifelike body helps the survivors to accept the reality of death is an open question. Funeral ceremonies tend to be costly. Before ordering a funeral service be sure you are fully aware of exactly what services will be included and what each will cost.

Do not simply accept a "package deal"! Some states have laws requiring funeral directors to provide customers with a written rundown on all costs and charges and also prohibiting crematories from insisting that remains be put in a casket for cremation.

The other type of death ceremony commonly used in modern society is a memorial service. This is, by definition, a service held after the body has been removed. In a memorial service the attention tends to be focused on the life of the person rather than on the dead body. It offers, furthermore, greater flexibility in choice of location and in timing and programming. Since the body is removed promptly after death, no embalming or cosmetic work is required, a simple container can be used instead of an expensive casket, and other expensive goods and services become unnecessary.

The use of a memorial service often can cut the expenses of a death to a fraction of what otherwise would be involved. If well handled, it can in most cases serve the human needs just as well or better than a funeral service.

Death Education

Before you can deal wisely with the financial aspects of death, you must be able to cope effectively with the philosophical, emotional, and social aspects. In this sphere, death education plays a key role. This education should take place before death occurs or becomes imminent, but whenever it occurs, it is valuable.

Death education which is restricted solely to the philosophical, emotional, and social aspects, however, and which omits instruction in the financial aspects of death, is deficient and not achieving its full potential.

An important by-product of death education—if, indeed, not a central purpose—is to promote the maturity of the individual, whatever his or her age may be, with relation to himself or herself and to society, and to refine his or her motives and priorities.

When you have completed reading this chapter you will have had a significant session in death education. If you wish to pursue this further, the Ernest Morgan "Manual" (see page 1093) will be a concise source of information and inspiration based on experience.

FUNDAMENTAL GUIDES

Be careful even of the advice given by your closest personal friends and dearest relatives. They may have the best intentions, but when in trouble you need help from people who have the full information and background to advise you.

If no prior arrangements have been made and if you are in a state of befuddlement, ask a sensible level-headed friend or relative, who knows what the family can afford, to help you with the arrangements. This person or these people will help find a licensed, reasonable funeral director who will co-operate in arranging for the type of funeral you want.

If a person dies at a distance and the body is to be shipped home, it may be transported in a private vehicle (assuming legal details are taken care of) or it may be sent by commercial carrier. Most airlines provide this service. Amtrak Express is less expensive and can provide service to some three hundred destinations.

If the body is cremated near the place of death, the small container of ashes can be mailed by parcel post or carried in a suitcase.

Get advice—from your lawyer, minister, friends—on the arrangements you will make *before* you authorize any given mortician to remove the body from home or hospital. Obviously, once a mortician takes custody of a body his bargaining power is multiplied. Note: Most large hospitals will keep a body for at least a day, and often longer, while you make arrangements.

If a bank or law firm is the executor of the deceased's estate, ask the appropriate officials to help arrange economical services.

If the funeral costs must be financed out of borrowed funds until any estate is settled, find out what interest rates will be charged by the funeral parlor or other lending source.

Check exactly what is included in the price tag on a casket. The casket alone? A complete range of services? Which? Don't permit a mortician to make you feel guilty or disrespectful if you try to economize.

• Steer clear of expensive frills such as costly "burial vaults" to enclose the casket, costing up to $150 or even more. Unless the cemetery requires these vaults, you can omit this expense altogether.

• If your family is in a serious financial squeeze, tell the facts to your funeral director. If he's reputable, he will make allowances for your circumstances.

• If you plan to buy a cemetery plot, find out if the cemetery participates in a nationwide Lot Exchange Plan under which, if you move to another area, you can trade one plot for another.

• If you want to donate your body (or part of it) for medical teaching purposes, transplants, etc., write to the medical or dental school of your choice and ask for details on how to go about it in your area. The above-mentioned manual lists names and addresses of U.S. medical schools and their rules covering bequeathal of bodies.

• Wait a few months or even years, until the shock is dulled and you've regained your balance, before you buy expensive markers or memorials.

Preplanning Saves Money and Minimizes Misery

By careful preplanning you generally can save 50 per cent to 75 per cent of the expenses with which you ordinarily are hit at time of death!

Equally important, the planning will help you accept the reality of death in advance so that when it does occur you will be able to cope with your own feelings more effectively. Then, too, the preplanning will help avert costly and painful misunderstandings within your family.

A practical way to preplan is to join a memorial society. You will find one of these co-operative, non-profit societies in 175 cities in the United States and Canada. You will be charged a one-time membership fee of $5.00 to $20 and your membership may be transferred from one city to another at little or no cost. The societies will provide you, a member, with the specific local information you need to plan effectively and in many cases they have advantageous contracts or agreements with funeral directors. As a member, you will normally pay from $150 to $350 for a cremation or a funeral. (Annual savings by the members run into millions of dollars.) Look for a complete list of the societies with their addresses in the Morgan Manual (see page 1093) or send a self-addressed stamped envelope to the Continental Association of Funeral and Memorial Societies, 1828 L Street N.W., Washington, D.C. 20036, and ask for a list.

You also may preplan without a society if you are prepared to make the effort and check with local funeral directors. Choose one who will make the preferred arrangements in advance of the inevitable event. You may calculate the costs now (subject to future price increases) or even may finance them in advance. If you do pay an advance be sure the money is put in a state-supervised trust and you can withdraw it if and as you decide to cancel the arrangements.

ABOUT BURIAL LAWS

There is a good deal of confusion about burial laws. There are patent lawyers, divorce lawyers, and corporation lawyers but who ever heard of a burial lawyer? Some funeral industry practices are required by law; many are not, and funeral directors often are not sure which are which. Hence they often are mistaken in the legal information they give their clients.

Laws governing burial are meant to protect public health and safety, but they commonly have the added purpose of promoting the business interests of funeral directors. For example, some states have a law that only a licensed funeral director may transport a dead body and one or two states actually require embalming!

Most state boards which regulate the funeral industry are composed entirely of funeral directors. Regulations made by these boards acquire the force of law.

The laws and regulations are almost continuously changing, and their interpretation and enforcement vary considerably from time to time and place to place. In some cases non-existent laws are observed by funeral directors and their clients. In other cases, unreasonable or selfishly motivated laws or regulations are quietly ignored.

The average family is best able to cope with this situation if it is affiliated with a memorial society or burial committee which knows its way around.

Funeral Benefits—Social Security, Veterans, and Other

A lump-sum death benefit is payable under Social Security upon the death of any worker who either is fully insured or has Social Security credit for as little as a year and a half out of the three years just before death.

This lump-sum death benefit of $255 may be collected by the surviving spouse even if there are no funeral expenses. If no spouse survives, it can be collected only to defray funeral expenses, or to reimburse persons who have advanced money for these expenses. It cannot be collected for funeral expenses if other specific provision, such as death insurance, was in force to cover those expenses. Hence any such insurance should be designated a "life insurance," not funeral insurance.

As in the case of other Social Security benefits, you must apply to get the payment. If a worker in your family dies, immediately get in touch with your nearest Social Security office.

Under the law, the lump-sum benefit is to amount to three times the worker's Primary Insurance Amount, but no more than $255. That $255 maximum has been in the law since 1954 and Social Security benefits have risen so spectacularly since then that the lump-sum benefit has become a flat payment of $255. Even the current minimum Primary Insurance Amount multiplied by three is more than $255.

Congress froze the maximum of $255 because of concern that increases would lead only to additional swelling in the costs of funerals. While in some quarters the belief is an increase in the maximum would not have the same impact on funeral costs as it would have had in earlier years, there also have been recommendations for the elimination of the lump-sum benefit altogether so that the money could be used to help finance other benefit improvements.

If the deceased person is a veteran, these are the key government funeral benefits:

• A basic $300 allowance will be paid toward the burial expenses of honorably discharged veterans, including veterans of peacetime service.

• Free burial will be permitted in a national cemetery in which space is available. Burial in national cemeteries is available, too, to an eligible veteran's wife or dependent children.

• For veterans who are not buried in a national or other U. S. Government cemetery, an additional "plot allowance" of up to $150 may be payable.

• If a veteran's death is service-connected, the total funeral expense allowance can go up to a total of $1,100.

- Headstone or grave markers will be available through the VA to the deceased, honorably discharged veterans.

You can get complete information on government burial benefits for veterans and their families at any VA office or veterans' service organization. Most post offices and funeral parlors are familiar with the benefits also, and can assist a beneficiary in applying to the appropriate government agency.

And there are many other types of death benefits.

For instance, some trade unions and fraternal organizations provide the payments for the families of their members. There are benefits for the survivors of any person who has been a railroad employee. Other employers may provide them as well.

If occupational factors were involved in the death, there may be Workers' Compensation benefits. There may be Automobile Club insurance; some auto insurance policies carry death benefits.

Depending on the circumstances of death, there may be liability insurance benefits. In some states, too, the families of state employees are entitled to survivor benefits.

And it is commonplace for the county to pay burial expenses for indigent families.

So many death benefits go unclaimed every year—usually not received by the persons most in need of them! Check out every angle with utmost care.

If You Are a Dependent Widow

Don't make an investment of any sort until your mind is working more normally and you have had ample time to get the advice of competent objective advisers concerned only with *your* welfare!

Don't buy securities.

Don't make loans.

Don't convert your insurance policies.

Don't buy annuities.

Don't make any investment.

You have a limited amount of money. It is now more important than ever. Take your time, get the best advice available to you before you take a single step.

Beware: Death Traps

Survivors, particularly widows, are frequent victims of vicious swindlers—often men or women who seem friendly and honest, but really aren't.

A favorite device is to collect a non-existent debt owed by the deceased, or to deliver merchandise (say, a Bible) that was never ordered.

- Another favorite of these gypsters is to inform the survivor of a non-existent life insurance policy on which a final premium must be paid before benefits can be collected, or some other "valuable asset" requiring a final payment of some kind.

• Widows are prime prospects for bad investments, and, when asked, even representatives of reputable investment firms will at times recommend changing stock portfolios merely for the sake of the commissions involved.

Moral: Be cautious, go slow, consult an experienced member of the family or other trusted business advisers, neither pay any unfamiliar debt nor sign any document before careful investigation and before you have recovered your balance.

21

YOUR GUIDE TO THE STOCK MARKETS

Introduction	1103
What Are Stocks?	1104
Should You Invest in Stocks?	1105
Key, Self-Revealing Questions	1106
What Causes Prices of Stocks to Change?	1108
What Are Dividends?	1109
How Big Are Dividends?	1109
How Do You Find Out What Stocks Are Doing?	1110
How Do You Get Information About Stocks?	1111
What Is the New York Stock Exchange?	1113
What Are Unlisted Securities?	1114
What Are Bull and Bear Markets?	1115
What About Brokers? Commissions?	1115
There's a Way to Buy Stocks Without Paying Any Commission	1117
But Where Do You Find a Broker Who Wants You?	1118
How Do You Detect a Swindler?	1118
Employee Savings Plans	1119
How to Start an Investment Club	1120
How to Beat the Stock Market Through "Dollar Cost Averaging"	1122
Investment Advice—Where Do You Get It?	1123
Professional Investment Management—Trend of the Future	1123

How Do You Chooose the Right Adviser for You?	1125
Way Out on the Horizon—Financial Supermarkets and Financial Planners	1126
Stock Market Letters	1128
How to Avoid the "Garbage" Stocks	1128
What About Regional and Second-Tier Stocks?	1129
How to Read an Annual Report	1130
What Is a "Blue Chip"?	1132
What Is a "Growth" Stock?	1133
What Is a "Special Situation" Stock?	1134
Should You Buy on Margin?	1135
Selling Short	1137
What Are Rights?	1138
Are You Better Off with Stock Splits?	1139
What Prices/Earnings Ratios Are All About	1140
Do Options Make Sense for You?	1142
For Your Protection—the SIPC	1145
Investment Bibliography	1147
the stock market and how it works	1147
learning to invest	1148
textbooks on theory and practice	1149
for the experienced investor	1149
newspapers and periodicals	1150
The Bafflegab of Stocks	1151

Introduction

Let's say that tomorrow you receive the news that you have a sweepstakes combination which gives you a chance to win from $50,000 to $200,000 net after taxes. Let's say your dream is to turn this into a million. How much of your possible winnings would you have to invest for how long, and in what ways, to reach this magic mark?

(1) You could invest $75,000 and be a millionaire within thirty years, if you could earn the 9.0 per cent a year which was the average rate of return on all common stocks listed on the New York Stock Exchange between the mid 1920s and the late 1970s. (The assumption was that you invested an equal sum of money in each stock each year and reinvested all your dividends.)

(2) You would have to put up $114,000 to become a millionaire in the thirty-year period if, instead, you put it into municipal bonds paying 7½ per cent (not the peak but fairly typical rate in the late 1970s).

(3) Or you would have to put up your entire $200,000 winnings plus $1,000 more—$201,000—to become a millionaire three decades hence if you invested in a passbook savings account paying the 5½ per cent rate prevailing in the 1970s, or $99,000 in 8 per cent long-term saving deposit certificates.

But let's come back down to earth: you're not due to win any wild contests or to get any financial windfall soon.

You may be, however, approaching your best earning years, or actually in them, and thus you may be ready to set aside fairly substantial sums. How much would you have to invest each year at 6 per cent to become a millionaire in one decade, two decades, three?

You could become a millionaire within thirty years by setting aside $12,649 a year if you could achieve the relatively commonplace yearly rate of return of 6 per cent—in stocks or bonds or real estate or some other investment medium.

You could become a millionaire within twenty years if you set aside $27,185 each year at 6 per cent.

Or you could become a millionaire in ten years if you invested $75,868 each year at 6 per cent.

These statistics were developed for me by the American Bankers Association and the New York Stock Exchange. They're drastically simplified, of course, since they do not take into account the inevitable tax bite on capital gains, dividends, or interest. And it's unrealistic to assume any set rate of return on stock or bond investments will continue indefinitely.

Nevertheless, a first key point is that, in today's society and at today's available rates of return on investments, it is within the realm of possibility that you can become the fabled millionaire. Right now, hundreds of thousands of American families have $1 million in assets. And there are several thousands families in the United States with assets of well over that.

A second key point is that the vast majority of these very wealthy have invested not with the goal of safety or liquidity or dividend income, but instead with the consistent aim of long-term capital gains. Most of the very wealthy look for returns of at least 10 per cent and usually 15 to 20 per cent a year in various types of enterprises, securities or real estate, or in the farther-out mediums of art works, antiques, commodities, etc.

A third key point underlined by the computations is that the faster you want to make your million the higher the return you must seek—which means the greater risk you must be willing to assume. The implication of this third fundamental point is that you must be able to afford to take the chance.

And a fourth point: not everybody aspires to be a millionaire. What most people want is an investment program that can help them reach some of their long-term family financial objectives: a comfortable retirement, a college education for the youngsters, perhaps a second home. For them, investing successfully can bring peace of mind and successful attainment of their goals even if they never come close to being millionaires.

What Are Stocks?

When you buy stock of a company you buy part of the ownership of that company. If, say, you buy a share of—let's call it the Widget Company—in effect you buy a part of Widget's plant, its output, and everything that company owns.

If the Widget Company has 10,000 shares of stock outstanding and you own 100 shares, you own 100/10,000 or 1 per cent. As a stockholder you are normally entitled to vote in the election of directors and to participate in other company affairs. Each share has one vote and big companies have millions of shares outstanding and many thousands of stockholders. For example, the American Telephone & Telegraph Company in the late 1970s had 2.9 million shareholders; General Motors had almost 1.3 million; International Business Machines had more than 580,000; and General Electric had more than 545,000. If the company whose stock you hold grows and increases its earnings per share, the prices of your stock should rise over the long run. The price also will fluctuate day by day based on ever changing supply-and-demand trends. It is a rare stock that stands still.

Should You Invest in Stocks?

Any well-balanced portfolio of investments should include stocks. But before you buy, consider these factors:

(1) *There is always an element of risk in stock ownership.* According to a survey of public attitudes toward investment conducted for the New York Stock Exchange in the late 1970s, most Americans resisted assuming the risks associated with common stock ownership. Whether because stocks have failed to keep up with inflation in recent years, disastrous previous experiences, or the attractiveness of other investments, stocks have plunged way down to ninth place—after life insurance, savings accounts, a home, and U.S. saving bonds—in investor popularity. The whipsaw, bull-and-bear markets of the late 1960s and 1970s have soured investors on the market. There is still money to be made in stocks, but you, an investor, must proceed with more caution than ever.

What degree of risk are *you* willing to assume?

(2) *Inflation is here to stay.* Stocks long have been considered a hedge against inflation. According to the Center for Research and Security Prices at the University of Chicago, an investment in a random cross section of stocks on the New York Stock Exchange from 1926 through 1977 would have increased in value to a degree giving you an average rate of return (before taxes) equal to 9 per cent a year compounded annually. To translate, an investment of $1,000 in 1926 compounded annually at 9 per cent would have grown to more than $80,000 in fifty-one years.

During bouts of extreme inflation, however, stocks may not be a good hedge. Late in the 1970s, the Dow Jones industrial average of thirty leading stocks was a numbing 8 per cent lower than its level ten years earlier! Investors who had taken for granted that an investment in the shares of America's largest companies automatically would keep up with inflation were disillusioned, disgusted, and determined to stick to a "never again" attitude.

Yet with proper research and timing, stocks can be excellent investments—even when the market as a whole does not keep pace with inflation. While many glamour issues on the New York Stock Exchange were declining in the late 1970s, for instance, smaller issues on the Big Board and on other exchanges were reaching new highs.

Often overlooked, too, is the fact that stocks are liquid investments. Real estate, while often appreciating faster than the rate of inflation, may be tough to sell. Other hedges, such as coins, stamps, art, and antiques, may be even more difficult to turn into cash (particularly when you need the money). Stocks, though, are readily bought and sold.

(3) *The economy is growing.* Inflation and recession may cloud the horizon, but the long-term trend of the U.S. economy is up. Stocks are a basic way for you to participate in this long-term economic growth.

The economic problems involved in energy and environmentalism, for instance, may adversely affect the stock performance of some companies. At the same time, these same problems create new opportunities for other companies. By buying shares in these corporations, you can participate in their future growth.

Key, Self-Revealing Questions

Can you afford to invest? Purchase stocks only after you have adequate life insurance and sufficient savings in cash or the equivalent to help you through an unexpected financial emergency. If you do not have this extra disposable income, you cannot afford to invest in stocks.

Have you determined a specific investment goal? Set a goal suited to your needs before you invest and be faithful to it until your circumstances change. If your goal is income, you'll want one type of stock; if it is growth, you'll want another; and if it is, above all, security of principal, you'll want a third.

If you're a young person earning more than enough to meet your family's current expenses and have set aside funds to cope with financial emergencies, your objective normally will be growth. Therefore, you'll buy stocks that promise to grow in price along with the economy's growth over the years. You may take greater-than-average risks in the hope of getting higher-than-average profits. Although you may lose on a stock in which you speculate, you can afford the risk at your age; you have time to recoup.

Do you have the emotional temperament to own stocks? As the New York Stock Exchange itself says, "Many persons should never buy stocks. The individual who can be seriously upset by a slight decline in price or who goes off on a spending spree when prices rise is better off out of the stock market."

That leads into the confession that one of the most embarrassing questions frequently put to me is, "What do you think the stock market is going to do?" And, usually before I can open my mouth, the questioner adds, "Boy, I bet you get plenty of inside tips! In your position, you probably clean up . . ."

When I answer that (1) I don't get many tips and the ones I do get I invariably ignore, and (2) I don't clean up, and what's more, have absolutely no desire to—the mildest reaction is disappointment.

It is true, though, for because of my temperament—my emotional attitude toward speculating in the stock market—I don't feel comfortable taking stock tips. I haven't the temperament to be a gambler in Wall Street. I don't clean up because I don't even try to. But I don't go broke either.

Without my being particularly aware of it, my activities in the stock market reflect my own personality. And the purpose of this confession is to emphasize to you the vital point that if your aim is to be a serene as well as a successful investor the first thing you must do is analyze your own personality.

To be even more specific, don't buy—or sell—stocks because it seems the thing to do: in the stock market, "conforming" doesn't pay off.

Don't buy stocks of a type or in amounts that give you anxiety and concern. If you are so nervous about owning stocks that you can't take a trip without worrying about what is happening to your stocks, stay out of the market.

Don't try to beat the professional traders unless you are willing to study enough to become a pro yourself.

In short, follow the fundamental rule: "know thyself."

Can you and are you willing to invest your time? It takes time to become informed about the stocks which interest you. If you don't have this time you may find yourself acting in response to tips or rumors, which, however intriguing, are usually wrong.

You wouldn't dream of buying a house simply on the basis of how it looks from the outside. You would examine the inside thoroughly, check on the reputation of the builder, the quality of the construction, and a hundred other aspects. The same thoroughness must be applied to buying stocks, for along with buying a house, investing in the stock market may be among the most important financial decisions you make.

You also probably wouldn't dream of trying to trade in and out of real estate and pit yourself against the real professionals in this field. Again, the same rule must apply to stocks. In the long run, you, as a novice investor, will almost surely make out better than an in-and-out trader.

One of the best ways to select a stock is on the basis of your own familiarity with (and respect for) the company's products or services.

Do you have the advice of an experienced and reputable broker who can help guide you?

Do you expect too much too soon? Many inexperienced investors become fidgety when their stocks rise only a little or decline soon after they buy them. They refuse to allow time for their stocks to perform as expected. Millions who have taken short-term losses would have shown handsome profits if they had had more confidence in their own judgment and were willing to give their stocks a chance to move.

The overall caliber of hundreds of the stocks listed on the NYSE is sufficiently high to bail you out of your errors most of the time, assuming you have the courage and capacity to hold on. The odds on gain are heavily against the individual trading blindly in and out of the market and heavily for the individual investing for the long term.

Can you adhere to your investment objectives? Many investors pay lip service to the objective of long-term growth and ask their brokers to recommend stocks to them that meet this criterion. Then they hear rumors and read stories about stocks that have doubled and tripled in a period of months. In envy and greed, they soon are badgering their broker to recommend speculative stocks in the hopes of also making tremendous gains. Be honest about your objectives. If you want long-term growth, buy and hold stocks that promise long-term appreciation. Don't be sidetracked into dangerously risky, speculative situations.

Are you fully aware that you buy stocks, not the stock averages? A common error of the amateur is to justify the holding of a "cat or dog" issue because the overall economy is growing or the stock averages are climbing. Even in the biggest bull markets, many stocks slide and, in this era's viciously selective and for so long deeply depressed market, what you own has been critical.

Do you have an overall family investment plan to protect you from falling into "hit or miss" investing? Most new investors overlook the importance of a diversified financial program that allocates funds to major types of investments—real estate (a home), stocks, bonds, etc., in addition to liquid savings in cash or its equivalent, life insurance, and similar vehicles.

There is no formula under which you can automatically put a proper percentage in each type of investment. The key point, though, is to avoid the error of "hit or miss" by diversification of your financial program.

What Causes Prices of Stocks to Change?

Once a company has sold its original stock to the public and the stock is freely traded in the market, the price of the stock will be set solely by what buyers are willing to pay for it and what sellers are willing to take. This is a classic case of how supply and demand operates in action.

Thus the market price of a stock is the reflection of the opinions of all the people who are buying or selling it. Among the key factors influencing the price people are willing to pay for a stock is the company's earnings. The more money a company earns, the greater the value attached to its shares. Obviously, selecting a profitable stock involves knowledge and judgment of the company behind it. How aggressive is its management? How popular are its products and services? What new products is it offering or planning? What about the industry in which it operates? Does it have a bright future? (The trolley car industry once was hot.) What about its competitors? How many and how strong are they?

Finally, what about the general business trend? Is it favorable or unfavorable to the industry in general and your company in particular?

What Are Dividends?

When a company earns a profit, it usually pays a part of its earnings in the form of dividends to its owners—its stockholders. Stockholders receive a certain amount for every share of stock they own. For example, if you own 100 shares of a company's stock and the dividend is $1.00 a share, you will get $100 in dividends. The rest of the company's earnings will be put back in the business.

The decision to pay a dividend on common stock and the amount of the dividend paid are determined by the directors of the company, who are elected by the stockholders. Many factors, including how much the company earned and how much should be retained in the business, influence the directors' decision about the dividend. Traditionally most companies distribute about 50 per cent of their earnings in the form of dividends. A study made in the early 1970s by the New York Stock Exchange showed that the 1,400 companies then listed on the Exchange paid out 51 per cent of earnings as dividends.

There are many companies that have paid dividends over a long span of years. In fact, on the New York Stock Exchange there are companies that have paid out some cash dividends to their stockholders every year for more than a hundred years. J. P. Morgan & Company has been paying dividends since 1840, the Singer Company has paid dividends since 1863. Also, the New York Stock Exchange lists 170 companies that have paid cash dividends quarterly for fifty years or more.

How Big Are Dividends?

The size of a dividend will depend on what a company earns in any given year. Most companies try to pay dividends regularly each year at a fixed annual rate such as $1.00 or $1.50 or $2.00 for each share of stock. In good years the rate may be increased or an extra dividend declared at the end of the year. In bad years a company may reduce its dividend or eliminate it completely. Interestingly enough, there are some major companies with fine records that don't pay any dividends. They plow back all the earnings they generate for future developments of new products and services. So, while the dividend payment is important for many who are looking for a yield every year on their investment, it does not carry so much weight with other investors.

One important term used in connection with dividends is yield. The yield of a stock is the yearly dividend divided by the cost of the stock. For example, if you paid $60 for a stock that pays $3.00 a year in dividends, your yield is 3/60 or 5 per cent. If you bought a $50 stock and it pays $1.00 a year in dividends, your yield is 2 per cent.

On an overall basis, dividends in modern times have provided yields from as high as 7.8 per cent in 1948 to as low as 2.6 per cent in 1968. This is the median yield on dividend-paying common stocks listed on the New York Stock Exchange, but the range of yields on individual stocks can be very sizable in a given year. For example, in the late 1970s, when the median yield on all NYSE stocks was 4.5 per cent, 136 stocks were paying yields of 8 per cent or better while 166 stocks were paying yields of less than 2 per cent.

How Do You Find Out What Stocks Are Doing?

That's easy! Just look in the financial section of your newspaper for the latest daily reading of any stock market indicator it publishes and see whether that indicator is up or down. The Dow Jones averages and Standard & Poor's indexes are the most familiar of these market "thermometers." The New York Stock Exchange also publishes a composite index that includes all its listed common stocks. The American Stock Exchange publishes one too and the over-the counter market has a composite NASDAQ index (see page 1114) which indicates the movement of stocks traded in this system. These indexes will tell you at once the price trends of large groups of stocks. In addition to these broad indicators, there are special indexes indicating how special industry groups—such as utilities stocks—have moved as a group.

If you are interested in finding out how a specific stock that you own or may want to buy is doing, you will find that most major newspapers publish detailed price information every day for stocks listed on the New York and American stock exchanges. They may also print condensed lists of stocks traded on regional stock exchanges and the over-the-counter market.

A chart showing you how to read a financial table follows.

Reading Newspaper Stock Tables

New York Stock Exchange Transactions—Day of Week, Date, Year

YEAR HIGH	YEAR LOW	STOCKS	DIV.	P.E. RATIO	SALES 100's	HIGH	LOW	CLOSE	NET CHG.
55	49¼	AT&T[1]	2.80	11	1362	51¾	51¼	51¾	–
9⅝[2]	6⅛[2]	AT&T wt[2]	–	–	1221	6⅜	6⅛	6⅜	–
75⅞	59½	Gen Elec	1.40[3]	19	1231	60½	57¾	59¼	–1¼
84⅝	70⅜	Gen Mot	4.45e[4]	9	797	71⅝	70⅝	71⅜	+½
78½	74⅝	Gen Mot pf[5]	5	–	15	75⅝	75	75⅝	+⅝
76⅞	59	McDonalds	–	63[6]	1048	60	58	59⅜	+¼
88⅞	77⅝	M.M.M.	1	34	444[7]	78⅜	77½	78⅛	–⅛
91	68¾	RCAcv.pf[8]	4	–	30	69⅞[8]	68¾[8]	69¾	+½
123¼	94⅞	Sears	1.40a	24	389	97⅝	94½	97[9]	+1⅝[9]

YOUR GUIDE TO THE STOCK MARKETS

1. Abbreviated name of the corporation issuing the stock. The stocks listed are common stocks unless an entry after the name indicates otherwise.
2. Wt stands for warrant. As with stocks, the price range indicates the highest and lowest prices per share paid for this warrant on the Exchange during the year—in this case, $9.62½ and $6.12½.
3. Rate of annual dividend—for this stock, $1.40. This amount is an estimation based on the last quarterly or semi-annual payment.
4. Letters following the dividend number indicate additional information. Here, for example, the "e" designates the stated amount as declared or paid so far this year. Other symbols are explained in tables appearing in newspapers.
5. "pf" following the name indicates a preferred stock.
6. The price of a share of stock divided by earnings per share for a 12-month period.
7. This column shows the number of shares reported traded for the day, expressed in hundreds—for this stock, 44,400. This number does not include stocks bought in odd-lot quantities, that is, in quantities less than 100 shares for most stocks. The letter "z" preceding an entry indicates the actual number of shares traded.
8. The highest price paid for this security during the day's trading session was $69.87½—the lowest, $68.75. Cv. pf. stands for convertible preferred.
9. The closing price or last sale of the day in this stock was at $97.00 per share. And this, the closing price, is $1.62½ more than the closing price of the previous day—as indicated by the "+1⅝."

If the newspaper doesn't print price information on the stock in which you are interested, chances are the stock is not popular or widely held. In that case, call your broker and ask the price of the stock. He will have a wide variety of reference materials from which he can get the answer.

How Do You Get Information About Stocks?

Whether you are among the tens of millions of us who already hold shares of publicly owned corporations and mutual funds or among the men and women who are considering becoming stockholders, most of you share this one characteristic: you want to learn more about the stock market and about individual stocks, but you don't know how to go about getting the information.

Okay, here are nine simple guidelines on how to inform yourself:

(1) Make an excellent start by enrolling in one of the courses offered through New York Stock Exchange member firms in major U.S. cities from coast to coast. Under this program, brokers offer lectures covering subjects such as: your investment objectives, investing for income, investing for growth, and methods of investing. Check with your local brokerage houses to find out what they have available and when they plan their next series.

(2) Take courses on investing at adult education institutions across the country. Investigate the sources in your neighborhood. Colleges and junior colleges in your area well may offer special credit and non-credit courses in investment. In New York, the New York Institute of Finance offers broad

training in finance to both amateurs and professionals. Some of these courses can be taken by correspondence.

(3) Ask your own broker or investment firm for literature on specific companies and industries as well as on the general stock market. Several hundred New York Stock Exchange firms alone are now turning out more than 400,000 pages of investment research a year—much of it exceedingly helpful.

(4) Get free copies from a local NYSE firm of the Big Board's basic educational pamphlets. You will learn plenty from such publications as *The Language of Investing* and *How to Get Help When You Invest.*

(5) Write to the Publications Department, New York Stock Exchange, 11 Wall Street, New York, New York 10005, for an "Investors' Information Kit" providing basic booklets for $2.50 (cost at end of 1970s).

(6) Use your public library. You will find dozens of useful books written for the amateur as well as for the more sophisticated investor. On pages 1147–50 there is a bibliography of good books on investing that you might want to read.

(7) Read the business and investment news in your newspapers and subscribe to one or more specialized business publications—such as *Barron's, Forbes, Financial World,* and *The Wall Street Journal.* Keep up with trends in the economy as well as with developments in individual industries and companies.

(8) Learn by doing. For instance, you might begin learning through an investment club. These clubs are groups of people who share a common interest, get together usually once a month to discuss securities, and invest small sums contributed by each club member in stocks selected by the group. Brokers often serve as advisers to these clubs and many of the best clubs are members of the National Association of Investment Clubs. Write this association for advice on forming a club. (A separate section on investment clubs follows.)

(9) Check your local educational television stations to see whether any are offering, as some do, a program or programs on general business news and on the stock market.

Any of these moves will help you. All of them will help make you well informed and ready to continue your education on your own. When you make decisions based on facts and your study of available information—plus the help of a qualified broker or adviser—you have gone through the process which distinguishes investing in stocks from gambling.

Your decisions will not always be correct, far from it, but you will at least have acted in a mature, intelligent way. And, being intelligent, you'll not only learn from your mistakes but also translate them into successes.

What Is the New York Stock Exchange?

Although there are tens of thousands of different stocks, the ones bought and sold most frequently are traded on the floor of the New York Stock Exchange. The New York Stock Exchange has a history going back to 1792, well over 185 years ago, when a group of brokers gathered under a buttonwood tree on Wall Street to make up rules of conduct as to how the business of trading in stocks could be done.

Since that humble beginning, the New York Stock Exchange has become the leading securities exchange not only in the United States but also in the world—and many of the world's other exchanges are patterned after its activities.

The Exchange is located in a historic building at 11 Wall Street at the corner of Broad and Wall streets in New York and physically encompasses a trading floor about the size of a football field. On that floor in the late 1970s, more than 2,100 common and preferred stocks were being traded, worth almost $800 billion in market value. In these stocks alone, the number of transactions often equaled 50,000 a day. To handle these transactions, about 2,700 people were involved on the floor of the Exchange.

As the 1980s neared, the Exchange was an organization consisting of 1,366 members who had bought Exchange memberships (commonly called seats) for prices that varied in the past ten to fifteen years from $35,000 to over $500,000. Most of these 1,366 members represent brokerage firms whose primary business is carrying out the orders of other people to buy and sell securities. These brokers are paid commissions for executing the orders placed by their customers.

In the late 1970s, there were nine stock exchanges in the nation: the New York and American (also located in New York City, at 86 Trinity Place), and seven regional exchanges—the Boston, Cincinnati, Intermountain (in Salt Lake City), Midwest (in Chicago), Pacific (with trading facilities in San Francisco and Los Angeles), Philadelphia, and Spokane.

As the decade of the 1970s neared a close, the American, Boston, Midwest, New York, Pacific, and Philadelphia stock exchanges began operating the Intermarket Trading System (ITS), an electronic communications network. The system enables brokers representing public customers to reach out electronically to another participating exchange to obtain a better price on dually or multiply listed stocks. In effect, ITS links the nation's major exchange trading floors to create a nationwide trading environment.

The Intermarket Trading System was a response to securities legislation passed by Congress in the mid 1970s that called for the creation of a national market system for trading securities. While the national market system is supposed to encourage competition, Congress did not spell out how this should be done or how the system should be structured. As a result, it may be many more years before the government and the securities industry hammer out a system that fully satisfies the congressional mandate. Blueprints for such a system range from one not unlike today's system of stock trading to such extreme proposals as a fully computerized stock exchange that would eliminate trading floors and traders.

At the approach of the 1980s, however, the New York Stock Exchange still dominates stock trading. It does the bulk of trading in listed securities because of the high caliber of its markets in the shares of its listed corporations: AT&T, IBM, General Motors, General Electric, etc. To be listed on the Big Board, companies have to meet the highest existing standards. These standards involve earnings, assets, number of shares outstanding, number of stockholders, and number of stockholders who held at least 100 shares. The standards for listing on the New York Stock Exchange also are raised periodically.

The listing standards of the American Stock Exchange (known as the Amex) were deliberately established at a lower level—and to the Amex went many young, smaller corporations not yet seasoned enough to meet the NYSE criteria.

Most regional exchanges traded in stocks that also were listed on the New York Stock Exchange. In fact, 90 per cent of their volume came from issues listed on the NYSE. In addition, the regional stock exchanges traded in local stocks. For instance, stocks of Chicago-based companies were traded on the Midwest Stock Exchange.

What Are Unlisted Securities?

Stocks listed on recognized exchanges are called listed stocks. Huge numbers of stocks and bonds, however, aren't listed on any exchange at all and are bought and sold in what is called the over-the-counter market.

The vast over-the-counter market is not a place. It is a method of doing business: by private negotiation among securities broker/dealers who communicate via an immense communications network rather than use a trading floor on which to buy and sell securities.

It is a market which in volume and variety of transactions dwarfs the listed exchanges. And it is a market which not only has no market place; it also has no ticker tape and not even any rigidly fixed hours of trading.

Most bank and insurance company stocks are traded in this market. So are U. S. Government bonds, municipal bonds, and as of the late 1970s the securities of some large, well-known companies (Anheuser-Busch, Bekins Company, Ethan Allen, Noxell). But unlisted securities in general are those of small companies.

The over-the-counter market offers investors a broad variety of issues ranging from the most conservative to the most speculative. Here investors will find many attractive growth stocks of companies which have not yet become popular because they operate in a regional area rather than on the national scene. Here the stocks are given time to "mature" before they are listed on one of the exchanges.

What Are Bull and Bear Markets?

When a lot of people decide at about the same time to buy stocks, this increase in buying interest tends to push up the average price of stocks. If the price rise of these stocks overall is substantial and prolonged it is called a bull market.

When a lot of people decide at about the same time to sell stocks, their more or less simultaneous selling tends to push down the average price of stocks. If the price decline is substantial and prolonged it is called a bear market. If the price decline is both substantial and precipitous, we run into the possibility of a panic.

To be bullish or bearish, then, simply means to think that stocks will go up or down. The reason the term "bull" is linked with those who expect an uplift in prices is probably the tendency of a bull to lift and throw up an object with his horns. The bear is usually more cautious in his fighting tactics and tries to knock down his opponent.

What About Brokers? Commissions?

If you are to do your buying and selling of stocks through a broker, it is obviously of vital importance to you to choose one who can service your account properly. But don't create a tough and unnecessary problem for yourself by expecting the broker you choose to be right all the time. For he won't be—and when he is wrong, you may be tempted to follow the tips of amateurs who intrigue you by claiming they are making fortunes. This way often leads to disaster and every day a dismally large percentage of Americans do take this course. Even the most astute professional will not be right all of the time. In fact, in some periods, his advice will range from indifferent to downright bad.

Choosing and recommending stocks is not a science. It is an art. Your broker should be right enough of the time to help guide you toward your investment objectives and help you to enhance your assets. You should be able to trust his experience, research, and judgment and you should feel comfortable with him. That's all. It's *your* money, *your* investment program. And basically your nest egg is *your responsibility*.

Here are five key rules to follow in selecting a broker.

(1) Choose a firm that is a member of the New York Stock Exchange. Of course there are non-member firms that also rank at the top, but you are a beginner and you probably have no sound information on these. The New York Stock Exchange in the late 1970s had about 470 firms including nearly

all the important firms doing business with the public, for an estimated 90 per cent of all the securities business in the country. Moreover, member firms of the New York Stock Exchange must meet the highest standards established to date—fulfill minimum capital requirements, undergo both an annual surprise audit by an independent CPA firm and spot financial checks by the Exchange. The member firm's brokers must complete a minimum training period of four months and pass an Exchange examination. These requirements give you at least some protection and it is only common sense to accept it.

(2) Examine the brokerage firm's commission schedule. Since May 1975 commission rates charged by Exchange member firms have been negotiable. Until that time, exchanges determined the commissions brokerage firms could charge.

Now that brokerage rates are unfixed, you can and should shop for the best available terms.

Most brokerage firms charge small customers rates similar to the old uniform commissions—but several so-called discount brokerage firms have emerged. While they provide few, if any, of the services you may expect from a brokerage firm—research, investment advice, a broad range of products and services—they will buy or sell stocks for you for fees which are frequently much lower than those of the major firms.

If you are an investor who knows exactly what you want to do and expect your brokers merely to carry out your orders, these discount brokers can be money savers. If you are an investor who needs or wants advice, counsel, and investment information, traditional brokerage firms may offer more value.

(3) Shop around as you would shop around for any service as important as this. Ask your friends, business acquaintances, and local banker for recommendations on which broker might be the best for you—particularly important in the uncertain conditions of the late 1970s. Call at least three or four brokerage firms in your area and talk to the manager of each. Tell each one about your investment goals, the amounts of money you can invest, and ask whether he can assign someone to your account with whom he thinks you will have good rapport.

(4) Ask each firm for its recommendations of investments for a person in your financial position and for its research reports on the companies suggested. Incidentally, the person who will eventually be assigned to you may be variously called a registered representative, a customer's man, or an account executive—but you will call him your broker.

(5) Select your broker on the basis of your comparisons of the firms and their advice to you. Then give the broker all the pertinent facts about your financial circumstances and goals. The more he knows about your situation, the better he can advise you. Be frank and honest. Ask what you should

reasonably expect in terms of capital gains and over what period of time. Find out how much service he can provide, how often you should expect him to call you, and how often he expects you to call him for information.

There's a Way to Buy Stocks Without Paying Any Commission

Q. Would you like to build your portfolio of stocks or add to good stocks you already own without having to pay any brokerage commissions at all—not even the "bargain" commissions offered by discount brokers?

A. Of course you would. And you can achieve this by accumulating your stocks through one of the dividend investment plans offered by some nine hundred of the largest, most widely held corporations in the United States as the 1980s opened.

And not only do these plans permit you to reinvest your dividends on extremely favorable terms, but many also give you an option under which you can invest additional cash (over and above what you receive as the dividend payment) for the purchase of the company's stock under similarly favorable terms to you.

The dividend reinvestment part of this is not new. An estimated 1.5 to 2 million individuals and institutions already are participating in these so-called "original issue stock dividend reinvestment plans." It has been estimated that each year in the late 1970s between $800 million and $1 billion was reinvested by stockholders under these plans.

The benefits of the plans are undeniable:

• You are provided a simple, convenient, and economical way to invest relatively small amounts, at substantial savings in brokerage commissions and administrative costs.

• The automatic reinvestment is, in effect, forced savings—and most of us need this discipline to keep us from dissipating the relatively small amounts we would get in cash dividends.

• The automatic reinvestment also is a form of "dollar cost" averaging (see pages 1122–23), which means you buy the stock in price downturns as well as upturns and "average out" your purchase prices. It's a superb way to avoid buying only at peaks, as so many do.

• The compounding effects that result from this periodic reinvesting produce larger dividends as your investment grows which in turn are reinvested, etc.

Significant new twists also are being developed.

• Some companies have started offering shareholders a 5 per cent discount with the purchase of shares through dividend reinvestment.

• The cash option is even more significant because it permits you to invest additional cash in the stock at specified times (generally quarterly or monthly) and within specified limits (generally a maximum of $3,000 per quarter) without payment of brokerage commissions or any administrative cost to you. All your invested dollars go toward the purchase of shares, none for expenses usually involved.

You might build a diversified portfolio including many of our nation's leading companies simply by making modest original investments in these companies—and then taking advantage of the dividend reinvestment privilege and the "cash" option plan.

The companies find the programs beneficial, too (or they wouldn't be offering them). And you could, over a reasonable span of time, accumulate a substantial portfolio of leading U.S. stocks, without paying any brokerage commissions on the major part of your holding. Not bad!

But Where Do You Find a Broker Who Wants You?

Let's say you don't participate in a dividend reinvestment plan but you do want to start buying stocks. However, you don't know any brokerage firms in your area with which to open an account and you're not sure where to turn. What do you do?

You send a postcard including your name and address to PIO Directory, Public Information Office, New York Stock Exchange, Inc., 11 Wall Street, New York, New York 10005. You will receive by return mail and without charge a small pamphlet giving you the names and headquarters addresses of hundreds of New York Stock Exchange member firms which say they are willing and able to handle your small account—and listing what minimum requirements and criteria each firm may have.

In the late 1970s these firms had 3,500 branch offices in more than 800 cities in all 50 states, of which more than 1,000 or 33 per cent were located in 24 major U.S. cities. More than nine out of ten of them say they do not have a minimum dollar requirement for the size of any buy or sell order they will accept from you. More than eight out of ten (or about 2,000 branch offices) say they will buy for or sell to you any stock traded on the major stock exchanges at any price—with no minimum price-per-share limitations either.

What the NYSE is obviously trying to do with this free pamphlet is to counter in part at least the very negative publicity Wall Street has received for its attitude toward and treatment of the small investor in the past several years.

How Do You Detect a Swindler?

Another key rule to follow in selecting a broker is: explore each of the following questions about any person who suggests stocks to you, even a broker at what you believe is a highly reputable firm—and *if any answer is yes, beware, for these are frequently the earmarks of a swindler.*

Does he plug one certain stock and refuse to sell you anything else? The crook always has a specific stock to sell and he'll not bother with you if you request another stock or ask for written information about the company he's plugging.

Does he promise a quick, sure profit? The legitimate broker never guarantees that the price of any given stock will go up. Nor will he attempt to guarantee you against losses.

Does he claim to have inside information? Second only to outright fraud, alleged "inside information" has cost investors more money than anything else. Most tips are phony, and furthermore, if he truly does have inside information, there is always the possibility that at some future date he might be sued by other investors because he improperly obtained the inside information and you too might be liable in a lawsuit if you use the inside information.

Is he in a hurry and does he urge you to buy "before the price goes up"? The legitimate broker doesn't try to stampede you into action.

Can you check his reputation? The crook will have no references except perhaps forged ones which won't stand checking.

Employee Savings Plans

An excellent way to enter the stock market and start creating your securities nest egg is via your company's employee savings plan—if it offers one.

The fundamental mechanism of an employee savings plan is simple.

(1) A participant voluntarily contributes part of his or her salary through payroll deductions. The most common contribution is 3 to 6 per cent of one's salary.

(2) The company then matches all or part of the participant's savings with a company contribution. The average is 50 cents by the company for each $1.00 the employee saves, but in some companies the corporation contribution is higher.

(3) The company and employee contributions are put into an employee trust fund to be invested and later paid out to the employees. In some cases, part of the funds are placed in the company's own common stock, but usually the investments are in a wide selection of stocks similar to the range of a mutual fund portfolio. And, generally speaking, the company turns over the management of these investments to a professional management company which oversees them.

A majority of employees in companies offering these plans take advantage of them. Most save at the maximum rate their plan permits. And most stay in their plan until they leave their jobs or retire. There are many benefits. First, the company is automatically boosting the chances you will get a profit from the savings program by the amount of money it has put in to match your contributions. Second, you get professional management of your funds at no cost to you and you also get a diversification of a portfolio which helps make sure that, over the long term, the overall fund will grow. And third, there are tax advantages arising from the fact that your employer's contribution is not taxable income to you in the year in which it is made. You pay no taxes on this money and only pay taxes on the contributions when you finally draw out your nest egg on leaving the company or retirement.

A variation on this program is company stock purchase plans. Under these, the company helps encourage employees to buy stock in the company. In the simplest version, an employee signs up to purchase stock in the company through payroll deductions every month and is credited over the period of his or her participation with buying shares of the stock. The company usually picks up the bill for any commissions or other fees involved in the purchase of the stock and keeps all the records indicating how many shares of stock the employee owns. Obviously, if you are having $50 or $100 a month deducted from your paycheck to buy stock, you will wind up with fractional shares of stock and this is permissible under these company stock purchase plans.

Use one of these plans if you get the opportunity. They are a superb plus for any employee eligible to save and invest this way.

How to Start an Investment Club

Let's say you feel that the only way you'll get started in the stock market is by being forced to invest a certain amount every month or so—and you want to do this via an investment club.

If so, you have plenty of company. In the late 1970s there were about 25,000 investment clubs across the nation with an estimated membership of more than 375,000. The majority of the clubs in operation for several years have been profitable, reports the non-profit National Association of Investment Clubs in Royal Oak, Michigan. Some 71,000 people belonged to clubs that were members of the NAIC and the track record on the investing of these clubs has in a surprising percentage of cases impressively surpassed the Dow Jones averages—not bad at all considering the fact that many professional managers of money didn't do nearly as well.

Basically, investment clubs are groups of ten, fifteen, or twenty people who work together, know each other socially, or belong to the same fraternal or business organization—and who then meet once a month to invest money regularly. In a sense, each club is akin to a small mutual fund with each club's members contributing $10, $15, $20, $25, or perhaps as much as $50 a month apiece into the club kitty for investment in stocks. Before stocks are purchased the club's members must make extensive investigations on the choices to be made.

If you are thinking of or are at the point of trying to start an investment club, you must recognize that you will be inviting a financial fiasco unless you know and manage your group according to the basic rules. Here are your ten guidelines:

(1) Limit your initial membership to ten or fifteen people. An investment club should be a long-term proposition and your members must be compatible not only personally but also in their attitudes toward investment.

(2) Understand, from the outset, that an investment club offers no avenue to instant riches. Instead, a get-rich-quick philosophy frequently is the cause for a club's failure.

(3) In an exploratory meeting with prospective members, try to arrive at an overall investment policy. For instance, what growth rate of your funds will you try to achieve? Will you invest every month?

(4) Set a reasonable goal for growth of your investments, including dividends and capital appreciation.

(5) Plan to invest a given sum each month no matter what the overall market conditions are. By buying shares of a selected company at both higher and lower prices, you average out the per-share cost over the long term.

(6) Plan also to reinvest dividends as they are issued.

(7) Aim for a diversified portfolio as protection against major swings in one segment of the economy or another. Strive, say, for shares in a dozen different companies per $10,000 invested.

(8) Seek guidance from well-qualified brokers, economists, security analysts, and established business publications. The amount of research and self-education members are willing to do and share with each other can mark the difference between a successful and an unsuccessful club.

(9) Before you formally establish your club, consult a qualified lawyer or tax adviser on how to get the biggest tax advantage for your club. Your club should have some legal status because brokers may refuse to do business with an informal organization. Usually, a partnership is the most economical form. If there are earnings in any given year, all members must report this on their income tax returns, of course.

(10) Also at the start, draw up a written agreement covering the club's investment policy; the maximum proportion any one member may own; which member will deal with the club's broker; how much information each will be expected to present monthly; what happens if a member wants to leave and wants to be paid out for his or her shares. Also make sure when you establish your club how much each will be expected to contribute monthly—and make sure, too, that the amount is a comfortable sum for each member.

Follow these rules, consult the NAIC for more detailed guidelines—and the likelihood is that your club will be profitable. Incidentally, there are many NAIC publications that you will find useful when trying to decide which stocks to buy. For illustration, the NAIC has and will send you samples of a fifty-page investor's manual, stock selection guides, and a portfolio guide ($6.00).

The NAIC's address is 1515 East Eleven Mile Road, Royal Oak, Michigan 48068.

How to Beat the Stock Market Through "Dollar Cost Averaging"

One way you can beat any viciously fluctuating stock market, put your money to work, and sleep well at night is through "dollar cost averaging"—a stock-buying method that many institutional as well as individual investors use in a logical attempt to acquire a stock at a reasonable price.

First, let's assume you don't have any convictions about where the stock market is heading in the next several months—but you feel strongly that the long-term trend of the U.S. economy is upward and stock prices will be much higher on the average ten years, fifteen years from now.

Let's also assume you've accumulated some extra cash and you earn enough to be able to accumulate cash for investment from time to time. Okay:

(1) Decide now how much money you can comfortably invest at regular intervals.

(2) Plan to invest the same fixed amount at regular intervals in the future —say, the fifteenth of each month or the fifteenth of every third month or the fifteenth of every sixth month, etc. Don't get fainthearted and hold back purchases if the market drops.

(3) Keep this up over the long-term, so your shares can grow with the economy's growth over five or ten or more years.

(4) Ignore the day-to-day fluctuations in the market, for you aren't trying to guess the bottom. You're averaging out your costs and the fundamental uptrend of the market over the long-term should carry you with it.

Here's an easy example of dollar cost averaging with a hypothetical investment of $50 a month. The price swings have been exaggerated and commissions have been eliminated to make the illustration stand out.

Date	Invested	Price per Share	Shares Bought
Jan. 15 1980	$50	$25	2
Feb. 15	50	20	2½
Mar. 15	50	15	3⅓
Apr. 15	50	15	3⅓
May 15	50	20	2½
June 15	50	25	2
July 15	50	30	1⅔

As you can see, you have bought fewer shares at the higher prices, more shares at the lower prices—with equal amounts of money. The average price of your shares on the seven dates is $21.43 per share. But with your $350 you have purchased 17⅓ shares, so each share has cost you $20.19.

In this hypothetical case, you would be showing a paper loss in April 1980, but you would be nicely ahead by July 15 (your cost per share, $20.19; the market, $30).

You can, of course, lose even with this system if your judgment is so bad that you buy a stock that doesn't realize its growth potential or if you are forced to sell out when the market value of your accumulated shares is less than your actual cost. So you can't commit funds to dollar cost averaging that may be needed for other purposes.

But I'm assuming that you'll follow these easy—but absolutely essential—rules. If so, history shouts that over the long-term you'll come out well ahead.

Investment Advice—Where Do You Get It?

Most investors expect, ask for, and get advice on buying and selling stocks from their stockbrokers. Most brokerage firms have research departments or access to professional research staffs and constantly feed their clients (you) with a stream of buy and sell recommendations. Some firms will even manage your portfolio on a non-discretionary basis—meaning you give the broker authority (discretion) to buy and sell without checking back for your approval. (Many brokers, though, shy away from such accounts.)

All you have traditionally paid for such services has been your commission fees—nothing more. But this is in the process of change—and this is just one of many great new changes taking place in the field of investment advice. Read on . . .

Professional Investment Management—Trend of the Future

When my husband and I accumulated a nest egg to invest in securities some years back, we entrusted it to a small, little-known, but top-notch investment counsel firm in Wall Street. We paid the firm an annual fee based on a small percentage of our portfolio's overall total value each year. In return, the firm took over all investment decisions and worked to increase the size of the portfolio and, thus, the size of its fee. When the firm was dissolved about a decade later and we reluctantly terminated our relationship, we were spectacularly ahead of the Dow Jones average. We couldn't possibly have done as well devoting a few hours (if that) a week to managing our money.

This type of professional management for a fee is now in a renaissance and breaking into entirely new areas. The investment manager who supervises the funds of the small investor for a fee is one of the financial trends of the future in our country. Brokerage companies have taken over or set up investment management subsidiaries which are wooing accounts in the up to $25,000 range. Some established investment advisers are cutting the minimum account they'll manage for a fee to $10,000. And a growing number of banks are taking accounts as small as $10,000 (and even under) to manage. Until fairly recently banks were interested only in $100,000-and-up accounts.

Also new on the scene are a growing number of small investment counsel firms which accept accounts as low as $5,000. These are the so-called "minicounselors" and the likelihood is there will be hundreds servicing the small investor in a few years.

The reasons for this unexpected movement to serve the small investor aren't hard to find. The market declines of the 1970s made millions of small investors brutally aware of how atrociously unprepared they were to manage their own money. They were also bitterly disillusioned by the performance of their go-go mutual fund shares. Simultaneously, many brokerage firms discovered just how profitable it could be to handle the small investors' business. What's more, trading in and out of stock to make commissions on small accounts came in for universal condemnation.

Here are several key characteristics of the investment counsel firms.

The firm will take responsibility for your entire investment portfolio, will buy and sell on your behalf to achieve whatever goals are consistent with your needs, and will generally aim for enhancement of your portfolio's value. These firms make no commissions on your transactions. Their earnings come from the set percentage fee—usually 1½ or 2 per cent or a minimum dollar amount—you pay on your total portfolio and thus they profit most when you profit.

Your fee will be tied to the size of your account. A typical fee might be 2 per cent of the total, or 2 per cent on the first $10,000 and a smaller percentage on amounts above $10,000. Others might charge a yearly minimum of $250. Fees are usually payable annually, although you may arrange otherwise. Of course, the fees are deductible on your federal tax return if you itemize.

You pay your own brokerage commissions in addition to the fee you pay. Sometimes you can ask the investment adviser to put your trades through your own broker, but generally you open a brokerage account with a firm suggested by your investment adviser.

You receive a statement—usually monthly—of all transactions and a list of securities you own and a periodic report on the progress of your account.

You may open your account with cash or securities or both. You usually give your adviser a limited power of attorney so he can make discretionary investment decisions for you. All securities are bought in your name and you alone can withdraw capital or securities from your account. You may cancel the power of attorney at any time.

Generally, you give your investment adviser discretion to make investments for you without consulting you every time he wants to buy or sell something for your portfolio. Some advisers, however, do consult with clients in advance of taking action, and still others do not want a discretionary account setup.

You may close out your account at any time on written notice. You may have dividends credited to your account or sent to you. You may withdraw a given percentage of your funds on a regular basis and you also may tell your adviser what stocks or industries you want to avoid.

But the central point of this is that in most cases you have no control over what securities are bought and sold for you. Your adviser takes over once your objectives are set. He's paid a fee to help you achieve your investment goals.

Of course, there are many variations in the way investment counseling is developing. Under the usual bank setup, the bank sends you a list of its recommendations on securities to be bought and sold. You then indicate if you agree and send the buy and sell order documents to your broker for execution.

Under the way most minicounselors operate, each client has his own account with an average of from five to ten or twelve stocks, depending on the size of the account. Thus, if the minicounselor has given you some very good advice and you hold a cross section of excellent securities in your portfolio, your whole portfolio can grow rapidly in value.

Obviously, you can't expect the fancy treatment given someone with a million-dollar account. You will not have long personal interviews; you may talk to your counselor only on the phone and even then not too much; you will not receive a portfolio designed just for you; you will find that your portfolio is quite similar to other accounts that the minicounselor manages.

But there is nothing wrong with any of this, for presumably the stocks recommended to you are the stocks in which the firm has confidence.

How Do You Choose the Right Adviser for You?

(1) Decide at the very beginning what *your* investment objectives are: Long-term growth? Current income? Maximum safety? Compare your objectives with the stated investment philosophy (if any) of each of the investment management firms you are considering.

(2) Explore the credentials of each firm's officers and research staff. Where does it get its investment research? Investment counseling has been an unregulated field in the past with no established standards for the counselors. It's only recently that the SEC has moved to set up some sort of standards.

(3) Ask the firm to provide you with references against which you can check these credentials—and follow up on them. Check with local banks and brokerage firms. Do not hesitate to query other clients to whom you are

referred. Question any friends or acquaintances who may have been clients or may have information.

(4) Pay particular attention to the performance records of the firm. How have the organization's actual accounts made out during the past five or ten years? (*Not* a selected "model" account!) If the firm hasn't been in existence that long, check back on the previous performance records of its individual members with other organizations. If the firm refuses to divulge its performance records, be skeptical about any of its claims.

(5) See what you can find out about the firm's performances in bear as well as bull markets. A firm should be able to demonstrate it has at least lost less than average in bear markets and surely gained more than average in bull markets.

(6) Make sure you differentiate between a firm's stated investment goal of a growth rate per account of, say, 10 to 15 per cent a year and its actual achievement.

(7) Try to interview personally at least one or two of the firm's officers and use this interview to discuss your investment goals and to ask such questions as these:

Are you permitted to specify the securities in which you want to invest? The answer should be no, or why pay your money for professional advice?

What is the procedure for withdrawing part or all of your funds to, say, meet an emergency? Can you do so immediately? How much, if any, of the fee is refundable if you cancel before completing a year?

How many different companies are in the portfolio of a typical account of the same size as yours. How often is your account reviewed?

At what intervals do you receive financial statements covering trading activity and progress reports on your portfolio? Who will have custody of your account?

(8) Before you make your decision among firms, compare the fees charged as well as their services and investment philosophies.

(9) Beware of any manager who pushes you to sign up. No reputable firm will use this type of hard sell. Take your time.

(10) But once you have selected a firm you consider competent, alert, and geared to your needs, don't try to second-guess the manager or push in turn. Let your investment counselor exercise the judgment you're paying for during a reasonable time span. Then reconsider, if need be.

Way Out on the Horizon—
Financial Supermarkets and Financial Planners

When the "financial supermarket" finally comes, it will be one of the most exciting developments on the U.S. financial scene: most, if not all, the major financial services you need available to you under one roof. And surely several emerging trends are telegraphing what is ahead.

Commercial banks are not only expanding their activities in the management of investment portfolios for both the little and the big fellow, they also are preparing income tax returns for a fee, aggressively promoting their extensive estate planning services, pushing innovations in paying of customer bills, creating new savings methods, and maintaining leadership in the overall lending field. Many banks are moving fairly close to one-stop financial centers even now.

Similarly, insurance companies are expanding the forms of insurance sold under one roof: life, homeowner's, health, etc. They are increasingly powerful factors in the making of personal as well as institutional loans. The insurance salesman who sells mutual funds is commonplace. Now an increasing number of insurance companies are planning stock brokerage subsidiaries.

Stock brokerage firms are studying the concept with utmost seriousness. Some brokers are diversifying by buying real estate and investment management companies. Many brokers now sell life insurance, some handle tax shelters (real estate, oil, and cattle deals). Although no brokerage firm is anything like a one-stop center, the giants are known to be working on it.

Still way out on the horizon is the organization which offers in one place *truly professional, high-caliber* assistance on services of such scope as: investment advice on stocks, bonds, mutual funds, other mediums; guidance on a sound overall insurance program; help in making out your income tax; financial planning for retirement; assistance in planning your estate and drawing up your will; bill-paying; on and on.

Why is the financial supermarket so easy to explain, so difficult to achieve?

The key stumbling block is the need for truly high-caliber professional experts. For such supermarkets can come into existence only when they are staffed by experts trained in each area, capable of giving you the assistance you want and guiding you, the individual. Although we have independent experts in each area, bringing them together in a constructive, profitable arrangement is something else again.

Another stumbling block is the establishment of standards for such a group, for in the long run this is imperative to protect the public. Several organizations are now at work to develop a professional category of "financial planner" and this should be a reality by the early 1980s.

Meanwhile, though, all over the country new small organizations are springing up to service on a completely different basis the overall financial needs of individuals. Their business takes a wholly different approach to the financial supermarket concept. These firms provide a broad range of financial counseling and advice to their clients but they usually *don't* offer any products.

What they do is analyze an individual's needs for insurance, savings, stocks, bonds, mutual funds; plan tax and estate strategy; and then come up with an integrated package of recommendations touching on about every aspect of the client's financial needs. But their work generally stops right there.

If the client wants to follow the firm's recommendations, he does it through his own broker, insurance agent, banker, accountant, and lawyer.

The financial planning organization gets a fee for the master financial program it presents and doesn't try to make any commissions from the stocks or mutual funds the client buys or legal or accounting fees the client pays to implement the recommendations on estate planning and tax strategy.

So far, only a handful of organizations provide such services and their fees are steep. It is not unusual for a plan tailored to an individual's requirements and needs to cost $2,000 to $4,000. As a result, most customers for this service are wealthy individuals; in some cases corporations pay the costs of such programs for their executives and consider it an additional fringe benefit.

However, these new-breed financial planning organizations are working on ways to cut the cost of their services so they can serve the needs of the many millions of you who need professional help but can't pay such staggering fees.

On one side, there is growing interest by major financial institutions in developing financial supermarkets. On the other, there is the growth of professional financial planning firms offering comprehensive financial programs.

Between these, it seems clear that the professional assistance and variety of financial services available to you in the future will be vastly superior to any existing today.

Stock Market Letters

If you don't want to go the investment adviser route, but want another source of investment advice besides your own broker, you might consider subscribing to one of the many stock market letters that are available. The letters range in quality from excellent to awful, so check with some of your business associates to get an idea of those that are highly regarded. The price tags on such letters can run from $25 to $1,000 a year and no one has yet proven that the price tag for such a market letter and the value of its advice go hand in hand.

One thing you should know: most market letter writers make their money from the *subscriptions they sell and not by using their own investment advice.*

How to Avoid the "Garbage" Stocks

It is not only in so-called hot new issues that you find "garbage" stocks that should intrigue only the wildest gamblers—who know what they are doing and can afford the risks. You can find these unknown "growth" stocks outstanding in the over-the-counter markets and listed on the smaller stock exchanges too.

How do you, an average speculator-gambler, protect yourself from this garbage? How do you speculate-gamble intelligently?

Here are ten questions to ask yourself which when answered honestly will be a superb guide to this sort of speculation:

(1) Is this a high-quality stock in its own industry? It should be. It could be a dominant company in a small industry. Or it could be number one but still a small company in a big, fragmented industry. Whatever, it should be at the top.

(2) Does it have a record of solid earnings even in adverse times? How, for instance, did it make out in 1969–70, in 1973–74, in 1976–77?

(3) Has it a history of steady, solid growth? Buy a company with a history unless you're willing to admit you're in a wild gamble.

(4) Is the company's product or service sufficiently appealing to make customers willing to pay a good price for it? You can check this one out by your own willingness to pay for the products or services.

(5) Is the company saddled with long-term debt? It's okay for it to be aggressive in sales, but it should be conservative in finance. A well-managed, growing company should be able to pay off its debts.

(6) Is it paying a dividend? It probably should *not* be. A strongly growing company can use that dividend money more profitably than you can. A no-dividend policy usually is a plus.

(7) Has it a high degree of profitability? Its per-share earnings should be rising each year by at least 9 per cent. Some professionals put the level for professional selections much higher than that, but for you, the amateur, 9 per cent should be the yardstick.

(8) Is the stock already popular or its product or service already a fad? Then beware: the stock is probably fully priced by now, and you want to beat the mob, not follow it.

(9) Is the company subject to government regulation? If so, avoid it. Regulatory agencies generally limit a company's gains, but they let it chalk up all the losses.

(10) Are you risking too much of your money in this speculation? Don't. The time-honored rule against putting all your eggs in one basket applies particularly to high-risk growth stocks. You could be wrong in your decision. Protect yourself by diversifying.

What About Regional and Second-Tier Stocks?

Most investors are interested in the big national companies with well-known products and names that are household bywords. And in the past the big brokerage firms concentrated their research efforts on analyzing these firms.

But in the late 1970s, attention turned to the so-called regional stocks—issues of companies that basically serve a small geographic area—and "second-tier" stocks—issues of smaller companies listed on exchanges or traded over the counter. Regional stocks, as their name implies, may be well known locally but their products and services aren't known nationally. Second-tier stocks are small but solid companies which may be known nationally, although not as well known as the giants.

What the security analysts discovered—and so did the public—is that many regional and second-tier firms had the makings to become major national companies, yet they were undervalued in price just because not many investors knew about them. In fact, many corporations that have become fairly well known in recent years started out as junior stocks. As a result, Wall Street firms now try to discover the smaller companies that might become the IBMs or Xeroxes of tomorrow.

So, as an investor, do not downgrade a recommendation to buy a stock just because it represents a company you never heard about before. It well may be easier for you to find a real growth stock among the outstanding regional and second-tier firms than on the lists of the national firms which have been carefully and repeatedly studied by countless numbers of analysts.

How to Read an Annual Report

Each year American shareholders receive more than 70 million annual reports from some 11,000 publicly owned U.S. corporations. But a shocking proportion of you will throw away these valuable documents without even opening the envelopes and many others of you simply will skim over the highlights.

If you are among these millions, you are junking the single most important account of the financial health of your company and your single best measure of how well (or how poorly) your savings now are invested. If you are also an employee of the company in which you own stock, your indifference is really inexcusable.

Why do so many stockholders, as many as 40 per cent according to one study, ignore this key document? What are corporations doing to win stockholders' confidence in their annual reports and to make the reports more readable?

Only a couple of decades ago the typical annual report did not contain even a table of contents to guide you through its maze of facts and figures. The typical report told the shareholder how the company did the previous year but gave no figures for other years to help you measure its long-term trends. The untrained shareholder was at the mercy of the professional corporation statisticians and accountants and considerable imagination went into the preparation of the balance sheets.

Now this has changed dramatically. Virtually all major corporations today provide not only detailed indexes in their annual reports but usually also a generous assortment of easy-to-read charts and summaries so you can judge at a glance your company's and its industry's progress. The crucially important ten-year summary of financial highlights, rare ten to fifteen years ago, is now commonplace. A growing number of corporations are printing financial highlights on the covers of their annual reports, to lure more readers to look inside and delve further into their figures.

In Europe, corporation financial reports frequently omit key figures, use outdated information, or fudge statistics beyond semblance of reality. In this country, though, today's shareholder can, with few exceptions, trust every fact, figure, and footnote in every annual report he receives. Helping to assure the accuracy and completeness of financial reports are the rules of the major U.S. stock exchanges, the regulations of the Securities and Exchange Commission, and the accounting principles established by the Financial Accounting Standards Board. Virtually all annual reports now contain a "stamp of approval" of a reputable outside auditing firm or a statement by this firm that it takes issue with some aspect of the report—and why.

Today even the unsophisticated investor can see through most efforts a company may still make to obscure bad financial news. In the words of one expert, "When the president's letter to shareholders begins with 'The year was a period of adjustment for your company,' you can assume it was a bad year." Or you can simply turn to the record itself and judge.

Despite the progress, though, it's not easy (and never will be) to understand a corporation annual report. Thus, here is a glossary of key items and the basic rules for interpreting them intelligently.

(1) *The president's letter to stockholders* is the first place to look for a summary of your company's financial highlights for the previous year, plus the reasons why profits were up or down. This letter or the subsequent text also should give you the company's own assessment of its short- and long-term outlook, with supporting facts.

(2) *The "income statement" or "earnings report"* is a summary of the year's sales volume, other income, costs, net profits or losses with comparative figures for the previous year. The crucial figure is the company's net income or net profit and this figure should be compared to profits over the previous five or ten years (usually summarized separately).

(3) *The "price-earnings ratio"* is a measure of how the overall investment community views your company. The ratio won't appear in an annual report, but you can calculate it by dividing the current market price of a share of your stock by the company's per-share earnings noted in the earnings report. A ratio well below the average for the company's industry or for business in general may reflect investor wariness of the future profit potential of the company and/or for the industry.

(4) *The "retained earnings statement"* tells you what share of company

profits is being returned to you in the form of dividends and what share is being held back. If the proportion going to you in dividends declines sharply, look for an explanation of how the extra funds are being reinvested.

(5) *Footnotes often reveal important information.* A footnote, for instance, might tell you that an unusually high profit stemmed from a one-shot ("non-recurring") financial windfall. It may be tedious, but read those footnotes!

If the annual report you receive does not contain at least these basic items of information, or the facts from which to calculate them yourself, ask your stockbroker for further details. Your broker also can provide you with the industry-wide record. This is the minimum you should know about the company and the industry in which you are investing your savings.

What Is a "Blue Chip"?

Ask a dozen stock market experts to define a "blue chip" and you may get a dozen different answers. I, though, stick to the original rules for spotting a blue chip—for they are basic, time-tested, and always have value.

To begin with, the name "blue chip" is traced easily to the game of poker, in which there are three colors of chips: blue, the highest value; red, next in rank; white, the lowest value.

Now here are four yardsticks for a blue chip:

(1) A long history of good earnings performance in recessions as well as in booms. This does not mean the company's earnings must be skyrocketing. It does mean the company must be turning in a record of solid profits year after year.

(2) A long history of cash dividend payments, and, again, the record must be consistent in bad times as well as good.

(3) Recognition as an established leader in an established industry. There can be several leaders in an established industry. For instance, General Motors and Ford in the auto industry or Eastman Kodak and Polaroid in the camera industry.

(4) A clear prospect for continued earnings growth and dividend payments in the years ahead: a solid—but not flashy—outlook.

Of course, today's red chip can become tomorrow's blue and today's blue can fade into tomorrow's white. The dividend yardstick alone produces some arbitrary divisions. It leaves out many solid and promising corporations operating in the United States today—in terms of recent earnings and dividend payments—simply because they don't have the "ancestry."

These very requirements may make a blue chip stock a dull investment. But, dull or not, the blue chip represents solidity, security, steady growth—precisely what millions of investors cherish most.

What Is a "Growth" Stock?

Several times I have suggested that you buy "growth" stocks for capital gains—but how do you define a "growth" stock? How do you find and invest in this type of stock?

Grasp one point from the start: a growth stock is *not* merely a stock that has gone up in price. A growth stock *is:*

(1) The stock of a company which has shown and is likely to continue to show a record of both consistent and *superior* growth in its earnings per share of stock.

Consistency means year after year, even in the face of business reverses. For instance, many years back the demand for color TV sets was so much larger than the supply that even the marginal producers were prospering. But if that sales pace had continued, there would have been four or five TV sets in every home! When the inevitable slowdown occurred, the stronger companies survived while the sales and earnings of the secondary ones collapsed.

Consistency means a year-in, year-out market for the company's products. Superior growth, in the opinion of many professional investment advisers, means a growth of better than 8 or 9 per cent a year in earnings per share. This on a consistent basis certainly narrows the field from the start.

(2) The stock of a company which dominates its market or is a leading company in a fast-growing field. One expert says he would rather have the stock of the number-one company breeding tropical fish than that of a little firm trying to make a better transistor.

(3) The stock of a company in an emerging field or a company developing new concepts in an established field.

(4) The stock of a company you are convinced is under strong management. You might buy IBM without personally knowing its management, but you should not buy stock in a tiny electronics firm without knowing something about the people running it. The smaller the company, the more crucial is its management's ability.

(5) And it is the stock of a company offering a high return on equity—meaning the company's net profit related to its stockholders' equity is high in comparison to that earned by other firms in the same industry. On an average in the United States today, for every dollar committed in a corporation, the stockholder gets a return on his investment of about 14 cents. The owner of a true growth stock might do better than this.

Admittedly, this merely touches the various aspects of a growth stock and there will be many disagreements with the definitions. But these rules are fundamental, and I trust you notice that each rule assumes that the company has a record to analyze and compare. This last hint alone will help protect you from a lot of "garbage" stocks that will be touted under the banner of "growth" stocks in the years ahead.

What Is a "Special Situation" Stock?

Attractive as a growth stock is, a "special situation" stock has even more potential for substantial appreciation. But again, how do you define, find, and invest in a "special situation" stock? These questions and answers will guide you:

Q. *What is a special situation stock?*

A. In the modern sense, it is a stock in which you're likely to make a profit as a result of a new or impending specific and unusual development either within the company or in the outside environment affecting the company. What makes this special is that few investors recognize the impending change, and the improvement has not yet been reflected in the price of the stock. In either case, the development is setting the stage for a substantial upsurge in company's earning—and usually you'll be able to make your profit no matter what the short-term swings in the general stock market.

Q. *How do you identify special situations?*

A. Although they can occur in almost any industry and kind of company, the overriding characteristic of them all is *change*.

The changes within the company itself might include: a new technological breakthrough; a major new process, product, or service; a shift in ownership control; a major acquisition; a fundamental switch in the management philosophy of a previously poorly run company.

Changes in the company's external environment might include: new favorable government action (such as tax breaks); favorable court rulings; new favorable legislation; a significant shift in technological or market trends in the company's industry or related fields; any change which could lead to a dramatic rise in demand for the company's product or service.

Q. *What are the dangers?*

A. You might not be able to analyze the new development or be reasonably sure of its outcome. If you can't do either, it's a sheer speculation, not a special situation.

Also, often, an external environmental change may not produce the expected outcome. If, for instance, you had bought stock of a land development firm which had bought raw land cheap hoping to cash in on the land boom but saw your hopes of a rise in the price of the stock disappear because of accounting practices, your purchase of this special situation stock would have been an expensive mistake.

Or a seemingly great new product may fail in the market place. As one expert points out, "Most potential Xeroxes turn out to be nothing more than an idea for 3-D motion pictures."

Q. *How can you avoid the dangers?*
A. Extreme selectivity and obviously intensive study of the nature of the external or internal changes are vital.

If it's a new management, look for a demonstrated record of superior previous achievement and whether the new managers have competence in the area involved. If it's a new product or service or process, look for some kind of previous track record by the company in introducing such products.

Some of the country's top investment research firms, for instance, rarely even bother to analyze a development until the product's commercial feasibility has been proven.

And whatever the development, it's truly a special situation only when the earnings breakthrough which results is of major proportions and is sustainable for at least several years.

Should You Buy on Margin?

Most of the country's millions of investors buy their shares outright and hold them for the long term—that is, they put up 100 per cent cash and hold on no matter what the market does. But there is a sizable minority of active investors and professional traders who use credit from their brokers to help finance their purchases. This, of course, gives the investor a lot more leverage and thus a bigger potential for profits—and losses too.

In the late 1970s individuals held some 950,000 margin accounts with their brokers. The amount of credit customers were receiving from their brokers for this purpose was as high as $12 billion as the decade neared a close.

Just how much credit you can receive from your broker depends on several key elements. First, the Federal Reserve Board sets initial margin requirements. This requirement has ranged from 50 to 100 per cent in the post-World War II period. Say the initial margin rate is 70 per cent. It means if you want to buy $10,000 worth of stock you have to put up $7,000 in cash to buy the stock; you can receive credit for the rest from your broker. Or you have to deposit securities with a loan value of $7,000 in order to purchase $10,000 worth of a listed stock. You must deposit the required cash or securities with your broker within five business days after the purchase to conform to Regulation T of the Federal Reserve Board.

The New York Stock Exchange also has a set of rules covering buying on margin. To open a margin account with a NYSE broker you must deposit at least $2,000 or its equivalent in marginable securities. And on top of this, individual brokerage firms may—and often do—set initial margin requirements higher than those of the Federal Reserve or the Exchange.

Q. *What do you pay for the money you borrow?*

A. The going interest rates vary from time to time but usually were in the 6 to 14½ per cent range in the late 1970s. The amount of interest will show up in the monthly or periodic statement you receive on your margin account.

Q. *How do you open a margin account?*

A. If you have the $2,000 cash deposit or equivalent in securities—or meet the higher standards that your broker sets—there is little problem or paperwork in opening an account. You simply sign a margin agreement and a securities loan consent form. The agreement gives your broker the power to pledge or lend securities carried for your account. All securities purchased on margin will be held by your broker in "street name." However, you'll be credited with all dividends received on them. Your broker also will send along to you all annual and quarterly reports on the company whose stock you are holding and he will vote your stock in proxy matters the way you direct him.

Once you open a margin account, you must abide by another set of regulations—margin maintenance requirements. The New York Stock Exchange requires that the margin equity of customers be at least 25 per cent of the market value of securities held in the account and some brokerage firms insist on percentages higher than 25 per cent. For example, say you bought that $10,000 worth of stock with an initial margin requirement of 70 per cent. You put up $7,000 and received credit of $3,000 from your broker. Now say the price of the stock drops to the point where it is worth $4,000. Since you owe your broker $3,000, your equity in the securities is only $1,000 and you are right at the 25 per cent limit.

Q. *What happens if the value of your stock approaches the minimum requirement line?*

A. You will get what is termed a margin call. The brokerage firm has a squad of margin clerks whose job is to keep track of the firm's margin accounts and to send out warning phone calls and letters if the value of your account is approaching the minimum requirement line. You'll be asked to put more cash into your account or to put up more marginable securities as collateral. Instead of doing either of these things, you might choose to sell some of the stock in your margin account and pay your broker back part of the money for which he gave you credit.

Q. *What is an undermargined account?*

A. Your account is undermargined when it has definitely fallen below the minimum requirements. If you don't move fast to put it back in order by a transfusion of more cash or securities, your broker has the right to sell the securities in your margin account to replace the credit he advanced to you.

Q. *Should you open a margin account?*
A. Probably not. Margin accounts are generally for individuals who are sophisticated investors, who are active in the market, and who understand the risks as well as the rewards of this type of account.

Also it is difficult to make a profit on small margin purchases. The amount of interest you pay on the borrowed money in your account, plus odd-lot differential charges and commission rates, easily can eat up small trading profits.

And though the leverage in purchasing power you get in a margin account can produce increased profits for you, it also can result in bigger losses if you have guessed wrong on the direction of either the market or an individual stock.

Selling Short

Once you start investing, somewhere along the line the question of whether you should sell short will come up.

What is short selling? It's a technique that reverses most normal attitudes about buying stocks. It starts off on the assumption that you think a certain stock is going to drop in value. So what you do is sell the shares at the current market price, borrow shares of the stock from your broker, and then wait in the hope that the price of the stock will go down. If it does, you buy the same number of shares at a lower price and use these shares to "cover" the stock you borrowed from your broker.

Obviously, the bigger the drop in the price of the stock, the more potential profit you can make. Sounds good? Well, don't jump into short selling, at least until you read on.

Actually, short selling has earned a bad name, mainly because questionable practices of short selling were used by such market manipulators as Dan Drew and Jay Gould in the nineteenth century. They deliberately drove down the prices of stocks in the hopes of buying them back cheap. And short selling still carries a negative, even unpatriotic, connotation. But as a result of some of these shady practices, there are several rules that now govern short selling, the most important of which is the so-called "up-tick" rule.

This means you can sell short only after the previous sale in the stock was one eighth point or more higher than the last sale price. No short sale is permitted except on a rising price. The goal is to make sure that repeated selling waves don't force prices into a down spiral.

At best, though, selling short is a risky business, better left to coldly sophisticated investors. To be specific, the risk is this: You can make money if the stock you are selling short takes a big drop. But what if, instead of dropping, the stock's price takes off in a sharp upturn?

Say you sell short 100 shares at $50 a share, hoping the stock drops, but instead it goes up to $70. You then have a $20-a-share loss which you must take if you then buy shares to cover the stock you've borrowed. And there's no limit at least in theory as to how large your losses can become—whereas in normal trading your loss can never exceed 100 per cent of your investment. Say the stock soars to $100 or $200 a share! Your losses could be catastrophic—200 per cent, 400 per cent . . .

Best bet: don't be tempted to sell short.

What Are Rights?

A few years ago one of the world's major enterprises, American Telephone & Telegraph Company, raised $1.2 billion in new capital. This was a goodly sum even for AT&T—many governments would have trouble raising as much.

AT&T raised the money through the offering of rights—a common technique employed by a wide range of corporations but, unfortunately, often overlooked by shareowners. A right, in essence, is a privilege given by the issuing corporation to buy its common or preferred stock or bonds or debentures, usually at a favorable price in relation to the price of the outstanding security.

The AT&T offering was a classic illustration of rights. Its several million shareowners were informed that they could buy one additional share for each twenty shares they owned. They would receive one "right" for each share they presently owned. To buy one share, the shareowner would have to have twenty "rights" and pay $100—although at the time of the announcement AT&T was selling at about $146 a share. The rights, of course, immediately acquired a value. (If you have the right to buy a security below its market value, this right has a value.) Theoretically, the rights were worth $46/20 or $2.30 apiece.

AT&T's shareowners had several choices. A shareholder could exercise his rights by paying the company $100 plus giving AT&T twenty rights for each share he wanted and was entitled to. Or he could sell his rights. Or if he owned, say, fifteen shares, and had fifteen rights, he could buy five additional rights, which would allow him to purchase one more share of AT&T at the favorable price.

When it issued the rights, AT&T went on the basis of the privileged subscription or pre-emptive right. Translated, this bafflegab means the company felt its shareowners should have the privilege of buying the additional shares before the stock was offered to the general public. Selling additional shares, of course, dilutes the proportionate equity of the original shareowners—unless the original shareowner has the opportunity to maintain his equity by buying the additional shares.

Rights are often confused with warrants, and admittedly, the difference is a bit hazy. In the broadest terms, a right is a short-term privilege to buy a security at a favorable price; the privilege derives from the security you already own. A warrant is the privilege, usually of a longer term, to buy a security at a specific price. This privilege is usually offered to facilitate the sale of a stock or bond which you do not own. You, the buyer, get the stock or bond plus the warrant.

Caution: check your broker before you ignore your rights or sell them.

Are You Better Off with Stock Splits?

If you buy stocks, you probably will find that over a period of time one of the stocks you own will split and soon you will be receiving additional shares from the company. Will these shares make you any richer? In theory, no. In fact, maybe.

To explain just what a stock split means, say you own 100 shares of the 1 million outstanding shares of the XYZ Company. The company votes to split its stock 2 for 1, increasing the number of shares to 2 million. Since you own 100, you get an additional 100 shares—1 for each you own—raising your stake to 200 shares. Before the split you owned 100 shares out of 1 million of the XYZ firm. After the split you own 200 out of 2 million shares of the company. Obviously, in terms of percentage ownership, your position hasn't changed one bit, and generally speaking, since company XYZ hasn't increased its assets in any way, the value of your holding shouldn't be affected.

If the shares sold at $1.00 each before the split the price should drop to 50 cents, making the 200 shares you now have after the split equal to the $100 market value of the 100 shares you owned before the stock split. Theoretically this would be true no matter what the ratio of the split—2 for 1, 3 for 1, 5 for 1, 6 for 1. Yet speculators and investors often respond with enthusiastic buying to news that companies plan to split their stock—and following are the two key reasons why:

(1) It is commonplace for a company to combine a stock split with an increase in its dividend rate. If company A pays 4 cents a year on each of your 100 shares before the split and now pays 3 cents on the split shares you are getting a 50 per cent increase in dividend—6 cents in place of 4 cents.

(2) Usually working to boost the value of split shares to more than the value of the shares before the split is the fact that many investors would rather buy lower-priced stocks than higher-priced stocks. Say, for instance, that you own 10 shares of a stock selling for $150 a share. Many investors will not buy a stock with that high a price simply for psychological reasons. But if your company splits its shares 2 for 1, you now have 20 shares at a market price of $75 per share. Historically, many more investors are interested in buying a stock at $75 than at $150.

And the increased investor demand alone well may help push up the price of the stock beyond its initial $75 level.

What Price/Earnings Ratios Are All About

An old Wall Street adage holds that a stock is worth what somebody is willing to pay for it. In stiffer words, the price at which a stock sells represents the buyer's opinion of its value at a particular time.

Investors use a wide range of yardsticks to try to arrive at this judgment on the worth of a stock. Among them are such factors as book value, net income per share, cash flow, dividend rate, several others. But probably the most widely used measurement is the price/earnings ratio, better known as the P/E ratio.

Q. *What is the price/earnings ratio?*
A. It is the ratio of the current price of the stock to its earnings over the past twelve months. Sometimes experts try to figure price/earnings ratios based on predicted earnings for the next twelve months, but that introduces a speculative element that just complicates matters for the average investor.

Putting an even greater emphasis on price/earnings ratio is the fact that, starting in early 1973, newspapers added price/earnings ratios to the New York and American Stock Exchange tables.

Q. *How do you calculate the price/earnings ratio?*
A. While you can get the ratios in the newspaper stock tables, it also is a simple do-it-yourself task. The current price is in the newspaper tables, and the earnings for the last twelve months are usually available in a Standard & Poor's or other reference work. Divide the current price by the earnings, and you get the P/E ratio. For example, a stock that currently sells for $40 and that earned $2.00 a share over the past twelve months has a P/E ratio of 20.

Another way of saying it is that an investor is paying $20 for each $1.00 of the company's most recent annual earnings.

Q. *How much do price/earnings ratios fluctuate?*
A. Although they don't fluctuate much for stocks in general, they do fluctuate tremendously for individual issues. In the 1960s the average price/earnings ratio for stocks traded on the New York Stock Exchange ran about 18. By the end of the 1970s, this figure had dropped to less than 10. But even as the average P/E ratio fell, ratios on some individual stocks soared and there have been stocks with P/E ratios above 100.

Q. *What can P/E ratios tell you?*
A. As you study price/earnings ratios, several points will soon become clear:

Stocks in a given industry tend to have about the same P/E ratio. For example, most auto companies or international oil companies have the same price/earnings ratios.

In broad market movements, the price/earnings ratios of stocks in an industry group tend to move up and down together. If chemical stocks become depressed, say, the P/E ratio of nearly all chemical stocks will move down.

Companies in growth industries—photographic equipment, computers—tend to have higher price/earnings ratios than firms in such established industries as utilities.

Cyclical stocks in general tend to have lower P/E ratios than companies with more stable earnings.

Obviously, the P/E ratio fluctuates with each change in price and earnings. It also depends on what people active in the market think of the industry's and the company's future earnings prospects.

Q. *Can P/E ratios help you spot bargains in stocks?*
A. Yes. Many analysts and experienced investors use P/E ratios as a tool to find undervalued situations in which they might want to invest.

As an illustration, say that you are interested in a machine tool company. You notice that when the machine tool business is in the doldrums this company's stock (as well as others in its industry) sells for a price/earnings ratio of 9. You also notice that when the industry moves into a favorable business cycle the price/earnings ratio for the company and the group runs around 14. Say the stock is currently selling for $18 and has earned $2.00 a share. You read that prospects for the machine tool industry are bright, and the earnings of the company you are watching are expected to move up to $2.50 next year. So you figure that even with the low P/E average the price of the stock could move up (based on $2.50 earnings) to $22.50. But based on the high P/E ratio of 14, and with $2.50 earnings, it could move as high as $35. Certainly, you now have one very helpful clue to the possible price potential of the stock.

By studying a company's pattern of earnings and P/E ratios you may ultimately see a pattern that will help tell you if you should invest in the stock —and when.

Q. *What about stocks selling at low P/E ratios?*
A. P/E ratios may also give you some idea of the relative profit/loss pattern in an investment. If a stock has historically never had a P/E ratio lower than 5, and its earnings seem headed up, you would seem to be taking little risk in buying the stock when its P/E ratio was 5. The likelihood that the stock will go down further seems fairly slim. On the other hand, the potential upward movement of the stock would seem very promising.

Now take the reverse situation. You are looking at a company which has never had a P/E ratio below 5 or higher than 18. Its earnings outlook appears modestly good, and it presently is selling at a P/E of 18. If you buy that stock when its P/E ratio is at its high point, you obviously are taking a bigger risk, for the likelihood that it will go up depends almost entirely on a sharp increase in its future earnings. On the other hand, the stock would slump before it reaches its historic P/E ratio low.

Huge numbers of investors and speculators have been badly hurt in recent years by buying growth stocks with astronomical P/E ratios. Only a handful of these stocks have been able to maintain their high P/E ratios over the years. The majority with ratios in the 40 to 80 category eventually slide down to realistic levels—but the slide is more akin to a crash for the many who paid fancy prices for the shares.

Q. *What's the safest policy then?*
A. It usually is safest to spot stocks which are selling at low P/E ratios and which are headed for substantial earnings growth. Your downside risk tends to be smaller and your upside opportunities can be very good.

Do Options Make Sense for You?

Basically, options are contracts in which a buyer pays a premium (the price of the option) for the right to buy or sell a certain stock at a set price (called the striking price or exercise price) within a set time period. Options to buy shares are termed "call" options; those to sell, "puts."

Option prices fluctuate daily based on the stock market performance of the underlying shares, that is, the shares upon which the options are based. Now that options are traded on exchanges, the expiration date, striking price, and size of each option (100 shares of the underlying stock) have been standardized. This uniformity has helped increase the liquidity of options trading, or the ease with which a buyer or seller of contracts can enter or leave the market.

Q. *Why do people buy options?*
A. There are many reasons, but the main one is that buying an option gives an investor who thinks a stock will move sharply up or down a chance to make a sizable profit while limiting the amount of possible loss.

Say you think that Ajax Mousetrap Company stock, selling for $50, may surge to $100 in three months. It would cost you $5,000 to buy 100 Ajax shares, and you may not want to risk $5,000 or you may not have $5,000 to invest. Still, you would like to take the chance that Ajax will jump in price and as a result will make you a large profit.

In this case, you might go the options route. You ask your broker to buy you one call option with a striking price of $50 and an expiration date three months in the future. Checking the options tables in your newspaper, you find that Ajax call option with a striking price of $50 and an expiration date three months hence, is selling at 3½. That means that the premium, or option purchase price, is $3.50 per share of Ajax stock, or $350 for an option to buy 100 shares. When searching the options tables, however, you notice prices for three calls with the $50 striking price. Of course, you find the option you've purchased—one with an expiration in three months—as well as options with expiration dates six months and nine months away. For example, there might be prices listed for Ajax/Apr/50, Ajax/Jul/50, and Ajax/Oct/50 contracts. All listed options contracts expire on the Saturday following the third Friday of the expiration month.

It is also possible to trade options sharing the same expiration date but having different exercise prices. The prices would reflect the differing expectations of movements in the underlying stock. For example, there could be Ajax 50s, 60s, and 70s all expiring in April. Higher or lower exercise prices are introduced by the exchanges when a significant change occurs in the market price of the underlying security. Normally, new exercise prices are introduced at five-point intervals for stocks trading below $50 a share, at ten-point intervals for stocks trading between $50 and $200, and at twenty-point intervals for stocks trading above $200 a share.

Q. *How can you make money with options?*
A. Go back to the option to buy 100 shares of Ajax stock at $50. Here are some events that could happen:

(1) Ajax stock takes off as anticipated and hits $90 within the option period. Now you exercise your option, buy the 100 shares at $50 per share, turn around and sell the shares you acquired on the market for $90 per share.

You have received $9,000 from the sale of the shares. From this subtract the $5,000 you paid for them, the $350 premium for the option and about $120 in brokerage commissions, and you wind up with a profit of more than $3,500.

(2) Now look at another scenario. You buy the option and three months later Ajax stock nosedives to $40. What do you do? You do nothing, and simply let your option expire. You have lost $370—the price of the option premium and brokerage commission. Compare that to a loss of $1,000—plus commissions—had you bought the Ajax shares at $50 and sold them at $40.

(3) Or suppose that a month after you bought your option, the price of Ajax stock rises to $55. The prices of calls sharing your option's expiration date presumably have become more attractive and the premium is bid, say, to $5.00 a share. You could sell your option, which cost $350, for $500, realizing a $150 profit, less commissions.

The $150 profit on a $350 investment—a 43 per cent return—illustrates the leverage it is possible to achieve through the purchase of calls. Had you instead bought 100 shares of Ajax common at $50 a share and sold it at $55, you would have received a 10 per cent return. For this smaller return, the stock buyer assumed a greater risk since the stock price could have gone down. The option buyer could have lost only the $350 price of the call.

Q. *Are there other ways to make money in options?*
A. Yes. One is through the selling, or writing, of call options. Just as call buyers have a double objective—leverage plus limited risk—sellers, or

writers, of calls also seek two basic objectives: additional income from their security investments, coupled with protection against a decline in the market price of those securities.

The call writer is the person from whom the option buyer purchases his option. The writer obligates himself to deliver 100 shares of the underlying stock for each option sold if and when the call is exercised. On delivery of the stock, the writer is paid the exercise price. This is in addition to the premium received.

Let's say an investor owns 100 shares of Ajax, for which he paid $50 a share. He notes that an Ajax call option can be written against the stock at a premium of $5.00 a share. He deposits the stock with his broker and instructs the broker to write an Ajax call option. Within a few business days, his account will be credited in the amount of $500, less commissions. This premium belongs to the writer of the call whether or not the option is ultimately exercised by the buyer. In this example, a $5.00 share premium represents a 10 per cent yield on the $50 investment in stock. In addition, the options writer always retains cash dividends earned on the underlying security during the time prior to exercise.

Writing options on stock you own may be a way to boost your overall return. But if the price of the underlying stock rises close to or above the exercise price, the call owner would exercise his option requiring the option writer to sell the underlying shares. Option writers, therefore, are betting against a rise in the price of their stock. If stock prices do not rise, the option writer increases his total yield; if stock prices exceed the exercise price, the call writer must sell his stock and miss out on the price appreciation. What if the call writer wants to hold on to his stock? He simply can *buy* an identical call at the current premium and close out his position. Even if the call option is exercised, he does not have to deliver the original stock. He can, if he prefers, buy new stock to deliver.

Q. *Are there any other strategies?*

A. Yes, but many are risky, for the same leverage which rewards some options traders wipes out others. One particularly risky maneuver involves writing "naked" options—an option written against stock you don't own. A sharp rise in the market price of the stock will lead to the exercise of the call. To satisfy your delivery obligation, you, the writer of the naked option, would have to acquire the stock in the market at a price substantially above the exercise price. This could result in a large net loss.

Other strategies involve writing and/or buying put options and writing and/or buying a combination of puts and calls. For example, one combination is termed a "straddle" and consists of simultaneously buying (or selling) both a put and a call on the same number of shares of the same stock with the same exercise price and expiration month. By purchasing a straddle, you have an opportunity to profit from either a substantial increase or a substantial decrease in the price of the underlying stock. Obviously, straddles and other complicated options strategies are not for novices. Before trading in options, therefore, arm yourself with as much information as possible!

Q. *Where can I find out more about options?*
A. Introductory material is available free of charge from the options exchanges. The Chicago Board Options Exchange (141 Jackson Boulevard, Chicago, Illinois 60604) offers a variety of pamphlets on options, options writing, options spreading, and tax considerations. The American Stock Exchange (86 Trinity Place, New York, New York 10006) offers similar booklets. Brokerage firms also offer material free of charge.

(Also see pages 1248–50 on commodity options trading.)

For Your Protection—the SIPC

The 1967–70 crisis in Wall Street came perilously close—far closer than was ever publicly acknowledged—to wiping out huge numbers of innocent investors who had entrusted their securities to the safekeeping of their brokers. But as a direct result of that nightmare the Securities Investor Protection Act of 1970 went on the statute books. In 1978, the act was amended to provide even greater protection.

The SIPC gives you protection against being hurt by the liquidation of the brokerage firm to which you have entrusted securities and cash almost in the same way that the Federal Deposit Insurance Corporation gives you protection against being hurt by the liquidation of the bank to which you have entrusted your deposits. The difference is that the SIPC is a federally chartered membership organization and the FDIC is an agency of the government.

The SIPC is one of the most important pieces of securities legislation of the past generation and of direct meaning to you. You must know its general outlines, so here goes:

Q. *What is the SIPC?*
A. The Securities Investor Protection Corporation is a non-profit, membership corporation created by Congress to provide financial protection for you —the customers of an over-the-counter broker/dealer or of a member of a national securities exchange. It is not, however, an agency of the U. S. Government.

Q. *What protection does it give you?*
A. Should a SIPC member firm fail, its customers first will receive securities which are registered in their names or which are in the process of being registered. Second, the customers will receive, on a pro rata basis, all remaining cash and securities of customers held by the firm. Third, the

SIPC's funds will satisfy the remaining claims of each customer up to a maximum of $100,000. On claims for cash, however, not more than $40,000 may be paid from SIPC's funds.

Q. *Is there any way I can get more than $100,000 protection?*

A. As of the late 1970s, you could have obtained more than $100,000 protection by maintaining accounts with more than one brokerage firm or by holding accounts with the same SIPC member in separate capacities; for example, as an individual and as a trustee for another person.

For more information on the SIPC, write to the Securities Investor Protection Corporation, 900 Seventeenth Street N.W., Suite 800, Washington, D.C. 20006.

Q. *Who are members of the SIPC?*

A. Automatically, members are all registered broker/dealers and members of national securities exchanges, including specialists. Firms excluded from membership are those doing only a mutual fund, insurance, or investment company advisory business—but they can apply for membership in the SIPC if they wish.

Q. *Who puts up the insurance funds for the SIPC?*

A. The securities industry itself. During the first years of the SIPC, assessments on member organizations created a fund of more than $150 million in cash. In 1979, a minimum assessment of $25 a year was imposed on each member. In addition to its $150 million reserve, the SIPC has a $1 billion line of credit with the United States Treasury in case it ever needs it. However, if this credit line is drawn upon, the brokerage firms who are members of the SIPC eventually must repay the Treasury for the loan.

Q. *How does the SIPC work?*

A. When it appears that a large SIPC member firm is in danger of failing to meet its obligations to customers, the SIPC will apply to the appropriate court for appointment of a trustee. Once appointed, the trustee will liquidate the firm, complete open securities transactions, deliver out customers' fully paid securities to the extent that they are on hand and can be identified, and then settle any customer claims up to a limit of $40,000 in cash.

In medium-size cases, the SIPC is permitted to act as a trustee. These are cases in which it appears that the obligations to general creditors and subordinated lenders will be less than $750,000 and there are fewer than five hundred customers.

In cases in which it appears that the claims of all customers will amount to less than $250,000, the SIPC is able to make payments directly to customers if it appears that such direct payments would cost the SIPC less than following the court-appointed trustee methods.

Q. *Who manages the SIPC?*
A. A seven-man board of directors including two representatives of the general public and three of the securities industry appointed by the President of the United States, and one each named by the Secretary of the Treasury and the Federal Reserve Board.

Q. *What does that $1 billion line of Treasury credit mean?*
A. It's an ultimate resource aimed at meeting a crisis far beyond any ever yet experienced. It is to provide for even the most remote danger of financial disaster. The SIPC is indeed for your protection—make sure the firm with which you are dealing is a member.

Q. *In sum, what do these changes mean to you?*
A. They mean that in the process of development is the most comprehensive regulatory program ever devised for the safekeeping of customers' funds and securities by brokerage houses.

Q. *Then can customers be confident of 100 per cent protection against brokerage firm failures?*
A. No, there is no system that is foolproof. For the vast majority of brokerage accounts, though, the $100,000 and $40,000 limits do amount to 100 per cent protection. And this is certainly a spectacular improvement over the defenses of only a few years ago.

Note: several large incorporated brokerage firms also provide insurance of their own that substantially raises the limit on payments to customers—some into the hundreds of thousands of dollars per account.

INVESTMENT BIBLIOGRAPHY

THE STOCK MARKET AND HOW IT WORKS

Dreman, David N. *Psychology and the Stock Market: Investment Strategy Beyond Random Walk.* New York: Amacom, 1977.

Klein, Frederick C., and John A. Prestbo. *News and the Market.* Chicago: Henry Regnery Co., 1974.

Malkiel, Burton G. *A Random Walk down Wall Street.* New York: W. W. Norton & Co., 1973.

Rosen, Lawrence R. *Go Where The Money Is.* Rev. ed. Homewood, Illinois: Dow Jones-Irwin, 1974.

Silk, Leonard. *Economics in Plain English.* New York: Simon & Schuster, 1978.

Sobel, Robert. *Amex: A History of the American Stock Exchange, 1921–1971.* New York: Weybright and Talley, 1975.

———. *Inside Wall Street: Continuity and Change in the Financial District.* New York: W. W. Norton & Co., 1977.

———. *N.Y.S.E. A History of the New York Stock Exchange 1935–1975.* New York: Weybright and Talley, 1975.

Wyckoff, Peter. *Wall Street and the Stock Markets: A Chronology (1644–1971).* Philadelphia, Chilton Book Co., 1972.

LEARNING TO INVEST

Blackman, Richard. *Follow the Leaders; Successful Trading Techniques with Line Drive Stocks.* New York: Simon & Schuster, 1978.

Darst, David M. *The Complete Bond Book; A Guide to All Types of Fixed-Income Securities.* New York: McGraw-Hill, Inc., 1975.

Engel, Louis (in collaboration with Peter Wyckoff). *How to Buy Stocks.* 6th rev. ed. Boston: Little, Brown and Co., 1976.

Gastineau, Gary L. *The Stock Options Manual.* New York: McGraw-Hill, 1975.

Graham, Benjamin. *The Intelligent Investor; A Book of Practical Counsel.* 4th rev. ed. New York: Harper & Row, 1973.

Hardy, C. Colburn. *Dun & Bradstreet's Guide to Your Investments.* New York: Thomas Y. Crowell, 1978.

Holt, Thomas J. *Total Investing.* New York: Arlington House, 1976.

Hoyt, Murray. *The Young Investor's Guide to the Stock Market.* New York: J. B. Lippincott Co., 1972.

Mader, Chris, and Robert Hagin. *The Dow Jones-Irwin Guide to Common Stocks.* Homewood, Illinois: Dow Jones-Irwin, 1976.

Mamis, Justin, and Robert Mamis. *When to Sell: Inside Strategies for Stock Market Profits.* New York: Farrar, Straus and Giroux, 1977.

Metz, Robert. *Jackpot!* New York: Simon & Schuster, 1977.

Newman, Joseph. *Stocks, Bonds and Mutual Funds.* Washington, D.C.: U.S. News & World Report Books, 1977.

Reilly, James F. *Too Good for the Rich Alone.* Englewood Cliffs, New Jersey: Prentice-Hall, 1975.

Rogers, Donald I. *How Not to Buy a Common Stock.* New York: Arlington House, 1972.

Rugg, Donald D. *The Dow Jones-Irwin Guide to Mutual Funds.* Homewood, Illinois: Dow Jones-Irwin, 1976.

Rukeyser, Louis. *How to Make Money in Wall Street.* Rev. ed. New York: Doubleday, 1976.

Sokoloff, Kiril. *The Thinking Investor's Guide to the Stock Market.* New York: McGraw-Hill, 1978.

Tobias, Andrew. *The Only Investment Guide You'll Ever Need.* New York: Harcourt Brace Jovanovich, 1978.

Train, John. *The Dance of the Money Bees: A Professional Speaks Frankly on Investing.* New York: Harper & Row, 1974.

TEXTBOOKS ON THEORY AND PRACTICE

Christy, George A., and John C. Clendenin. *Introduction to Investments.* 7th ed. New York: McGraw-Hill, 1978.

Cohen, Jerome B. *Investment Analysis and Portfolio Management.* 3rd ed. Homewood, Illinois: Dow Jones-Irwin, 1977.

Dougall, Herbert E. *Investments.* 10th ed. Englewood Cliffs, New Jersey: Prentice-Hall, 1978.

Latane, Henry A. *Security Analysis and Portfolio Management.* 2nd ed. New York: Ronald Press, 1975.

FOR THE EXPERIENCED INVESTOR

Blotnick, Srully. *Winning; The Psychology of Successful Investing.* New York: McGraw-Hill, 1978.

Blumenthal, Earl. *Chart for Profit; Point and Figure Trading.* Larchmont, New York: Investors Intelligence, 1975.

Brealey, Richard A. *Security Prices in a Competitive Market; More About Risk and Return from Common Stocks.* Cambridge, Massachusetts: M.I.T. Press, 1972.

Cootner, Paul H., ed. *The Random Character of Stock Market Prices.* Rev. ed. Cambridge, Massachusetts: M.I.T. Press, 1964.

Dines, James. *How the Average Investor Can Use Technical Analysis for Stock Profit.* New York: Dines Chart Corp., 1972.

Edwards, Robert D., and John Magee. *Technical Analysis of Stock Trends.* 5th ed. Springfield, Massachusetts: John Magee, Inc., 1966.

Fosdack, Norman G. *Stock Market Logic; A Sophisticated Approach to Profits on Wall Street.* Fort Lauderdale, Florida: The Institute for Econometric Research, 1976.

Fried, Sidney. *Fortune Building in the 70's with Common Stock Warrants and Low-Price Stocks.* New York: RHM Press, 1974.

Granville, Joseph E. *Granville's New Strategy of Daily Stock Market Timing for Maximum Profit.* Englewood Cliffs, New Jersey: Prentice-Hall, 1976.

Hardy, C. Colburn. *Investor's Guide to Technical Analysis.* New York: McGraw-Hill, 1978.

Noddings, Thomas. *How the Experts Beat the Market.* Homewood, Illinois: Dow Jones-Irwin, 1976.

Thomas, Conrad W. *How to Sell Short and Perform Other Wondrous Feats.* Homewood, Illinois: Dow Jones-Irwin, 1976.

U. S. Industry and Trade Administration. *U.S. Industrial Outlook with 5-Year Projections for 200 Industries* (annual). Available in many libraries. Also, for sale by the Superintendent of Documents, U. S. Government Printing Office, Washington, D.C. 20402.

NEWSPAPERS AND PERIODICALS

Bank and Quotation Record. (monthly magazine) New York
Barron's: National Business and Financial Weekly. (weekly newspaper) New York
Commercial and Financial Chronicle. (weekly newspaper) New York
Dun's Review. (monthly magazine) New York
Finance. (monthly magazine) New York
The Financial Analysts Journal. (bimonthly magazine) New York
Financial Times. (daily newspaper) London
Financial World. (semi-monthly magazine) New York
Forbes. (biweekly magazine) New York
Insiders' Chronicle. (weekly magazine) New York
Investment Dealers' Digest. (weekly magazine) New York
Journal of Commerce. (daily newspaper) New York
M/G Financial Weekly Market Digest. (weekly newspaper) Richmond, Virginia
Money. (monthly magazine) Chicago, Illinois
Money Manager. (weekly newspaper) New York
O-T-C Review. (monthly magazine) Oreland, Pennsylvania
Official Summary of Security Transactions and Holdings. (monthly magazine) Washington, D.C., SEC
Statistical Bulletin. (monthly magazine) Washington, D.C., SEC
Stock Market Magazine. (monthly magazine) Yonkers, New York
Wall Street Journal, The. (daily newspaper) New York
Wall Street Transcript. (weekly newspaper) New York

THE BAFFLEGAB OF STOCKS

The language of Wall Street is colorful and enriched by many idioms. Some of the words and phrases go back more than a century; others are as up-to-date as this year's music. Here is a guide through the bafflegab. I have selected only terms which you will come across fairly frequently and, thus, which you should understand.

ARBITAGE A technique which takes advantage of a temporary price difference between a security or commodity traded on two or more exchanges; or a temporary price difference between new and old securities of the same company; or a temporary price difference between convertible securities and the securities into which they are convertible. The arbitrateur's profit lies in taking almost simultaneous opposite action in two markets to take advantage of the price differentials. You must have detailed technical knowledge of the different prices, excellent communications, be able to take major risks, and be fairly sophisticated in finance to

YOUR GUIDE TO THE STOCK MARKETS 1151

be an arbitrateur. It's not for amateurs. Rather, it is practiced mostly by brokers who are members of exchanges and not subject to their customers' usual commission costs.

AT THE MARKET An order to buy or sell a stated number of shares at the most advantageous price your broker can get when the order is executed. You are ordering immediate execution of your order "at the market," not specifying any price. Also called a "market order."

AVERAGES Yardsticks for measuring broad trends in stock prices. The best-known is the Dow Jones average of the prices of thirty outstanding industrial stocks listed on the New York Stock Exchange. Other widely used market indicators, known as indexes, are issued by Standard & Poor's and the New York Stock Exchange.

The Dow Jones average generally gives you the trends in well-established blue chip stocks but not in stocks of service companies, smaller companies, or glamour issues. The New York Stock Exchange index includes *all* common stocks listed on the NYSE and is most representative of the market. The Standard & Poor's indexes of 425 industrial stocks and of 500 stocks (including utilities and rails)—all listed on the NYSE—are also excellent yardsticks.

BEAR An investor who thinks that a stock's price, or the market as a whole, will fall. A bear market is a sharply declining market. See page 1115.

BID AND ASKED The "bid" price for a stock is the highest price that anyone has declared he is willing to pay for a share of the stock at a given time. The "asked" price is the lowest price at which anyone has declared he is willing to sell this same share at a given time. The actual price at which you buy or sell the share usually will be somewhere between the bid and the asked price. "Bid and asked" is usually called a quote.

BIG BOARD Wall Street nickname for the New York Stock Exchange, Inc.

BLOOD BATH In the stock market, this means a horrendous loss suffered by many investors due to a sharp market decline. "Taking a bath" means taking a terrific loss, usually a personal loss but not necessarily a widespread market drop.

BLUE CHIPS Stocks which, like poker chips, have the highest "rank" in terms of: a long history of earnings in both good times and bad times; an unbroken history of paying quarterly cash dividends, for twenty-five years or more, in recessions as well as booms; established leadership in an established industry; a clear, solid prospect for continued earnings, growth, and dividend payments.

BLUE SKY LAWS A securities industry expression for the laws of various states designed to protect the public against securities frauds. These state regulations prescribe the requirements which must be met for intrastate issue and sale of securities. The term is said to have come into being when a judge ruled that a particular stock had the value of a patch of blue sky.

BOOK VALUE A company's total assets (exclusive of such intangibles as good will) less its liabilities and the liquidating value of its preferred stock divided by the number of shares of common stock outstanding to put the figure on a per-share basis. Book value is not the same as market value and generally has little or no relation to it.

BROAD TAPE   Wall Street slang for the Dow Jones & Company news ticker displayed in many brokerage houses as a large rectangular screen with lines of copy rolling upward, while the American and Big Board ticker tapes are displayed as narrow rectangles with copy running horizontally from right to left.

BROKER   An agent who executes your orders to buy and sell shares of stock, other securities, or commodity futures contracts for a commission. The word "broker" can refer to the partnership or corporation with whom investors have accounts and, by extension, to its sales employees. A securities salesman is more accurately known as a registered representative, account executive, or customer's man.

BULL   A person who thinks a stock's price, or the market as a whole, will go up. A bull market is a sharply advancing market. See page 1116.

CALL   An option contract that entitles the holder to buy a number of shares of the underlying security at a stated price on or before a fixed expiration date. Calls were the first option contracts to be listed for trading on option exchanges. See PUTS.

CALLABLE   Stock, usually preferred shares, which may be bought back (redeemed) or called by the company, at the option of the company's board of directors, at a certain price within a certain time span and under certain agreed-upon conditions. It is much more usual for bonds and debentures to be callable than stocks. Shares traded on exchanges are usually non-callable.

CAPITAL GAIN (OR LOSS)   Profit (or loss) on the sale of any capital asset, including securities. A long-term capital gain is a gain achieved after the securities have been held for a set period under the law: as of 1978, the period was "more than one year." Long-term gains are taxed at a lower federal rate than short-term gains, which in 1978 were gains achieved in "one year or less." A capital loss occurs when you sell stock (or other capital assets) at a loss. This loss also can be short-term or long-term, and each type is treated differently in income tax reporting.

CATS AND DOGS   Highly speculative and usually very low-priced stocks.

CHURNING   An extraordinary, excessive—and therefore suspicious—amount of trading in a customer's account without adequate or proper justification and probably done only to generate additional commissions for an unscrupulous broker. Such improper conduct is subject to disciplinary action by various regulatory organizations.

CLOSED-END INVESTMENT COMPANY   First, let's define an investment company. This is a company which invests in the securities of other companies, holds a diversified list of these securities, and buys and sells them for the purpose of making profits and earning income. It is, in short, a mutual fund.

The closed-end investment company is an investment company with a fixed capitalization and usually a fixed number of shares outstanding which may be traded on a securities exchange. You buy shares of a closed-end investment company in the open market from another owner and sell your shares to another buyer exactly as you would trade in other stocks. In contrast, the familiar open-end investment company (or mutual fund) constantly issues new shares and its capitalization is "open." You buy new shares from the mutual fund itself and redeem them by selling them back to the mutual fund. See Chapter 22 "Mutual Funds" for details on both types.

COMMISSION The broker's basic fee for purchasing or selling securities or property as an agent.

COMMISSION BROKER An agent who executes the publics orders for the purchase or sale of securities or commodities.

CONFIRMATION A form you receive from your brokerage house after you buy or sell securities informing you that your buy or sell order has been executed, the number of shares traded, at what price, in what market, the standing of your account, and the settlement date.

CONGLOMERATE A corporate "supermarket" which has grown externally by rapidly acquiring many unrelated companies primarily through the use of borrowed money and the exchange of securities. In one sense, buying stock in a conglomerate is similar to buying an entire portfolio of different stocks—but at the top a conglomerate, like any other company, is run by a single management team. Basically, therefore, this team's competence and the ability of a conglomerate to grow in size and in earnings per share through both good and bad economic times will determine the prospects for the company as a whole.

CONVERTIBLE A bond or debenture or preferred stock which not only provides a fixed rate of return (in interest or dividends) but which you can also convert into shares of the same company's common stock at a later date if it is to your advantage to do so. Conversion terms often change and are governed by the indenture (contract) covering the original underwriting.

CORNER Buying of a stock or commodity on a scale large enough to give the buyer, or buying group, control over the price. A person who must buy that stock or commodity—for example one who is short—is forced to do business at an arbitrarily high price with those who obtained the corner. Corners are rare these days, since registered exchanges have the power to prevent them.

COVERING A SHORT POSITION What happens when a person who has sold short buys shares of the stock he has "shorted" so he can deliver the shares to the broker from whom he has borrowed the shares. He thereby "covers" his short position. See page 1137.

CURB EXCHANGE Former name of the American Stock Exchange. Now known as the Amex.

CURRENT YIELD The dividends or interests paid on a security by a company expressed as a percentage of the current price. A stock with a current market price of $40 a share which has paid $2.00 in dividends in the preceding twelve months is said to return 5 per cent ($2.00÷$40.00). The current yield (also called return) on a bond is figured the same way. A 3 per cent $1,000 bond selling at $600 offers a return of 5 per cent ($30÷$600). Figuring the yield of a bond to maturity calls for a bond yield table.

Yields vary tremendously from stock to stock and often they may be misleading. To illustrate, a very low yield may be a good, not bad, sign, for it may reflect the fact that a company is putting most of its earnings into its own future business and buyers of its stock are banking on that future. A high yield, on the other hand, may be a bad sign, for it may suggest that the company may in time cut the dividend and that investors question its future growth potential.

CUSTOMER'S MAN Another name for a registered representative, account executive, or securities salesman. See BROKER.

CYCLICAL STOCKS Stocks which go up and down with the trend of business (the business cycle)—climbing fast in periods of rapidly improving business conditions and sliding fast when business conditions deteriorate. However, cyclical stocks might also follow special cycles related to their own industry which might not parallel the business cycle.

DEALER An individual in the securities business who acts as a principal, in contrast to a broker, who acts as an agent. A dealer buys securities for his own account and then sells to you, the customer, from his own holdings. His profit or loss is the difference between the price he paid for a security and the price at which he sells the security to you. At different times, an individual or firm may act either as a broker or as a dealer. But he has to alert you to the capacity in which he is acting.

DEBENTURE A promissory note backed by the general credit of a company and usually not secured by a mortgage or lien on any specific property. See CONVERTIBLE.

DEFENSIVE STOCKS Stocks which tend to be more stable, in terms of dividends, earnings, and market performance, in periods of recession or economic uncertainty than a general cross section of the market. When the market seems to be entering a major bear phase, portfolio managers and experienced investors attempt to switch from high-growth and speculative stocks to quality stocks, hence the term "defensive."

DISCOUNT A reduction in market price from the face value or original price of a security. In contrast, a premium means an increase in market price above the face value or original price of a security. Much more commonly used in the bond than the stock markets. For instance, a bond selling at a discount is selling below its face value or original price while a bond selling at a premium is selling above its face value or original price. See Chapter 23 "Your Guide to the Bond Market . . ."

DISCOUNTING THE NEWS When the price of a stock or the level of a major market indicator rises or falls in anticipation of a specific development—good or bad—and then scarcely moves when the actual development takes place and is announced, this stock, or the market, has "discounted the news." Sometimes the stock or the market moves in a direction opposite to the bullish or bearish news when it is actually published.

DISCRETIONARY ACCOUNT An account in which you, the investor, give your stockbroker or other agent full or partial authority in writing to buy and sell securities or commodities for you without requiring your specific approval on each transaction. The discretion will include selection, timing, and price to be paid or received for the securities.

DIVIDENDS A payment distributed to share owners on a proportional basis in amounts and at times voted by a company's board of directors. A dividend may be in cash, additional shares of the company's own stock, or in the securities of another company it owns.

On preferred stock, the dividend amounts are usually fixed. On common stock, dividends may vary throughout a year and from year to year—or may be omitted entirely.

DOLLAR COST AVERAGING A system in which you invest a fixed amount of money regularly in a given stock or stocks. See pages 1121–22.

DOW THEORY A theory of market analysis based upon the performance of the Dow Jones industrial and transportation stock price averages. The theory says that the market is in a basic upward trend if one of these averages advances above a previous important high, accompanied or followed by a similar advance in the other. When the averages both dip below previous important lows, this is regarded as confirmation of a basic downward trend. The theory does not attempt to predict how long either trend will continue, although it is widely misinterpreted as a method of forecasting future action. Whatever the merits of the theory, it is sometimes a strong factor in the market because many people believe in the theory—or believe that a great many others do.

EARNINGS (OR INCOME) STATEMENT A company's statement to shareowners which may appear in an annual, semi-annual, or quarterly report, of its net profits (or "net income") or losses after taxes and expenses, for the period covered by the report.

EQUITY FINANCING Since stock represents ownership or equity in a company, equity financing is the obtaining of funds by a company through the sale of stock.

EX-DIVIDEND Means "without dividend" and is usually indicated by the symbol "X" after the company's name in the stock tables. If you buy a stock when it is selling ex-dividend, it means you will not receive a just-declared dividend. Instead, that dividend will go to the previous owner (the seller), who was the stockholder of record.

EX-RIGHTS Means "without rights" that a corporation may have offered stockholders to subscribe to new or additional stock. If you buy a stock selling "ex-rights," you are not entitled to the rights; these remain the property of the seller.

EXTRA The short form of "extra dividend." A dividend in the form of stock or cash in addition to the regular or usual dividend the company has been paying.

FALL OUT OF BED A crash in stock prices. For instance, "the market fell out of bed on the news" means the market declined very sharply.

FISCAL YEAR A company's accounting year, which may coincide with the calendar year or may span some other period—typically July 1 through June 30.

FLOOR The trading area of any of the world's stock exchanges; as of the late 1970s, most particularly the huge trading area where common and preferred stocks were bought and sold on the New York Stock Exchange. Bonds were traded on the New York Stock Exchange in a separate small Bond Room in the building's basement.

FLOOR BROKER A member of an exchange who in the late 1970s executed orders to buy or sell listed securities on that floor.

FOREIGN EXCHANGES Refers to securities exchanges operating in other countries. For instance, the London Stock Exchange is a foreign (securities) exchange.

FORMULA INVESTING An investment technique. One formula calls for the shifting of funds from common shares to preferred shares or bonds as the market, on average, rises above a certain predetermined point—and the return of funds to common share investments as the market average declines.

GOING PUBLIC The underwriting process whereby a privately owned company offers its own stock for sale to the public for the first time and makes it available for trading in the over-the-counter market or an organized exchange.

GROWTH STOCKS Stock in a company with superior prospects in earnings which historically have exceeded the growth rate of the economy or of corporations on the average.

HEDGE In the securities and commodities markets, to hedge means to try to minimize or eliminate a risk by taking certain steps to offset the risk.

HOLDING COMPANY A non-operating company which owns the securities, and usually holds voting control, of another company which does sell products or services. Hence, "holding company."

IN-AND-OUT Buying and selling a stock within a short period of time. In-

and-out speculators strive for profits resulting from hour-to-hour and day-to-day stock price changes.

INSIDER Directors, officers, and principal securities holders of a corporation. The latter can be companies or individuals who are beneficial shareholders of 10 per cent or more of a publicly traded company's stock. The Securities and Exchange Commission requires insiders to report their initial position and details of any significant change in their holdings.

INSTITUTIONAL INVESTOR An organization or company with substantial funds invested in securities—i.e., a bank, insurance company, mutual fund, university, labor union, pension plan.

INVESTOR ADVISER OR COUNSEL Individual (or firm) who supervises or manages funds of investors for a fee.

INVESTMENT BANKER (OR UNDERWRITER) Middlemen between companies needing capital and the investing public. To illustrate, when a company wants capital for expansion or modernization, it may sell its securities to an investment banker or underwriter; this firm, in turn, will sell the securities to the public.

INVESTMENT CLUB A group of ten to twenty people who meet regularly and invest together. Most clubs have formal rules and defined investment goals.

INVESTMENT COMPANY Current meaning refers usually to an open-end or a closed-end mutual fund. See Chapter 22, "Mutual Funds."

INVESTOR An individual, owning securities, whose main goals are relatively long-term growth of his principal and/or dividend income. He differs from a speculator in his goals, expectations, risks, and temperament.

LAMB An amateur speculator who blindly follows the flock, buying or selling on tips and rumors, and is easily "fleeced" by the pros or by his own naïveté and greed.

LETTER STOCK A type of unregistered stock—often issued by new small companies to avoid the cost of a formal underwriting—that is sold at a presumed discount to mutual funds and experienced investors specializing in such speculative investments. Letter stock usually carries a proviso that it may not be resold for a considerable period of time.

LIMIT ORDER An order to buy or sell a stated amount of a security at a specified price, or a better price if obtainable, after the order has been placed.

LIQUIDATION Dissolution of a company; process of converting securities and other assets into cash.

LIQUIDITY Capacity of the market in a particular security to absorb a reasonable amount of buying and selling at reasonably limited price changes. An "illiquid" market in a security means you cannot buy or sell with reasonable freedom at reasonable price changes.

LISTED STOCK Stock traded on a national securities exchange. Both the stock and the exchange have been registered with the Securities and Exchange Commission. Detailed information on such stock has been filed with the SEC and the issuing company has met the listing standards of the exchange upon which it is being traded.

LOAD Sales charge which a buyer of mutual funds must pay on top of the actual net asset value of the shares—unless the mutual fund is a no-load fund (meaning the fund is sold without any sales charge to the buyer). See Chapter 22, "Mutual Funds."

LOCKED IN An investor who will not sell stocks in which he has a substantial profit because he would have to pay capital gains tax on the profit. He has a "paper" profit which he is reluctant to take because the tax will consume a good part of it and thus he is "locked in."

LONG Means simply that you have bought a certain number of shares of a stock and hold them in anticipation of higher prices (are "long" of it) or for whatever other goals you have in mind.

MAKING A KILLING Make a spectacular profit.

MANIPULATION Illegal buying and selling of securities in order to create false impression of active trading, or to drive prices up or down as a lure for others to buy or sell while the manipulators are taking profits.

MARGIN Minimum proportion of the purchase price you must pay when you wish to use your broker's credit to buy a security. Initial margins are regulated by the Federal Reserve Board and have ranged in recent years from 50 per cent to 100 per cent of the stock purchase price. A 100 per cent margin means no borrowing is permitted.

You buy on margin when you want to purchase more stock than your cash on hand would permit. You get credit for the balance from your broker at current interest rates because obviously you are hoping to increase your gains. A 50 per cent margin means you put up only 50 per cent of your cash to buy a stock; you get credit for the rest. The New York Stock Exchange also has strict margin maintenance rules that its member organizations are expected to enforce in customer accounts.

MARGIN CALL A call from your broker asking you to put up additional cash (or collateral) in order to bring your equity in your account at least up to the margin maintenance requirements stipulated by the exchange. You might get this call if your stock declines sharply instead of rising. If you don't meet the call and bring up your equity to the requirement, your stock will be liquidated by your broker.

MARKET ORDER Order to buy or sell a stated amount of a security at the best price obtainable in the market at the time.

MARKET PRICE The last reported transaction price of a security.

MEMBER FIRM A securities brokerage firm organized either as a corporation or a partnership and having at least one executive or general partner who is a member of an exchange.

NASD The National Association of Securities Dealers, Inc., an association of brokers and dealers in the over-the-counter securities business. The Association has the power to expel members who have been declared guilty of unethical practices. The NASD is dedicated to—among other objectives—"adopt, administer and enforce rules of fair practice and rules to prevent fraudulent and manipulative acts and practices, and in general to promote just and equitable principles of trade for the protection of investors."

NET ASSET VALUE Most often used by mutual funds which report their net asset value per share every day. The NAV represents the market value of the securities the fund owns on that day plus the cash it holds divided by the total number of the shares the mutual fund has outstanding. "Load" mutual funds charge a sales charge in addition to their net asset value per share. "No load" mutual funds simply sell their shares at the NAV per share.

NEW ISSUE New stocks or bonds sold for the first time to raise money for just about any purpose. The issuers range from the U. S. Government and foreign governments to the most risky small corporations and cities. If a new issue is in heavy demand and its price rises to a premium over the issue price immediately after the offering, it is called "hot."

NEW YORK STOCK EXCHANGE The nation's largest securities exchange in the late 1970s was the New York Stock Exchange.

The NYSE is a not-for-profit corporation which does not own the securities traded and does not set prices. Nor does it make or lose money when securities rise or fall. It provides a marketplace for the purchase and sale of securities.

ODD LOT An amount of stock normally less than the 100 shares which make up a "round lot." In seldom-traded "inactive" stocks, 10 shares make up a round lot, and 1 to 9 shares make up an odd lot.

OPTION A right to buy or sell specific securities, commodities, or properties at a specified price within a specified time.

OVER-THE-COUNTER By far the biggest securities market in the world, where stocks and bonds which are not listed on securities exchanges are traded. It is the principal area for the trading of U. S. Government securities and municipal bonds. The O-T-C is not a place but mostly a communications network of stock and bond dealers doing business chiefly on a principal basis. This area is supervised by the National Association of Securities Dealers, Inc., which has the power to expel members who have been declared guilty of unethical practices.

PAPER PROFIT Amount of profit you, the holder of a security, have "on paper" and *would* make *if* you sold this security. Paper loss is the amount of loss you *would* take *if* you sold the security.

PAR VALUE In a common stock, its nominal value. But many common stocks today are issued without par value, and par value has little meaning to buyers of common stock. Although it has no relation at all to market value or book value, par value for common stock does have legal and corporate significance. In a preferred stock, par value has meaning to the investor because dividends are normally paid on the basis of par value. (A 5 per cent preferred stock might pay that percentage on a par of $100 or a $5.00 dividend.) In a bond, par value is also important to the investor, because par is its face value, the principal on which interest is paid. (A 5 per cent bond might pay that percentage [or $50] every year, usually on a par value of $1,000.) Par value is also the amount usually repaid at the maturity of a bond by the borrower.

PENNY STOCKS Superspeculative stocks, often of mining companies, which usually sell for $1.00 a share or less.

POINT In stock prices, one point equals a change of $1.00 and a one-point rise or fall means a $1.00 rise or fall in the stock's price. A half-point rise or fall means a 50 cents change; one quarter means 25 cents, etc.

In bond prices, though, one point equals a change of $10 and a one-point rise or fall in the price per $1,000 face value of bond means a $10 rise or fall in the price of that bond. A two-point change means a $20 change per bond, etc. See Chapter 23, "Your Guide to the Bond Markets . . ."

PORTFOLIO The collection of securities held by an individual or institutional investor (such as a mutual fund). Term is especially applicable when these securities have been carefully researched and assembled in a deliberate fashion, regarding proportions of: bonds to stocks, growth to income, cyclical to non-cyclical, and speculative to conservative issues.

PREFERRED STOCK A category of stock which is subordinate to the debt a company owes but which has a claim ahead of the company's common stock upon the payment of dividends or the assets of the company in the event the company is liquidated. (Hence the name "preferred stock.") Preferred stock is usually called a "senior" security and its dividend usually is at a set rate—both characteristics similar to those of bonds.

A key difference between preferred stock and bonds is that bonds almost always have a final maturity date (when a bond becomes due and payable), while preferreds do not because these stocks represent ownership. A preferred stock will remain outstanding indefinitely unless called for redemption at a price fixed by the company at the date the stock was issued. Most preferred stocks also are cumulative—meaning that if their dividends are omitted they build up in arrears and then the company must pay these arrears plus current preferred stock dividends before it can pay common stock dividends.

Some preferred stocks are convertible into common stocks just as some bonds are.

PREMIUM The amount by which a preferred stock or bond may sell above the par value. See DISCOUNT.

PRICE/EARNINGS RATIO The relationship between the price at which a stock is selling and the company's earnings per share.

PROFIT TAKING Selling stock which has appreciated in value since purchase in order to realize the profit. The term is often used to explain a downturn in the market following a period of rising prices.

PROSPECTUS One of the documents filed with the Securities and Exchange Commission by a company when it is planning an issue of securities for public sale totaling $500,000 or more. It is a selling circular containing highlights from the full registration statement, subject to the SEC's disclosure rules, and used by brokers to help investors evaluate the new securities before or at the time of purchase.

PROXY Authorization you give to a company official or other representative to vote your shares for you at a shareholders' meeting.

PUTS Options to sell a fixed amount of a specific stock at a specified price within a specified period of time.

QUOTATION Often shortened to "quote." The highest bid to buy and the lowest offer to sell a security in a given market at a given time. If you ask your broker for a "quote" on a stock, he may come back with something like "45¼ to 45½." This means that $45.25 was the highest price any buyer wanted to pay at the time the quote was given and that $45.50 was the lowest price which any seller would take at the same time.

RALLY A sharp rapid rise in stock prices or in the price of one particular stock, following a decline.

RED HERRING A preliminary prospectus. It carries a cautionary statement on the first page, printed in red, which gives rise to the term "red herring."

REGISTERED REPRESENTATIVE A securities salesman employed by a brokerage firm who has passed certain tests and met certain standards set by the New York Stock Exchange and/or the National Association of Securities Dealers. Also called an account executive, customer's man, a stockbroker, or simply a broker.

REGISTRATION Before a public offering may be made of new securities offered by a company, or of outstanding securities by controlling stockholders—through the mails or in interstate commerce—the securities must be registered under the Securities Act of 1933 and a registration statement must be filed with the SEC by the issuer. This statement must disclose pertinent information relating to the company's operations, securities, management, and purpose of the public offering. Securities of railroads under jurisdiction of the Interstate Commerce Commission, and certain other types of securities, are exempted. On securities offerings involving less than $500,000, less information is required.

Before a security may be admitted to dealings on a national securities exchange, it must be registered under the Securities Exchange Act of 1934. The application for registration must be filed with the exchange and the SEC by the company issuing the securities. It must disclose pertinent information relating to the company's operations, securities, and management. Registration may become effective thirty days after receipt by the SEC of the certification by the exchange of approval of listing and registration, or sooner by special order of the Commission.

RIGHT   A short-term privilege to buy additional shares at a specified, advantageous price for a short, limited time given to the shareholders on a proportional basis by the issuing company. Rights are often offered by a company seeking to raise additional capital, and may involve bonds, especially debentures. Rights are offered to existing shareholders so that they will continue to hold the same equity position after the change in capitalization has taken place. You, the shareholder receiving rights, have two choices: (1) to buy the security on the terms offered (for example, 1 share for each 20 shares owned); (2) to sell the rights, which, because of the favorable price of the offer, have a value of their own. Failure to exercise or sell your right results in a loss—through dilution of the value of your existing holdings by the issuance of the additional stock. Therefore, you should either exercise your rights or sell them during the allotted time span.

ROUND LOT   A unit of trading in a security. Usually 100 shares for active stocks; 10 shares for inactive stocks.

SEAT   Membership in a stock exchange which entitles the owner to buy and sell securities on that exchange. Big Board seat prices have ranged from $35,000 to $515,000 in recent years.

SEC   The Securities and Exchange Commission, the federal agency established by Congress to help protect investors. The SEC administers the Securities Act of 1933, the Trust Indenture Act, the Investment Company Act, the Investment Advisers Act, and the Public Utility Holding Company Act.

SECONDARY DISTRIBUTION   (Also known as a secondary offering.) The redistribution of a block of stock sometime after it has been sold by the issuing company. The sale is handled off the NYSE by a securities firm or group of firms and the shares are usually offered at a fixed price which is related to the current market price of the stock. Usually the block is a large one, such as might be involved in the settlement of an estate. The security may be listed or unlisted.

SETTLEMENT DAY   The deadline by which a buyer of securities must pay for securities he has purchased and a seller must deliver certificates for securities he has sold. In regular trading, settlement day is the fifth business day after execution of an order.

SHORT POSITION   Stocks sold short and not covered as of a particular date. On the NYSE, a tabulation is issued once a month listing all issues on the Exchange in which there was a short position of 5,000 or more shares and issues in which the short position had changed by 2,000 or more shares in the preceding month. Short position or interest also means the total amount of stock an individual has sold short and has not covered as of a particular date. See SHORT SELLING.

SHORT SELLING   The reverse of the usual transaction, for instead of buying a stock first and selling it later, the short seller sells it first, then borrows the stock and buys it back later to complete the transaction.

"SMART MONEY"   Refers to the so-called professional and sophisticated traders who supposedly exploit alleged "inside" information to make profits at the expense of other investors. In other words, the term implies exceptional contacts, knowledge, timing, and forecasting ability, the special knack of finding the most profitable deals, and use of the newest financing or investing techniques and media.

SPECIALIST   A member of an exchange who has two functions. The first is to maintain an orderly market, as far as reasonably practicable, in the stocks in which he is registered as a specialist. In order to maintain an orderly market, the exchange expects the specialist to buy or sell for his own account, to a reasonable degree, when there is a temporary disparity between supply and demand. The second function of the specialist is to act as a broker's broker. When a commission broker on the exchange floor receives a limit order, say, to buy at $50 a stock when selling at $60, he cannot wait at the post where the stock is traded until the price reaches the specified level. So he leaves the order with the specialist, who will try to execute it in the market if and when the stock declines to the specified price. There were some 380 specialists on the NYSE alone in the late 1970s

SPECULATOR   A person whose goal in buying and selling securities is to multiply his capital quickly and who is willing to take greater risks than an investor to attain this objective. Differs from an investor in goals, risks, temperament. See IN-AND-OUT.

SPLIT   A division of a company's outstanding stock: i.e., if a company has 1 million shares outstanding, currently priced at $50 per share, and splits its stock two for one, it has 2 million shares outstanding which will sell at $25 per share. If you own 100 "old" shares at $50, after the split you own 200 "new" shares at $25. Theoretically, the new shares are worth only half the amount of the old shares, but in actual practice prices tend to rise when a stock is split—at least temporarily. Reason: investors generally are more interested in buying relatively lower-priced stocks than high-priced stocks, hence buying frequently increases after a stock is split.

SPREAD   The difference between two prices, between bid and asked or between purchase and sale price.

STOCK DIVIDEND   A dividend paid by a company to its stockholders in the form of additional shares of the company's stock instead of in the form of cash (when it is a cash dividend).

STOCK OPTION   A privilege, often conferred as a fringe benefit by a company to its executive and key employees, to buy stock in the company at a specified presumable favorable price, within a specified period of time, and on advantageous terms.

STOP ORDER Standing instructions to your broker to sell your shares automatically if the price drops to a specified level. The aim is to assure yourself that profits don't disappear or your losses don't exceed a given amount. There is no guarantee that a stop order will be executed exactly at its "trigger" price, because when a stop is activated it becomes a market order and allows the broker to get the best possible price then available in a market. Stops can be used for buy orders too.

STREET The New York financial community in the Wall Street area.

STREET NAME Securities left by the owner in his broker's name and custody. Often investors leave all their securities in street name as a matter of choice and convenience, but securities bought on margin must be left in street name.

SYMBOL The single capital letter or combination of letters given to a company when it is listed on an exchange and by which it is thereafter identified on the tape. For instance, U. S. Steel is "X"; General Motors is "GM"; American Telephone & Telegraph is "T."

TAKEN TO THE CLEANERS In the stock market, this means the same thing as taking a bath or blood bath. In short, it means being hit by one or many whopping losses.

TENDER In stock market language, a tender means an offer to acquire a security you own or to exchange stock which you own for stock in another company. Usually a tender is made by a corporation or individual to gain control of a company or to simplify the corporate structure of the company.

THE STREET Wall Street. But "Wall Street" is not just a street in New York City bounded at one end by a river and at the other by a graveyard. It has been broadened to include all the financial institutions, securities and money markets, and investors on all the Main Streets of the United States from coast to coast.

THIN MARKET A market in which there are comparatively few bids to buy or offers to sell or both—or an illiquid market. The phrase may apply to a single security or to the entire stock market. In a thin market, price fluctuations between transactions are usually larger than when the market is liquid. A thin market in a particular stock may reflect a lack of interest in that issue or a limited supply of stock in the market.

TICKER The instrument which prints prices and volume of security transactions in cities and towns throughout the United States and Canada within minutes after each trade on the floor. In recent years it has been complemented by thousands of visual display units on tops of brokers' desks.

TIPS Recommendations of stocks to buy or sell often given to novices by other novices on the false basis of alleged "inside" information about the stock. Tips may be accurate too, and given in entirely good faith—but these are in a slim minority as far as the general public is concerned. Tipping could be illegal. A tipster, of course, is a person who gives tips.

TRANSFER AGENT A transfer agent, usually a bank, keeps a record of the name of each registered shareowner, his or her address, the number of shares owned, and sees that certificates presented for transfer are properly canceled and new certificates issued in the name of the transferee.

TURNOVER The volume of trading on a stock exchange—or in a particular security, or in the entire securities market—on a given day or in a given period.

UNDERWRITER See INVESTMENT BANKER.

WARRANT A privilege to buy a security at a specified price—within a specified time limit or perpetually. Usually a long-term offer made by a corporation to pave the way for the eventual sale of stocks or bonds to persons who do not already own its securities. As a rule, it is offered as an inducement to get investors to buy the other securities. A warrant is similar to a right but it normally has a much longer life.

"WHEN ISSUED" Term used to describe a new issue of securities that has been authorized but not actually issued to purchasers and that is being bought and sold in the market with all transactions settled only when, as, and if the securities are finally issued. "WI" is the label for these issues in the newspaper stock tables.

YIELD The percentage of return per year on a security. To find the current yield on a stock, you divide the current annual dividend rate by the current price of the stock. (If you bought the stock at $100, and it is paying $3.00 a year in dividends, your current yield is 3 per cent.) Figuring yields on bonds is more complex and determining yields to maturity requires the use of bond tables.

YO-YO STOCKS Volatile, usually high-priced specialty issues, which fluctuate wildly.

22

MUTUAL FUNDS

What Are Mutual Funds?	1168
What Fund for You?	1169
Why Should You Buy Mutual Funds?	1169
Types of Mutual Funds	1171
What Is the Investment Record of Mutual Funds?	1172
Load and No-Load Funds	1177
Ways to Buy and Use Mutual Funds	1178
How Mutual Funds Help in Other Ways	1180
How to Buy Mutual Funds Professionally	1182
Open-end Funds Versus Closed-end Funds (Publicly Traded Investment Funds)	1185
Sources of Information on Mutual Funds	1186
The Bafflegab of Mutual Funds	1187

What Are Mutual Funds?

Probably the best known of the many different types of so-called investment companies, mutual funds are a medium through which you invest your money in a diversified list of stocks and bonds chosen by professional investment managers.

You buy shares in a mutual fund which in turn uses your money to buy the securities of other companies. You can buy and sell mutual fund shares at prices that are calculated once or twice a day on any days that the securities markets are open.

There are "load" and "no-load" funds. There also are the closed-end funds (now known as publicly traded investment funds) and unit trusts, plus many others, most of which are discussed separately later in this chapter. The load funds are sold by salespeople through elaborate marketing systems, and on these shares there is a sales charge (load). The no-load funds have no salespeople, no elaborate distribution systems, and no sales charge. You are not "sold" these shares; you must "buy" them. You usually learn about a no-load fund from another investor, from a banker, a lawyer, an investment adviser, an ad in a financial news section, or from a discussion such as this.

Q. *How many mutual funds are there?*
A. In the closing years of the 1970s, there were more than 700, of which about 255 were no-load funds.

Q. *Who buys mutual funds?*
A. Individuals. Also many institutional investors have in recent years become large holders of fund shares. All together, some 8.5 million individuals and firms had invested in funds as the 1980s neared.

Q. *Where are the prices on mutual funds quoted?*
A. In the financial pages of the major daily newspapers, which usually have a section giving bid and asked prices on mutual funds. On the no-load funds, you will find the same price quoted under "bid" and "asked." On the load funds you will find a higher price under "asked" than under "bid" because the "asked" price will reflect the sales charge. For example, if the bid on Fund A is $10.50 and the asked is $11.20, the sales charge is 70 cents.

Also many major newspapers use the designation "NL" (no-load) next to this type of fund, thereby making it easy to find the no-load funds.

What Fund for You?

Every investor certainly should investigate funds. Many of you will find the funds are suitable for achieving your investment goals.

To help you determine the kind of mutual fund that is best suited for you, here are broad guidelines.

Specifically, if you are:

• *Single,* earning under $15,000, with a savings-oriented (conservative) temperament: you should own an income fund with a dual goal of providing some longer-term capital growth.

• *Single,* earning under $15,000, with a chance-taker's (aggressive) temperament: yours should be a "total return" fund, concentrating on high-growth common stocks or a long-term growth fund.

• *Married,* with two or three dependents, earning $15,000 to $25,000, with a conservative temperament: the best for you would be a blue-chip, common stock fund, for long-term growth of both capital and income.

• *Married,* with two or three dependents, earning $25,000 and up, with a growth-oriented temperament: yours should be either a pure "income" fund, a "money-market" fund, or a bond fund.

• *Working couple,* earning $25,000 and up, with growth-oriented temperament: obviously, a growth fund is for you, so the investments can help you accumulate resources for future tuition needs, travel and other recreation, retirement, etc.

• *Older person,* income coming from Social Security and some savings, with a conservative temperament and a goal of preservation of capital and more current income: ideally, the medium should be an income fund of the more conservative type which pays dividends and has some appreciation possibilities. Or a money-market fund which will preserve capital and offer a satisfactory yield.

Why Should You Buy Mutual Funds?

If I were to tell you that the investment advice given to the small investor in the United States is far inferior to that given to the big guy, and that the men and women who give that advice agree the above is true, wouldn't you be deeply disturbed? Okay, I'm telling you that this is the opinion of an overwhelming percentage of the nation's security analysts. According to a recent survey:

• A shocking seven out of ten security analysts have "reservations about the advice available to the small investor as compared with that given the large one."

- Only one in three believes that "the quality of investment advice now available adequately serves all types of investors."
- Nearly half favor "some form of blanket registration of security analysts" (in short, greater control).

This is a serious indictment of investment advice by the advice industy itself.

By itself, this report would be sobering enough. It becomes even more so in view of the forecasts dramatized in the previous chapter on investing in stocks: first, the fees you pay for Wall Street's service are on the rise while fees the funds pay are declining; second, commissions you pay are more and more determined by the level of the investment advice you request; and third, an investment manager has emerged who supervises the funds of the small investor for a fee on top of the commissions the investor must pay to buy and sell.

What does all this mean to you?

It means you must recognize that you will not get the same high-quality research and advice as an institutional investor and certainly not at the same time the pro gets it—unless you pay extra for it. This in turn means that one possible solution for you lies in joining the pros via buying mutual fund shares.

Here are some of the major advantages of mutual fund ownership versus personal selection by the amateur of a portfolio of stocks and bonds.

Diversification. In general, the greater variety of stocks, bonds, and other types of investments selected by mutual funds lessens the risk of loss due to your making one big mistake in selecting individual stocks.

Mutual funds have to diversify. By federal law, except in instances of special exemption disclosed in the prospectus, they may not invest more than 5 per cent of their assets in the securities of any single issuer. Funds may not own more than 10 per cent of any class of securities issued by a single company.

Professional management. All of the major mutual funds are managed by professionals backed by substantial facilities for research, statistical analysis, and economic research.

Federal regulation. Mutual funds are closely regulated by federal and state laws designed to guard against abuses. By law, mutual funds ordinarily must distribute at least 90 per cent of their net income to shareowners each year. Moreover, there are tight federal restrictions on the amounts of money a mutual fund may borrow.

Convenience. Obviously, it's much simpler for you, the shareowner, to have one single certificate representing your ownership (through a mutual fund) in one hundred or more stocks. Mutual funds have a fine record in handling the paper work of their customers. Many take care of the paper work completely.

Services and easy purchase plans. There are many different, easy, and new ways in which you can buy—and enjoy the ownership of—mutual funds today. This includes automatic reinvestment plans, periodic purchase plans, retirement plans, ordering by telephone, free exchange between funds in "families" of funds, withdrawal plans, and the like.

Liquidity. It's very easy to sell a mutual fund. Nearly all funds will repurchase fund shares at the bid price, and the sell order can be conveniently arranged.

Variety of funds. There are dozens of different types of mutual funds to choose from—including stock, bond, and money-market funds, as well as growth, balanced, income, speculative funds—which means there's probably at least one fund that can meet your specific needs.

What Is the Investment Record of Mutual Funds?

Of course, the performance varies from fund to fund depending on the objective of the fund (growth versus income, for instance) and on the excellence of management. But over the long term, the records of mutual funds compare favorably with the familiar stock averages.

Over the short term, though, the performances of mutual funds can be startlingly good or abysmally poor. For example, in the 1960–74 period, many of the fund shares chalked up dreadful records. Their performance came in for particular criticism in view of the fact that the funds are managed by professionals at a handsome fee and the fact that at a minimum their goal is preservation of capital plus income while, at a maximum, their aim is significant enhancement of capital plus income.

This was the period in which the "go-go" performance funds went into their downward spin. Some of the star fund performers of the 1960s—such as the Manhattan Fund, Mates Investment Fund, Enterprise Fund, and Neuwrith Fund—plummeted from the list of top performers to the also-ran category. It was painful testimony of the extent to which so many of the funds had changed from being a safe, sane haven for the small investor wanting long-term growth into a playground for the fast-moving speculator seeking instant performance.

I repeat, however, that this is short-term, and, in general, mutual funds are much more suited to the long-term investor rather than the trader.

In the latter part of the 1970s, fund managers, stunned by the poor performance earlier in the decade and the investor disenchantment reflected in several consecutive years of net redemptions for the industry, set about developing products, services, and management investment practices designed to win back investor confidence in mutual funds and the basic values mutual funds offer—portfolio diversification, professional management, relatively low entry costs. As a result, fund sales again started to rise, and in the second half of the 1970s mutual funds as a whole were once more outperforming the broad market averages.

On balance, the long-term record of the funds shapes up impressively in the investor's favor.

It would be self-defeating to submit statistics to you at this date to document the excellent long-term performance of mutual funds compared with other forms of investing and saving as well as against other key stock market indexes. You would be only confused as prices of various investment mediums and the returns you can earn fluctuate from month to month. Sources that instead will quickly supply you with up-to-the-minute figures are listed on pages 1186–87 in this chapter.

There may be or may not be a modest charge involved in obtaining the information. Or you may want to subscribe to one or more of the reporting services.

Types of Mutual Funds

As the 1980s begin, you can buy shares in literally dozens of different types of mutual funds—many of them new and little known and many of them highly specialized. These, of course, are in addition to the "old" types of funds, part of the industry since it emerged in the 1920s.

For instance, you can invest your money in shares of a mutual fund specializing in chemical stocks or energy companies. You can choose a fund that gambles in ultra-risky speculative securities, or you can settle for a fund with a conservative investment philosophy. You also can buy shares in funds specializing in tax-exempt short-term securities or bonds, utilities, Canadian securities, options, commodities, the stock market indexes, insurance and bank stocks, or in foreign securities. You even can buy shares in a mutual fund carrying built-in insurance against any loss in your investment—assuming you're willing to pay an insurance premium cost (in addition to the sales charge, if the offering fund is a load fund type).

Mutual funds have now diversified to the point where you can actually lose your way in this financial industry without a guide. Quietly but rapidly, whole new classes of mutual funds have been developed. For example, it was as recently as 1970 that the bond and money-market (liquid asset or cash reserve) funds jumped into the popular class.

To the old-line definitions, it is thus essential to add explanations of some of the new types of funds. In alphabetical order, here is a guide through "old" and "new":

Balanced Funds: among the more conservative funds, with investment portfolios "balanced" at all times among bonds, preferred stocks, and common stocks—as a protection against a roller-coasting stock market. This type of fund is for a person who is seeking safety of principal plus a regular income and who, to get this, is willing to settle for relatively modest growth of his investment.

Bond Funds: funds that invest in portfolios of various types of senior

MUTUAL FUNDS

securities to produce relatively high yields. In recent years, the yields on such funds have often substantially outstripped those of savings accounts or even large certificates of deposit. Another attraction of such funds is the possibility of eventual capital gains if some of the bonds in the portfolio were bought at discounts below face value.

Closed-end Funds: see Publicly Traded Investment Funds.

Commodities Funds: funds that seek capital gains through a portfolio consisting of holdings of commodities, as opposed to stocks and bonds.

Common Stock Funds: funds that have limited their portfolios to common stocks. They range from ultra-conservative funds investing primarily in the highest-quality blue chip common stocks to ultra-risky funds investing in speculative stocks.

Convertible Funds: are aimed at producing current income and capital gains by investing in convertible preferred stocks and convertible bonds.

Dual-purpose Funds: type of funds offering two kinds of shares: income shares and capital shares. In most dual-purpose funds, each class of investor at the outset stands to get double his money's worth. The capital shareholder will reap gains (or losses) on the income shareholder's money as well as his own. The income shareholder collects the capital shareholder's dividends. To obtain this form of leverage, the income shareholder must usually give up all claim to capital appreciation and the capital shareholder must forfeit all income. There are only a handful of such funds and they haven't operated long enough to get a good reading on their performance. They have a long and successful history in England and Holland.

Fund of Funds: these are funds ("multifunds") which invest in shares of other mutual funds, thereby offering shareholders a highly diversified type of investment.

Growth Funds: funds concentrating on purchase of growth stocks. Growth funds involve relatively more risk than income or balanced funds. A growth fund should give you a return ranging from at least 8 per cent to 12 per cent annually over a five-year period or it's not worth the risk.

Hedge Funds: began as private pools of speculative funds formed by groups of wealthy investors, but now there are hedge funds for anyone who wants them. These funds use such unorthodox (for mutual funds) techniques as borrowing against their own stocks in order to buy more shares, speculating in put and call options, and selling shares short in order to profit from stock price declines as well as rises (thus, "hedge" funds). Their major objective is capital gains.

Millions of dollars were put into hedge funds in the 1960s, and until 1969 some turned in dazzling performances. But in the 1969–70 crash, many of the leading hedge funds lost as much as 40 to 50 per cent in value and their reputations were seriously tarnished. Many went out of business. Hedge funds are usually not for the small investor.

Income Funds: the principal goal of these is income to be achieved by investment in high-yielding stocks and bonds. Only an incidental objective is capital gains. These funds tend to be the most conservative—and their popularity swings up and down depending on shifting investor interest in income versus long-term growth.

Index Funds: this type of fund invests in a portfolio that duplicates the Standard & Poor's 500 Stock Index. Through an index fund, the investor is —in effect—buying a prorated interest in all the stocks that make up the S&P Index of Stocks listed on the New York Stock Exchange. By so doing, this type of fund can be expected to about match the performance of the stock market as a whole.

Junk Bond Funds: these funds invest in high-risk corporate bonds and therefore offer investors high yields coupled—inevitably—with high risks. Junk bond funds are not for the conservative!

Letter Stock Funds: highly speculative funds that invest your money in stocks of companies not yet registered with the Securities and Exchange Commission. This stock is called "letter stock" because a buyer (in this case, the mutual fund) must sign an "investment letter" promising not to resell the stock for a specified short-term period and pledging instead to hold it for a longer term. This type of stock is generally sold by small, fledgling companies to finance research, development, expansion.

Look upon any investment in mutual funds specializing in letter stocks as sheer speculation. This is definitely too risky for most mutual fund buyers and the funds virtually disappeared in the market breaks of the early 1970s.

Money-market Funds: funds that invest in short-term money-market instruments. Investors can buy these shares in comparatively small amounts and thus get the same advantages of the relatively high rates on these instruments that big investors get when they buy large blocks in the open market. By the late 1970s, more than $20 billion had been invested in money-market funds by individuals and institutions.

Be sure the money-market funds fit in with your investment objectives. The funds are not meant to be long-term investments nor the keystone of an individual or institutional investment program. But the funds do provide a haven to put your cash to work easily and efficiently at the highest returns consistent with safety.

They invest in short-term money-market paper, are highly conservative, offer returns that usually will rise and fall with the ups and downs of short-term interest rates. Their principal values will show relatively minor changes, reflecting moves in interest rates and credit risks. They usually are used as a safe place to keep money at work that is temporarily out of the stock market or that you must keep in the most liquid form.

Even in this narrow field, investment goals, portfolio policies, and investor services may vary.

Some funds tend to anticipate short-term interest rate fluctuations and change their investments accordingly. Others merely try to maintain their investments at the highest available short-term rates and do not attempt to outguess rate fluctuations.

Some limit themselves to the highest quality U. S. Government securities. Others rely heavily on different types of short-term instruments, such as bank certificates of deposit, commercial paper, other short-term paper of high quality. See "Your Guide to the Bond Markets," Chapter 23. Some impose rigid quality restrictions on their own investments. Others will buy below the highest quality to get a relatively higher yield.

You must check out the funds themselves. Particularly, you must examine the prospectus of each fund for clues to the knowledge, reputation, experience, and resources of the organization and the fund's portfolio managers.

Services the money funds offer include: check writing privileges, immediate phone or wire redemption, exchange privileges, automatic redemption, accounting.

Municipal bond mutual funds: tax-exempt funds popularly called munifunds may be for you *if* income exempt from federal taxes is what you're looking for. That could be if you report at least $16,000 in taxable income on a joint return, or $12,000 on a single return, earn enough to maintain a regular investment program—*and* avoid undue risks by restraining your greed for the highest possible annual returns and vow instead to invest only in quality funds.

• A municipal bond fund follows the basic strategy of buying and selling its investments, just as a stock mutual fund does. The funds are "managed," and your return can vary along with the protection you are given against loss of principal.

Munifunds first appeared in late 1976 and immediately took off, with dozens of investment companies in the field now and others being regularly developed.

If you're a couple filing a joint return on a taxable income in the $20,000–$24,000 bracket, a tax-free 5½ per cent return is the equivalent of a taxable 8.09 per cent; if your bracket is the $28,000–$34,000 range, the 5½ tax free is equal to 9.02 per cent. In the 50 per cent bracket, of course, it's equal to 11 per cent a year. (See Chapter 23 on investing in bonds.)

• Never forget that municipal bond funds can decrease as well as increase in value. The cheapest fund may not be the most stable or the best managed; the fund offering the highest return may be investing in very poor bonds. You *can lose* money.

• Profits from increases in asset value are taxable as capital gains.

In munifunds, there are both "load" and no-load funds.

• Before you put up a penny, decide on your goals. And restrain your greed!

Option and Option Income Funds: these funds promise high income and appreciation by investing in options on stocks. This is a relatively new and untested type of fund. Only a few exist. Great caution should be exercised before investing in an option fund.

Publicly Traded Investment Funds: popularly called closed-end funds, these operate like open-end mutual funds except that they issue only a fixed number of shares and will not usually buy back their shares. Shares are bought and sold on the stock market but hardly ever at a price equal to the net asset value per share. As a result, they either sell at a "premium" over their asset price or at a "discount" below it.

Special-purpose Funds: these aren't new, but their number is multiplying. They invest primarily in one specific type of stock or bond or in one particular industry to take advantage of the anticipated faster growth in that area or industry. For example, there are the funds that invest heavily in chemicals, energy, gemstones, minerals, geographic regions or countries—or only in United States Government securities. Within this special-purpose category, too, there are funds adhering to a special stock market forecasting theory or technique.

If you invest in a special-purpose stock fund, a wise precaution would be to seek a fund with an investment portfolio widely diversified among key beneficiaries of any major advance in its chosen area or industry.

Tax-free Exchange Funds: a limited number of funds have been specifically organized to exchange individual securities for a diversified holding of stocks, without incurring immediate taxes. This so-called tax-free exchange through organizations of a mutual fund type of operation was prohibited by the Internal Revenue Service in 1967.

Unit Trusts: UITs were established as far back as 1961. While securities in a mutual fund are actively managed, securities—usually bonds—placed in a unit trust simply remain there for the limited life of the trust or until the bond reaches maturity. Therefore, there is no conventional management role in the performance of a unit trust.

Each UIT is actually a separate trust, with a fixed portfolio of bonds. Though bonds may be sold from the portfolio, if credit-worthiness is adversely affected, no new bonds can be bought to replace them. In short, once the UIT acquires the bonds, it holds them to maturity, thereby assuring you a stable—known in advance—rate of return.

If you have enough of a nest egg to meet the usual minimum investment requirements of $1,000 to $5,000—*and* you also strictly obey the basic rules on greed and quality—UITs may be worth investigating.

UITs charge a one-time sales fee of 3 to 4½ per cent included in the price, but no annual management fee.

Venture Capital Funds: funds that usually invest in securities of smaller companies that are little known and with stock often not yet registered with the Securities and Exchange Commission. These restricted securities cannot be sold publicly until they have been registered. Venture capital funds often provide new and young companies with seed capital. Nowhere is an investor betting more on a manager's ability and judgment than in venture capital funds. Generally, these funds are higher risk investments and should be considered only by more sophisticated investors.

Load and No-Load Funds

A load fund will usually be sold to you by a salesperson or selling organization and, for this, you will pay a sales charge, or a "load." A no-load fund you will have to seek out and buy on your own. There are no salespeople, no sales charges—and thus the description "no-load." This is the sole distinction.

Among the no-load funds you will find the same wide selection as among the load funds—in investment goals, in size, in investment record, in quality of management, etc. You can get the same services with no-loads as with loads: systematic purchasing plans, withdrawal plans, dividend reinvestment, retirement plans, payroll deduction, check writing, exchange privileges, and insurance plans. You can sell them easily just by telling the fund's home office you want to redeem your shares. (A few have a redemption charge, usually less than 2 per cent.) The tax status is the same in both cases and so are the SEC's regulations.

Since no-loads have no sales organizations, further information must be obtained by writing directly to the fund, or contacting the No-Load Mutual Fund Association, Valley Forge, Pennsylvania 19481.

When you buy a load fund, you pay the net asset value plus the sales charge. This is generally around 8½ per cent, which translates into something over 9 per cent above the asset value. The charge, however, can range from 1 per cent to more than 9½ per cent. In short, the minute you buy a load fund, the worth of your holdings is less than what you put in. For example, if you buy $1,000 worth of a load fund, you may only get $910 in asset value; $90 went for commission.

With no-loads, all your money goes to work. This gives the no-load investor a head start. Here's why.

Let's assume two $10,000 investments: one in a load fund, the other in a no-load. In the case of the load fund, 8½ per cent, or $850, is deducted, the remaining $9,150 is invested. If both funds grow at the same rate—10 per cent per year, for example—the no-load will be worth $11,000 at the end of the first year, while the load fund will be worth only $10,065. The no-load investor is now $1,000 ahead; the load fund investor is about even. But let's look closer. Originally the no-load investor had $850 more working for him than did the load fund investor. Now the differential is $935 ($11,000 vs. $10,065). What has happened is that the $850 paid out as commission in one case, but invested in the other, is also growing. And over the years this sum will continue to grow and compound, widening the differential. By the end of twenty years, the no-load investment will be worth close to $6,000 more, if both funds continue to grow at the same 10 per cent rate per year.

The long-term records of the no-load funds compare favorably with those of the load funds. The lack of a sales charge has nothing to do with the caliber of the fund's management.

In recent years, no-load funds have become increasingly popular as investors have become aware that they are around and that they provide a savings in commissions. But you well may decide that a specific load fund is right for you and thus you'll ignore the sales charge. The crucial thing is that the specific fund meets your investment goals. Moreover, in time the amount of commissions on "load" funds will go down—in response to the competitive pressure from the "no-loads" plus increasing pressure from the SEC and Congress.

Since this could be your biggest single investment medium for now and the future, the only sensible move is to explore the whole field of loads and no-loads.

Ways to Buy and Use Mutual Funds

There are not only many different types of mutual funds to choose among, there are also many easy and new ways in which you can buy mutual funds. Just how you buy them depends in part on the way you plan to use them ultimately, for, say, extra regular income, building a retirement fund, or creating a college education fund.

Here's a simple guide through some of the investor programs now available.

Automatic Dividend Reinvestment: under this program all dividends and capital gains distributions are automatically reinvested. In the late seventies, roughly 3 million dividend reinvestment plans were in force.

Withdrawal Plan: an arrangement under which investors in mutual funds can regularly receive monthly or quarterly payments of a specified amount. This may be more or less than the actual investment income.

Letter of Intent: with a pledge to purchase a sufficient amount of mutual fund shares within a limited period of time, you can qualify for the reduced selling charge that would apply to a comparable lump sum purchase.

Periodic Purchase (or Accumulation) Plans: under these, you simply send in checks to invest regularly (usually monthly but sometimes bimonthly or quarterly) in mutual fund shares or you can authorize your bank to invest for you and to deduct the costs from your monthly bank statement. In the late seventies there were about 4 million such plans in force. The minimum investment under these plans is typically between $25 and $50, though some funds have no minimum and some substantially higher; also, in most plans, you can change the dollar amount at any time or stop investing altogether, if you so decide.

A key point here is that, while you're investing identical amounts at regular intervals via these periodic purchase plans, you are also getting the advantage of dollar-cost-averaging—meaning you get more shares when stock prices are depressed and less shares when they are rising. Thus, you average out your costs, which is, as I repeat and stress, an excellent way to invest in stocks over the long term.

403(B) Plans: individuals employed by school districts, hospitals, municipalities, and other non-profit organizations or associations may be eligible to adopt 403(B) plans which will reduce current tax liability and permit earnings in the plan to compound on a tax shelter basis.

Corporate Retirement Plans: many funds make available pension or profit-sharing plans in prototype form for use by corporate employees. Check with your company to find out if it offers this type of plan and the terms for participation.

Keogh Plan: this plan is for the self-employed individual who may contribute 15 per cent of earned income, up to a maximum of $7,500. A retirement plan can be set up by making tax-deductible contributions and at the same time shelter current income dividends and capital gains distributions from current tax liability.

Defined Benefit Keogh: a newer type of Keogh plan that lets you defer income taxes of up to $10,800—a tax deferment on substantially higher income than the $7,500 maximum allowed on regular Keoghs.

Simplified Employee Pension Plan: permitted by the 1978 Tax Reform Act, a SEP eliminates much of the paper work associated with traditional pension plans. Under a SEP an employer contributes to an Individual Retirement Account in the employee's name. The maximum contribution is 15 per cent of earned income, not to exceed $7,500. If your employer's contribution amounts to less than $1,500, you may make up the difference and take that figure as a deduction on your income taxes.

Exchange Privilege: some funds will permit you to shift your investment from one fund to another by telephone. This is permitted only among funds under the same management or with an outside fund under a mutual agreement between the funds. This is a convenience for the shareowner whose investment objective or current needs change.

Individual Retirement Accounts: IRAs were created by passage of the Employee Retirement Security Act of 1974. Individuals not covered by formal corporate, government, or other retirement plans may set up tax-shelter retirement programs of their own with annual funding of 15 per cent of your gross wages, up to a maximum of $1,500 as of the late 1970s, plus an additional $250 is permitted to cover a non-working spouse. And the maximum permissible investment per individual is almost certain to go up.

The Variable Annuity Separate Account: investment vehicles offered by life insurance companies as a means to combine the protection of insurance with the potentials of equity investments.

IRA Roll-over Plan: this permits distributions from a qualified pension or profit-sharing plan to be reinvested within sixty days from the date of the distribution in a qualifying individual retirement account. The amount so invested is not subject to the $1,500 annual IRA limit of the late 1970s. Further, such funds may be later transferred back to a qualified pension or profit-sharing plan, all without incurring a tax liability.

Payroll Deduction Plans: these are among the most rapidly growing fringe benefits offered by U.S. corporations—and, as you might suspect, the payroll plans are being aggressively pushed by the mutual fund industry. Often, by investing this way through your company you will pay a lower load charge —or no sales charge if the plan invests in no-load funds.

Life Insurance-Mutual Fund Plans: you can combine purchase of mutual fund shares and life insurance or invest in a type of plan that will buy X number of shares of a given mutual fund, and then the dividends plus capital gains on your shares will pay your life insurance premiums. If, however, the value of your mutual fund shares drops substantially, you may have to pay your life insurance premium costs out of capital you have invested—or out of your pocket.

Group Life Insurance: some funds offer group life and accident insurance. In this case, you, the shareholders, will be given the opportunity to purchase insurance at special, low group rates, with premium costs being paid optionally from the proceeds of your mutual fund investment or an additional direct payment of the periodic premium cost.

Plan Completion Insurance: also provided optionally by some funds, is a means of ensuring that an intended plan will be completed in the event that the plan holder should die.

Insured Redemption Value Plans: offered by selected funds to protect an investment in a mutual fund against long-term loss. If the total value of your investment at the close of the period, including the value of shares received from reinvested income dividend and capital gains, is less than the insured investment, including the amount of the premium, the insurance company makes up the difference. You, the shareholder, do not have to redeem your shares to collect.

How Mutual Funds Help in Other Ways

You will find a wide variety of uses for mutual funds to help you in planning for your own and your family's financial well-being. To illustrate:

• If your income is at the level suggesting some tax-sheltered income would be valuable, mutual funds that invest in tax-exempt bonds issued by states, cities, and other local governments can be exceedingly attractive. The interest obtained from these bonds is passed through to shareowners free of federal tax.

- If you want to invest in equities but avoid the chance of poor fund management, a fund with a portfolio structured to duplicate the Standard & Poor's 500 Stock Index can be expected to do at least as well—or as poorly—as the stock market as a whole.
- If you want to put your idle cash to work harder for you, you may want to invest some in a money-market fund. Through these so-called liquid asset type funds, you can enjoy competitive interest yields from portfolios that invest primarily in such short-term instruments as those issued or guaranteed by the U. S. Government or its agencies, bank certificates of deposit, commercial paper and short-term corporate obligations. With a money-market fund you can withdraw all or any part of your money at any time for any purpose without penalty, and redemptions often can be accomplished by a simple telephone call. You can use your redemption checks as immediate cash and your investment will still be earning interest, until the checks clear. Money funds are a way to keep your extra savings working for you until the instant they are needed.
- You can buy shares for your children under the "uniform gifts to minors" act and arrange to have dividends and capital gains automatically reinvested to build a college fund. There are significant tax angles, so check them. One major advantage is that you usually have to pay taxes on your fund dividends and capital gains distributions and your youngster doesn't.
- If you are self-employed, you can use mutual funds (among other investments) to create a retirement nest egg for yourself. As of the late seventies, you could contribute up to $7,500 a year under the Keogh law—with the total amount deductible for income tax purposes—and until you retire you need not pay any income tax on any dividends or capital gains distributions paid into your account.
- You can arrange for a second income from your mutual fund shares by setting up a voluntary withdrawal plan. Typically, users of these plans have shares valued at a minimum of $7,500 to $10,000. If you own $10,000 worth of shares and elect to withdraw a typical 6 per cent a year, you'll get about $50 a month. If your shares grow by more than 6 per cent a year, you'll be able to withdraw $50 a month and keep your assets intact.
- You can switch programs. Often so-called families of mutual funds, several of which are run by the same management, permit the owner of one fund to switch to another without paying additional load charges. For example, if a young man buys a growth fund and continues investing in it and then wants to switch to an income fund as he reaches retirement age, he could do this usually without paying additional load charges—if he is investing in load funds—to acquire the income fund. Most no-load fund families offer exchange privileges without any charge for this service. The restriction is that the income fund be in the same "family" as the growth fund. Federal income taxes, though, are applicable on such a switch.

How to Buy Mutual Funds Professionally

There is far more to the purchase of mutual funds than a simple decision that this is the prudent way for you to invest. There is much more to the wise selection of a fund than a cursory comparison of records and a quick look at a fund's portfolio of investments. Behind a fund's investment record, portfolio makeup, investment philosophy, and investment objectives are many crucial considerations and facts with which you should be thoroughly familiar before you can reach a decision on which fund is the most suitable for you.

Most of the selling of mutual funds focuses on points that *all* funds have in common: management, diversification, services, etc. No one fund has anything unique here. Most mutual fund literature you will see contains similarly persuasive text, photos, and charts. This section is designed to help you become professional in your selection of a fund—so you can, in fact as well as theory, choose the right fund for your needs. You won't get this sort of talk from the average mutual fund salesman; he probably doesn't even know it. Nor will you get it in the average mutual fund literature; it isn't there.

Here are six basic factors in addition to the sales charge to consider before choosing a fund.

(1) *Your own situation.* Don't be deceived by the seeming simplicity of this, for it is the most fundamental consideration of all. Too often, mutual fund salesmen pay only lip service to your circumstances—financial and otherwise. And don't mislead yourself in your eagerness for quick and big profits. Keep in mind that if you pick a fund with the wrong objective and then decide to switch to another fund, it can be costly.

Analyze your own needs and objectives. Do you want a fund for forced savings? College tuition for your child? Long-term financial security? A monthly income supplement? What? Based on these factors, decide on your investment strategy and stick with it in good times and bad.

(2) *Your investment objectives.* This isn't as simple as it sounds either. It's much more complex than finding a fund that has objectives matching yours.

Size of a fund, for instance, can be crucial to whether and how your investment objectives are achieved. A small fund may be less successful in achieving the goals of stability of income than a large fund, for the large fund can buy a more diversified and extensive portfolio and may be able to grow in a more orderly way than the smaller fund. On the other hand, a large fund is likely to be less successful in achieving the goal of big capital gains than a small fund, for it cannot concentrate as a small fund can on a few small companies which have explosive growth potentials. In a small portfolio, say of $10 million to $25 million, two or three hot stocks can do wonders for performance.

Risk. Comparative risk is another factor crucial to weigh in deciding which of the many funds—all with the same investment objectives—is right for you. A fund that diversifies its holdings among many industries and companies is likely to have a less spectacular short-term record than one that concentrates on relatively few industries and companies with spectacular possibilities. The diversified fund's longer-term record, though, can be far superior—particularly if the limited fund's management runs into a period of bad judgment. To illustrate, in 1968 some of the smaller growth funds chalked up superb records—but in the devastating bear markets that followed, these very same funds faded away.

To capsulize, the lesson of the tortoise and the hare should be required reading for mutual fund investors! Size and portfolio makeup are vital in analyzing performance.

(3) *The time factor*. The original idea of the mutual fund was to provide a means by which the small investor could acquire a diversified investment portfolio under constant management. A fund can produce large gains—or losses—over any short-term period, but it *never* was intended for short-term speculation, and if you try to use it, you are misusing it. Funds are meant for long-term investing objectives.

This leads to the key point that, in buying mutual funds, "timing" of your investments to catch tops or bottoms is much less significant than "consistency" in making your investments. Since the fund's managers are investing to produce continuing results over the long term, whether prices are high or low at a given moment is far less important than your ability to maintain a buying program through good times and bad. (This, again, is the professional approach to dollar-cost-averaging.)

Another point on timing: a fund that raises lots of money from new investors during a bull market will have a hoard of cash which it will feel compelled to invest. This can become a minus factor the instant the markets dip. Thus, "timing" ranks with earlier points as a far more complex and subtle factor than most investors suspect.

(4) *The structure of the management*. Some funds are pretty much one-man operations—and, as with any one-man business, the built-in risks are obvious. Other funds have created strong management teams with diversified brains at the top and with a strong backup in research and other tools essential for successful management of a securities portfolio. You owe it to yourself to find out precisely what sort of management you are buying when you buy mutual fund shares. Since you're buying your shares for the long term, you should make sure your fund has a management structure that can operate successfully over the long term.

In short, an investment program worthy of the name does not consist of just "name" personalities! Many of the famous portfolio managers of the late 1960s have left the business. Also, you may buy into a fund because you understand it has top portfolio managers and find they have left to go to another firm. If you're a truly professional investor in mutual fund shares, you'll do your homework in areas such as this.

(5) *The investment record*. On the face of it, it seems simple enough to say that Fund X has performed better than Fund Y and therefore you should buy X. But as any professional would tell you (and remember, you're trying to become a professional, too), there is far more to an investment record than the simple comparison of percentage gains or losses (which salesmen love to stress when the comparison is in their favor).

To illustrate, for what periods are the investment records being compared? If it is a short-term period, what was the market environment? Was it a market in which speculative issues dominated on the up side? If so, was Fund X, as opposed to Fund Y, in a position to take advantage of this environment?

In recent years, much has been made of the short-term investment record of a limited number of mutual funds. But ask: what actually produced the results? Was it, for instance, the fact that the fund had a very small portfolio with a limited number of holdings and a couple of these happened to be star performers? Or did the fund come on the scene just when a bull market was starting? Was it because the fund emphasized a given "hot" industry that may soon cool? Was the fund using borrowed capital? Was it invested in highly speculative—and to a great extent unmarketable—securities?

If the answer to any of these questions is in part or in whole yes, proceed with caution. For you must avoid being deluded by short-term percentage figures. Ask and get clear, unqualified answers to such hard questions as I've posed here. The central question is: what has been the fund's long-term record? The importance of this cannot be overemphasized, for you want to see how the fund performs through bad markets as well as good. To the extent that your fund produces relatively favorable results through down markets as well as up markets, you can feel reasonably confident in the management's ability. Figure on a ten-year performance record as a minimum to compare it with another.

And what about the age of the fund? The benefit of a long life is that the fund has had the obvious advantages of navigating through both down and up markets. Its management has become seasoned. A fund that has prospered only in up markets is unseasoned. The acumen of its management must remain open to question. It's generally a good bet to stay clear of mutual funds that have been in business less than five years.

(6) *Makeup of the portfolio*. This point will give you vital clues to the operating philosophy of the fund's management as well as to its investment goals. Among the factors you should analyze in this area are: whether the portfolio includes a great many holdings or just a limited number; the fields of investment in which the fund is primarily involved; the relative emphasis

on investments in each of these fields; the size of companies in which the fund invests; the balance between seasoned companies and unseasoned companies; the holdings (or lack) of bonds, preferred stocks, cash.

It is this knowledge and understanding of the portfolio makeup of a fund that will help you assure yourself that this is indeed the fund in which you wish to invest your nest egg and current earnings.

If you'll abide just by the guidance in these pages, you'll be on your way to investing successfully the way the real pros do. You'll also sleep well at night.

Open-end Funds Versus Closed-end Funds
(Publicly Traded Investment Funds)

Closed-end (publicly traded) funds have been around a long time, but they have never been as popular as the open-end funds—even though these funds operate the same way as open-end mutual funds in terms of diversified portfolio, professional management, and various investment objectives.

The difference is that there are a fixed number of shares in a closed-end fund and their price fluctuates up and down (past its net asset value) just as ordinary common stocks fluctuate up and down on the stock exchanges or in the over-the-counter market. Many closed-ends, in fact, have sold historically at discounts from their net asset value. This has made them at times attractive to some investors who felt they would profit if the discount eventually disappeared.

What are the pros and cons of publicly traded funds or closed-ends as compared to open-end funds?

- If you buy open-end shares, you know precisely on a given day that you can sell your shares back to the mutual fund for the net asset value. If you own publicly traded fund shares, you don't know what price you'll get for your shares on any given day. The price you get can be higher or lower than the net asset value.

- Because closed-end funds do not have to worry about investors redeeming their outstanding shares, they can invest for the long term without some of the concerns that an open-end fund may have.

- On the other hand, the fixed number of shares makes it difficult for publicly traded or closed-end funds to trade their portfolios as aggressively as some open-end mutual funds. Before buying a new stock, a closed-end fund must frequently sell a current holding.

- No one has really solved the mystery of why most closed-end funds sell at a discount. The explanation could be merely that securities salesmen push open-end mutual funds on which they can earn perhaps an 8½ per cent commission rather than closed-end (publicly traded) funds on which there is only a regular (and fluctuating) stockbrokers' commission.

- Open-end funds offer investors a greater flexibility, and range in buying options. There are many more open-end funds from which to choose, and, for instance, they offer more programs as automatic reinvestment and withdrawal plans than do closed-end funds.

• As for whether a closed-end fund selling at a large discount from its asset value is a real bargain, yes, in many cases this is true. However, if you buy a fund for this reason, there is no guarantee that when you sell it other investors will realize it is such a bargain and you might have to sell your shares at the same discount at which you bought them—or worse. Moral of the story: a "bargain" is only a bargain if other investors think it is and ultimately push its price up.

Sources of Information on Mutual Funds

Also to help you with your own homework on mutual funds, as well as to prepare you to discuss your goals intelligently with any adviser or mutual fund salesperson, here are top sources of detailed information on the industry and individual funds. Check what is available in your local library.

(1) *Wiesenberger Financial Services* (210 South Street, Boston, Massachusetts 02111), a division of Warren, Gorham, Lamont, which publishes each year a voluminous book on mutual funds performance—past and present—entitled *Investment Companies*. It also publishes *Wiesenberger Investment Companies Service,* a monthly report on statistics and news, which can be very helpful.

(2) *Moody's Investors Service, Inc.* (99 Church Street, New York, New York 10004), which publishes *Moody's Bank and Finance Manual*—a compendium of details on the hundred largest mutual funds in the United States.

(3) *The Investment Company Institute* (1775 K Street, N.W., Washington, D.C. 20006)—trade organization of the majority of the funds, which publishes industry statistics, *Mutual Funds Forum,* a bimonthly newsmagazine, and an annual *Fact Book.*

(4) *No-Load Mutual Fund Association, Inc.* (Valley Forge, Pennsylvania 19481—trade organization of the no-load mutual fund industry, which publishes an annual free directory and investor information book.

(5) *Computer Directions Advisors* (8750 Georgia Ave., Silver Spring, Maryland 20910)—statistical services available in brokerage offices or by $300 annual subscription.

(6) *Forbes Magazine* (60 Fifth Avenue, New York, New York 10011)—annual mutual fund performance issues.

(7) *Lipper Analytical Distributors, Inc.* (74 Trinity Place, New York, New York 10006)—statistical services on the fund industry, available in many brokerage offices.

(8) *Donoghue's Money Fund Report* (Box 540, Hollister, Massachusetts 01746)—publishes a newsletter covering the money-market fund industry.

(9) *Association of Publicly Traded Investment Funds* (666 Fifth Avenue,

New York, New York 10019)—trade organization for the closed-end funds, publishes a membership directory and descriptive information which is useful in understanding this type of fund.

(10) *Investment Dealers Digest Mutual Fund Directory* (150 Broadway, New York, New York 10038)—a semiannual directory of investment companies.

(11) *The Hirsch Organization, Inc.* (6 Deer Trail, Old Tappan, New Jersey 07675)—publishes *Mutual Funds Scoreboard,* a quarterly, and the annual *Mutual Funds Almanac.*

In addition, there are other weekly, biweekly, and monthly publications devoted to mutual funds which are written for the public and which often contain valuable data. They are frequently advertised in your daily newspaper's financial pages.

The Bafflegab of Mutual Funds

ACCUMULATION PLAN An increasingly popular arrangement under which you may buy mutual fund shares on a regular basis in small or large amounts—either on your own or through an automatic payroll deduction plan such as a company employee savings plan. Automatic reinvestment of dividends and distributions is commonplace. Many investors are using this type of plan to accumulate funds for retirement, for emergencies, or for the college education of their children.

ASKED OR OFFERING PRICE The price at which a mutual fund's shares can be purchased. The asked or offering price means the net asset value per share plus the sales charge, if any. For no-load funds, the net asset value is the "asked" price.

ASSET VALUE PER SHARE The worth of a share—as you see it quoted in the newspaper financial pages under the heading "bid"—based on the market value of the fund's entire portfolio of stocks and other financial assets, minus the fund's expenses and liabilities, divided by the number of shares that have been issued by the fund. Same as net asset value per share, or NAV.

BID OR REDEMPTION PRICE The price at which a mutual fund's shares are redeemed (bought back) by the fund. The bid or redemption price usually means the net asset value per share.

BLUE SKY LAWS Laws of the various states governing the sale of securities, including mutual fund shares, and the activities of brokers and dealers within the particular states.

BOOK SHARES A modern share recording system which eliminates the need for mutual fund share certificates but gives the fund's shareowner a record of his holdings.

BROKER-DEALER A firm that retails mutual fund shares to the public.

CAPITAL GAINS DISTRIBUTION A distribution to shareholders by the mutual fund from the net long-term capital gains the fund has taken on the sale of securities from its portfolio. Many investors choose to have such distributions automatically reinvested in additional shares of the fund.

CAPITAL GROWTH   An increase in market value of a mutual fund's securities which is reflected in the net asset value of fund shares. This is a specific long-term objective of many mutual funds.

CASH EQUIVALENT   Includes U. S. Government securities, short-term commercial paper, and short-term municipal and corporate bonds and notes.

CHECK WRITING REDEMPTION PRIVILEGE   Some municipal bond and most money-market funds offer redemptions through free check writing privileges.

CLOSED-END INVESTMENT COMPANY   See pages 1186–87.

CONTRACTUAL PLAN   A type of accumulation plan under which the total amount you intend to invest is stated and you commit yourself to invest regular amounts monthly or quarterly for a specified pay-in period until you reach the total. A substantial amount of the sales charge covering the entire total is sometimes deducted from the first year's payments; this is called a front-end load.

CONVERSION PRIVILEGE   See exchange or switch privilege.

DEALER   A person or a firm who, as part of a regular business, buys from and sells securities to others. Load mutual fund shares are usually purchased through dealers; no-load shares are usually purchased directly from the fund's distributor.

DISTRIBUTIONS   Payments to shareholders from capital gains realized by the fund or dividends paid from the fund's net investment income.

DOLLAR-COST-AVERAGING   Investing equal amounts of money in regular intervals regardless of whether the stock market is moving upward or downward. This reduces average share costs because more shares are purchased in periods of lower securities prices and buys fewer shares in periods of higher prices.

DUAL-PURPOSE FUND   A type of investment company designed to serve the needs of two distinct types of investors: (1) those interested only in income, and (2) those interested solely in possible capital growth. To accomplish these purposes, this type of fund has two separate classes of shares and an investor can purchase the class of shares in which he or she is interested—the class of shares that seek income or the class of shares that seek possible capital gain.

EXCHANGE PRIVILEGE   The right to exchange the shares of one mutual fund for shares of another fund under the same sponsorship at either little or no cost or a reduced sales charge. However, you are liable to federal taxes on profits realized from first fund.

EXPENSE RATIO   The proportion of annual expenses to average net assets of the fund.

FRONT-END LOADS   Plans under which the investor enters into a contractual investment plan calling for the payment of regular installments for his shares. Sales charges can range up to 50 per cent in the first year.

INVESTMENT ADVISER The organization that is employed by a mutual fund to give professional advice on its investments.

INVESTMENT COMPANY A company that invests the funds it obtains from buyers of its shares in a diversified list of securities.

INVESTMENT COMPANY ACT OF 1940 The basic federal law governing the registration and regulation of investment companies.

INVESTMENT MANAGER The company that provides administrative services for a fund and often also serves as investment adviser to the fund.

INVESTMENT OBJECTIVE A capsule description of the fund's investment objective, described in greater detail in each fund's prospectus.

INVESTMENT POLICY A brief description of the policy followed by the investment adviser in aiming at the stated objectives.

INVESTMENT TRUST Same as Investment Company.

KEOGH PLAN A retirement program for self-employed persons under which they can save on income taxes while regularly investing funds for their retirement via mutual funds, savings bonds, savings accounts, insurance, etc.

LETTER OF INTENT A pledge to purchase a sufficient amount of mutual fund shares within a limited period of time in order to qualify for the reduced selling charge that would apply to a comparable lump sum purchase.

LOAD The sales charge imposed on a mutual fund investor by load funds to cover the costs of the elaborate sales organizations maintained by the majority of the funds. Added to the asset value of the fund's shares (the offering price).

MANAGEMENT FEE The amount that the managers of mutual fund portfolios charge for their management services—in both load and no-load funds.

MULTIFUNDS See fund of funds (page 1173).

NO-LOAD FUNDS See pages 1177–78.

PAYROLL DEDUCTION PLAN An arrangement whereby an employee may accumulate shares in a mutual fund by authorizing his employer to deduct and transfer to the fund a specified amount from his salary at stated times.

PERIODIC PAYMENT PLAN Same as Accumulation Plan.

PORTFOLIO The stocks, bonds, and other assets held by a mutual fund at any given time—and thus, held indirectly by the fund's shareowners.

PORTFOLIO TURNOVER The dollar value of purchase and sale of portfolio securities, excluding transactions of U. S. Government obligations and commercial paper.

PROSPECTUS The official document that describes the mutual fund and offers the shares for sale. It contains information as required by the Securities and Exchange Commission on such subjects as the fund's investment objectives, its policies, services, investment restrictions, officers and directors, how shares can be bought and redeemed, its charges and its financial statements.

PROXY STATEMENT A written power of attorney that stockholders give to another person to vote their stock if they are not present at stockholders' meeting.

PUBLICLY TRADED INVESTMENT FUNDS See page 1176.

QUALIFIED RETIREMENT PLAN A private retirement plan that meets the rules and regulations of the Internal Revenue Service. Contribution to a qualified retirement plan are—in almost all cases—tax deductible and earnings on such contributions are always tax sheltered until retirement.

REDEMPTION FEE About twenty funds charge shareholders a small fee—usually less than 2 per cent—when shares are redeemed.

REDEMPTION IN KIND Redemption of investment company shares for which payment is made in portfolio securities rather than cash.

REDEMPTION PRICE The price at which a holder of mutual fund shares may redeem his shares. In most cases of open-end shares, it's the current net asset value per share. Sometimes there is a redemption charge of 2 per cent or less. In the closed-end companies, this would be the highest price offered for the shares in the exchange market, which may be either a premium over or a discount from the net asset value per share.

REINVESTMENT PRIVILEGE A privilege under which your mutual fund dividends may be automatically invested in additional shares of the fund, without the payment of a sales charge, except for some loads.

SEPARATE ACCOUNT A portfolio completely separated from the general account of the insurance company, since the assets are generally invested in common stocks.

SPECIALTY FUNDS A mutual fund specializing in the security of certain industries, special types of securities, or in regional investments.

SPLIT FUNDING A program that combines the purchase of mutual fund shares with the purchase of life insurance contracts or other products.

STATEMENT OF POLICY A guide issued by the Securities and Exchange Commission to assist issuers, writers, and dealers in complying with the statutory standards as applied to advertising, sale, literature, reports to sales, and other communication addressed to or intended for distribution to prospective investors.

TELEPHONE REDEMPTION Some funds allow liquidation by telephone where prearranged and approved agreements have been signed.

TRANSFER AGENT The organization that is employed by a mutual fund to prepare and maintain records relating to the accounts of its shareholders.

TURNOVER RATIO The extent to which the portfolio of securities owned by a mutual fund is changed (traded or turned over) within the course of a single year.

UNDERWRITER OR PRINCIPAL UNDERWRITER The organization that acts as the distributor of mutual fund shares to broker dealers and the public.

VARIABLE ANNUITY An annuity contract under which the dollar payments received are fixed but fluctuate more or less in line with average common stock prices.

VARIABLE ANNUITY SEPARATE ACCOUNT The funding vehicle for an insurance company's variable annuity contract.

VARIABLE LIFE INSURANCE A contract or plan under which the death benefit and the cash fluctuate in tandem with the investment performance of a separate account generally composed of common stock.

VOLUNTARY PLAN A flexible accumulation plan in which there is no definite time period or total amount to be invested.

WITHDRAWAL PLAN An arrangement under which investors in mutual funds can regularly receive monthly or quarterly payments of a specified amount. This may be more or less than the actual investment income.

YIELD Income received from investments, usually expressed as a percentage of market price, and also referred to as return on the investment.

23

YOUR GUIDE TO THE BOND MARKETS

Obligations of the U. S. Treasury, Federal Agencies, Guaranteed or Partially Insured Mortgage Pools, States and Cities, U.S. Corporations—Short- and Long-Term

A New Force in the Financial Market	1194
Basic Facts on Bonds and Money Market Instruments	1195
"M1?" "M2?"—"M What?"	1200
How to Buy Bonds	1202
The Corporate Bond Market	1203
The Market for Mortgage-Pool Pass-through Certificates and Mortgage-backed Bonds	1204
pass-through issues	1205
mortgage-backed bonds	1205
The Tax-exempt Municipal Market	1206
The United States Government Securities Markets	1209
The Market for Federal Agency Securities	1215
Lower-Quality Bonds—or "Junk" Bonds	1217
Pitfalls for the Small Investor	1217
A Bank or a Bond? Which for You?	1218
Financial Futures	1218
What Should Be Your Policy on Bonds?	1220
The Bafflegab of Bonds	1221

A New Force in the Financial Market

In the early 1970s, a profoundly important new force entered the financial market. It was the historically high interest rates which investors—big and small, institutions and individuals—could earn on bonds, even the highest-quality bonds. This development created competition of the toughest caliber for the stock market. Many investors switched out of common stocks and growth mutual funds and put their money into U. S. Treasury securities, corporate bonds, tax-exempt bonds, new bond and money market funds. Money in savings accounts, too, was shifted into money market instruments and bonds on an impressive scale. And professional investment managers returned to what was a once fashionable investment technique of "balanced" portfolios with both stock and bond holdings.

To understand this fascinating turnabout, you must realize that in the 1940s yields on stocks were about twice those of bonds. By the early 1970s yields on bonds were about twice those of common stocks!

High interest rates have an understandable appeal to investors. If you can invest your money in a bond that pays 9 per cent and if you let the interest accumulate, your nest egg will double in about eight years. If you invest it at 7 per cent, it will double in about ten years. This assumes that you will be reinvesting at the same interest rate and omits tax factors.

These—and higher—fixed annual returns have been available in the bond and money markets of the United States in recent years. Obviously, at these interest rates, high-quality fixed-income investments—in the obligations of the U. S. Treasury, federal agencies, guaranteed or partially insured mortgage pools, our states and cities, U.S. corporations—take on some of the characteristics of "growth" securities. You can also buy low-interest coupon bonds selling at a discount and make long-term capital gains as the bonds rise to their par value.

An investment that can double in ten years is growing by any definition. At the same time this type of investment retains the advantages of its fixed annual return and offers greater protection against adverse economic conditions than do stocks. (It is not without hazards, though. And, of course, steep inflation rates which cut deeply into the buying power of fixed dollars can offset and even eliminate the "growth" entirely.)

If buyers can get these high rates, they can count on them every year until their bonds are called or finally mature and that can be five, ten, fifteen, twenty, or even thirty years from purchase date.

Let me be more specific. If a high-grade corporate bond provides an 8 per cent return, it is rivaling the long-term return record for common stocks. Not so many years ago typical interest rates on top-rated corporate bonds were 3½ to 4 per cent.

What will be the level of interest rates on fixed-income securities when *you* are reading this chapter I do not know—and only a fool would pretend to have the capacity to forecast precisely—for the forces which determine interest rate trends are varied and exceedingly complex. However, it is reasonable to assume that in the decade of the 1980s we will maintain a level of interest rates which, regardless of temporary market fluctuations, should be high enough to provide a "living wage" to all investors—meaning the coupons should cover the anticipated annual rise in living costs as well as the income tax bite out of the interest. Under these circumstances, you will need basic information on the fixed-income securities markets so you can carry on to get whatever additional facts you want. And so the following is your *primer on bonds.*

Basic Facts on Bonds and Money Market Instruments

Q. *What's a coupon interest rate on a bond?*

A. This is the specified amount of money the issuer promises to pay you during the life of the bond in return for the use of your money throughout the period. The issuers (borrowers) may be: the federal government, federal agencies, state and local governments, corporations, foreign governments, individuals seeking mortgages.

The interest may be payable to you every six months or every year and in a few cases every month. Or, as in U. S. Government E or EE savings bonds, the interest may accumulate during the life of the bond and be payable to you only when you cash in the bond or when it reaches final maturity date.

Q. *What's the difference between a bond and a stock?*

A. When you buy a bond you are lending your money to its issuer, and thus you become a creditor. When you buy shares of common stock in a corporation you are becoming a part owner of the corporation.

When you buy bonds you expect to earn a fixed rate of return (the interest) as long as you own this type of obligation. When you buy common stocks, you expect to share in the company's profits via the dividends the company pays you—which may vary from year to year. You also own a pro rata share of retained earnings, which can lead to capitalization of earnings in the form of stock dividends or stock splits, hopefully leading to higher values for your stocks—but you can make capital gains on bonds as well as on stocks.

Q. *What's the key to bond prices?*

A. Interest rate levels. When interest rates *rise,* bond prices *fall*—and vice versa. Suppose, for instance, that you held a $1,000 bond paying 6 per cent interest. Because of a variety of factors, interest rates available on new bonds of the same type rise to 7 per cent. Now, your bond will sell for less than $1,000, for if someone can invest $1,000 at 7 per cent by buying a new bond, why should he or she pay you $1,000 for your old bond, which returns only 6 per cent? The lower price and the fixed payment of $60 a year brings the return to about 7 per cent.

Or suppose interest rates fall, so that the rate available on new bonds of this type is now 5 per cent. Your 6 per cent bond will now be worth *more* than $1,000; for if someone can get only 5 per cent interest by investing $1,000 in this type of bond, why should you sell your 6 per cent bond at that $1,000 price?

Interest rates doubled in the last five years of the decade of the 1960s, reached the highest levels in more than a century, then spiraled even higher in the mid—and again in the late—1970s. These upswings have driven down prices of bonds issued at much lower interest rates in earlier years.

Short-term interest rates tend to fluctuate much more violently than long-term interest rates—reflecting the fact that short-term rates primarily respond to Federal Reserve System maneuvers in fine-tuning monetary policy, while long-term rates primarily respond to investor expectations about inflation well into the future.

But while short-term rates tend to fluctuate more widely, short-term obligations are in a sense much safer than long-term securities. The reason is that an equal change in short-term and long-term rates will have a much larger impact on prices of long-term obligations than on prices of short-term obligations. For instance, a 1 per cent across-the-board rise in interest rates will lower the price of a five-year $1,000 bond about $2.00; on a $1,000 thirty-year bond the cut will be about $12.

Q. *What moves interest rates up or down?*

A. What usually determines the price of any product or service? The demand for and supply of it. When the demand for loans is greater than the available supply of credit, the price for loans (the interest rate) goes up; when the supply of credit is greater than the demand for loans, the price (interest rate) goes down. Expectations of higher or lower interest rates also influence the direction of rates—meaning psychology plays an enormous role too.

But this is by no means the whole story, for a key factor determining the supply of credit in the United States is the monetary policy of the Federal Reserve System (the central bank) of the United States, which regulates the flow of money and credit into our economy.

There is no point in this primer in going into the tortuously complicated, technical details on how the Federal Reserve System attains its credit goals. Suffice it to say that through various devices and operations the Federal Reserve pursues its objective (not always successfully, by any means!) of trying to put just enough credit into the economic stream to promote orderly, sustained growth over the years.

Q. *Why have interest rates risen so much in recent years?*
A. Because, starting in the mid-1960s, the demand for credit exploded—reflecting the prolonged business boom, the Vietnam war, the development of a deep inflation psychology.

At the same time the Federal Reserve tried to curb inflation via the orthodox means of limiting the supply of credit available for expansion. With the demand for loans soaring and the supply of credit restricted, interest rates had to skyrocket.

Q. *Should we all own bonds?*
A. It would be ridiculous for me to claim that bonds are an appropriate investment for all of you: there are so many different maturities, so many different grades that even the simple word "bonds" becomes a misleading generality. It also would be utterly out-of-character folly for me to make so superficial a recommendation.

Nevertheless the money and bond markets since the start of the 1970s have appealed to an extraordinarily broad cross section of income and age groups. Many individuals in the $15,000-to-$30,000-a-year income brackets have for the first time ventured into bonds. In fact, in the 1970s many stock brokerage salesmen made a good part of their income selling bonds and money market securities of all types rather than stocks to individuals. That's why this chapter is giving you the fundamentals so you can find out the details on your own.

Q. *What about the income tax factor?*
A. This is vitally important, for you must pay income taxes on interest you earn. Of course, this cuts into your net return and the higher your income bracket the more the cut—except on tax-exempt bonds. For example, if you are in the 40 per cent tax bracket and collect $100 a year in interest on your bonds, you'll pay out $40 of the $100 in taxes, will keep only $60.

Q. *What about inflation?*
A. In judging what your real net rate of return will be on a fixed-income security, you also must consider the erosion in your dollar's buying power caused by the likely annual rate of rise in living costs in coming years.

To illustrate, let's say you buy a $1,000 bond carrying an interest rate of 8 per cent and that the annual rate of inflation in the years ahead turns out to be 6 per cent. Your "real" rate of return—bond interest rate less rate of inflation—would be 2 per cent.

Q. *What about your age?*
A. Of course, this is a vital consideration, for if you are young and can look forward to many years in which you can recoup losses on your investments, you can properly assume more risks in the stock market and speculate for big long-term capital gains. But if you are in the older age brackets, bonds yielding 8 to 10 per cent have indisputable appeal.

Q. *How are bonds quoted?*
A. As a percentage of their par value or face amount—usually in denominations of $1,000. However, many U. S. Government, federal agency, and state and local government issues are now sold with minimum denominations of $5,000 or $10,000. A price of 98 for a $1,000 par value bond means that $980 would be the actual cost (plus any accrued interest).

Since interest is paid on the par value of the bond, your actual percentage return may be more or less than the interest rate specified on the coupon by the issuer of the bond.

To illustrate, say you buy a bond just issued that pays 9 per cent interest or $90 at a price of exactly $1,000. That gives you $90 a year interest on a $1,000 investment or an actual yield of 9 per cent.

But say the bond has already been issued and has been on the market some time and you buy it at 95, or $950. This means your current yield is more than 9 per cent. Current yield is determined by dividing the interest by the price paid for the bond. This means 90/950 or 9.47 per cent.

Or say you bought the same bond for 105, or $1,050. This means your yield is less than 9 per cent. It would be 90/1,050, or 8.57 per cent.

Q. *Is this what is meant by yield?*
A. This is what is meant by current yield. It is interest divided by the price you paid for the bond—that rate of return you receive on the amount of money it cost you to buy the security.

Q. *What's the difference between current yield and yield to maturity?*
A. Yield to maturity takes into consideration the price at which your bond is paid off (redeemed) at maturity as well as the interest coupon it bears and the price at which you bought the obligation.

For example, suppose you bought the 9 per cent bond at a premium, say 105, or $1,050. In figuring yield to maturity it is necessary to amortize the premium until the maturity date. In this case, the yield to maturity will be less than the 9 per cent coupon rate and less than the 8.57 per cent current yield.

In the case of a bond purchased for $950, or at a discount, the yield to maturity will be the coupon rate of 9 per cent, plus the $50 additional money the holder will receive when the bond matures. In this case, the yield to maturity will be greater than 9 per cent and greater than the 9.47 per cent current yield. A reference volume, generally referred to as the *Basis Book*, accurately computes yield to maturity.

Q. *How do you collect interest on your bonds?*
A. There are two major ways you collect your interest. If you own a coupon bond or "bearer" bond you clip a coupon attached to the bond and collect the money by depositing the coupon as if it were a check with the issuer's paying agent or your own bank. If you own a registered bond, your name appears on the bond and also is registered with the issuer. Interest is usually paid by check. Registered bonds offer greater protection from theft than coupon bonds. However, they are tougher to sell because of the bother and delay in arranging transfer of ownership on the registrar's books.

Q. *Do the terms "fixed income" and "bonds" mean the same thing?*
A. Yes, a bond is a fixed-income obligation, but a large percentage of the obligations available to you aren't bonds at all. By definition, they're "notes," "debentures," "certificates," or "bills." And a large percentage aren't traded in the bond markets either. They are bought and sold in the money markets —which are part of the vast over-the-counter markets to start with.

Q. *What are money market securities?*
A. They are the short-term obligations of various borrowers: the U. S. Treasury, federal agencies, state and local governments, banks, corporations of all types.

In general, these are the most marketable, the most liquid, the least risky of fixed-income obligations. Among the obligations in which you might be interested and which you can readily buy and sell in the money markets are:

U. S. Treasury bills, due in up to one year and considered the virtual equivalent of cash.

Short-term federal agency issues, which next to Treasury bills are the most marketable of securities.

Short-term tax-exempt obligations, highly liquid too.

Also traded in the money markets are large ($100,000 and over) commercial bank certificates of deposit; large ($100,000 and more) denominations of commercial paper notes of corporations; bankers' acceptances in denominations of $25,000 and up; Eurodollars; and federal funds (not for individuals, however).

Q. *How can small investors buy in such big amounts?*
A. The smaller investor was effectively barred from the often higher-yielding money market instruments and restricted to the lower-paying "consumer" certificates available from commercial banks and savings institutions for many years, but as interest rates on large certificates of deposit spiraled upward in the 1970s, enterprising firms found ways to get around that patently unfair discrimination against the little fellow.

The concept was simple: the funds of many small investors were "pooled" until the amounts in the pools were large enough to meet the minimums imposed. The "pools" took various forms. Also, as short-term interest rates hit historic peaks in the 1970s new mutual funds came into existence to specialize in these money market instruments and offer small investors a way to share in the juicy returns by purchase of fund shares. The funds were both no-load and load variety—taxable and tax-exempt—and they lured hundreds of millions of dollars out of savings institutions. In 1978, banking regulators allowed banks, savings and loans, and credit unions to issue six-month certificates which can yield up to the same as the latest six-month Treasury bills. (See pages 1194–95.)

Q. *What are bond markets?*
A. In the bond markets, longer-term obligations of various issuers are traded. In turn, the bond markets subdivide into the market for corporate bonds; for U. S. Government bonds and notes and for longer-term federal agency issues; and for tax-exempt municipal bonds. Newer instruments include federally guaranteed Government National Mortgage Association passthrough mortgage pool certificates and private pool certificates.

In only a few places in the 1970s (such as the Bond Trading Room of the New York Stock Exchange) could you visit and watch bond trading in action. Most bonds are handled in the over-the-counter market, where securities are bought and sold by dealers and brokers located all over the nation, communicating with each other via an intricate and immense telephone network and video display terminals.

Q. *What is meant by underwriting syndicates?*
A. These are groups of investment bankers (syndicates) which commit their capital to buy new issues of securities from borrowers at set prices. By doing this, the bankers "underwrite" the issue—provide the total funds at once to the corporation, state, city, or other type of borrower. Then the group reoffers the securities at a higher price to institutional and individual investors. The difference (spread) between what the underwriting syndicate pays for the securities and the higher price at which the group reoffers the securities to you represents the bankers' or syndicate's profit after expenses. Of course, the underwriting syndicate loses money when the bankers misjudge the market and are forced to resell the securities at a lower price than they paid the issuer.

"M1?" "M2?"—"M What?"

Item: Every Thursday shortly after 4:10 P.M. (New York time), financiers in private and government policymaking positions in money centers all over the globe stop whatever they are doing to crowd around their ticker tapes and listen to the tickers clatter out the latest news on M1 and M2 from the Federal Reserve Bank of New York's powerful trading desk.

YOUR GUIDE TO THE BOND MARKETS

These weekly reports have assumed enormous significance throughout the world as direct clues to the monetary policy of the Federal Reserve System: whether the U.S. central bank is tightening credit to fight inflation and support the dollar more vigorously; or whether it is easing credit to spur the economy and reduce joblessness more vigorously; or whether it is just standing pat.

"M1?" "M2?" Countless millions of you must have heard of the bafflegab. How many of you honestly can define it?

Item: At a business luncheon of ten men and women from widely varied fields, a Midwestern banker next to me said he thought the growth in M1 in the past few months had been far too rapid and it was contributing to the speedup in inflation in the closing years of the decade. I answered that M1's growth had slowed down substantially, that its weekly gyrations were getting too much attention anyway, and that the concentration on the monetary aggregates from week to week was out of hand.

As we argued, my eyes went around the table. The others listening to us—prominent business leaders, professors in fields outside economics, the like—seemed glassy-eyed.

"How many of you can define M1 or M2?" I asked.

Not one person at the table answered.

"M1?" "M2?" What part do they play in your life?

Item: "When it comes to definitions, money is a little bit like sex appeal," said an analysis in the economic review of the Federal Reserve Bank of Richmond some time ago. "Everyone has a fairly clear intuitive idea of what it is, but defining it in precise language is difficult. Economists have been arguing about the best way to define money for centuries."

Then the Richmond Fed went on to try, for it emphasized that "the concept of money lies at the core of both monetary theory and monetary policy."

Okay, then, I'll rise to the challenge, too. Herewith the accepted definitions of the various "M's" in my simplest language.

• M0. That's just U.S. currency, the dollar bills (of any denomination) and coins in your possession. There's lots of currency circulating in our country today, some for completely legitimate reasons of business and commerce, some for "dirty" deals where tax evasion is a goal.

• M1. That's the total of all U.S. currency in circulation plus the demand deposits all of us—as individuals and organizations—have at commercial banks from coast to coast. This is also known as the "narrowly defined money supply," for it covers a minimum of the money supply affecting our economy and others.

• M1+. Introduced as a "new" measure of the money supply in late 1978 by the Federal Reserve Board in an attempt to offset distortions caused by the development of automatic transfers of funds from savings to checking accounts. Created as only an "interim measure" and immediately dubbed in the sophisticated money markets as "the cold remedy," M1+ consists of M1 (demand deposits and currency) plus savings accounts at commercial banks, NOW (negotiable orders of withdrawal) accounts, checkable deposits at thrift institutions. The purpose of M1+ is to include deposits that are readily usable in transactions for payments to third parties, which is a key aspect of money as distinct from savings.

• M2. That's M1 (defined above) plus all our time deposits at commercial banks, but not including large negotiable certificates of deposit (which usually are bought and sold by very big investors, individuals and institutions). Time deposits include any savings accounts or savings certificates or savings shares you have—but only at commercial banks. The narrowly defined money supply has now been substantially broadened.

• M3. This is M2 (defined directly above) with the additions of all mutual savings bank deposits, savings and loan association shares, and credit union shares. Now the money supply total is truly being broadened.

Now let's say you are thinking for the first time about buying fixed-income securities as an investment . . .

How to Buy Bonds

Q. *How do you buy outstanding fixed-income securities?*

A. Go to your broker, place your order, and pay the principal amount plus the required commission. It usually will run about $10 per $1,000 face value bond, but it can be more, particularly if you buy just one or two bonds. If the investment banker already *owns* the bond, you pay no straight commission, but you do pay the "spread" between the bid and asked prices on the bond. This is often $20 per $1,000 face value if you're buying less than $25,000 worth. If you don't have a broker, establish a relationship with a reputable firm which maintains a retail bond department. Ask questions about commissions and which types of fixed-income securities would be right for you. Or you can buy bonds through your bank but you'll probably pay more in commissions and fees, particularly if you buy a corporate bond that the bank is not permitted to deal in.

Q. *How do you buy new fixed-income securities?*

A. You can subscribe to new issues of corporation or muncipal bonds through a firm which is a member of the underwriting group distributing the new issue to the public. If your order is accepted, you'll pay no commission. The issuer of the securities pays the investment banking house through the spread between the selling price and the amount turned over to the issuer.

You can subscribe through your broker or banker to new U. S. Treasury issues and pay a service charge for the convenience. Or you can subscribe to new U. S. Treasury issues through your district Federal Reserve Bank and pay no commission. You'll have to learn the details about forms, minimum deposits required, etc., but they're not difficult.

And you can subscribe to new federal agency issues through the firms which belong to the selling group customarily distributing new agency securities. You'll pay no commission but you'll probably have to pay a service charge if yours is a small subscription.

Check out the details with a broker, bank, or bond dealer who knows you and who will give you a fair deal.

Q. *What firms might you go to?*
A. Some of the great, world-famous investment banking firms won't take your orders. They deal only in large transactions with institutional investors or with wealthy individuals. But many brokerage firms do maintain bond departments and readily accept individual orders. If you're now a customer of one of these firms, ask your own broker about the firm's policy before you go elsewhere. In some areas, however, you might find it more convenient to do business through a bank.

THE CORPORATE BOND MARKET

The corporate bond market is where a lot of the action has been in recent years. Here is where our nation's leading industrial and utility corporations, and finance companies, have borrowed tens of billions of dollars for modernization, expansion, and working capital too. Here is where, during the 1970s, interest rates spiraled up to the highest levels in more than a hundred years. And here is where individual investors began in 1970 to invest aggressively in fixed returns for the first time in decades.

Q. *How many types of corporate bonds are there?*
A. At least a dozen. But the types which will be of most interest to you are:

First mortgage bonds. These are bonds secured by a mortgage on all or a portion of the fixed property of the issuing corporation. These are among the highest-grade corporate bonds because they provide a prime, clear and indisputable claim on the company's specified assets and earnings. Most utilities issue mortgage bonds.

Debenture bonds. These are bonds backed by the general credit and full faith of the issuing corporation. In short, they represent a pure IOU, a promise to pay. Many of the nation's big, well-established corporations issue debentures. Under the classification of debentures are *subordinated debentures,* which have a claim on a corporation's assets only after senior debt claims have been met, and *income debentures,* on which interest is payable only if it is earned. These are of lower quality than the more senior securities.

Convertible debentures. These are bonds which give the owner the extra privilege of converting the debenture into a certain number of shares of common stock of the same corporation under specified conditions. In other words this is a hybrid, combining some of the features of both a stock and a bond. Convertibles yield less than straight bonds but the conversion sweetener adds speculative appeal because the owner has the chance of making an additional profit if the stock of the issuing company goes up. This makes the conversion privilege more valuable. Of course, the stock can also go down.

Q. *Should I buy only first mortgage bonds, then?*
A. Of course not. The overall strength of a corporation is the key. A debenture of a great, prosperous industrial corporation is far more desirable than a first mortgage bond of a shaky third-rater.

Q. *How can I find out about the quality of bonds?*
A. The quality of bonds ranges from the very highest to the riskiest—with the judgments on the creditworthiness of the various obligations being made by various independent services, such as Moody's and Standard & Poor's. The ratings starting from the top are: Aaa (Moody's) or AAA (Standard & Poor's), Aa or AA, A, Baa or BBB, Ba or BB, B, Caa or CCC, Ca or CC, C. If you're anxious to avoid risks of default, you'll not go below ratings of A. Most dealers will quote the bond ratings along with prices and yields.

Q. *What about call provisions?*
A. This is a key point—for if interest rates decline sharply below the levels at which corporations have sold their bonds they will try to call them in and replace them with new issues bearing lower rates. Thus, you want to make certain that your bond will be protected against redemption by the corporation for a specified period. Usually you can get protection against a call for ten years from issue date on industrial bonds. Treasury bonds and notes are frequently not callable.

Also check with care the price at which the corporation reserves the right to call in its bonds, for this will place an effective ceiling on the price to which your bond can rise in the open market. One way of beating this is to buy bonds that are non-callable.

The Market for Mortgage-Pool Pass-through Certificates and Mortgage-backed Bonds

In the 1970s, a new type of debt obligation involving mortgaged-backed securities rapidly gained investor acceptance. To understand this type of investment, suppose you lend money to a friend to purchase a house—the same as a bank does, with the house mortgaged as security. You know that mortgage loans of this character pay handsome interest, and that your security (residential housing) will tend to retain its value over time. But still, you're nervous; you worry about risking so much of your nest egg on just one person.

Now you have a way to invest money in different mortgages—indirectly. The procedure is this: a bank or institution which lends mortgage money to many home buyers can sell the mortgage IOUs to others. Eventually, the holder of a large total of mortgages can pool these mortgages and sell participations in the pool to you, a public investor. A trustee holds the mortgage pool and passes along interest and principal payments to you.

The mortgage holders which issue mortgage-backed securities can be government agencies or private institutions. The best-known is the Government National Mortgage Association (GNMA, or "Ginnie Mae"). Another is the Federal Home Loan Mortgage Corporation (FHLMC, or "Freddie Mac"). Private institutions include mortgage lenders such as banks and savings and loans.

There are two distinct types of mortgage-backed securities: "pass-through" securities and "mortgage-backed" bonds.

PASS-THROUGH ISSUES

Pass-through issues consist of pools of mortgages which have been sold to a trustee. You, the investor, buy a participation in the pool. The institution continues to collect monthly interest and principal payments that it receives on its pool of mortgages, and after skimming a small fee passes the money through to you, the security holder—each month. Unlike most fixed-income securities, if you are an investor in pass-through certificates, you are paid interest *and* principal regularly, instead of just interest (with the principal paid at the end).

Most pass-through certificates are backed by pools of mortgages of thirty-year duration, but you should not view them as thirty-year obligations. In fact, pass-throughs usually trade as if they were a unique form of twelve-year obligation. The assumption is that the principal on the certificate is paid down monthly—half before twelve years, the remaining after twelve years—for an average twelve-year life.

Why would this assumption be made?

Because it's the historical experience with mortgages. Often, for instance, houses on which owners still owe money are sold before the mortgages are paid off. So the mortgages end up being prepaid long before the thirty-year expiration date. As far as pass-through certificates are concerned, each pool of mortgages will have a different record of prepayment of principal. The fact that a pass-through *trades* as if it has a twelve-year prepayment doesn't mean that it can't be paid down well before, or after, the twelve-year mark.

MORTGAGE-BACKED BONDS

Mortgage-backed bonds are sold in minimum amounts of $10,000 with $1,000 increments. In short, you can buy $11,000 worth—but not $1,000 worth. The maturities of these bonds run five years and more.

Mortgage-backed bonds are much like other bonds—they pay the investor a series of interest payments with a final interest-and-principal payment at the end. They are issued by mortgage-lending institutions, and are obligations of the institution itself. But they are collateralized with large numbers of mortgage IOUs, often a larger dollar amount of mortgages than the total dollar amount of the bonds.

One important fact of which you must be aware if you are considering these bonds: some are government-guaranteed, some not.

The mortgages backing Ginnie Mae pass-through pools are insured by the Federal Housing Administration or the Veterans Administration. In addition, the Ginnie Mae securities themselves are backed by the full faith and credit of the U. S. Government—the same as Treasury obligations. If any mortgages default, the Treasury makes up the payments to the investor.

Freddie Mac mortgages are *not* government-backed, although the FHLMC puts its own guarantee on its securities—which makes them safer than most private mortgage-backed securities. The private pass-through securities, however, often have their mortgage pools insured. These securities are rated by Standard & Poor's and Moody's.

A problem: these securities frequently are marketed in huge dollar chunks. GNMA and private-issue pass-through securities are issued in principal amounts of $25,000; FHLMC pass-throughs are issued in principal amounts of $100,000. But it is possible to buy these pass-throughs for substantially less than the original principal amount, because as the principal amount of the mortgages is paid off, the remaining principal amount shrinks. So you might be able to buy a GNMA pass-through certificate originally issued at $25,000 that now has only $15,000 worth of principal left.

THE TAX-EXEMPT MUNICIPAL MARKET

The great factor favoring purchase of municipal bonds or other tax-exempts is that interest on these obligations is exempt from federal income tax —and if you are a resident of the issuing locality, often from state and local taxes as well. That's the major reason why individuals now own about one third of all the tax-exempt bonds outstanding. A second reason is that tax-exempts of the top-rated issuers have a high degree of safety.

Even if you're only in the 30 per cent tax bracket, a 6½ per cent tax-free return is equal to a taxable rate of 9.29 per cent. And in the 55 per cent bracket, it's the equivalent of a 14.44 per cent return!

There's no doubt that new municipal bonds will be pouring into the market in coming years, for the borrowing needs of states, cities, and towns across the land are and will be enormous. There's no doubt too that this will help place a floor under the rates you can earn and that you'll have a wide variety of types of bonds, of quality of bonds, and of maturity dates from which to choose.

Q. *What are municipal bonds?*
A. These include any obligation issued by a city, town, or village and also by states, territories, U.S. possessions. In addition, they include obligations issued by housing authorities, port authorities, and local government agencies providing and maintaining community services ranging from schools to waterworks. They are all tax-exempt and are all nicknamed "municipals."

Q. *What sets the interest rates on municipals?*
A. First, the general level of interest rates. After that, the credit rating of the issuer—determined by the rating services. Triple A, of course, is the best. I repeat: if you wish to avoid risks of default, don't go below their ratings of A.

Q. *What types of municipals are there?*
A. *General obligation bonds,* secured by the full faith and credit and general unlimited taxing power of the municipal authority. Many bonds of big cities are in this category.
Limited tax or special tax bonds, backed by a limited portion of the issuer's taxing power, or payable only from the proceeds of a single tax.
Revenue bonds, secured by the revenue of a particular municipal department or a special authority created to operate a self-supporting project. Included in this category are toll road and turnpike authority bonds; hospital bonds; many electric and water utility bonds; and housing authority bonds.
Leased revenue bonds, backed by the lease payment made by a governmental unit to a special authority which builds a project (such as a civic center) and issues it back to the municipality.
Industrial revenue bonds, issued by a municipality or authority but secured by the lease payments made by the corporation using the facilities financed by the revenue bond issue. The best quality and most marketable of these are pollution-control issues backed by the creditworthiness of large corporations.

Q. *What are the special characteristics of municipals?*
A. Some are in denominations of $1,000 and up—although the $5,000 minimum denomination is the most common. Most are bearer bonds. The owner's name is not on record with the issuer and if you *hold* the bond the presumption is you *own* it. Usually you'll clip a coupon every six months and collect interest from a paying agency or through your own bank.
You must safeguard bearer bonds as you would cash, for if "your" bonds are in someone else's possession, how can you prove they are yours? If your bearer bonds are stolen, you may be completely out of luck—just as you would be if your cash was stolen. Each bond does have a serial number which may be some help in locating stolen securities.
Most are serial bonds. A certain number will mature each year, will be paid off and retired. The range of maturities may be five, ten, fifteen, twenty

years or perhaps thirty or forty years, which means you can decide the date on which you want your capital back and then choose a maturity that fits.

Q. *What about the tax exemption?*
A. You may be able to get eye-popping rates of return—tax-free—on low-quality municipal bonds. But I will not suggest anything second-class—not in this investment area.

The tax advantages are not just for the wealthy! Tax exemption can benefit you to a lesser extent in the lower tax brackets as well. The returns are more attractive than you probably realize, particularly if you're among the millions of us who are subject to state and local as well as federal income taxes.

To the single individual with $15,000 to $18,200 of taxable earnings in a moderate 30 per cent income bracket (including state and local taxes), a tax-free 5 per cent bond equals 7.14 per cent on taxable interest; 6 per cent equals 8.57 per cent on taxable interest; 6½ per cent equals 9.29 per cent; and 7 per cent equals 10 per cent.

TAX-EXEMPT INCOME VS. TAXABLE INCOME

TO EQUAL A TAX-FREE YIELD OF:

JOINT RETURN	SINGLE RETURN	TAX BRACKET	5%	5½%	6%	6½%
$ 20,200- 24,600		28%	6.94%	7.64%	8.33%	9.03%
	$ 15,000- 18,200	30%	7.14%	7.86%	8.57%	9.29%
$ 24,600- 29,900		32%	7.35%	8.09%	8.82%	9.56%
	$ 18,200- 23,500	34%	7.58%	8.33%	9.09%	9.85%
$ 29,900- 35,200		37%	7.94%	8.73%	9.52%	10.32%
	$ 23,500- 28,800	39%	8.20%	9.02%	9.84%	10.66%
$ 35,200- 45,800		43%	8.77%	9.65%	10.53%	11.40%
	$ 28,800- 34,100	44%	8.93%	9.82%	10.71%	11.61%
$ 45,800- 60,000	$ 34,100- 41,500	49%	9.80%	10.78%	11.76%	12.75%
$ 60,000- 85,600		54%	10.87%	11.96%	13.04%	14.13%
	$ 41,500- 55,300	55%	11.11%	12.22%	13.33%	14.44%
$ 85,600-109,400		59%	12.20%	13.41%	14.63%	15.85%
	$ 55,300- 81,800	63%	13.51%	14.86%	16.22%	17.57%
$109,400-162,400		64%	13.89%	15.28%	16.67%	18.06%
$162,400-213,400	$ 81,800-108,300	68%	15.63%	17.19%	18.75%	20.31%
$215,400 & Over	$108,300 & Over	70%	16.67%	18.33%	20.00%	21.67%

Q. *What is a moratorium on municipal securities?*
A. Suspension (postponement) by a state or municipality of repayment of principal on a maturing debt. Moratoriums are declared when a debtor hasn't the cash to pay off its obligations when due, even though it continues to pay interest owed on time.

Q. *Is the tax-exempt feature of these bonds safe?*
A. New federal legislation has been proposed from time to time to author-

ize states and localities to issue taxable bonds—if they so desire—with the federal government providing subsidies to offset the added interest cost to them. The goal: to attract investors who have no incentive now to buy tax-exempts.

Sale of these taxable bond options will not disturb the tax-exempt status of outstanding securities or any new tax-exempts the issuers prefer to sell instead of taxables.

Q. *Aren't some municipals insured to guarantee payment?*
A. Yes, several governmental authorities have taken out insurance to guarantee payment of interest and principal on their obligations in the event of default. The insurance does *not* cover loss due to market fluctuation during the life of the insured bond.

The two major insurers of municipal bonds are the Municipal Bond Insurance Association (MBIA) and the American Municipal Bond Assurance Corporation (AMBAC). An issue that has been insured by the MBIA receives an AAA rating from Standard & Poor's, and an issue insured by the AMBAC receives an "AA" rating. (Moody's does not take account of the insurance coverage in its ratings of municipals.)

The AMBAC also insures mutual bond funds and individual portfolios.

In sum there are three ways to obtain the security of insurance on your tax-exempt bond investments: (1) purchase bonds that the issuing government or underwriter has had insured by the MBIA or AMBAC; (2) purchase shares in a mutual fund that has had its portfolio insured by the AMBAC; (3) insure your own portfolio with the AMBAC.

The United States Government Securities Markets

One fixed-income securities market in which the question of quality doesn't even come up is the market for U. S. Government securities. Default on the U. S. Treasury's issues is unthinkable.

Q. *What about U.S. savings bonds?*
A. These are non-marketable bonds and are covered in the following pages.

Q. *What are the marketable types of U.S. securities?*
A. (1) U. S. Treasury bills, the most marketable fixed-income securities in the world, are issued on a discount (sold at less than face value) basis with maturities of three, six, and twelve months and are redeemed at face value at the specified maturity dates. The difference between the lower issue price and the higher maturity price represents your interest. Or if you sell them in the open market before maturity, your income is the difference between the issue price and your sale price.

There are also cash management bills which mature on tax dates and are attractive to investors with large incomes.

(2) U. S. TREASURY NOTES, by definition, securities with maturities of one to ten years. These carry specified coupons.

(3) U. S. TREASURY BONDS, by definition, obligations maturing in more than ten years. Many Treasury bonds outstanding today were sold many years ago at much, much lower than prevailing interest rates. Because of their comparatively low coupons—3 to 4¼ per cent—they sell at deep discounts from par value. Some long-term Treasury bonds issued in recent years, though, carry coupons up to 9⅜ per cent or higher.

Q. *Is buying discount bonds a good idea?*

A. It's a way of helping to guarantee yourself a capital gain if you hold the bond to maturity. You can run a risk of loss if interest rates rise sharply in the meantime and the price of your bonds is down to an even deeper discount if you sell before maturity. Conversely, you can achieve capital gain if interest rates decline and you sell at a profit before maturity. Also, a limited number of U. S. Treasury bonds which can be bought at a discount from par and which are held at death of the owner can be redeemed at par and accrued interest for payment of estate taxes. Of course, you can't have it both ways: these so-called "flower bonds" will be valued in the estate at par for inheritance tax purposes too. (See page 1223.)

Q. *How are Treasury securities issued?*

A. Treasury notes and bonds are issued in registered, bearer, and in book entry form. Treasury bills are available only in book entry form.

Q. *How do you buy outstanding U. S. Treasury issues?*

A. You can buy them through your broker or banker and pay the market price plus the current commission or service charge.

A convenient way to obtain the safe returns comparable to those on U. S. Treasury obligations—without actually buying Treasuries—is to substitute an investment in bank "savings certificates," described on page 1200. Savings certificates are covered by U.S. government agency insurance for up to $40,000 per account. But there are substantial penalties for pulling your money out early. Thus you may be better off buying Treasury securities outright, since they are easily marketable at any time.

Q. *How do you buy the new U.S. issues which the Treasury offers to raise cash?*

A. You can submit tenders through your broker or banker and pay whatever service charge is asked. Or you can submit a tender offer through the Bureau of the Public Debt, Securities Transaction Branch, Washington, D.C. 20226 or your district Federal Reserve Bank—and pay no commission.

Q. *What are the minimums you can buy?*

A. At the start of the 1970s, the Treasury raised the minimum purchase on Treasury bills to $10,000 in an obvious move to eliminate the nuisance of the small investor and to protect savings banks from massive deposit withdrawals. The minimum on some Treasury notes and on bonds remained at $1,000 although higher minimums are fixed on most issues.

Q. *If you have the $10,000 minimum, how do you buy U. S. Treasury bills?*

A. You can submit a tender through the Federal Reserve Bank, bank branch in your district, or Bureau of the Public Debt, Securities Transaction Branch, Washington, D.C. 20226. Assuming you're buying less than $500,000 worth, you can buy at the non-competitive tender (bid)—meaning you won't compete with the professionals but will accept the *average* price. The non-competitive bid is the best for you.

Either go in person to your Federal Reserve Bank or branch or write and ask for a "non-competitive tender" covering the bill maturity you want: three, six, or twelve months. Fill out the total you want ($10,000 minimum) and enclose payment in full (face amount). Pay either by certified personal check, bank check, cash, or through Treasury bills you own which mature by the new issue date.

The discount on the bills—the difference between the *average* bid submitted (and the price at which you will therefore buy your bills) and the $10,000 you sent—is your interest. It will be refunded to you on the date the bills are issued. On the maturity date of your bills, when they are worth par or $10,000, you'll either redeem them for cash or exchange them—"roll them over"—for more new bills.

Occasionally the Treasury also offers cash management bills at a discount from face value which you may use at face value to pay income taxes. Once you learn the technique of buying ordinary Treasury bills, you'll find it a cinch to buy these—if you can use them.

Q. *Where do you find a Federal Reserve Bank?*

A. Here are the twelve Federal Reserve Banks, their twenty-nine branches, addresses, and phone numbers. Choose yours.

FEDERAL RESERVE OFFICES

BOARD OF GOVERNORS
  Twentieth and Constitution Avenue N.W., Washington, DC 20551
  (202) 452-3000

ATLANTA
  104 Marietta Street N.W., Atlanta, GA 30303
  (404) 586-8500

Birmingham Branch
   1801 Fifth Avenue, North (P.O. Box 10447), Birmingham, AL 35202
   (205) 252-3141

Jacksonville Branch
   55 Julia Street, Jacksonville, FL 32203
   (904) 632-4400

Miami Branch
   3770 S.W. Eighth Street, Coral Gables, FL 33134 (P.O. Box 520847, Miami, FL 33152)
   (305) 445-6281

Nashville Branch
   301 Eighth Avenue, North, Nashville, TN 37203
   (615) 259-4006

New Orleans Branch
   525 St. Charles Avenue (P.O. Box 61630), New Orleans, LA 70161
   (504) 586-1505

BOSTON
   600 Atlantic Avenue, Boston, MA 02106
   (617) 973-3000

Lewiston Office
   1775 Lisbon Road, Lewiston, ME 04240
   (207) 784-2381

Windsor Locks Office
   Windsor Locks, CT 06096
   (203) 623-2561

CHICAGO
   230 South LaSalle Street (P.O. Box 834), Chicago, IL 60690
   (312) 322-5322

Detroit Branch
   160 Fort Street, West (P.O. Box 1059), Detroit, MI 48231
   (313) 961-6880

CLEVELAND
   1455 East Sixth Street (P.O. Box 6387), Cleveland, OH 44101
   (216) 241-2800

Cincinnati Branch
   150 East Fourth Street (P.O. Box 999), Cincinnati, OH 45201
   (513) 721-4787

YOUR GUIDE TO THE BOND MARKETS

Pittsburgh Branch
  717 Grant Street (P.O. Box 867), Pittsburgh, PA 15230
  (412) 261-7800

DALLAS
  400 South Akard Street (Station K), Dallas, TX 75222
  (214) 651-6111

El Paso Branch
  301 East Main Street (P.O. Box 100), El Paso, TX 79999
  (915) 544-4730

Houston Branch
  1701 San Jacinto Street (P.O. Box 2578), Houston, TX 77001
  (713) 659-4433

San Antonio Branch
  126 East Nueva Street (P.O. Box 1471), San Antonio, TX 78295
  (512) 224-2141

KANSAS CITY
  925 Grand Avenue (Federal Reserve Station), Kansas City, MO 64198
  (816) 881-2000

Denver Branch
  1020 Sixteenth Street (Terminal Annex, P.O. Box 5228), Denver, CO 80217
  (303) 292-4020

Oklahoma City Branch
  226 Northwest Third Street (P.O. Box 25129), Oklahoma City, OK 73125
  (405) 235-1721

Omaha Branch
  1702 Dodge Street, Omaha, NB 68102
  (402) 341-3610

MINNEAPOLIS
  250 Marquette Avenue, Minneapolis, MN 55480
  (612) 340-2345

Helena Branch
  400 North Park Avenue, Helena, MT 59601
  (406) 442-3860

NEW YORK
: 33 Liberty Street (Federal Reserve P.O. Station) New York, NY 10045
: (212) 791-5000

Buffalo Branch
: 160 Delaware Avenue (P.O. Box 961), Buffalo, NY 14240
: (716) 849-5000

PHILADELPHIA
: 100 North Sixth Street, Philadelphia, PA 19106 (P.O. Box 66, Philadelphia, PA 19105)
: (215) 574-6000

RICHMOND
: 100 North Ninth Street (P.O. Box 27622), Richmond, VA 23261
: (804) 649-3611

Baltimore Branch
: 114–120 East Lexington Street (P.O. Box 1378), Baltimore, MD 21203
: (301) 539-6552

Charleston Office
: 1200 Airport Road (P.O. Box 2309), Charleston, WV 25311
: (304) 345-8020

Charlotte Branch
: 401 South Tryon Street (P.O. Box 300), Charlotte, NC 28230
: (704) 373-0200

Columbia Office
: 1624 Browning Road (P.O. Box 132), Columbia, SC 29210
: (803) 772-1940

ST. LOUIS
: 411 Locust Street (P.O. Box 442) St. Louis, MO 63166
: (314) 444-8444

Little Rock Branch
: 325 West Capitol Avenue (P.O. Box 1261), Little Rock, AR 72203
: (501) 372-5451

Louisville Branch
: 410 South Fifth Street (P.O. Box 899), Louisville, KY 40232
: (502) 587-7351

Memphis Branch
: 202 North Main Street (P.O. Box 407), Memphis, TN 38101
: (901) 523-7171

SAN FRANCISCO
   400 Sansome Street (P.O. Box 7702), San Francisco, CA 94120
   (415) 544-2000

Los Angeles Branch
   409 West Olympic Boulevard (P.O. Box 2077, Terminal Annex), Los Angeles, CA 90051
   (213) 683-8323

Portland Branch
   915 S.W. Stark Street (P.O. Box 3436), Portland, OR 97208
   (503) 221-5900

Salt Lake City Branch
   120 South State Street (P.O. Box 30780), Salt Lake City, UT 84125
   (801) 355-3131

Seattle Branch
   105 Second Avenue (P.O. Box 3567), Seattle, WA 98124
   (206) 442-1376

THE MARKET FOR FEDERAL AGENCY SECURITIES

Ranking a mere step below the direct obligations of the U. S. Treasury are the obligations of the federal agencies. They are not direct obligations of the U. S. Treasury itself but in one way or another they involve federal government guarantees or sponsorship. They are not outstanding in anywhere near the volume of U. S. Treasury issues but tens of billions of dollars of agency issues already are being traded in the open market and the volume keeps climbing.

What's more, just because they are *not* direct Treasury obligations, the returns available on federal agency issues are usually higher than on Treasuries. As a general rule, at any given time the yield on an agency issue will be above the yield on a Treasury issue of similar maturity.

Q. *Just what are federal agency issues?*
A. They are securities issued by federal agencies created by Congress over the years and operating under federal charter and supervision.

Among the federal agencies concerned with financing the agricultural industry are: the Federal Intermediate Credit Banks (FIC), the District Banks for Co-operatives (Co-ops), and the Federal Land Banks. These are marketed as Consolidated Farm System issues.

Among the agencies concerned with the housing industry are the Federal Home Loan Bank; the Federal Home Loan Mortgage Corporation (Freddie Mac); the Federal National Mortgage Association (FNMA or Fannie

Mae); the Government National Mortgage Association (GNMA or Ginnie Mae).

Also, to illustrate the variety and scope among other agencies, there are the Tennessee Valley Authority (TVA) and the Export-Import Bank (ExIm), the Small Business Administration, and more. In addition, new agencies are created from time to time and they too will sell their obligations in the open market—or will have their securities sold for them by the U. S. Treasury.

Q. *What are the minimums on purchases and maturities of the agency issues?*

A. A $10,000 minimum was set in the early 1970s on some federal agency issues also to eliminate the small "nuisance" subscriber. A $5,000 denomination is still fairly typical among the agencies, though, and the minimum on Federal Land Bank issues is $1,000. The maturities of agency issues generally run from a few months to over fifteen years.

Q. *What do federal agency and Treasury issues yield?*

A. Check your daily newspaper for the bid and asked quotes and yields available or call your broker or bank. The quotations and yields change from day to day.

Q. *How do you subscribe to new issues of federal agencies?*

A. Each of the federal agencies has a fiscal agent in New York City which puts together a nationwide selling group when it has a new issue to sell. In the group will be securities dealers, brokerage houses, and dealer banks. The sale will be publicly announced in the newspapers and other media one or two days prior to the offering.

Each of the firms which is a member of the selling group will accept subscriptions from investors on the established terms—and assuming your order is accepted, you will pay no commission on your purchase. You will pay a clearing fee or service charge, however, and this will cut your net return. You must check these details, as stressed over and over in this chapter, with a broker, dealer, or banker who knows *you* and will give you a *fair* deal.

Q. *How do you buy outstanding federal agency issues?*

A. The same way you buy other fixed-income securities trading in the open market: through a broker or banker with whom you have an established relationship. If you buy in the open market, you'll pay the prevailing commission or the offered price.

Q. *In what form are agency securities issued?*

A. Usually in bearer form. You have to assume the responsibility of safeguarding them, collecting interest, and redeeming them at maturity. This can be done through your broker or bank.

Lower-Quality Bonds—or "Junk" Bonds

On these, you can really earn some juicy returns. The rate just below A is Baa according to Moody's and BBB according to Standard & Poor's. And these are not low ratings, for those categories go down to Ba or BB, Caa or CCC, Ca or CC, or C. In some of these areas, bonds will return a yield ranging up from 10 per cent. But I warn you. Bonds of this caliber *can* turn out to be very risky and you may deeply regret reaching for the rich returns.

"Junk" bonds are risky not only because of the possibility of default by the issue. Their price fluctuations also are sharper and faster than those on higher-quality issues. When interest rates fall—that is, when bond prices rise —most junk bonds appreciate much more than the average fixed-income security. But when interest rates *rise*—and bond prices fall—junk bonds often plummet. The reason is fairly obvious: if you, an investor, can get fairly high yields on good-quality bonds, why should you bother with junk?

At the same time, there has been powerful demand for top-rated obligations, which has widened the spread in interest rates between the quality and the junk.

There has been no mistaking the message: conservative investors clearly prefer the safety of top-caliber obligations at lower rates to the higher income available on lower-quality bonds appealing to speculators. Smaller investors who are willing to take the junk bond risk for the high return can diversify by purchasing high-yield mutual funds, either taxable or tax-exempt.

Pitfalls for the Small Investor

Q. *But what if you don't have a big account or a working relationship with a bank?*

A. Unless you have a most extraordinary relationship with your bank, you'll not be able to buy outstanding short-term issues of the U. S. Treasury and federal agencies without meeting some rigid requirements. Specifically:

• You must have a hefty total of cash in your account or be a regular customer. You can't just walk into any bank with a check.

• You must invest at least $100,000 or you'll be considered an odd-lot buyer and have to pay a service charge. You must make sure this service charge doesn't eliminate the interest rate advantage.

• You must meet the minimums—$10,000 on Treasury bills; $5,000 to $10,000 on federal agency issues, depending on the agency. The usual minimum for commercial paper you buy through your bank is $100,000.

• You must keep track of your maturity dates, for if you fail to reinvest your money when your obligations mature, you lose future interest.

Q. *And what about brokers?*
A. You'll have to meet the same rigid requirements. Most brokers also consider you a nuisance to avoid and will slap on a service charge of $20 or more per order. This can more than offset your interest rate advantage.

In short, these are sophisticated markets. You have to seek them out, you have to do your homework, you have to have money, and you have to assume responsibilities.

A Bank or a Bond? Which for You?

What should you do if you have a fair-size sum to invest and what you primarily want is safety and income?

Should you simply put your money in a corner bank or savings institution, take no risks of the market place at all, and get whatever returns the financial institution offers?

Or should you go into the open market, accept some risks of price fluctuations, and freeze for yourself some of the return available there?

To get your answer, ask yourself:

• How long do you want to freeze your savings in fixed-income mediums? You will certainly not buy long-term bonds if you plan to keep the money invested in the bonds for only a short time—not unless you're trading in and out for quick profits. And that kind of trading is an entirely different matter from what I'm covering in this section.

• What are your investment goals? If all you want is absolute safety and a fair interest rate, you might as well put your money in a nearby savings institution. It's simple and satisfactory.

• What is your age? You can afford to take more risks at a young age.

• What is your judgment on the future pace of inflation? You will want to feel confident that your interest coupon will more than cover the annual loss in the purchasing power of the dollars you have invested.

• Do you have enough money to go into the open market? You must consider the commission charges on buying a few bonds and, of course, there also are the minimums required on many investments.

• How willing are you to accept responsibility for managing your savings in the market? Investing in any of the securities I have discussed in the preceding pages takes more knowledge and responsibility on your part than does a simple deposit in a local bank or savings institution.

These questions will guide you to the proper decision for yourself.

Financial Futures

If you are to invest in bonds or other fixed-income securities, you also must study what might be called the "futures market for interest rates," or "financial futures." Futures are a highly speculative type of investment (more on pages 1248–50), historically associated with such commodities as wheat, corn, copper, etc. In briefest summary, a future is a contract—a contract for a future delivery or purchase at a predetermined price. A typical copper futures contract might require a buyer to purchase 25,000 pounds of copper from the seller next July at X cents a pound. If copper prices have gone up in the meantime, the buyer has a bargain—or if down, vice versa.

There are futures contracts in fixed-income securities, too. The concept behind futures is to hedge against coming price movements—or to place a bet on the way you think the price will go.

A large bond dealer, for instance, may hold a huge supply of U. S. Government bonds paying attractive interest rates; nevertheless, the dealer wants to be protected against a further rise in interest rates—which would cause his supply of bonds to tumble in price. So he sells contracts to deliver U. S. Government bonds in the future. If interest rates do rise, his bonds will be worth less, but he'll make a nice countervailing profit on his futures contracts. Why? Because if bond yields have increased and prices have fallen, he can fulfill the agreement of his futures contract and buy bonds at a lower price for delivery than that at which he originally contracted to sell. Conversely, if interest rates fall, he'll lose money on his futures, but will make a profit on his bonds. (This goal is to guarantee himself the attractive interest payments without fear of capital loss.) The buyer of the contract just may be a speculator betting that interest rates will fall—that is, bond prices will rise or the other participant may be an arbitrageur.

Interest rate futures as the end of the 1970s neared included: Treasury bond and commercial paper futures and two types of GNMA futures, traded on the Chicago Board of Trade; three-month and one-year Treasury bill futures, traded on the International Money Market of the Chicago Mercantile Exchange; and a GNMA certificate delivery contract on the American Commodities Exchange affiliate of the American Stock Exchange. New varieties of similar types of contracts are in the making, and may be actively trading as you read this.

The lure of futures—as opposed merely to buying bonds—is that leverage is tremendous. A tiny change in interest rates will yield a huge profit—or it may wipe out your investment.

For this reason alone, you should trade in *financial futures* only if you are an *experienced investor* able to risk ample sums of money not essential to your well-being!

To suggest how overpowering this leverage is, consider that the typical interest rate futures contract calls for the buyer to buy (and the seller to sell) $100,000* to as much as $1 million† worth of fixed-income instruments at some date in the future. Yet you can buy or sell one of these contracts by

* For Treasury bond futures and GNMA futures.
† For T-bill futures.

putting up a deposit of only around $1,500, which is called the "margin." If interest rates move even slightly, the value of the tens of thousands of dollars of bonds involved in the contract can change enough to wipe out your $1,500 deposit—or double your money. (In the case of Treasury bond futures, a fluctuation of only .12 of a point in interest rates would change the value of a single contract by $1,500; in the case of GNMA futures, .12 of a point; in the case of Treasury bill futures .6 of a point.)

By now you may be wondering: Suppose I *do* earn a profit on a $1,500 deposit. Where would I get the money to fulfill a contract calling for me to buy or sell thousands of dollars worth of bonds? Don't worry; very few futures speculators ever have to take over or make "delivery" on their contracts. (To see why, consult pages 1248–50.)

But be warned: even the most sophisticated futures speculators do lose their shirts in this most esoteric of markets.

And the amateurs? I shiver . . .

What Should Be Your Policy on Bonds?

Let me put it bluntly: unless you know your way around the bond markets, and can afford to take the risks, go and stay first-class.

Don't go into these sophisticated markets blindly.

Don't buy low-grade bonds which might default and wipe you out.

Unless you have at least $5,000 to invest *don't* buy individual bond issues even where there are no minimums. (The alternative here might be to buy into a bond fund, described earlier.)

Don't try to diversify too much when you are buying just a few bonds. Commission charges on buying or selling one or two bonds can be steep and in addition the spread on the bid and asked when you are buying just one or two bonds can also be sizable. Some brokers might quote you a spread as much as five points ($50 on a $1,000 par value) if you buy a single bond. If you can, buy several of one issue. You'll probably get a better price and pay less in commissions.

Don't try to make a killing by trading on thin margins.

Do get guidance from a broker or banker you respect and who knows you, your circumstances, and the bond market.

Do make sure you are dealing with a reputable firm. In the 1970s there were far too many scandals in connection with high-pressure bond salesmen in the "Sunbelt" area especially where so many retire with cash to spare and time to fill. Among the shoddy as well as illegal sales tactics were charging excessive prices; quoting deceptive maturities and ratings; providing misleading descriptions of issues.

Do learn the basics of bond yield, maturity, discounts, and ratings before taking the plunge.

Do use your head and curb your greed.

The bond markets are great for wise and cool investors. They can be murder for fools.

The Bafflegab of Bonds

ACCRUED INTEREST   Interest which has accumulated on a bond from the last interest payment to the present day. When you buy a bond, you must pay the interest which has accrued from the last interest payment to the seller of the bond. When you in turn sell a bond, the buyer must pay you the interest accrued from the last interest payment. Not all bonds trade with accrued interest. Those in default trade *flat,* and income bonds usually pay interest only when and if it is earned.

AMORTIZE   Fixed periodic charges or credits are scheduled for the specific purpose of adjusting purchaser's cost to redemption.

BASIS   This is another word for yield. The basis of a bond is its yield to maturity. In the financial futures world, though, it is the difference between the price of a nearby contract and the price at which the underlying security can be bought in the cash market.

BASIS POINT $1/100$ of 1 per cent or 0.01. Used in finely describing the yield of a bond.

BEARER BOND   Bond on which the owner's name is not registered with the issuer and thus, in some ways, is equivalent to cash in your possession.

BLUE LIST   Daily trade publication for dealers in municipal bonds listing the names and amounts of municipal bonds that dealers all over the country are offering for sale to other dealers. Printed in blue ink on blue paper, hence *Blue List.* The *Blue List* also includes coupon price, and yield, of offerings.

BOND   Promissory instrument to obtain credit on which principal is to be repaid in usually more than ten years after the loan is made. Interest is to be paid periodically. Bonds are issued by federal, state, and municipal governments as well as corporations and are usually marketable. All nongovernment bonds are covered by a contract (trust indenture) held by a trustee who—in case of serious violation of the indenture by the bond issuer—can take action to protect the rights of all the bondholders.

BOND MARKETS   Markets in which longer-term debt securities of various borrowers are traded.

CALLABLE BOND   Bonds which include a call provision stating that the issuer may redeem them before their maturity date under specified conditions. Usually the call price is at a premium over par. For example: A corporation has a $10 million bond issue outstanding which carries a 9 per cent coupon maturing in twenty-four years and which is callable at 105. If interest rates drop to, say, 6½ per cent, and the corporation can be assured by its investment bankers that this lower rate is available, it is obvious that the corporation can benefit by paying the slightly additional cost involved in calling the bonds at 105 and floating another loan at a coupon rate so much lower than 9 per cent. Most issues prohibit call to take advantage of lower interest rates in the early years of the issue life.

COMPOUND INTEREST Interest paid on accumulated interest as well as on the principal and computed on both the accumulated interest and the principal. Over the life of a bond, compounding interest can be equal to more than half the total of realized return.

CONVERTIBLE DEBENTURE Bond issued on the general credit of the corporation which may be converted into common and sometimes preferred stock of the same corporation at a specified price under stated conditions.

CORPORATES Corporation bonds.

COUPON The piece of paper attached to a bearer (or coupon) bond which is evidence that interest is payable on the bond, usually every six months. The coupon rate is the rate of interest which the issuer has pledged to pay you, the bondholder, annually. The coupon amount is the dollar amount you will receive when this paper is submitted to a bank or through your broker for collection.

CURRENT YIELD The interest paid by a bond expressed as a percentage of the coupon to the current market price. Example: a 3 per cent $1,000 bond selling at $600 offers a current return of 5 per cent ($30/$600).

DEBENTURE A type of corporate bond which is backed only by the general credit of the issuing corporation and not by any pledge of property.

DISCOUNT Difference between the lower price at which a bond may be trading and its higher value (par value) at issuance or normally at maturity.

DISCOUNT BOND Bonds quoted at a price below their face (or par) value. For example: a bond selling at par would be shown in a newspaper bond table at 100, a discount bond would be shown below that (99, 62, 73, etc.).

DISCOUNT RATE The interest rate the Federal Reserve System charges banks belonging to the Federal Reserve System for loans. It is considered a basic interest rate of the nation because it is the rate banks themselves pay to borrow money. As a result, changes in the discount rate by the Federal Reserve affect all other interest rates in the nation.

EASY MONEY See TIGHT MONEY.

FEDERAL AGENCY ISSUES Securities issued by federal agencies created by Congress over a long span of years and ranking in caliber right below U. S. Government securities themselves. Some are obligations of the government; some are backed by the agency.

FEDERAL RESERVE SYSTEM Established under the Federal Reserve Act of 1913 to regulate the banking system of the United States and to set monetary policy of the country. See MONETARY POLICY.

FINANCIAL FUTURES Contracts traded on major commodities exchanges for the future delivery of large amounts of fixed-income instruments—including Treasury bonds, Treasury bills, GNMA pass-through certificates, and commercial paper.

FIRST MORTGAGE BOND A type of corporate bond which is secured by a mortgage on all or part of the fixed property of the issuing corporation.

FIXED-INCOME SECURITIES Securities which return a fixed income over a specified period. Fixed-income securities may be bonds, notes, bills, preferred stocks, or mortgage-backed securities and pools.

FLOWER BOND Nickname for certain U. S. Treasury bonds which can be turned in at par or face value for payment of federal estate taxes if the bonds are actually owned by the decedent at the time of death. However, because of changes in the tax laws, some of the tax advantages may not be as great as was once the case.

If these bonds can be bought at a deep discount from par, the bonds can be helpful in estate planning. Under a recent law, no more bonds with the special par redemption provision for estate tax purposes will be issued, so the supply of the bonds is limited and growing smaller as the bonds mature or are turned in. Here are flower bonds still outstanding and their maturities as the 1980s neared:

COUPON	MATURITY
4	2/80
3½	11/80
3¼	6/83
3¼	5/85
4¼	5/85
3½	2/90
4¼	8/92
4	2/93
4⅛	5/94
3	2/95
3½	11/98

GENERAL-OBLIGATION BOND The major type of municipal bond backed by the full faith and credit of the issuer. These differ from limited-obligation bonds, which rely upon special assessments and specific sources of revenue, and from revenue bonds, which have no call on taxing power.

INTEREST Money paid for the use of money.

INTEREST RATE A percentage determined by the amount of money the borrower pledges to pay to the lender of money for the use of the total borrowed. If you pay $80 interest per year on a loan of $1,000, you are paying an 8 per cent interest rate.

INVESTMENT BANKERS Financial organizations, but usually not commercial banks, raising funds for various types of borrowers often by buying all of the securities and selling them through a selling group of broker-dealers to institutional and individual investors.

LIMITED TAX OR SPECIAL TAX BOND Also a type of municipal bond.

MATURITY Specified date on which the stated value of a bond—the principal—becomes payable in full to the bond's owners. Also called due or maturity date.

MONETARY POLICY Set by the Federal Reserve Board to influence the supply of bank credit and other monetary conditions in the U.S. economy. Monetary policy, therefore, is a key factor in the trend of interest rates and the direction of the entire U.S. economy. Since interest rate changes send the bond and money markets up or down, monetary policy is also obviously a crucial force in these markets. See FEDERAL RESERVE SYSTEM.

MONEY MARKETS Markets in which the short-term securities of various borrowers are traded.

MORTGAGE-BACKED BONDS Bonds issued by a bank or institution which lends mortgage money to homeowners. Mortgage-backed bonds have as collateral a sizable amount of mortgages—usually a larger dollar amount than the total dollar amount of the bonds.

MORTGAGE BOND See FIRST MORTGAGE BOND.

MORTGAGE PASS-THROUGH CERTIFICATE A certificate of participation in a pool of mortgages that a mortgage-lending institution has sold to a trustee. Investors in pass-through certificates receive monthly payments of interest and principal as the mortgages in the pool are paid off.

MUNICIPAL BONDS Any obligations issued by a city, town, village, state, territory, U.S. possession, etc. All are exempt from federal income taxation as of the laws in the late 1970s (and under certain conditions sometimes from state and local taxes too), and all are called municipals.

NATIONAL ASSOCIATION OF SECURITIES DEALERS, INC. A non-profit membership corporation, established in 1938 by Congress and including thousands of securities dealers and brokers throughout the United States. The NASD is responsible for self-regulation of the over-the-counter securities markets and also, in turn, to the Securities and Exchange Commission.

OBLIGATION In Wall Street, an IOU, a bond, a note, or a bill.

OFFERING Principal amount of an obligation or the face value at which an obligation is issued and on which interest is paid. Usually $1,000 or $5,000 per bond.

POINT In bonds, one point represents a $10 change in the price per $1,000 (face value) bond—in contrast to stocks, where one point is a $1.00 change in price. The reason a point is $10 is that a bond price is quoted as a percentage of $1,000: 1 per cent of $1,000 is $10, 5 per cent is $50, etc., and so one point is $10, five points is $50, etc. To illustrate further, a quotation of 92 is $920 and a five-point rise to 97 would be equal to $50 or a rise to $970.

PREMIUM Difference between higher price above par at which a bond may be selling and the lower price recorded at the time it was issued or to be received at maturity date.

PRINCIPAL Face value of a bond on which interest is paid.

PRUDENT-MAN RULE A standard for investments. Under this standard, states having "prudent-man laws" permit trustees managing other people's money to diversify their investments and include high-quality stocks as well as the highest-quality bonds in the portfolios they manage.

RATINGS The informed judgments of independent rating services (the two major ones are Moody's and Standard & Poor's) on the quality of various obligations. Obligations are ranked from the very highest Aaa (Moody's) and AAA (S&P's) to C and even lower. The ratings of these two services play a key role in evaluating the quality of bonds to investors.

REAL RATE OF RETURN Annual yield derived from fixed-income securities reduced by per cent of yearly rise in cost of living. Sometimes quoted on a pre-tax basis and sometimes on an after-tax basis.

REDEEM Repayment of the par value of a bond at maturity or at the price that has to be paid if the bond is being redeemed earlier at a call date.

REFUNDING The replacement of an outstanding and redeemed obligation with a new obligation. When interest rates decline, an issuer may in advance of maturity date decide to call in securities it sold at higher interest rates and refund them into new lower-interest bonds.

REGISTERED BOND A bond registered in the name of the owner with either the issuer of the bond or the issuer's agent. The owner is mailed a check when interest is due and the bond can be transferred only by endorsement of the certificate. See BEARER BOND.

RETURN Also known as yield. The rate of income derived from an investment—interest in the case of bonds, dividends in the case of stocks.

REVENUE BOND A type of municipal bond relying upon revenues generated by some public facility (bridges, tunnels, roads, transit, etc.) rather than taxes. Industrial revenue bonds are a special sort issued by a government and therefore pay tax-exempt interest to finance a corporate facility. Their main security is the lease rental paid by the industrial corporation.

ROLLOVER Another word for refund, commonly used when the Treasury replaces its short-term bills at their maturity dates with new short-term bills, or a bank replaces maturing certificates of deposit with proceeds of new CDs.

SELLING AT A DISCOUNT A bond selling at a price below its face value. See DISCOUNT.

SELLING AT A PREMIUM A bond selling at a price above its face value. See PREMIUM.

SERIAL BONDS Issues which are redeemed on an installment basis in sequential—usually annual—order. A predetermined amount carry chronological maturity dates so that bonds fall due every period until the full amount is paid up.

SIMPLE INTEREST Interest that is paid only on the principal and computed only on the principal.

SINKING FUND A pool of money created through periodic payments by an issuer of bonds that must be used to retire (call in) a certain fixed (or variable) amount of its outstanding bonds at specified intervals. See AMORTIZE.

SPREAD Difference between two prices. Between bid and asked; or between the price at which an investment banking syndicate buys an issue from the issuer and the price at which the syndicate sells the issue to the public; or between the prices at which top-rated bonds are quoted and the prices at which second-quality bonds are quoted; or just between different types of bonds.

SYNDICATES Groups of investment bankers formed to underwrite and distribute issues of securities.

TAX-EXEMPTS Slang name for all types of municipal obligations which are exempt from federal income tax and sometimes from state and local taxation.

TERM Length of time that a bond is outstanding. A term bond, in comparison with a serial bond, has only a single maturity date.

TIGHT MONEY Financial conditions that develop when the Federal Reserve adopts a monetary policy under which it restrains the supply of credit and thereby encourages higher interest rates. As the supply of credit becomes more limited while demand remains unaffected, the availability of the credit to would-be borrowers shrinks and there is a feeling of "tightness" in the markets. Easy money describes financial conditions that develop when the Federal Reserve adopts a monetary policy under which it expands the supply of credit and thereby encourages lower interest rates. The policy usually follows a decline in demand for funds, reflecting a slowdown in business activity.

TREASURY Nickname for the securities of the United States Government: bonds, notes, and bills.

TREASURY BILLS Short-term marketable U. S. Treasury obligations maturing from ninety days to one year and offered on a discount basis. T-bills are considered in the investment community almost as liquid as cash or as savings in the bank. Minimum denomination is $10,000.

UNDERWRITING SYNDICATES Groups of investment bankers who buy and market new issues to public.

UNITED STATES GOVERNMENT SECURITIES MARKET Generally speaking, the vast over-the-counter market in which bills, notes, and bonds of the U. S. Treasury are bought and sold. (Some are listed on the New York Stock and American Exchanges too.)

VARIABLE RATE The term applied to certain special loans or debt obligations, the interest rates on which vary with overall interest rates or some specific interest rate. Also called Floating Rate notes.

YIELD TO MATURITY Total, true rate of return you are slated to receive on a debt instrument, taking into consideration the price you paid, the interest to be received, and the price at which your bond will be paid off at its maturity date. This is an exact calculation that must be worked out with aid of specially prepared mathematical tables.

24

YOUR GUIDE TO UNITED STATES SAVINGS BONDS

INTRODUCTION	1230
KEY QUESTIONS ON SAVINGS BONDS	1231
HOW TO USE THE TAX ADVANTAGES OF SAVINGS BONDS TO CREATE A TAX-FREE EDUCATION FUND	1235
A FINANCIALLY INTELLIGENT ATTITUDE TOWARD BUYING AND HOLDING SAVINGS BONDS	1236
CHANGES IN THE 1980S	1236
SERIES EE BONDS	1237
SERIES HH BONDS	1237
SERIES E AND H BONDS IN THE 1980S	1238
THE BAFFLEGAB OF SAVINGS BONDS	1242

Introduction

"On New Year's morning, my husband and I vowed to save $50 a month, a minor per cent of his take-home pay. But in the past few weeks an unexpected bunch of expenses has wiped it all out. This has happened over and over again to us, with the result that we haven't accumulated one extra dollar in the past five years. Is there any cure for the habitual non-saver?"

This typed plea for help, sent to me, is far more typical of Americans than any figures on total savings suggest. This is the sort of letter, in fact, which highlights the fact that, despite our ever-rising volume of overall savings, a full one third or more of U.S. families have no savings at all—in the form of bank deposits, stocks, bonds, etc.—and for millions of other families the savings total is less than $500.

If you are among the millions who feel unable to stick to voluntary savings plans, your best answer will be a form of "forced savings." There are literally dozens of different ways to discipline yourself into saving and I've analyzed many of the techniques in these pages. But among the very, very *best* ways to force yourself to save is to buy United States savings bonds under a payroll savings plan at the place where you work—or via a bond-a-month plan at your corner bank. And in fact a fantastic total of approximately 9 million Americans in the early 1980s were buying bonds via these savings plans at their offices or plants or factories.

This advantage is not to be underestimated in any way! By buying savings bonds via these plans, you discipline yourself into saving money you otherwise might easily fritter away. By authorizing regular small deductions from your paycheck, you build over the years a sizable total of savings. By enrolling in a payroll savings or bond-a-month plan you tend to become "frozen" to the savings program and to keep building your nest egg through good times and bad.

This is the "heart" of the United States savings bond program. This is the "magic" by which a few dollars put aside regularly every week becomes hundreds of dollars saved over a year. This is the secret of the program's continuing popularity, for as one of the leading industrialists of the country said to me a while ago:

"Many employees wouldn't save at all unless they were enrolled in a payroll savings plan. It is a lot better to get only a mediocre interest rate on something than a sensational interest rate on nothing!"

To put it another way, there may be better ways to invest—and there are—but there is no better way to save. It's a subtle but significant distinction.

Okay, the above explains why the savings bond program has survived so long. Now what are these bonds?

Key Questions on Savings Bonds

There are two series of U.S. savings bonds currently on sale—Series EE and Series HH. E and H bonds are no longer sold, but they continue to earn interest for their owners. Since savings bonds were originally issued many years ago, the Treasury raised the interest rate paid in successive stages until by early 1980 you could earn up to 7 per cent on EE bonds held to 11-year maturity. It is highly likely the interest rate on U.S. savings bonds will go up again in the relatively near future. With that in mind, check your local bank for the latest interest rates.

Q. *What are the characteristics of savings bonds?*

A. The familiar EE bond is an appreciation-type security. This means you buy it at a discount from its face amount, and the gradual increase in the value of the bond, from your purchase price to its face amount (or redemption price), represents your interest.

The less familiar Series HH bond is a current-income security. This means you buy it at par (face value) and you receive interest in the form of semi-annual checks from the U. S. Treasury.

Both types of bonds are non-marketable bonds—non-negotiable, not acceptable as collateral for loans. Series E and EE bonds may be redeemed by the Treasury or one of its authorized paying agents (most banks and other financial institutions are authorized paying agents and will redeem your bonds). H and HH bonds may be redeemed only by the Treasury or any Federal Reserve Bank branch.

Q. *How do you earn the interest rate?*

A. Series E and EE bonds increase in redemption value monthly from the third to the thirtieth month after issue, and semi-annually after that. Your interest, represented by these increases, is compounded semi-annually. Your overall rate of return increases on a graduated scale, from 4.54 per cent for bonds redeemed after one year to 6 per cent for bonds held five years after issue. The following table shows you your return on E or EE bonds with issue dates beginning September 1, 1976, if you cash them in before or at original maturity.

E or EE Bonds

Cashed in After	Yield
1 year	4.54 (annual)
1½ years	4.69
2 years	4.76
2½ years	4.86
3 years	4.95
3½ years	5.03
4 years	5.32
4½ years	5.80
5 years	6.50

Series EE bonds held for 11 years earn 7 per cent interest. Series E bonds held for 11 years after their first interest period in 1980 earn 7 per cent for the 11 years between 1980–91.

The following table shows you your return on H bonds—with issue dates beginning December 1, 1978—if you cash them in before or at original maturity.

(See pages 1237–42 later in this chapter for facts on HH bonds.)

H Bonds Cashed in After	Yield
½ year	4.20%
1 year	5.24
1½ years	5.58
2 years	5.76
2½ years	5.86
3 years	5.93
3½ years	5.98
4 years	6.01
4½ years	6.04
5 years	6.06
5½ years	6.14
6 years	6.20
6½ years	6.25
7 years	6.29
7½ years	6.33
8 years	6.37
8½ years	6.39
9 years	6.42
9½ years	6.44
10 years (maturity)	6.50

YOUR GUIDE TO UNITED STATES SAVINGS BONDS

Q. *Has the rate been increased for older bonds?*
A. Yes. Beginning with 1959, the yields on outstanding savings bonds have been improved several times, bringing them in line with current issues.

The latest increase was effective January 1, 1980, or at the beginning of the first semi-annual interest period thereafter.

Q. *How do the various extensions of maturity apply to E and H bonds?*
A. E bonds, with original maturities ranging from five years to ten years, have been granted one or more ten-year extensions.

Date of Issue	Extended Maturity	Life of Bond
May 1941–Apr. 1952	May 1981–Apr. 1992	40 years
May 1952–Jan. 1957	Jan. 1992–Apr. 1996	39 years, 8 months
Feb. 1957–May 1959	Jan. 1996–Apr. 1998	38 years, 11 months
June 1959–Nov. 1965	Mar. 1997–Aug. 2003	37 years, 9 months
Dec. 1965–May 1969	Dec. 1992–May 1996	27 years
June 1969–Nov. 1973	Apr. 1995–Sep. 1999	25 years, 10 months
Dec. 1973–June 1980	Dec. 1998–June 2005	25 years

For H bonds, the extended maturities are as follows:

Date of Issue	Extended Maturity	Life of Bond
June 1952–Jan. 1957	Feb. 1982–Sep. 1986	29 years, 8 months
Feb. 1957–Dec. 1979	Feb. 1987–Dec. 2009	30 years

Q. *Is there any advantage in redeeming older E or H bonds to buy new bonds?*
A. Absolutely none. They all pay the same interest rate schedule. And in fact there is a good reason not to cash in—if the interest for Series E bonds has not been reported each year as it accrued—for then you would be required to report the accumulated interest (the gain in value) for federal income tax purposes during the year you cash in. In addition, the new bonds purchased with the proceeds would initially accrue interest at a lower rate than the bonds that were cashed.

Q. *Are the rates guaranteed?*
A. Yes. The bonds are backed by the full faith and credit of the U. S. Government and the rates are guaranteed to maturity. You can, though, cash in your bonds as you wish after a short time. Interest may be increased but not decreased, once the rate for an extension has been published.

Q. *How do I sell my bonds?*
A. You don't sell savings bonds. You cash them in or redeem them at guaranteed values. E or EE bonds may be redeemed at most banks and other financial institutions at their current redemption value.

At your, the owner's, option, H or HH bonds may be redeemed at any

Federal Reserve Bank or Branch, or at the Bureau of Public Debt, Securities Transactions Branch, Washington, D.C. 20266, at any time after six months from issue date. H bonds received during the month preceding an interest payment date will be held for redemption until that date.

Q. *What about cash-in restrictions?*
A. Savings bonds are, I repeat, liquid assets which may be cashed in after their minimal holding periods.

Q. *What if a bond is lost or stolen?*
A. Savings bonds are "indestructible." Any bond which is lost, stolen, mutilated, or destroyed will be replaced by the U. S. Treasury upon your application without charge to you. A record of each bond sold is maintained by Social Security account number for those issued on or after October 1, 1973.

The record is kept by the Bureau of Public Debt. More than 3.6 million U.S. savings bonds, valued at more than $294 million—either lost, stolen, damaged, or destroyed—have been replaced by the Treasury, over the past three decades, without charge to their owners.

Q. *You mean all bonds are registered?*
A. Yes. And you have a choice of registration. The bonds may be issued in one name only, in the names of two persons as co-owners, or in the name of one person with a second person as beneficiary (payable on death).

If bonds are registered in co-ownership form, during co-owner's lifetime either of you may cash the bonds, but a co-owner's name cannot be removed without his or her consent. If registered in beneficiary form, during owner's lifetime only he or she may cash an E bond and beneficiary's name cannot be removed without the beneficiary's consent. On an EE bond, this consent clause has been eliminated.

Savings bonds cannot be transferred, sold, or used as collateral.

Q. *How do I make a claim if my bonds are lost?*
A. Write to the Bureau of Public Debt, 200 Third Street, Parkersburg, West Virginia 26101. Provide as much information as you can about the lost, stolen, damaged, or destroyed bonds; serial numbers, issue dates, names and addresses on bonds. The Bureau of Public Debt will send you a special form to execute to receive your "duplicate" bonds. Keep your bonds in a secure place, such as a safe deposit box. *In another location,* maintain a list of your bonds, with their serial numbers, denominations, and dates issued. Get a "Personal Record of Ownership" from any local savings bond division office.

Q. *What about taxation of savings bonds?*
A. Interest on savings bonds is exempt from all state and local income or

personal property taxes. Interest on savings bonds is subject to federal income tax, but the tax may be deferred on E and EE bonds until the bonds are cashed, otherwise disposed of, or finally mature. This tax-deferral privilege permits you to create and build up education, retirement, disability funds (or funds for whatever your objective) which—under certain circumstances—may be tax-free. This aspect is also a major "plus" for E and EE bonds.

You cannot similarly postpone paying income tax on interest you earn on marketable Treasury obligations or other taxable obligations. H or HH bond interest, paid semi-annually by Treasury check, must be reported annually for federal income tax purposes.

Q. *Any other important characteristics?*
A. Yes. Unless administration is required for other purposes, probate is not required in order to dispose of a decedent's savings bonds. The Treasury provides special forms, depending on the amount involved, which may be used for the purpose. Bonds registered in co-owner or beneficiary form belong to the survivor and are not a part of the decedent's probate estate; their value may be included in computing the size of the estate for estate and inheritance tax purposes, whether federal or state.

How to Use the Tax Advantages of Savings Bonds to Create a Tax-free Education Fund

The fact that you need not report the interest you receive on E or EE bonds until you cash in the bonds is a vital tax benefit for you. And you can increase these tax savings when you buy the bonds as gifts for your children.

For instance, as a means of saving for your child's education, buy the bonds in your child's name and designate yourself as beneficiary (*not* co-owner). File a federal income tax return in your child's name and state thereon that the child elects to report the interest annually. But it is not necessary that the election to report interest annually be made in the first year the bonds are purchased. You may do that at any time. In the year the election is made, all the interest earned to date on all E or EE bonds held must be declared as interest income for that year. Also the first return should state that it is being filed to establish the taxpayer's intent to be an accrual basis taxpayer for savings bonds under Section 454 of the Internal Revenue Code. A tax return is only required in future years (reporting only that year's bond interest accrual) if your child's total unearned (investment) income exceeds his or her personal exemption *or* his total income exceeds his personal exemption plus his standard deduction.

Thus, when your child cashes his or her bonds to meet the costs of college, all the accrued interest on the bonds will be free from federal income tax. And the interest is also exempt from all state and local income taxes and personal property taxes.

Or you might buy the bonds in your child's name, with yourself as beneficiary, and not file a federal income tax return until your child starts college and begins to cash in the bonds for his or her educational expenses. Your child then would file a tax return each year and report the full amount of interest on the redeemed bonds as income.

As of the tax laws of the late 1970s, if the total amount of your child's investment income was less than $1,000 a year, no income tax would be due. (The tax-free income of the child could increase considerably more if the child had "earned income" in addition to his investment income. In this regard, earned income does not include interest or dividends.)

If you use the first Tax-Free Education Plan, be sure you keep a copy of the tax return you file to prove "intent."

A Financially Intelligent Attitude
Toward Buying and Holding Savings Bonds

If you buy the bonds via payroll savings, they are a superb way to force yourself to save small amounts regularly and, by so doing, to accumulate a basic reserve. But a rate of 6.5 and 7 per cent did not cover the erosion in your return from spiraling living costs and steep income taxes in the late 1970s and early 1980s.

If inflation is to be our way of life in the rest of the twentieth century as it has been in the past, the Treasury will not be fair to buyers of its bonds until it offers a purchasing power guarantee—e.g., a bond with a dollar value that would rise as the cost-of-living index rose.

This is not a new idea—and, in fact, in the United States in recent years we have been moving closer and closer to purchasing power guarantees to give major segments of our population some automatic protections against steadily rising prices. Social Security benefits are now automatically tied to increases in the Consumer Price Index. Cost-of-living escalator clauses have become commonplace in union wage contracts. The record high interest rates of the 1970s reflect, in part at least, efforts to protect investors in marketable fixed-income securities from the erosion of inflation.

The very least the Treasury should do is give the subject the exhaustive study it demands but since even the study is still in the future, once you've accumulated your nest egg, maintain only a modest proportion in savings bonds.

Divide the balance among sound investments which will grow as our economy grows and, thereby, put and keep you well ahead.

In essence, savings bonds will help you create a nest egg. Other investments will help you enhance it.

CHANGES IN THE 1980s

In 1980, significant changes occurred in this great savings program. Briefly, on January 2, 1980, the Treasury introduced:

YOUR GUIDE TO UNITED STATES SAVINGS BONDS

• A series EE bond to replace the series E bond that has been on sale since 1941.

• A series HH bond, to replace the current series H bond that has been on sale since 1952.

• An exchange offering, under which owners of E bonds, EE bonds and savings notes can exchange them, with a tax-deferral privilege, for series HH bonds.

SERIES EE BONDS

The series EE bond—so named because it will double in value between its purchase and maturity dates—will retain the tax-deferral advantage of the present E bond.

The new features are:

• The purchase price is one half the face value, e.g., $25 will buy a $50 (face value) bond.

• The lowest available denomination is $50, face value. Other denominations are $75, $100, $200, $500, $1,000, $5,000 and $10,000.

• The interest rate of 5 per cent (for five or more years) remains the same as E bonds, while the term of maturity will be eleven years. There is a ½ per cent "bonus"—or 7 per cent rate—for EE bonds held to eleven-year maturity.

• The annual limitation on purchases is increased from the present $7,500 (issue amount) to $15,000 (issue amount).

• The new EE bonds can be cashed in six months after purchase.

• The requirement that a bond beneficiary must consent to a change in the bond is eliminated.

Although the familiar $25 savings bond ($18.75 purchase price) no longer is available, the new series EE $50 bond can be purchased for $25, an increase of only $6.25 in the minimum purchase price.

SERIES HH BONDS

The series HH bond has these new features, as compared to the long-outstanding H bond:

• Interest payments are a level 6½ per cent from day of purchase, rather than the present graduated scale.

• Bonds purchased for cash (rather than through exchange of other savings bonds) are subject to an interest penalty if redeemed before maturity.

• The annual purchase limitation is increased from $10,000 (face amount) to $20,000 (face amount).

The new series HH bonds can be bought for cash or obtained in exchange for the present series E or EE bonds or savings notes, singly or in combination, in multiples of $500. The new HH bond has the same maturity period as the H bond and the same denominations.

SERIES E AND H BONDS IN THE 1980s

Changes which affect owners of the present E and H bonds are:

• The earliest E bonds—bought between 1941 and April 1952—will not be extended again when they fall due between 1981 and April 1992, after forty years of interest-bearing life.

• Series H bonds bought from June 1952 through May 1959 will receive no further extensions. These bonds reach final maturity between February 1982 and May 1989.

• Owners of E bonds, EE bonds and savings notes can exchange them for the new HH bonds. This can be done up to a year after final maturity of the old E bonds. This exchange carries the same tax-deferral privilege as the present E to H bond exchange.

The changes should dispel any uncertainty about the Treasury's position on the final maturity of outstanding E and H bonds. Holders of the 1941–52 series E bonds thus will have the opportunity to decide well in advance of their bonds' final maturity whether to redeem them for cash or exchange them for HH bonds.

Get this key point straight: E and H bonds, although no longer sold, are still earning interest for their owners, and most bonds will continue to do so for years. When older E bonds do stop earning interest, you can either redeem them for cash at your local bank or exchange them for HH bonds for federal tax purposes. The amount of deferred interest will be shown on the face of your new HH bond.

COMPARISON OF TERMS AND CONDITIONS OF
SERIES H AND SERIES HH
CURRENT INCOME-TYPE SAVINGS BONDS

	SERIES H BONDS	SERIES HH BONDS
Offering date	Terminate December 31, 1979	Begin January 2, 1980
Denominations	$500, $1,000, $5,000, $10,000	Same
Issue price	Face amount	Same
Maturity	10 years with guaranteed 20-year extension	10 years
Interest	Payable semiannually by check	Same

YOUR GUIDE TO UNITED STATES SAVINGS BONDS

	Series H Bonds	Series HH Bonds
Yield curve	4.7% first 6 months, 6.3% next 4½ years, 7% final 5 years to yield 6.5% if held to maturity. During extension, uniform-payments based on rate prevailing when bond enters extended maturity.	Payments based on 6½% level rate; however, bonds sold for cash will have an interest penalty applied against redemption value, if redeemed prior to maturity. Bonds issued on exchange will not be penalized for early redemption.
Retention period	Redeemable any time after 6 months from issue date.	Same
Annual limitation	$10,000 face amount	$20,000 face amount
Tax status	Interest is subject to federal income tax reporting in year it is paid. Bonds subject to estate, inheritance and gift taxes — federal and state — but exempt from all other state and local taxes.	Same
Registration	In names of individuals in single, co-ownership or beneficiary form; in names of fiduciaries or organizations in single ownership only.	Same
Transferability	Not eligible for transfer or pledge as collateral.	Same
Rights of owners	Co-ownership: either owner may redeem; both must join reissue request. Beneficiary: only owner may redeem during lifetime; both must join reissue request.	Co-ownership: same. Beneficiary: same except that consent of beneficiary to reissue not required.
Exchange privilege	Issuable on exchange from Series E bonds and savings notes, in multiples of $500, with continued tax deferral privilege.	Issuable on exchange from Series E, EE, and savings notes, in multiples of $500, with continued tax deferral privilege.

	SERIES E BONDS	SERIES EE BONDS
Offering date	Close over-the-counter sales December 31, 1979; close payroll sales June 30, 1980	Begin January 2, 1980; phase in payroll sales through June 30, 1980
Denominations	$25, $50, $75, $100, $200, $500, $1,000, $10,000	$50, $75, $100, $200, $500, $1,000, $5,000, $10,000
Issue price	75% of face amount	50% of face amount
Maturity	5 years with guaranteed 20-year extension	11 years and 9 months
Interest	Accrues through periodic increases in redemption value to maturity	Same
Yield curve	4% after 2 months, 4.5% first year, increases gradually thereafter to yield 6% if held 5 years	4% after 2 months, 4.5% first year, increases gradually thereafter to yield 6½% if held 5 or more years and 7% when held to maturity.
Retention period	Redeemable any time after 2 months from issue date	Redeemable any time after 6 months from issue date
Annual limitation	$7,500 issue price	$15,000 issue price
Tax status	Accruals subject to federal income and to estate, inheritance and gift taxes — federal and state — but exempt from all other state and local taxes. Federal income tax may be reported (1) as it accrues, or (2) in year bond matures, is redeemed or otherwise disposed	Same
Registration	In names of individuals in single, co-ownership or beneficiary form; in names of fiduciaries or organizations in single ownership only	Same
Transferability	Not eligible for transfer or pledge as collateral	Same

	SERIES E BONDS	SERIES EE BONDS
Rights of owners	Co-ownership: either owner may redeem, both must join reissue request. Beneficiary: only owner may redeem during lifetime; both must join reissue request	Co-ownership: same Beneficiary: same except that consent of beneficiary to reissue not required
Exchange privilege	Eligible, alone or with savings notes, for exchange for Series H bonds in multiples of $500, with tax deferral privilege	Eligible, alone or with Series E bonds or savings notes, for exchange for Series HH bonds in multiples of $500, with tax deferral privilege

COMPARISON OF THE TERMS AND CONDITIONS OF
CURRENT INCOME BOND EXCHANGE OFFERINGS

	SERIES H EXCHANGE	SERIES HH EXCHANGE
Offering date	Terminate December 31, 1979	Begin January 2, 1980
Eligible securities	Series E Bonds and Savings Notes, singly or in combination	Series E Bonds, Savings Notes, and Series EE Bonds, singly or in combination; E Bonds must be received no later than one year following their final maturity date
Minimum amount	$500 current redemption value of accrual-type securities	Same
Annual purchase limitation	Exempt	Same
Exchange security	Series H Bonds including all terms and conditions thereof	Series HH Bonds, including all terms and conditions thereof except that bonds redeemed prior to maturity will not be subject to the interest penalty
Eligible owners	Registered owners, co-owners and persons entitled as surviving beneficiaries or next of kin or legatees of deceased owners	Same

	SERIES H EXCHANGE	SERIES HH EXCHANGE
Tax treatment	Accrued interest on retired securities may be (1) reported on federal income tax return for year of exchange (or maturity, if earlier), or (2) deferred to the taxable year in which the current income bonds are redeemed, disposed of or mature. Amount of deferred accruals will be shown on face of new bonds	Same
Registration of bonds issued on exchange	Tax deferred: new bonds will be in name of owner and in same forms as securities submitted except that principal coowner, as defined in Circular, may change, add or eliminate co-owner or beneficiary. Non-tax deferred: any authorized form	Same
Cash adjustments	If securities submitted for exchange have current value which is not an even multiple of $500, subscriber may add cash to reach next highest multiple or receive payment of amount in excess of next lower multiple. In the latter case, amount of refund must be reported currently for federal income tax purposes	Same

The Bafflegab of Savings Bonds

ACCRUAL-TYPE SECURITY This is the E or EE bond type—a bond sold at a discount and which gradually increases to above its face amount at maturity. The difference between the purchase price and the amount received for the bond when you redeem it is your interest.

ACCRUED INTEREST Interest that has been earned on savings bonds but has not been collected, because the bond has not been redeemed by the holder.

APPRECIATION-TYPE SECURITY Same as Accrual-type Security, above.

CHAIN-LETTER SCHEMES Illegal get-rich-quick schemes which frequently are built around Series E savings bonds. If you purchase savings bonds as an innocent participant in a fraudulent chain-letter deal, you may request a refund of your money. Get and use Treasury Form PD-2966, available at any local bank.

COLLATERAL Securities or other property pledged by a borrower against the payment of a loan. Savings bonds cannot be used as collateral for loans.

YOUR GUIDE TO UNITED STATES SAVINGS BONDS 1243

CURRENT-INCOME SECURITY This is the H or HH bond type. A bond sold at face value (par value) on which a specified amount of interest is paid semi-annually.

DENOMINATION Face amount of various savings bonds. Both the E and EE bonds have eight denominations, up to $10,000. The H and HH bonds have four, up to $10,000.

EXTENDED MATURITIES Extension by the U. S. Treasury of original maturity date on savings bonds for an additional ten-year period. Owners need do nothing to take advantage of the extension of maturity. Just hold the bonds.

FREEDOM SHARES U.S. savings notes sold from 1967 through mid-1970. No longer on sale. However, the original savings notes were granted a twenty-year extension beyond their initial four-and-a-half-year maturity date at the 6½ per cent current interest rate.

ISSUE PRICE Price actually paid for bond by the buyer. Differs from denominations in E and EE bonds and Freedom Shares, because issue price is at a discount from the denomination, and that difference is the interest which accrues on the bond or share until it finally matures or is redeemed, in advance of final maturity.

NON-MARKETABLE BONDS Non-negotiable securities which cannot be sold or bought in the open market. Savings bonds are non-marketable securities.

PURCHASE LIMIT Maximum of savings bonds which can be bought by one owner in a single year.

REGISTERED BOND Bond with its owner's name recorded on the books of the issuer. With savings bonds, the owner's name is recorded by the United States Treasury.

SAVINGS STAMPS No longer issued by the U. S. Treasury. If you have or find any of these 10-cent to $5.00 stamps, cash them in at your post office or bank (if it will redeem stamps) or add enough cash to acquire a small-denomination E bond.

TAX DEFERMENT Postponement of taxes. Payment of federal income tax on interest accrued on E bonds may be deferred to redemption, other disposition, or final redemption of the bonds.

WAR BONDS Also called Defense Bonds. Series A, B, C, D, F, G, J, K are no longer being issued and are no longer earning interest. If you hold or find any of these series, redeem them at once. Send them by registered mail to the Federal Reserve Bank or branch in your district or to the Bureau of Public Debt, Securities Transactions Branch, Washington, D.C. 20226. Many banks are not qualified to handle this redemption for you. (E and H bonds also no longer are issued but they continue to earn interest.)

25

YOUR GUIDE TO THE EXPLODING COMMODITY MARKETS —FOR SPECULATORS AND HEDGERS

The Two Categories of Traders	1246
Powerful Forces Behind the Boom	1247
How Commodities Are Traded	1248
Market Analysis	1251
fundamental analysis	1251
technical analysis	1252
what is the value of charts?	1252
The Great Pitfalls, How to Identify and Avoid Them	1254
Managed Accounts and Commodity Funds	1256
Where to Get Information on Commodity Trading	1258
Commodities Swindles—Biggest Investment Fraud of the 1970s	1259
the pitch	1260
what's wrong with this pitch?	1260
the con man	1261
the victims	1262
how to protect yourself	1262
The Bafflegab of Commodities	1264

The Two Categories of Traders

How would you like to buy 5,000 bushels of soybeans, or 38,000 pounds of pork bellies, or 1,000,000 Swiss francs? Does this seem more exotic and "far out" to you than buying, say, American Telephone & Telegraph shares or settling for an account in a nearby savings institution?

If the thought of trading such provocative items does appeal to you, you merely would be joining mounting millions of other Americans in all income and age brackets, at all levels of education, men and women, married and single, living in areas scattered throughout the United States who in the 1970s discovered and became active in the commodity futures markets.

Futures trading boomed during the 1970s and the explosive growth shows no signs of slowing, much less ending.

Commodity traders fall into one of two broad categories—hedgers and speculators—and both groups began their spectacular expansion at the start of the 1970s.

Hedgers are individuals or corporations who use the futures markets in the course of their business operations to protect themselves against adverse price fluctuations. Commodity prices can and do fluctuate dramatically, and these changes can have a significant impact on profit margins. When producers and users of commodities can free themselves from worry in this sphere, they can concentrate on running their businesses more efficiently, and this increased efficiency is of general public benefit. Stripped of all hopped-up hoopla, this probably is the most important reason for the existence of futures exchanges.

The number of hedgers has increased sharply for two important reasons: (1) the heightened volatility of commodity prices during the 1970s made hedge protection especially desirable and, in some industries, virtually indispensable; (2) more and more businessmen have learned both the mechanics and the benefits of hedging. Later in this chapter, you'll find references to several publications that discuss this subject in depth for you.

The speculator category is loaded with individuals (qualified or utterly unqualified) who trade commodities because they hope to make money by so doing. Doctors, lawyers, businessmen, accountants, and just about every other occupational group are among the swelling ranks of futures speculators.

Powerful Forces Behind the Boom

Why have so many millions turned on to futures trading in recent years? Among the most powerful forces behind the commodity boom:

(a) The combined impact of accelerated inflation and intermittent worldwide shortages of a wide variety of agricultural and industrial items have sparked substantial price moves in many commodities. These increasingly volatile price changes have been widely publicized, alerting more and more people to the profit opportunities open to those who can accurately forecast commodity prices.

(b) Commodity trading is done on relatively small margin requirements. As a general rule, a speculator must post only about 5 to 20 per cent of the value of the commodity traded. This substantial leverage allows huge sums to be made (or lost) very quickly. It is not at all unusual for a commodity speculator to double or lose all his trading capital within a few weeks.

(c) Futures contracts can be sold short in exactly the same manner as they are bought. Thus it makes no difference whether prices are rising or falling—a trader who can predict correctly how prices will change can profit with equal ease in both bull and bear markets.

(d) The number and variety of futures contracts has multiplied dramatically in recent years. In addition to such traditional items as corn, sugar, and soybeans, the futures spectrum now includes such varied "commodities" as gold, silver, live cattle, foreign currencies, and U. S. Treasury Bills (and by the time you read this, there even may be a futures contract based on the Dow Jones Industrial Average!). If you have a firmly held opinion in any economic arena you probably can find a futures contract that will allow you to put your ideas to the toughest test: risking your whole nest egg.

(e) Commodity market information is easy to obtain. Securities traders have trouble finding up-to-the-minute news on any but the most active of the more than three thousand companies listed on the New York and American exchanges alone. Commodity traders have no such trouble. Only about 35 commodities have active futures contracts, and current information on all of them is readily available. Everyone involved with commodities has access to the facts. Whether you succeed or fail depends on whether you know how to understand and use those facts.

(f) Commission costs for futures transactions are very low—usually amounting to much less than 1 per cent of the value of the underlying commodity. What's more, these charges apply only when a position is closed out, not when it is initiated.

Intriguing, isn't it? If you like action and have a few thousand dollars or more with which to *play*, then the commodity futures markets could be for you. But futures trading can be a bewildering and costly experience if you try it without at least a basic concept of what makes it tick. So here goes . . .

How Commodities Are Traded

Commodities are traded on commodity futures exchanges. These exchanges are located in major U.S. cities, plus London, Paris, Hong Kong, and other cities around the world. The biggest of the dozen or so U.S. exchanges is the Chicago Board of Trade (CBOT), which accounts for about half of all the trading done on U.S. futures exchanges. The Board of Trade was founded in 1848, and is the home of trading in the all-important midwestern agricultural commodities, among the most significant of which are wheat, corn, and soybeans. The Chicago Mercantile Exchange (CME) is the second largest commodity exchange, and in recent years has been the fastest growing. It is the hub of the nation's huge livestock activity, and has active futures contracts in live cattle, live hogs, and frozen pork bellies (bacon), among others. The CME also has a subsidiary exchange known as the International Monetary Market (IMM) which trades futures in eight different foreign currencies. The U.S. dollar's well-publicized battering during the late 1970s helped spark interest in these challenging contracts. Both the CBOT and CME also offer interest rate futures contracts, which became increasingly popular among both financial institutions and speculators after their inception in the mid-1970s.

The Commodity Exchange, Inc., of New York offers futures contracts in gold, silver, and copper, and is the third largest U.S. commodity futures exchange. Other important New York exchanges include: the Coffee, Sugar & Cocoa Exchange, Inc., the New York Cotton Exchange, and the New York Mercantile Exchange. The Kansas City Board of Trade and the Minneapolis Grain Exchange offer futures contracts in types of wheat different from the CBOT. The Mid-America Commodity Exchange (MACE) in Chicago offers "mini-contracts" in several major commodities. For instance, the MACE soybean contract consists of one thousand bushels compared with the CBOT's five-thousand-bushel contract. Outside the United States, the major futures markets are in London. The most important of these are the London Metal Exchange, the London Cocoa Terminal Market, and the London Sugar Exchange.

Despite the rich variety of commodities and locations, all futures markets operate in much the same fashion. Commodity exchanges, like stock exchanges, are membership organizations. Most members are either engaged in the producing, marketing, or processing of commodities, or are brokers whose principal activity is to execute orders for others. Non-members trade through brokerage firms, which hold memberships through partners or officers. The exchanges are supported by dues and assessments on members.

The basic unit in commodity trading is the futures contract. Futures contracts are standardized in terms of quantity, quality, and location and require delivery of the commodity during a specified month in the future. Thus if you, a trader, buy one contract of December soybean oil, you know that you are taking responsibility for sixty thousand pounds of soybean oil that will be delivered in Decatur, Illinois, or at a specified alternate delivery point, sometime in December. Actually, only 1 or 2 per cent of all futures contracts are settled by physical delivery. The rest are offset by an opposite futures transaction prior to maturity.

Commodity futures trading in the United States is strictly regulated both by the exchanges themselves and by the Commodity Futures Trading Commission (CFTC), which is an agency of the federal government. The long history of active trading and the steady growth of participation in futures are evidence of the diligent supervision by both exchange and government personnel.

Most prospective commodity traders have had experience with securities, and the chances are that their own securities firm also handles futures transactions. In addition to the major, full-service brokerage firms, there are firms which specialize in commodities and handle little or no business in other areas. Some brokerage houses require a minimum initial deposit (usually $3,000 to $5,000) to open a commodity account. Others have no minimums and will accept accounts as small as several hundred dollars.

Once your account is opened, trading commodities becomes a simple matter (at least as far as the mechanics are concerned!). You need only call and tell your broker how many contracts of a particular commodity you wish to buy or sell, and at what price. The broker then will relay your order to the trading floor of the appropriate exchange. After it is executed, the brokerage firm's representatives on the trading floor will report back to your broker, who will relay the information to you. Often, this entire procedure takes no more than several minutes. Within a few days of every transaction, you will receive a written confirmation of your activities.

Every time you initiate a futures position you will be required to post a specific amount of margin money with your brokerage firm. Commodity margins are really performance bonds that guarantee the customer's willingness to accept any profits or losses. In general, you, the customer, are asked to put up an original margin deposit equal to 5 per cent to 20 per cent of the total value of the commodities involved. Minimum margin requirements are set by the commodity exchanges themselves, but brokerage houses are free to require higher margins if they wish. Margin requirements are always specific dollar amounts rather than percentages—e.g., $1,000 per contract of copper or $2,500 per contract of soybeans. Unlike the securities market, there are no interest charges on the difference between margin and full cost.

Another unique feature of futures markets is the existence of daily trading limits. To lessen the likelihood of an overly extreme market response to unusually dramatic news, all U.S. (and most foreign) exchanges have adopted maximum fluctuation limits beyond which prices cannot move in the course of a trading session. For example, the daily limit on silver is 20 cents. Thus if July silver closes at $5.50 one day, its permissible range the following day will be $5.30 to $5.70. If there are no bids at or above the lower end of this range or no offers at or below the upper extreme, no trading will take place.

Minimum price fluctuations also are set by the exchanges, and although these usually appear small, the quantities of the various commodities involved are large enough to make even minor price changes significant.

For instance, the minimum price fluctuation for wheat, corn, and soybeans is ¼ cent per bushel. Doesn't sound like much, does it? But multiply that by 5,000 bushels (the size of a single futures contract) and you'll find that you, as a trader, make or lose $12.50 every time the price changes by the minimum amount—which it often does several times a minute! And if that's not fast enough action, you can always trade five, ten, fifty, or more contracts at a time! To give you a clearer idea of what commodity price changes mean to you in terms of real, out-of-pocket dollars, the following table shows the *effects of a 1-cent price move* (up or down) in a variety of the more actively traded items:

Commodity	Exchange	Contract Size	Effect of 1¢ Price Change
Cattle (Live)	Chicago Mercantile	40,000 lbs.	$ 400
Cocoa	New York Cocoa	30,000 lbs.	300
Copper	COMEX (NY)	25,000 lbs.	250
Corn	Chicago Board of Trade	5,000 bushels	50
Cotton	New York Cotton	50,000 lbs.	500
Hogs	Chicago Mercantile	30,000 lbs.	300
Pork Bellies	Chicago Mercantile	38,000 lbs.	380
Potatoes	New York Mercantile	50,000 lbs.	500
Silver	COMEX (NY)	5,000 troy oz.	500
Soybeans	Chicago Board of Trade	5,000 bushels	50
Sugar	New York Coffee & Sugar	112,000 lbs.	1,120
Swiss francs	IMM of CME	125,000 francs	1,250
Wheat	Chicago Board of Trade	5,000 bushels	50

Market Analysis

Commodity traders usually divide market analysis into two general categories—fundamental and technical. Fundamental analysis deals with the basic forces of supply and demand, production and consumption. The fundamentalist wants to know how much is being grown, how much eaten, how much exported, and so forth. He attempts to predict prices by applying basic economic principles to the commodities being traded.

Technicians (or chartists, as they are often called) believe that past market behavior holds the key to successful forecasting. The technician's most important tool is a chart of price action which reflects the interaction of all the various forces of supply and demand. By analyzing various price patterns on their charts, technicians attempt to identify the current trend and project it into the future. Chart analysis has been around since the late nineteenth century, but became especially popular among commodity traders beginning in the mid-1960s.

FUNDAMENTAL ANALYSIS

As a futures trader, you must pay at least some attention to market fundamentals. You may follow only the most general statistics relating to national or international supply and demand considerations. Or you may analyze fundamentals in as much detail as you can, looking at local weather conditions, daily changes in wholesale prices, etc. A general rule is that short-term price movements may depend heavily on minor or localized changes in the supply/demand picture, while long-range trends will be determined by broader forces.

A major attraction of the commodity markets is the fact that so much fundamental information is so readily available. Market news flows from the U. S. Government, the futures exchanges, private research organizations, trade and industry groups, brokerage firms. Through its Departments of Agriculture and Commerce, the U. S. Government is easily the most important source of raw commodity data, releasing huge amounts of data relating to crop production, imports, exports, livestock numbers, etc. Most of the U. S. Government's statistics are carried on the various financial newswires, and the major new releases are printed in the financial section of the big-city newspapers.

Because the output of commodity data is so voluminous, nearly all traders rely to some extent on professional analysts to collect the various pieces of information and put them together in proper perspective. Of the oldest and most respected publications dealing with market fundamentals, two are put out by Commodity Research Bureau, Inc., 1 Liberty Plaza, New York, New York 10006. CRB's Commodity Year Book has been published annually since 1939. The Year Book contains separate statistical sections for each of more than a hundred commodities, more than a hundred charts of long-term price trends, and a wide range of articles each year on subjects of interest to commodity traders.

Commodity Research Bureau also has published a weekly newsletter called Futures Market Service, since 1934, popularly known as the "blue sheet." The blue sheet discusses the current fundamentals affecting each of more than twenty commodities and each week carries an in-depth analysis, complete with charts, of provocative market situations.

Brokerage houses are another worthwhile source of fundamental market information. Most brokerage firms publish weekly or biweekly market letters, and some of the larger firms have internal newswires in each of their branch offices with a portion of the space devoted to commodity news. In addition, nearly every brokerage house branch office that takes its commodity business seriously has at least one of the two major commodity newswires —Reuters and Commodity News Service (CNS). Both of these wire services carry commodity information exclusively and are essential for brokers and traders who want to stay abreast of current market developments. The two services carry virtually the same information, and many brokers choose between them more for reasons of style than substance.

The futures exchanges themselves publish useful information for fundamentally oriented traders as well. The various major exchanges maintain their own statistical departments, which compile and release figures pertinent to their particular futures contracts. Most exchanges publish daily printed market reports disclosing the most important of these statistics along with a summary of the day's trading activity. These letters are available to you, the public, at relatively modest cost.

TECHNICAL ANALYSIS

The central problem which fundamentally oriented traders must face is deciding when a market will respond to the various pieces of its supply/demand puzzle. Few experiences are as frustrating as correctly diagnosing the fundamental outlook and losing money anyway because of poor market timing. After being too early a few times, and too late a few other times, if you are typical of most traders you will turn to technical analysis for assistance.

WHAT IS THE VALUE OF CHARTS?

Here there is a considerable difference of opinion. Some experts hold that price changes in broad, liquid markets are strictly "random" and that price behavior of the past has no relationship whatever to price changes of the future. Others regard charting as some sort of magic key to trading profits, and refuse even to give a passing glance to fundamentals.

The truth must lie somewhere in between. Technical analysis is neither a complete waste of time nor the road to instant wealth. It is an important and valuable forecasting technique used by large and growing numbers of hedgers, speculators, analysts, and others whose businesses require them to anticipate market trends. Technical analysis "took off" in popularity among futures traders starting in the early 1960s, and today even the most diehard fundamentalists pay at least some attention to the charts—even if only to see what the technicians are likely to do next.

The purpose of technical analysis is to measure the relative strengths of buying and selling pressures. The actual forecasting process consists of identifying and interpreting various chart "formations" which, over the years, have correlated with subsequent price moves in a particular direction. Vertical line charts are the most frequently used technical tool. On these charts, each day's price action is represented by a vertical line connecting the high and the low of the session. A short cross line marks the closing price.

Commodity chartists are particularly concerned with identifying *trends*, which play a key role in futures trading. Commodity futures markets have a well-established reputation for extensive moves in one particular direction. Since charts make it possible for you to visualize the presence or absence of a clear trend, no wonder they are popular! The chartist's main objective is to identify the existence of a prevailing trend as quickly as possible after it begins, and to trade with the trend until there is evidence of a reversal.

Do not be dismayed by the following financial bafflegab, but technicians also pay special attention to *support and resistance levels, continuation patterns,* and *reversal formations.*

In simplest explanation, support and resistance areas are price regions in which previous trading activity was especially heavy or meaningful. Because traders have a penchant for "getting even," prices are likely to have difficulty moving above a resistance area or below a support level.

Continuation patterns are pauses of several days to several weeks that usually are followed by a resumption of the previous trend.

Reversal formations, as the name implies, signal major trend changes.

Because constructing charts for the dozens of active futures contracts is such a laborious process, almost all technicians subscribe to a professional chart service. By far the most popular of these services is Commodity Chart Service, published weekly by Commodity Research Bureau, Inc., and containing over two hundred futures charts, analytical comments, and a variety of additional statistical information. As a subscriber you are given (free) booklets explaining the basic principles of chart analysis.

If you want to learn more about chart analysis, you can consult several excellent books on the subject. The so-called bible is *Technical Analysis of Stock Market Trends* by Robert D. Edwards and John Magee (John Magee, Springfield, Massachusetts). While this book deals almost exclusively with securities, most of the technical principles also can be applied to futures.

The same is true of William L. Jiler's *How Charts Can Help You in the Stock Market* (Trendline, New York, New York), a more recent work than that of Edwards and Magee. Jiler is president of Commodity Research Bureau and one of the most widely known and respected authorities on the technical analysis of futures markets.

Though there are "pure" fundamentalists and "pure" technicians, if you are to be like nearly all successful traders you will employ a blend of these two techniques.

Thus, if you think the supply/demand picture for wheat points to significantly higher prices, you would be wise to check whether the wheat charts also look bullish before laying any cash on the line.

Even complete agreement between charts and fundamentals cannot ensure profits, but if you avoid market situations where the two approaches disagree markedly, you will have a useful safeguard against catastrophe.

The Great Pitfalls, How to Identify and Avoid Them

Let's say you are intrigued rather than frightened by the pitfalls that confront all futures traders, you are willing to spend the time learning, say, where soybeans are grown, and you've figured out such bafflegab as the difference between an uptrend line and a symmetric triangle. Now you think you are ready to grab the challenges and make your fortune in grains or livestock or precious metals.

But wait! You are *not* ready unless you also have thoroughly grasped the basic rules of successful commodity trading and have taken a solemn, unbreakable vow that you will respect and obey them always. The rules that follow won't *guarantee* you success (no rules can) but they will give you at least a fighting chance to avoid losing your entire capital and even a chance to win.

(1) Before you trade a single commodity futures contract, make a list of several actively traded commodities whose movements you would like to follow. Learn everything you can about these markets—via United States Department of Agriculture publications, brokerage house letters, and independent advisory services such as Futures Market Service. Keep up-to-date on all basic forces affecting the prices of each item—weather, crop forecasts, consumption trends, etc. You need not know as much as the experts to trade successfully, but even if you rely heavily on the advice of others, you should be able to understand and draw your own conclusions about the advice.

(2) Trade through a reputable brokerage firm that is financially sound and has solid experience in the markets in which you plan to trade too. Most of the major stock brokerage firms have commodity divisions and are well qualified on this score. There also are several well capitalized and highly regarded specialized commodity firms that have national branch office networks.

(3) Do not trade with money that you cannot afford to lose! Commodity trading can be enjoyable, stimulating, and sometimes very profitable. But it is always a *risky* venture. Speculate only with money you can afford to lose without affecting either your financial state or your peace of mind.

(4) Before you begin to speculate, decide on an overall plan and stick to it. Are you a fundamentalist or a technician? Will you be looking for short-term or long-term price moves? How much are you willing to risk before reappraising your trading approach? Answer these and other similar questions as honestly as you can before you risk a single dollar on a futures position.

(5) Be faithful to the old guide: "Cut your losses short and let your profits run." This is the *cardinal* rule of futures trading. The most spectacularly successful commodity speculators have more losing than winning trades, but they come out ahead in the long run because their average profits far exceed their average losses. Many speculators who consistently make money actually profit on only about one third of their trades. Bob Feduniak, now senior vice-president of Commodity Research Bureau, ran the managed commodity account program for one of the largest Wall Street brokerage firms from late 1973 to early 1976. Feduniak told me that during that period he made 215 trades. Of that number, *only 72, or 33 per cent, were profitable,* but his typical account, starting with $15,000–$25,000 showed a net profit of more than $20,000. Taking small losses quickly is the best protection you can have against the one or two ruinous defeats that could remove you from the trading game permanently. Letting profits run is the best way to make the trending tendency of commodity prices work for you rather than against you.

(6) Use stop-loss orders as your most effective safeguard against letting your losses balloon. These orders instruct your broker to offset your position once prices have reached a specified adverse level. Your broker can tell you more about "stops" as they are called, and guide you in placing them. And never—*never*—move your stop order even one penny in the direction of further risk.

(7) Don't try to pick tops and bottoms. While it's only human to try to buy things at their cheapest and sell at their most expensive, in commodity trading that temptation can be suicidal. To repeat it once again, the reason is that futures prices often trend in a particular direction much longer than most people expect. When you spot a trend, ride with it—don't try to guess when it will reverse.

(8) Don't be in the market all the time. Nobody—not even the most astute, full-time professional traders—can understand what is happening in a market day in and day out. At times, fundamentals are confusing, charts look fuzzy, and you can't tell pork bellies from soybean oil. When these times come, as they do for everyone, you belong on the sidelines. Save your

money and your energy for the time ahead when you feel confident about where prices are headed.

(9) Don't trade inactive markets. On some futures markets, average daily trading volume totals ten thousand, twenty thousand, or more contracts. On others, only a handful of contracts are traded each week. Learn which markets are which (the newspapers publish volume statistics) and restrict yourself to the most actively traded commodities. You will find thinly traded markets difficult to move into and out of, and the lack of interested traders usually makes it hard to get vital information.

(10) Don't overtrade. No matter how convinced you are that the price of a particular commodity is headed up or down, resist the temptation to risk a large portion of your trading capital on a single position. Any number of unforeseen events, ranging from hurricanes to wars, can violently change a price outlook literally overnight. *There is no sure thing in commodities*, so always try to diversify into at least two or three markets.

(11) Never trade on the basis of tips or rumors. Base your trading on the best factual information you can find, and ignore the advice of anyone doing you a "favor" by offering "inside information."

(12) Approach commodity trading as an avocation and not a one-shot deal. Realize that commodity trading is an exceedingly complex business, and view your first year or two as an educational period. Pace your trading so you'll be able to learn from early errors and still have enough capital left to take advantage of what you will have learned.

Managed Accounts and Commodity Funds

If by now you're really impressed by the potential rewards of commodity trading and still undaunted but you lack the time or inclination to follow the markets yourself and you fear making your own decisions, then professional account management may be the answer for you. A sizable and growing number of brokerage firms and private traders will handle futures transactions on a strictly discretionary basis. That is: you put up the money, they do the trading. Not surprisingly, the various programs and managers span the spectrum from excellent to fraudulent, so if you are considering this route, you must investigate each situation with utmost caution before laying any cash on the line.

The two most common ways for you to arrange to have your commodity trading handled by someone else are via (1) managed accounts and (2) commodity funds.

A managed account is simply an ordinary commodity account over which you give the manager limited power of attorney. This allows the manager to transact business in your account without consulting you, while you retain responsibility for all profits and losses.

A commodity fund is similar to a securities mutual fund. Each participant owns shares of the fund (or, more typically, units in a limited partnership) and trading is done in the account of the fund rather than in the accounts of the individual participants.

The principal advantages of a commodity fund are limited liability and increased flexibility. As a limited partner, your losses cannot exceed your original investment, whereas in an ordinary commodity (or security) margin account you are liable for any deficits that might occur. Also, since limited partners' funds are pooled, the trading account has the usual advantages of diversification and handling which very large traders also enjoy.

The main advantage of a managed account over a fund is your retention of some control. In general, limited partners have no say in how their fund is handled and can withdraw only at specified times since the secondary market for these units is virtually non-existent. But as the owner of an individual account, you can close the account or revoke power of attorney at any time—giving you greater continuing voice in the handling of your futures money.

The costs of professional money management in commodities are comparatively reasonable. Several of the large brokerage firms maintain internally run managed programs and impose no charges at all beyond the usual commissions. Private managers generally charge a fee of around 1 to 1½ per cent per quarter of an account's equity, plus 5 to 15 per cent of any profits. Most reputable firms require that managed accounts be of a specified minimum size—usually in the $15,000 to $25,000 range.

Smaller accounts usually don't generate enough commissions or fees to offset handling costs unless they are overtraded, so beware of anyone who says that he will "professionally manage" accounts of only a few thousand dollars. Limited partnership units, however, frequently sell for around $1,000 each, and can provide a way for you to get into futures trading with smaller amounts of risk capital.

Paying a professional to trade commodities for you is an easy and potentially profitable way to participate in these exciting markets, but the admonition *caveat emptor* applies with brutal force.

If you are considering a fund or limited partnership, read the prospectus carefully.

Pay particular attention to the backgrounds and qualifications of the managers, and to their prior trading records.

If you are looking at individual managers, ask each for a written (and preferably audited) record of his actual trading results for other clients.

Beware of "hypothetical" or "simulated" track records, since these have a way of losing their luster under real-life market conditions.

Where to Get Information on Commodity Trading

As emphasized earlier, the best sources of commodity information are the United States Department of Agriculture, private research organizations, brokerage houses, and the various futures exchanges.

The Chicago Board of Trade and the Chicago Mercantile Exchange offer the widest selections of basic information of all the exchanges. Write to them at the addresses below for lists of what is available.

Commodity Research Bureau, Inc., with its several publications already discussed, is the leading private publisher of commodity information. CRB offers a wide variety of books, charts, market letters, statistics, and computerized data for all types of traders. You can obtain a complete list of the CRB's products by writing your request to 1 Liberty Plaza, New York, New York 10006.

The USDA publishes vast quantities of commodity material, most available to you free of charge. For catalogs of the most important reports, along with information on ordering them, write to: Crop Reporting Board, U.S.D.A. Room 005, South Building, Washington, D.C. 20250; and to: U.S.D.A. ESCS Information Staff, Publications Unit, Room 0054-South, Washington, D.C. 20250.

Another source of information is the Association of Commodity Exchange Firms, Inc., 1 World Trade Center, New York, New York 10005.

Here are the addresses of the major exchanges to which you might write for additional material:

Chicago Board of Trade
141 West Jackson Boulevard
Chicago, Illinois 60604

Chicago Mercantile Exchange
444 West Jackson Boulevard
Chicago, Illinois 60606

Commodity Exchange, Inc.
4 World Trade Center
New York, New York 10048

New York Coffee and Sugar
  Exchange, Inc.
4 World Trade Center
New York, New York 10048

Kansas City Board of Trade
4800 Main Street
Kansas City, Missouri 84112

New York Cocoa Exchange, Inc.
127 John Street
New York, New York 10038

New York Cotton Exchange
4 World Trade Center
New York, New York 10048

New York Mercantile Exchange
4 World Trade Center
New York, New York 10048

Mid-America Commodity Exchange
175 West Jackson Boulevard
Chicago, Illinois 60604

Minneapolis Grain Exchange
400 South Fourth Street
Minneapolis, Minnesota 55415

Many books are available that cover the various facets of commodity markets and futures trading in some detail, and are worthwhile reading if you want to pursue the subject more deeply. Among the best and most popular are:

Modern Commodity Futures Trading, by Gerald Gold (Commodity Research Bureau, Inc., New York, New York)

The Commodity Futures Game, by Richard J. Teweles, Charles V. Harlow, and Herbert L. Stone (McGraw-Hill, Inc., New York, New York)

The Economics of Futures Trading, by Thomas Hieronymus (Commodity Research Bureau, Inc., New York, New York)

Most daily newspapers provide no more than sparse coverage of commodity news in their financial sections. Beginning in the mid-1970s, however, the *Wall Street Journal* significantly expanded its coverage of futures markets, and its commodity page is worthwhile daily reading for anyone interested in or involved with futures.

COMMODITIES SWINDLES—BIGGEST INVESTMENT FRAUD OF THE 1970S

The fraudulent sale of London commodity options was one of the giant telephone swindles of the late 1970s. Falsely touted as "investments" these speculations turned into nightmares for countless thousands of the defrauded victims.

The fraud was so widespread that in mid-1978, the industry's regulator, the Commodity Futures Trading Commission, actually banned the sale of London commodity options in the United States! But the profits of fraud were so great that many of the promoters easily modified their boiler-room, hard-sell campaigns and started selling either diamonds or managed commodity accounts. (For the diamond scheme, see pages 1299–1302.) As the price of gold soared in this period, the con men moved quickly into fraudulent sales of the leveraged gold contract and the deferred delivery gold contract.

Even though you may be totally disinterested in and ignorant of commodities or metals, options or managed accounts, you still may be the target of some of the cleverest con men who ever have operated in the United States marketplace.

Your ignorance and gullibility can easily betray you. Your greed will steal your savings!

So when your phone rings in early evening and a fast-talking pitchman tells you in glib terms about the fortunes being made in managed commodity accounts, or leveraged gold contracts, be on guard! First some basics.

Some commodities—such as sugar, coffee, copper—are bought and sold in large quantities in auction markets in London and the United States. That is what this whole chapter has been about. And as stressed, it's complicated.

Playing with commodities is only for you if (1) you are a sophisticated speculator, (2) you are more than typically familiar with the intricacies of the market, and (3), most important, you can afford to lose all the money you put up.

If this chapter convinces you merely of these three points and compels you to be cautious, I will have achieved my goal.

THE PITCH

In New York, in Florida, in Ohio, all over the Midwest and West Coast, London commodity options were pushed by such sales pitches as the following hypothetical come-on:

"Hello, Mr. Wilson, I'm calling from ZYX Commodities Co. We sell London options. You know what the price of coffee has done lately and we think sugar is about to do the same thing. But I'm not calling to sell you anything. Just to tell you about commodity options. These are an amazing investment opportunity now available to the American public for the first time.

"As an example, several months ago, we were recommending the purchase of $2,000 copper options. Within one month, the option our clients bought was worth $6,000. That's a killing! I will mail you all the facts so you can see in black and white how you can double and triple your money. The sugar move is already on its way..."

About eight days and seven calls later, another call:

"Mr. Wilson, you've already made $110. I bought you an option for $2,500, today it went to $2,610. Wire me the money right away to pick up your option in London.

"My commission? Only 10 per cent. Check us out with the Commodities Futures Trading Commission (CFTC). We're registered. And if you want a banking reference, call..."

WHAT'S WRONG WITH THIS PITCH?

(1) Again, the often prestigious sounding but meaningless company name; the wild claims of gains across the board—possible, but highly improbable; the con man's comment that he has reserved an option for you in their London office. There probably isn't even a London office.

(2) As for the 10 per cent commission—not likely! Instead, the commission is likely to be at least double. Commission, fees, overhead, and *profits* may take 60 per cent of your outlay. Buying an option from someone else would be a lot, lot cheaper.

(3) Registered with the CFTC? Yes, by law the firm had to be. But some companies operated without registration. The CFTC found enforcement of its regulations to be exceedingly tough and finally just outlawed London commodity options. What's more, registration with the CFTC did not mean

you could believe a telephone pitch. And of course, the company will have a pile of money in the bank (perhaps, including yours).

Beware! The biggest commodity sold in these instances is deception.

THE CON MAN

While obviously the convicted felons operating in the London commodity options market are in a minority, the con man element is a large one. Who are some of these con men?

• One high-pressure promoter working for a company denied registration by the Commodities Futures Trading Commission (CFTC) is a felon who was released from jail in mid-1976 after having been convicted of defrauding gullible investors out of hundreds of thousands of dollars in a "business opportunities" scheme in New Jersey. While in options, he advertised for a "partner" to invest $10,000 in a new venture, claiming in his ad that after the partner put up the $10,000, he would earn a salary of $800 a week.

• The principal of another option company, with offices in New York and Florida, was the subject of action by the Florida attorney general while operating a Florida land resale rip-off. This slippery swindler took money from landowners for assistance in helping them to sell their land, then went out of business, leaving the property owners stuck with their land but without their cash. After options he switched into diamonds but that company folded leaving rent unpaid. Present whereabouts? Unknown.

• A Massapequa Park, New York, resident, a former salesperson for a New York options firm, now bankrupt, pleaded guilty in New York State Supreme Court to a felony arising from her securing her salesman's registration without revealing that she had been permanently enjoined previously from offering or selling securities and commodities within and from New York State. In another, an individual who had been convicted for stealing securities first went to work as a salesman for an options house and, when it folded, formed his own options firm, which failed a few months later. He "accomplished" all of this while on parole!

• *The pattern is clear:* the salespeople and boiler-room organizers travel from options house to options house after the firm for which they are working goes out of business leaving large debts to customers. Often their first entrance into commodity options is when the marginal securities house in which they had been employed goes out of business.

• Record-keeping at these firms is, at best, inadequate and, at worst, horrendous and chaotic. Investigators have discovered that even normal books of accounts used by any business aren't established or maintained. Sending confirmations to customers and mailing checks to customers often are delayed for unreasonable periods or, in many instances, never sent.

In one firm, an employee was able to forge his signature to company checks and received more than $80,000 based on the forged checks without being detected. In documented cases, customers who did receive payments due them actually were receiving funds that had been put into the firm by more recent customers—a modern-day version of one of the oldest swindles in finance.

• Salesmen for the firms are practicing "boiler-room" techniques—swindles that most of you almost surely thought were past history by now. Individuals who had been permanently enjoined from dealing in the offer or sale of commodities and securities have been found working for commodity options firms. Some salesmen have had records of felon convictions for interstate transportation of stolen securities, arson, bad checks, assault charges, etc.

There is a thread which ties together many of these gypsters—and they appear to move almost as a group from one area to another, from securities to diamonds to London commodity options, Scotch whisky, or silver.

THE VICTIMS

Who are the victims of commodity options fraud? Who is likely to be ripped off? Is there a chance that you—if you are typically gullible and typically greedy—will get involved?

"I purchased two sugar options at a total price of $7,300 and, as you know, lost the whole thing," wrote a small-town Michigan businessman to the Better Business Bureau in Metropolitan New York. (He expressed no regret.)

"My father-in-law received ten phone calls in ten days from the same saleslady," a bank executive in Ohio reported. The saleslady claimed that the profit on a $6,500 copper option could easily range from $12,000 to $13,000.

A typical victim:

(1) Is not wealthy but has a nest egg in savings;

(2) Is a middle-aged male operating his own business, quite probably in a rural area;

(3) Has little or no experience making his own investment decisions; and

(4) Before the pitchman phoned, had never heard of London commodity options.

Recognize yourself? Or a close friend or relative?

HOW TO PROTECT YOURSELF

It's your nest egg that's at stake. You must know not only what you are buying, but from whom you are buying as well.

How can you protect yourself from the con men preparing right now to defraud you?

And be warned: London commodity options and phony "managed accounts" in commodities were just the favorites in the late 1970s. In past years, Scotch whisky, diamonds, and silver have been favorites; in the next decade solar energy, insulation, and others will undoubtedly emerge.

Most of you who will get the telephone sales pitch shouldn't be speculating in commodities, and certainly not risking your life's savings.

Because of the volatile nature of the commodity markets, the trading of commodity futures or options was not and is not suitable for most members of the public. You should not, I repeat again, purchase a commodity contract or an option unless you are prepared to sustain a total loss of your commitment.

Here are some simple rules to remember if and when a salesman calls:

(1) Don't discount your own common sense, skepticism, experience. If a stranger promises you over the phone to double your money in several months, ask the obvious question: "If it is so easy to make so much money so fast, why is he letting me in on it?"

(2) Refuse to make an important investment decision over the phone. In the real world, big-time deals transacted over the phone are between people who may never see each other but who know and have respect for each other's credentials. Again, ask the obvious: "If it's so easy to make so much, why does this stranger have to phone me?"

(3) Ask for references for both the salesman and the company. What was the salesman selling last year? For whom did he work in the past? If he was in the business of advising on securities, what was he promoting and how did his recommendations work out? (Don't accept mere verbal assurance; get this in writing.) Compare the answers to your questions with your own knowledge (or the advice of experts) on what actually did happen to the securities he recommended and, again, double-check the answers. If you are an utter innocent in this sphere, move away fast.

(4) Educate yourself in the basics before you risk your savings in any kind of investment—particularly anything as speculative as commodities. Don't be taken in by the alluring promises of a pitchman. Use your head.

(5) Ask any phone salesman at least these questions: How did you get my name? What is the total price I will pay for this option? Commissions, fees, other charges?

(6) Be sure you also are fully aware of how much money you will get back (if any) if the market moves against you or if you will have to put up any more money during the life of the contract. And get it in writing. You can't trust the spoken word!

(7) Ask questions, be tough and persistent in demanding answers in writing on company letterheads signed by a company officer whose credentials you can and you *do* check. That still doesn't protect you completely, but at least it's a starter.

(8) Be on guard from the beginning about prestigious-sounding company names and references. The names may be meaningless; they certainly may

be misused. As for excellent banking references, con men usually have solid bank deposits (other people's money).

(9) Freely admit your own gullibility and ignorance. You wouldn't put thousands of dollars in a local bank without asking several key questions. How can you put the money in diamonds and options without seeking at least some fundamental facts?

(10) If you have a question about commodity options, call the CFTC's hotline at (800) 424-9838. You may get a tape message. Leave your name and phone number and your call will be returned.

(11) Never speculate on impulse. Never confuse "speculation" with "investment." An investment carries a modest or minimal risk, offers some return, some degree of security. Inherent in speculation is a "major chance of loss." Never confuse a con game with either.

THE BAFFLEGAB OF COMMODITIES

ACCUMULATION Building up of either a long or short position in a given commodity by buying or selling contracts over a period of time.

ACTUALS (Spot commodities): Physical commodities. Goods available for immediate delivery, as opposed to futures contracts.

ARBITRAGE Simultaneous buying and selling of the same commodity in two different markets to profit from a temporary price discrepancy.

AT THE MARKET Order to buy or sell a contract at whatever is the best price available at the time the order reaches the pit (or market). Also called "Market Order."

BASIS The price difference over or under a designated futures contract at which a given cash commodity is quoted.

BID Price offer made by a buyer for a specific quantity of a commodity.

BOT Abbreviation for "bought," widely used in the stock and bond as well as commodity markets.

BREAK Sharp price decline for a given commodity.

BULGE Sharp price advance.

BUY ON CLOSE To buy at close of a trading session at a price prevailing at that time. Buying on opening means to buy at a price within the range at the opening of a trading session.

CARRYING CHARGE Charges incurred in carrying the actual commodity including interest, insurance, and storage.

CASH COMMODITY Same as actuals.

CCC Commodity Credit Corporation. Wholly government-owned corporation established in 1933 to assist agriculture through price support programs and other measures.

CFTC Commodity Futures Trading Commission. The federal agency which regulates trading on the commodity exchanges in this country and also administers the Commodity Exchange Act.

COMMISSION HOUSE A concern that buys and sells actual commodities or futures contracts for the accounts of customers.

CONTRACT A unit of the commodity being traded. The amount of the unit is set for each commodity by the exchange where it is traded.

COVER Shorts are said to "cover" when they buy back the contracts they had previously sold, thereby liquidating their position.

CROP YEAR Period from harvest of a crop to the same period in the following year. Thus the United States wheat crop year is June 1 to May 31.

DAY ORDERS Orders that are to be executed the day for which they are effective and are automatically canceled at the close of that day.

DELIVERY MONTH The calendar month during which a futures contract matures.

DELIVERY NOTICE A notice of intention to deliver a stated quantity of a commodity in settlement of a futures contract.

DISCRETIONARY ACCOUNT Account under which you specifically authorize your broker to place buy and sell orders for you—without your having to give the broker your consent prior to each order. Your broker, in short, has "discretion" over your account.

FILL OR KILL ORDER Order which requires that it be either executed at once or that it be canceled.

FUTURES CONTRACT Agreement to buy and receive or to sell and deliver a commodity at a future date and in accord with the established rules of a futures exchange.

HARD SPOT Period of strength in a commodity market usually due to heavy buying.

HEDGE In its simplest form, a hedge is a sale of a commodity futures contract against a purchase of actuals, or vice versa. It is a medium through which offsetting commitments are employed to eliminate or minimize the impact of an adverse price movement on inventories or other previous commitments.

LIMIT Maximum fluctuation in the price of a futures contract permitted during one trading session as fixed by the rules of a contract market.

LONG Person who is on the buying side of the futures contract.

MARGIN The amount which you deposit with your broker as a guarantee that you will fulfill your financial obligation in cases of losses on contracts being carried or to be carried by the brokers. In the commodity market, margins generally range between 5 and 20 per cent of the actual value of the contract.

MARGIN CALL Demand by your broker for additional funds to cover losses in the event of a price decline in the commodity for which you own a contract—in order to restore your deposit to original level required or maintenance requirements. Or a margin call may be the demand to deposit the original margin at the time of the transaction.

MARKET ORDER   Order to your broker to buy or sell a futures contract at the best possible price as soon as received.

OPEN INTEREST   The number of outstanding futures contracts. It refers to the total quantity of unliquidated purchases or sales, and never their combined total.

OPEN ORDER   Buy or sell order which is considered good unless and until you cancel it.

OPEN OUTCRY   Method of registering all bids and offers in the pits.

PAPER PROFIT   Unrealized profit that a holder of a commodity contract has and that can be realized by offsetting his open position.

PITS   Platforms (locations) on the trading floor of a commodity exchange on which traders and brokers stand as they trade in particular commodities.

POSITION   Your stake in the commodity market—via long or short ownership of a futures contract.

PURCHASE AND SALE STATEMENT   A statement sent by a commission house to a customer when his futures position has been wholly or partly offset. It generally shows the quantities and prices involved, the gross profit or loss, commission charges, and the net profit or loss. (Frequently referred to as a P and S.)

PYRAMIDING   Using profits of open or unliquidated positions to add to your original position.

RANGE   The difference between the high and low price of a futures contract during a given period (often a single trading session).

RING   Same as "Pits," above.

ROUND TURN   Completion of your order to buy a futures contract and, later, to sell it as well. Or, vice versa, completion of both a sale and purchase order.

SHORT   Person who is on the selling side of a futures contract.

SPOT COMMODITIES   Same as "Actuals," above.

SPREAD (also STRADDLE)   The simultaneous purchase and sale of two different but related futures contracts. The objective is to profit by forecasting changes in price relationships rather than in absolute price levels.

STOP-LOSS ORDER   Order to buy or to sell a futures contract when the market reaches a given price. Primarily used as a protection to limit your losses or protect profits.

VISIBLE SUPPLY   Amount of a particular commodity in store at trading centers.

VOLUME   The number of futures contracts traded during a particular period (usually a single session).

26

YOUR MOST SIMPLE GUIDE TO BUYING LAND

WHAT DO YOU WANT?	1268
WHAT ARE YOU BUYING?	1269
HOW CAN YOU FIND IT?	1269
WHERE ARE THE BARGAINS?	1270
BUYING LAND—PROS AND CONS	1271
DISADVANTAGES OF BUYING LAND	1271
ADVANTAGES OF BUYING LAND	1271
TEN RULES FOR INVESTING IN LAND	1272
YOU MUST READ THE PROPERTY REPORT	1273
ARE YOU BEING HUSTLED?	1274

What Do You Want?

For profit and as a hedge against inflation over the years, you want desperately to buy land. You are scarcely unusual! *But:*

Know your objectives. Capital appreciation or income? Living space—primary residence, or vacation home?

Know your financial limitations. Investment or speculation? Security or risk?

Do you plan to live on the land? Or do you want to turn a nice profit in seven years without your ever tending it? Or a little of both? Your objective will determine the kind of land you purchase.

If you want to live on the land, it should be habitable and near a job if you need one. If a campsite or a weekend retreat is your objective, *commute* the distance several times in both good weather and bad *before you buy*.

If speculation is your goal, then you must know far more than these few pages will tell you. If the money with which you are speculating is an essential part of your net worth, then stop right here. If you are speculating in land, nothing you read in these pages should be new to you. If you are reading any angles here for the first time, you don't know what you are doing. Put your money elsewhere.

Whatever your objectives in buying land, write all the facts on paper in your own words. Put down the numbers; initial cash outlay; interest charges on the loan; attorney's fees; filing fees; title search. Now add in the costs of using the land: an access road, both building and maintenance costs; site clearing costs; water, sewer, and power installation costs; structural costs; travel expense to and from the location. And the kicker: calculate the interest you would have made had you merely left your initial cash outlay in a savings institution and avoided all the additional expense you have just tallied. Add some reasonable amount for the dollar value of the man-hours you and your family will devote to owning this property.

Put aside all these figures and read them again tomorrow. Make sure you and your family clearly understand your objectives and the costs of achieving them before you buy.

What you are reading is just a brief outline of the kind of careful examination you must make before you proceed with a major purchase in land.

And this is designed only for one person or family buying one residential piece of property. Any investment in commercial real estate is far too complex a subject for treatment here. If commercial real estate investment or speculation is what you are seeking, then the basic information in this chapter cannot possibly prepare you to make an intelligent decision. Unless you want to master the material yourself by enrolling in several real estate courses at a university-level business school in your vicinity, or unless you want to try to graduate from the school of hard knocks, you must get professional advice.

What Are You Buying?

Get a map. A good topographical map will give you a tremendous amount of information about a piece of land before you even see it. It should show natural features such as ground coverage, swamps, lakes, streams, deserts, plus man-made features such as roads, power lines, dams, cultivated land, and towns and building. Check with the United States Geological Survey for the map of the proper section. By studying the map several times prior to visiting the site you should be prepared to make a thorough and efficient on-site examination.

Plan to spend some time on the site. Perhaps a couple of visits at different times of day would be good over a weekend. Concentrate on critical features: drainage; winds; easements; layout of your planned buildings; septic tanks and water sites on adjacent lots, and the ones you plan for yours.

A pretty view should be a secondary consideration. Other nearby property probably has the same or a similar view.

Make sure *you buy* and are *not sold*. Land developers offer few bargains. Assume a real estate salesman will not tell you the negative characteristics of the property you are looking at. You must know enough to ask the right questions, evaluate the answers, pursue an independent inquiry. But test your real estate salesperson by letting him talk first. Then ask your questions and see how clear and forthcoming his answers are. If his replies concur with the information you get from independent third parties, give him credit. You have an honest real estate salesperson.

How Can You Find It?

Bargains are rarely advertised. Land is no exception and may be worse than most retail purchases. The bigger the land developers' promotion, the less of a bargain you are getting. You pay for everything: the advertising, the fancy brochures, the dinners, the trips to the development, the free gifts and "vacations," the stock offering and the salesman's hefty commission.

So make sure you understand that a land promotion in which the sellers woo you will rarely turn out a bargain for you.

So, how do you find the bargains? With difficulty. Talk to local people: the mailman, the gas station attendant, the bread man, the milk man, if they still come to the house. They regularly tour the neighborhood. They know the changes, who's moving, who has died, where building is going on. Check the local paper's obituary columns for the last six months. Subscribe to the local paper if you know you want to buy property in a local town or county. Drive out to see a particular site that attracts you and then visit the county courthouse to check the assessor's records for ownership.

Where Are the Bargains?

If you're an amateur, a good place to begin your search for sound investments in land is in your own "back yard." The reasons are obvious. You've been living with local trends in real estate. Here is where you've watched the process of buying and selling among neighbors, friends, and outsiders. You undoubtedly know quite a bit about prices now being paid and about how those prices dwarf those paid five or ten years ago. You have a good idea of what is and what isn't a bargain.

If you live in any major suburb, you almost surely have seen prices climb steeply to levels often double or triple those of the early 1970s (the prices are astronomical in some wealthy suburbs, and thus the dollar totals don't mean much). What's more, there is no sign of anything more than an interruption in these trends in the years directly ahead.

Here, according to the National Association of Real Estate Boards and other key sources, are some of the best places to shop for reasonably priced raw land with a good profit potential:

(1) In the suburbs. Although prices in many areas seem dreadfully inflated, reasonable buys still do exist—and with more than 70 per cent of our expanding population continuing to congregate in the nation's major metropolitan areas, the likelihood is for sustained price advances in the years ahead. Consult local real estate agents on going prices for various types of land in this category; on zoning matters affecting property which appeals to you; on current population growth trends; plans for new or expanded public services, schools, hospitals, bus lines, recreational facilities, etc.

(2) Areas just beyond the suburbs.

(3) Exurbs—areas beyond the suburbs but still accessible to major city facilities—into which increasing numbers of corporations have moved, followed, of course, by the movement of employees and their families, with obvious impact on land values. If you are investing in land with the objective of later resale for industrial use, though, be warned: *musts are adequate transportation facilities,* appropriate utilities, labor sources.

(4) Recreational areas—particularly "water-oriented" land near lakes, rivers, fishing brooks and streams, shorelines within three to five hours' drive of major metropolitan areas.

(5) Commercially zoned real estate near airports and with good accessibility to the airports. Industrial parks are burgeoning in these areas as reliance on air freight increases.

(6) Any land within the boundaries of any U.S. megalopolis with some very special attribute: a beautiful view, woodlands, a tempting body of water, a very attractive location. You'll have to pay extra for these special aspects. But the future profit potential also is likely to be much greater than the potential for an ordinary parcel of land.

(7) Properties already in the process of change and upgrading by others —through the installation of new public facilities, planned new roads or highway interchanges, parking facilities, an urban renewal or rural beautification project, a new town, a reservoir or park or man-made lake.

Buying Land—Pros and Cons

DISADVANTAGES OF BUYING LAND

(1) In all parts of the country, property taxes have soared—and taxes, of course, are a major part of the cost of land-ownership. Moreover, property taxes tend to leap with each sale.

(2) High interest rates add heavily to the cost of real estate you buy with borrowed money.

(3) To invest in real estate, you generally must be prepared to commit a sizable sum of money—say $10,000 or more—in order to turn any significant profit. You can obtain a stake in securities with much less.

(4) Real estate is one of the least liquid of all investments, and it may take months or years to dispose of a property at a price you approve. Realtors' commissions, when you sell, can cost 10 per cent or more of the selling price.

(5) Some forms of real estate—such as land slated for recreational purposes—are highly vulnerable in any period of business recession. So an investor in this type of land must be prepared to accept such risks and be prepared to sit out a prolonged downturn. In the depression of the 1930s there was simply no market at all and several times in the 1970s the market became exceedingly "sticky." (The "advantage" side of this was that you could pick up tremendous bargains at tax auctions.)

(6) There is no formal market for buying and selling real estate, as there is for trading securities. And there is no really solid way for the small investor to investigate and compare values in various parts of the country.

ADVANTAGES OF BUYING LAND

(1) The key advantage, of course, is the relatively high return you can achieve over the long term on any sound investment in real estate.

(2) By investing in real estate and making your profit on land, you can

get favorable tax treatment when you sell because your land profits are treated as capital gains.

(3) You can get the great benefit of "leverage," for you may be able to borrow between 60 and 75 per cent of the cost of the property and thus tie up only a small amount of your own capital. To illustrate how leverage works, let's say you invest in a $10,000 parcel of land with a $3,000 down payment; you get a ten-year mortgage for the remaining $7,000 at 8 per cent interest a year. And let's say you're able to resell at $15,000 after two years, which isn't an unrealistic achievement. Your monthly mortgage payments on the $7,000 loan are $85 and after two years you've paid off $1,000 in principal and $1,040 in interest (tax-deductible). Your net profit on the deal is $3,960 ($15,000 less $11,040)—but your total outlay has been just $5,040. That's an 80 per cent profit in only two years!

(4) Finally, debt in itself is a hedge against inflation because you borrow "expensive" dollars, repay with increasingly "cheap" dollars over the years.

Let's assume you feel the advantages win. Let's assume, therefore, that even though you're a complete amateur you have decided to try a modest investment in land.

Ten Rules for Investing in Land

What I have given you in this short chapter is only a primer—for if you are going into investing in land in a serious way, what you need most at this beginning stage is an easy-to-read guide outlining the most basic points for you in broad strokes. Then you carry on to find the facts which will tell you whether your specific investment is the right one for you.

What, then, are the fundamental rules for investing in land for you, an amateur?

(1) Before you invest, get answers to this key question: How can the land actually be used when you sell it? For housing? Fishing? Hunting? Swimming? Enjoying a good climate? Skiing? Shopping center? Retirement homes? Summer vacations? Winter vacations? Industrial parks? Your profit when you resell the land will depend largely on the uses to which the buyer can put it.

(2) Also, before you invest, find out from local census statistics, local Realtors, gossipy individual citizens, other sources in the area: Are there local shortages of housing and available land? How fast is the section which interests you growing? (This rate could be obscured by the growth rate for the area as a whole.) Is the land suitable for building? What have similar properties been selling for?

(3) Calculate how much money you would have to invest to turn the property into one which you could resell at a maximum profit. Or will time alone probably bring you adequate profits on a resale? An investment could

be brutally costly, entail bringing in telephone lines, building a road, cutting views, clearing, finding and drilling for water, on and on.

(4) Study the possibilities of making the land earn money during the period in which you are waiting to resell. Among the choices: planting trees, raising some other crop, selling timber rights, charging admissions to hunters and campers, renting pasture land. Other ideas will be suggested by what nearby owners do.

(5) If you intend to resell a part of the property right away, sell the less valuable parts first. The more desirable parts of the land tend to grow more rapidly in value.

(6) Be on guard if a property is advertised as a "distress sale." However, notes Don G. Campbell, author of *The Handbook of Real Estate Investment*, "hell hath no fury like a property owner whose love affair with a piece of real estate has flagged"—so at least investigate the "distress."

(7) Try to gauge what the effect of various national economic developments will be on the value or salability of any land you buy. For instance, if a business recession, fuel shortages, or similar misfortunes dampened sales of vacation properties, could you hold on until the nation was again in a strong upturn?

(8) Shop for the best possible financing deal—a fundamental point which becomes particularly important in any period of high or rising interest rates. If you can arrange a comparatively favorable mortgage rate and if you can pass on this mortgage to a future buyer, this could be a real "plus."

(9) Avoid ultra-cheap, undeveloped land in the middle of nowhere—especially if it's being pushed in high-pressure promotions. There are millions of acres of raw land that are just as unwanted and undeveloped now as they were two hundred years ago.

(10) And study books about land as an investment. Get the most expert advice you can find (and be willing to pay for it). Treat this investment with the respect it demands!

You Must Read the Property Report

Because of the great land frauds in the 1970s, more states require registration of land offerings within the state. In addition, the United States Department of Housing and Urban Development requires that interstate land offerings comply with the Interstate Land Sales Full Disclosure Act. In the past, many victims simply have not bothered to read the information available to them.

The property report is like a prospectus in a stock offering: it should contain all the material facts about the land development and the proposed sale. In the late 1970s, HUD streamlined the property report because the public found it too difficult to understand. But if you're dealing with a land developer, whether selling land intrastate or interstate, you must read the offering statement or propery report.

You may find that many of the improvements in the development which the salesman mentioned are in early planning stages and that the developer has no obligation to carry them out. Nor has financing been arranged. The promotional literature might convey a different impression.

You may find that the well-known company whose name is used in the promotion actually has no corporate connection with, nor financial responsibility, for the success of the development.

You surely should be fully aware of the fact that an offering is registered with the state or HUD does *not* mean that the state in any way recommends or endorses the offering.

You also should read that, under certain conditions, you may have forty-eight hours to revoke the contract without penalty.

You may find, too, that there is no regular water service to the land tract; that purchasers must obtain water from private sources at their own expense.

You may learn that the United States Government has a perpetual right to overflow the banks of the river in the development in order to facilitate irrigation operations.

You may discover that temporary structures are prohibited and that no campers will be allowed for permanent residence.

These are just a few of the items that you might find in a property report or offering statement. Never sign a document stating that you have read the property report until you have not only read it but studied it with utmost care as well!

Never sign a document waiving your right to cancel within forty-eight hours.

And never rely on someone else's summary of a property report or offering statement.

If you are unwilling to take the time to read the report yourself, then you are not investing your money to buy land. You are giving your nest egg away.

Are You Being Hustled?

During the 1970s, countless thousands of Americans were swindled out of millions of dollars when con men sold them desert land as an investment. Few of those con men ever went to jail. Few of the companies had to pay back any substantial percentage of the money they made in the form of fines. There was little restitution to any of the victims.

Old people, young people, middle-aged people were sold thousands of acres of desert land as vacation homes, retirement homes, or "great" investments. But their dollars blew away with the sand. The promoters made a killing selling a fraction of an acre for $2,000 to $5,000 after they had bought the land for next to nothing.

Therefore, when you are dealing with a land developer who is pressing you hard to make a cash outlay, be alert to the likelihood that you are being hustled!

- Be suspicious if you get an unsolicited phone call inviting you to a dinner to hear about a great land offering.
- Never sign a contract at a dinner or any other kind of promotional gathering designed to stimulate your emotions and dull your judgment.
- Never buy land without visiting the property.
- Never buy land in another state before thoroughly examining the "property report" which the developer must give you to be in compliance with the Interstate Land Sales Full Disclosure Act.
- Always check on the financial position of the developer by asking for an audited financial statement.
- Determine what improvements, if any, the developer will provide.
- Never make your decision to buy during the first inspection to the site when you're being pitched by a salesman, but don't have adequate time to make a thorough inspection or evaluate the offer.
- Learn the names of the principals and officers of the development and how long they have been associated with this firm or similar firms.
- Before closing any deal, retain an attorney who has had experience in land transactions.
- Never sign an installment contract without fully understanding the interest charges, the monthly payments, the total of the monthly payments, and your ability to maintain them.
- Get a written statement of the consequences if you miss a payment, or several payments. If you miss a payment, do you forfeit your right to own the land or lose any credit for installments already paid?
- Always be suspicious of any high-pressure sales tactics, elaborate promotional dinners, glossy brochures, and starlet-filled movies.

None of these has anything to do with investing in land! Rather, in the past, they have been the hallmarks of the land hustle.

27

YOUR GUIDE TO OFF-BEAT AND ON-TARGET

Where the "Smart Money" Has Been Going	1279
If You Want to Buy Gold, Here's How	1279
Five Methods	1280
Beware the Gold Bug! It Bites!	1281
The Pitfalls in the Pitch	1282
How to Protect Yourself	1283
Or Gold Jewelry	1285
Shop the Stores	1285
Karats, Other Terms	1285
How to Buy "Collectables"	1287
Be on Guard	1287
And "Nostalgia" Collectables	1288
Antiques as an Arena	1289
An Insatiable Taste	1289
Key Forces	1290
Fundamental Rules	1290
Four Categories for Bargains in Antiques	1291
The Lure of Oriental Rugs	1292
Up 10–15 Per Cent Annually	1292
Pitfalls for Sellers and Buyers	1293
Guidelines	1293
Coins Not for Spending	1294
Spectacular Upsurge	1294
How to Appraise Your "Collection"	1295
If You Are a Beginner	1295

Diamonds: a Dilemma	1296
dizzying spiral	1296
caution!	1297
if you buy	1297
how to spot a diamond gyp	1298
the future	1299
diamond gyps over the phone	1299
what's wrong with the pitch?	1300
a few additional guidelines	1301
Feverish Boom in Art	1302
all price records broken	1302
forces at work	1303
ten rules to guide you in art investing	1304
five types of art for rapid "growth"	1305
Prints Roar On Too	1306
big winner	1306
factors behind buying explosion	1306
basic rules for buying prints	1307
seven categories for investing	1308
what determines values of prints?	1309
Stamps as Investments	1310
upswing year after year	1310
three levels of investment	1311
do's and don'ts for investing in stamps	1312
Books Not for Reading	1313
one of the richest eras ever	1313
basic rules for neophytes	1314
Vintage Cars—for Fun and Profit	1315
another love affair with cars	1315
pitfalls!	1317
three classifications	1317
guidelines	1318
How to Choose an Appraiser	1319
who are the appraisers	1319
questions to ask	1320

Where the "Smart Money" Has Been Going

In the late 1960s, stock prices across-the-board stumbled into a plunge so prolonged and at times perpendicular that Wall Street earned the unenviable reputation of being a disaster area. Since then tens of billions of dollars of "smart money" have moved in mounting volume into the off-beat investment spheres.

Among them: coins which are not for spending . . . books which are not for reading . . . paintings which are not for viewing . . . stamps which are not for postage. All are beyond the traditional mediums, involve possibilities for profit and risks for loss that would challenge any imagination. And challenges the mediums have been indeed, and still are in every sense of the word.

In fact, the old gag about the wheeler-dealer who tried to unload a railroad car of rotten sardines on a skeptical buyer was even more appropriate at the end of the 1970s than at the start. For protested the fast-talking salesman:

"These are not *eating* sardines, these are just *buying* and *selling* sardines!"

If off-beat areas intrigue you, the following pages are designed specifically to help you turn your sense of the unusual into maximizing your profits and minimizing your losses . . . as well as having fun . . .

If You Want to Buy Gold, Here's How

As the worldwide demand for gold as a haven of safety continued powerful and undiminished into the late 1970s, the number of ways you could buy the precious metal multiplied. Some ways make it simpler to buy; others make it less expensive to hold; all are designed as lures to draw you into the gold market.

But do not permit yourself to be lulled into overconfidence by any of the appeals. Gold buying is a speculation; as is true of all speculations, there are traps for the uninformed, pitfalls for the unwary. And while it is indisputable that gold was a great buy in the 1970s—as the new decade neared, its price had more than quintupled since gold was torn from its long-standing peg of $35 an ounce—it was an utterly sterile and costly holding for a prolonged span of time before the upward move finally began.

FIVE METHODS

Here are five of the ways you can participate in ownership of gold—if you want to despite all the warnings and the determination of many major governments around the world to minimize the role played by gold in the international monetary system:

(1) You can, if you have a hefty bankroll, take part in the periodic auctions of gold held by the United States Government. The smallest amount you can buy is a 400-ounce bar. Merely to submit a bid, you must place a $10-an-ounce deposit. Purchasers at these auctions have been primarily European banks.

(2) You can buy "gold deposit certificates," a new instrument introduced at the end of the 1970s.

You can buy the certificates in minimum units of $2,500, representing an undivided but specific interest in gold bullion with a minimum fineness of 0.995. The metal is registered and stored in bulk at a depositary bank in Zurich. The potential return to you, the buyer of the certificates, lies solely in the market increase in the price of gold. If the price of the metal falls, you, as a gold deposit certificate holder, are the loser.

(3) You can buy "common" gold coins, such as the South African Krugerrand (1.0 ounces), the Mexican 50 peso (1.2057 ounces), and the Austrian 100 crown (0.9802 of an ounce). These coins are attractive solely because of their gold content in contrast to numismatic coins which sell for large premiums over their gold content. American gold coins minted before 1932 sell for a 200 to 300 per cent premium over their gold content. You must have expert guidance and be cautious in buying them.

Common gold coins are rarely counterfeited, are quickly recognizable, and are bought and sold by most dealers at a narrower spread or markup than on small gold bars.

(4) You can buy gold bars, but here you must trade only via a reputable dealer who will guarantee that he will buy back the bars at a fixed markup. It's difficult to sell gold bars to strangers, which accounts for the need to have an advance commitment from the dealer as a protection. Assaying bars before sale can be (and is) cumbersome, time-consuming, and expensive.

(5) You can buy shares of gold mining companies. With the exception of Homestake Mining, located in South Dakota, however, this choice involves buying shares of Canadian or South African mines. And here, there is a clear political risk. But these shares often pay dividends averaging 15 per cent a year—a major advantage over holding gold itself, which can be costly and pays nothing.

I must confess to a long-standing prejudice against gold as an investment (much less, a speculation). But I also agree that gold is sought eagerly when people don't trust paper currency, and the 1970s has been a decade of deep mistrust. Although gold has been officially downgraded in the monetary system, it still constitutes 45 per cent of central bank reserves in the free world. And the supply of gold is not only limited but also it is so widely owned that its price cannot be manipulated by any one country.

So, I bow out of the debate—and leave it up to you—except for the following warning:

BEWARE THE GOLD BUG! IT BITES!

If you are thinking about buying gold as a good investment and as a hedge against inflation, watch out!

Hundreds of telephone con men are luring you to part with your money. The bait includes such exotic speculations as "leveraged gold contracts," "supervised gold accounts," and "deferred delivery gold purchases." Many of these speculations are sold fraudulently by boiler-room, watts-line con men representing firms that were not in business last year and may not be here tomorrow.

Any of these contracts can be legitimately sold as a speculation and most companies selling actual gold or gold stocks are legitimate. But beware of the tipster touting a speculation as a sure thing.

Sound complicated? *It is!* London commodity options were complicated too, yet thousands of you were swindled out of tens of millions of dollars in the late 1970s, despite all warnings.

The same con men with the same boiler rooms then moved into diamonds, art, managed commodity accounts and gold.

Here's how it works:

You get three calls on one day from a pitchman touting gold. He tells you his firm is a gold specialist with dozens of experts watching the minute-by-minute movements in the gold markets and computing and charting future price action. He reminds you that "gold has done well in the recent past and his firm thinks that it will keep reaching new highs year after year."

His firm offers a unique program that, for the first time, makes the profitability of gold available to the small investor with limited risk. The chances are excellent that you can make twice your money in a few months.

You are skeptical but interested. The pitchman sends you the firm's promotional literature, which includes some expensive glossy brochures and numerous reprints from leading business publications. The firm's name sounds prestigious and the address is in New York City's Wall Street area. The company claims to be a leader in the field and lists references, including well-known New York City banks, several commodities exchanges, and even a federal government agency.

Several days later you get another call from the firm. This time the pitchman tells you that "if you had invested last week, you would have made

$400 by today. You better get in right away before the price rises. Your investment of $4,000 will control ounces of gold worth over $20,000. We invest the money for you in a supervised account . . . My commission? No commission. We make money when you make money. We take 25 per cent of the profits we make for you . . ."

THE PITFALLS IN THE PITCH

• The glossy promotional literature may look impressive but usually tells you few facts about the firm or the sale.

• The firm is not a "gold specialist" but a telephone sales specialist. Their help-wanted ads reveal their real specialist: "telephone pro . . . heavy closer . . . $2,000 to $4,000 per week."

• Contrary to the pitchman, the chances are not excellent that you will double your money in the following few months. The chances are excellent that you will lose your entire cash outlay.

• The reprints from well-known publications are nearly always used without the publication's authority. References are often misused and are always dangerous to take at face value.

• As for commissions, a hefty percentage of your cash outlay, sometimes as much as 50 per cent, goes immediately to the firm for fees, commissions, and other charges. The claim that the only cost is 25 per cent of the profits is nearly always a lie. One pitchman allegedly told a Missouri farmer that there was no commission and reiterated it in a second call the same day. The same salesman was telling a Better Business Bureau investigator a few hours later that he had fully disclosed that commissions and fees would take $2,400 of the farmer's $5,000 initial cash outlay.

• What about the "unique program" and the "dozens of experts . . . watching the gold market . . ."? The experts are bucket-shop pros keeping a close eye on their commissions and the "unique program" is being touted by more than a dozen boiler-room operations in New York.

As for the claim that gold will keep hitting new highs, it might happen. But the past is no guide to the future.

Are the con men successful? Yes, they always are. Many of you are sending in thousands of dollars without even knowing what you are buying. Here are the profiles of some pitches and some purchases from people who contacted the New York City Better Business Bureau.

• A California dairy farmer and his wife sent $9,000 to a New York City firm for 200 ounces of gold. They did not know whether they had bought an option, a deferred delivery contract, or the actual gold. They did not consult their broker, banker, or lawyer. A few days later, the salesman called them back with the good news that the price of gold had increased and they had already made money. Didn't they want to invest more? They sent another $13,500. Finally a concerned daughter-in-law called the New York City Better Business Bureau. More than two months after wiring their money bank-to-bank in the overnight federal funds market, the Californians were embroiled in a dispute to get back their $22,500. The company insisted it went for "selling costs."

• A coal mine superintendent in Ferron, Utah, sent $9,500 to a different company. He was unable to get written confirmation of his purchase or even to get anybody at the company, including his salesman, to talk to him. When he contacted the company he was told the salesman had suffered a nervous breakdown and was in the hospital. The same evening, a company spokesman told the Better Business Bureau investigator that the same salesman was on the telephone. Most of the $9,500 went to fees and commissions but the miner was not told that before he sent in his cash.

Fortunately, few who get calls send money. A construction company owner in Shawnee, Oklahoma, got a pitch to buy $55,000 worth of gold contracts. A messenger would come around in person to pick up the check. A few hours before the messenger's planned arrival, he called the New York City Better Business Bureau. "We told him we had known of the firm three weeks. After a few questions, this man realized he did not know what he had agreed to buy nor how much he was paying for it," said the New York City Better Business Bureau, adding:

"Most people don't know what they are buying, from whom, on what terms, or at what cost. Nearly all are taking savings to buy, at best, a speculation or, at worst, a swindle. To say they are being made fools of may seem unkind. Unfortunately, it's true."

HOW TO PROTECT YOURSELF

When the phone rings and a promoter starts talking about gold contracts, why you should buy one, how much money you can make, and why gold is going to reach new peaks per ounce, let him talk. Follow these suggestions and you will learn a good lesson in how to protect your savings and future earnings from the telephone con men who will swarm all across the nation in the 1980s.

While he is talking, you take notes. Jot down key phrases from his telephone pitch that you can check later. Take notes under these headings: The commodity (gold), the company, the references, the salesman, the cost, the contract, the market. After you are finished, your notes should look something like this:

• The commodity—gold: gold will go to $? by the mid-1980s, Arabs requiring gold clause in oil payment contracts, political unrest in South Africa.

• The company: a subsidiary of a Connecticut firm, long established, one of the biggest in the street, offices in Geneva and London for fourteen years, used to be in the jewelry business.

• The references: trade on all commodity exchanges, major New York City banks, licensed by the federal government.

- The cost: no commission to me, take 25 per cent of the profits, no margin calls, risk limited to initial investment.
- The contract: you own the gold but defer delivery, you can get out at any time, store the gold for you and pay 8 per cent interest.
- The market: gold will skyrocket in months ahead.

When the pitchman has finished, casually work into your conversation with him his statements you want to confirm.

Then begin your interrogation. *This* man wants $4,000 of your money. At those rates, you are entitled to ask a lot of questions.

- . . . "gold will skyrocket." Why? You get an answer that is a litany of canned con: "The OPEC nations are requiring payment in gold for oil, the United States dollar is no longer No. One, inflation continues, South Africa is very unstable, there are new mining difficulties with gold . . ." "But why?" you ask again. And you observe that gold has had its slumps as well as its swings in recent years. "Why won't that repeat?" you ask. Silence from the promoter. You have marshaled a fact. He has no retorts.
- "Mother company in Connecticut has the gold." What is the name, address, and chief executive officer? Is your firm a subsidiary? Affiliate? "Oh, no connection." How long has your firm worked with this firm? (A call to the "mother company" may tell you that there is no connection and the promoter asking for your $4,000 is just a cash-paying customer of the so-called "mother company" or may even be misusing their name.) A check on the "mother company's" reputation may reveal that it was recently accused of fraud by a federal regulator.
- "Firm in business since early 1970s." At what address? Under what name? Same ownership? Who were and are the officers? Same telephone listing? (Check telephone information where the firm is based. You may find the firm has a new listing.)
- "Company has offices in Geneva and London." Where in Geneva and London? Addresses and phone numbers.
- "Trade on all exchanges." What is the exchange name and address? Is the firm a member? How long? If not a member, does the firm trade through a member firm? Who? Name, address, and chief executive officer? (Write to confirm a long-standing satisfactory relationship between the promoter firm and the exchange member.)
- "No commission." How can you live solely on a percentage of unknown profits? (Newspaper ads for "telephone sales pros, heavy closers" often claim annual incomes of $50,000 to $100,000 per year. Something is not right.) How much is the contract price really? But what about the contango fee? The brochure says the $4,000 is the non-refundable contango fee. What about that?
- "Risk is limited to $4,000 investment." If it is an investment, just how risky is it? What is the security? If the risk is limited to $4,000, what is the cost? Is there any additional charge such as a storage fee, an incentive fee

based on paper profit, a monthly management fee? Is there any additional cash required from me anytime? (There usually are additional fees over the life of the deferred delivery or leverage gold contract. Get details in writing.)

As you go through the claims of the pitchman, and your notes, you will have basic information that you can check directly with third parties of your choosing, or, as is more likely, you will have a list of vague responses and non-answers. But in either case, you will have spent nothing out of your pocket. You will have developed a technique for foiling the telephone con man who usually triumphs in today's fast-paced market place.

It's your money. You have to protect it. There are a thousand-and-one ways to lose it. Most Americans who are making stupid mistakes think they can beat inflation through gambling.

In fact, they often lose everything. Gold glitters—but don't let it blind you!

Or Gold Jewelry

SHOP THE STORES

But you, amateur investor, need not even try to play the awesomely risky, complex world gold markets. You can get a sense of the glitter of gold merely by shopping at your local jewelry store to buy gold jewelry. And that you obviously have been doing.

Sales of gold jewelry have been in a spectacular upsurge.

In the greatest boom ever has been gold jewelry for men—attributed not only to the appeal of gold but also to the return of an era of elegance in men's attire and of romanticism.

KARATS, OTHER TERMS

You, a would-be-buyer, cannot go safely into the gold jewelry market, however, without some basic knowledge of what you're buying in terms of karats, finishings, alloy, etc.

(1) For instance, the karat mark identifies the percentage of gold in an item. (Carat, though, spells out the stone weight in figuring the weight of diamonds.)

If an item is marked 24 K, it means it is made of 100 per cent pure gold, with each karat representing $\frac{1}{24}$ parts gold. Pure, solid gold is 24 karats—too soft to be used by itself in jewelry. It must be alloyed with other metals for strength and hardness.

If a piece of jewelry is marked 14 karat, or "14 K," it has 14 parts of pure gold to 10 parts of alloy. Or as a percentage, it is 58.5 per cent gold. If the jewelry is 18 karat gold, it contains 18 parts of pure gold to 6 parts of alloy. Nothing less than 10 karats can be called "gold," or "karat gold," under

U. S. Government regulations. England allows the sale of 9 K "gold" jewelry. Nothing less than 18 karat can be sold in some countries, such as France. Many experts agree that below 10 karats, the metal loses the special characteristics of gold.

There are times when a piece of jewelry will carry the mark "585" or "750." Some Europeans—notably Italians—use this karat marking. It expresses the gold karatage in percentages of 1,000 (750 equals 18K; 585 equals 14K) rather than in the American fractions of 24.

(2) An alloy is a metal composed of two or more metallic elements and it is used to improve its properties. Most alloys are obtained by fusing a mixture of metals.

Gold is an exceedingly versatile metal, and many shades can be made by alloying it with special metals. Karat golds are available in yellow, red, pink, green, and white—with the color variations made by varying the proportions of copper, nickel, zinc, and silver in the alloy. The proportion of pure gold is unchanged.

(3) Fashion jewelry may be gold-plated, gold-electroplated, or gold-washed. These items are defined by law, according to the percentage of real gold in the jewelry—and if you are not familiar with the terms, you could wind up beguiled into paying "karat gold" prices for gold-plated jewelry.

(4) Gold-filled jewelry, also known as "gold overlay," is rated between karat and costume jewelry and is made by mechanically bonding a gold layer or layers to a base metal such as copper.

It must have a fineness of 10 karats or better; the outer layer must be at least $\frac{1}{20}$ the total weight. Thus, if a 14-karat layer has been used, the jewelry should be marked "14 K gold filled," or "14 K G.F."

(5) Rolled gold plate describes high-quality costume jewelry. Manufactured by the same method as gold-filled jewelry, the gold layer is less than $\frac{1}{20}$ the total weight. Look for the markings that tell you the ratio of gold to the metals used: "$\frac{1}{40}$ 12 K Rolled Gold Plate," or "$\frac{1}{40}$th 12 K R.G.P."

(6) Gold electroplate is jewelry that has been electrolytically coated with at least seven millionths of an inch of karat gold. If the gold coating is thinner, the jewelry should be labeled "gold washed" or "gold flashed." If it is a thicker karat gold label—at least 100 millionths of an inch—the manufacturer can mark the product "heavy gold electroplate."

Preferred in our country in fine jewelry is 18-karat gold, representing 75 per cent pure gold. As for durability, the more karat gold in a piece of jewelry, the longer it will last. King Tutankhamen's gold has survived for thousands of years. Jewelry with a very thin layer isn't meant to endure; it is designed to have a short life-span.

The important point when considering gold jewelry: look for the karat stamp. Only karat gold jewelry is real gold.

How to Buy "Collectables"

BE ON GUARD

The popularity of "collectables"—so-called "limited edition" medallions, coins, records, ingots, plates, spoons, statuary, you-name-it—has rocketed to such peaks in recent years that the mass market has become crowded to the point of saturation. Your chances of finding a "winner," therefore, are steadily diminishing. The signal to you as the 1980s begin is: be on guard!

New editions of artistic pieces that have caught the public's fancy have flooded the market in a flow estimated at more than a thousand a year! Increasing numbers of manufacturers are entering the "limited edition collectables" market. A chilling appraisal by Aetna Life and Casualty, one of the nation's largest insurers of personal property and "objets d'art" is that 80 per cent of all collectables are worth less now than on the day they were purchased.

Reflecting this deterioration in the market's attractiveness was the report in the late 1970s that the Kennedy Memorial medal was still at $40 to $50, higher than the $25 issue price, but no higher than a listing a few years earlier.

A set of fifteen gold medals for the prime ministers of Canada that came out in 1971–72 at $570 was ranging from $1,100 to $1,250 in the late 1970s. That was a gain, obviously, but not so sensational considering what $570 would have earned at 7 per cent simple interest in the same span of time. In fact, not sensational at all.

But of course, some "instant collectables" do and will continue to climb significantly in value over a period. For instance, a limited edition Franklin Mint sterling silver plate, which sold in 1970 for $100, was being offered by one dealer for $550, less than a decade later!

But such increases in value are becoming extremely rare.

(1) There is no established market through which to resell limited edition collectables—which means no established prices and no simple ways to bring potential buyers and sellers together.

(2) With markups at 240–270 per cent on many collectables, you have virtually a built-in loss if an item sells for only the worth of the material from which it is composed.

(3) Manufacturers widely advertise the charms, plates, commemorative coins, statues, etc., in Sunday newspaper supplements but, cautions Aetna, often with incorrect appraisals and sometimes at prices dramatically higher than true market values. Consequently, Aetna, for one, will not insure such items for more than their actual purchase price. In its words, "the price obtainable when the collector decides to sell is often a small fraction of the so-called market price used for appraisals of the collectables."

(4) Despite what you might think, silver—the raw material of many

collectables—is not recession-proof. Silver sold at 24 cents an ounce in the mid-1930s, during the Great Depression, its lowest price in a century.

(5) If you are a fledgling collector, you must be wary of outright fraud, when a so-called "floater" will try to sell a replica of famous originals to innocent collectors as the "real thing." "Limited editions" produced after expiration of the production cut-off date also have been foisted upon unsuspecting collectors by unscrupulous manufacturers.

The question you must face is: how much will an assortment of instant collectables, bought today, be worth five years from today? "It is practically certain the collectables advertised will be worth less than they cost, with no market in which to sell," Aetna says bluntly. You, an owner, will be lucky to salvage half your investment if you sell the piece.

In essence, you must heed the time-honored cliché of "let the buyer beware." Aetna suggests you, as a newcomer:

• Buy what pleases your own esthetic taste.

• Buy only from a manufacturer, mint, or dealer whose reputation and integrity you have verified.

• Buy what fits your pocketbook and under no circumstances borrow to purchase the piece.

• Do not view commemorative art as a hedge against inflation or protection against deflation—but rather as a speculation. Some collectors, suddenly pressed for cash and forced to sell, have had to accept as little as 30 cents on the dollar for their collections.

• Insure your collectables against a wide range of losses by an "all risks hobby collection policy," available on listed "collectables" at $15 per $1,000 of insurance coverage for one year. This type of policy provides much broader coverage than you could get under a homeowner's policy.

AND "NOSTALGIA" COLLECTABLES

These are the items that used to be junk—Shirley Temple dolls, windup toys from the 1920s, and, later, old postcards, political campaign buttons, and glass from "nostalgia" collectables.

For instances, those tin boxes in which cigarettes were packed in the early 1930s—the Lucky Strike "flat fifties"—sold to nostalgia buyers for $8.00 and up in the late 1970s. A tin "Li'l Abner" windup toy that retailed at $2.98 in 1946 sold for $40 nearly twenty years ago and is up to more than $250 in the original package. The value of any nostalgia item increases if it is preserved in its original box. A "Mickey Mouse" watch which sold for $2.50 in 1932 was valued at over $300 with the original box as the 1980s neared.

If you are thinking of taking a flier in the nostalgic collectables, be warned: this is a fad business!

It is virtually impossible to guess the next fad that will catch the public eye and by the time a new buying mood becomes general knowledge, it's usually too late to make money.

Some areas that could have promise are:

burlesque-house posters;

early paperback books;

plaster Kewpie dolls—the kind given away at carnival shooting galleries;

glass;

baseball cards, which can range over $1,500 for a Honus Wagner card and have long-lived appeal.

In the "nostalgia" collectables market as differentiated from the new "limited edition" collectables, a big factor in values can be rumor. And that knowledge should be sufficient for you to move with caution.

Antiques as an Arena

An Insatiable Taste

Of the $2 million raised by a Henry Ford II sale of French furniture and decorations in the late 1970s, half went to individual private Americans bidding against fierce foreign competition.

Dramatizing what is becoming a virtually insatiable thirst for antiques among Americans was the $65,000 paid by a private U.S. collector for a Queen Anne carved walnut highboy, a startling three times the presale estimate. While the antique was of rare, small size, and had belonged to a descendant of General "Mad" Anthony Wayne of Revolutionary War fame, it set a record for a Philadelphia highboy and for miniature American furniture.

Bids for Victorian International have been setting new high marks month after month. Decorative nineteenth-century porcelain, silver, furniture and bronzes, rugs, tapestries, clocks, vertu, etc., again have become fashionable—reflecting the glitter of Victorian International.

A few years ago an eighteenth-century American Paul Revere tea set brought $70,000 at Sotheby's in New York. This was double the amount experts predicted. A five-inch sugar tongs fetched an amazing $5,250. Prices of some antique American silver pieces have doubled in the last ten years and gone on to increase again.

Exceptional pieces of eighteenth-century French furniture were being sold in the late 1970s for more than $100,000. Single eighteenth-century French chairs which brought $5,000 to $10,000 in the early 1970s were going as high as $20,000 with the coming of the 1980s.

Between 1950 and 1980 Chinese porcelain multiplied twenty-three times in value and no end was in sight.

A chief auctioneer at Sotheby Parke Bernet in North America observed: "We can thank American bidders for putting us into a whole new orbit in attracting fine property for sale."

And should you want a translation of that judgment into dollars, antiques have been rising in value at more than 10 per cent a year—against the "round trip" movements during the 1970s of stocks, bonds, commodities, other more familiar investments.

As still another confirmation, in the face of tough bidding by dealers representing the Mideast and European markets, twelve of the fourteen top prices were paid by Americans at a Sotheby Parke Bernet sale, a while back. Not only was the sale a record for Victorian International, but it was claimed to have been "the most international sale ever to have taken place in America."

What's behind the soaring market for antiques?

KEY FORCES

As always, a key force is the obviously limited supply. In addition, the sophisticated investing public is buying.

It is against this traditionally favorable background of restricted supply and expanding demand that price peaks are tumbling and each record sale brings new buyers stampeding into the market.

Even the summer auction trails have been setting new marks. Prices along the remote country lane locations have been higher than ever. In the straw hat shopping market of rural America, furniture of the 1800s has been appreciated as much as 15 per cent yearly. Tiffany glass has been going up an astounding 25 per cent yearly.

Mechanical toys, vintage photo equipment, and tools dating to the late 1800s have zoomed through the roof (or barn) in price. And more increases are expected in the years ahead. Antique mechanical banks have soared an astronomical 1,000 per cent in the past ten years! And more price increases are predicted.

A longtime collector characterized the market succinctly: "Antiques are better than blue-chip stocks." The observation was made to include lower-price items found on the country circuit.

Thus, every class, period, and price range encompassed the market with the coming of the 1980s.

FUNDAMENTAL RULES

How do *you* get into the antiques arena? What are the fundamental rules you must learn and never disobey?

- As a beginner, advises Sotheby's, concentrate on a specific category—American silver, French tapestries, whatever.
- Read as much available literature in the field of your choice as you can find.
- Attend auctions. Survey dealers for prices. Go to the previews or showings at auctions before the sale.
- If in doubt, hire a dependable dealer or connoisseur to represent you at the auctions—and pay the fee required. (You can save as much as 25 per cent or more by buying at auction vs. retail.)
- Look for quality (is it a good example?); authenticity (can its origin be verified?); condition; rarity; age (is the piece dated and can its date be verified?); area and era (is it from a country and period considered valuable?).
- Buy the best examples. Don't be afraid to go to a major international house because you're a "small" buyer. The average "lot" at one top New York auction house sells for $500.
- In bidding at auctions, first pick a reputable firm. Some sell on consignment—some from their own accounts. Shun the house with a no-touch policy on furniture. The better houses will have experts on the floor for consultation during exhibitions.
- Find out when items you're seeking will go up for bids. You often can leave a bid but this can get sticky. Reputable firms frequently will designate employees to bid for customers. Don't necessarily try to put in a rock-bottom price; most houses have so-called "reserve" prices below which there is no sale.
- Watch—without bidding—the first auction, and look for the dealers who often gather in little knots. In the absence of dealers, be wary.
- Check out trucking arrangements and insurance, storage charges, pickup terms, payment terms, surcharges, and attendant fees. Bring a tape measure when you go to an auction, to make sure the item is in scale with your furnishings and is appealing in your home—in addition to its inherent investment value.

FOUR CATEGORIES FOR BARGAINS IN ANTIQUES

Here are four categories in which experts at New York's Sotheby Parke Bernet Galleries believed bargains still existed in the late 1970s:

(1) Late American Federal (or "Empire") furniture—from the 1830–50 period. In pre-1830 early fine American Federal furniture, too, relatively lower-priced pieces still are available.

(2) Early American textiles, including quilts and flags with some historic association.

(3) Other Americana, such as early hand-carved duck decoys, New Eng-

land tinware, utensils of the post-Civil War period; late nineteenth-century decorative objects such as candelabra, fixtures, art pottery, and porcelains.

(4) Indian miniatures, often of as fine a quality as Persian works, yet sell for a fraction of the cost. Fine nineteenth-century examples cost a few hundred dollars. Quality eighteenth-century paintings only bring a few thousand at best.

There are disadvantages to antiques as an investment. Among them:

>they are perishable;

>may be costly to maintain properly;

>may have a retail markup of 100 per cent or more;

>are subject to price fluctuations based on fashion;

>cannot necessarily be sold quickly at top prices.

But the key advantages of investing in antiques are that—aside from the strong chance of substantial increase in values—you also can develop a happy hobby of collecting and you can decorate your home at least temporarily with the antiques you buy.

The Lure of Oriental Rugs

UP 10–15 PER CENT ANNUALLY

Whether you are a collector, connoisseur, or window-shopper, mounting numbers of you have been turning to Oriental rugs as investments, with a handsome and perhaps spectacular promise of gain.

Never has the boom in Orientals in the United States been greater. The market for fine Orientals is now appreciating at an annual rate of 10 to 15 per cent and . . . no end appears in sight.

Skilled workers on new Orientals are shifting to other areas of employment throughout the world. Supplies of used Orientals are being snapped up by dealers and at auctions. Sales and auctions—once limited to such major centers as New York and Chicago—are now spreading all over the country. While the big wave of U.S. interest in Orientals dates back only to the past five years or so, experts predict that values of higher-quality rugs easily could double in the next five years.

And on top of the investment appeal, the Western world long has been fascinated by the designs and craftsmanship of Oriental carpets and the visions of the exotic that they inspire.

But while the opportunities for gain in Orientals (particularly used Orientals) seem solid over the next decade, most industry experts agree, there are major pitfalls for the unwary and uninformed. On the resale side, for instance:

PITFALLS FOR SELLERS AND BUYERS

• You should be fully aware that investments in Oriental classics are not for the overnight, get-rich-quick speculator. You must hold for the long-term—up, say, to ten years or more.

• You may have a major liquidity problem since, depending on the market place, a satisfactory sale could take as much as six months to a full year.

While fine antique and semi-antique rugs are expected to increase in value year after year far into the new decade, many so-called "new" Orientals could have limited upside potential value. These are Middle East rugs that are under twenty years old.

For example, new Kirmans are said to be coming in lacking the quality of ten years ago. Sarouks, too, are inferior to the quality of a few years back. The poorer quality is ascribed to the fact that weavers have been reported not applying the same time as in the past. This, in addition to the fact that the older weavers are dying off.

Even in the face of the fact that values of most better-quality rugs are expected to double in the early-mid 1980s, buying in the market still requires skill. It's really an art.

• Because sales are generally made through dealers or at auction houses which work on a consignment basis with a commission from 25 per cent and up, you must have a satisfactory built-in profit to compensate for your net shrinkage from the market value.

GUIDELINES

On the buying side, there are similar warnings:

• No matter how much knowledge and experience you gain as an amateur in your early stages of studying Orientals, you will have difficulties in judging a rug. You must learn such factors in evaluating an Oriental as the knot count, the quality of the wool used in the pile, the kind of dye employed, the period and place from which the rug came.

• The guidelines will be altered for knot density, design type, and wool quality depending on the region from which the Oriental originated. For instance, a carpet with high knot density could be less valuable than one with low knot density from the same period, depending on the skills of the area where it was produced.

• Learn how to test for the quality of the warp and woof. Fold the carpet face-in; then jerk the fold slightly. If it cracks, hesitate about buying. The warp and woof could be faulty.

• Learn how to value a rug's condition. The better the condition, the more valuable can be the rug. Check for evenly clipped pile, luster of wool along with the quality of the color dye. Examine the rug in full daylight.

• Avoid so-called bargain sales. Pick your dealer with utmost care, for this is the expert in position to consider all factors relative to valuation. Shop several dealers, for prices and advice will vary. As a novice, you must move slowly. Do extensive homework in advance, possibly preparing for a full year before entering the actual market for a purchase.

• Inquire if a dealer has a policy permitting you to buy on approval. Most reputable dealers want you to be satisfied, will allow you to make an exchange if you ask within a reasonable time.

• Study estate sales as a source; these sales ads frequently appear in the Sunday newspapers.

• If you're a beginner, start in a price range of from $500 to $3,000. Stay away from the high end of the price spectrum. If you're attending an auction, get expert opinion and evaluation in advance; the tempo is fast at an auction sale. Never forget you're bidding against professionals in many cases and restrain your eagerness.

Orientals may be grouped as new, used, semi-antique, and antique. Antique rugs are said to be at least a hundred years old; semi-antiques at least a half century; and used rugs can mean just about anything.

Age and name are not necessarily the requisites for guarantee of quality. Regardless of the style or vintage, the condition of the rug can make the big difference. Condition in Orientals can be as vital as condition in a fine painting.

• Learn about maintenance, possible summer storage (if there is any threat of deterioration from bright light), washing, and repairs. The basic of basics is *study*.

• And while you consider your Oriental rug as a valuable investment, treasure its beauty and functionalism as well.

Coins Not for Spending

SPECTACULAR UPSURGE

In Chicago a short while ago, a coin collection of 1,530 pieces, one of the most important in the nation, was auctioned off piece by piece for $2.25 million, well above the experts' expectations. A $5 gold piece, 1825-over-1824, went for $140,000 to a coin dealer. Even though only two such coins are known to exist, the price paid was characterized as "way over the estimated value."

This was merely the latest manifestation of the big boom during the 1960s and 1970s in coins not meant for spending, along with the upsurge in books not meant for reading, paintings and sculptures not necessarily for viewing.

Do you own a 1964 50-cent piece, minted in honor of President John F. Kennedy the year after he was assassinated? It was worth $2.00 or four times its face value at the close of the 1970s, a 100 per cent increase just since 1974 when it was worth twice its face value.

Or a 1940 quarter from the Philadelphia mint, all silver and never circulated? It commanded $9.00, or thirty-six times its face value, up from $7.50 just from the mid-1970s.

And how about a 1950 Jefferson nickel, minted in Denver in limited quantities? That nickel would have brought you an astronomical increase of 220 times its face value—or $11. And a 1909 penny V.D.B. (Victor D. Brenner series) uncirculated? This one would have shown a 1,250 times increase over face value, or $12.50. As recently as 1975, it sold at a hefty 500 times its face value.

HOW TO APPRAISE YOUR "COLLECTION"

But how do *you* find out if that box of collected coins in your attic has any real value?

The chances are your "collection" is only an "accumulation," say the experts. But to make sure:

(1) Take the collection to two or three respected dealers, ask each what it would pay for the entire collection, not just best pieces. Dealers will charge for a formal, written appraisal. (A New York-based dealer, for instance, charges a fee of 1 per cent of the total value of your coins, with a minimum fee of $25.) The appraisal is refunded—if you sell the collection through that dealer.

(2) Do not make your own inventory of the coins to present it to a dealer for appraisal. The dealer wants to see the coins.

(3) Under no circumstances, try to clean the coins! A poor cleaning job can drastically slash a coin's value. Using pencil erasers, silver polish, or baking soda won't make the coins more valuable. You can only harm them.

(4) Rare coins, like other antiques, are most desirable in their original condition. What could be a seemingly dirty coin just might appear beautiful to a dealer.

(5) If you are told you have expensive coins, do not keep them at home. Even when insured, put them in a safe deposit box.

IF YOU ARE A BEGINNER

And if you are a beginner in coin collecting?

• Don't try to collect every type of coin. Specialize. Read extensively. Get the advice of acknowledged specialists.

• Buy the best examples of coins you can find. Over the long run, the better coins are likely to climb the most in value.

• Don't succumb to coin "fads." In recent years, as an illustration, foreign governments have been selling virtually worthless proof sets in coins in fancy packaging for as much as $30. The prices then have fallen back to the $5.00 range.

- Don't invest for the short-term. Collections are to be designed for long-term investments.
- Beware of coins which appear grossly underpriced. They almost surely are not "super bargains," but just gyps.
- Don't buy or sell through unknown mail-order coin dealers; obey the prime rule of patronizing only the reputable firms.
- Don't hoard on the basis of rumors. Treasury $1.00 silver certificates were redeemed in 1968 for as much as $1.85. In 1979, they could not be redeemed above the face value.
- Beware of coins that are overgraded. Unless the true condition of the coins is described, you are heading for trouble.
- Finally, note that the value of coins does not depend on the age of the coin, its face value, or the price originally paid. Rather, value is based on rarity, condition, demand, date, mint mark, and authenticity. These are your never-to-be-forgotten yardsticks.

Diamonds: a Dilemma

DIZZYING SPIRAL

Diamonds soared to such dizzying price levels in the late 1970s that some of the world's largest diamond retailers as well as the world's greatest diamond cartel warned publicly that diamond prices had been driven too high.

New York's West Forty-seventh Street—hub of the United States diamond industry—became the center of excitement. A one-carat top stone which had wholesaled, for example, a few years back at roughly $7,500 had doubled or more as the 1980s rolled in. Your cost as a consumer would be double this amount.

What caused the spectacular price run-up? A measure of the impetus came from the action of the world's giant diamond marketing cartel—De Beers Consolidated Mines, Ltd. The company, with next to total control over worldwide "diamond rough," i.e., uncut and unpolished stones, boosted prices 40 per cent. De Beer's action partially came as the result of reduced output which resulted in a cutback on the stones it could market.

Beyond the De Beers action, other factors behind the astronomical increase in the prices of diamonds included:

- Spiraling demand for polished diamonds for investment purposes.
- Diamonds are portable and can be secretly removed if it is necessary to flee a homeland.
- Diamonds are an inflation hedge or a defense against currency devaluation.

So immense and intense has been the interest in diamonds that some stock brokerage firms have been exploring ways to offer customers the opportunity to participate in diamond-investment programs.

CAUTION!

If you, an individual, are intent on buying for investment, proceed with caution.

The big drawback is that those who make profits in diamonds are primarily dealers in the gems who *buy from you at wholesale and sell to you at retail*—a vast disadvantage considering the diamond retailer's markup ranges from 30 to 125 per cent over the wholesale price.

Add to this local sales taxes and annual insurance premiums and it becomes apparent that even with the big increase of the late 1970s, if you bought for a quick profit, you could easily be burned.

There also is the very real possibility that future processes for producing imitation diamonds could undercut demand for and depress the prices of real diamonds.

Then, you must realize that, of the two thousand separate categories of diamonds, an overwhelming 99 per cent have shown gains of less than 15 per cent a year—and only the top 1 per cent of quality grades appreciate at faster rates. Many firms claiming to sell this high-quality merchandise are in actuality selling the lower-quality gems.

IF YOU BUY

Have the grade of the diamond analyzed by a bonded and insured gem laboratory, with qualified and trained personnel. Be sure the lab guarantees the accuracy by international standards of the grade supplied or guarantees your money back. These are essential protections. In addition:

• Buy only diamonds of the very finest qualities and be aware of the importance of the size you select. Large diamonds appreciate faster than smaller diamonds, but in very top qualities, large diamonds are extremely expensive and often not very liquid. Very fine diamonds of from one-half- to two-carat sizes are the most liquid when you wish to resell all or part of your diamond assets.

• Deal only with companies established in the real diamond industry. If a company says it sells diamonds wholesale, ask if it sells to jewelry stores. Obtain references in the jewelry industry which the company claims to service. Check with the Jewelers Board of Trade, in Providence, Rhode Island, and the Jewelers Vigilance Committee in New York City, to find out if the company is a member of either organization. Ask your local Better Business Bureau if it has any data on the firm.

• Shop and compare prices and grade categories. Do not buy diamonds sealed in plastic or containers which make examination hard.

• Be sure the diamond is sold according to specifications set by the Gemological Institute of America, an international grading standard. If the seller does not have its own gemological lab (bonded and insured), have the diamonds appraised by an outside lab.

- Buy only from companies which guarantee to repurchase the diamonds if you are not totally satisfied—and the guarantee should be unconditional. Many reputable sellers offer this guarantee.
- If you're buying diamonds as a collector, buy merchandise of the highest clarity grade, under GIA grading criteria, in the colorless spectrum of G-H color or better, and of very fine proportion and finish. Only about 1 per cent of all diamonds fall into this high band of excellence. If any one of the scales of quality is lowered even slightly, the merchandise is much less rare, much more abundant, and appreciates at a much, much lower rate. Although many companies advertise that they have ample supplies of this merchandise, few firms in the United States actually do have many gems of this grade.
- Get full disclosure of fees at your initial purchase of the diamond for collection, and in advance of your purchase, full disclosure of fees and charges to resell the diamond at a future date. Avoid any seller unwilling to make, or who is vague about, these disclosures.

HOW TO SPOT A DIAMOND GYP

No agency of the law—federal, state, or local—or any Better Business Bureau or any jewelers' trade association could possibly stringently police the individual sale of diamonds through retail outlets. Even so-called "reputable" jewelers have been known to palm off inferior diamonds to an unknowledgeable consumer, hiding the deception by incorrect and collusive appraisals. Your fundamental guide is obvious: buy only from an established jeweler whose reputation you can trust.

You also may be able to detect an unscrupulous dealer if he tries to sell you:

(1) A perfect blue-white diamond, unless it is truly colorless and flawless. Because the term "blue-white" has been misused so much, most reputable dealers do not use it.

(2) An artificially colored diamond. This is a genuine diamond of poor color. The diamond may be painted or coated to disguise its yellowish color. In either case, a jeweler must state in writing before the diamond is sold what treatment was used, under penalty of fine and jail.

(3) A piggyback diamond. This is a small diamond placed in close proximity to another, with the mounting hiding the separations of the stones and making the two small diamonds look like one large one. Dishonest jewelers will try to sell this as, say, "one carat in diamonds" or some other deceptive advertising.

(4) An imitation or simulated diamond which will look like the real thing. Its chemical term, though, will be "colorless synthetic sapphire," or "synthetic rutile," or "strontium titanite."

When you shop, keep constantly in mind the traditional four "C's" of the trade—color, clarity, carat, and cut—which deeply affect prices.

Carat weight. This is a weight unit for diamonds and other gems. It comes from "carob"—seeds of the Mediterranean trees used in ancient bazaars to balance the scales because they were so uniform in weight. The metric carat of 200 milligrams is standard in most of the world. Some dealers suggest carat weights between one carat and three carats per stone. The majority of carats mined are under one carat. As noted, diamonds over three carats are not as liquid.

Color. A diamond's body ranges from colorless to yellow scale. The absence of color is an important factor in investment of quality diamonds. The most valuable color grades are those diamonds that are colorless.

Clarity. This identifies the relative position of a diamond on the flawless-to-imperfect scale. A number system is used to grade diamonds. Probably the most common begins with flawless or perfect; very, very, slightly imperfect; very slightly imperfect; slightly imperfect; and imperfect.

Cut. These are the facet angles and proportions mathematically calculated to achieve maximum brilliance consistent with a high degree of fire in a round brilliant which is considered the ideal cut.

THE FUTURE

What about the future of diamonds in view of the lofty price peaks already reached?

Dealers are optimistic that prices will rise at a rate matching the pace of inflation in the 1980s. An added hedge is the tremendous role played by De Beers. During the forty-plus years that De Beers has played a dominant role in the industry, it has *never* reduced prices. When demand declined, the company simply withheld stones from the market.

DIAMOND GYPS OVER THE PHONE

The pitch below is a hypothetical sales pitch. Tomorrow you may get one just like it.

It's early in the evening when your home phone rings. "Hello, Mr. Jones, I'm the head buyer with ZYX Gems Exchange in New York City. I would like to talk to you about diamonds. Did you know that investment quality diamonds have increased at a rate of 30 per cent a year for the past ten years? Most people don't. Instead, they buy diamonds at exorbitant retail prices.

"Here at ZYX Gems we are trying to let the average American get in on what professional investors have known all along. That is, you can make your fortune in diamonds. The price always goes up! One company mines 80 per cent of the diamonds in the world and that company controls diamond prices.

"We are calling *you* to offer the highest-quality investment grade diamonds at wholesale prices. We deliver directly to you. The diamonds come with a forty-five-day money-back guarantee. If for any reason you don't like them, just send them back and we will give you your money back . . . And since the diamonds always increase in value, if you want to sell them, we will buy them back. We can resell while you wait on the phone.

"Trust me. You can't go wrong . . ."

How true are these claims?

They are typical of the most deceptive claims used by the few but pervasive high-pressure promoters selling diamonds over the phone. During the 1980s countless thousands of Americans will realize that they have lost millions of dollars to con men touting diamonds as a "sure thing."

WHAT'S WRONG WITH THE PITCH?

The name of the company sounds prestigious enough. But in fact, the company is not an "exchange" in the sense of an auction market; it is not "international" in the sense that it has operations in many countries; and it has been in business for only a short time.

The "head buyer"? He is really a pro, but not at diamonds. He is likely to be what the telephone sales trade calls a "heavy closer," a boiler-room high-pressure professional. To you, he is selling diamonds; last year it was silver; next month it may be sugar options; a few years ago it was Scotch whisky.

Diamonds *in general*, as emphasized earlier, have *not* been increasing in value at the spectacular rate of 30 per cent a year even in this era.

This company is not offering the "highest-quality investment grade" diamonds but frequently is pushing diamonds that are seriously flawed and less than a carat in weight—and that is not investment quality.

The "forty-five-day money-back guarantee" is limited by terms and conditions, such as the fact that the container seals must remain unbroken. How can you examine the stones to see whether or not you want to exercise the money-back guarantee?

The "buy-back agreement" usually is fictitious. The company may try to resell your diamonds—meaning a "best efforts try"—but it doesn't guarantee the resale or the price. And it will charge a commission for the service.

And that giveaway con man's line about "trust me, you can't go wrong"—don't fall for it. A TV repairman in Oklahoma who got that pitch laid out $12,000—and now he has learned his diamonds are worth only a fraction of what he paid for them.

You may call back, find the company's phone is disconnected, and the "trust me" salesman is off on a new venture.

One large New York City diamond promoter may have deceptively sold grossly overpriced diamonds of dubious value to more than five thousand customers, from whom the company grossed in excess of $10 million in ten months. At this writing, the company has been under investigation by federal agents for over a year and a half. Some of the customers may get back a pittance, but they will wait a long time to retrieve even a small percentage of what they so invested because they were so gullible.

Who are these victims? A cross section: the fellow across the back alley, the lady down the block, the person you work with, *and you*.

"I should have my butt kicked!" exclaimed a hospital executive in Ohio when told that he had been swindled out of most of the $2,257 that he had paid for diamonds sold to him over the phone.

"The $8,000 I put up was about 98 per cent of my lifetime savings," moaned a rubber stamp manufacturer in a rural Washington State area when he found out that the company which had sold him the diamonds was no longer in existence to honor its buy-back agreement.

"Most of the people who get pitches to buy diamonds or options have no experience in either," emphasizes the New York Better Business Bureau.

And, says the New York BBB, during the late 1970s, dozens of companies employing hundreds of telephone hucksters operated nationwide. So it was not surprising that diamonds were a top big-ticket phone fraud. Even if you never bought diamonds, and don't trade in stocks, you still may become the victim of a smooth-talking pitchman who will reach you by phone and convince you to take thousands of dollars out of your savings deposits or bonds and buy diamonds.

Gems traditionally glitter in the eyes of the average individual. And all of us have some degree of larceny within ourselves which tends to make us believe we can pile up a fortune by risking a small stake. The con man's success is built on our greed and gullibility.

Of course, there are legitimate companies selling diamonds to the public all over the United States!

But most of you who will get a telephone sales pitch will lack two fundamentals for successful diamond investing: knowledge to measure quality and access to a resale market. If you want to buy diamonds for investment or speculative gain, make sure you can tell the difference between the swindlers and legitimate sellers.

A FEW ADDITIONAL GUIDELINES

• Never buy diamonds over the phone from a company and salesman utterly unfamiliar to you. This is downright stupid.
• Before you buy any diamonds, check and double-check with local, long-established, highly reputable jewelers. You will get sound guidance from these jewelers; they know the market, they know prices, they will be reliable.
• Never clean out your savings account to put the money in diamonds. It

has happened. According to one fraud investigator, "People who shop weeks to save $300 on an automobile will send $8,000 for diamonds to a company they never heard of, based on the promises of an unknown salesman they never will even meet."

• Find out about boiler-room markups. All retail markups are hefty. Do a thorough comparative shopping job and give other gem dealers a detailed description of the stone you are considering buying. Describe it in detail by the grading characteristics: clarity, carat, cut, and color. But don't be impressed by a pitchman's expertise when he uses these four C's with seeming authority. These words are in his first lesson. Make sure you are buying quality goods in each grading category. Slightly inferior quality in any one category can have a great adverse impact on the value of the stone.

• Don't kid yourself about any get-rich-quick potential. To make significant profits, you will have to hold your diamonds for at least two or three years of generally rising prices.

• If you get a pitch or think you have been defrauded, write all details to your local U. S. Attorney and to your local BBB. Don't delay. If you have received the diamonds, make sure they are what you actually ordered. Take them to a registered gemologist and have him appraise them. He can give you some kind of an estimate, probably by looking through the container, without breaking the seal.

• If they are not worth what you paid, complain at once. If they are what you ordered, and were sold without misrepresentation, deception, and at a reasonable price, then you might put them away safely and in several years see what you can get for them. You may have made a little money, but make sure you measure what you made in diamonds against what you would have made on your money in a savings account or in a high-yield bond.

• And back to the basics: if you receive a phone call from a stranger who promises get-rich-quick profits in diamonds, shrug him off and hang up the phone!

Feverish Boom in Art

ALL PRICE RECORDS BROKEN

In all history, there never was a more monumental period for the world of art than the end of the 1970s.

In London, bidders from all over the globe poured out a record $34.1 billion at Sotheby Parke Bernet's auction of the Baron Robert von Hirsch collection of splendid art. Walter Feilchenfeldt, a Zurich dealer, paid the highest price ever at auction for a watercolor by any artist—$1,177,600 for an Albrecht Dürer work. "I was amazed at the prices here," said Feilchenfeldt, "but I paid them because we will never have another chance at some of these things."

In New York City, Sotheby Parke Bernet reported the sale of the Garbisch collection of Impressionist and modern art at $14.8 million and the setting of an all-time record for sales at auction by payment of $6.4 million for J. M. W. Turner's "Juliet and Her Nurse."

In Los Angeles, a new high was set for any American work of art—$980,000 for *The Jolly Flatboatmen,* by George Caleb Dingham, circa 1848. A world peak was reached for an American portrait with the $265,000 sale of a Thomas Eakins.

Sales of paintings of major importance in the $1 million range actually became commonplace! A Van Gogh sold for $1,300,000, a Rembrandt self-portrait, for $1,519,200. These prices were hundreds of thousands of dollars above the levels they would have commanded only a few years back and, if brought again to the feverish auction market, the odds are they would bring substantially more.

Among individual artists, the upsurge also was sensational for Renoirs, Monets, Picassos, and Braques.

You can find art prices published weekly in many newspapers and art departments in big-city department stores.

Franchised art galleries have been set up across the nation. While art investment funds have not multiplied as expected in Paris and in New York, investment counselors are offering advisory services in investment in art works.

Adding to the frenzy is the entrance of the young American into the investment-in-art sphere, investing thousands of dollars a year in paintings and sculptures, for aesthetic as well as moneymaking potentials.

Then there are the corporations—not only the famous giants who display contemporary sculpture and paintings in and around most, if not all, of their buildings, but also small companies following the lead in investing for gain as well as for status.

FORCES AT WORK

What are the key forces behind this raging art boom?

(1) Inflation, obviously. During this whole phase of rapidly climbing living costs, favorite investments have been tangible, rare, valuable assets—ranging from rare books to old wines.

(2) The growing American sophistication along with the funds to satisfy the yearning for culture. As museums and universities buy art works, they, too, help drive up prices.

(3) And there are the basics behind every price upspiral: a growing demand coming head-up against a steadily shrinking supply of the acknowledged, familiar masters.

TEN RULES TO GUIDE YOU IN ART INVESTING

Say "art" is your choice of the wide variety of areas covered in this chapter. Here are ten rules to guide you.

(1) Before you put down a penny, invest as much time as you can reading art catalogs in the field which interests you, visiting galleries to see what works are available and how much they cost, inspecting art works before auctions, attending auctions to get the feel of them. You even might subscribe to art auction catalogs published by major galleries in the field of your interest.

Many of these catalogs will give you, after each auction, prices paid for each item which appeared in the pre-auction catalog. Keep these catalogs for later comparisons of prices for various items.

Try to read all the scholarly books you can find on your specialty to help give you a feel for "good," "better," and "best" in quality and value.

(2) When you decide to buy, be cautious at least to start. Don't spend all you have on one item you think is a good buy.

(3) Make sure you have, also before you buy, a really special feeling about a painting or sculpture—a sense which tells you it has quality. Or have somebody who has this type of instinctive feeling represent you as a buyer or bidder at an art auction.

(4) Deal with a top gallery or art dealer. Don't be afraid to frequent the very best. Also, a top dealer is interested in earning and holding your patronage. If you are not satisfied, he will make every effort to resell anything you bought for at least what you paid. Some dealers and major galleries will guarantee the authenticity of the art works they sell, in fact, so check this point as well. Don't patronize galleries or dealers whose large ads proclaim their merchandise to be "art investments" (they often are not).

(5) Have an understanding with your dealer or gallery about trading up—so he'll repurchase or resell your works as you have more money to invest in high-quality art. Also find out whether he'll let you and your prospective purchase have a "trial marriage"—by taking a picture home for a week or so before you make a final decision.

(6) Be wary of works by modern artists in current fashion. Inflated prices easily can result from an exhibit by a single major museum. But after the excitement of the show has subsided, prices tend to drop as well. Buying art works because they are a current rage is akin to buying stocks on tips at a cocktail party.

(7) If there is a museum director or curator in your community, ask for his advice on buying. Or use the services of specially assigned personnel at large art galleries whose job is to guide you.

(8) Decide, before you buy, how much money you can afford to invest and stick to that ceiling. If you find a more expensive work irresistible, arrange to pay for it over a period of time.

(9) Unless you are an expert, spread your financial risks by investing in the works of a variety of different artists. But try at the same time to maintain a theme or unifying force in your collection.

(10) Buy the best examples you can afford in any category. For buyers with limited funds, a good drawing by a given artist may be a better buy than a poor painting. You well may find artists who were overshadowed by the greats in the era in which they lived a better buy than new artists who have not been tested by time.

FIVE TYPES OF ART FOR RAPID "GROWTH"

As a newcomer, what types of art should you seek? What is expected to grow at a relatively rapid rate in the years coming up? These, according to spokesmen for Sotheby's, New York, are among your best bets:

(1) Old master paintings or drawings. Their value is virtually guaranteed to continue rising, despite today's high prices. However, they'll probably increase in value at a slower rate than other art categories. While there are still some excellent old master drawings ranging up to $50,000 and more, a substantial number are available at a fraction of this amount. Always turn to a reputable dealer for counsel on what good drawings by superb artists can be bought at reasonable prices.

(2) Almost any good American painting of unusual historical, social, or geographic interest. Bargains may still be had, dealers say, in late nineteenth- and early twentieth-century paintings by respected American artists of the Hudson River School (Thomas Cole, Thomas Doughty, Asher Durand, and their associates) and in good marine paintings by many American artists. Prices range from $1,000 to $10,000 and up.

(3) German artists of the nineteenth century. Good examples of their works are said to be worthwhile buys at prices ranging from $600 to $6,000.

(4) Primitive art works. Authentic African wood carvings, pre-Columbian works, such as sculptured figures, vessels, and ceramics, are regarded as good investments. Go only to top-name galleries for these items. Prices will vary from a few hundred dollars to a few thousand. Primitive oceanic carvings from the Southwest Pacific islands range from $50 to $100 and into the thousands for the more elaborate, large carvings. Beware of modern reproductions and fakes, which have flooded the market.

(5) Classical antiquities. These include small bronzes, pottery, and sculptures from the Mediterranean which should appreciate. You can create a fairly large collection of significance for about $50,000 today. Only five years ago, a collection could have been established for around $30,000. You can still buy most individual art objects in this area for an investment of a few hundred dollars or so.

A crucial guideline: specialize in a specific field and become acquainted with other art lovers in it.

Prints Roar On Too

BIG WINNER

"Art used to be a place to spend extra money," said the president of Associated American Artists, in New York, as the 1980s neared. "Now taxi magnates are investing their profits in art."

And high on the list of winners in the art market are prints—which have moved way out of what was once second-class status into an artistic niche of their own. To illustrate:

• A Picasso linoleum cut, entitled "After Cranach," went for $600 in 1960, commanded $60,000 in the late 1970s.

• A Toulouse-Lautrec print, entitled "La Grande Loge," soared to world record of $175,000, while Rembrandt etchings startled the art world with price runups as high as $80,000 to an almost incredible seven figures.

• In the early 1960s, an original, signed Matisse lithograph entitled "Seated Odalisque" from an edition of 50, was priced at $350, rocketed to the $50,000 range.

FACTORS BEHIND BUYING EXPLOSION

Why the churning of prices in the print explosion?

(1) Print dealers have been multiplying. In turn, they have bought up prints to build their inventories. The impact on prices has been obvious. For example, in the early 1960s, there were no more than twenty top print dealers in the United States. Today, they number in the hundreds. This includes not only galleries and print shops but also department store boutiques, bookstores, picture frame and gift shops.

(2) The ranks of collectors have been greatly expanded by young Americans who find the tag for paintings and sculptures by major artists prohibitive. They have added immensely to the demand and, in doing so, have lifted prints out of a second-class status into an artistic niche of their own. Status has become identifiable by a collection of fine prints.

(3) Art investors and art funds have been flocking to the print market. This has opened competition with the collectors of art.

(4) Availability of material from the old masters has been diminishing. Prints done from the fifteenth to the eighteenth century have grown in value due to their antiquity and rarity. There has been a tremendous drain on the old masters by institutions augmenting or beginning new study collections.

(5) Middle East oil wealth has upped prices. For example, Iran, in opening a museum, has bought paintings, sculpture—anything in the market place of artistic value. This material will never return to the market place. In the United States, universities continue to develop important museums.

(6) The absence of a property tax has been an important consideration in contributing to demand for art, also. Another appeal to many people is the fact that, in contrast, say, to real estate, prints are portable and virtually maintenance free.

BASIC RULES FOR BUYING PRINTS

The print market—like other similar markets—is plagued by its share of fly-by-nights, forgers, and unscrupulous dealers. Hundreds of Chagall "original" lithographs have been clipped out of books and French publications, dressed up with fake signatures and "limited edition" numbers, and sold for ridiculously inflated prices.

High-pressure auctioneers have been known to offer examples from large editions (300 to 400 impressions) by artists who are described as fabulous and famous by the auctioneers—but who are, in fact, unknown to the rest of the art world.

How then can you avoid paying big sums for forged prints and other non-originals? How can you find etchings, engravings, lithographs, or other types of prints to adorn your living-room walls and at the same time see your purchases grow in value in coming years?

A fundamental point is that prints can be either originals or reproductions. An original print, as defined by the prestigious Print Council of America, comes from a plate, block, stone, or other medium on which an image has been created by the artist himself. A reproduction, however, is a copy of a print or other art work made by photographic techniques, seldom under supervision by the artist.

Here are the basic rules for buying prints, both for their artistic rewards and for their profit potential:

(1) Before buying, consult established sources of information, including auction catalogs, art books, and "catalogues raisonnés," which are comprehensive, well-annotated compilations of all the prints of various artists. Also, to get a basic education, visit museum print cabinets. Often you must make an appointment to do so but don't fail to do this, for many of the finest examples of prints are to be found today in museums.

(2) Browse in galleries and shops, both in the United States and abroad, to get an idea of the range of prints available and prices being charged by various outlets for similar works. Try to find an era or an artist or a school of artists really attractive to you and then focus your interests and attention on your choices.

(3) When you are ready to buy, stick to established print dealers—preferably those who have been in business at least five years. Seek their guidance on the quality and authenticity of the prints you are considering purchasing.

(4) Avoid one-shot print exhibitions in hotel suites and sales by unknown

auctioneers. Frequently, experts say, fly-by-night auctioneers will hold up a page which has been torn out of an art book, announce flatly, "This is worth $250 but let's start the bidding at $25"—and succeed in selling it for a distinctly non-bargain price of $50.

"Small-time auctions," dealers warn, "can be a great place to buy prints, but only if you know exactly what you are doing." A cardinal rule on this type of auction is to attend the exhibition beforehand and examine the prints, since they are generally sold "as is."

(5) Also avoid the "bargains" advertised in your neighborhood picture frame shop unless the dealer has an established reputation in the field of prints and you know what you want.

(6) Be on the lookout for "restrikes"—which are reruns of the original plates. These plates may have been rediscovered long after an artist's death, sometimes with cancellation lines drawn through them by the artist so that further prints supposedly could not be made.

(7) Finally, examine catalogs at auctions and art print exhibitions. Descriptions of individual prints should include whether or not they are signed by the artist, the condition and quality of each print, the number of impressions in the entire edition (for modern prints), the print's size and date, the process or processes used. Reputable dealers also should be happy to put whatever descriptive data you wish on the invoice or give a certificate of authenticity.

SEVEN CATEGORIES FOR INVESTING

With these basic rules for shopping for profit firmly in mind, what might you find the most provocative areas for investing in the print market? Seven specific categories underlined by leading dealers are:

(1) French nineteenth-century artists such as Jean Baptiste Camille Corot, Jean François Millet, Adolphe Appian, Albert Besnard, Félix Buhot, and Charles François Daubigny. In the late 1970s, you could buy good Corots and Millets for $300 to $600 and good examples of others for $20 to $200—a fraction of the prices which were paid for other major artists of this era such as Toulouse-Lautrec, Manet, Cézanne, Renoir.

(2) American early twentieth-century artists and especially those who worked in the 1930s. Good prints by Thomas Hart Benton, John Steuart Curry, Grant Wood, George Bellows, John Sloan, and Reginald Marsh could be bought for $300 to $1,500.

(3) The celebrated British "triumvirate" of the 1920s—D. Y. Cameron, Muirhead Bone, and James McBey. Works by these once fantastically popular artists were available in the closing days of the 1970s for only 10 per cent of the prices they commanded a half century ago ($200 to $3,000 in the expensive dollars of the 1920s). "Whether the prices for works by these artists will ever come back to the levels of the 1920s is anybody's guess,"

says one print dealer. "But they might possibly be an interesting school to explore." Similarly, works by Seymour Haden, Whistler's brother-in-law, well may start to rise on Whistler's coattails. Prices of major Whistler prints have passed the $3,000 mark.

(4) High-quality works by lesser-known printmakers of the fifteenth, sixteenth, and seventeenth centuries—e.g., Lievens, Hollar, Waterloo, to name just a few. Outstanding examples of prints by these artists could be bought in the late 1970s for $50 to $500. But choosing among these lesser-knowns takes expert knowledge and if you don't possess it consult someone who does have the required know-how.

(5) Other lesser masters with appeal—Van Leyden, Callot, Adriaen Van Ostade, and Raimondi. Outstanding examples of these artists are now $2,000 to $3,000. However, you can buy fine examples of these lesser-known artists in the $100 to $500 range as opposed to the outstanding examples.

(6) Ultramodern art. This can be riskier, for time has not tested the durability of many of today's avant-garde. Among the most important contemporary artists are Robert Motherwell, Jasper Johns, Helen Frankenthaler (one of her prints fetched over $3,000 at auction as the 1980s neared), David Hockney, Richard Estes, Andy Warhol, and Jim Dine (his etchings have passed the $2,000 mark).

(7) Old masters. Price increases notwithstanding, there are still some attractive investment areas. Prints from the old masters such as Rembrandt and Dürer are in big demand, bringing $10,000 and up. Old masters require a vast amount of expertise. Beware of buying an old master that was printed in the nineteenth century—even though it was from an original plate. It could be of minor monetary value and hardly worth the investment.

WHAT DETERMINES VALUES OF PRINTS?

Print values in all categories are based on these four factors: the artist, the image or subject of the print, the rarity of the print, and the print's condition.

But an artist's standing as an oil painter or a sculptor has little to do with his stature as a printmaker. Aristide Maillol, for instance—whose sculptures are valued in the tens of thousands of dollars—is considered a minor printmaker.

Rarity is the key to the upswing in prices for fine examples of prints by such artists as Rembrandt, Dürer, Cranach, Callot. And a print from an edition of only fifty may cost four times the price of an example from an edition of two hundred, everything else being equal.

As an illustration of the importance of a print's condition, a Toulouse-Lautrec poster which normally would sell for $7,000 might fetch less than $2,000 if it is torn or wrinkled or otherwise in poor condition.

If you are considering buying an old master, shop and consult with an expert. One fine print by Dürer may be worth upward of $25,000. Late impressions of the same print in poor condition may be worth less than $1,000. This rule applies particularly to Rembrandt. Late impressions can be worth only a fraction of the value of early impressions.

If you invest in lesser prints, don't underestimate the problem of liquidity. You may have to wait for years to get the price that you believe is fair for such prints. Auctions are getting choosy and are turning down the hard-to-sell items.

Before you buy, study sources of information on the category of prints which interests you, e.g., museum print cabinets, print galleries, auction catalogs, art books, and "catalogues raisonnés"—the latter are complete compilations of all the prints of a single given artist.

Be on guard against today's ever-broadening array of questionable print offers such as one-shot print exhibitions in hotel suites, small-time auctions conducted by unknown auctioneers, and books of prints by well-known artists offered at grossly inflated prices.

Buy only from established dealers who will be your best guides to quality, authenticity, and fair prices.

Beware of vendors who indicate "regular price $1,000, special price $500" on a print. In all probability, the $1,000 is exaggerated and the $500 is overpriced. Beware of such terms as "Fine Arts Print," "Museum Quality Print." These have little to do with the print's intrinsic value.

A final guide: If you do decide to choose prints as an investment medium as well as a source of great personal pleasure, avoid the hottest print fads and concentrate on the temporarily less fashionable but still high-quality artists and epochs. In fact, here—among the less fashionable eras and less fashionable artists—is where you'll find real price bargains.

Stamps as Investments

UPSWING YEAR AFTER YEAR

While the stock market was mostly a disaster area during the 1970s and stock values lagged far behind inflation's erosion of your dollar's buying power, stamps continued to climb as much as 20 per cent year after year. In many instances, the upsurge in values was even more spectacular—and no reversal in the escalation is foreseen.

Item: A top-quality inverted U.S. airmail 24-cent stamp, familiar to generations of collectors and considered among the world's fifty most valuable, was auctioned in the late 1970s for $100,000 and another similar stamp went for $72,500. As recently as the mid-1970s, the upside-down airplane was quoted at $35,000 to $40,000—and even conservative experts predict this stamp's price could range up to $120,000 in the 1980s.

Item: A New Orleans stamp dealer paid $380,000 for a couple of 1847 one-penny stamps from the Indian Ocean island of Mauritius a few years back. The Mauritius stamps epitomized all the elements that go into the value of stamps: rarity, demand, and good condition.

Item: Since World War II, classic U.S. stamps have risen in value an average of 20 per cent a year. Other increases have been even more spectacular. A British Guiana 1-cent stamp, for example, was sold in 1940 for $45,000. Thirty years later it went at auction for $280,000. In the early 1980s it had soared to an astronomical $850,000 in value!

Item: A new force behind the spiraling of stamp prices has been the emergence of the big-money syndicate. Added to the approximately one million serious individual stamp collectors in this country, the big-money syndicates put high leverage on prices as well as provide a price floor. The stamp market has moved way beyond the hobby of grade school and high school youngsters and into the area of major investments.

THREE LEVELS OF INVESTMENT

There are three levels of investment in stamps.

(1) $500 to $1,000. While they have no great lure as big money-makers, if you invest wisely by investing in ten or so items costing around $50 each, you can have a nice appreciation potential. You should avoid stamps in the $2 to $10 area and new issues that are mass produced.

(2) $1,000 to $10,000. Here is where more expensive stamps show their greater rapid appreciation. Concentrate on issues costing from $100 to as high as $5,000. Intensive research and a bit of luck could get you a real money-maker. Develop a specialty in buying at these prices. You can get burned with random buys.

(3) $10,000 to $50,000. Here you enter the real investment arena with stamps involving outlays of $100 to $500 or more. In assembling a collection in this area, concentrate on a philatelic theme. Your rewards could be healthy. Or, limit yourself to a limited number of rare items that could range from $5,000 and up. In this price range the emphasis is on scarcity for ultimate significant appreciation.

Postage stamps have long been considered a traditional hedge against inflation and economic-political catastrophe.

Their small size makes them easy to hide.

Stamps are readily convertible into cash.

Many wealthy foreign investors—frightened that they will be subjected to government seizure of their assets—have been turning to stamp acquisitions as a way to handle their resources. Wealthy South Africans, for instance, are extensively "plowing money into stamps," reported the chief executive officer of the American Stamp Dealers Association in New York City. "It's a seller's market," he adds.

DO'S AND DON'TS FOR INVESTING IN STAMPS

How then can you, the amateur, intelligently invest a portion of your capital in stamps to protect your savings against inflation and probably to make substantial profits too?

(1) Do start as a general collector, investing only small sums. Then develop a specialty—such as stamps of one type—airmail stamps or classic stamps, stamps from a particular country or region, stamps from a particular era. Study as much reliable literature as possible and attend as many auctions in your area as you can. Join a local stamp club and learn from experienced collectors.

(2) Don't waste your money on cheap packets of stamps. The odds that you'll find a valuable one are virtually nil because these packets are put together by experts who almost surely have snagged any valuable stamps before they get into the packet. The wholesale price of a typical collection of five thousand stamps may be only $12.50.

(3) Don't buy up whole sheets of ordinary new stamps from this or that country—where a currency devaluation could slash their value. This goes for the United States too: the value of post-1943 U.S. stamps as collector's items has remained at or below their face value and their sole use as postage.

(4) Do stick to the higher-price specimens and avoid the typical 50 per cent retail markup on inexpensive examples. The big increases in values are taking place today in this high-priced category—particularly, nineteenth-century quality stamps and early airmail stamps.

(5) Do, if you find an old stamp collection in the attic and want to sell it, take it to one or two reputable stamp dealers and/or auctioneers. Ask each how much he considers the whole collection to be worth. If the stamps are attached to the original letters, don't remove them, or you may slash their value to next to nothing. A stamp professional may legitimately charge you for an assessment of your collection, if you do not end up selling it to him. Typically an auctioneer will charge you a commission of 20 per cent of the sale price of the collection for auctioning it, less if the collection is very valuable.

To make sure a stamp dealer is reputable, check names with the American Stamp Dealers Association in New York City or one of its chapters in other big cities.

(6) Do, if you know nothing about stamps but still want to invest for profit, employ a knowledgeable dealer or other expert to advise you, to buy stamps for you at auction, or simply to sell you stamps he deems investment-worthy. Such agents today are representing increasing numbers of investors; their fees generally run about 5 to 10 per cent of the cost price of stamps bought. Serious collectors and top stamp auctioneers can steer you to good advisers or, in the case of some auctioneers, advise you.

(7) Do beware of improbable "bargains" of any sort. Errors and varieties

YOUR GUIDE TO OFF-BEAT AND ON-TARGET

can be manufactured and apparent quality improved by a "stamp doctor" for the sole purpose of fleecing the unwary. On such "bargains," get advice from a reputable dealer, a trusted expert friend, or a reputable committee of stamp experts (usually part of the large philatelic societies) which issues certificates of stamp authenticity.

Stamps are not for the short-term investor. Experts agree that the key to success for the amateur collector is to follow up on top-grade stamps and establish a specialty. In this environment, you should achieve impressive appreciation in three to five years.

Books Not for Reading

ONE OF THE RICHEST ERAS EVER

For the first time in more than a half century, individual collectors had a chance to bid at auction in the late 1970s for a Gutenberg Bible, the book of books that rare book collectors covet beyond all others as the greatest masterpiece of printing in world history. It fetched $2.2 million.

It was the second example of the work of Johannes Gutenberg (the fifteenth-century inventor of moveable type) to have changed hands in the late 1970s. A New York-based rare book dealer had earlier sold his copy to the Gutenberg Museum in Mainz, West Germany, for $1.8 million.

This was one of the richest eras ever for rare book collectors and dealers, with the marketing of such coveted rarities as a fifteenth-century Flemish Book of Hours; a first edition of Mark Catesby's *The Natural History of Carolina, Florida, and the Bahama Islands,* the earliest known book on American birds with colored illustrations; Ezra Pound's first book, *A Lume Spento,* plus a large collection of Ernest Hemingway correspondence.

Never had interest in this type of investing been so acute, reported the president of Swann Galleries, New York, largest specialty rare book auctioneers in the United States. The signs: increased membership in the industry trade association, the Antiquarian Booksellers Association of America (ABAA); mushrooming of new dealers; multiplication of book fairs; accelerating auction activity.

Long neglected by the public, rare book collecting has been viewed in the past as a classical form of investing, a rich man's hobby. While old coins, stamps, and art have boomed, rare books have climbed in value at a steady but unspectacular price.

But now . . . a copy of James Joyce's first edition of *Ulysses,* in good condition, one of a hundred, and signed by Joyce, was auctioned at $10,000 in the closing years of the 1970s against $2,100 in 1968. William Faulkner's first book, *The Marble Faun,* published in 1924, inscribed, sold for $6,250. An art book by Chagall, published as recently as the 1950s for $35, sold for $1,000.

While the soaring value of rare books and manuscripts rarely make the front page or the business news, book collecting for profit has become so attractive that it now ranks third in popularity behind stamps and coins. It is a solid, relatively low-risk investment that requires less cash outlay than, say, art and antiques, and there is every likelihood that values will continue to climb in the next five to ten years.

The biggest profits are made in anticipating what collectors will want at some future date. For example, Ian Fleming, the late British author of the popular James Bond books and one of England's leading book collectors at his death, collected manuscripts by Karl Marx. These items ultimately proved to be the most valuable in his impressive collection.

Similarly, some prices shift. The reason in not quite clear. An illustration is Edward S. Curtis' *The North American Indian,* a 20-volume set, with twenty portfolios of illustrations, published in 1935. The set sold for $20,000 in 1972, was auctioned for $60,000 five years later, was down to $50,000 as the 1980s opened. The reason? Either the unusually sharp rise of the Curtis set pushed the volumes out of reach of collectors, or it motivated other owners to offer their copies. Hence, the element of supply and demand possibly entered to lower the set's value.

BASIC RULES FOR NEOPHYTES

If you are a neophyte, don't enter this area to make a quick killing. Buy rare books and manuscripts first for the love of the items, the pleasure of ownership—and view moneymaking as a corollary, after you've educated yourself on how to collect.

You can collect in many fields: paperbacks (the first Penguin Paperback is now worth over $100); mysteries, science, telephone books, directories (the first New York City Directory sold a short while ago for more than $1,000).

The most active areas of book collecting are first editions, books of Chinese and Japanese art, medical books, maps and atlases, children's books, travel, cooking and wine books. Also, books on geology, crime, whaling, the American Indian, and early works on scientific subjects.

You can create your own field. "Why not collect every book published in Cleveland in 1931, for instance?" asks one expert.

Another area might be imprints. "I've known people who collected Swedish cookbooks published in France or books on a variety of subjects published in the year of their birth," the expert adds. "There are no limits to individual taste or interest."

Or:

(1) You may specialize in scientific and medical papers describing vital discoveries and inventions. *De Revolutionibus,* Copernicus (1543), went from $11,000 in 1963 to $40,000 in 1974, is now over $100,000. H. D. W.

Smyth's report, heralding the Atomic Age, published in 1945 is now at the $1,000 mark.

(2) Modern first editions. In addition to Faulkner, other hot authors are F. Scott Fitzgerald, John Steinbeck, and Ernest Hemingway. (Hemingway's high school yearbook of February 1916, containing his first published story, "Judgment of Manitou," recently sold for $1,000.)

(3) Press Books, with examples of fine printing. Important names are Doves Press, Kelmscott Press, The Limited Editions Club.

(4) Children's books with "a certain eternity." A first edition of *Pinocchio* by Carlo Lorenzini, published in Italian in 1883, and in English in 1892, sells for $500 to $800. Lewis Carroll's *Alice's Adventures in Wonderland* sells for $10–20,000. These high values can be ascribed to the fact that perfect copies of children's books are rare.

(5) Books on photography, maps, atlases, and nineteenth-century literature in fine condition command good prices.

(6) Limited and signed art books. In addition to Chagall, Picasso, Calder, and Dali books draw premiums.

(7) Comic books. If you want to save these, make sure your copies are in perfect condition.

In general, for the uninitiated, the watchwords are condition and collection. Therefore, as a newcomer, buy the best you can afford. Bargain hunting is false economizing when condition is so important a factor. One prime book is better than a room full of instant libraries which will have little appeal to knowledgeable dealers later.

Value lies in the collection. The more complete it is, so much the better. Single copies seldom bring much money on resale, since the market wants collections.

If you try collecting first editions, handle with care! If the pages are uncut, don't cut them. Don't remove the dust jacket. Wrap them in plastic and carefully put them away. Don't touch (much less read).

Form a good relationship with a dealer and book collector, particularly one who specializes in the subject you've chosen. The guidance you receive can pay huge dividends in the long run.

Finally, educate yourself. You can't go it alone. Read dealer and auction catalogs. Attend courses on rare books being offered across the country.

Vintage Cars—For Fun and Profit

ANOTHER LOVE AFFAIR WITH CARS

How would you treasure an investment of $30,000 that doubled itself in the next five years? And, then increased again by more than your original outlay in the second five years?

What would you think of doubling your money on a $6,000 investment by the mid-1980s?

Would you be happy if your investment of $12,000 today is worth $20,000 in the next five years?

Hard to believe? Got to be a catch? Not at all.

These are the past and projected growths in the value of restored collector cars—vintage automobiles for which the boom also appears relentless. Spurred by America's thirst for the nostalgic and couples with a love affair with the automobile, thousands of car buffs are finding fortunes in vintage autos.

Residents on Main Street and in mansions, alike, have taken to this profitable and fascinating hobby in unprecedented numbers. Collecting vintage cars looms as the great social "leveling" influence of a generation of Americans in the 1980s.

As with all booms, speculators have entered the field in numbers that virtually guarantee price spiraling and warn you to be on guard. Add to that a new breed of car counterfeiters whose clandestine operations span the Atlantic, and who copy original parts, assemble them to a bogus body, fake in manufacturer's serial number identity—then sell the finished item for $25,000 to $30,000 and up.

Conversion of expensive sedans into rare, limited editions of exotic models through counterfeiting of parts is not unknown, either.

An estimated 800,000 vintage-car buffs swelled demand for these cars in the 1970s. Now, it is predicted that the ranks will be enlarged by another 200,000 in the 1980s.

Lovers of nostalgic cars fan out to club rallies and car shows—all turned on by a hobby that has become rich bounty for old-car hunters. Their vocabulary is spiced with references to "antique cars," "classic cars," and "milestone models."

An important factor in the expansion of the vintage-car market was the national obsession that swept the country in the late 1970s for anything that reflected nostalgia. From collecting of antiques to the exchange of old bubble-gum baseball cards, millions of Americans have found new pleasure in turning back to yesteryears.

Whole new industries have sprung up in recent years to mirror the American obsession. In automobiles, of course, it could only be the real thing. And that meant turning back to the "Rembrandts" of the car world, the vintage car.

A second spur to the soaring market for cars of a bygone era has been the attraction of this hobby for the very wealthy. The polo set of the 1920s found a new hobby in the 1970s in the assemblage of a stable of cars from the turn of the century, or later. The result: dwindling supplies of the "good oldies" established a hydraulic lift of base market prices.

Latter-day self-made millionaires also have embraced vintage-car collecting. A Nevada casino operator was noted for his outstanding assemblage of these automobiles as museum pieces.

But the contagion of vintage-car collecting has not been limited to the wealthy. For the millions of American men who envision themselves as "tire kickers," the appeal of owning (and driving) a refurbished old car with a patent-leather shine and dazzling polished hardware has proved a strong lure too.

In fact, the boom in vintage-car collecting reflects not only a yearning for the past, but also the American identity with the automobile and the highway which began with the burgeoning of the Ford assembly line and the guaranteed $5.00 per day minimum salary.

All of this has been stimulated even more by the gathering of the car buffs; the explosion of antique-car societies; the regional and national meets; and the mushrooming of periodicals reporting enthusiastically about the field.

Collecting the cars is only a part of the busy world of the vintage-car owner and prospect. Restoration has become an important business.

PITFALLS!

The financial and aesthetic appeal of the vintage-car market can become magic. But, to the unwary, its pitfalls are risky. For the impatient it can be downright dangerous, since this is a hobby that requires expert knowledge, careful appraisal, and controlled bidding.

While big profits are being made by the informed, racing into this fascinating field for pure "moneymaking" can be very treacherous. You can get stung—perhaps badly—because, as a neophyte, you fail to take time to study the field.

A fun-filled avocation with the potential of profits can turn into a financial mudhole. The uninitiated can be caught in an escalating price market against a background of misleading advertising, revved-up salesmanship, and overpriced restoration jobs.

Restoration poses particular problems for the uninitiated, according to those experienced in the vintage-car market. Old-car buffs admonish beginners to watch with care the balancing of costs against maintenance of authenticity in the car's restoration.

THREE CLASSIFICATIONS

The vintage-car market actually covers three classifications of nostalgic cars:

Antiques. Can be traced to the beginning years of this century through World War I. The market turned lackluster on this category in the late 1970s.

Classics. Cars that span the era of the 1920s and 1930s. These have attracted substantial totals of sophisticated money in the past few years. Prices have been climbing, and experts agree that they could advance smartly into the mid-1980s.

Milestones. Post-World War II models with their preponderance of heavy metal trims. Interest has been great in cars from a quarter of a century ago —these gas-guzzling models of the 1950s. For the buyer with $10–$15,000 to invest, milestones have been particularly attractive, with appreciation possibilities still good.

GUIDELINES

Getting into the collectable car hobby requires homework. If you are tempted by this field of investing for fun and profit, here are a few guidelines to set you on the right road:

(1) Absorb as much education as possible. Read magazines in the field. Read the catalogs, anything to learn the market. Do research. *Hemmings Motor News* often is cited as a major source. *The Old Car Value Guide* is another important source.

(2) Develop a "feel" for ads. Knowing the values inherent in the market will be especially helpful in helping you to negotiate a price.

(3) Join local vintage-car clubs, a popular meeting place for old-car buffs. You can get a wealth of information from your associates in the field.

(4) Train yourself to be thoroughly familiar with the basic values in vintage cars. Become a student of rarity, condition of the car, engineering and aesthetic excellence as you also gain knowledge on makes and models. You should, for example, know that any classic car which was regarded as a masterpiece when it was built is still highly thought of by the old-car buffs. Convertibles could rise steadily in price if they fail to appear again in significant numbers from the Detroit assembly lines. Open cars such as roadsters are considerably more valuable than sedans.

(5) Approach auction markets with caution. Certainly until you learn your way around this field, take along an experienced friend. Watch out for the high-pressure auctioneer. Vintage-car auctions can turn out to be sheer folly for the untried and uninitiated shopper. Inspect cars ahead of sale and put a limit on your bidding budget. Don't allow yourself to be swept away. Consider bringing along a professional car restorer who can be retained for a fee in the $100 range to make an inspection of the car you have under consideration.

(6) Ask the advice of established dealers on types and prices of cars before you invest. Again, if you have a particular car in mind, get a professional appraisal.

(7) Undertake vintage restoration only if you are prepared to devote an inordinate amount of time to the job. It can be a big task and consume

five hundred to two thousand hours of your so-called "free" time depending on the size of the car and how mechanically expert you are. Be warned: not only will your ability be involved, but you also may need costly special tools.

(8) If you restore—don't overdo. Being sensible is as important as being authentic.

(9) Consider a professional restorer. Depending on your car and its condition, restoration costs could run well into five figures. You could sink more into the restoration than you will ever recoup on a resale—even in a rising market. Restorers frequently will take monthly payments of a quarter to a third of the price of the job.

(10) Make sure that you are adequately covered by liability and collision insurance. Some policies will cover you for parading your vintage cars at a show or similar festive event—but you could be banned from driving on major highways. Understand the limitations and restrictions of your policy.

Finding vintage cars outside the established market place can be fun and potentially profitable for the neophyte shopper. Consider making a few car-searching trips into the countryside, for the cars still could be sitting in some barns. Try touring the back roads. Keep looking for a potential bonanza that might be rusting away in some yard. Ask local residents about old cars: some could be abandoned; some could be on blocks.

Search for semi-restored cars which their owners halfheartedly gave up midway through the spruce-up job.

Pass the word among your friends to be on the lookout for you. This way you'll have several emissaries working in your behalf.

And above all, go slow! Don't be overeager. Learn the rules. Abide by them. Vintage cars can be a great hobby. But you must study the cars and the market—as you would any investment.

How to Choose an Appraiser

WHO ARE THE APPRAISERS

An accurate appraisal of any asset you own (all those mentioned in this chapter, for example) often is imperative—if only for your own protection. And certainly this will be the case if you're selling or buying, if taxes are at stake, if estate values are involved. How much do you know about this vast area?

Who are the appraisers? How are they organized, educated, monitored? When you need their services, how do you find and select the right one?

• There are five leading, nationwide testing/certifying appraisal societies in the United States, with an estimated 30,000 members of whom perhaps 15,000 have been tested and certified as being professionally expert and experienced. In addition, about 25 national, regional, local groups represent appraisal practitioners; and there are about 100,000 non-organized, or non-affiliated practitioners.

- Since the early 1900s, United States appraisers have been trained and monitored mainly by these five major societies, together with "in-house" training by some government agencies. Seminars, guidelines, tests, similar learning tools have been prepared by their educational leaders. A code of ethics has been published and is enforced by each of the five societies.
- But few states bother with monitoring appraisers. And there are *no* states which license, certify, or register appraisers in personal property appraising (or machinery/equipment, utilities, etc.). Only a couple specifically license even real estate appraisers.
- Your growing awareness, however, is stimulating appraisers to look seriously at themselves and some are taking steps to improve their educational, monitoring, and public service programs. As one example, the Washington-headquartered American Society of Appraisers is involved in a nationwide effort to create for the first time in the United States a valuation sciences degree program under which the education of appraisers will be placed with colleges and universities. As of the late 1970s, five colleges were offering the program.

This action will facilitate access to the most current data on statistics, economics, data processing, ethical criteria, and reporting techniques, says the ASA's executive officer, and it "will emphasize the great need for participation in appraising by minority members, whose participation we need to strengthen our professional ability to serve the public.

"Some form of licensing/certification/registration should be legislated," the ASA stresses, "for the benefit of the public, and all appraisers should be included in all fields."

The ASA also has adopted a "recertification concept," which would require continuing education criteria for every designated appraiser.

Thus, appraisers are moving to improve their profession, upgrade educational methods, encourage minority participation, require continuing education.

QUESTIONS TO ASK

But—how do you learn to select the best service you can? By asking these questions of the appraiser before you hire him or her:

What are your special qualifications to appraise this particular property? Are you a member of an appraisal society? Have you been tested by written exams? How long is it since you have been examined? May I see a list of clients for whom you have worked?

Ask for the name of the appraisal society. Call the organization for a double check.

The names and addresses of the five major societies, each with chapters and members in major cities from coast to coast, are:

American Society of Appraisers, Dulles International Airport, P.O. Box 17256, Washington, D.C. 20041; American Society of Farm Managers and Rural Appraisers, P.O. Box 6857, Denver, Colorado 80206; American Institute of Real Estate Appraisers, 430 North Michigan, Chicago, Illinois 60611; National Association of Independent Fee Appraisers, 7501 Murdoch Street, St. Louis, Missouri 63119; Society of Real Estate Appraisers, 7 South Dearborn Street, Chicago, Illinois 60606.

28

KNOW YOUR RIGHTS!—AND HOW TO USE THEM!

The Consumer Movement at the Start of the 1980s	1326
Helping You to Help Yourself	1327
Consumer Rights Quiz	1327
State and Local Government Protections for You	1329
How to Complain—and Get Action!	1329
basic rules on complaining	1330
why you never get your money back	1331
how to file a formal complaint	1334
how to write your representatives	1335
How to Avoid Mail Order Agonies	1335
rules for shopping by mail	1336
what to do with unordered merchandise	1336
What Is a Warranty Worth?	1337
what is a warranty?	1337
traps in a written warranty	1338
key questions to ask about warranties	1339
what you must do to make your warranty work	1339
How to Get the Most Out of Your Car Warranty	1340
guides before going to court	1341
used car warranties	1342
Shopping for Legal Services	1342
lawyers allowed to advertise	1342
basic rules for finding and choosing a lawyer	1343
if you cannot afford the fee	1344

Shopping for Legal Services (Contd)

HOW TO SLASH LEGAL COSTS	1344
UNDERSTAND THE FEES!	1345
WHICH LEGAL SERVICES DO YOU NEED?	1347

Your Rights as a Borrower — 1347

SHOPPING FOR CREDIT	1347
CLOSED END CREDIT DISCLOSURES	1348
OPEN END CREDIT DISCLOSURES	1348
CREDIT ADVERTISING	1349
OTHER PROTECTIONS UNDER TRUTH IN LENDING	1349
YOUR REMEDIES	1350
LEASING VS. BUYING ON CREDIT	1350
APPLYING FOR CREDIT	1352
WOMEN AND CREDIT	1352
CREDIT AND THE ELDERLY	1354
CREDIT AND MINORITIES	1354
REMEDIES	1355

Your Right to an Honest Credit Rating — 1355

HOW TO REVIEW YOUR OWN FILE	1356
CREDIT HISTORIES FOR WOMEN	1357
DEBT COLLECTION PROTECTIONS FOR BORROWERS	1358
WAGE GARNISHMENT PROTECTIONS	1358
IF YOUR CREDIT CARD IS LOST OR STOLEN	1359
BILLING ERRORS	1359
HOW TO ARGUE WITH A COMPUTER	1360
FASTER ERROR RESOLUTION	1361
PROTECTION AGAINST DEFECTIVE OR SHODDY GOODS OR SERVICES	1361
DISCOUNTS ALLOWED FOR CASH-PAYING CUSTOMERS	1362

Your Rights as a Veteran — 1362

VETERANS' BENEFITS	1363

Your Rights as a Hospital Patient — 1364

WHAT IS HAPPENING	1365
THE "PATIENT ADVOCATE"	1366

Your Rights as a Disabled Person — 1367

YOUR RIGHT TO EMPLOYMENT	1367
YOUR RIGHT TO EDUCATION	1368
YOUR DISABLED CHILD'S RIGHT TO EDUCATION	1368
IF YOUR RIGHTS ARE NOT RESPECTED	1368

Your Rights as a Taxpayer — 1369

HOW TO FIGHT THE IRS	1369

KNOW YOUR RIGHTS!—AND HOW TO USE THEM!   1325

- Your Rights as a Taxpayer (CONTD)
  - WHAT TO DO   1370
- Your Rights as a Worker   1372
  - YOUR RIGHT TO A JOB   1372
  - YOUR RIGHT TO A MINIMUM WAGE   1373
  - YOUR RIGHT TO JOIN A UNION   1373
  - YOUR RIGHTS AS AN OLDER WORKER   1373
  - EQUAL EMPLOYMENT OPPORTUNITY   1373
  - WOMEN'S RIGHT TO EQUAL PAY   1374
  - YOUR UNEMPLOYMENT INSURANCE PROTECTION   1375
  - YOUR RIGHT TO WORKER'S COMPENSATION   1375
  - IF YOU LOSE YOUR JOB THROUGH COMPETITION FROM IMPORTS   1376
  - YOUR RIGHT TO SAFE AND HEALTHFUL WORKING CONDITIONS   1377
- Your Rights as a Vocational School Student   1378
- Your Rights as a Franchisee   1378

The Consumer Movement at the Start of the 1980s

As the 1980s begin, the consumer movement is being viewed by millions of Americans with a new mix of disappointment and suspicion. Ironically, the aggressive consumer advocacy of the past decade has itself contributed to the disillusionment.

For "consumerism" has moved beyond the easy black-and-white issues of banning flammable children's sleepwear and into the gray areas that do not inspire your instant support or lead to quick solutions.

It is hard, for example, for average citizens to get excited about legislation that would enable public interest groups to take part in government proceedings. And there is no clear or easy answer as to where the line should be drawn between the constitutionally protected right of commercial free speech and invasions of an individual's privacy. This is the sticky issue which the Federal Communications Commission and other state government bodies are up against as they weigh whether and how to control unsolicited "junk" phone calls.

In many respects, the consumer movement has evolved from a crusade against blatant outrages into an attempt to change the way institutions work, to open them up, to make them more responsive to a variety of viewpoints and interests.

But in this maturing process, the consumer movement has made serious mistakes.

It has failed to celebrate its successes with the same relish that it has cataloged its failures and unfinished business.

It also has failed to make clear that its major goal is not "more government" or a form of "big brother" protectionism but to establish rules of conduct in the market place which enable you to help yourself, to make your own choices and decisions based on information that is accurate and easy to understand.

In 1962, President John F. Kennedy outlined in a consumer message to Congress four basic consumer rights that underlie today's consumer advocacy and which warrant repetition:

• The right to safety—to be protected against the marketing of goods and services which are dangerous to your health, life, or limb.

KNOW YOUR RIGHTS!—AND HOW TO USE THEM!

• The right to be informed—to know enough to guard yourself against fraudulent advertising, inaccurate labeling, unfair and deceptive practices, and to have facts which enable you to get full value for your dollar.

• The right to choose—to have, as far as possible, access to a variety of products at reasonable prices.

• The right to be heard—to obtain legal redress of complaints and grievances when the market place fails.

One of the basic challenges facing the consumer movement in the 1980s is to re-emphasize these original goals and to make clear that its aim is to disperse power and information to you, the individual, not consolidate it within a bureaucracy.

Helping You to Help Yourself

Do you know what your rights are when you have a dispute with the automobile repair shop?

Are you aware that you can take legal action against a dealer in any type of merchandise who unjustifiably threatens your credit rating?

Do you know what protection the law gives you if you receive unsolicited goods in the mail?

Test your ability to take care of yourself in today's market place, your awareness of important consumer rights, by answering this consumer rights quiz. True or False:

Consumer Rights Quiz

(1) Mail order firms generally must fill orders within thirty days or offer your money back. (True)

(2) Parents and students over eighteen have the right to see most school records and get inaccurate information corrected. (True)

(3) A consumer in Small Claims Court in all states must be represented by a lawyer. (False)

(4) Food labels must list their contents in order of quantity. (True)

(5) If your credit card is lost or stolen, you are liable for any amount until you notify the issuer. (False. You're liable until you notify the issuer or up to a maximum of $50, whichever is less.)

(6) There is a thirty-day cooling-off period on door-to-door sales contracts. (False. There's a three-day cooling-off period during which you can cancel door-to-door sales.)

(7) All wearing apparel selling for more than $3.00 is required to carry care labels. (True)

(8) Anyone seeking classified data from the government must receive a reply to his or her inquiry within ten working days. (True)

(9) If a moving company fails to pick up and deliver your household goods when it agreed to and as a result your family incurs motel and dining expenses, the moving company almost always will pick up the bills if you submit a breakdown of your expenses. (True)

(10) If you complain about an error in your bill to a creditor and don't hear from him for two months, you are entitled to keep the disputed amount up to $50, whether or not an error has been made. (True)

(11) If you have overpaid or returned an item and forgot you have credit outstanding, the store can pocket the money after thirty days. (False. You must be sent a refund or a notice of your credit during each billing period.)

(12) A creditor can ask if you are divorced or widowed if you're seeking individual credit. (False. A creditor may only ask if you are married, unmarried, or separated.)

(13) The Consumer Leasing Act requires leasing companies to tell you the facts about the cost and terms of their contracts, when you lease cars, furniture, appliances, and other personal property (not apartments or houses) for more than four months. (True)

(14) If you are covered by a private pension plan and have worked long enough to get a pension, it will automatically go to your spouse if you should die before retirement. (False. It will be so directed only if your plan has early retirement provisions, you opt for a surviving spouse reduction, and you have reached a certain age.)

(15) The Federal Wage Garnishment law limits the amount of your wages that your employer may withhold to repay a creditor to whom you owe money. (True)

(16) The Fair Debt Collection Practices Act prohibits anyone from harassing or abusing you, calling you repeatedly at odd hours, or telling anybody other than you that you owe money. (False. It applies only to debt collectors who regularly collect money for others, not the creditor himself or his lawyer.)

(17) If you are turned down for credit, insurance, or a job, you have the right to be told the name and address of the consumer reporting agency that prepared the report which resulted in the turndown. (True)

(18) If you are "bumped" involuntarily from an overbooked airline flight and the airline puts you on another flight to your destination within minutes you are still entitled to receive a refund. (True)

(19) With a few exceptions, no law prevents a private organization from demanding your Social Security number, but no law says you have to provide it either. (True)

(20) Federal law sets the minimum interest rates which banks, credit unions, and savings and loans must pay on deposits. (False. The maximum is set by law.)

How did you score?

If you found that you did poorly, review the quiz and the basic protec-

KNOW YOUR RIGHTS!—AND HOW TO USE THEM!

tions which federal law provides you, and which are discussed in virtually all the chapters of this book.

Also check what types of consumer protection rules your state and city now have on the books.

State and Local Government Protections for You

Various states and localities, for instance, prohibit:
• Selling used goods (such as demonstrator cars and worn furniture floor models) as new.
• Presenting you with a non-itemized repair bill.
• Stating that an item has been "marked down" when it normally has been priced at its current level.
• Changing the term of an advertised guarantee when you come to the store to look over the item.

Some areas also require that:
• All grocery items be marked with their individual prices, regardless of whether the store has an automated computer checkout system.
• All trade schools and auto repair shops be licensed or registered.
• Landlords place rent deposits into escrow accounts that cannot be used as income until disposition of the deposit is determined.
• Mobile home park tenants must be given a sixty-day written notice if the management wants to evict you, the tenant, and you must be told why.

A survey comparing laws and regulations in all fifty states and the District of Columbia on fifteen consumer issues disclosed that California and Massachusetts rated the highest, Wyoming and North Carolina the lowest.

How to Complain—and Get Action!

The fact that we in the United States are the owners of more than one billion home appliances, small and large, is convenience carried to a new dimension. But the miseries of repairing and servicing all these appliances also can be agony in a new dimension.

When was the last time you brought home some brand-new gadget, found it to be a lemon, then struggled through the utterly frustrating experience of having the dealer who sold it to you pass the buck to some huge and distant manufacturer, who maintained a stony silence for weeks before even acknowledging your complaint, much less fixing the appliance?

When was the last time you registered a complaint during the warranty period, then watched the dealer welch out of the warranty because he failed to cope with the problem before the warranty ran out?

But do you know what to do about these infuriating situations? Do you know how to complain—and get action?

BASIC RULES ON COMPLAINING

Here's what—and how:

(1) Go back to the dealer who sold you the product, or to the service agency to which he directs you, and complain—loudly. Take the ailing product with you (unless it's a refrigerator or a stove or some other monolith) and the original sales slip. Give the dealer all such pertinent details as the date of the purchase, the date on which the problem arose, a description of the problem and, if you could not take the appliance for any reason, the identification number of the machine. Don't threaten; this will only turn people off. Let the facts speak for themselves. And don't accost an innocent salesgirl who has neither the know-how nor the authority to handle your problem. If you document your case well, the normal channels of complaint usually will work.

(2) If the dealer or service agency refuses to help, then write or telephone the manufacturer's customer relations department. Again, state the key facts clearly—including dates, serial numbers, place of purchase, amount paid, what went wrong. Send photocopies of canceled checks and previous correspondence if you can. *Never, never send your only and original documents.*

(3) If this doesn't produce results, write to the company's president, again coldly stating the facts. Indicate at the bottom of your letter that copies are being sent to a variety of consumer organizations. If you do not know the name of the company president or the address of the company, ask your state or local consumer protection agency how and where you can find this information. Or go to your local library and look them up in Poor's Register of Corporations, Directors, and Executives or Moody's Industrial Manual. If these directories are not available in your local library, ask for the "directory" issues of such business publications as *Fortune, Business Week,* or *Forbes.*

(4) Send copies of your letter to your local consumer protection organization and also to such organizations as the Office of Consumer Affairs in Washington, Consumers Union, and your local Better Business Bureau. (See pages 1381–1403, for addresses of agencies and organizations which are eager to hear about your problems and in *some* cases prepared to assist you.)

When the Better Business Bureau receives a complaint, it contacts the company involved and tries to arrange a settlement. In some cases, arbitration is used. Because the Better Business Bureau makes contact with a company's top managers, reasonable complaints are fairly often settled satisfactorily.

However, there are limits to what the BBBs can or will do.

A BBB can only be a negotiator, not a judge.

It cannot force a firm to make an equitable settlement.

It can rarely even negotiate a settlement of a complaint with an unscrupulous enterprise, and it cannot force it out of business.

KNOW YOUR RIGHTS!—AND HOW TO USE THEM!

It will not handle complaints involving legal matters, credit matters, collection of accounts, or wages owed.

It will not pass judgment on prices or quality of goods or services.

To make the best use of a Better Business Bureau, request a Bureau report on a company—summarizing its past methods of operation—before committing yourself to any expensive proposition.

(5) Be constructive all along the line. If you have a suggestion on how the company or the dealer or the manufacturer could avoid the problems you are complaining about, include this suggestion in your correspondence. Propose a specific remedy. Do you want a refund? Repairs? Replacement? An apology? Be fair and realistic about what you propose.

(6) Don't try to be an amateur lawyer or insist on your "rights." The company or person to whom you are complaining probably knows a lot more about your rights than you do.

(7) If you are complaining in writing for the umpteenth time, give the dates of previous complaints.

(8) If you have bought the unsatisfactory or undelivered merchandise on a charge account, tell the store you don't intend to pay for it until a fair adjustment has been made.

(9) If it's an appliance, and if the manufacturer is unresponsive, send all pertinent information to the Major Appliance Consumer Action Panel or "complaint exchange" operated by the Association of Home Appliance Manufacturers in Chicago. MACAP has a staff of consumer specialists equipped to get action on your complaints on both small and large appliances. Also appeal directly to a local consumer organization, and if no such organization exists, ask the Consumer Federation of America in Washington for help in locating one.

(10) Tell your problem to your local newspaper in the form of a letter to the city editor, a tip to the consumer "action line" desk, a telephone request for help. Don't exaggerate, don't dramatize: just tell it the way it is. If your problem is real and other consumers also are victims, most newspapers or TV or radio stations will rise to your defense. There is no more powerful weapon than publicity.

Above all: Don't fail to complain if you feel you have a valid gripe—not only about a money loss but also about rude salespeople, deceptive advertising, late deliveries, confusing warranties, or outright gyps. It may be embarrassing to admit you've been had, but your complaints—if you make them fairly and coolly—will win better products and better service over the long range not only for yourself but also for other shoppers.

WHY YOU NEVER GET YOUR MONEY BACK

The 1980s will have the unenviable reputation as a bonanza decade for the nation's schemers and probably will be the worst decade ever for the millions of you who will become victims of your own ignorance and greed.

Equally dismaying, you'll not even have the excuse that you have been the target of a "new" gyp. The most successful of the rackets are and will be perennials that you should have learned to recognize and avoid in elementary school, and that I have tried to warn you about repeatedly throughout this book.

And worst of all, despite the growing numbers and power of consumer protection bureaus, law enforcement agencies, regulatory bodies at all levels of government, if you become a victim, the odds are overwhelming you won't get one cent—not one—of your money back.

But, "I want my money back!" is understandably the anguished cry that almost always comes after a victim of a consumer fraud discovers he/she has been ripped off and his/her precious "investment" has simply vanished.

Q. *Why do you rarely get it back?*
A. Because your money is, in fact, gone. Many schemes have profit margins no higher than their legitimate business counterparts. (Racketeers are not usually good money managers.) If a promoter does make a bundle, he/she siphons it off, so it's hard to find or recover.

Q. *"Where did the company go?"*
A. Bankrupt or closed. Or unknown to you, the gypsters start up again in a new city/town under a new name while you try (without a chance of success) to recover from the defunct firm.

Q. *"I'll get the law involved!"*
A. "Money back" still requires a voluntary agreement, usually under pressure, or a suit and a court order. Either requires a thorough investigation. A court order requires prosecution. Since few law enforcement agencies have adequate resources, they pick among frauds to investigate and prosecute. Your individual complaint may be neither carefully investigated nor prosecuted.

Q. *"But can't the court order restitution?"*
A. Yes, but far, far too often it is not paid. Con men frequently are "judgment proof." Unlike most of us who own property, a car, a house, etc., they have no assets that can be seized.

Q. *"But fraud is a crime!"*
A. Yes, even though these schemes seem outright frauds to you and me, it's tough to prove to a jury "beyond a reasonable doubt" that the intent of the defendant was to defraud. While it may be easy to show that you, a victim, have lost, this is not proof of fraud. The defense attorney simply may argue the business failed.

Q. *"He's convicted. At least send him to jail!"*
A. He may or may not go to jail. But no one gets any money back unless

KNOW YOUR RIGHTS!—AND HOW TO USE THEM!

the judge orders restitution as part of the sentence. And often the judge does not so order.

Q. *"Any other reasons why I don't get my money back?"*
A. Yes. You won't get your money back from the 1980s' record total of consumer frauds unless you, the victim, complain loudly enough. A veteran postal inspector says that even in fraud cases fewer than 5 per cent of the victims complain. And often if you do complain, you are up against a professional con man.

On a scale beyond anything ever known in the United States, the "con man" will be spreading out across the nation in the 1980s—snaring countless numbers of you as victims in the market place. The circumstances of the 1980s will be made to order for these shrewd, slippery swindlers: tens of millions itching to use their nest eggs to get-rich-quicker side-by-side with steep unemployment and other millions desperately seeking ways to earn a living wage.

If you are caught in a con man's web, the odds are he (or she) will escape unpunished and free to go on to other schemes. The odds also are you'll rarely, if ever, recover a single penny.

Your only real protection is being sufficiently informed to be on guard. Below, therefore, is a profile of a real-life con man, L.D., who has been operating throughout the 1970s without ever being put away by law enforcement agencies.

(1) In 1972, working out of New Jersey, L.D. touted a nationwide consumer discount buying service to alert members to ecological hazards, unsafe products, misleading ads, and even frauds. In reality, L.D.'s scheme was a straight distributorship and he, with his accomplices, conned more than $500,000 from hundreds of victims. The promoters misrepresented earnings, told distributors to claim they were making a survey in order to pitch other distributors, failed to disclose that so-called "account manager" jobs had to be purchased, and pressured the gullible into falsifying loan applications at banks. In 1974 a New Jersey court ordered L.D. to pay restitution of $503,000 plus fines and costs of $10,000. For itself, the state collected less than $1,000. Not one of the 312 victims got a cent.

(2) In 1975, L.D. crossed the Hudson to a swanky Central Park South cooperative apartment/office in New York City. His business-opportunity ads claimed: "Tired of working for someone else? Tired of giving all of yourself and not receiving? Call us . . . We Can Help! . . . A product every motorist needs. No competition. Guaranteed location and buy back." The product was a tire sealant to be vended from ten gas stations. But there was no merchandise. There were no locations. A promotional quote from a Chicago banker who headed "the nation's 2nd largest bank" was a complete fabrication. Neither the bank nor banker existed. In November 1976 a New

York state court ordered the return of $36,000 to victims of the scheme plus payment of $4,000 in state courts. L.D. has paid zero.

(3) The U. S. Government was next in the web, through the Commodity Futures Trading Commission (CFTC), a federal agency which was then fighting the nation's biggest investment swindle—the fraudulent sale of London commodity options. L.D. registered with the CFTC as a salesman (omitting mention of his phony schemes in his application). The CFTC has since revoked his license and fined him $10,000. But as of this writing, the CFTC is waiting for its $10,000. (And it always will be waiting.)

(4) In late 1977, L.D. advertised for an "associate or partner, $40,000 1st year guaranteed with better potential the second year. My marketing firm is growing . . . I am seeking a working partner with $10,000 to invest. Serious inquiries only." Among his victims was a Long Island business products salesman who grabbed a distributorship selling artificial flowers made of silk to be sold from display racks. The victim's loss: $4,500.

The law affords little protection and less recourse. So:

• Avoid any promise of quick money which involves your putting up cash first. That combination is almost always lethal.

• Don't be fooled by plush offices, handsome clothes, an expensive car. Victims' money bankrolls the con man, and his bank accounts are usually newly opened. Check the longevity of the account; it's more important than the balance.

• Never take references, even the most impressive, at face value. Ask the promoter what they mean, then check the references. You may get two entirely different stories.

• Don't be impressed either by such words as "national," "international," "consumers," etc. How many cities does "national" mean? Which ones? Be skeptical about any claims of affiliates, subsidiaries, suppliers, customer relationships. They may not exist. Get letters, names, addresses, question every claim.

• Insist on any promise in writing. Even then, be wary. Once a con man parts you from your money, you're out. But L.D.? He's still around, with several schemes going at once.

HOW TO FILE A FORMAL COMPLAINT

If you are filing a formal complaint with a government agency—say the Food and Drug Administration—be reasonably sure there is a violation of a law for which that agency has responsibility to avoid wasting your and the agency's time. (See pages 1381–1403 on where to get help, for the addresses of all key federal agencies you might want to write or call.)

To be effective, your complaint should be prompt and should contain the following information:

• Your name, address, phone number, and directions to your home or where you work.

- A clear description of the problem.
- A description of the label on the product and any code marks on it (such as the numbers stamped on a tin can).
- The name and address of the store which sold you the product, and the date you bought it.

Save whatever is left of the offending product, and save any unopened containers, for your doctor's use or for possible inspection by the agency.

Also report the suspect product to its manufacturer, the packer or distributor shown on the product label, and to the store where you bought it.

HOW TO WRITE YOUR REPRESENTATIVES

Finally, you may strongly support current consumer legislation to protect you and others in the future. If so, the first thing to do is to write your representatives—both in your state legislature and in Washington. Good, thoughtful, constructive letters may have a great impact on your senator's or congressman's thinking, and ultimately on legislation.

Here are five key rules for writing your representative:

(1) Identify the issue or bill that concerns you—by either its official or its popular title.

(2) Write as soon as possible after a bill has been introduced—but in any event before it comes out of the committee that is holding hearings on it and is responsible for shaping it into the form in which it will be put before the entire Senate or House.

(3) Make your comments constructive: if you oppose a bill, offer sound alternatives; if you approve, say why.

(4) If you are especially knowledgeable in the area about which you are writing, or if you have significant personal experience related to the legislation to report, share your knowledge and your experience.

(5) Keep your letter short—and clearly written.

The addresses at which you write (or telegraph) all senators and representatives are:

The Honorable ———— ————   The Honorable ———— ————
Senate Office Building   House Office Building
Washington, D.C. 20510   Washington, D.C. 20515

How to Avoid Mail Order Agonies

One of the convenient but also potentially the most agony-laden ways to shop is by mail either from mail order catalogs or in response to advertisements. Among the worst agonies are late deliveries, non-deliveries, broken merchandise, and refusal to honor warranties on products which do not perform as they are supposed to.

RULES FOR SHOPPING BY MAIL

You can avoid this type of bitter disappointment, though, by following these basic rules:

• Order at least three to four weeks before the date on which you want delivery—particularly during the Christmas season. Look in the catalog for a notation on the deadline for guaranteed delivery for Christmas.

• Be explicit in your instructions. Be sure to include your name and address (surprisingly, many don't), and any other information required. Also tell the store how to include your name if the gift is being sent by you to a friend.

• Don't rely solely on the picture of the merchandise you want to order. Read the description of its size, dimensions, weight, contents. And if key dimensions are missing, skip it.

• Look into the conditions of sale and/or guarantees. Are all sales final? Are products guaranteed to satisfy? To grow? To work? What will the company do if you are not satisfied—especially with expensive items? Give your money back? Replace the item? Or, least desirable, give you credit toward another purchase? Do you have anything specific to get the guarantee fulfilled—such as keeping the shipping label?

• Pay by check or money order, not cash. If you are ordering from a department store, charge the order if you can, then pay promptly after you have received your order intact and on time. If you must return an item, do so promptly, stating your reasons in a letter attached to the package. Give your name, address, account number, date of your order, description and cost of the item. If you complain "properly," most reliable companies will replace unsatisfactory merchandise or refund your money. And if your order does not arrive until after the time when you need it, the company will almost always accept return of the merchandise.

• Inspect mail order packages as soon as you receive them to be sure no parts are missing and to confirm the contents.

• If your complaints don't get a response within a reasonable period of time, write the Postal Inspection Service of the U. S. Postal Service in Washington to start an investigation into possible fraud, the Bureau of Consumer Protection, Federal Trade Commission, Washington, D.C. 20580, and the Direct Mail Marketing Association Consumer Service Director, 6 East 43rd Street, New York, New York 10017. This trade association will bring pressure on any member violating its standards of ethics.

In sum, be at least as wise a shopper by mail as you are in a store.

WHAT TO DO WITH UNORDERED MERCHANDISE

What should you do if you receive, say, a clutch of ugly neckties either through the mail or delivered to your door, which you have not ordered, do not want, and certainly do not wish to pay for? You also do not want to go

KNOW YOUR RIGHTS!—AND HOW TO USE THEM!

to the trouble of rewrapping them, trundling them to the post office, and paying return postage to return them to their sender.

You have no obligation to accept the merchandise, return it, pay for it, or give it any special care. So feel free to ignore any dunning letters for payment for any unordered merchandise you may receive. If you receive any such merchandise C.O.D. through the mail this is a postal violation and should be reported immediately to your post office.

Of course, first be sure that the merchandise was not sent to you by a merchandiser—such as a book or record club—which has signed you up for "negative option" selling. Under this arrangement you, the member of the "club," must return a reply card to the company if you do not want the merchandise, and are obligated to pay for the items if you fail to return the card within the allotted time. Under a Federal Trade Commission "Trade Regulation Rule," dating back to the mid-1970s, you have at least ten days in which to return the form rejecting an offer of merchandise. The FTC also requires the merchandiser to tell you "clearly and conspicuously" on all promotion materials:

> how to reject the offer of a selection;
>
> whether you are required by your agreement to buy a certain number of items in a certain time;
>
> that you have the right to cancel your membership in the plan at any time.

If you would like to reduce the volume of unsolicited mail you receive, write to the Direct Mail Marketing Association and request a form to remove your name from the mailing lists of their 1,600 member firms.

What Is a Warranty Worth?

WHAT IS A WARRANTY?

You buy a new TV set from a neighborhood store, the set is "guaranteed," and it breaks down within the guarantee's time limit. Who is responsible for repairs—the store or the manufacturer?

Will you have to pay labor costs and other charges which would amount to the bulk of the repair bill?

Does the guarantee cover all the parts, or will you find out that the part which broke down wasn't warranted?

Do you have to send the product a long distance to be repaired and at whose cost?

If you are promised "satisfaction or your money back," do they really mean they'll give you a refund if the product is defective?

And how much red tape do you have to endure before you get your money?

If an appliance is guaranteed for a "lifetime," what does "lifetime" mean?

Does the guarantee cover problems rising from faulty installation or only the manufacturer's defects?

What if the installer and manufacturer disagree on the cause of the problem?

These are merely a few of the annoying, often frustrating questions facing you when one of those sixteen appliances in your "average" household quits, collapses, or goes up in flames. It's no more than common sense to inform yourself about the basic provisions of warranties and on the fundamental rule for protecting yourself against worthless "guarantees."

Consumer product warranty law now gives you a basic floor of warranty coverage and requires that all warranties on virtually all types of products "mean what they say and say what they mean."

There is no difference between a warranty and a guarantee. They are the same: a maker or seller backs the product you buy. But there are two main types of warranties: an "express" warranty and an "implied" warranty. The usual express warranty is the one you see in writing—the type you find on most automobiles, small and large appliances, other household and around-the-house equipment. The implied warranty, which goes automatically with all purchases (except "as is") that you make, is the *unwritten* protection *implied* by the seller when he offers to sell to you. It is created by law. It simply says that when you buy something, it should perform the job it is supposed to perform, whether there is a written warranty or not. If it doesn't work, it's up to the seller to repair it or replace it or give you a refund.

TRAPS IN A WRITTEN WARRANTY

With any express or written warranty, what is *not* covered often tends to be more important than what *is* covered. In one study by a Presidential Task Force, no fewer than thirty-four different types of disclaimers were found on appliance warranties! A toaster you buy, for instance, may have a single defective part which is costly to replace or have repaired. That part may be excluded from coverage.

Be skeptical about products advertised as covered by an "unconditional guarantee" or a "lifetime guarantee." "Lifetime" guarantees almost never refer to the life of you the buyer. A product with a "lifetime" warranty is usually warranted for *its* own life (whatever that means!) or for the life of the product with which it is used (such as a muffler on a car), or for as long as the first purchasers continue to own the product. You also often may be led to believe a "lifetime" guarantee means the product is especially durable. This isn't necessarily so. Manufacturers are well aware how soon you're likely to sell, say, a car or lose a bicycle.

KEY QUESTIONS TO ASK ABOUT WARRANTIES

Here are the key questions you should ask about *any* warranty or guarantee:

Who will be responsible for repairing the product? The dealer? A service agency? The manufacturer? A repairman designated by the manufacturer? Does whatever source responsible have a good reputation for living up to warranties?

Does the warranty cover the entire product—or only certain parts? Are any kinds of failures excluded? Once you know the scope of the warranty learn its terms.

Is it a full warranty or a limited one? What do you get if the warranted product is defective?

Is labor included or only replacement parts?

Is there a provision for prorating the guarantee—e.g., paying only an allowance toward replacement of an item such as the motor of a year-old food blender which has somewhat depreciated?

If the product you have bought is defective and must be removed from your home for repair, will the dealer or manufacturer substitute an equivalent appliance in the interim?

Do you have to pay to return it to the shop or pay shipping charges to the factory?

How and by whom would the warranty be honored if you should move? Is there an authorized service agency at your destination which could perform the needed repairs?

Note: In warranties offered on many cars, tires, bikes, furniture, and appliances, there may be two different sets of rules—one set covering the first year and the other set covering the remaining one, two, four, or nine years.

WHAT YOU MUST DO TO MAKE YOUR WARRANTY WORK

You, the buyer, must protect your warranty coverage by informing yourself thoroughly and *before you buy* about what a product's warranty does and does not cover. Consider the warranty coverage offered on products made by different manufacturers as you comparison shop. And do *your* part to keep the warranty valid.

Most important, keep your sales slip. You almost always have to prove the date of purchase. If you must mail a special warranty card before the warranty is valid, do so, although very few companies insist on this; they use these cards mostly for marketing information. Keep any guarantee you may have seen in an advertisement. Don't lose the guarantee card which may have come with the product. It tells you what you get and how to get it. If you must submit the product for special inspections or servicing to make the guarantee good, do so.

Also, be sure to keep a written record of the dates you request service and your service receipts so that if your warranty period runs out before repairs are performed, you'll be able to establish the fact that the problem started while the warranty was still in effect. If it did, it is covered under the warranty.

And be on guard:

"Do-it-yourself" repairs on an appliance within the warranty period will probably make the warranty invalid. So leave such work strictly to the seller or his authorized service company.

Put in a file the exact name and address of the company or individual making the guarantee or keep the warranty.

How to Get the Most Out of Your Car Warranty

There are probably few problems quite as frustrating as those you encounter if and when you find yourself stuck with a car that's a "lemon." One Chicago woman, for instance, was forced to take her new expensive model car back to the dealer eight times to be repaired. The car was two months old. Despite her efforts, the car's transmission did not move in gear, it leaked oil, died frequently, and was infested with so many ants her seven-year-old son was afraid to ride in it!

If you are typical of many new-car buyers, you believe you are stuck with a "lemon" so long as the dealer continues to try to repair the defects.

This isn't so.

By law, all products, including cars, have an "implied warranty" that there are no defects interfering with the use and value of the product.

An "implied warranty of merchantability" is yours automatically by law when you buy any product, except one at an "as is" sale. As applied to cars, it basically guarantees that your automobile will be fit for safe, efficient, and trouble-free transportation. It covers defects that exist in the car at the time of sale and show up then or any time thereafter.

There is a catch to this "protection," though. Most states (with a few notable exceptions) allow dealers and manufacturers to limit the "implied warranty" to the duration of the written warranty. Say, for instance, one month after your 12,000-mile or 12-month written warranty runs out, your car's engine explodes. Under the manufacturer's written warranty you are out of luck. But under the "implied warranty of merchantability" if you bought your car in a state which does not limit it, you still have the right to file suit to have your engine replaced. In other states you may be stuck, although people in other states have sued—and won—in such cases.

If you or your lawyer are considering legal action, send for a free fact sheet on private consumer remedies, prepared by the staff of the Federal Trade Commission and available from Room 130, FTC, Washington, D.C. 20580. Another helpful booklet is "The Down Easter's Lemon Guide," from

KNOW YOUR RIGHTS!—AND HOW TO USE THEM! 1341

the Bureau of Consumer Protection, State House, Box 692, Augusta, Maine 04330. It is free to Maine residents, but if you live out of state, it cost $1.00 in the late 1970s.

GUIDES BEFORE GOING TO COURT

But before you consider going to court be sure that:
- Once you have bought a car, you do your part by maintaining it according to the schedule in the owner's manual. Have the shop doing the work note it in the schedule.
- You keep copies of all work orders to show when you first had problems and whether or not they were fixed properly.
- If you believe that you have a problem covered under the warranty, you take the car to the dealer from whom you bought it. Get a written estimate on what must be done and on whether or not the work will be covered by the warranty—*before* you authorize the dealer to proceed with it. Give him adequate time to do the necessary repairs.
- If you do not get satisfaction, you write or call the manufacturer's zone manager or factory zone manager. You can get his name and address from the dealer (simply asking him for this may make him more cooperative). A courteous and objective letter—giving full, appropriate details—will have the best chance of success. Be clear about what you want—a repair, replacement, refund, loaner car, etc.
- If your car is out of warranty but the problem arose during the warranty period, you mention this and that you are well aware the company is obligated to fix it. The firm cannot get out of its responsibility by saying "sorry your car is out of warranty." The same applies if your problem was "fixed" once and reoccurred. The company has to keep trying to repair the defect.
- You keep in mind, too, that many problems are the result of faulty design and may result in recalls. If the problem affects the safety of the car, you might want to call the Department of Transportation's toll-free hotline (800-424-9393) for recall information and to report safety problems.
- You realize that in many places you can take your problem to a small claims court, magistrate's court, county court, etc., where you do not need to be represented by a lawyer. You should use these courts for disputes involving cars if:

(1) the problem is repairable but the shop hasn't made the repairs.

(2) the shop or dealer charged you for the repair but shouldn't have.

(3) you went to another repair shop to have work done that should have been done under warranty but wasn't.

- You take advantage of the fact that you can work through a local consumer group to spur a dealer to act by, say, running an ad in your local newspaper detailing how the dealer shortchanged you. But *don't* attempt this on your own without legal advice. You can get into major legal trouble.
- You consider writing to the Federal Trade Commission, Warranties Di-

vision, Washington, D.C. 20580, telling the agency of your problem. Do not expect the staff, however, to help you directly or to get involved in your case. They cannot do so.

• You inform the dealer that you are doing all this.

• You are fully aware that court action is your last resort. It's here that "lemons" get replaced or money refunded. It does happen, and federal warranty law allows the court to require that your lawyer's fees be paid by the warrantor. One more guide: often manufacturers settle after a lawsuit is filed. Fear of a court battle frequently is enough to make them act.

USED CAR WARRANTIES

In some states, used car dealers must offer a guarantee that their cars will pass state inspection. In others used cars must pass inspection before they leave the lot. But most states leave the condition of a used car offered for sale pretty much up to the dealer. Any used car warranty has the same remedies as one supplied on a new car, but implied warranties on used cars are all but worthless.

If you financed your car *through the dealer,* however, you can stop payment until he honors the warranty. Before you do this, contact the bank or finance company where you make payments and the dealer to inform them you'll not be making any additional payments until the problem is resolved.

This step, as well as those outlined above, should improve your chances of fair treatment.

Shopping for Legal Services

LAWYERS ALLOWED TO ADVERTISE

Each American adult will have at least three serious legal problems in a lifetime. Yet 30 per cent of adult Americans have *never* consulted a lawyer and an additional 30 per cent have talked with a lawyer only once, according to an American Bar Association report in the late 1970s.

Why, when law schools are graduating thirty thousand lawyers a year?

Because millions of you simply do not know how to find the right lawyer for you. You are utterly befuddled about which lawyers specialize in handling what types of problems and at what prices.

This was the prime reason for a 1977 Supreme Court decision striking down state and local bans against lawyers' advertising. As one result, you now can get more facts than ever before about lawyers—their availability, specialties, and fees—through TV, radio, newspaper, and magazine advertisements.

Another significant result has been the development of legal clinics—supermarket-like law firms that specialize in offering routine legal services at cut-rate prices. As the 1980s neared, there were a thousand of these clinics in operation throughout the country and more are springing up all the time. They often are located in shopping centers and offer their services during evenings and on Saturdays. Because they handle so many clients, use paralegals to do much of the work, and concentrate on such relatively simple matters as uncontested divorces, personal bankruptcy cases, and uncomplicated wills, their fees almost always are lower than those of individual lawyers associated with big law firms or practicing alone.

Many lawyers still are reluctant to advertise but this resistance undoubtedly will be whittled down as more prominent firms take the plunge. Some state bar associations already have begun to set aside advertising budgets to stimulate business for the whole profession and to encourage widespread use of lawyers' services.

BASIC RULES FOR FINDING AND CHOOSING A LAWYER

The wisest time to decide who will be your family lawyer is *before* you need one. If you are new in town or have never before used the services of a lawyer, there are a variety of ways you can find a lawyer to meet your needs.

Check the Yellow Pages for the number of your local bar association. Many bars have prepared lawyer directories—books which list lawyers by their specialties: criminal law, general practice, consumer law, etc. The directories also contain information about the lawyer's education, whether he speaks any foreign languages, and his fees. Many lawyers give details on how much they will charge for an initial consultation.

• Instead of or in addition to these directories, even more local bar associations maintain lawyer referral services. The best of these advise you whether your particular problem actually requires legal help. This alone can solve your case immediately. If your problem does require a lawyer, the service then refers you to one, or perhaps several lawyers, who have indicated experience in your problem area. The referral service also may help you arrange an appointment, and often can tell you about other legal services and social service organizations in your area which might be able to assist you. The fees for such referral services usually range between $5 and $25.

• Ask your friends, doctor, minister, bank officers, or your company lawyer for suggestions. Any of these may have had some experience with your kind of problem and can refer you to an appropriate lawyer.

• Investigate local public interest groups which may provide legal services in certain specialized areas of law. If they cannot help you directly, often they will know of lawyers who are the most experienced in the field of your problem.

• When asking for referrals, be as specific as you can about the nature of your problem and be honest about the limits of your ability to pay.

IF YOU CANNOT AFFORD THE FEE

But what if you cannot afford to pay the fee a lawyer asks to help you solve a serious legal problem? Then . . .

• Go to one of the nation's five-hundred-plus Legal Aid Society offices. Look in the Yellow Pages under "Legal Aid" or "Lawyers" or call the local bar association for the address and phone. These societies are backed by community funds and offer legal aid at low or no cost. (In criminal cases, the best source of free help is the Public Defender.)

• Ask for help at one of the many federally funded Legal Service Corporation offices around the country. The LSC is the largest provider of legal aid to the poor and indigent. To locate an office near you, also look in the Yellow Pages under "Lawyers," call your local bar or write directly to the Legal Service Corporation, 733 Fifteenth Street, N.W., Washington, D.C. 20005.

• Find out if any local law schools have set up legal service facilities for ordinary consumers or low-income groups.

• Check whether your company or labor union offers free legal advice or group "lawyer insurance." As the 1980s approach, few do. Premiums for these services are deducted from your paycheck. You may be able to buy a prepaid legal plan on the open market, too. These are similar to health insurance plans. If you would like to join a prepaid plan or have questions about a specific one, write to the National Resource Center for Consumers of Legal Services, 1302 Eighteenth Street, N.W., Washington, D.C. 20036.

HOW TO SLASH LEGAL COSTS

To keep your legal costs to a minimum, first find the best lawyer you can afford to handle your problem, and check with all potential lawyers to whom you are referred through any of the sources previously mentioned. Call and talk to several of them before you make your first appointment.

When you phone, find out if the lawyer has experience with your kind of case. Learn what he charges for an initial interview, if anything. If you believe your matter is routine, ask if he has a standard fee and what it covers. If your problem is more complicated, ask what the lawyer's hourly fee is. Inquire if the lawyer provides written agreements describing the fees and the services he will give in return.

Consider these answers from each of the lawyers, then make an appointment with those whose replies suit you the best.

During your first interview, keep in mind that the attorney works for you. He or she should be anxious to help you solve your problem in the best way possible—which well might mean avoiding court action. Your lawyer also should be able to explain simply what he can do for you and how he will accomplish it. You should feel that you can tell the lawyer everything about your problem, including information that might be unfavorable. He can only assess your problem and his ability to solve it accurately if you are completely honest and straightforward.

When talking about your case, it will save you time (and therefore money) if you are as organized as possible. Prepare in advance a clear summary of your needs. Bring with you the names and addresses of all parties involved, their attorneys and insurance companies, if you know them. Have all pertinent documents—medical bills, receipts, contracts, etc.—in order too. Some lawyers may ask you for these before your interview so they can review them in advance of your actual meeting.

If you have decided to seek an interview with a law firm, ask who will actually be working on your case. If the firm uses paraprofessional help (law students, paralegals, etc.) to prepare certain routine legal documents or background information, decide if you should talk directly with those people. Increasingly, such individuals are doing more routine legal work. Their hourly rate is considerably less than an attorney's, so if they handle much of the work on your problem you should know it and the cost should be less.

If you want to be actively involved in your own case, you should be allowed to be. Make this clear to the lawyer at the first interview and tell him you want to:

• Receive copies of all documents involved in the case or have them available to you at his office.

• Be told of all developments in the case.

• Be consulted before decisions in the case are made and the major instances in which you can make these decisions yourself.

• Ask the lawyer for a list of events that are likely to occur in your case and a timetable for them. You should have some idea of how long he will need to resolve the matter.

UNDERSTAND THE FEES!

Perhaps the most common cause of dissatisfaction between lawyers and their clients revolves around fees.

It is essential—even if the lawyer is your friend or is taking the matter on a reduced-fee basis—to understand fully his fees and how you will pay them.

Most lawyers charge on an hourly basis, with fees ranging from about $20 per hour to more than $100, as the 1980s approached. You can see about a reduced rate if the lawyer you want to hire normally charges more than you can afford. You also can ask that a lawyer not exceed a certain amount of time or amount of money on your case without first getting your permission.

More and more, both clients and lawyers are spelling out fee agreements in writing to avoid possible misunderstandings. Make sure that your agreement not only explains the fees your lawyer charges but also expenses that he's likely to incur and for which you will pay and the services he will provide in exchange.

Some lawyers require an advance fee called a retainer. It usually represents a number of hours of the attorney's time at his usual hourly rate. If the time your lawyer spends on the case exceeds the amount paid for by the retainer, he will bill you for the additional charges. You both should agree beforehand on how billing and payment for such excess will be made. If the attorney spends less time than is covered by the retainer, you both should agree that a refund will be made.

If the retainer is for a flat fee, covering the entire cost of the case no matter how much or how little time it takes, you may be unable to get a refund.

In accident or personal injury and some other types of cases, some lawyers agree to accept as their fee a percentage of the money you may get if you win. If you lose, you pay the lawyer only for the expenses associated with the case—telephone calls, court costs, postage, copying costs, etc. Cases handled on such a basis are called contingency fee cases.

If you agree to such an arrangement, be certain you understand what portion of the recovery you and your lawyer will each receive and how expenses will be covered.

The Citizens Advisory Committee to the Washington, D.C., Bar has prepared an excellent guide, "Finding and Hiring a Lawyer" (available by writing D. C. Bar, 1426 H Street, N.W., Suite 840, Washington, D.C. 20005). The guide recommends you ask your lawyer the following questions regarding any type of legal fee arrangement:

- Can you prepare for me an estimate of how much this legal problem will cost?
- Can you give me a written fee agreement which sets forth not only my obligation to pay but also exactly what you will do for me?
- How often will I be billed? Will you agree to let me know when a specific dollar amount of your time has been spent on my case so that I can authorize further payments?
- Can you estimate how much court costs, witness and deposition fees and other costs will run, aside from your fees? How will I be required to pay these costs?
- When will I have to pay? (Explain to your lawyer the payment schedule which is best suited to you.)

In your final analysis of any lawyer you should trust your own common sense and feelings as you judge a lawyer's personality, experience, how you communicate with one another.

These aspects are well outside of the money area, but fundamentally may be just as important as, or even more important than, the fees you will have to pay.

KNOW YOUR RIGHTS!—AND HOW TO USE THEM!

WHICH LEGAL SERVICES DO YOU NEED?

Inquire about what services and specialties are and are not provided by the law firm as a whole. If services important to you are not provided, ask whether the lawyer or firm has access to top-notch outside legal specialists.

Here's a list of five legal services a family lawyer should be able to provide.

(1) Deed preparation, title searches, and other details in real estate transactions. (See chapter on housing for description of legal mechanics of home buying.)

(2) Drawing up a will and perhaps later serving as executor or legal adviser for your estate. (See "What You Should Know About Wills, Estates, and Trusts.")

(3) Representing you in and out of court if you should be arrested or sued or if you should decide to sue someone else.

(4) Preparing a separation agreement and other documents associated with a divorce and, if necessary, representing you in a divorce court. (See chapter on "Sex and Money" for discussion of can you afford a divorce?)

(5) Steering you to a competent insurance agent, tax adviser, accountant, and other experts whose fees are favorable to you or who will make special arrangements with you.

Your Rights as a Borrower

SHOPPING FOR CREDIT

The 1968 Truth in Lending Act is one of the most important consumer protection measures ever signed into law. It requires creditors to provide you with information that tells you exactly what credit will cost. With these facts you can compare the *real* cost of credit from Lender A with that available from Lender B. Furthermore, the act also covers professional services, such as those provided by your physician, dentist, or lawyer, if you pay for them in more than four installments.

In order to help you comparison shop, the law requires that the same terms be disclosed by all creditors. The two most important disclosures required are the *finance charge* and the *annual percentage rate*.

The finance charge is the amount of money you pay to get credit. It includes interest as well as such other charges as loan or finder's fees, points, service charges, or premiums for required credit life, accident/health, or property insurance.

The annual percentage rate (APR) is the charge for credit expressed as a percentage. The lowest APR is always the best credit buy, *regardless* of the amount of the debt or the length of the time over which payments are to be made. Comparing the APR on credit deals and choosing the lowest one gives you the most for the least amount of money.

The APR is not always the same as the interest rate. Like the finance charge, it also includes other charges which may increase the cost to you and expresses them in a manner which allows you to compare one deal with another.

Basically, you, a consumer, can obtain two major types of credit.

One type is called "closed end" credit. It is frequently used to finance the purchase of such relatively expensive items as cars, furniture, TV sets, or for personal loans. You usually ask for this type of credit for a specified period of time and agree in advance on the amount, number, and due dates of payments, as well as the dollar amount of the finance charge.

The second major type of credit is called "open end" credit. You generally use this sort with revolving charge accounts or credit cards to pay for such less costly items as clothes, meals, and hotel rooms. Another example of "open end" credit is the overdraft checking account. With this type of credit, you pay finance charges periodically on your unpaid balance, and you may obtain new extensions of credit at any time.

Depending on the type of credit you get—open or closed end—the Truth in Lending Act requires you be provided with certain facts. Here is a sampling of the information you must be given for each type of credit:

CLOSED END CREDIT DISCLOSURES

All closed end credit disclosures must be given to you *before* any credit agreement is made. You must be given a copy of the document on which the disclosures appear. Below is what you *must* be told:

• The total finance charge—the amount of money the credit will cost you.
• The annual percentage rate.
• The number, amount, and due dates of payments, plus the sum total of all the payments.
• The amount or method of figuring out what penalty fee you may be charged if your payments are late.
• A description of any security interest and clear identification of the property to which it applies.
• A description of any penalty charge that you might have to pay if you pay off your account before the agreed-upon time limit.
• A statement of whether you will get any rebate of unearned finance charges for early payment and, if so, the method used to compute the amount of such a rebate.

OPEN END CREDIT DISCLOSURES

Before any transaction is made on an open end credit account, creditors must disclose a number of important facts to you. Among these are:

KNOW YOUR RIGHTS!—AND HOW TO USE THEM! 1349

• A description of when a finance charge may be imposed and the time within which you can pay without having to pay any finance charge.

• The method the creditor will use to determine the balance on which a finance charge may be imposed, as well as how he'll determine the amount of the finance charge.

• The periodic rate or rates which he will use to compute finance charges and the range of balances to which each rate applies, and the corresponding annual percentage rate.

• The minimum periodic payment required.

• A notice describing your rights under the Fair Credit Billing Act (see pages 1360–61).

When you open a new open end account, you must be given this information. In addition, you also must be sent a periodic statement (usually monthly) that tells you: your previous balance, the date and amount of each of your purchases, a recognizable description of each item you charged, credits for returns, the amount of the finance charge for the period, the address to which billing inquiries should be mailed, and other items.

If, under the open end credit plan, you can avoid a finance or other charge by repaying any portion of your new balance before a certain time has elapsed, your periodic statement must be sent to you at least fourteen days before the cutoff date.

CREDIT ADVERTISING

The Truth in Lending Act regulates credit advertising, too, including deals with no finance charges but payable in more than four installments. If a creditor or seller advertises any specific credit term in newspapers, magazines, radio, television, promotional material, or on the price tags attached to merchandise, he must include other pertinent credit information. For example, he may not simply say that "you'll pay only $30 a month" without telling you such facts as the "cash price," the "cash down payment required" (even if zero), the annual percentage rate, and other pertinent information.

OTHER PROTECTIONS UNDER TRUTH IN LENDING

In any credit transaction in which your home is to be used as security, a creditor must give you three business days during which you can back out of the deal and cancel the contract you have signed.

You must be given a written notice explaining you have the right to this "cooling off" period.

If you decide not to go through with the transaction, you must tell the creditor in writing. This three-day cooling off or "rescission" period applies to such credit arrangements as second mortgages and home repair or home improvements loans (some of these involve mechanics' and similar liens; see pages 278–79 for a description of such liens).

The right to cancel does *not* apply to a first mortgage loan used to purchase your home.

YOUR REMEDIES

If a creditor fails to give you any of the information outlined above (except the disclosures required in credit advertisements), you have the right to sue.

You can sue for damages plus twice the amount of the finance charge (not less than $100 or more than $1,000). You can also be reimbursed for court costs and attorney's fees if you win the lawsuit.

However, even if you should win, you still must pay off the debt, including the finance charges. Creditors who deliberately violate the law may be hit with criminal charges, including fines of up to $5,000 or a maximum of one year in prison, or both.

LEASING VS. BUYING ON CREDIT

When shopping for your next car or furniture for an apartment that you plan to use for only a short time, you well may wonder if you should buy on credit or lease. The Consumer Leasing Act, which became law in 1977, will help you decide. It will also help you compare the terms of one leasing arrangement with another.

As with credit transactions, there are two main types of leases: "open end" and "closed end."

In an open end lease you run the risk of owing extra money depending on the value of the property when you return it. This payment is called a "balloon payment."

In a closed end lease you are not responsible for the value of the property when you return it and will not have to make a balloon payment. Consequently, closed end leases usually have higher monthly payments than open end leases.

The Consumer Leasing Act applies to both open and closed end leases. It requires that certain facts be disclosed to you, the individual, when you lease property for more than four months for your personal, family, or household use.

Before you sign a lease you must, for instance, be told:

• The amount of any advance payment or security deposit.

• The amount and dates of regular payments and the total amount of those payments.

• The kind of insurance you'll need, who is responsible for maintaining and servicing the property, and whether or not you can buy the goods, when and at what price.

• The amount you must pay for taxes, license, registration.

• How you or the leasing company may cancel the lease and what the charge is for doing so.

KNOW YOUR RIGHTS!—AND HOW TO USE THEM!

If you choose an open end lease, the leasing company also must tell you that you may face a balloon payment and how it is determined. You have the right when such a lease is over to get an independent appraiser's estimate of what the property is worth. Both you and the leasing company must abide by the estimate.

Say, for instance, you sign an open end lease for a car. At the end of the lease, the leasing company figures the car will be worth $2,000. If, when you return the car, the leasing company claims it is worth only $1,500, you can ask an outside appraiser to determine the car's value. If he agrees with the leasing company, you probably will have to pay a balloon payment of $500.

There are limits on the size of balloon payments, however. The law says that in an open end lease they may not exceed three times the average monthly payment, unless you agree to make a higher payment or have, in the case of a car, driven more than average mileage. The leasing company may seek a bigger payment by going to court. If it does go to court, it must pay your attorney's fees, whether it wins or loses.

To compare the cost of buying on credit with the cost of open end leasing, you will need to know:

The annual percentage rate you must pay on your loan and the finance charge;

The total amount for which you are responsible under the lease—that is, total periodic payments, the estimated value of the property at the beginning and end of the lease, and the difference between the two.

All of this information must, by law, be given to you.

To illustrate, here is a rundown on a three-year open end car lease. The lease might show:

36 monthly payments of $125	$4,500
+Estimated value of car at lease end	2,000
Amount for which you are responsible	$6,500
—Value of car at beginning of lease	5,800
Difference	$ 700

If you bought this same $5,800 car and financed it over a period of thirty-six months by obtaining a loan with an annual percentage rate of 12¼ per cent, you would pay a finance charge of about $1,160. Compare this finance charge figure with the difference shown in the example above. This permits you to compare the two costs.

Of course, the costs of buying the car on credit depend on the annual percentage rate of your loan. The higher your credit costs, the more appealing leasing may seem. But before making up your mind, take into account the cost of insurance, maintenance, and other special fees associated with both leases and loans.

APPLYING FOR CREDIT

Credit—the right to incur debt and to defer paying for goods and services—is an important privilege, not a right. Banks, department stores, gasoline companies, credit unions, and other creditors set their own standards for judging your creditworthiness or ability and willingness to repay.

Under the Equal Credit Opportunity Act, however, they cannot deny you credit on the basis of your sex, marital status, religion, natural origin, or (with limited exceptions) your age.

In general, creditors assess your ability to repay your debts by asking how much money you earn; if you have other outside income, say from such investments as stocks and bonds; and if your earnings are steady. Often creditors inquire how long you have held your present job. Usually you have to be employed for at least six months before a creditor will consider you sufficiently reliable to receive credit.

The best indication of your willingness to repay your debts is your credit history—whether you've paid your credit card bills and loans on time, any outstanding debts you may have, if you've ever gone bankrupt or had actions taken against you by a collection agency, etc.

Creditors also will ask about your assets: whether you have a savings and/or checking account, a home, a car. They use other criteria to judge your stability: your occupation, whether you own or rent your home, how long you have lived at your present and previous address, whether you have a telephone.

Many firms, particularly large ones, have replaced the above more traditional, rule-of-thumb measures of an applicant's creditworthiness with a mathematically developed credit scoring system.

These systems are based on the information in a particular creditor's own accounts, and certain characteristics which have been selected to predict your financial trustworthiness. Whether you are considered a good risk or bad depends on your total score.

While these systems have been praised for their statistical accuracy, they also have been criticized by some legislators and consumer groups for being incomprehensible.

For example, when an applicant has been turned down by some creditors using such systems, he has been told that the "reason" for denial was geographical area, occupation, type of residence, or other explanations which give him no chance to take corrective action in order to qualify for credit. These incomplete and ambiguous statements have led some critics to charge that creditors are still practicing discrimination.

WOMEN AND CREDIT

Until relatively recently, many creditors discriminated against women, not because they lacked steady jobs or were burdened with debts, but simply because they were women. The Equal Credit Opportunity Act, which became law in 1975, makes discrimination on the basis of sex or marital status illegal. The act gives women these important protections:

• A creditor may not refuse you credit because you use your maiden name, a combined or hyphenated last name, or your first name with your husband's last name that you have assumed—"Anne Smith," for example, rather than "Mrs. John Smith."

• If you are married, divorced, widowed, or separated or change your name, a creditor may not require you to reapply for credit because of this change. He may not require you to change the terms of your account or stop reporting your credit history.

• Creditors cannot ask any questions regarding your childbearing or birth control practices. They may not assume that because you are of childbearing age and statistically apt to stop working that your income will fall, and for that reason deny you credit.

• A creditor may not refuse to consider alimony, child support, or separate maintenance payments as income for you as long as the payments are regular or reliable. Each creditor has a different idea of what constitutes reliability for this sort of income, so you should ask what evidence or proof he might want (copy of a court order or checks sent to you) before you apply. However, you do not have to reveal that some of your income comes from these sources unless you think you won't obtain credit without them.

• A creditor may not refuse to consider your income because it comes from regular part-time work.

• A creditor cannot require your husband to co-sign or guarantee credit or a loan, unless you are depending on his income to support your application or jointly held property is being put up as collateral for a secured loan.

• Creditors cannot ask you what your marital status is if you are applying for a separate, unsecured account unless you live in a community property state (Arizona, California, Idaho, Louisiana, Nevada, New Mexico, Texas, and Washington). In fact, if you don't live in one of these states, are not relying on your spouse's income, alimony, or support payments and your spouse will not be using the account, creditors cannot ask for any information about your spouse.

Many private groups and public agencies have written excellent, easy-to-understand booklets about women's credit rights. Among these are:

"Equal Credit Opportunity" and "Women and Credit Histories," available free from the Federal Trade Commission, Legal and Public Records, Room 130, Washington, D.C. 20580.

"A Woman's Guide to Personal and Business Credit" by Susan Ingram ($2.95) from Pilot Books, 347 Fifth Avenue, New York, New York 10016.

"New Credit Rights for Women" ($2.00) from The Consumer Credit Project, Inc., 267 Kimberly, Barrington, Illinois 60010.

"Borrowing Basics for Women," free from the Public Affairs Department of Citibank, Box 939, Church Street Station, New York, New York 10008.

"How Woman Can Get Credit" (20 cents) from National Organization for Women, 2000 P Street N.W., Washington, D.C. 20036.

"Women to Your Credit," free from your nearest Commercial Credit office or Commercial Credit Corp., 300 St. Paul Place, Baltimore, Maryland 21202.

"The Credit Handbook for Women," free from the American Express Co., American Express Plaza, New York, New York 10004.

CREDIT AND THE ELDERLY

You have just turned sixty-five and receive a notice to reapply for credit at a local department store. You are seventy-eight years old, still have a steady job, a savings and checking account, home and car, yet your application for a major credit card is turned down.

Experiences such as these led to the 1977 amendments to the Equal Credit Opportunity (ECOA) Act. These amendments extend the ban on credit discrimination to include race, national origin, religion, receipt of public assistance, as well as age.

The ECOA permits creditors to consider age only if:

You are too young (usually under eighteen) to sign contracts;

You are sixty-two years or older and the creditor provides special credit help or consideration because of your age;

The creditor uses a statistically sound credit scoring system which *favors* applicants sixty-two years old and over. (See "Applying for Credit" for an explanation of credit scoring systems.)

Because age has its economic consequences, creditors can use it to consider factors that clearly bear on your ability and willingness to repay a debt. They may, for instance, determine if your income is about to drop because you are close to retirement.

However, creditors may *not:*

• Refuse to consider your retirement income (money from a pension or annuity plan) in rating your credit application.

• Require you to reapply, change the terms, or close your account just because you reach a certain age or retire.

• Deny you credit or close an account because credit life insurance or other credit-related insurance is not available to someone your age.

CREDIT AND MINORITIES

The ECOA prohibits you from being denied credit because of your race, color, religion, and national origin, because you receive income from any public assistance program or because you have exercised your rights under consumer credit laws.

Under the law, too, lenders may not consider the race or national origin of the people who live in the neighborhood where you want to buy or fix up a home with the help of a loan.

You also might want to know where most lending institutions in your city make mortgage and home improvement loans. The Home Mortgage Disclosure Act requires most major lenders in metropolitan areas to make this information available annually. You can ask to see the disclosure statement at your bank, credit union, or savings and loan association.

REMEDIES

If you believe you have been the target of discrimination, you can sue for actual damages and up to $10,000 in punitive damages. Before taking legal action, complain to the creditor. Let him know you are aware of your rights. Request the reason for your denial in writing. If still unsatisfied, speak with the credit manager or loan officer.

If the problem cannot be solved, you can file a complaint with one of a number of federal agencies which have enforcement responsibility.

If the creditor is a retail store, small loan and finance company, gasoline or travel card firm or state-chartered credit union, contact the Federal Trade Commission, Equal Opportunity Division, Washington, D.C. 20580.

If the creditor is a bank, write to one of the bank regulatory agencies. (See pages 1386–88 for a discussion of which agencies are responsible for which types of banks.)

If the creditor is a federally chartered credit union, alert the regional office of the National Credit Union Administration.

Your Right to an Honest Credit Rating

Because of the Fair Credit Reporting Act, which became effective in 1971, you can take action if you believe you have been denied credit, insurance, or a job or had difficulties obtaining any of these due to a consumer report on you.

There are two basic kinds of consumer reports. The most common is a credit report or credit history assembled by a credit bureau. It contains information about your credit accounts and bill-paying habits, which comes from creditors who use the services of the credit bureau. This type of consumer report costs little, and merchants, banks, credit card companies, and other creditors request thousands of them on applicants every day.

The other type of consumer report is an investigative report. It usually is requested by insurance companies or employers. This type of report involves personal interviews with third parties who may know something about the consumer's character, general reputation, or style of living. As a rule, the consumer is entitled to be told when he is the subject of such a report. These investigative reports are costly and relatively rare.

The Fair Credit Reporting Act is designed to protect consumer privacy and safeguard the accuracy of credit bureau reports. Under the Act you have the right:

• To learn the name and address of the consumer reporting agency responsible for the report which caused you to be denied credit or a job.

• To discover upon request and proper identification of yourself the nature and substance of the information (except medical) that a credit bureau or other consumer reporting agency has on file about you.

• To know the sources of such information, except for investigative-type sources.

• To get the names of all who have received reports on you within the last six months or within the past two years if the report was furnished for employment reasons.

• To have incomplete or incorrect information reinvestigated and, if it's found to be inaccurate or cannot be checked, to have it removed from your file.

• To have your side of a disputed fact or story included in your file and credit bureau (at no cost to you) notifies those firms which you name of the inaccuracies.

• To have your side of a disputed fact or story included in your file and future reports, if a disagreement between you and the agency cannot be resolved.

The law forbids reporting agencies from sending out adverse information about you that is more than seven years old, although bankruptcies may be reported for fourteen years. There are no time limits for sending information on you if you apply for a loan or insurance policy of $40,000 or more or apply for a job with a salary of $20,000 or more.

HOW TO REVIEW YOUR OWN FILE

It is simple to learn what is in your credit file. You may visit in person or possibly receive the information by mail or over the phone.

Check the Yellow Pages under such headings as "credit" or "reporting agencies" to get the name and address of the major credit bureau in your area. Or call your bank or department store and ask which credit bureau it uses.

Call to arrange a personal or telephone interview. Some, but not all, bureaus will send you a report by mail once you send them a release form and probably a small fee ($2.00 to $5.00). Technically, you have the right to be told what is in your file, not to receive a copy of it.

If you visit the credit bureau, have some personal identification with you. You also may bring one person with you when looking over or discussing your file. That person must furnish identification, too, and you may have to give the bureau written permission for his or her presence. If you have any questions, the law requires that the credit bureau provide you with a trained counselor who can help you read and understand your file.

CREDIT HISTORIES FOR WOMEN

Frequently when women are rejected for credit, the reason is "lack of sufficient credit history." In the past, credit accounts often were recorded only under the husband's name, even though the wife used the accounts and took charge of paying the monthly bills.

If you are a woman—single, married, divorced, separated, or widowed—you owe it to yourself and your family to establish a credit history in your own name!

Why? Because the chances are very high that at some point in your life you will want and need to get a mortgage loan, department store charge account, or credit card. The day almost surely will come when you will be on your own with an income of some sort and obtaining credit will be important to you. To obtain it, you will need to establish your creditworthiness.

To develop your own credit record, take these steps:

• Open a checking and/or savings account in your own name (e.g., "Mrs. Susan Smith," not "Mrs. John Smith," which is a social title and could possibly refer to more than one woman. You may use your maiden name, a hyphenated last name or whatever name you wish and use legally). Establishing a separate checking and/or savings account doesn't mean you have to close out a joint account that you share with your husband. Just open a new one for your own use. Don't overdraw on it.

• Apply for a retail, bank, or credit card in your own name. This is one of the least expensive ways to start a credit history, since you can use the cards without paying any interest if you pay your bills within a certain period of time. You may have to accept a limited credit line until you prove your willingness to repay. You don't have to borrow on these lines of credit. They will appear on your credit history and establish you as soon as they are approved.

Don't apply for too many accounts at one time. Some creditors may deny your application if they think you are opening too many new accounts in a short space of time. If you are turned down, though, the Equal Credit Opportunity Act gives you the right to request the specific reasons why.

Make certain that your local credit bureau has complete and accurate information about *you* in a file in *your* name, if you have had credit before, alone or with your husband. (Look in the Yellow Pages under "credit" or "credit rating" or "reporting agencies" for the name and address of major credit bureaus in your area. Contact them and arrange to find out what is in your file. The bureau may charge you a small fee, but it's worth it.)

• Be sure that the creditor is reporting information on any shared accounts in both spouses' names, if you opened an account with your husband after June 1977. This is the law under an ECOA amendment.

• Ask to have any accounts opened before June 1977 added to your file—

if these accounts were reported only in your husband's or former husband's name, whether the accounts are active or closed.
- Notify the creditor that you want the account history reported to the credit bureau in your name, if the accounts are still open.
- Ask the bureau to add them to your file, too, if the accounts are presently closed.
- Give a creditor any information which shows that a derogatory credit history from your marriage should not be used against you.

DEBT COLLECTION PROTECTIONS FOR BORROWERS

The Fair Debt Collection Practices Act prohibits debt collectors from harassing, oppressing, or abusing you, from using any false statements, such as implying that they are attorneys or work for a credit bureau, and from engaging in such unfair practices as making you accept collect calls or threatening to take your property without the right to do so.

The law applies to any personal, family, or household debts—money owed for a car, for charge accounts or medical care. It covers debt collectors who regularly collect debts for others, not the creditor himself or his lawyer.

The law forbids debt collectors from contacting you at inconvenient times or places—before 8 A.M. or after 9 P.M., unless you agree. A collector may not contact you at work if your employer disapproves, and he must not tell anybody other than you that you are behind on your bills. He may contact other persons about your debt only in order to find your whereabouts, and he generally must not talk to a second party more than once.

Once you tell a debt collector in writing to stop trying to reach you, he must stop except to let you know he will not be in touch again or that he or the creditor will take some specific action on which he usually carries through.

You have the right to sue a debt collector within one year from the date the law was broken. You may recover up to $1,000 for any violation, as well as money for actual damages, court costs, and attorney's fees.

If you wish to learn more about this act or wish to complain about collectors other than banks and other financial institutions, write to the Federal Trade Commission, Debt Collection Practices, Washington, D.C. 20580 or to one of its regional offices.

WAGE GARNISHMENT PROTECTIONS

The Federal Wage Garnishment law, in effect since July 1970, limits the amount of your earnings that your employer may withhold to repay a creditor to whom you are in debt.

The amount is limited either to 25 per cent of your after-tax (disposable) weekly earnings; or the amount by which your disposable earnings exceed thirty times the federal minimum hourly wage, whichever is less.

For example, if the minimum wage is $2.90 an hour, an employee's earn-

KNOW YOUR RIGHTS!—AND HOW TO USE THEM! 1359

ings may not be garnisheed at all if his disposable earnings in a given week are $87.00 or less. (If you are paid on a monthly basis, the figure is $374.10; on a semi-monthly basis, it is $188.49.) If your weekly disposable earnings amount to more than $87.00 but less than $116, only the sum above $87.00 may be garnisheed. (As the federal minimum wage rises, naturally so will these numbers.)

An employer may not fire you because your earnings have been subjected to garnishment for a single debt, regardless of the number of garnishment proceedings brought to collect the debt. Anyone willfully violating this law may be fined up to $1,000 or imprisoned for as long as one year, or both. State laws with more restrictive provisions take precedence over the federal law.

If you believe any portions of this law have been broken, contact the Labor Department's Wage and Hour Division. The nearest office should be listed in your telephone directory under the Labor Department in the U. S. Government listing section.

IF YOUR CREDIT CARD IS LOST OR STOLEN

Under the Truth in Lending Act, it is illegal to mail or otherwise issue unsolicited credit cards. This protects you against credit card thieves who steal and use credit cards that you didn't even know had been issued in your name. If this happens, you are not responsible for any charges made with the card.

You also are protected from *unauthorized* use of credit cards that you have accepted. If you lose your card or it is stolen, you are liable only for the lesser of $50 or the amount charged before you report the loss to the card issuer. The $50 maximum applies even if you fail to discover and report the loss or theft for months. However, if the credit card company failed to provide you with a notice of the potential $50 liability or neglected to give you a self-addressed postage-paid notification form, you have no liability at all. You also are not liable if the card issuer provided no method to identify you as the person authorized to use your card, such as by signature or photograph on the card. (For discussion of your liability for lost or stolen debit cards used to make electronic fund transfers see Chapter 15 on "Your Personal Banking Business.")

BILLING ERRORS

The computer at the local department store bills you for goods you have returned to the store or fails to credit your account for payments made. How do you get that computer to listen to reason?

Your credit card company's computer makes a mistake in figuring your finance charge. How should you approach this problem?

Or you are billed $90 for two tires you never bought. Or the bank's electronic billing brain raises the price of a $25 loan on your overdraft checking account to $250.

Billing errors are a common and major nuisance. But as a result of the Fair Credit Billing Act (FCBA), much of the onus for clearing up disputes is now on the creditor—provided you, the customer, take certain steps. Furthermore, you can fight over a bill that you believe is unfair with reasonable protection of your credit rating.

HOW TO ARGUE WITH A COMPUTER

Under the Fair Credit Billing Act, which went into effect in the fall of 1975, you have sixty days from when the first bill containing the error is mailed to *write* the store, credit card company, or bank about a billing error. This notice need not be long. Just identify yourself and your account number; indicate that your bill contains an error. State the amount involved and briefly explain why you think a mistake has been made.

Do not send in your copy of a sales slip or other document unless you have a duplicate copy for your records.

Send this letter to the address given on your bill for billing error notices. It's wise to send the letter by certified mail with a return receipt requested, so you have proof of the date it was mailed and received.

The notification letter is essential. It triggers protections provided by the Fair Credit Billing Act, and shifts the burden of resolving the dispute from you to the creditor.

The creditor has thirty days to let you know that he has received your letter, and two billing cycles (not more than ninety days) to resolve the dispute by correcting your account or explaining why he felt it was accurate.

Once your letter is received, the creditor cannot:

- close your account;
- send you collection letters;
- threaten to damage your credit rating or sue you;
- report the disputed amount as delinquent to a credit bureau (although it can be reported as in dispute);
- turn the matter over to a collection agency or attorney.

Furthermore, once you have sent this letter, you do not have to pay the amount in dispute or make any minimum payments or finance charges connected with it until the matter is resolved. (You are still obligated, however, to pay all parts of the bill that are not questioned.)

If it turns out that the creditor or his computer is in the wrong, you won't have to pay any finance charges on the disputed amount. If the reverse is true—you have made an error—then you may have to pay for any finance

KNOW YOUR RIGHTS!—AND HOW TO USE THEM! 1361

charges which accumulated on the amount in question and you will have to make up any minimum payments on the disputed amount that you missed.

If the creditor fails to follow these rules, he may not collect the amount indicated by the customer to be a billing error, up to $50, and finance charges, even if the bill turns out to be correct. You also have the right to sue for actual damages, and twice the amount of any finance charges, not less than $100 or more than $1,000, plus reasonable attorney fees.

FASTER ERROR RESOLUTION

While it is important to write a letter about a suspected error in your bill in order to preserve your rights under the FCBA, you may want to use the telephone as well. Most questions and disputes involving major credit cards are handled over the phone. (Usually there is a toll-free customer service number given in your monthly statement.)

These credit card company telephone lines tend to be busiest Monday mornings. So call in the afternoons and at the end of the week, if you can. Get the name of the person to whom you are talking.

But caution! Using the telephone does not preserve your legal rights—only a letter does that.

Two other tips: keep your own receipts when you make charges, and check them against your monthly statements. And be sure to check large bills, especially ones for hotel rooms, before charging them. Hotel and airline bills are sources of many arguments.

PROTECTION AGAINST DEFECTIVE OR SHODDY GOODS OR SERVICES

Before the FCBA took effect, if you used a credit card to buy an item that you later discovered was a piece of junk, you might have been required to continue making payments to the bank or credit card issuer, while trying to seek satisfaction from the seller—sometimes a fly-by-night operator who had since skipped town or gone out of business or who simply was unwilling to make good on defective merchandise.

While the FCBA does not treat such cases as "billing errors" subject to its resolution requirements, it may allow you to withhold payment from the credit card issuer, *if* you first try in good faith to return the goods or to convince the merchant to correct the problem.

There are two limitations on this right: first, the purchase price must be more than $50; second, you must have made the purchase within your home state or within a hundred miles of your current address. These limitations do not apply if the retailer is owned or operated by the creditor—a department store on whose charge you made a purchase, for instance, or if the creditor sent or participated in an advertisement for the goods or services that you bought.

This protection against poor goods and services is important and useful, especially in certain instances. An example: because automobile repair work is the source of many consumer complaints, some consumers try to insure themselves satisfaction by paying for such repair work with a credit card. If they discover, as many car owners do, that no repairs have been made or that they have been done improperly or inadequately, they withhold payment. Of course, you first must earnestly request the car repair shop to meet its obligations. You also should notify the credit card company of the dispute, so it won't report the disputed amount as delinquent until the matter is settled.

DISCOUNTS ALLOWED FOR CASH-PAYING CUSTOMERS

The law also allows stores, hotels, restaurants, and other retailers who honor credit cards to give discounts of up to 5 per cent to customers who choose to pay by cash or check. Previously, many credit card issuers had prevented member merchants from giving these discounts. Such agreements are now prohibited.

Nothing requires merchants to give discounts to customers paying cash, but if they do, they must post signs telling you about it. Presently, few stores offer their customers cash discounts. But it's probable the granting of discounts will spread during the 1980s, as prices continue to rise and more cash-paying people question why they have to finance the cost of a credit system that they do not use.

Your Rights as a Veteran

In the late 1970s, about 100 million Americans, including veterans, their families, and survivors of deceased veterans, were eligible for benefits distributed by the Veterans Administration—ranging from low-cost life insurance to VA hospital and medical care, VA-guaranteed home loans, GI Bill benefits for education and training, disability and death compensation, pension payment.

Details on most of these are in other sections of this book—covering life insurance, college scholarships, loan programs, funerals, pensions—and you'll find a full range of veterans' benefits spelled out in a VA booklet entitled "Federal Benefits for Veterans and Dependents." Listed too are the locations of VA offices, hospitals, drug treatment centers, national cemeteries, and veterans' programs administered by other government agencies, such as the Civil Service Commission's federal job preference (to veterans) rules, and loan programs run by the Small Business Administration. Copies of the booklet are available for a small sum from the Superintendent of Documents, Washington, D.C. 20420.

Every eligible veteran (man or woman) has a right to these benefits. But among the most important rights a veteran has are those connected with the job he or she left to enter military service.

If you are a veteran now re-entering the job market, it will be crucially important for you to be thoroughly aware of these rights to your former job, as well as to promotions, fringe benefits, seniority, etc.

Under the law, if you apply within ninety days after discharge you are entitled to get back the job you left to go into service—with the same pay, seniority, and status. This rule also applies if you can't do your old job because of physical disability or because the job has been changed. It doesn't matter if the company has been sold, as long as the business still goes on.

If your employer has a seniority system—in a contract or in practice—you must be credited with seniority for your time in service. If there has been a general pay raise or increase in benefits, you are entitled to these too. If promotions are automatic, based on length of employment, you are entitled to any promotion you would have received if you hadn't been in service. If fringe benefits depend on length of service, you must be credited for the time you were away. If your right to a pension or a longer vacation depends on the period of your employment, your military service must be counted. For other benefits, you're like any other employee who has been on leave. You also share in pay losses or changes in working conditions which occurred while you were away.

You can't be fired or demoted for one year (six months in the case of National Guardsmen) except for misconduct or other good reason. Your seniority and other rights last as long as you stay on the job.

If your employer refuses to rehire you, you can bring a lawsuit in a federal district court and ask the United States Attorney to represent you. You can get help or further information at the Office of Veterans' Reemployment Rights, which is part of the United States Labor Department and has offices in cities all over the United States. Also, you can go to the local VA, state employment service, or any veterans' organization for guidance. To make sure you know and get all your job rights, register with one of the state employment service offices throughout the country. By law, you will get preference and priority in both job counseling and placement.

Check with your nearest Veterans Administration regional office on your rights and eligibility for a wide range of education, employment, and training programs. These change frequently; keep up to date.

And most important: do not ignore or downgrade the full range of benefits available. Make sure you explore all the possibilities.

VETERANS' BENEFITS

The Veterans Administration pays a dependency and indemnity compensation to widows of veterans who died while in service or from a service-connected disability, based on the husband's pay grade while he was in service. In the late 1970s this ranged from $297 to $760 a month for a widow, with an additional $35 a month for each child under age eighteen.

If your husband died while on active duty (including training) or within 120 days after discharge and from a service-connected cause, there also is an award of a six months' death gratuity. This is a lump-sum payment of six times the veteran's monthly pay, but not more than $3,000 or less than $800, payable by his military service.

Under the law after the amendments of 1978, the surviving spouse of a veteran could qualify for a Veterans Administration "death pension" in an amount sufficient to bring her (or his) income up to $2,379 per year, to $3,116 for a surviving spouse and one child, and with $600 added for each additional child. If the surviving spouse is so disabled that he or she is confined to the home, there is an extra allowance of $1,427 per year to cover needed aid and attendance.

These survivors benefits, like veterans' pension benefits (see pages 1054–56), are to be increased to keep up with the cost of living.

There also is a burial expense grant of $300 for veterans whose death was not service-connected, and up to $1,100 if the death was service-connected. (See pages 1098–1100 for more details on veterans' death benefits.)

If the funeral director does not alert the VA insurance division of your husband's death, contact the nearest VA center.

Unremarried widows of men who served in World War II, the Korean war, or the Vietnam war and who died in service or from service-connected disabilities also may qualify for GI home loans and educational benefits. (See pages 211–12 for more on the GI home loan program, and also pages 1098–1100 on financing an education.)

In addition, widows are entitled, until they remarry, to special preference when applying for Civil Service positions. If the widow is the mother of a veteran who lost his life or became totally disabled, she also is entitled to special preference.

For answers to other questions you may have, or assistance you may need, write, phone, or visit your nearest VA regional office.

Your Rights as a Hospital Patient

The American Hospital Association a few years ago adopted the first nationwide "Patient's Bill of Rights"—a milestone for you in view of the probability that sooner or later you'll be hospitalized for one reason or another and, if you're unlucky, you'll be confronted with a long series of unnecessary indignities, confusion, secrecy, arrogance, and frustrating lack of responsiveness to your needs.

Yet you, the patient, are the one paying the nation's multibillion-a-year health care bill—with a huge share of this for hospital services. Your life and limb and comfort are at stake—not anybody else's. You, therefore, have every right to insist on certain basic rights while you're hospitalized—even if they are not specifically spelled out in any lawbook.

According to the American Hospital Association's Bill of Rights you, the patient, should have the right:

KNOW YOUR RIGHTS!—AND HOW TO USE THEM!

(1) To considerate and respectful care.

(2) To get complete information from your physician concerning your diagnosis, treatment, and prognosis, in terms you understand.

(3) To receive whatever information is necessary for you to give your informed advance consent for any procedure and/or treatment.

(4) To every consideration for your privacy concerning your medical care program.

(5) To refuse treatment to the extent permitted by law, and to be informed of the medical consequences of your action. (This would mean that, as an adult, you have the right to die if your condition is hopeless.)

(6) To expect that all communications and records pertaining to your care will be treated as confidential.

(7) To expect a hospital to respond, within reason, to your request for services.

(8) To get information about any relationship between your hospital and other health care and educational institutions in so far as your care is concerned and to get information (including names) on the existence of any professional relationship between individuals who are treating you. (This means that you, the patient, have the right to know whether you are being treated by a member of a university hospital or by your physician's student.)

(9) To be advised if the hospital proposes to engage in or perform human experimentation on you in the course of your care or treatment.

(10) To expect reasonable continuity of care.

(11) To examine and receive an explanation of your bill, regardless of the source of payment.

(12) To know what hospital rules and regulations apply to your conduct as patient.

WHAT IS HAPPENING

What has happened in the years since the Hospital Association made its formal move?

Only a fraction of the nation's hospitals have offered all the rights to their patients, although "a few have made it a policy to distribute copies of the AHA's Bill of Rights" to patients—and some others have developed their own statements of rights.

The State of New York Hospital Code mandates the posting of a Patient's Bill of Rights and states that it also must be made available to individual patients upon request.

Meanwhile, other major moves on behalf of us as patients are being made. For instance, state legislatures are now considering a variety of bills giving terminally ill or injured people the right to order doctors to permit them to die.

The United States Department of Health, Education and Welfare in the mid 1970s issued a major set of regulations to protect subjects of medical research experimentation financed by the federal government in or out of hospitals. Under the regulations, would-be subjects must be fully informed of the risks, discomforts, and benefits of the experimentation. Special review committees in research institutes must consist not only of reviewers from within the institution but also of outsiders who might well be more objective.

Ralph Nader's Health Research Group has issued a guide to choosing a dentist and is promoting the preparation of local directories of physicians.

In the late 1970s, the Health Research Group published *Getting Yours: A Consumer's Guide to Obtaining Your Medical Records*.

The book notes that patient access to health records enables you to protect your privacy by knowing what is there. In addition, access improves patient education and understanding of medical conditions.

It improves the patient-doctor relationship and also continuity of care.

There are step-by-step, state-by-state instructions for getting patient records. All patients in federal facilities such as VA or Public Health Service hospitals, it points out, are entitled to see their records under the federal Privacy and Freedom of Information Acts. In only fourteen states, however, did patients have the right of direct access to medical records held by physicians or hospitals or both, in the late 1970s.

Getting Yours, available from the Health Research Group, Dept MR, 2000 P Street N.W., Washington, D.C. 20036, for a moderate price, tells how consumers might work to change state laws to provide for freer patient access.

The surgery releases which hospitals require patients to sign waiving any liability on the part of hospitals for surgical bungling—and more—are being challenged by consumer protection lawyers. Says one of these lawyers: "A court would never enforce this type of contract."

THE "PATIENT ADVOCATE"

Another aspect of consumer choice is going through dramatic change.

Prior to the 1970s the physician's legal obligation to disclose information to his patient was measured by a professional community standard. The doctor could be held liable for non-disclosure only if he revealed significantly less than other doctors would have disclosed under similar circumstances. A court case in the early 1970s changed that. In the case of Canterbury vs. Sponce, the United States Court of Appeals for the District Court Circuit set the stage for a shift to a patient-based standard. Under the Canterbury decision and the large number of state court opinions which it influenced, the doctor must reveal all that a "reasonable patient" in the position of the person he is treating would consider "material" to his decision as to whether to accept the doctors proposed treatment.

If you or a loved one have been hospitalized recently, you may have encountered a new type of consumer representative known as the "patient advocate." About 20 per cent of all hospitals now employ such ombudsmen to try to help humanize the hospital, to enable patients to get action on their complaints, and to recommend changes in policy or procedure which will benefit patients.

Some of these patient advocates simply try to enforce the Patient's Bill of Rights; others have considerable authority, including the power to adjust bills. Some have been criticized as merely cosmetic attempts to smooth over problems. They are gaining a stronger foothold, though, and their organization, the Society of Patient Representatives, is the most rapidly growing professional society affiliated with the American Hospital Association. Their supporters point out that they can help to head off malpractice suits, have improved hospital billing and collection procedures—and even meal menus.

Your Rights as a Disabled Person

Taking a leaf out of the book of the civil rights activists of the 1970s, the nation's 30 million disabled—the blind, the deaf, the crippled, and all those with other physical or mental handicaps—are now demanding a place in society. Backed by federal law, they are demanding improved access to education and jobs and easier physical access to public buildings and transportation.

Under Section 504 of the Rehabilitation Act of 1973, all institutions and agencies that accept federal aid in the form of funds, services, or property must make their programs accessible to the handicapped—or risk having the federal aid withheld.

Another law, the Education for All Handicapped Children Act, assures a disabled child's right to a free appropriate education and gives the parent of the child a right to participate with the public school in planning and evaluating the education programs.

The Rehabilitation Act identifies a handicapped person as anyone with a physical or mental disability that substantially impairs or restricts the person in one or more of such major life activities as walking, seeing, hearing, speaking, working, or learning. Epilepsy is considered to be such a condition; so are perceptual handicaps such as dyslexia, minimal brain dysfunction, and developmental aphasia. The U. S. Attorney General has ruled that alcoholism and drug addiction are physical or mental impairments that are handicapping conditions if they limit one or more of life's major activities.

YOUR RIGHT TO EMPLOYMENT

An employer who is receiving federal funds or other federal assistance may not discriminate against you, the disabled person, in hiring, promotion, demotion, transfer, layoff, or rehiring. You must be given an even break with the non-disabled in job assignments and on career ladders—as well the same treatment on leaves of absence, sick leave, training programs, etc.

Once you have been hired, your employer must take reasonable steps to take account of your disability, supplying a reader if you are blind, for example, and reading is essential to the job, or giving you adequate workspace and a way of getting to it if you use a wheelchair.

YOUR RIGHT TO EDUCATION

Your disability cannot be a factor when you apply to enroll in any private or public educational institution that receives assistance from the Department of Health, Education and Welfare.

Your application must be considered on the basis of your academic or other school records.

Once you are enrolled, the college is not required to lower its standards or degree requirements, but it may have to give you more time to earn a degree. It also must provide braille books or other aids you may need if they are not obtainable from another source.

YOUR DISABLED CHILD'S RIGHT TO EDUCATION

Under Section 504 of the Rehabilitation Act, your state and local school districts are responsible for providing an appropriate elementary and secondary education for your physically or mentally disabled child.

The type of disability and the severity of the disability do not alter this responsibility. Further, the education must be provided at a cost to you that is no more than the cost to parents of children who are not handicapped.

You and your public school district decide whether it shall be:
* A regular public school classroom
* A special education program of the public school
* A boarding school if the public school has no appropriate program
* Appropriate education in a hospital if the child is a long-term patient

The Education for All Handicapped Children Act is even more specific. The public school is required by that legislation to develop with your advice and consent a tailor-made education program for your child and to give you in writing a list of the special aids that will be provided, such as braille books or a desk that can be used with a wheelchair.

You also must be given a schedule for the periodic review of your child's progress and an explanation of your rights, including your right to a written notice of major changes proposed in your child's program or the location of that program.

IF YOUR RIGHTS ARE NOT RESPECTED

If you believe that your rights as a disabled person (or the rights of your disabled child) have been violated by any business, hospital, physician, school, college, or any other institution which receives federal funds from the Department of Health, Education and Welfare, write to the Office of Civil Right in the HEW Regional Office in your part of the country. Submit full details.

Your local post office or your nearest Social Security Office can give you the address.

Your Rights as a Taxpayer

You have just come home from an infuriating afternoon at the local office of the Internal Revenue Service—during which you tried with increasing desperation to convince an IRS agent that you *do not* owe an extra $300 on your latest income tax return. But the IRS agent won't concede a dollar, even though you are convinced of your right to deduct $1,000 of disputed contributions to your church. Further appeals within the IRS have been abysmal failures.

You are incensed. You want to fight the IRS, not to give in with a whimper. What do you do? Your basic right, as a taxpayer, is to pay *only* the federal income tax which you actually owe—and to pay not one cent more. To protect this basic right, you, as a taxpayer, have a distinct and formal set of legal procedures you can use.

HOW TO FIGHT THE IRS

You may fight the IRS—via the Small Tax Case procedure of the U. S. Tax Court, the court which Congress created specifically to help you, the taxpayer, and which came into existence in 1971 under a minor provision of the Tax Reform Act of 1969.

The provision authorized the Tax Court to hear and decide small claims—now defined as any dispute about income, gift, or estate taxes involving not more than $1,500. You argue your own case without a lawyer and without filing any technical and time-consuming forms. Under the Small Tax Case procedure, the technical rules of evidence are off and the dominant rule instead is informality. However, if you wish, you may hire a lawyer or file a brief or do both.

You have no worries about strangulating red tape or masses of paper work. Both are at a minimum. You will not be placed at an immediate disadvantage by being forced to travel far from your home for your informal hearing and the decision. A hearing on your case will be held as near your home as the court finds possible, and you'll get advance notice of when your case is coming up. The Tax Court judges hold hearings in more than a hundred cities across the nation each year. You won't have to wait long for a decision either. The judge hearing your case probably will decide whether you win or lose against the IRS within thirty days.

Of course, since this is a Tax Court procedure, you can fight your own case there without first paying the tax deficiency claimed by the IRS. Only if and when you lose or settle will you have to pay up. If you were to use the other courts—a district court or the Court of Claims—you would have to pay the deficiency claimed by the IRS first and then bring suit for a refund to get that money back.

You can be relaxed when telling your side of the dispute, trusting the judge hearing you to give you any benefit of the doubt. In fact the judge probably will help you to bring out points in your own favor which, in your innocence, you might overlook or shrug off on your own.

Moreover, the decisions of the judge are not subject to review by any other court. This means that neither party—neither the taxpayer nor the IRS —can appeal the decision to any higher court. This encourages the judges to rule more speedily and freely, for they do not face the possibility of being overthrown by another court.

And the fact that the decisions set no precedents means that a judge's ruling in one case will have no effect on future cases in any court. This encourages judges to be more lenient with taxpayers, for they need not fear that their rulings will open the way for cases which would cost the Treasury countless tens of millions of dollars.

So, what if you are the reasonable taxpayer described above and you want to fight the IRS's claim that you owe $300 more on your last year's taxes?

WHAT TO DO

Here's what you do:

(1) Get a ninety-day letter (its official name is a "notice of deficiency") from the IRS office that is handling your case. You must start your case in the Tax Court within ninety days after the date on which that ninety-day letter is mailed to you. If you do not, you lose your right to litigate in the Tax Court.

(2) Write to the Clerk of the Court, U. S. Tax Court, 400 Second Street N.W., Washington, D.C. 20217, and ask for a Small Tax Case kit. The clerk will send you this kit, which includes an instruction pamphlet, a return envelope, and four copies each of these two forms:

Form 2, Petition (Small Tax Case);

Form 4, Request for Place of Trial.

(3) Fill out the forms. They are very simple.

In paragraph one of Form 2 Petition fill in the taxable year or years for which the deficiency is claimed and the city and state of the IRS office that sent you the ninety-day letter.

To illustrate, in your case it would read: "John and Mary Doe, Petitioners v. Commissioner of Internal Revenue, Respondent. Petitioners request the court to redetermine the tax deficiency for the year 19 . . . , as set forth in the notice of deficiency, dated (blank), a copy of which is attached. The notice was issued by the Office of the Internal Revenue Service at 120 Church Street, New York, New York 10007."

In paragraph two, fill in your Social Security number and your spouse's if a joint return is involved. In your case, it would read: "Petitioner's taxpayer identification (e.g., Social Security) numbers are 012-34-5678 and 876-54-3210."

In paragraph three, tell how you disagree with the IRS deficiency notice. In your case, it would read: "Year, 19 . . . Amount of deficiency disputed, $300."

In paragraph four, state briefly where you think the IRS agent went wrong in claiming you owe more taxes. In your case you might write: "The Commissioner of Internal Revenue made the following error in determining this tax deficiency: he mistakenly disallowed the entire $1,000 amount that I deducted as a charitable contribution."

Also, give facts to support your claim that the Commissioner was wrong. In your case, you might write: "We have witnesses who saw me give $1,000 in cash to my church as part of a special fund-raising drive on May 6, 19 . . ."

Now you sign the petition, with your spouse if it is a joint return, and give your present address. For example:

"John Doe, 105 Main Street, New York, N.Y. 10010
"Mary Doe, 105 Main Street, New York, N.Y. 10010."

The official form has this paragraph above your signatures: "Petitioners request that the proceedings in this case be conducted as a 'small tax case' under section 7463 of the Internal Revenue Code of 1954, as amended, and Rule 172 of the Rules of Practice of the United States Tax Court."

There also is room for the signature and address of your lawyer if you retain one—but I'm assuming you're battling the IRS in this instance all on your own with a minimum of expense and red tape. For that's the central idea of this Small Tax Case Division. And don't mark an "X" in the box at the bottom of the petition, because that would make your case a regular Tax Court Case instead of a Small Tax Case.

Now make three identical copies of the Petition and set them aside. Attach a copy of your deficiency notice to the original of the Petition.

(4) Turn to Form 4 Request for Place of Trial, of which you also have four copies. Fill out one form by listing the city and state in which you would like to have your trial and by signing it where required.

To illustrate in your case, the form would read: "John and Mary Doe, Petitioners v. Commissioner of Internal Revenue, Respondent. Petitioners hereby request that trial of this case be held at New York City, New York State. (Signed) John Doe, husband, Mary Doe, wife." And that's all there is to it!

Make three identical copies of this form too.

(5) Make out a check or money order for $10 payable to "Clerk, U. S. Tax Court."

(6) Mail this check together with the original and two copies of your Petition and the original and two copies of your Request for Place of Trial to:

United States Tax Court, 4 Second Street N.W., Washington, D.C. 20217.

Keep one copy of each form for yourself.

(7) The Commissioner will answer your petition and, almost surely, will make some concession or compromise suggestion—assuming you have a fairly reasonable case.

If there is still a disagreement between the IRS and you after the commissioner's answer, your case will be set for trial at a time and place of which you will be notified by the court.

(8) The size and location of the city you have selected for trial will determine whether the Tax Court will be able to comply with your request in your Form 4. (New York City is a cinch). But, if the court cannot comply, it will pick a place that is as close and convenient to your choice as possible and it will then notify you.

A crucial point is that the judge will try to persuade you to settle the case without going to trial if your case has any validity. If you are satisfied with any settlement offer, that will end the case. A fat majority of taxpayers, incidentally, do settle before trial.

A caution, however: even though the Small Tax Case procedure is informal, easygoing, relaxed, and designed to help *you*, the taxpayer, you still must have a reasonable case to win.

Your Rights as a Worker

Today there are federal and state laws covering just about every aspect of work—minimum wage laws, equal-pay-for-equal-work rules, overtime pay requirements, on-the-job safety and health standards, wage garnishment protections, and many others. Because there are so many such laws and enforcement of them is spread over dozens of separate state and federal agencies, departments, and divisions, many are neglected or violated. Thus, you, the employee, must be the watchdog of your own workplace. To help you, here is a brief rundown on major employee protection laws:

YOUR RIGHT TO A JOB

The Employment Act of 1946 and its successor, The Humphrey-Hawkins Full-Employment Act of 1978, make the federal government responsible for fostering general economic and financial conditions that will promote high employment. These laws are not really enforceable but resemble proclamations of good intentions. The Humphrey-Hawkins Bill, for instance, sets the government goals of bringing the unemployment rate down to 4 per cent by 1983, and the overall inflation rate to 3 per cent by the same date.

KNOW YOUR RIGHTS!—AND HOW TO USE THEM!

YOUR RIGHT TO A MINIMUM WAGE

A federal law signed in November 1977 set a uniform minimum wage for virtually all workers. As of January 1, 1979, this wage was at $2.90 an hour and it will jump to $3.10 in 1980 and to $3.35 in 1981, unless amended by Congress.

The law also requires that workers receive one and a half times their regular pay if they work overtime—more than forty hours a week. Some states have higher minimum wage laws, and these supersede the federal law. Any questions or complaints regarding wages should be directed to the U. S. Department of Labor, Wage and Hour Division, Washington, D.C. 20210, or your state employment office.

YOUR RIGHT TO JOIN A UNION

The 1934 National Labor Relations Act and amendments guarantee employees in private industry the right to organize, to bargain collectively, and to strike.

YOUR RIGHTS AS AN OLDER WORKER

Employers of twenty or more workers cannot fire or refuse to hire individuals age forty to sixty-five simply because of their age, unless the job—say, modeling dresses—requires someone within a certain age range. Firms cannot favor younger workers in pay, promotion, and fringe benefits, and unions cannot deny membership to older persons or refuse to refer them to jobs.

Furthermore, employment agencies cannot refuse to refer a job applicant to an opening because of his or her age. "Help-wanted" ads, too, cannot contain such statements of age preference as "Boy Wanted," "Girl Wanted," or "Only under thirties Need Apply."

The 1978 Age Discrimination Act also protects most workers from mandatory retirement before age seventy. (See pages 992–93.) These protections are enforced by the Labor Department's Wage and Hour Division, Washington, D.C. 20210.

EQUAL EMPLOYMENT OPPORTUNITY

Women and minorities receive most of their equal employment protection under Title VII of the Civil Rights Act. It specifically bans job discrimination in private employment on account of race, sex, religion, or national origin. It also prohibits discrimination against anyone who wants to join a union or who seeks the services of an employment agency. It bars discrimination in help wanted ads, pay scales, fringe benefits, promotions, and other aspects of employment.

A 1978 amendment to the Civil Rights Act, the Pregnancy Discrimination Act, provided specific protections for pregnant workers. It said that pregnant women who are able to work must be permitted to do so on the same conditions as other employees. When they are unable to work for medical reasons they must be given the same rights, leave privileges, and other benefits as disabled workers. The condition of pregnancy may not be singled out for reduced coverage in medical, sick leave, or disability benefit plans.

However, the law permits abortions to be excluded from employee health insurance plans, unless the abortion was necessary to save the life of the mother. This exception applies to health insurance only. Employers are required to provide sick leave and disability benefits as they would for any other disability. Furthermore, they must cover health costs involved in treating medical complications that result from non-therapeutic abortions.

Complaints of discrimination by private employers, unions, or employment agencies should be directed to the Equal Employment Opportunity Commission, Washington, D.C. 20606.

Discrimination complaints involving the federal goverment should first be taken to the individual agency's equal employment office. If it cannot be resolved within the agency, contact the Board of Appeals and Review, U. S. Civil Service Commission, Washington, D.C. 20415.

Firms which have contracts with the federal government are subject to special non-discrimination and affirmative action requirements. Complaints involving the employment practices of companies with federal contracts should go to the Office of Federal Contract Compliance, U. S. Department of Labor, Washington, D.C. 20210.

WOMEN'S RIGHT TO EQUAL PAY

Your key defense against salary discrimination on the basis of sex is the Equal Pay Act of 1963 and its amendments. This law requires that men and women performing under similar working conditions receive the same wages, overtime pay, and benefits when their jobs demand "substantially" equal (not "identical") skill, effort, and responsibility. It is enforced by the Equal Employment Opportunity Commission, Washington, D.C. 20506.

Despite this law and despite the increasing number of women doctors, lawyers, construction workers, and astronauts, women still earn only around 60 per cent of the money that men do. This proportion has been relatively constant for the last twenty to thirty years. Today, the median (half above, half below) salary of full-time working women is $166 a week. The median salary for full-time working men is $272 a week.

The major reason for this pay gap is that the majority of women still hold lower-paying and traditionally "female" jobs as secretaries, service workers, salespeople, and household helpers.

Some women's groups feel that many jobs routinely filled by women are "comparable" to higher paying ones usually held by men. They argue that a nurse, for instance, exercises as much skill and responsibility as a factory manager and should earn as much. Their arguments have not as yet been upheld by the courts. But "comparable pay for comparable work" may become the rallying cry for working women in the 1980s just as "equal pay for equal work" was in the 1960s and '70s.

YOUR UNEMPLOYMENT INSURANCE PROTECTION

And if you lose your job?

An important source of between-job financial assistance for workers in all pay brackets is unemployment insurance benefits. To qualify for this aid you usually must have left your job involuntarily and be able, willing, and looking for work. With some exceptions, most states do not provide unemployment insurance benefits to workers on strike.

Basically, unemployment benefits are paid for twenty-six weeks, but in some states under certain conditions they are stretched out an additional thirteen weeks. The size of your benefits depends on the amount of your earnings, your marital status, and the number of dependents you have.

In the late 1970s, covered out-of-work Americans were getting benefits ranging from a low of $10 a week in Mississippi to a high of $183 a week in Connecticut. The national average payment in fiscal year 1978 was in the $80 to $90 per week range. And the unemployed averaged twelve to thirteen weeks on the federal insurance program.

Unemployment insurance benefits were tax-free until 1979. They are now subject to federal taxes and to taxation in some states. Each state operates its own unemployment compensation system. To find out if you qualify for benefits and if so, how to apply, contact your local unemployment insurance office. It is listed in your telephone directory under the heading for state government agencies.

If you are an executive and lose your job, your former employer almost surely provides for some amount of severance pay. In addition, the company planning to lay you off may permit you to continue working until you have located a suitable new job, and thus keep you covered by its group insurance plans.

YOUR RIGHT TO WORKER'S COMPENSATION

Since the first workman's compensation law was passed in 1911, an increasing number of workers (and their survivors) have become entitled to receive benefits in the event of a job-related injury, disability, or illness.

With the exception of three groups of workers—federal employees, coal miners, and harbor workmen and longshoremen—each state administers its own workman's compensation program. These programs vary enormously.

Several states provide coverage for all job related injuries or diseases, while a few recognize only certain occupational illnesses. Some states exempt employers with a small number of workers. Some fail to cover such categories of workers as farm laborers or domestics. The amount of compensation that you, an injured worker, may receive also varies widely as does the time it takes to process an injury or disability claim.

Basically, compensation claims fall into three major categories: temporary, permanent, and death.

If you are injured and are out of work temporarily as a result, most states provide you with benefits equal to a maximum of 66⅔ of the average weekly wage in your state. In the late 1970s, this maximum ranged from about $60 a week in Oklahoma to about $600 a week in Alaska. Some state laws provide no benefit payments for the first three to seven days you are off the job, unless your time off exceeds a certain period, ranging again from four to forty-one days.

If you are disabled permanently—say, you've lost an arm or have contracted a lung disease from inhaling factory dust—both the size of the benefits you receive and the period for which you'll receive them depend on the laws in your state. If your injuries are permanent and you lived in Alabama in the 1970s, you could get a maximum benefit of $120 per week. In Maine you could get a maximum of $220 a week. The loss of an arm might be worth two hundred weeks' worth of compensation. Partial loss of your arm might entitle you to fifty weeks' worth of benefits. Again, the "schedules" vary, as do the size of death benefits, maximum burial allowances, and the ways in which the programs are administered.

If you are injured or contract a disease through a job-related activity or exposure, you should take the precaution of reporting your claim to your state worker's compensation commission. You may be required to support your claim with medical data. Also report your injury or illness to your employer. In most instances, he in turn will file a report with the appropriate state agency and/or his private insurer.

The amount of time you must wait until your claim is processed depends on where you live, your claim, your doctor's medical reports, whether your employer disputes the claim, and other factors.

Although each state has jurisdiction over its own worker's compensation program, the U. S. Department of Labor's Office of Workers Compensation (within the Employment Standards Administration) has a state standards division. This division is trying to coordinate state programs and has offices within each of the Labor Department's ten regional bureaus.

IF YOU LOSE YOUR JOB THROUGH COMPETITION FROM IMPORTS

If you lose your job because of increased competition from abroad—in short, from imports—you may be entitled to adjustment assistance from the Department of Labor.

Under the 1975 Trade Act, groups of three or more workers or their union representative may petition the Secretary of Labor for various types of aid. By writing the Office of Trade Adjustment Assistance, Bureau of Inter-

national Labor Affairs, U. S. Department of Labor, Washington, D.C. 20210, you may receive:
- employment training assistance
- relocation allowances
- employment counseling, testing, and job placement help
- cash trade adjustment allowances amounting to 70 per cent of your average weekly wage, up to a maximum of about $230 a week. You can obtain such funds for as long as fifty-two weeks and up to seventy-eight weeks if you are sixty years of age or older or enrolled in a qualified training program.

At the end of 1978, about 400,000 American workers—many of them from the steel, automobile, electronics, and shoe industries—had received a total of $560 million under the Trade Adjustment program. Like unemployment insurance benefits, these trade adjustment payments are newly subject to federal income taxes. They, too, are administered by your state employment security office.

YOUR RIGHT TO SAFE AND HEALTHFUL WORKING CONDITIONS

When the Occupational Safety and Health Act was passed in 1970, and the Occupational Safety and Health Administration (OSHA) established to run and enforce it, they were hailed as the most important sources of protection for U.S. workers in this half of the twentieth century.

Nearly ten years later, OSHA is the prime contender for the title of most disliked government agency. From one side, business groups complain its standards are costly and even ridiculous (one spelled out how "exit" signs were to be designed). From the other, public interest and union groups charged the agency had done little to implement the 1970 law, which promised "as far as possible every working man and woman in the nation safe and healthful working conditions." By May 1977, OSHA had issued only seventeen health standards.

Despite its poor record to date, OSHA has stepped up its action on major health hazards. It has grouped suspected cancer-causing agents according to importance, required warning notices in the workplace and on products, and proposed that much tougher penalties be levied on firms that violate safety rules. In addition, the National Institute for Occupational Safety and Health (NIOSH) that acts as a research agency has been authorized to inform workers who have been exposed to certain dangers on the job. NIOSH can obtain the names and addresses of affected workers from the Internal Revenue Service.

Among the obvious potential hazards for which you should be on guard in your workplace are: dust, fumes, gases, vapors, and mists that you breathe; asbestos; microwaves; lasers; drugs and hormones; molds; parasites, or bacteria from animals or animal products; materials that irritate your skin; and excessive noise.

OSHA has several hundred inspectors in the field, and if you report a complaint it is up to the agency's representatives to visit your plant or office, explore the details, and set in works the machinery to right the situation. Inspectors are supposed to arrive unannounced, and you can ask to have your complaint kept confidential. OSHA's main address is Department of Labor, Washington, D.C. 20210; phone: 202-523-8141.

Your Rights as a Vocational School Student

If you, a vocational school student, decide for any reason to quit your pilot training, secretarial, beautician, or any other trade course, the school must give you your money back. It is permitted to keep only a $75 enrollment fee and a portion of your tuition covering the lessons you have completed.

If, however, you drop out of the school within *fourteen days* of signing your enrollment agreement, the school must refund *all* your money. Furthermore, at the time you sign up you must be told that you have fourteen days during which to cancel and receive your money back.

These important protections are part of a Federal Trade Commission rule in effect in January 1980. The rule covers all seven thousand of this country's vocation schools, including those which provide correspondence courses.

The only sort of instruction excluded from the rule's requirements are self-improvement courses and ones leading to either high school equivalency certificates or standard college-level degrees.

Also under the rule, you must receive the following information from the vocational school:

• the number of students who have dropped out, as well as the number or percentage who have graduated.

• the rate at which the school has actually found jobs for its graduates and their earnings. This information must be given you, if the school makes any claims about the availability of jobs or earning potential of its graduates. (It might, for instance, advertise "Our grads earn $20,000 a year or more.")

If you pull out of a vocational school, be certain to return any equipment that the school may have supplied you as part of the course. If you don't return it, the school may charge you for it. If the course has started when you cancel, the school may keep a portion of the equipment charge based on how long you have used it, even if you return it.

Schools which fail to comply with this rule can be required to pay $10,000 per violation and damages to injured students.

Your Rights as a Franchisee

If you ever thought about owning your own business, you probably have toyed with the idea of buying a franchise.

Franchises often provide your business with instant name-recognition, and good operations supply quite a lot of advertising and technical support. It is possible to buy a small franchise operation for as little as $1,500. Or you can spend as much as $500,000 for a popular restaurant franchise.

The biggest mistake that people make in buying a franchise is failing to investigate the business thoroughly. They also neglect to spend time with people already in business to find out where potential pitfalls and problems lie.

A new Federal Trade Commission rule, effective in mid-1979, goes a long way toward helping you, potential franchisees, by requiring franchise operators to give potential investors the following facts:

• A list of key executives in the operation and their employment background.

• A rundown on all lawsuits and bankruptcies involving the company.

•A full description of any financial help that the franchiser has given to the franchisee.

• A complete disclosure of all money that the franchisee has to pay both at the start and during the life of the business.

• A list of all suppliers with whom the franchisee must do business and the amount of money these suppliers pay to the franchise operator.

• A clear explanation of why your franchise might be revoked. Generally, you risk losing your business if you don't make the kind of profit the franchiser expects.

If you are misled by a franchiser, complain to the FTC. It won't be able to help you get your money back. You have to go to court for that. But your complaints will help the agency build a case against the franchiser.

For background information on nearly eight hundred franchise operations, write to the U. S. Department of Commerce, Industry and Trade Administration, Room 1104, Washington, D.C. 20230. Their franchise booklet is free. For more information on this topic, see chapter on your job, career, or business of your own.

29

HOW AND WHERE TO GET HELP

A Record Number of Allies for You 1382
Nationwide Organizations 1382
State and Local Consumer Protective Organizations 1384
Where to Take Your Problem: by Category or Subject 1384

A Record Number of Allies for You

Never before have you had so many allies to assist you in finding your way through our increasingly gargantuan, endlessly complex market place and in dealing with your complaints. Numerous public interest organizations, specializing in areas ranging from the overall environment to the individual problems of the disabled, have been started in recent years. These groups initiate and pursue research projects, testify before Congressional committees, participate in federal agency proceedings, bring lawsuits, publicize issues, pinpoint problems, distribute newsletters and other information. Not all handle your complaints as an individual, but some do, and many can give you valuable advice.

Directly below are the names of the broadly based, nationwide private groups and government agencies which are concerned with many types of problems.

This is followed by a list of agencies and organizations which concentrate on one or a few categories of issues, broken down so you easily can find the subject of importance to you. Neither list is by any means exhaustive.

But by contacting one or more of the organizations mentioned, you have a head start toward solving your problem or at least learning how to begin.

Nationwide Organizations

Bureau of Consumer Protection, Federal Trade Commisssion, Washington, D.C. 20580. Rides herd over deceptive advertising, illegal sales tactics, violations of the Truth in Lending law, and a host of other consumer frauds, deceptions, unfair sales, and trade practices. Telephone: (202) 523-3727.

Center for Science in the Public Interest, 1755 S Street N.W., Washington, D.C. 20009. Specializes in promoting food and health safety, energy conservation, and good nutrition through publications and participation in government proceedings. Telephone: (202) 332-9110.

Center for the Study of Responsive Law, P. O. Box 19367, Washington, D.C. 20036. Subjects of study range from mental health to aviation to coal mining. This is Ralph Nader's working address. Telephone: (202) 833-3400.

HOW AND WHERE TO GET HELP

Citizen Action Group, 1346 Connecticut Avenue N.W., Washington, D.C. 20036. Helps students and citizens organize state and local consumer action groups and public interest research groups. Telephone: (202) 833-3935.

Common Cause, 2030 M Street N.W., Washington, D.C. 20036. Largest citizen's lobby in the country. Concentrates on "structure and process" issues to improve function and accountability of government. Also, in the late 1970s, key issues were tax reform, energy policy, consumer and environmental protection. Telephone: (202) 833-1200.

Congress Watch, 133 C Street S.E., Washington, D.C. 20003. Lobby groups which keeps tabs on voting records, committee performance, and responsiveness by senators and representatives to their constituents and to the public generally. Telephone: (202) 546-4936 or (202) 546-4996.

Consumer Opposed to Inflation in the Necessities (COIN), Suite 413, 2000 P Street N.W., Washington, D.C. 20036. A coalition of consumer, labor, senior citizen and other public interest groups dedicated to fighting inflation in food, energy, health and housing. Telephone: (202) 659-0800.

Consumer Federation of America, Suite 406, 1012 14th Street N.W., Washington, D.C. 20005. Private, non-profit national federation of hundreds of state and local consumer groups which helps groups organize and act, testifies and lobbies on any proposed consumer legislation, and publicizes important issues. Telephone: (202) 737-3732.

Consumers Union, 256 Washington Street, Mount Vernon, New York 10550. Publishes *Consumer Reports* magazine, the classic shopper's guide, which includes results of Consumers Union tests of products ranging from cars to contraceptives—for safety, convenience, effectiveness. Also participates in lawsuits on behalf of consumers. Telephone: (914) MO4-6400.

Corporate Accountability Research Group, 1346 Connecticut Avenue N.W., Washington, D.C. 20036. Contests corporate power, violation of antitrust laws, seeks to make corporations accountable to shareowners and the public. Telephone: (202) 833-3931.

Council of Better Business Bureaus, 1150 17th Street N.W., Washington, D.C. 20036. Headquarters of the well-known Better Business Bureaus. Can put you in touch with the right local Bureau for you. Telephone: (202) 862-1200.

Disability Rights Center, 1346 Connecticut Avenue N.W., Washington, D.C. 20036. Works to strengthen rights of the disabled through legal action and monitoring of federal actions. Telephone: (202) 223-3304.

Energy Action, 1523 L Street N.W., Washington, D.C. 20005. Consumer oriented group that watches federal energy legislation and publishes a newsletter. Telephone: (202) 737-6220.

Office of Consumer Affairs, 626 Reporters Building, Washington, D.C. 20201. The consumer's "man in Washington"; government agency concerned with all kinds of consumer problems, consumer education and legislation.

Telephones: consumer complaints (202) 755-8820; state and local programs (202) 755-8892.

Public Citizen Litigation Group, 7th Floor, 2000 P Street N.W., Washington, D.C. 20036. Initiates lawsuits against corporations, government agencies on behalf of the public. Telephone: (202) 785-3704.

STATE AND LOCAL CONSUMER PROTECTIVE ORGANIZATIONS

All states—and many cities and counties as well—now have a central department or agency to deal with consumer fraud and also with less dramatic problems and gripes. Frequently this office is a part of the state attorney general's office. Or it may be listed under: Department (or Division) of Consumer Protection; Consumer Affairs Bureau; Consumer Protection Agency; Department of Weights and Measures; or perhaps some other name.

Each state also has at least one privately sponsored consumer organization. It may be called Consumers Council or Consumer Association or Consumer Information Center. Most states have a Ralph Nader-affiliated Public Interest Research Group, which may be called CALPIRG (in California) or VPIRG (in Vermont)—depending on the state.

Look for the agencies and organizations in your city or state—both government and non-government—under "Consumer . . ." in the government agencies section of your telephone book, as well as in the regular telephone listings.

In addition to seeking help from these organizations, you may find it helpful to get in touch with:

> your city department of consumer affairs (see the telephone directory, or call City Hall to find out whether there is such an agency);
>
> your local chamber of commerce;
>
> your local Better Business Bureau;
>
> the "Action Line" of your local newspaper, radio, or TV station;
>
> the Consumer Education Department of a local college or university;
>
> the Extension Service of the U. S. Department of Agriculture.

WHERE TO TAKE YOUR PROBLEM: BY CATEGORY OR SUBJECT

Aging. See Retirement.

Air Travel. If you have a complaint which you have been unable to resolve with an airline—about mishandled baggage, or failure to deliver you to your

HOW AND WHERE TO GET HELP

destination, or being illegally "bumped" off a flight, or being overcharged on a fare—write: Bureau of Consumer Protection, Civil Aeronautics Board, 1825 Connecticut Avenue N.W., Washington, D.C. 20428. Telephone: (202) 673-5482.

Or you may use the CAB hot line, (202) 673-5158, at any hour of the day or night. You will be billed for a three-minute call, but after that the CAB will call back to finish discussing your problem.

Aviation Consumer Action Project (ACAP), 1346 Connecticut Avenue N.W., Washington, D.C. 20036, works on problems in air carrier safety and regulation as well as passenger treatment.

Appliances. First try to settle your complaint with the dealer or manufacturer. Among the toll-free lines that you may be able to use are Whirlpool: (800) 253-1301; Westinghouse: (800) 523-5222.

If the appliance dealer, manufacturer, or serviceman fails to act on any legitimate complaint you have, write: Major Appliance Consumer Action Panel (MACAP), Complaint Exchange, Room 1500, 20 North Wacker Drive, Chicago, Illinois 60606.

Or telephone MACAP at: (312) 984-5858.

Auto Insurance. See Insurance.

Automobiles. Owners can write:

American Motors Corporation, 14250 Plymouth Road, Detroit, Michigan 48232; telephone: (313) 493-2344; or, in Canada, 350 Kennedy Road South, Brampton, Ontario.

Chrysler Corporation, P.O. Box 857, Detroit, Michigan 48231; telephone: (313) 956-5970; in Canada, the Chrysler Center, Windsor, Ontario.

Ford Motor Company, Owner Relations Department, Park Lane Tower West, Dearborn, Michigan 48126, about warranty problems; telephone: (313) 322-8055.

General Motors car owners should contact the appropriate division's Consumer-Relations Manager. Division addresses are:

Buick Motor Division, 902 East Hamilton Avenue, Flint, Michigan 48550. Telephone: (313) 766-1240.

Cadillac Motor Car Division, 2860 Clark Avenue, Detroit, Michigan 48232. Telephone: (313) 554-5536.

Chevrolet Motor Division, 3044 West Grand Boulevard, Detroit, Michigan 48202. Telephone: (313) 556-5219.

Oldsmobile Division, 920 Townsend Street, Lansing, Michigan 48921. Telephone: (517) 373-5546.

Pontiac Motor Division, 1 Pontiac Plaza, Pontiac, Michigan 48505. Telephone: (313) 857-1321.

AUTOCAP is an automobile owner complaint service of the National Automobile Dealers Association. Programs are located throughout the country. To find out if an AUTOCAP is in your area, contact National Automobile Dealers Association, 8400 West Park Drive, McLean, Virginia 22101. Telephone: (703) 821-7070.

Auto Safety. If your complaint has to do with automobile safety (or lack of safety)—which may affect other car owners as well—address your question, gripe, or suggestion to:

National Transportation Safety Board, U. S. Department of Transportation, 400 7th Street S.W., Washington, D.C. 20591.

Director, Office of Public and Consumer Affairs, Department of Transportation, Washington, D.C. 20590. Telephone: (202) 426-4570.

National Highway Safety Administration; toll-free hotline (800) 424-9393; in Washington, D.C., call (202) 416-0123.

National Highway Traffic Safety Administration, Public Affairs, Room 5232, 400 7th Street S.W., Washington, D.C. 20590. Telephone: (202) 426-9550.

Center for Auto Safety, 1346 Connecticut Avenue N.W., Washington, D.C. 20036. Telephone: (202) 659-1126.

If you are a truck or bus driver and would like to contribute information and ideas for improved truck or bus safety, contact: Professional Drivers Council (PROD), 7th Floor, 2000 P Street N.W., Washington, D.C. 20036. Telephone: (202) 785-3707.

Borrowing. If you suspect a store, a dealer, a finance company, or a small loan company of violating the federal Truth in Lending law—for example, by not clearly stating the true simple annual interest rate on an installment loan or a purchase agreement on time—call or write the nearest regional office of the Federal Trade Commission. National headquarters of the FTC is Washington, D.C. 20580 (address complaints and inquiries to the Bureau of Consumer Protection).

The FTC's regional offices are at these addresses:

John F. Kennedy Federal Building
Government Center
Boston, MA 02203

Federal Building
26 Federal Plaza
New York, NY 10007

6 Pennsylvania Avenue
Washington, DC 20580

55 East Monroe Street
Chicago, IL 60603

2001 Bryan Street
Dallas, TX 75201

450 Golden Gate Avenue
Box 36005
San Francisco, CA 94102

HOW AND WHERE TO GET HELP

Suite 500
The Mall Building
118 St. Clair Avenue
Cleveland, OH 44114

1718 Peachtree Street N.W.
Atlanta, GA 30308

Federal Building
11000 Wilshire Boulevard
Los Angeles, CA 90024

915 Second Avenue
Seattle, WA 98101

1405 Curtis Street
Denver, CO 80202

If you have any reason to believe that your *bank* is not clearly spelling out full details of the loan you are negotiating, and if it's a national bank, check with Consumer Affairs, Office of the Comptroller of the Currency, Washington, D.C. 20219. Telephone: (202) 566-2000.

Or if it's a state-chartered bank which is a member of the Federal Reserve System get in touch with the Truth-in-Lending Officer of the Federal Reserve Bank in the city closest to you. Federal Reserve Banks are located at these addresses:

600 Atlantic Avenue
Boston, MA 02106

230 South LaSalle Street
Chicago, IL 60690

33 Liberty Street
New York, NY 10045

411 Locust Street
St. Louis, MO 63166

100 North Sixth Street
Philadelphia, PA 19105

250 Marquette Avenue
Minneapolis, MN 55480

1455 East Sixth Street
Cleveland, OH 44101

925 Grand Avenue
Kansas City, MO 64198

100 North Ninth Street
Richmond, VA 23261

400 South Akard Street
Dallas, TX 75222

104 Marietta Street N.W.
Atlanta, GA 30303

400 Sansome Street
San Francisco, CA 94120

NON-MEMBER INSURED BANKS. If it's a bank which is not a member of the Federal Reserve System but is federally insured contact the Office of Bank Customer Affairs, Federal Deposit Insurance Corporation, Washington, D.C. 20429. Telephone: (202) 389-4427.

Or call the FDIC Supervising Examiner for the district in which bank is located.

If it is a federally insured savings and loan association get in touch with the Federal Home Loan Bank Board's Supervisory Agent in the district in which the association is located. Or write Office of the General Counsel, Federal Home Loan Bank Board, N.W., Washington, D.C. 20552. Telephone: (202) 377-6000.

Addresses of the FHLBB's twelve districts are:

(Connecticut, Maine, Massachusetts, New Hampshire, Rhode Island, and Vermont): P.O. Box 2196, Boston, Massachusetts 02106.

(New Jersey, New York, Puerto Rico, and Virgin Islands): 1 World Trade Center, Floor 103, New York, New York 10048.

(Delaware, Pennsylvania, and West Virginia): 4th Floor, 11 Stanwix Street, Gateway Center, Pittsburgh, Pennsylvania 15222.

(Alabama, District of Columbia, Florida, Georgia, Maryland, North Carolina, South Carolina, and Virginia): P.O. Box 56527, Atlanta, Georgia 30343.

(Kentucky, Ohio, Tennessee): P.O. Box 598, Cincinnati, Ohio 45201.

(Indiana and Michigan): 2900 Indiana Tower, 1 Indiana Square, Indianapolis, Indiana 46204.

(Illinois and Wisconsin): 111 East Wacker Drive, Chicago, Illinois 60601.

(Iowa, Minnesota, Missouri, North Dakota, and South Dakota): Second Avenue at Center Street, Des Moines, Iowa 50309.

(Arkansas, Louisiana, Mississippi, New Mexico, and Texas): 1400 Tower Building, Little Rock, Arkansas 72201.

(Colorado, Kansas, Nebraska, and Oklahoma): P.O. Box 176, Topeka, Kansas 66601.

(Arizona, Nevada, and California): P.O. Box 7948, San Francisco, California 94120.

(Alaska, Hawaii and Guam, Idaho, Montana, Oregon, Utah, Washington, and Wyoming): 600 Stewart Street, Seattle, Washington 98101.

FEDERAL CREDIT UNIONS. If it is a federally chartered credit union, write National Credit Union Administration, 2025 M Street N.W., Washington, D.C. 20456. Telephone: (202) 254-9800.

Or contact the NCUA's regional office serving the area in which the federal credit union is located. Regional offices are located in Boston, Atlanta, Toledo, San Francisco, Harrisburg, and Austin.

If it is a state-chartered credit union, get in touch with the appropriate state supervising agency—either the Department of Banking or the Finance Department or the state agency covering credit unions.

Another federal agency enforcing various aspects of the Truth in Lending law is the Civil Aeronautics Board, Bureau of Enforcement, 1825 Connecticut Avenue N.W., Washington, D.C. 20428.

And if the problem involves interstate transportation (trucking companies and railroads that cross state lines), write the Office of Proceedings, Interstate Commerce Commission, Constitution Avenue and 12th Street N.W., Washington, D.C. 20423.

Finally, if you believe you have been illegally fired or otherwise harmed because your wages have been garnisheed—a possible violation of the Truth in Lending law—contact the Labor Department's Wage and Hour Division, which is in charge of enforcing this part of the law.

HOW AND WHERE TO GET HELP

Broadcasting. Send your complaints about radio or television broadcasting or business practices to: Federal Communications Commission, 1919 M Street N.W., Washington, D.C. 20554.

The National Citizens Committee for Broadcasting, 1028 Connecticut Avenue N.W., Washington, D.C. 20036, tries to encourage citizens and groups to take a more active role in the media and regulation of these forms of communication.

Action for Children's Television (ACT), 46 Austin Street, Newton Center, Massachusetts 02159, tries to reduce offensive TV ads aimed at child viewers. Telephone: (617) 527-7870.

The Consumer Assistance Office, Federal Communications Commission, also may deal directly with your complaints as a consumer. (Address above.) Telephone: (202) 632-7000.

Civil Liberties. If you believe there has been a serious infringement of your civil liberties, contact: American Civil Liberties Union, 22 East 40th Street, New York, New York 10016. (See also Discrimination.)

Counseling. If you need counseling on subjects ranging from wage garnishment to problems in your child's school to psychiatric needs, call a local voluntary Family Service agency. For names and other specifics on such agencies in the area where you live, write: Family Service Association of America, 44 East 23rd Street, New York, New York 10010.

Or contact: Office of Human Development, Department of Health, Education, and Welfare, 300 Independence Avenue S.W., Washington, D.C. 20201. Telephone (202) 472-7257.

Or get in touch with your local YMCA or YWCA. For the address of the branch nearest you, write: Young Men's Christian Association, 291 Broadway, New York, New York 10007, or the Young Women's Christian Association of the U.S.A., 600 Lexington Avenue, New York, New York 10022.

For counseling on runaway children, call the National Runaway Hotline: toll-free (800) 621-4000. In Illinois, call (800) 972-6004.

Credit Rating. If you are unfairly rated a bad credit risk, write for help directly to: Associated Credit Bureaus, Inc., 6767 Southwest Freeway, Houston, Texas 77036. Telephone (713) 774-8701. Or appeal to the nearest office of the Federal Trade Commission, which enforces the Fair Credit Reporting Act.

If you need help setting up a program to repay your debts and manage your finances properly in the future, visit a credit counseling service in your area. (See Yellow Pages for addresses of a local service.) Or write the National Foundation for Consumer Credit, Inc., 1819 H Street N.W., Washington, D.C. 20006, for names and addresses of credit counseling services convenient to where you live.

Discrimination. If you believe you are the victim of illegal discrimination—on the basis of race, age, sex, or national origin—at your job, in your pay, in your search for housing, in trying to borrow money, in the courts, or in any aspect of your constitutional rights, there are a number of organizations ready to help you.

If your problem is racial discrimination:

National Association for the Advancement of Colored People, 1790 Broadway, New York, New York 10019.

NAACP Legal Defense and Education Fund, 10 Columbus Circle, New York, New York 10019.

American Civil Liberties Union, 22 East 40th Street, New York, New York 10016 (or your state's branch of the ACLU).

If the problem is sex discrimination, in jobs, credit, pay:

Women's Bureau, United States Department of Labor, 200 Constitution Avenue N.W., Washington, D.C. 20210.

Center for Women's Policy Studies, 2000 P Street N.W., Washington, D.C. 20036. Telephone (202) 872-1770.

National Organization for Women, 705 G Street S.E., Washington, D.C. 20003. Telephone (202) 347-2279.

If your problem is discrimination in housing, call the housing discrimination hotline: (800) 424-8590. In Washington, D.C. call (202) 755-5490.

If your problem is employment discrimination:

Equal Employment Opportunity Commission, Washington, D.C. 20506 (or any of the EEOC field offices).

Wage and Hour Division, Employment Standards Administration, U. S. Department of Labor, 200 Constitution Avenue N.W., Washington, D.C. 20210 (or any of the 350-plus field or regional offices listed under "United States Government—Department of Labor, Wage and Hour Division" in the telephone book).

If you are an applicant, trainee, or apprentice in a program covered by federal regulations, and you believe you have been discriminated against: Bureau of Apprenticeship and Training, United States Department of Labor, Washington, D.C. 20210.

If your employer is a federal government contractor or subcontractor: Office of Federal Contract Compliance, Employment Standards Administration, United States Department of Labor, Washington, D.C. 20210, or: Assistant Attorney General, Civil Rights Division, United States Department of Justice, Washington, D.C. 20415.

You can also address a complaint to your state Fair Employment Commission or Human Rights Agency or your city's Commission on Civil Rights.

If you feel immediate action is in order, report the matter to the nearest office of the Federal Bureau of Investigation or to your nearest United States Attorney.

If your complaint goes unanswered or if you don't get satisfactory action, write or call: United States Commission on Civil Rights, 1121 Vermont Avenue N.W., Washington, D.C. 20425. Telephone: (202) 655-4000.

Door-to-Door Sales. If your problem or dispute involves a door-to-door salesperson, or the goods or services he is selling: Direct Selling Association, 1730 M Street N.W., Washington, D.C. 20036.

Drugs. See Food and Drugs.

Electronic Equipment. If you haven't been able to resolve a problem involving a TV, stereo, or calculator, the Electronic Industries Association, 2001 I Street N.W., Washington, D.C. 20006, will forward the complaint to the company involved and follow up for you until you receive a response.

Environment. If you believe court action is warranted against a person or corporation destroying some aspect of your environment, go first to your local environmental board or write Office of Public Affairs, Environmental Protection Agency, 401 M Street S.W., Washington, D.C. 20460. Telephone: (202) 755-0707. If you fail to get satisfaction, get in touch with one of these groups of lawyers and scientists dedicated to preserving a healthful environment through court action: Environmental Defense Fund, 1525 18th Street N.W., Washington, D.C. 20036; or: Natural Resources Defense Council, Inc., 122 East 42nd Street, New York, New York 10036.

For advice on how to change your buying habits to minimize their adverse environmental effects: Concern, Inc., 2233 Wisconsin Avenue N.W., Washington, D.C. 20007.

If you want to share in efforts to prevent further pollution or depletion of the earth's natural resources, among the leading environmental and conservation organizations you can join:

Environmental Action, Inc., 1346 Connecticut Avenue N.W., Washington, D.C. 20036. Publishes biweekly *Environmental Action.* Lobbies and educates for stronger laws and enforcement.

A good source of environmental news is the weekly *Environmental Action Bulletin* (Rodale Press, Emmaus, Pennsylvania 18049).

Friends of the Earth, 620 C Street S.E., Washington, D.C. 20003. Publishes monthly *Not Man Part,* publicizes issues, lobbies, brings suits.

National Audubon Society, 950 Third Avenue, New York, New York 10022. Publishes monthly *Audubon* magazine, educates, researches environmental problems.

National Wildlife Federation, 1412 16th Street N.W., Washington, D.C. 20036. Publishes bimonthly *National Wildlife* and *International Wildlife.* Concerned with all environmental problems affecting wildlife.

Sierra Club, 530 Bush Street, San Francisco, California 94108. Publishes monthly *Sierra Club Bulletin*. Local chapters sponsor outdoor activities, lobbying, legal action.

Wilderness Society, 1901 Pennsylvania Avenue N.W., Washington, D.C. 20006. Publishes quarterly *Living Wilderness*, lobbies, educates, sues, conducts outings.

If your environmental problem involves solar heating, one advice source is the National Solar Heating and Cooling Information Center, Box 1607, Rockville, Maryland 20850. Toll-free hotline: (800) 523-2929. In Pennsylvania: (800) 462-4983.

Flammable Fabrics. Use the Consumer Product Safety Commission's hotline, (800) 638-2666, to report cases of dangerously flammable fabrics on the market or to get safety-related information on fabrics you suspect of being dangerously flammable—including names of offending brands and retailers.

Food and Drugs. If you find you have bought any contaminated or otherwise harmful food, drugs, or cosmetics, report it to your nearest FDA regional or district office or resident post.

The FDA's national headquarters is: Consumer Inquiry Section, Food and Drug Administration, 5600 Fishers Lane, Rockville, Maryland 20852. Telephone: (301) 443-3170.

The FDA's district offices are:

District Office	Address	Area Code and Number
Atlanta, GA 30309	880 West Peachtree Street N.W.	(404) 881-3576
Baltimore, MD 21201	900 Madison Avenue	(301) 962-3731
Boston, MA 02109	585 Commercial Street	(617) 223-5857
Brooklyn, NY 11232	Room 700 850 Third Avenue	(212) 965-5529
Buffalo, NY 14202	599 Delaware Avenue	(716) 846-4483
Chicago, IL 60607	Room 1222, Main Post Office 433 West Van Buren Street	(312) 353-7126
Cincinnati, OH 45202	1141 Central Parkway	(513) 684-3501
Dallas, TX 75204	3032 Bryan Street	(214) 749-2735
Denver, CO 80202	721 19th Street U. S. Customhouse Room 500	(303) 837-4915
Detroit, MI 48207	1560 East Jefferson Avenue	(313) 226-6260
East Orange, NJ 07018	20 Evergreen Place	(201) 645-3023
Kansas City, MO 64106	1009 Cherry Street	(816) 374-3817

District Office	Address	Area Code and Number
Los Angeles, CA 90015	1521 West Pico Boulevard	(213) 688-3771
Minneapolis, MN 55401	240 Hennipin Avenue	(612) 725-2121
New Orleans, LA 70122	4298 Elysian Fields Avenue	(504) 589-2401
Philadelphia, PA 19106	Room 900 2nd and Chestnut	(215) 597-4390
San Francisco, CA 94102	Room 568 United Nations Plaza Federal Office Building	(415) 556-2062
San Juan, PR 00905	P.O. Box S 4427 Old San Juan Station	(809) 967-1221
Seattle, WA 98104	Room 5003 Federal Office Building 909 First Avenue	(206) 442-5304

The Health Research Group, 2000 P Street N.W., Washington, D.C. 20036, is a consumer advocate group concerned with occupational safety, food and drugs, and health care delivery.

The Community Nutritional Institute, 1146 19th Street N.W., Washington, D.C. 20036, provides information and technical aid on a wide range of food programs and policy issues.

The Children's Foundation, 1028 Connecticut Avenue N.W., Washington, D.C. 20036, monitors federal food assistance programs and helps eligible women and children to participate.

(Also see Health Care.)

If you have reason to believe that your butcher's or supermarket's or grocer's scales are rigged to show a heavier weight for meats, fruits, vegetables, or other products—or that the weight of a product you have bought is misstated on the label—alert your state Bureau of Weights and Measures or: Office of Weights and Measures, National Bureau of Standards, Washington, D.C. 20234, or Assistant Secretary for Food and Consumer Services, U. S. Department of Agriculture, Administrative Building, Room 2018, Washington, D.C. 20250; telephone: (202) 447-4623.

Furniture. If you cannot clear up a dispute with a furniture dealer within a reasonable time:

Furniture Industry Consumer Advisory Panel (FICAP), P.O. Box 951, High Point, North Carolina 27261. Telephone: (919) 885-5065.

The National Association of Furniture Manufacturers, 8401 Connecticut Avenue N.W., Washington, D.C. 20015, represents more manufacturers than the Consumer Advisory Panel. Telephone: (202) 657-4442.

Health Care. If you have a problem or question or serious complaint about medical service, tell it to:
- your state's office of Consumer Health Affairs (if there is one);
- your local and/or state Health Department;
- your state or county Medical Society;
- the local private Health and Welfare Council (in major cities);
- the local chapter of the Medical Committee for Human Rights based at P.O. Box 7155, Pittsburgh, Pennsylvania 15213 (but with chapters in other major cities);
- the nearest Comprehensive Health Planning agency;
- your state insurance commissioner;
- state or local consumer protection agencies;
- your state's Public Interest Research Group;
- the local offices of the Blue Cross and Blue Shield organizations, Social Security Administration, the Welfare Department;
- or to one of these key national organizations:

American Medical Association
535 North Dearborn Street
Chicago, IL 60610

American Dental Association
211 East Chicago Avenue
Chicago, IL 60611

American Psychiatric Association
1700 18th Street N.W.
Washington, DC 20009

American Public Health Association
1015 18th Street N.W.
Washington, DC 20036

National Medical Association
1720 Massachusetts Avenue N.W.
Washington, DC 20036

United States Public Health Service
5600 Fishers Lane
Rockville, MD 20852

American Hospital Association
840 North Lake Shore Drive
Chicago, IL 60611

Find out whether the hospital has a patient advocacy system or any other type of grievance mechanism.

Get a copy of the American Hospital Association's Patient's Bill of Rights (see pages 1364–65) and show it to hospital authorities.

A few states have special "grievance panels" which function as alternatives to malpractice suits. Inquire about whether your problem could be handled by such a panel.

For quick referral to a nearby specialist who can give you a second medical opinion about your problem, call HEW-funded (800) 325-6400.

If venereal disease is your worry, call VD, toll-free hotline (800) 523-1885. In Pennsylvania, call (800) 462-4966.

Finally, you can get a variety of excellent "Shopper's Guides"—to sur-

HOW AND WHERE TO GET HELP

gery, dentistry, and health insurance—published by the Pennsylvania Insurance Department. If you are a Pennsylvania resident, send a self-addressed 9×12-inch envelope with 20 cents postage per guide to the Pennsylvania Insurance Department, Harrisburg, Pennsylvania 17120. Non-residents can get copies of these and other guides for $1.00 each from Consumer News, Inc., 813 National Press Building, Washington, D.C. 20045.

Immigration and Naturalization. If your problem is in this area, your source for help is: Information Services, Immigration and Naturalization Service, 425 I Street N.W., Washington, D.C. 20536. Telephone: (202) 376-8449.

Information. For help in prying loose government information under the Freedom of Information Act: Freedom of Information Clearinghouse, 2000 P Street N.W., Washington, D.C. 20036.

If you need advice or information on such close-to-home matters as child care, gardens, nutrition, health, clothes care, food storage, "do it yourself" projects, farm subsidies, financial problems, or dozens of other subjects, three superb sources of pamphlets, instructions, and guidance are: Extension Service, U. S. Department of Agriculture, 14th Street and Independence Avenue S.W., Washington, D.C. 20250; Superintendent of Documents, U. S. Government Printing Office, Washington, D.C. 20402; and Consumer Information Center, Pueblo, Colorado 81009.

Of the three, the Center is your best one-step source for getting low-cost or free publications on subjects ranging from warranties to myths about vitamins. You can get a free Consumer Information Index, listing the more than 250 publications available, by writing the Consumer Information Center, Pueblo, Colorado 81009. The Index is also available in Spanish. It is published four times a year.

To get information quickly about which federal, state, or local agency can help you with a problem or to obtain help directly, the General Services Administration in co-operation with the Civil Service Commission operates Federal Information Centers in cities across the country. They also have toll-free numbers linking nearby cities to the centers. Here are the toll-free numbers:

ALABAMA
- Birmingham (205) 322-8591
- Mobile (205) 438-1421

ARIZONA
- Phoenix (602) 261-3313
- Tucson (602) 622-1511

ARKANSAS
- Little Rock (501) 378-6177

CALIFORNIA
- Los Angeles (213) 688-3800
- Sacramento (916) 440-3344
- San Diego (714) 293-6030
- San Francisco (415) 556-6600
- San Jose (408) 275-7422

COLORADO
- Colorado Springs — (303) 471-9491
- Denver — (303) 837-3602
- Pueblo — (303) 544-9523

CONNECTICUT
- Hartford — (203) 527-2617
- New Haven — (203) 624-4720

DISTRICT OF COLUMBIA
- Washington — (202) 755-8660

FLORIDA
- Fort Lauderdale — (305) 522-8531
- Jacksonville — (904) 354-4756
- Miami — (305) 350-4155
- Orlando — (305) 422-1800
- St. Petersburg — (813) 893-3495
- Tampa — (813) 229-7911
- West Palm Beach — (305) 833-7566

GEORGIA
- Atlanta — (404) 221-6891

HAWAII
- Honolulu — (808) 546-8620

ILLINOIS
- Chicago — (312) 353-4242

INDIANA
- Indianapolis — (317) 269-7373

IOWA
- Des Moines — (515) 284-4448

KANSAS
- Topeka — (913) 295-2866
- Wichita — (316) 263-6931

KENTUCKY
- Louisville — (502) 582-6261

LOUISIANA
- New Orleans — (504) 589-6696

MARYLAND
- Baltimore — (301) 962-4980

MASSACHUSETTS
- Boston — (617) 223-7121

MICHIGAN
- Detroit — (313) 226-7016

MINNESOTA
- Minneapolis — (612) 725-2073

MISSOURI
- Kansas City — (816) 374-2466
- St. Joseph — (816) 233-8206
- St. Louis — (314) 425-4106

NEBRASKA
- Omaha — (402) 221-3353

NEW JERSEY
- Newark — (201) 645-3600
- Trenton — (609) 396-4400

NEW MEXICO
- Albuquerque — (505) 766-3091
- Santa Fe — (505) 983-7743

NEW YORK
- Albany — (518) 463-4421
- Buffalo — (716) 842-5770
- New York — (212) 264-4464
- Rochester — (716) 546-5075
- Syracuse — (315) 476-8545

NORTH CAROLINA
- Charlotte — (704) 376-3600

OHIO
- Akron — (216) 375-5638
- Cincinnati — (513) 684-2801
- Cleveland — (216) 522-4040
- Columbus — (614) 221-1014
- Dayton — (513) 223-7377
- Toledo — (419) 241-3223

OKLAHOMA
- Oklahoma City — (405) 231-4868
- Tulsa — (918) 584-4193

HOW AND WHERE TO GET HELP

OREGON
Portland (503) 221-2222

PENNSYLVANIA
Allentown/
Bethlehem (215) 821-7785
Philadelphia (215) 597-7042
Pittsburgh (412) 644-3456
Scranton (717) 346-7081

RHODE ISLAND
Providence (401) 331-5565

TENNESSEE
Chattanooga (615) 265-8231
Memphis (901) 521-3285
Nashville (615) 242-5056

TEXAS
Austin (512) 472-5494
Dallas (214) 749-2131

Fort Worth (817) 334-3624
Houston (713) 226-5711
San Antonio (512) 224-4471

UTAH
Ogden (801) 399-1347
Salt Lake
City (801) 524-5353

VIRGINIA
Newport
News (804) 244-0480
Norfolk (804) 441-6723

WASHINGTON
Seattle (206) 442-0570
Tacoma (206) 383-5230

WISCONSIN
Milwaukee (414) 271-2273

One good source of more addresses of organizations which stand ready to help you and accept your help is:

Help: The Useful Almanac (available for $4.95 from Consumer News, Inc., 813 National Press Building, Washington, D.C. 20045, or at a reference library), which lists and describes hundreds of private and government agencies across the country. A detailed guide to what you can *do* to secure your rights is *A Public Citizen's Action Manual,* by Donald Ross ($1.95 from Grossman Publishers, 625 Madison Avenue, New York, New York 10022).

Insurance. If your question is about insurance, an insurance agency, or insurance salesman, write direct to the State Insurance Department in your state capital, or to one of these private trade associations:

FOR LIFE INSURANCE
American Council of Life Insurance
1850 K Street N.W.
Washington, DC 20006

FOR CRIME INSURANCE
Federal Crime Insurance
P.O. Box 41033
Washington, DC 20014
Free hotline: (800) 638-8780

FOR AUTOMOBILE AND LIABILITY INSURANCE
Insurance Information Institute
110 William Street
New York, NY 10038

1266 National Press Building
529 14th Street N.W.
Washington, DC 20004

400 Montgomery Street
San Francisco, CA 94104

You can get excellent, no-nonsense advice on how to buy insurance by sending small sums for *Shopper's Guide to Term Insurance; Shopper's Guide to Cash Value Life Insurance; Shopper's Guide to Health Insurance;* and *Shopper's Guide to Mobile Home Insurance* (Consumer News, Inc., 813 National Press Building, Washington, D.C. 20045). *The Shopper's Guidebook* by Herbert Denenberg also is available from this source ($3.50).

FOR FLOOD INSURANCE
National Flood Insurance,
Department of Housing and Urban Development
Washington, DC 20410
Toll-free hotline: (800) 424-8872

Job Safety. If you think you are being exposed to a hazardous substance or other dangerous condition in your workplace, contact the nearest field office of the Occupational Safety and Health Administration, listed in the phone book under "United States Government, Department of Labor." The main office address is: OSHA, Department of Labor, Washington, D.C. 20101. Employees covered by the law can request inspection of their workplace, and the OSHA must agree not to reveal the names of any complainants to employers. Also, contact the Health Research Group, 2000 P Street N.W., Washington, D.C. 20036, which has written about how workers can become involved in OSHA proceedings.

Job Training and Employment. Check your phone book under "State Government" for your State Employment Service. Or write Employment and Training Administration, Department of Labor, Washington, D.C. 20201.

Legal Services. The National Consumers Center for Legal Services, 1302 18th Street N.W., Washington, D.C. 20036, gives information about legal service plans. The National Legal Aid and Defender Association, 2100 M Street N.W., Washington, D.C. 20037, helps provide the poor with quality legal services. The Legal Services Corporation, 733 15th Street N.W., Washington, D.C. 20005, is federally funded and is the largest provider of legal aid to the poor and indigent. Also call your local bar association, Legal Aid Society office, law school, or legal clinics for referrals.

Life Insurance. See Insurance.

Magazine Action Line. This organization resolves complaints about any magazine. It is a service of Publishers Clearing House, a large direct-mail, discount seller of subscriptions. Address: 382 Channel Drive, Port Washington, New York 11050.

Mail Order. If you suspect mail fraud of any description or if you receive unordered merchandise through the mails, or even if you simply receive a piece of highly deceptive advertising, ask your local post office whether a formal complaint is in order, or write: Office of the Chief Postal Inspector, U. S. Postal Service, Washington, D.C. 20260. Telephone: (202) 245-5445.

If you have complaints about postal service (e.g., packages lost or damaged, surly clerks, long lines), take them first to your local postmaster. If he can't help you, write: Consumer Advocate, at the United States Postal Service, Washington, D.C. 20260. Telephone: (202) 245-4514.

If you have an unresolved disagreement with a mail-order house or would like to reduce the amount of junk mail you get, write: Consumer Service Director, Direct Mail Marketing Association, 6 East 43rd Street, New York, New York 10017. Telephone: (212) 689-4977.

Mortgages. If you have problems about a home mortgage insured by the Veterans Administration or the Federal Housing Administration, or a home improvement contractor who is working on a project involving a federally guaranteed loan, ask your bank for the address of the nearest office of the VA or FHA. The FHA's national headquarters are: Federal Housing Administration, Department of Housing and Urban Development, 451 7th Street S.W., Washington, D.C. 20410.

The VA's headquarters are: Veterans Administration, 810 Vermont Avenue, Washington, D.C. 20420.

All HUD field offices give free counseling to people who have housing problems.

Moving. Send your complaints about movers to: Bureau of Operations, Interstate Commerce Commission, Constitution Avenue and 12th Street N.W., Washington, D.C. 20423, or call the ICC on its hot line: (800) 424-9312. In Washington, D.C., call (202) 275-7301. In Florida, call (800) 432-4537.

Occupational Health. See Health Care and Job Safety.

Pensions. The Department of Labor keeps tabs on pension plans and has legal responsibility, under the 1974 pension reform law to initiate action to correct abuses. If you have a complaint about your pension plan, send it to the Office of Communications and Public Services, Pension, Welfare and Benefit Programs, 200 Constitution Avenue N.W., Room S4522, Washington, D.C. 20216. It also has a representative at your nearest area office of the Labor-Management Services Administration. Or send your complaint to: Administrator of Pension, Welfare, and Benefit Programs, 200 Constitution Avenue, N.W., Room S4522, Washington, D.C. 20216.

The Internal Revenue Service also regulates pension plans and can terminate a plan and split its assets among the participants if it is being improperly administered. So send a copy of your complaint to: Office of Employee Plans and Exempt Organizations, Internal Revenue Service, 1111 Constitution Avenue N.W., Washington, D.C. 20224.

If you're thinking of taking a pension case to court, you or your lawyer may want to contact: National Senior Citizens Law Center, Suite 201, 1636 West Eighth Street, Los Angeles, California 90017, or: National Senior Citizens Law Center, 1200 Fifteenth Street N.W., Washington, D.C. 20005, or Pension Rights Center, 1346 Connecticut Avenue N.W., Washington, D.C. 20036. The latter publishes excellent "Pension Fact Sheets" that you can receive for 25 cents upon request.

Another group concerned with your pension rights is:

American Pension Conference, 358 Fifth Avenue, New York, New York 10001.

See also Social Security and Veterans' Benefits.

Pollution. If you believe that a local industry or individual is illegally polluting the air or water in your community, check with one or all of these agencies:

The state or local Environmental Control Board or pollution control board;
The state or local Health Department;
The U. S. Environmental Protection Agency, 401 M Street S.W., Washington, D.C. 20460.

Consumer Protection and Environmental Health Service, Public Health Service, Department of Health, Education and Welfare, 5600 Fishers Lane, Rockville, Maryland 20852.

Product Labeling. See Food and Drugs.

Product Safety. If you have found an unsafe product of almost any kind, get in touch with the Consumer Product Safety Commission Team, 1750 K

HOW AND WHERE TO GET HELP

Street, N.W., Washington, D.C. 20207. Toll-free hotline: (800) 638-8326. In Maryland, call: (800) 492-8363.

Addresses and phone numbers of the commission's regional offices are:

1330 West Peachtree Street, N.W.
Atlanta, GA 30309
(404) 881-2259

100 Summer Street
Boston, MA 02210
(617) 223-5576

230 South Dearborn Street
Room 2945
Chicago, IL 60614
(312) 353-8260

Room 410-C
500 South Ervay
P.O. Box 15035
Dallas, TX 75201
(214) 749-3871

Suite 938
Guaranty Bank Building
817 17th Street
Denver, CO 80202
c/o Food and Drug Administration
(303) 837-2904

Room 1500
1125 Grand Avenue
Kansas City, MO 64106
(816) 374-2034

Suite 1100
3660 Wilshire Boulevard
Los Angeles, CA 90010
(213) 688-7272

Room 1905
911 Walnut Street
Kansas City, MO 64106
(816) 374-2034

Room 650
Federal Building, Fort Snelling
Twin Cities, MN 55111
(612) 725-3424

International Trade Mart, Suite 414
2 Canal Street
New Orleans, LA 70013
(504) 527-2102

Building 1, 8th Floor, Bay 7
830 Third Avenue
Brooklyn, NY 11232
(212) 788-5000, Ext. 1166

Continental Building, 10th Floor
400 Market Street
Philadelphia, PA 19106
(215) 597-9105

Room 558
50 Fulton Street
San Francisco, CA 94102
(415) 556-1816

1131 Federal Building
909 First Avenue
Seattle, WA 98104
(206) 442-5276

DEB Annex 21046
Brookpark Road
Cleveland, OH 44135
(216) 522-3886

For Alaska, Hawaii, Virgin Islands, and Puerto Rico, phone (800) 638-8333.

Retirement. Here are key organizations and agencies concerned with the special needs of elderly citizens (see pensions too):

Your state's Commission on Aging

United States Administration on Aging

National Council of Senior Citizens
1511 K Street, N.W.
Washington, DC 20005

Social and Rehabilitation Service
Department of Health, Education and Welfare
Washington, DC 20201

National Council on the Aging, Inc.
60 East 42 Street
New York, NY 10010

Senate Special Committee on Aging
Senate Office Building
Washington, DC 20510

American Association of Retired Persons
1909 K Street, N.W.
Washington, DC 20006

Social Security. If you have any questions about Social Security, contact your local Social Security office first (look for it in the phone book under "United States Government"). If the local office cannot or will not resolve your problem, contact: Social Security Administration, 6401 Security Boulevard, Baltimore, Maryland 21235.

If you disagree with a decision on a claim for Social Security benefits or for Supplemental Security Income (SSI), you have sixty days from the date you are notified of the decision in which to request a reconsideration.

You can file your request at any Social Security office, but it must be in writing, either in a letter, or on a form your Social Security office can supply.

If, after you have received the results of that reconsideration, you still are not satisfied, you may ask for a hearing before an officer of Bureau of Hearings and Appeals. This request, too, must be made within sixty days of the time you receive notice of the reconsideration decision.

If, when you have been notified of the hearings officer's decision, you still disagree, you may ask for a review by the Appeals Council. The hearing decision notice will show how much time you have to file for that review.

Claimants who disagree with an Appeals Council decision may take the final step and bring suit in Federal Court.

Stocks and Securities. If you are the victim (or even suspect you may be the victim) of a shady deal involving a transaction in securities, get in touch with the nearest regional office of the Securities and Exchange Commission, or write: Securities and Exchange Commission, 500 North Capital Street N.W., Washington, D.C. 20549.

Taxes. If you have a question or complaint about your federal income tax, call your local Internal Revenue Service office. To learn where this office is, check your Form 1040 Instructions, or contact: Internal Revenue Service, 1111 Constitution Avenue N.W., Washington, D.C. 20224.

Or use one of the IRS's toll-free information numbers. These are listed on the Form 1040 Instructions, and in many telephone books under "United States Government." You also can get the number for your area by calling "Information."

For information on tax court procedures, contact: Clerk of the Court, United States Tax Court, Washington, D.C. 20217.

If you feel you have been the victim of inequities or abuse in any aspect of the tax system—sales, property, income, etc., contact: Tax Reform Research Group, 133 C Street, S.E., Washington, D.C. 20003.

Tenants' Rights. If you are, for any reason, served with an eviction notice, consult your lawyer. Or, if you don't have a lawyer and can't afford to hire one, go to the local tenants' association for advice on what to do about it. Or get in touch with: National Tenants Organization, 1025 Fifteenth Street N.W., Fifth Floor, Washington, D.C. 20005; telephone: (202) 783-0711.

Toy Safety. See Health Care and Product Safety.

Unemployment Insurance. To sign up for benefits or to resolve a problem concerning benefits, go to the nearest state employment service office (look for the address in the telephone book under the listing for your state government).

Utilities. If you are dissatisfied with the service or business policies of your phone, gas, water, or electricity company and cannot resolve the matter with the company itself, complain to your state utility regulating body. This may be called the public utility commission, the public service board, or some similar name; its address will be under the state government listing in the capital phone book.

Warranties. If your warranty is not honored, contact your regional office of the Federal Trade Commission or its main office, Division of Special Statutes, FTC, Washington, D.C. 20580; telephone: (202) 523-3598.

EPILOGUE

How Much Do *YOU* Know About Your Economic System?   1406
   MONEY   1406
   ECONOMIC TERMS   1407
   CONSUMERS   1407
   WORK AND WAGES   1407
   THE ANSWERS   1408
The Hidden Threat to America's Economic System   1409
   THE THREE FUNDAMENTAL POINTS   1409
   OUR ECONOMIC ILLITERACY   1409
   THE HARSH DOCUMENTATION   1410
   "GRASSLAND"   1410
   THE HEART OF THE MATTER   1411

How Much Do *YOU* Know About Your Economic System?

The subject really isn't nearly as confusing as it might seem, once you understand the fundamentals. Test your knowledge of our system with the following quiz. There is just one right answer to each question. Answers appear at the end of the quiz, along with a brief explanation of some points.

Give yourself one point for every correct answer. If you score between 13 and 16, you are indeed well informed on economic matters. If you score between 9 and 12, you are above average and you can probably debate the issues with just about anyone. If you score between 5 and 9, you're average. But if you score 6 or less, you might want to make an effort to learn more about the United States economic system and the forces that often play tug-of-war with your family income.

MONEY

1. The value of the U.S. dollar is determined by
(a) the amount of government-held gold reserves
(b) the amount of goods and services the dollar will buy
(c) the Federal Reserve

2. Of the total American money supply, checking account money represents about
(a) 75 per cent
(b) 45 per cent
(c) 30 per cent

3. The "prime rate" refers to
(a) the interest that banks charge on business loans to their best corporate customers at a given time
(b) the going rate most banks and savings and loans charge on residential mortgages
(c) the highest interest rate banks are permitted to pay on savings deposits

4. A Federal Reserve Bank is any bank that offers checking and savings accounts. True or false?

ECONOMIC TERMS

5. Our gross national product refers to
(a) the total market value of goods and services produced by the United States in a given period of time
(b) the total amount of goods and services sold by the United States in a given period of time
(c) the total market value of goods and services exported by the United States in a given period of time

6. The consumer price index measures changes in prices paid for goods and services by urban consumers. True or false?

7. When the dollar is "down" against the Japanese yen, it takes fewer yen to equal one dollar. True or false?

8. Baseball great Babe Ruth was able to earn $80,000 at the depth of the Depression when millions of other Americans were unemployed. This illustrates the economic principle of
(a) supply and demand
(b) scarcity and choice
(c) income distribution

CONSUMERS

9. The buying public largely determines the type and amount of goods and services produced in the U.S. economy. True or false?

10. The availability and widespread use of consumer credit helps make possible a higher standard of living for all Americans. True or false?

11. A shortage of business capital has little effect on the average consumer. True or false?

12. When you invest money in something, your "return on investment" is the total profit you make on the transaction, or your gain. True or false?

WORK AND WAGES

13. The U.S. standard of living is closely tied to worker productivity. True or false?

14. If a company goes bankrupt, stockholders are among the first in line to divide up available assets. True or false?

15. Of all American workers, those who belong to a union represent
(a) 1 out of 4
(b) 1 out of 2
(c) 1 out of 3

16. Your "disposable income" is
(a) your annual salary
(b) your take-home pay after income taxes
(c) money you spend on entertainment and recreation.

THE ANSWERS

1. (b)

2. (a)

3. (a) The prime rate tends to rise and fall with the cost of money banks must borrow from the Federal Reserve and other sources to meet the corporate credit demand.

4. (False) All national banks and many state-chartered banks are members of the Federal Reserve System. However, Federal Reserve Banks are "central banks" that conduct business mainly with the federal government and with their member banks, rather than with the general public.

5. (a)

6. (True)

7. (True)

8. (a)

9. (True)

10. (True) With credit, consumers are able to purchase many more goods than they could pay for with cash. Therefore, more goods are produced, more factories are built, and more jobs are created.

11. (False) A scarcity of business capital affects your life as a worker and consumer in important ways. When business has difficulty building new plants, it may be forced to manufacture products at greater per unit cost with outdated equipment. This means productivity is restricted even though consumer demand for some goods may be on the increase. As always, when demand is high and supply is low, prices go up and *you* feel the pinch in your pocketbook.

12. (False) Don't forget taxes. Your actual "return on investment" is your profit *after* you've paid Uncle Sam and any other state or local taxes that might be applicable.

13. (True) As productivity increases, more goods and services flow into the market place, and availability of these products helps reduce cost. The amount of goods and services produced by the average American worker continues to increase at a rate of almost 3 per cent a year, and innovations in production methods, along with the discovery and use of cheaper resources, allow families to buy more goods and services and enjoy a higher standard of living.

14. (False) Stockholders go to the rear when a company goes under. Bondholders have the better chance of recovering all or part of their investment by claiming a share of any available assets.

15. (a) At present, union memberships account for nearly 23 million workers, or about 25 per cent of the entire American work force.

16. (b)

SOURCE: Continental Illinois National Bank and Trust Company of Chicago.

The Hidden Threat to America's Economic System

THE THREE FUNDAMENTAL POINTS

Out of a lifetime specializing in my chosen field of economics-financial reporting, I have learned these three fundamental points:

The first fundamental point is that the American market place is an economic jungle. As is true of all jungles, this market place easily can destroy all who are ignorant of the basic guides for survival. Millions of you easily can fall into dangerous traps from which you cannot escape unharmed if you are not on the alert and aware of the maneuvers to avoid them. But you also can come through safely, in fine shape, and can even conquer the jungle —if you learn the rules, heed them, and refine them for your own use.

My second fundamental point is that we are a nation of economic illiterates and our illiteracy is a threat to the survival of the system we profess to love so much.

My third fundamental point follows the second and leads to the fear I've always had that if our system ever dies, it will be because in our ignorance we didn't know it was dying—or that we were killing it.

OUR ECONOMIC ILLITERACY

In our Congress, policies vitally affecting the survival of our form of economic system have for decades been made by economic illiterates, and probably still are being made.

In the executive suites of great financial and business concerns and in union headquarters across the nation, decisions directly involving our paychecks, profits, and prosperity have been made and probably still are being made by men and women who have only the vaguest idea of what creates paychecks, profits, and furthers prosperity.

In most of our high schools and colleges, the future leaders of America are either being taught nothing about our economic system or given courses woefully superficial, appallingly inadequate.

We are a nation of economic illiterates.

Few students in our high schools learn anything at all about our economic system in their classrooms.

The vast majority of American adults are not only ill informed on economic issues: worse, just because they are ignorant, they don't care about being better informed.

Most of our lawmakers are loaded with misconceptions about the economic issues on which they are passing laws.

And this indictment goes to the very top of our nation at this start of the 1980s, a time when more than ever before, understanding of our own economy and what's right with it, what's wrong with it, what might be done to make it stronger, more virile, more productive of basic values and of everyday things that make life more comfortable—such understanding has been and is absolutely imperative.

Harsh words? They certainly are. And I could make them even harsher.

THE HARSH DOCUMENTATION

Heed these simple dreadful statistics:
* Less than four out of ten U.S. high schools offer separate courses in economics—and only about two out of ten of those require students to take the course.
* The total time spent in high schools is about 3,557 hours. Thus, those students who *do* take the economics course will devote only a little over 1 per cent of their total hours in high schools to studying economics.

Only about 65 per cent of the colleges with teacher trainees require economics of social studies majors—the teachers usually assigned to teach economics. Where economics is not required, rarely does more than one out of ten take it voluntarily.

As an illustration of how this frightening lack of teaching and training works out, consider this test statement about a hypothetical country:

"GRASSLAND"

"Grassland is a country in which there is very little government ownership of farms and businesses. People may train for jobs and start businesses as best they can. The government does not usually control prices and wages."

What type of economic system does Grassland have?

The shocker here is that only a minority of students in 13,000 junior high school systems confronted with this statement by testers for the Joint Council on Economics Education recognized Grassland's as a "capitalistic" system. The majority opted for "communistic," "socialistic," "co-operative"—or "don't know."

As other illustrations of economic ignorance:
* A test was administered to over 21,000 high school students by a professor at Georgia State University. Over half did not know that the U.S. economy is based upon private enterprise.
* The New York University Center for Economic Education administered a test (twelfth-grade level) to several hundred students in community colleges in the New York area. The majority missed questions on: (a) government and freedom of choice in a free enterprise economy; (b) the characteristics of communism and free enterprise; (c) the relationship between productivity and wages.
* The same test used with the New York Community College students was given to 540 college students in Rhode Island with these partial results: 85 per cent did not understand the impact of inflation on creditors; 82 per cent did not understand the relationship between changes in business spending

and recessions; 81 per cent did not understand the simple opportunity cost concept.

• The same test was administered to a group of young adults employed by a major U.S. bank. All were college graduates but had not taken economics. Their overall knowledge of economics was no better than that of high school students who had not taken a course in economics. Indeed, most of them missed questions of the functions of the Federal Reserve and on the differences between capitalism and communism.

Enough. Research studies underline the almost incredible ignorance of the so-called man in the street—but what about *educated* adults whose formal education did *not* include economics? The best example is the large group of bank employees tested. All were college graduates (with top scholastic records); all were in positions of responsibility (relations with important bank clients); all were picked by their supervisors as being "the best" in their departments. All claimed to be interested in economic matters and all read such papers as the New York *Times*. Results:

The average score on the test of economic understanding was little better than that of the average high school student who had taken no economics.

The majority missed questions on money and banking (origin of commercial bank deposits)!

The majority missed questions of functions of the Federal Reserve!

The majority did not understand the balance of payments problem.

THE HEART OF THE MATTER

And that brings me to the heart of my message about the "real" world in which you live.

Both "pure" and consumer economics are horribly neglected fields—and the neglect you pay it and others pay it is dangerous, terribly dangerous.

Behind every war, there is an economic cause. Never have wars been fought strictly for ideological reasons or for political reasons or for religious reasons.

Behind every social change, there is an economic cause. It's simply impossible to understand the modern world and its trends without understanding the key part economic changes are playing in our lives and our futures.

Now: Whose fault is it that of all the spheres in our lives, the sphere of economics is the least understood, the least covered, and certainly the least attractively presented?

First, I admit it is the fault of the individual reporter and commentator, people in positions like mine—and, I repeat and re-emphasize, of the education system that produced us.

Since our teachers cannot and do not begin to give us the fundamental information to help us understand our economy, and do not even teach the fundamentals of family finance, when you, the student, graduate, you haven't even the elementary facts to guide you to understanding. As a result, few of you think of economics as the very core of your lives.

Or those who do try to teach you often are economists who turn to writing as an afterthought. They cannot write; they do not even begin to recognize the extent to which simplicity is an art. They write down to you; they hide their own confusions behind fancy words, incomprehensible jargon, what I call bafflegab.

Second, it is the fault of the educators who belittle this type of news or who are bored to death with it or who don't understand.

In too many instances, editors cater to tastes you've already developed or which are obviously there—juicy scandals, personal or political.

It's not so obvious that what is happening to your dollar and jobs and savings is mighty important and interesting—to you—too.

The need is there, the taste is there—but it cannot be met and will not be until and unless the need and taste are fully appreciated (as my entire life and this book symbolize my appreciation).

Let me give you a personal anecdote that illustrates the general lack of appreciation in a painful way.

In the late 1970s, the head of a nationwide organization phoned to tell me that a blue-ribbon volunteer committee had been formed to help combat public ignorance of how our system works. It had plans to distribute millions of pamphlets, each dealing with a frequently misunderstood aspect of our economy. The gentleman offered me the story on an exclusive basis because he knew of my dedication to fighting economic illiteracy.

"Will the pamphlets be free?" I asked.

When he said that there would be a small charge, I responded that if he could work out a way to distribute them free, I would enthusiastically help publicize the effort. He got the permission for free distribution, so I asked him to send me copies of the pamphlets at once.

When I saw the pocket-size booklets, I was appalled. The looking-down-the-nose approach was so apparent that my first reaction was embarrassment plus resentment. The effort to achieve simplicity had led only to a "cutesie-tootsie" result.

End of my effort to help as originally planned. As for the pamphlets, I don't know where they are.

"Cute" writing must never be confused with simplicity. Simplicity of writing or talking about economic matters, I often have thought, can be compared to an iceberg. Two-thirds is beneath the surface, only one-third is visible.

And incidentally, how much do *you* really know?

The average U.S. citizen thinks corporation profits amount to 28 cents out of every sales dollar and even stockholders think after-tax corporation profits average 23 cents on the sales dollar, according to an opinion research corporation poll.

The average actually ranges between 3 cents and 5 cents out of a full dollar.

I guess I could boil all this down to two four-word sentences.

You have to understand. You have to care.

And that's what this whole book has been designed to help you do—understand, protect yourself. And care enough to fight the hidden enemy of our system—before it does indeed destroy us.

INDEX

Abandoned or unclaimed property: forgotten money and, 901–2; life insurance benefits, 1050–52
Abortion, 842–46; costs, 843; insurance, 845; reducing costs, 843–44; referral services, 844; tax tips, 846
Absentee fathers, tracing, 862–63
Absenteeism, alcohol abuse and, 547–48
Abstract of title (title search), 192, 194, 216, 218
"Academic apprentice" program, federal, 590
Acceleration contract clause, 967
Accessories (*see also* specific items, kinds, problems): auto options, 351–55, 359; bicycle, 458; household, 228 (*see also* specific kinds); jewelry, 780–88; wedding, 825
Access rights, disabled persons and, 1367–69
Accidental death and dismemberment policy, 487
"Accidental death benefit" insurance, 1040, 1052
Accident and health insurance, 1042, 1048
Accidents, 511–13 (*see also* specific aspects, problems); automobile, 405–12 (*see also* Automobile accidents); bicycles and mopeds, 459–61; health insurance and, 481ff.; medical emblems and, 569–70; motorcycles, 455; workers' compensation, 511–14, 1375
"Accrual basis" money management, 20–21
Accrual-type (appreciation-type) securities, 1231, 1238, 1242
Accrued interest, bond, 1221
Accumulation (periodic purchase) investment plans, 1119–20, 1178–79, 1187, 1188
Additives, food, 83, 126, 129; labels, 98; organic foods and, 125–26, 128–29
Additives, gasoline, 395
Add-on contract clause, 967
Add-on interest rate, 953–57
Administrator (administratrix), 1087
Adoption, child, 852–53
Advanced Placement Examinations, 598–99
Advertisements, 59–68; auto repairs, 384, 386; beef bulk buying, 116–17; "cents off" coupons, 54–55; credit, 62–63; credit, consumer rights and, 1349; deceptive and honest, 59–68; "earn money at home," 750–53; electric appliances, 61; employment agencies, 667–68, 669–70; energy and fuel savings claims, 60–63; executive counseling, 712–14; food savings and, 54–55, 80–86 *passim*; furniture (furnishings), 226, 227–28, 231–32, 235–36; health hoaxes, 558–66; home improvement gyps, 283–92; jobs and, 666–67, 707; key questions to ask, 753; life insurance, 1048–49; mail-order, 63–65, 504–8 (*see also* specific kinds); organic foods, 125–26; reading to save money, 59–68; retirement homesites, 1062–64; sales, 59–68 (*see also* specific kinds); self-improvement books, 63–65; small business gyps, 728–29, 730, 731–35, 738ff.; terminology, 65–68; tires, used cars, 425–26, 429, 438–39, 440; weight reduction, 558–59

Age (age bracket): aging and retirement (*see* Elderly, the; Retirement); alcoholism and, 547; auto costs, 336, 340; auto insurance and, 368–71, 374; bonds and, 1197–98; contact lenses, 574; credit and consumer rights, 907, 908, 916, 1352, 1354–55; disability benefits, 509–11; education costs and savings needed, 583; "empty nest," 682–83; equal rights opportunity, 714–15, 1373; health insurance and, 487, 499–504; hearing loss, 566–68; home ownership and, 152–53, 165; insurance and, 340; job discrimination, 714–15, 1373; job success and, 694–98; Medicare and, 499–504; mental health care and, 540–41; mopeds and, 460–61; motorcycles and, 455–56; physical exams and, 521, 524; Social Security and, 499–504, 509–11; working women and, 1024
Age Discrimination Act, 1373
Aging (the aged). *See* Elderly, the
Agricultural commodities, futures and, 1246–66
Agriculture, jobs in, 632, 633, 637, 650, 654
Agriculture Department (USDA), 81, 88, 1393; beef-cut charts, 113–14; beef grades, 111; "Calories and Weight" guide, 81; and commodity futures, 1251, 1258–59; Extension Service, 1384, 1395; and fast foods, 142; "Food and your

INDEX

Weight" bulletin, 80; and food labels, 98; key food publications, 88, 111; meat inspection stamp, 98; and organic foods, 126
Aid to Families with Dependent Children program, 862–63
Air bags, auto, 354
Air conditioners, 56; auto, 351–52; central, home buying and, 172, 183; checking EERs, 61, 312; energy savings and, 307, 310, 311–12, 320, 321; filters, 312; when to buy, 56
Air travel, 465–71, 790ff., 811–12; bumping protection, 470–71; caution on medications, 793; charters, 791–92; complaints, 1384–85; do-it-yourself planning, 801ff.; first-class coach fares, 465–66, 467, 469–70; handicapped people and, 793–94; off-season, 795; overseas, 466–67, 468–70; package tours, 791–92, 796–801; "scheduled charters," 467; super-saver rates, 467–68; travel agents, 799–801
Alarms (alarm systems): burglary, 262–63; smoke detectors, 256–57
Alcohol abuse and alcoholism, 486–87, 520, 521–22, 547–48, 557, 1367; and auto accidents, 405; cost of, 547–48; health insurance and, 487; help for, 548, 561; statistics, 547
Alimony, 856–57, 858, 861, 862–63; for husbands, 857
Allowances, personal: children, 31–32; college students, 33–34; money management and, 21, 31, 34, 36, 38–40, 42; and saving method, 34, 36, 38–40
"All risks" insurance policy, 221
Alternative mortgage instruments (AMI-ers), 6, 213ff.
American Association of University Women (AAUW), 684
American Bankers Association, 829, 1104
American Board of Family Practice, 518
American Cancer Society, 562
American cheese, 111
American Civil Liberties Union, 1389, 1390
American Council of Life Insurance, 1049, 1051, 1397
American Dental Association, 496, 536, 1394; Directory, 495
American Express credit card, 942, 943, 944
American Gas Association Laboratories, Blue Star Seal of, 238, 254
American Hospital Association, 1364–65, 1367; and "Patient's Bill of Rights," 1364–67, 1394
American Institute of Real Estate Appraisers, 169–70
American Medical Association, 536, 537, 559, 569, 1394
American Municipal Bond Assurance Corporation, 1209
American Mutual Insurance Alliance, 417
American National Standards Institute (ANSI), 187
American Psychiatric Association, 1394
American Society of Appraisers, 1320, 1321
American Stock Exchange (AMEX), 1110, 1113, 1114, 1145, 1154, 1219, 1247

American Youth Hostel, 807; and bike trails, 808; and bus passes, 807–9
Amortization, home mortgage loans and, 216, 217
Amtrak, 463–64, 794, 801, 812; body shipments by, 1096; "Tickets to Anywhere," 464
Annual financial reports, corporate, 1130–32
Annual percentage rate (APR), 952; disclosure, 1347–48, 1351, 1386
Annuities, 1045–46, 1052; new types of, 1046
Antifreeze, 384, 412
Antique furniture, "honest copies" of, 231
Antiques, 1289–92; art, 1303–10; bargain categories, 1291–92; books, 1313–15; buying rules, 1290–91; Oriental rugs, 1292–94
Anti-Rollback Odometer Law, 378, 420, 424, 440–41
Apartment residences, the elderly and, 306–7, 550
Apartments, 177–79; burglary protection, 260–63; buying vs. renting, 155–57; check list, 269–70; condominiums, 179–82; co-ops, 177–79; energy-saving guide, 309–28; equipment for, 225–27; finding, 151; fire protection, 253–58; home insurance, 218ff.; kitchen remodeling, 282–83; leases, 266–70; moving, 298–305; painting, 280–82; renting, 151, 152; second homes, 263–70; tenants' rights, 1403; utilities, saving on, 250–53
Apple juice, "organic," 130
Appliances, household, 236–50 (see also specific kinds, problems); "bargain," 239; color TV, 244–45; consumer rights and complaints, 1329ff., 1386, 1390; credit and, 913, 950, 951; cutting repair costs, 239–42, 245–47; energy-saving guide, 309–28; fire protection, 253–58; getting the best deal, 242; home buying and, 172, 174, 189, 190; life expectancy of, 238; name brands, 237; no-frill models, 237, 244–47; repairs, 238, 239–42; rules for buying, 236–37; safety seal, 237–38; sales ads, 61; second-hand, 239; sound equipment, 247–50; space and floor for, 237; TV repairs, 245–47; utility bill savings, 250–53; warranties and guarantees, 1337–42; when to buy, 56, 57–58
Application letters, job hunting and, 671–72
Appraisals (appraisers): auto insurance, 375; choosing, 1319–21; home buying and, 169–73, 216; home insurance and, 219; societies, 1321
Apprenticeship programs, job training and, 675–76; complaints, 1390–91; information sources, 676
Arbitage, 1150–51
Architects, 195–97; fees, 196, 197; finding, 196–97
Art, investing in, 1302–10
Arthritis, 564–66; "cures," 64, 564–66
"Artificially sweetened" food, 82
Art supplies, when to buy, 56

INDEX 1417

ASPIRA Educational Opportunity Center, 593–94
"Aspirations, era of," 11–12, 19
Aspirin, 537–38
Assessments, home buying and, 159–60, 216; special, 159–60
Assets, 974 (*see also* specific kinds); appraising, 1319–21; co-ownership, 1072, 1081–84; credit rating and, 915; divorce and, 858; net worth and, 46–47; "separate property," 1083; student aid and, 585–87; wills, estates, and trusts, 1067–90
Asset value per share (NAV), 1159, 1187
Assigned-risk (auto insurance) plans, 374, 375
Assorted interest accounts, 887
Attestation clause, 1074, 1087–88
At the market (market order), defined, 1264
Attics, energy savings and, 320, 321–22; home buying and, 171
Auctions: antiques, 1290, 1291; country, 1290; government sales, 69; Oriental rugs, 1292; prints, 1308; vintage cars, 1318
Automatic bill-paying, 894
Automatic deduction savings plans, 27, 895
Automatic dividend reinvestment, 1117–18, 1178
Automatic fuel adjustment clause, 6
Automatic line of credit, 829, 868, 874, 894–95, 925–26
Automatic payroll service, 895
Automatic savings, 27, 895. *See also* specific kinds
Automatic teller machines (ATMs), 896
Automatic (power) transmission, auto, 352, 397–98; checking in used cars, 436–37
Automation, 633
Automobile accidents, 404–12; bad weather, 412–14; breakdowns, 410–12; consumerism and costs, 391–94; costs of, 404–12; drinking and, 405; equipment, 411, 414; insurance (*see* Automobile insurance and liability); obtaining copy of report, 406; precautions, 405, 410–12; report form, 408–10; reporting, 406; statistics, 405, 425–26; what to do in case of, 406ff.
Automobile buying and ownership, 334–453; accidents and costs (*see* Automobile accidents); average cost per mile, 337; buying a new car, 348–62; buying a used car (*see* Used car buying); car (van) pools, 418, 453; car theft, 415–17; "cash-flow" costs, 344–45, 422; cents-per-mile costs, 338; choosing size and model, 348–49ff., 361; commuting and, 418–19, 464–65; consumer rights and complaints, 1340, 1386; cost differences in car sizes, 345–47; costs to run, 335ff.; credit ads, 62–63; depreciation, 337, 338–40, 343, 421, 430; duty-free, 797; elements of vehicle costs, 338ff., 421ff.; expenses, budgeting, 26; figuring own costs, 343–45; financing and interest costs, 341–42, 343–44, 362–65, 393, 431; fixed and variable expenses, 338, 340ff.; garage, parking, and tolls, 52, 266, 341, 418–19; gas mileage and costs, 61, 350–51, 359, 395–98; gyps on the road, 388–89; insurance (*see* Automobile insurance and liability); leasing, 62–63, 1350–51; leasing vs. renting, 442–53, 467–68; mechanics and repair shops, 382–84ff.; price ranges, 348; real purchase price, 338–40, 429; recalls and "lemons," 392–94, 405; resale value, 338–40; safety, 394, 402–12; selling (trading) your car, 377–78; "shopping" for a dealer, 355–57, 426–27, 429; shopping for options, 351–55, 359, 360; special rules for economy cars, 357–62; tires (*see* Tires, auto); trade-in price, 339–40; used car selling, 377–80; vacation travel and, 802, 804, 811; vintage cars, 1315–19; warranties, 355–56, 357, 381–82, 399–400, 403, 1340–42; when to buy, 57, 58; year-by-year costs, 422
Automobile dealers, 355–57ff., 427–28; consumer rights and, 1340–42, 1385–86; economy cars, 357–62; and financing, 362–65; and insurance, 371–72; markup and profit, 362–64; recalls and "lemons," 392–94; and tires, 399–400, 403–4; used cars and, 426–27, 429–30ff.; warranties and, 355–56, 357, 1340–42
Automobile insurance and liability, 340, 365–77, 450–52; accidents and, 406ff.; age and, 368–72, 374; crash repair controls, 366; discounts, 368–72; federal controls, 366–67; foreign travel and, 802; information, 1398; leasing ads, 62–63; non-renewal, 373–74; policies, 366ff.; premium rates, 365ff.; reducing costs, 367–74; rented cars, 450–52; rise in costs, 365–66; stolen cars, 415–17; terminology, 375–77; used cars and, 432
Automobile repairs, saving on, 380–91; accident prevention and, 405; age of car and, 380–81; auto mechanics and, 382–84ff.; breakdown prevention, 411–12; corrosion, 390–91; dirty tricks away from home, 388–89; do-it-yourself, 384; gas mileage and, 395–98; insurance, 366; myths, 387; recalls and "lemons," 392–94; shopping for big-ticket repairs, 386–87; warranties and, 381–82
Auto Safety Hotline, National Highway Traffic Safety Administration, 394
Awnings, 319

Babies (*see also* Birth control; Children): adoption, 852–53; costs of having, 846–54; family planning and, 830–54
Baby food labels, 98
Backyard gardens, 131–32
Bacon, 107, 111, 115
Bad risks, auto insurance and, 374, 375
Bait and switch tactic: bulk beef buying, 120, 121–23; home improvements, 284; swimming pools, 289; TV repairs, 246; used cars, 439
Balanced mutual funds, 1172
Baldness gyps, 1061–62
Ball, Robert M., 1017
Balloon note, used car, 438–39
Balloon payments, 912, 967; consumer rights and, 1351

INDEX

Bank checks, 37
Bankers' acceptances, 1199
Bankruptcy: corporate, 1407, 1408; personal, 973–74
Banks (banking), 867–902 (*see also* specific aspects, kinds); and bonds, 1203, 1204–6, 1218; cash-machines and, 880–82; checking accounts (*see* Checking accounts); commercial, 867, 870; comparison shopping among, 867–69; computer technology and, 872, 873, 880–84, 893–96; consumer rights and protection and, 1355, 1359–60, 1387–88; credit cards and, 942–49; economic illiteracy and, 1406–13; establishing credit and, 828–29, 264; insurance and money "safety," 896–99; interest on savings, 890–93; jobs in, 644, 651; and loans, 205ff., 264, 363–64, 604–5, 922ff.; money management and, 28, 33, 34–40; mutual savings, 871; safe deposit boxes, 899–901; savings accounts, 37–38, 884–93; savings certificates, 1199, 1210, 1225; "special purpose" accounts, 37, 38; and stock investing, 1123–24; and student loans, 604–5; treasury rate certificates and, 888; unclaimed money in, 901–2; and wills and estates, 1075
Bar associations, 1343; and divorce fees, 856
Bargains (*see also* Discounts; specific items, kinds): beauty care, 785–88; calendar for, 53, 56–58; car rental, 448–49, 453; clothes, 764–65, 775; college education financing, 597–98; credit card use for, 829; food, 84–89, 109–11, 112ff.; home shopping, 167–68, 191; land, 1269–70; whiskey and wine, 134–35, 141
Basements: construction, 171, 172; gyps, 286–87
Basic Educational Opportunity Grant (BEOG), 588–89
Bathing, energy savings and, 315, 316–17
Bathrooms: energy-saving guide, 315, 316–17; home buying check list, 176
Batteries, auto, 56, 388–89, 413
Bear and bull stock markets, 1115, 1151, 1152
Bearer ("coupon") bond, 1199, 1216, 1221
Beauty care, 785–88, 1059–60 (*see also* Cosmetics); gyps aimed at the elderly, 1059–60
Beds (bedding), 56, 227–28, 231
Beef, buying, 74–76, 88, 106–17; bulk buying, 113ff.; cuts (chart), 113–16; grades, 111–12; home freezers and, 117–23; labels, 97, 100–2; warnings, 120–23; yield grades, 114, 116
Behavior therapy, 542
Belted bias ply tires, 400, 401, 403
Beneficiary: defined, 1088; insurance, 487; "primary," 1052
Bequests, 1073, 1088
Best's Insurance Guide, 1037
Better Business Bureaus, 62, 65, 183, 189, 197, 239, 246, 285, 289, 290, 292, 389, 391, 429, 734, 740, 1330, 1331; complaints and, 1330, 1383, 1384; Council, 1383

Better Hearing Institute, 568
Beverages (drinks), 83, 85, 134–35, 136–42 (*see also* specific kinds); eating out and, 142–43; saving on liquor, 134–35, 136–42
Bias ply tires, 400, 401, 403
Bicycles, 456–60; accessories, 458; bike trails, 807–9; certification seal, 457; courtesy, 460; kinds, 457; mopeds, 460–61; safety, 459–60; tips for buying, 456–60; used, 458; when to buy, 56
Bid and asked price, 1151; mutual funds, 1168–69
Bidding (bids): government sales, 69; insulation contracts, 326
Bid (or redemption) price, 1187, 1190
Billing errors, 1359–61
Binder, defined, 216
Bird, Caroline, 1023
Birth control, 830–46; abortions, 842–46; methods and comparative costs, 831–46
Blacks (*see also* Minorities): and jobs, 634
Blackwell, Kate, 1006
Blanket (batt) insulation, 324–25, 326
Blind, the (blindness): Social Security and, 509; vacation travel and, 794
"Blind" ads, 707
Blood lipids, 557
Blood pressure, 519, 520, 521, 522, 557
Blood tests, 523, 524
Blue Cross Association, 488, 527, 530, 845
Blue Cross plans, 482, 483–84, 486, 504, 516, 530–31, 533, 534, 535, 545, 548, 552, 859; abortion coverage, 845; HMOs, 489–94
Blue Shield plans, 482, 483, 504, 534, 535, 536, 570, 858; abortion coverage, 845
Blue sky laws, 1151, 1187
Boats (boating, yachting), 471–75, 810; choosing and buying, 472ff.
Boat (steamship) vacation travel, 801, 810; tipping on winter cruises, 806
Bodily injury liability insurance, 373, 375, 450
Bologna, 107, 111
Bonds and money market instruments, 1194, 1226; banks or, 1218; basic facts, 1195–1202; buying, 1202–3; corporate bonds, 1203–4; federal agency securities (*see* Federal agency securities); financial futures, 1215–20; lower-quality, 1174, 1217; mortgage-pool pass-through certificates and mortgage-backed bonds, 1204–6; mutual funds, 1172, 1175–77; pitfalls for small investors, 1217–18, 1220–21; tax-exempt municipals, 1206–9; terminology, 1221–27; U.S. government securities market, 1209–15; U.S. savings bonds, 1230–43
Books: ads, 63–65, 67; rare, investing in, 1313–15; self-improvement, 63–65; when to buy, 57
Book value, stocks and, 1151–52
Borrowing, 906–79 (*see also* credit, Debts; Loans; specific items, kinds): basic do's and don'ts, 911–13; consumer rights, 1347–62, 1386–88; credit rating and, 829; establishing a credit rating, 829, 913–17; holding down costs, 959–61; interest charges, 952–59ff.; loan sources,

918–25ff.; pitfalls and traps, 961–67; terminology, 974–79
Bottled waters, 135–36
Brakes (braking): auto, 397, 412, 413, 436; bicycle, 457, 459
Bread, 87, 89; storage, 96
Breakdowns, auto, 410–14; preventing, 411–12
Breslow, Dr. Lester, 521–22
Broadcasting: complaints, 1389; jobs in (*see* Radio and television jobs)
"Broad form" insurance policy, 221
Brokers (stock brokers), 1107–8, 1111, 1112, 1113, 1115–20, 1121, 1123, 1124, 1128, 1152, 1153, 1154, 1187; banks as, 1127; bond, 1200, 1202, 1218, 1220; commissions, 1115–20; commodity futures, 1249, 1251–52, 1254, 1256; detecting swindlers, 1118–19; loans from, 933–34; margin buying, 1135–37; selecting, 1115–20; and short selling, 1137
Budget (flexible) charge account, 951
Budgets (budget keeping), 19–49; average family and, 19, 21, 47–48; clothing, 763–68; in college, 33–34; day-to-day expenses, 20, 28–31; family income and, 22–23; fixed expenses, 23–27; food, 74, 76ff.; four simple forms for, 22–31; his-and-hers, 40–46; net worth and, 46; role of children, 31–34; savings and, 23, 26–27, 33, 34–40; where to keep your money, 34–40
Building your own house, 193–204ff.; chart for estimating costs, 204; choosing an architect, 195–97; choosing a contractor, 197–98, 199; construction loans, 206; cutting high costs, 198–204; doing it yourself, 200–4; energy-saving guide, 309–28; expandable houses, 200; finding right site, 194–95; fire protection, 255; home improvements, 270–94; home insurance, 218–25; labor savings, 200; "manufactured" house, 199; mortgage shopping, 205–15
Bulbs (lamps), 58, 231, 317
Bulk buying, 53, 120; food co-ops, 92–93, 95; home freezers and, 117–24; meat, 107, 113–17ff.; unit pricing, 102–4
"Burglar pins," 262
Burglary, 260–63; home insurance, 223, 224; home protection, 260–63; rental leases and, 268
Burials (funerals): expenses (*see* Funeral and burial expenses): wills and, 1072, 1073–74
Buses (bus travel), 461–63; handicapped people and, 794; passes, 807–8
Business (white collar) crime, 737–38ff.
Business life ("key man") insurance, 1052
"Business opportunities" swindles, 738–43
Buying (how to buy), 52–69 (*see also* specific items, kinds); advertising terminology, 65–68; borrowing and credit and, 1064–79; calendar for bargains, 56–58; "cents off" coupons and, 54–55; clubs, 92–94, 95; deceptive and honest ads, 59–68; dozen wise rules for, 53–54; federal government's property sales, 68–69; key weapons against rising costs, 52

Buying power, inflation and, 4–15. *See also* Inflation
Buy on close (buy on opening), 1264

Caesarean delivery, 847, 848
Calendar for bargains, 53, 56–58. *See also* Seasonal buying
Callable: bonds, 1203, 1221–22; non-callable, 1203; stocks, 1152
Call and put options, 1142–45, 1152
Calories, 83–84; diet food, 80–82; low-calorie food, 81–82; and meat, 107, 109–10, 111; USDA bulletins, 81; and weight loss, 559 (*set also* Overweight)
Campers (vehicles), 454, 809–10
Camping trips (campgrounds), 57, 809–11, 813
Cancellation (termination) auto insurance, 375
Cancellation clause, leases and, 267
Cancer, 519; quackery, 562–63
Canned foods, 99; labels, 98; meats, 107; seafood, 125; storage, 96
Canterbury vs. Sponce case, 1366
Cantor, Eddie ("Eddie Cantor clause"), 1021–23
Capital gains (losses), 1104; bonds, 1175; distribution, 1187–88; stocks, 1152
Capitation fees, health care, 493
Car and van pools, 418, 453
Career counselors, 667, 669–70, 707, 711, 712–14, 715
Careers, 631–753 (*see also* Employment; Jobs; specific aspects, kinds); changing and job hunting, 698, 705–15ff.; choosing, 631–32ff.; college grads and, 642–44ff.; compensation, "perks," and fringe benefits, 698–704; education and, 642–47; foreign language skills and, 640–42; franchises, 721–28; goals for women, 683–85; guides for parents, 648–49; guides for women, 683–85; guides to occupations, 647–48; information sources by listed occupations, 650–61; job hunting, 661–74; job satisfaction, 704–5; job training programs and sources, 675ff.; key trends in, 634ff.; layoffs and, 708ff.; opportunity areas, 636–42; options for dropouts, 649ff.; promotion and success guides, 694–98ff.; quitting and, 697, 705–15ff.; raises, 674–75; self-employment, 717–53; women and, 680–93; working at home, 749–53; workweek changes, 634–36
Carpeting and rugs, buying and care of, 233–36
Carriers, household moves and, 300–2
Carte Blanche credit card, 942, 943, 944
Car theft, 415–17
Cash loans, 918–25ff.; sources of, 918–25ff.
Cash-machine cons and errors, 880–82
Cash management bills, 1210, 1211
Caskets, 1094–95, 1096
Cassette players, 248, 249
Catalogs, "phony," 733–34, 735
Catalyst, 684, 686
Catastrophic coverage, health care, 493
CAT scanner, 528

INDEX

Caulking, 284, 310
CB (citizens band) radio, 353
Cemetery plots, 1096, 1098
Center for Science in the Public Interest, 1382; "Nutrition Scoreboard" of, 99–100
Center for the Study of Responsive Law, 1382
Center for Women's Policy Studies, 1390
Cereals, 85, 87, 89; breakfast, 79, 85, 129
Certificate of title, 216
Certificates of deposit (CDs), 886–87, 898, 1199, 1210; consumer, 886–87; rollover, 1225
CETA, 678
Chagall, Marc, 1307, 1313, 1315
Chain-letter schemes, 741–46, 1242
Chain referral home improvement gyps, 285–86
Chairs, 229–30, 231; reupholstering, 229, 230
Chapter XIII bankruptcy, 973–74
Charge accounts, 768, 912, 914, 915, 951 (*see also* Installment buying); billing errors, 1359–61; consumer rights and complaints, 1348–62, 1386–88, 1389; credit cards as, 941–50; saving on, 53; teenagers and, 32–33
Charge off, 974
Charitable trust, 1088
Charters: air travel, 467, 791–92; bus, 462
Charts (technical market analysis), 1251, 1252–53
Chattel mortgage, 974–75
Check credit plans, 975
Checking accounts, 35, 867, 868, 870, 872–80 (*see also* Checks); balancing checkbook, 882–84; bill-paying services, 874, 894; combination savings and, 35, 38–39, 41; computer technology and, 893–96; credit and, 829, 925–26; fees, 867, 872–73, 874; forgeries, 879; insurance and "safety," 896–99; interest-bearing, 867, 868, 871; joint, 35; loans, 922–23, 924; money-market funds, 876; money orders, 875–76; NOW accounts, 874–75; overdraft feature, 829, 874; ready credit, 925–26; regular, 873–74; separate, 36–37, 873, 874, 895; telephone transfers, 875, 895
Checks (*see also* Checking accounts): answers to key questions on, 878–79; canceled, discarding, 982–83; depositing, 876, 877; endorsing, 877; forgeries, 879–80; stopping payment, 878–79
Check verification, computer, 896
Checkwriter maintenance frauds, 730–31
Chemicals (*see also* Drug addiction; Medications): additives and organic foods, 125–30; detergents, 316, 318; GRAS, 128; household, and food storage, 96
Chemosurgery (face peeling), 1061
Chest X-rays, 523, 524
Chicago Board of Trade, 1248, 1258
Chicago Board Options Exchange, 1145
Chicago Mercantile Exchange, 1248, 1258
Chicken, buying, 97, 107, 108, 109, 111, 123
Children, 31–34; adopting, 852–53; allowances, 31–32; bicycles, 456–60; birth control and, 830–54; broadcasting complaints, 1389; budgeting, for college, 33–34; clothing, 57, 58, 758–59, 764–65, 768, 775; costs of having or adopting, 846–54; day-care centers, 690–92; disabled, education rights and, 1368–69; disinheriting, 1080–81; divorce and child support, 856–57, 858, 861, 862–63; family planning, 830–54; financing education, 582–625; fire protection, 254; health insurance, 487; hearing loss, 566–67; home buying and, 152, 153, 160, 161, 181, 188; immunization records, 985–86; life insurance and, 1029–42; life insurance on, 1044–45; mentally retarded, psychoquacks and, 563–64; money management and, 31–34; moving and, 300; mutual funds and, 1181; runaway, 1389; school savings accounts, 888–89; shoe sizes, 775; soaring costs of rearing, 853–54; Social Security benefits, 509–10, 1015, 1017–18, 1023, 1026, 1057–58; walk-in surgery, 533; wills, estates, and trusts, 1067–90; working mothers and, 680, 681–83, 685, 690–92
Children's books, collecting, 1315
Chimneys, 171, 172
Cholesterol, 108, 124, 520, 522, 524, 557
Christmas: Club plan, 38; duty-free shopping, 796–97; gifts, when to buy, 57; mail-order deliveries, 1336; trees and fire hazards, 257–58
Churning, stocks and, 1152
Cigarettes. *See* Smoking
Circulatory diseases, 557
Circumcision fees, 765, 768
City governments. *See* Local governments
Civic organizations (*see also* National organizations): and scholarships, 593; and student loans, 604
Civil Aeronautics Board (CAB), 470, 790–92, 1385; complaints to, 1385, 1388
Civil liberties complaints, 1389, 1390
Civil Rights Act, Title VII, 1373
Civil Service jobs, 590, 632, 655, 666, 690, 715; retirement pensions, 1019; veterans' preference, 1364; workers' benefits, 1056, 1058
Claims (*see also* Complaints; specific kinds): auto insurance, 366–67ff., 375; health insurance, 487; moving and, 305
Cleaning products (detergents), energy savings and, 316, 318
Clearance sales, 56–58
Clinics: abortion, 841–43; family planning, 830, 831; legal (*see* Legal services); maternity, 849; mental health, 543; service credit, 951; smoking, 561
Closed end credit disclosures, 1348
Closed-end funds. *See* Publicly traded investment funds
Closed-end leasing, 1350–51; auto, 62, 443, 444–45
Closing, home buying and, 209–10, 216
Clothes (clothing), 756–78; baby and maternity, 847–48, 850, 852; budgets, 763–68; care and maintenance, 759–62, 772–74; furs, 776–78; jewelry and, 780–88; labels, 759–62, 774; money

INDEX

management and, 29, 36, 48, 53, 56, 57; office attire, 768–69; seasonal buys, 764–65; sewing machines, 769–72; sizes and fit, 757–59; shoes, 774–75; wardrobe planning, 763; workmanship and, 763
Clothes dryers, 238; common problems, 240–41; energy savings and, 318–19, 320; when to buy, 57
Clothes washers, 240, 318–19
Codicils, wills and, 1071, 1072, 1088
Coins: collecting, 1294–96; common gold, 1280, 1294; "limited editions," 1287
Co-insurance, 484–85, 487
Coitus interruptus (withdrawal method), 840, 841
"COLAs," 6
Cold weather driving, 412–14
Collard greens, 99, 100
Collateral, 917, 923, 960, 961, 975, 1242; life insurance as, 1029
Collectibles, buying, 1287ff.
College and university education (college and university graduates), 581–622; Advanced Placement Exam, 598–99; career options for dropouts, 649ff.; CLEP, 598; Co-operative Education Programs, 600–1, 678; cost cutting and financing, 581, 582–86ff., 596ff.; costs at selected colleges, 610–12; deferred tuition payment plans, 599; divorce and, 859; economic illiteracy and, 1409–11; employment and, 581, 633, 642–47ff., 696 (*see also* Careers; Employment); external degree program, 599–600; financial aid programs, 582ff.; grants, loans, and scholarships, 588–96, 599–600, 602–12, 923, 930–32; helpful publications, 623; home study gyps, 622–23; job success and, 696; job training and, 679; money management and budgets, 33–34; shopping for, 597ff.; special payment plans, 599–600; "tuition budget" plan, 931; vacation colleges, 612; vacations at, 812; women and, 154, 684–85
College-level Examination Program (CLEP), 598
College Work-Study Program, 589–90
Collision auto insurance, 365ff., 450; defined, 375
Combination savings and checking accounts, 35, 38, 41
Comic books, collecting, 1315
Commercial banks, 867, 870; auto loans, 363; checking accounts, 872–79; credit cards, 942–49; as financial "supermarkets," 1126–28; home mortgage loans, 205, 211; insurance and money "safety," 896; loans, 922–26, 960; student loans, 604–5; what they are and do, 870
Commercial paper notes, 1199; futures, 1219
Commissions (fees), 1115–20 (*see also* specific kinds, services); bonds, 1202–3, 1221; commodity futures, 1247, 1257, 1260; executors and, 1088; lawyers, 856, 1344–47; mutual funds (load), 1177–78, 1189; stock brokers, 1115–20, 1153, 1202
Commodity Exchange, Inc., The, 1248, 1258

Commodity futures, 1246–66; contracts, 1249; exchanges, 1248, 1250, 1252, 1258; gold, 1281–85; hedgers and speculators, 1246; how traded, 1248; information on, 1247, 1251–52, 1258–59; managed accounts and funds, 1172, 1256–57; market analysis and, 1251–53; pitfalls, 1254, 1256; swindles, 1259–64; terminology, 1264–66
Commodity Futures Trading Commission, 1249, 1259, 1260, 1264, 1334
Commodity Research Bureau, 1251, 1254, 1255, 1258
Common Cause, 1383
Common-law marriage, 818
Common stock funds, 1173
Community, buying or renting a home and, 152, 156, 157, 158–64, 167, 169; character and convenience of, 161–62; check list, 163; condominiums and co-ops, 177, 179; house building and, 200; mobile homes, 184–91; new towns, 184; property taxes, 159–60; schools, 160–61; zoning and planning, 162–63
Community and home gardens, 131–32
Community banks, 870. *See also* Commercial banks
Community colleges, and jobs, 679
Community education schools, 624
Community health resource services, 525–26; elderly people and, 550–51; HSAs, 529–31; mental health clinics, 544
Community property, 1083, 1088
Commuting: cars and, 418–19, 464–65; convenience and home buying, 161; costs, 161; mopeds, 460–61; train, 464–65
Company stock purchase plans, 1120
Compensation, workers' disability, 508–14
Complaints (where to complain), consumer rights and, 1329–31; basic rules, 1330–31; disabled persons and, 1368; employment discrimination, 1374; formal filing, 1334–35; franchises, 1378–79; getting help, 1382–1403; information sources, 1395–97; mail-order problems, 1335–37; nursing homes, 556; taxpayers and, 1369–72; veterans and, 1363; warranties, 1337–42
Compounding of interest, 890, 891–93; defined, 1222
Comprehensive auto insurance, 375–76
Comprehensive Employment and Training Act (CETA), 678
Comprehensive health care, 493, 529; what is included in, 493
Computer-assisted check-out systems, 6
Computer field, jobs in, 646, 652, 653, 750
Computerized credit reporting, 913–17
Computer technology, financial, 872, 873, 880, 893–96, 913–17; billing errors, 1360–61; electronic fund transfer system, 882, 894–96; protections, 880–82
Conditional sales contract, 975
Condom, use of, 838, 841
Condominiums, buying, 177, 178–82, 216, 220, 264, 275
Confession of judgment, 963
Congress Watch, 1383

1422　INDEX

Conservation: jobs and, 652; tourism and, 811–13
Construction and building materials: check list, 173–77; home improvements and, 270, 271–72, 273, 277, 278, 279ff.; house building and, 199, 200, 201, 202, 203–4; house buying and, 171–72; insurance and, 219
Consumer certificates of deposit, 886–87
Consumer Credit Counseling Service, 42
Consumer Credit Protection Act (Truth in Lending Act), 62, 63, 278, 949, 952, 959, 961, 1347–51, 1359, 1382; complaints, 1387, 1388; disclosure rules, 62
Consumer Federation of America, 1331, 1383
Consumer Information Center, 1395; Index, 1395
Consumerism (consumer movement, consumer rights and protection), 1326ff. (*see also* specific agencies, aspects, organizations, problems); auto costs, 391–94, 429; borrowing, credit, and debts, 960–67, 971–74, 1347–62; complaints and action, 1329–31, 1334, 1336–37; contracts, 1349–50; disabled persons and, 1367; franchises, 1378–79; frauds and restitution, 1331–34; getting help, 1382–1403; health care, 528, 529–30, 535–37, 1364–67; hospital patients, 1364–67; information sources, 1395–97; interest rates, 952–59; legal services, 1342–47; legislation, 1326–29, 1335, 1337, 1338, 1347–62; mail-order problems, 1335–37; state and local government protection, 1329; taxpayers and, 1369–72; Truth in Lending Act, 1347–51; unordered merchandise, 1336–37; used car buying and, 429; veterans and, 1362–64; vocational schools, 1378; warranties and guarantees, 1337–42; workers and, 1372–78; writing to legislators, 1335
Consumer Leasing Act, 1328, 1350–51
Consumer Price Index, 5, 345, 1407, 1408
Consumer Product Safety Commission Team, 1400–2
Consumer Reports, 349, 430, 763, 1383
Consumers (*see also* Buying; Consumerism; specific aspects, items, kinds, problems): and budgets and money management, 19–49; defined, 1407; and economics and economic illiteracy, 1406–13; inflation and, 7, 11–12 (*see also* Inflation)
Consumers Opposed to Inflation in the Necessities, 1383
Consumers Union, 763, 1383; ratings, 237
Contact lenses, 573–76, 577
Continental Trailways, 794, 801; Eaglepass, 808
Contingency legal fees, 1346
Continuing education programs, 679, 684
Contraception, 831–46 (*see also* specific aspects, methods); abortions, 842–46; methods and costs, 831–46
Contractors (builder contractors), 169, 197–98, 199, 277–79ff., 325–27, 328 (*see also* Developments); being your own,

280; cautions, 183; choosing, 277–78; contracts, 277, 278–79; gyps, 283–92; home improvements and, 270–71, 275, 277–80ff.; house building and use of, 197–98, 199
Contracts, 278–79; car rental leases, 442–44, 445–47; conditional sales, 975; consumer protection, 1349; credit traps, 967; discarding copies of, 983, 984; franchising, 725, 728; futures, 1219, 1248–49; gold, 1281–85; home improvements, 277, 278–79; job counseling, 713; key rules and warnings, 279; life insurance, 1043; new cars, 357; "rescission" right, 278, 979, 1349; selling your home and, 296; used cars, 431
Conventional (non-FHA, non-VA) mortgages, 212
Convertible debentures, 1203–4, 1222
Convertible funds, 1173
Convertible stocks, 1153
Convertible term insurance, 1032, 1036
Cooking (*see also* Food): changed eating habits and, 84; energy-saving guide, 313–14; meat, 107; microwave ovens, 132–33
Cooperative community gardens, 131–32
Co-operative Education Programs, 600–1, 678
Co-operatives, food, 92–94, 95
Co-ops (co-operative apartments), 177–79, 216, 220
Co-ops, health, 493
"Core" hours of work, 635
Corporate bonds, 1194ff., 1203–4; buying, 1203–6; lower-quality, 1217; ratings, 1204; types, 1203
Corporation (companies, industry), 1129–32 (*see also* specific aspects, kinds, problems); annual financial reports, 1130–32; and "business opportunities" swindles, 738–53; career success and, 694–98ff.; consumer complaints and (*see* Consumerism); economic illiteracy and, 1343; and employees' education programs, 677ff.; and employees' savings plans, 27, 1119, 1230–31 (*see also* specific plans); and franchising, 726–27; investing in stocks of (*see* Stocks)
Correspondence courses and schools, 622–23
Cosmetics, buying and use of, 785, 786, 787–88; consumer complaints, 1392–93; gyps aimed at the elderly, 1059–60; labels, 98
Cost of living: budgets and money management and, 19–49; inflation and, 4, 10 (*see also* Inflation)
Cost-push inflation, 5
Costume jewelry, 57, 782, 783–84, 1286
Cost weight table, unit pricing and, 103
Couches, 226, 227; convertible, 226, 231
Counseling, 1389 (*see also* specific agencies, kinds); getting help and, 1389; investing and, 1123–28, 1157; job, 667, 670, 707, 711–14, 715
Coupon credit charge plan, 951
Coupon interest rate, bond, 1195, 1222
Courts (*see also* Laws; Lawyers):

consumer rights and, 1332, 1333, 1341, 1369–72; and Small Tax Case procedure, 1369–72; and wills, 1076, 1085
Credit, 906–79, 1347–62 (*see also* Borrowing; Debts); advertisements and protection, 62–63, 1349; applications, consumer rights and, 1352–55; auto loans, 362–65; automatic line of, 829, 868, 894–95, 925–26; bankruptcy and, 973–74; basic do's and don'ts of, 911–13; basic types and maturities of loans, 917–18; billing errors, 1359–60; "closed end," 1348; complaints and remedies, 1355–62, 1386–88, 1389; consumer rights and, 1347–62, 1386–88, 1389; credit cards, 941–50; elderly persons' rights, 1354; Equal Credit Opportunity Act, 1352–55, 1357; establishing and maintaining credit rating, 828–30, 913–17, 970–71; Fair Credit Reporting Act, 1355–58; honest rating right, 1355–58; inflation and, 937–38; interest rate charges, 952–59ff.; leasing vs. buying on, 1350–51; legislation, 913, 916, 927, 949, 952, 959, 963, 1347–62; life insurance and, 364, 1029; and living standards, 1407, 1408; loan sources of, 918–25ff.; minority rights and, 1354–55; "open end," 1348–49; overextended, 968–70, 971–74; pitfalls and traps, 961–68; right and wrong reasons for use of, 908–11; Truth in Lending Act and, 1347–51, 1359; women's rights and, 1352–54, 1357–58
Credit bureaus, 913–17; consumer rights and, 1355–58, 1389; reviewing your own file, 1356
Credit cards, 829, 908, 923–24, 941–50; advantages and disadvantages of, 943–44; billing errors, 1359–61; cash loans, 944–45; consumer rights and, 1348, 1352–62, 1389; convenience and loans, 946–48; getting, 943; how to use, 946; lost or stolen, 948–50; mail-order and phone-order, 945–46; protecting, 948–50
Creditors, bankruptcy and, 973–74
Credit rating, 1355–58; consumer rights, 1355–58, 1389; establishing, 828–30, 913–16; maintaining or restoring, 970–71
Credit reports (credit history), 916–17; consumer rights, 1355–58, 1389; reviewing your own, 1356; women's rights and, 1357
Credit sale disclosure statement, 976
Credit unions, 205, 867, 868, 871, 926–28; auto loans, 363–64; computer technology, 893–96; consumer rights, 1347–62, 1387–88; insurance and "safety," 896–99; loans, 205–6, 604–5, 926–28; share draft accounts, 867, 868, 871, 874; what they are and do, 871
Cremation, 1092–93, 1094–95, 1097
"Crew switching" home improvement gyp, 286
Crime (*see also* Burglary; Deceptions; Theft): business (white collar), 737–38ff.; home insurance and, 220, 223, 224; insurance information, 1397–98; stealing from the boss, 737–38; trends, buying a home and, 162, 184

Cromwell, Cynthia, 126
Cruise ships, tipping on, 806
Current-income securities, 1231, 1238–39, 1243
Curtesy rights, 1081
Custody, divorce and, 861
Cyclical stocks, 1154

Dance studio gyps, 1060
"Dating, open," 101–2
Day-care centers, 690–92; jobs, 653
Day hospitals and treatment centers, 550
Dealers (*see also* specific items, kinds): auto (*see* Automobile dealers); consumer complaints and, 1330–31, 1386, 1393; and frauds (*see* Deceptions)
Death, 1092–1100; estate taxes, 1068–72, 1075, 1083–86, 1088; funeral and burial expenses, 1092–1100; survivors' emotional needs and, 1094; veterans' benefits and, 1363–64
Debentures: bonds, 1203, 1222; stocks, 1154
Debt collectors, 961–67, 973; consumer rights, 1358
Debt pooling (debt adjusting), 962
Debts (indebtedness), 906–79; bankruptcy and, 973–74; borrowing and credit and, 906–79; cash loans, 918–25ff.; collectors and pitfalls and traps, 961–67, 972, 1358; counseling, 972–74; credit cards, 941–50; how much is too much, 967–70; limits and guidelines, 969–70; problems and help, 968–70, 971–74; wills and, 1085–86
Deceptions (frauds, gyps, swindles), 8, 59–68, 283–92 (*see also* specific items, kinds); advertising and, 59–68; aimed at the elderly, 1059–64; auto repairs, 388–89; beauty care, 788; "business opportunities," 738–50; "carpet sharks," 235–36; cash machines, 880–82; commodity futures, 1259–64; consumer rights and protection, 1331–34, 1382–1403; credit, 961–67; "death traps," 1099–1100; diamonds, 1298–99, 1299–1300; dieting, 558–60; executive counseling traps, 712–14; furs, 778; getting help, 1382–1404; gold, 1281–85; health hoaxes and medical quackery, 504–8, 558–66; home improvements, 270, 283–92; home study courses, 622–23; insulation contracting, 325–27; job ads, 666; land buying, 1274–75; organic foods, 129–30; retirement homesites, 1062–64; sewing machines, 771–72; small businesses, 728–36, 738–49ff.; stealing from the boss, 737–38; stock investing, 1118–19; tires, 399–400; used cars, 429, 438–41; vocational schools, 615–17; weapons against, 291–92; working at home, 750–53
Decreasing term insurance, 1032–33, 1038
Deductibles (deductible insurance), 221, 224, 376, 382; autos, 367–68, 372, 376; major medical, 484, 485, 487, 514; Medicare, 500, 545; private disability, 514
Deeds: condominium, 179; home buying and, 192, 216, 218; quitclaim, 218

Default judgment ("sewer service"), 962–63
Defective or shoddy goods or services, consumer rights and, 1361–62
Defensive stocks, 1154
Deferred tuition payment loan, 600, 602
"Defined benefit" pension plans, 1001; Keogh, 1178
Demand loan, 917
Demand-pull inflation, 4, 75
Dental care (dentists), 494–99, 786–87, 951; insurance, 495, 497–98; jobs, 636, 644, 653, 750; looking for, 494–96; prepaid, 497–98; preventive dentistry, 497
Department stores (*see also* Stores; specific items, kinds, problems): billing errors, 1360–61; charge accounts and credit cards and, 941–42, 946, 951; consumer rights and, 1326ff., 1336, 1360–61, 1386–88
Deposit ("earnest money"), 191, 217
Deposit term insurance, 1033
Depreciation: auto, 337, 338–40, 343, 421, 430; defined, 217
Developments (developers), housing, 166, 182–84ff. (*see also* Contractors; specific aspects, kinds); buying check list, 182–84; buying in, 182–84; cautions, 183–84; condominiums, 180–81, 182; land buying, 1269–75; mobile homes, 184–91; models and, 183; retirement homesite gyps, 1062–64
Diabetes, 520; food labels, 82; medical emblem, 569
Diamonds, 780, 782–83, 1296–1302; cautions, 1297, 1299–1302; engagement and wedding rings, 821–22; future of, 1299; gyps, 1298, 1299–1302
Diaphragms, contraceptive, 834–37, 841
Dictionary of Occupational Titles, 647
Diesel-engine autos, 351
Diet (diet food), 80–82, 87; definitions, 81–82; health and pill hoaxes, 558–60
Diners Club card, 942, 943, 944
Direct deposit service, 895
Direct dialing, 250, 252
Direct Mail Marketing Association, 1399; Consumer Service, 1336, 1337
Directory invoice gyp, 729
Disability insurance and benefits, 508–14, 1017–18, 1027, 1367–68, 1383 (*see also* Health and accident insurance; Health insurance); "insured salary continuance," 483, 485, 486, 487; private coverage, 513–14; Social Security, 509–11, 513; workers' compensation, 511–13, 1375–76
Disability Rights Center, 1383
Disabled persons' rights, 1367–69, 1383
Discount bonds, 1154–55, 1210, 1222, 1225
"Discount cards," phony, 734
Discount interest rate, 953–57
Discount rate, 1222
Discounts (*see also* Bargains; specific items, kinds): air travel, 790; auto, 338, 356–57; auto insurance, 368–73; beauty care, 788; brokerage, 1116; clothing 765–67; drugstores, 537; food, 91–92, 107; sound equipment, 249
Discretionary accounts, 1155, 1265

Discretionary spending (discretionary purchasing power), 11, 48
Discrimination (*see also* specific groups, kinds): age and, 1373; civil rights, 1389, 1390; complaints and remedies, 1355, 1389–90; credit, 1352–55; equal employment protection, 1373–74, 1390; equal pay, 1374–75, 1390; housing, 1390; women and minorities and, 1023–27, 1373–75
Dishwashers, 172, 312–13; common problems, 241–42; energy savings and, 312–13, 317, 318, 320; life expectancy of, 274, 317
"Disposable income," meaning of, 1407, 1408
"Distress sales," land, 1273
Distributorship swindles, 738–53
Dividends, stock, 1109, 1155; automatic reinvestment, 1117–18, 1190; cash option, 1117–18; extra, 1156; in stock, 1163; yield and, 1109–10, 1165
Divorce, 828, 855–63; alimony and child support, 856–57, 859, 860–63; corporate success and, 697–98; do-it-yourself, 856; "hidden costs" of, 858; legal fees, 856, 859–60; new trends, 860–61; and property ownership, 858–59, 860–61; Social Security and, 1016–17; statistics, 855; uncontested, 860
DOC (Drive Other Cars) insurance, 376
Doctors. *See* Physicians
Do-it-yourself: auto repairs, 384; auto selling, 377–80; divorce, 856; home improvements, 270–74, 280ff.; moving, 301–2; painting, 280–82; travel planning, 801–13; wills, 1076–77
Domestic Independent Tour (DIT), 800
Doors: burglary and, 261, 262; energy savings and, 310, 311, 312, 321, 323; insulating, 310; storm (*see* Storm windows and doors)
Door-to-door sales and complaints, 1391
"Double indemnity" insurance, 1040
Douching, contraceptive, 840
Dower rights, 1081
Dow Jones averages, 1110
Down payments: auto financing, 363, 364; home mortgage loans and table for, 207–8, 212
"Downsizing," 7–8
Dow Theory, 1155
Drapes and curtains: energy savings and, 312; when to buy, 57
Drawers, judging furniture and, 230
Drive shaft, auto, dropped, 411–12
Driveway resurfacing, 284–85
Driving, automobile: accidents, 404–12; bad weather and, 412–14; breakdowns, 410ff.; courses, 370–71; increasing gas mileage and, 395–98; safety (*see* Safety: auto); winter driving tips, 413–14
Dropouts, jobs and, 667; career options for, 649ff.
Drug addiction, 1367
Drugs (medications). *See* Medications
Dual-purpose fund, 1173, 1188
Duty-free shopping, 796–97

INDEX 1425

"Earnest money," home buying deposit and, 191, 217
Earnings, 5, 10 (*see also* Assets; Income; Pay; Salary; Wages); garnishment and protection, 979, 1358–59, 1388; inflation and, 5–6, 10–11, 12–15; money management and budgets and, 19–49; pension plans and, 1002–3, 1011ff. (*see also* specific plans); Social Security and, 1018–21ff.; women and, 688–90, 854, 1024, 1025–26
Earnings, corporate, investing and, 1103, 1108–9, 1131, 1132, 1155; annual reports, 1131, 1132; price-earnings ratio, 1131, 1140–42; profits, 1412; retained earnings, 1131–32
Ear problems, 566–68
Eating (*see also* Diet; Food; Nutrition): in restaurants, 142–43
E (EE) bonds. *See under* Savings bonds, United States
Economics (economic system), 1406–13 (*see also* Inflation; Money); hidden threat to, 1049ff.; illiteracy and, 1409–13; quiz, 1406–8; terminology, 1407
Economy cars, new, buying, 357–62; criteria, 358; gas mileage, 396–97; key rules, 358–60; optional accessories, 359, 361
Economy size, 87; bulk buying, 53; liquor, 140–41; unit pricing, 103–4
Education, 581–625 (*see also* College and university education; Schools; specific aspects, kinds, schools); and careers, 642–47; co-operative, 677–78; correspondence schools, 622–23; cutting costs, 582ff.; disabled persons' rights, 1368; elderly people and, 623–25, 991; helpful publications, 623; home study gyps, 622–23; income by class and, 8–9; inflation and, 11; and job hunting, 663; and job success, 696; loans (*see* Loans, education); money management and, 29, 33–34; need for community education schools, 624; on-the-job programs, 675–80; teaching jobs (*see* Teaching jobs); trade and vocational schools, 613–22; working women and, 681, 684–85
Eggs, 80, 97, 111
Elderly, the, 549–56, 990–1064; and annuities, 1045–46; and auto insurance, 368–70; and credit rights, 1354; and employment rights, 1373; and financial independence and personal security, 990–1064; gyps aimed at, 1059–64; and health care, 534, 533–40, 549–56, 995, 998, 1059–62; home care programs, 533, 549, 550; housing and education needs, 306–7, 623–25, 991; key federal agencies for (listed), 1402; life insurance and, 1028–54; new ways of caring for, 550–52; nursing homes, 550, 551, 552–56; pensions and pension complaints, 1000–8, 1400 (*see also* specific kinds); retirement homesite warnings, 1062–64; retirement planning, 991ff. (*see also* Retirement); Social Security and, 1011–28 (*see also* Social Security)
Electrical circuits (electrical wiring), 170; fire protection, 254–58; fraudulent "repairmen," 287–88; storms and, 259–60
Electric appliances, 236–50 (*see also* specific items, kinds); buying, 236–38; common problems, 240–42; energy requirements and operating costs, 320; energy-saving guide, 310–28 *passim;* fire protection, 253–58; sales ads, 61
Electric heating, 202–3 (*see also* Heating systems); energy-saving guide, 310–28 *passim;* house building and, 201–4
Electric meters, reading, 252
Electrocardiogram (EKG), 521, 523, 524, 532
Electronic banking, 869, 874, 876, 880–82. *See also* specific aspects, kinds
Electronic fund transfer system (EFTS), 882, 894ff.
Elimination period, health insurance, 488
Emergency reserve saving fund, money management and, 26, 27, 885
Emission control devices, auto, 396
Emotional Assessment Exam, 522, 524
Employee Retirement Income Security Act (ERISA), 1004, 1006
Employees (*see also* Careers; Employment; Jobs; specific aspects, kinds, problems): and disability, 508–14, 1368; group insurance, 701; investment plans, 702; and job hunting (*see* Job hunting); and pensions and retirement, 992–95, 1000–8, 1017–21ff., 1059 (*see also* Social Security); and stealing from the boss, 737–38; unemployment insurance, 1375, 1403; women and minority rights and, 1373–75, 1390; workers' rights and complaints, 1372–78, 1390–91, 1398
Employee savings plans, 27, 1119, 1230–31. *See also* Payroll deduction plans
Employers (*see also* Employees; Employment; Jobs): cash loans from, 921–22; and use of employment agencies, 716–17
Employment, 631–753 (*see also* Careers; Employees; Jobs; specific aspects, kinds, problems); agencies (*see* Employment agencies); buying a home and, 153–55; career choices, 631ff.; changing, 632ff.; education and, 581, 642–47; job hunting and, 661–74; key trends, 634ff.; opportunity areas, 636–42; self-employment or, 717–53; trade or vocational schools and, 613ff.; women and, 153–55 (*see also* Working women); working at home, 749–53
Employment agencies, 667–71, 707, 711–17; employers' use of, 716–17; fees, 667–68; getting the most out of, 668–71; over-forty-five and, 714–715; private, 667–71, 707, 711ff.; private, 667–71, 707, 711ff.; state and federal, 647–48, 667, 676, 707, 715
"Empty nest," 682–83
Endicott, Frank C., 674
Endorsements, checks and, 877; blank, 877; in full, 877; restrictive, 877
Endowment insurance, 1034, 1053
Energy (energy and fuel costs), 15, 57, 60–61, 132–33, 250–53, 309–28, 740–41

(*see also* Utility bills); ads, 60–61; energy-saving guide, 309–28; gasoline, 395–98 (*see also* Gasoline); house building and, 201–2; house buying and, 168, 170–71, 172
Engagement and wedding rings, 821–22
Engines, automobile: checking in used cars, 434–36, 437; gas mileage and, 395–98; idling, 434–35; motor replacement, 387; oil changes, 384, 388; overheating, 412; repairs, 386, 387; size, 351–52; starting problems, 414
Entertainment, saving on, 42, 52
Environment: employment and, 634, 643, 645, 652; protection and rights, 1391–92, 1400; volunteer work, 1391
Epilepsy, medical emblem use in, 569
Epoxy glues, 284
Equal Credit Opportunity Act, 1352–55, 1357
Equal employment opportunity protection, 1373–74, 1390
Equal Pay Act and amendments, 1374–75
Equitable distribution statutes, divorce and, 858, 860–61
Estates, wills, and trusts, 1067–90; life insurance and, 1029ff.; savings bonds and, 1235; taxes and, 1068–71, 1075, 1083–84, 1088
Estrogen pill, 832–33
Eurodollars, 1199
Exchange privilege, 1179, 1181, 1188; savings bonds and, 1236–41
Ex-dividend, defined, 1156
Executive (job, career) counselors, 667, 669, 707, 711, 712–15; traps to beware of, 712ff.
Executives, corporate, promotion and success guides, 649–98ff.; compensation, "perks," and fringe benefits, 699–704; dishonesty and, 737–39; divorce and, 697–98; quitting, layoffs, and job hunting, 705–15ff.
Executive search firms (executive recruiters), 711–12, 717
Executors, wills and estates and, 1067–68, 1073–74, 1075–76, 1078, 1085
Exercise, health and, 557
Expandable houses, 200–1
Expenses, money management and, 19–49; "average" spending patterns, 47–49; budgets, 19–49; buying wisely and, 52–69; day-to-day, 20, 28–31; fixed, 23–27
Extended coverage, home insurance, 224
Exterminators, termite swindles and, 288–89
External degree program, 599
Eye care, 570–77; contact lenses, 573–76; exams, 570–71, 576; eyeglasses, 570–73; group plans, 573; sunglasses and fun glasses, 571–72, 576–77

Fabrics (*see also* Fibers): clothing, 761, 768, 771, 774; convertible couches, 227; flammable, complaints, 1392; ironing, 318; reupholstering, 229–30
Facial skin care. *See* Beauty care
Factory outlet: clothing, 766; use in ads of, 66

Fair Credit Billing Act, 1349, 1360–62
Fair Credit Reporting Act, 1355–58
Fair Debt Collection Practices Act, 1328, 1358
Families (*see also* specific aspects, members, problems): borrowing and credit and, 906–79; buying and saving and (*see* Buying); divorce and (*see* Divorce); and "empty nest," 682–83; family planning and (*see* Family Planning); and income (*see* Household income); and money management (*see* Money management and record-keeping, 982ff.; working women and, 680–82
Family doctors, 517–18, 529
Family expense health insurance policy, 488
"Family income" policy, 1034–35, 1038, 1053,
Family planning, 830–54; birth-control methods and costs, 831–46; child adoption and, 846–54; costs of having or adopting a baby, 846–54; elderly people and, 990 (*see also* Retirement); life insurance and, 1028–54; low-cost or free help in, 830–31
Family plan policy, 1035, 1053
Family Practice program, 518
Family Service Agencies, 972
Fans, ventilating, 57, 315, 320; when to buy, 57
Farmer Home Administration (FmHA): home improvement loans, 276–77; mortgage loans, 212
Farm (rural family) loan, 938
Farms (farmers): auto insurance discount, 372; direct marketing, 94–95; home gardening, 131–32
Fast food restaurants, 142; franchises, 721
Fat content of meat, 108, 109–10
Faucets, leaky, 315
Federal agency securities, 1194, 1198, 1199, 1203, 1207, 1215–16, 1222; buying, 1216, 1217; types and issuing agencies, 1215–16
Federal Communications Commission (FCC), 1326, 1389; and CB radio, 353
Federal Crime Insurance, 1397
Federal Deposit Insurance Corporation (FDIC), 868, 870, 897, 898, 1145, 1387
Federal Employees Compensation Act, 511
Federal government (*see also* specific agencies, aspects, investments, plans, problems, programs): and consumer rights and protection, 1326–29, 1335, 1347–62, 1382, 1387–88, 1389, 1392ff.; elderly people and, 549, 550–51, 552–54, 623; employment service, 647, 667, 676; health care and insurance, 490, 492, 497, 511–13, 565–66; information sources, 1395–97; and personal property sales, 68–69; and retirement and pensions, 1004–6, 1008–10, 1011–28; and Social Security, 1011–28; and student aid, 582ff., 588ff.; and taxes, 10–11, 12–15, 183–86, 198–99 (*see also* Taxes)
Federal Home Loan Mortgage Corporation ("Freddie Mac"), 1205, 1206, 1215
Federal Housing Administration (FHA), 179, 185, 190, 209, 211–12, 217, 264; and

"DSI" list, 198; and house building, 194, 198, 199
Federal job training programs, 678
Federal Land Bank issues, 1215, 1216
Federal Reserve Board, 1135, 1147
Federal Reserve System (and Banks), 1196, 1197, 1201, 1202, 1222, 1406, 1411; addresses of offices, 1211–15; and borrowing and credit complaints, 1386–87; and monetary policy, 1222, 1224, 1226, 1406; and tight money, 1266
Federal Savings and Loan Insurance Corporation (FSLIC), 868, 870, 897
Federal Trade Commission, 187, 230, 536–37, 565, 617, 760–61, 778, 964, 1336, 1341, 1378, 1379, 1386, 1389; Bureau of Consumer Protection, 1382, 1386; Debt Collection Practices, 1358; Equal Opportunity Division, 1335; regional offices, 1386–87; "Trade Regulation Rule," 1337
Fellowships, graduate, 595–96
"Female heads of families," 681
Fertilizer(s), 126, 127, 129, 292
Fibers (*see also* Fabrics): clothing, 761; rugs and carpets, 203
Fiduciary account, 888
Finance charges, 952–53, 959; billing errors, 1359–61; consumer rights, 1347–48, 1360–61, 1386–88; disclosure, 1347, 1348–49
Finance companies: auto, 364; student loans, 604–5
Financial aid programs, education, 582–96; college work-study program, 589–90; costs (expenses) and, 582–87ff.; determining need, 587; federal programs, 588–90; Financial Aid Form, 585, 589; graduate fellowships, 595–96; GSLP, 590–91, 602, 606ff.; hunt for, 582ff.; minorities and women and, 593–94; NDSL loans, 590, 602; needs analysis, 585, 587, 593; protection of assets, 585–86; scholarships, grants, and loans, 588–96; state programs, 591; tips on what you will pay, 587; trade and vocational schools, 615; veterans and, 595
Financial futures, investing in, 1218–20, 1222–23
Financial institutions, 867–902 (*see also* specific aspects, kinds*)*: cash-machine cons and errors, 880–82; checking accounts, 872–80; comparison shopping among, 867; computer technology, 872, 873, 880–82, 893–96; consumer credit rights, 1347–62, 1386–88; credit cards, 943–50; insurance and money "safety," 896–99; loans, 922ff.; savings accounts, 884–93; stock investing and, 1123–25, 1126–28; treasury rate certificates, 888; types, 869–71; unclaimed money, 901–2
Financial reports, annual corporate, 1130–32
Financial responsibility laws, 376
Financing (*see also* Borrowing; Credit; Debts; Loans; specific aspects, kinds): autos, 341–42, 343–44, 362–65, 393, 431; home improvements, 276–77; home mortgages, 205–8; house building and, 194, 198; mobile homes, 185–86, 189
Fireplaces, 172, 311, 321, 322
Fire protection, home, 253–58: extinguishers, 254; flammable fabrics, 234, 1392; insurance, 218, 221, 224; mobile homes, 186, 187; safeguards, 254–55
First editions, buying, 1315
First mortgage bonds, 1203–4, 1223
Fish, buying, 111, 124–25
Fishing in the National Park System, 810
Fixed expenses, 23–27; auto, 337–38, 340ff.; money management and, 23–27
Fixed-income securities, 1194ff. (*see also* specific kinds); buying, 1202–3; defined, 1199, 1223
Fleet operators ("fleet cars"), 421; and leasing or renting cars, 442–53; used car buying and, 428–29, 431
Flexible premium—deferred annuity, 1046
Flextime job concept, 635–36, 685
"Floater policy," home insurance, 222
Floods (disasters), 259–60, 1398; insurance, 221, 1398
Floors: house building and, 171, 204; house buying and, 171; insulated, 322
Flower bonds, 1210, 1223
Flowers, buying, 141, 824
Flow restrictors, water, 315
Fluorescent lighting, 317
Fly-drive vacations, 811
Foam, vaginal, 834, 835, 836, 841
Foam mattresses, 228
Food, buying and saving on, 74–143; basic rules, 84–89; beef and, 74ff. (*see also* Beef); budgeting, 20, 28, 29, 30, 36, 37, 45, 48; bulk buying, 113–17ff.; buying clubs, 92–94, 95; calendar for bargains, 56, 57; consumer rights and protection, 1392–93; cost of feeding a family, 76–77; discount stores, 91–92; eating out and, 142–43; gardening and, 131–32; general money-saving hints, 106–17; home freezer use, 117–23; "nutritional return" and, 99–102; organic foods, 125–30; "paying more for less," 80–83; reading labels, 96, 97–102; saving on meat, 106–17; shopping list and, 84, 89–91; size of family and, 77; substitutions and, 52, 75, 86; "trading down" and, 89–91; "Truth in Meat" label, 100–1; unit pricing, 103–4; whiskey and wine, 134–35, 136–42
Food and Drug Administration, 81–82, 95, 133, 135, 538, 559, 565, 567; Consumer Inquiry Section (district offices), 1392; and organic foods, 126
"Food and Your Weight," 81
Food labels (and standards), reading, 96, 97–102
Food, travel, and entertainment credit cards, 942ff.
Forced savings, 889–90, 1117, 1230–31. *See also* specific kinds, plans
Foreclosures, mortgage, buying a home and, 167
Foreign Car Prices, 349
Foreign children, adopting, 853
Foreign language skills, jobs and, 640–42
Forgery frauds, 730–31; checks, 879–80

INDEX

"Forty-plus Club," 715
Four-day workweek, 634–35
403 (B) plans, 1179
Franchising (franchises), 721–28; "business opportunities" swindles, 738–53; check list, 725–28; companies, 726–27; contracts, 724, 727–28; fees, 725; guide, 722–25; investigating and check list of sources, 723–24; most rapidly growing fields, 721–22; profit potentials, 725; rights as a franchisee, 1378–79; sources for advice, 728
"Free," use in ads of, 60, 236, 239
Freedom of Information Act, 198, 1395
Freedom shares, 1243
"Freeway runners," auto gyps and, 389
Freezers, home. See Home freezers
Freud, Sigmund, 542
Friends, cash loans from, 920–21
Friends of the Earth, 1391
Fries, Dr. James F., 521
Fringe benefits, job, 700–4
Front-end load, 1181, 1189
Frozen foods, 79, 85, 87, 99, 100, 125; home freezers, 117–23; storage, 96, 97, 117–23; when to buy, 57
Fruit, buying, 79–80, 83, 84, 85, 87, 88, 93, 94, 99; gardening, 131–32; labels, 98; organic, 125–30; "reduced calorie," 81
Fuel. See Energy; Gasoline; Utility bills
Fuel adjustment clause, automatic, 6
Full coverage, auto insurance, 376
Full-maintenance car leasing, 444, 445–46
Fundamental market analysis, futures and, 1251, 1252
Funds of funds ("multifunds"), 1173
Fund raising, "phony," 731, 732
Funeral and burial expenses, 1092–1100; benefits, 1098–99; care and disposition of body, 1092–94; death education and, 1095; "death traps" (gyps), 1099–1100; guides, 1095–96; laws, 1097–98; "package deals," 1095; survivors' social and emotional needs and, 1094–95
Fun glasses, sunglasses and, 576–77
Fur buying, 57, 776–78
Furnaces, 274, 310–11; common problems, 241; energy savings and, 310–11, 312; and fires, 354; house building and, 201–3; house buying and condition of, 171, 189, 190; phony "inspectors," 287
Furniture (furnishings), 225–33 (see also specific kinds); antiques, 1289–92; bargains, 231; best stores, 231; buying on time, 230–31; complaints, 1393; delivery time, 232; guarantees and warranties, 232; guides to good quality, 230; guides to wood, 231; interior designers, 232–33; mobile homes and, 189, 190; rugs and carpets, 233–36, 1292–94; storm damage, 259–60; when to buy, 57
Furniture Industry Consumer Advisory Panel, 232, 1393
Futures, financial, 1218–20, 1222–23 (see also Commodity futures); interest rates, 1218–20

Games People Play (Berne), 543
Garages, 172, 266, 341, 418–19; door openers, 262; theft prevention, 415
Garage sales, 300
"Garbage debts," 911
Garbage disposal appliances, 237; common problems, 242
Gardening and landscaping, 292–94; backyard gardens and grow-your-own trend, 131–32; buying supplies, 57, 292–94; lawns and mowers, 293–94; traps, 290–91
Gas appliances (see also Appliances; specific kinds, uses): buying, 236–50; common problems, 240–42; energy-saving guide, 310–28; fire protection, 254–58; utility bill savings, 253
Gas-forced air heating, 202, 203. See also Furnaces; Heating systems
Gas meters, how to read, 252–53
Gasoline (gas mileage), auto, 395–98; check list of fuel savers, 395–96; consumption measurement, 395; driving habits and, 395–98; frozen line, 414; how to increase mileage, 395–98; illegal fuel tanks, 396; mileage and costs, 343, 350–51, 359, 395–98; saving devices ads, 61–62
General obligation bonds, 1207, 1223
General Services Administration, 1395; property sales by, 68
Gestalt therapy, 542
Get-rich-quick books, 65
Getting Yours: A Consumer's Guide to Obtaining Your Medical Records, 1366
"Ghosts," TV, 245
GI Bill benefits, 1362, 1364; Junior Bill, 595
Gifts, 30; duty-free, 796–97; estate taxes, 1083–84, 1085; wedding, 827–28
Glaucoma, 524, 576
"Gliding" workday, 635
Gold buying, 781–83, 1279–89; bars, 1280; certificates, 1280; coins, 1280, 1294; jewelry, 781–83, 1285–88; karats and alloys, 781–82, 1285–86; "limited edition" collectables, 1287–88; shares of stock, 1280; terminology, 781–82; warnings, 1281–85
Golden Eagle Passport card, 810
Gold overlay (gold-filled jewelry), 1286
Goods and services (see also specific items, kinds, problems): borrowing and credit and, 906–79; buying and saving on, 52–69; consumer rights and, 1326ff.; defective or shoddy, 1361; health care and, 481–577; inflation and (see Inflation): money management and (see Money management); productivity and living standards and, 1407, 1408; small businesses and franchises, 717–53; warranties and guarantees, 1337–42
Government. See Federal government; Local governments; State governments
Government National Mortgage Association (GNMA, "Ginnie Mae"), 1200, 1205, 1206, 1216, 1219–20
Grace period(s): credit, 960; insurance, 1053; savings accounts, 891
Graduated payment mortgage (GPM), 213
Graduate fellowships, 595–96
Grandparents' visitation rights, 861

INDEX

GRAS (Generally Recognized As Safe), 128
Greyhound Lines, 794, 801; Ameripass, 808
Grievance panels, health care, 1394
Gross National Product, 1407; cash value of women's housework and, 688, 689
Ground beef, 107, 108, 114. *See also* Hamburger
Ground-fault circuit interrupter (GFCI), 283
Group insurance: employee, 701; health and medical, 483, 484, 486, 494, 545, 845, 848; lawyers, 1344; life, 1037, 1053, 1180
Group practice, physicians and, 493
Group vision care plans, 573
Growth funds, 1173, 1194
Growth stocks, 1133–35, 1156
Guaranteed insurability option, 1045
Guaranteed renewable insurance, 376
Guaranteed Student Loan Program (GSLP), 590–91, 602, 606–9; information sources (by state), 606–9
Guarantees, 1337–42 (*see also* Warranties); auto repairs, 385, 387; furniture, 278, 289, 290, 292; home improvements, job, vocational schools and, 617; purchasing power, 1236; sales ads and, 60–61, 64; TV, 243; used cars, 431
Guardians, and wills, estates, and trusts, 1073, 1077
Gutters and downspouts, home buying and condition of, 172

Hair care, 786–87; baldness gyps, 1061–62
Ham, 108, 109, 111, 115
Hamburger, 75, 99–100, 108, 109, 111, 113–14, 142
Handicapped, the (*see also* specific aspects, kinds): disabled persons' rights, 1367–69, 1383; legal definition, 1367; and vacation travel, 793–94
Harassment, debts and, 964
Hatchback autos, 355, 359, 362
H (HH) bonds. *See* Savings bonds, United States
Health and accident insurance, 1042–43, 1048
Health and safety, workers' rights and, 1377–78
Health care (health and medical care and services), 477–577 (*see also* specific agencies, aspects, plans); abortions, 842–45; alcohol use and, 547–48; childbirth, 846–49, 852; choosing a physician, 516–18; community services, 525–26; consumer complaints, 1394–95; contraception (*see* Contraception); dental care, 494–99; elderly people and, 534, 538–40, 549–56, 995–96, 998–99, 1059–62; eyeglasses and contact lenses, 570–77; family doctors, 517–18; family planning, 830–54; hearing loss, 566–68; high costs and cutting bills, 481ff., 515ff., 527–29ff., 557; HMOs, 489–94; home care programs, 533–34; hospital patient's rights, 1364–67; hospitals and cost cutting, 515–16, 527–29 (*see also* Hospitals); HSAs, 527, 529–31; insurance (*see* Health insurance); keeping records, 985–86; medical emblems, 569–70; mental problems, 540–47; PAT, 531–32; personal habits quiz, 557–58; physical exams, 519–25; quackery and hoaxes, 558–66, 1059–62; second opinions, 495, 534–35, 1394; shopping for a hospital, 515–16; smoking and, 560–61; surgery (*see* Surgery); vacation travel and, 793
Health Care Provider, 493
Health Co-Operative, 493
Health, Education, and Welfare Department (HEW), 566, 594, 615, 616, 636, 840, 853, 862, 863, 985, 1365–66, 1368; National Flood Insurance, 1398; Office of Civil Rights, 1368; Office of Human Development, 1389
Health field, jobs in, 637–38, 645, 655–56, 686–88, 849
Health foods, 127. *See also* Organic foods
Health insurance (medical insurance), 481–87, 529 (*see also* Major medical expense insurance; specific kinds): abortions, 845; auto insurance and, 372; childbirth, 848; costs, plans, policies, 482–87; coverage types, 482–83; disability, 509–14; divorce and, 858–59; elderly people and, 552–56; exclusions, 487; HMOs, 489–94; hospitals and (*see under* Hospitals); mail-order, 504–8; Medicaid (*see* Medicaid); Medicare, 499–504; mental health and, 545–46; money-saving tips, 485ff.; prepaid dental, 497–98; second opinions, 534–35; shopping for, 483ff.; sterilization and, 845–46; terminology, 487–88, 492–94
Health Maintenance Organizations (HMOs), 488–94, 523, 536; check list for services, 492; fees, 490
Health Research Group, 1366, 1393
Health Risk Profile, 522
Health Systems Agencies, 527, 527–31
Hearing loss, 566–68; aids, 567–68
Heart disease, 519, 522, 524, 557
Heating systems, 310–28 (*see also* specific kinds); baseboard, 202, 203; energy-saving guide, 310–28; fire protection, 253–58; gyps, 287; hot water, 171; house building and, 201–31; house buying and, 171, 172, 189–90; kinds, choosing, 201–3; storm damages and, 259; utility bill savings, 252–53
"Heat pump" systems, 311
Hedge funds, 1173
Hedges (hedging), 1156, 1173, 1265; art, 1302; commodity futures, 1246, 1265; diamonds, 1296–1302; financial futures, 1218–20; gold, 1279–86; land, 1268; vintage cars, 1315–19
Help: The Useful Almanac, 1397
"High risers" (children's bikes), 457
High school graduates: and AP exams, 598; and college education, 581–622 (*see also* College and university education); and economic illiteracy, 1410, 1411; and jobs, 632, 633, 642–47 (*see also* Careers; Jobs); and trade or vocational schools, 613–22
His-and-her budgets, 40–46
Holder in due course, 965–67

INDEX

Holidays: burglary protection, 261; paid, 701; sales, 56–58, 60; second homes, 263–70; vacation travel, 790–813
Holographic (handwritten) wills, 1076, 1088
Home and community gardens, 131–32
Home appliances, 236–50 (see also Appliances; specific kinds); consumer rights and complaints, 1329ff., 1385, 1391; warranties and guarantees, 1337–42 (see also Guarantees; Warranties); when to buy, 57
Home freezers, 117–23 (see also Refrigerators); costs of operation, 118–19; dishonest plans, 120–21; energy savings and, 313, 320; food storage, 97; life expectancy of, 238; space for, 237; when to buy, 58
Home health care programs, 533–34, 550, 551, 552; women and jobs in, 686–87
Home improvement loans, 276–77, 923, 924
Home improvements, 270–94. See also Remodeling
Home insurance, 156, 198, 218–25; adequate coverage, 222–24; amount, 219–20, 221; basic guidelines, 218ff.; kinds and savings, 221; mobile homes, 185; mortgage, 210–11; title, 192–93
Home mortgages, 205–15, 217, 907, 923, 924, 925, 935–38; affordability, 205, 206–7, 208; closing costs, 209–10; condominiums, 179–80; consumer rights, 1349–50, 1399; co-ops, 178; costs, 205–6; down payment, 207–8, 211–12; home improvements and, 276, 923, 924; income formula for, 206–7; insurance, 211; interest rates, 155–56, 159, 205–6, 207–15, 952, 959; length of term, 208; main types, 211–15; mobile homes, 185, 189; monthly payments, 205, 206, 209; open-end, 211; points, 209; prepayment, 210; problems and complaints, 1399; refinancing, 936–38, 973; second homes and, 264; shopping for, 205–15
Homeowner's policy, 224
Home Owners Warranty (HOW), 183, 198
Home repairs (home improvements), 273–76ff. (see also Remodeling); contractors and contracts, 270–71, 275–76, 277–79; deceptions and gyps, 283–92; do-it-yourself, 273–74, 280ff.; warranties, 274–76
Homes (housing, shelter), buying, 145–307; affordability, 165–66, 205, 206–7; apartments (see Apartments); appraising the house, 168, 169–73; bargains, 167–68; building instead of, 193–204; burglary protection, 260–63; buying or renting, 155–57; comparing specific houses (check list), 168–69, 173–77, 182–84; co-ops and condominiums, 177–82; deed, 192; demand for, 165; developments and developers, 182–84ff.; down payment, 207–8; elderly people and, 306–7, 622–23, 998; energy-saving guide, 309–28; equipment, 225–50; fire protection, 253–58; fraudulent "repairmen," 283–92; hunting for, 164–65ff.; income and, 206–7; income formula for ownership, 206–7; insurance (see Home insurance); legal mechanics, 191–93; mobile homes, 184–91; mortgage shopping, 205–15; neighborhoods and, 158–64, 167, 169, 178; new or old, 157–58, 168; new towns, 184; property taxes, 159–60; real estate terminology, 216–18; Realtors and, 164–65, 167; remodeling and (see Remodeling); renting (leases), 266–68; resale value, 169; second (vacation), 263–70; selling your home, 294–98; taxes, 155–57, 159–60; title insurance, 192–93; title search, 192–93; utility bill savings, 250–53, 309–28
Homes for the aged, 550
Homesites (lots): building and, 194–95; buying a house and, 176–77, 182, 187, 190; retirement, warnings on, 1062–64; survey, 194
Home study programs, 622–23; and college degrees (CLEP), 598; gyps, 622–23; women and, 685
Honeymoons, 826–28
Hospitals (hospitalization), health care and, 515ff.; abortions, 843–44; childbirth, 846–49, 852; cutting costs, 515–16, 527–29ff.; and day-care centers, 691; day of week to enter, 516; elderly people and, 551–52, 553–56; and Family Practice programs, 518; HMOs and, 488–94; insurance, 481ff., 488, 499–504, 516, 1048; Medicare, 499, 500–4; "patient advocate," 1366; "Patient's Bill of Rights," 1364–66; Pre-admission Testing, 531–32; psychiatric care, 545–46; service credit, 951; shopping for, 515–16
Hosteling, 807
Hotels, 795–96; air travel, 468, 469–70; cutting bills, 803–6; do-it-yourself planning, 801ff.; "family plan," 803–4; package plans, 796, 797–801; tipping and, 804–6; travel agents and, 799–801; vacations and travel and, 795–96; weddings, 825, 826
House brand liquor, 134
Household income (family income), 22–25; and budgets and money management, 19–49; characteristics of class and, 8–9; and food, 74–76; and health care, 477ff.; and housing, 48, 165–66, 205, 206; and inflation, 1–15; and insurance, 1035, 1038, 1053; working women and, 681–82
Housewives (homemakers), 688–89 (see also Wives); cash value of, 688–89; and Social Security, 1024–27
Housing and Urban Development (HUD), 182, 186, 187, 198, 1399; Federal Insurance Administration, 220
Housing developments. See Developments (developers)
Housing discrimination complaints, 1390
How Charts Can Help You in the Stock Market, 1253
How to Abandon a Burning House Without Panicking, 258
How to Buy a Used Car, 430
"How to Choose a Career—and a Career School," 617

INDEX

Humidifiers, 312, 320
Humphrey-Hawkins Full Employment Act, 1372
Husbands-and-wives, budgets and money management and, 34–44; bank accounts, 35–39; his-and-her budgets, 40–46; savings methods, 34ff.
Hypertension (high blood pressure), 519, 520, 522, 557
Hysterectomy, 839

IFBs, 69
Ignition system checking, 413
Illiteracy, economic, 1409–13
Illness. *See* Health care
Immigration and Naturalization Service, 1395
Immunization records, 985
"Implied warranty," 279
Import quotas, food costs and, 83
Impulse buying, 53, 86; food, 86; clothes, 763
Income (*see also* Earnings; Pay; specific kinds): auto ownership and, 335–36, 348, 367; budgets and money management and, 19–49; and credit, 829–30, 907, 908–9, 947, 968–70, 971; financing college and, 581, 585, 589, 590, 600, 602ff.; and health care, 496–97; and home ownership, 153, 165, 206–7; household (*see* Household income); and rental formula, 266; retirement (*see* Income, retirement); and spending patterns, 48; tailored paychecks, 698–700
Income, retirement, 1008–64; annuities, 1045–46; estimating needs, 999–1000; expenses and needs, 995–96; getting, 1008ff.; life insurance and, 1028–54; pension plans, 1000–8, 1009–10, 1011–28; rate of return and duration of fund for, 1010–11; Social Security and, 1011–28
"Income insurance for the breadwinner's wife," 486
Income statement, annual corporate, 1131
Income tax, federal, 10, 12–15, 1175, 1180 (*see also* Internal Revenue Service); condominium ownership and, 181; and munifunds, 1175, 1180; savings bonds and, 1234–35, 1236, 1238–41; self-employment and (*see* Self-employment); tax-exempt municipals, 1175, 1206–9; taxpayers' rights, 1369–72, 1403; and tax shelters (*see* Tax shelters)
"Inconvenient venue," 963
Independent Inclusive Tour (IIT), 800
Index funds, 1174, 1181
Indian Affairs Bureau, 594
Individual ("personal") health insurance, 448
Individual Retirement Accounts (IRAs), 1006–7, 1008–9, 1179; roll-over plan, 1180
Individual savings account, 888
Industrial life insurance, 1053
Industrial loan companies, 934–35
Industrial revenue bonds, 1207
Inflation, 1–15, 339–40; annual rate, 5; budgets and money management and, 19–49; buying (shopping) and, 52–69

(*see also* specific items); characteristics of class and, 8–9; "constant dollar" figures, 339; economic illiteracy and, 1410; effect on morality of, 6–8; "era of aspirations" and, 11–12; expectations and psychology of as self-fulfilling prophecies, 5–6; and feeling "broke" despite highest pay ever, 10–11; impact at annual rate of 8 per cent, 5; overall definition, 4; taxes and, 10–11, 12–15; two types of, 4–5
"Inflation guard endorsement," home insurance and, 222
Inheritance tax, 1084
Injuries (*see also* Accidents; Health care): and health insurance, 481ff.; workers' compensation and, 511–13, 1375–76
Inspection stickers, auto, 405, 431
Installment buying, 906–79 (*see also* Borrowing; Credit); basic do's and don'ts, 911–13; charge accounts and, 951 (*see also* Charge accounts); consumer rights and complaints, 1386–88; credit cards, 941–50; holding down costs, 959–61; installment loan, 917–18, 925; interest rate charges, 952–59ff.; pitfalls and traps, 961–67; retail credit, 951–52
Installment loan, 917–18, 925
"Instant cash" plans, 960
Insulation, 324–27; ads, 60–62; blanket-type (batt), 324–25, 326; energy savings and, 310, 311, 316, 321–22, 324–27; fringe contractors, 325–27; house building and, 203; house buying and, 172; how to judge, 324–27; loose-fill, 324–25, 326; R-values, 324–25, 326
Insurance (*see also* specific agencies, items, kinds, plans, problems, programs): auto (*see* Automobile insurance and liability); consumer information, 1397–98; health (*see* Health insurance); home (*see* Home insurance); jobs in, 655; life (*see* Life insurance); motorcycle, 455–56; moving and, 302; storing policies, 900; trip cancellation, 801; "wife," 689
Insurance companies, as stock brokers, 1127
Insurance Information Institute, 1398
Integrative therapy, 542
Interest (interest rates), 952–59ff., 1223 (*see also* specific items, kinds); compounding, 890, 891–93; consumer rights and protection, 952–59ff., 1347–62, 1386–87; defined, 1223; economic illiteracy and, 1406; Federal Reserve System and, 1200–2, 1224, 1406, 1408
Interest (interest rates), auto financing and, 341–42, 344, 362–65
Interest (interest rates), bond and money market instruments and, 1194–95ff., 1207–9; futures, 1218–20; savings bonds, 1231–35, 1237–39
Interest (interest rates), borrowing and, 952–59ff.; add-on and discount calculation methods, 953–57; basic types and maturities, 917, 918–19ff.; consumer protection, 952–59ff., 1347–62, 1386–87; credit cards, 941–50; fundamentals of, 952–59; Rule of 78s, 953–54; "true interest" and, 953–59; typical annual rates

INDEX

and maturities, 924–25ff.
Interest (interest rates), financial institutions and, 867, 868, 869, 871, 885, 887, 888, 890–93; borrowing and, 952–59ff.; compounding, 890, 891–93; "highest" on savings, 890ff.
Interest (interest rates), home mortgage loans and, 155–56, 159, 205–6, 207–15, 952, 959; amount, 208–9; mobile homes, 185; monthly payments, 209; points, 209; prepayment, 210
Interior designers, 232–33
Intermarket Trading System (ITS), 1113–14
Intermediate-term loan, 918
Intermedic, 793
Internal Revenue Service (IRS), 996–97, 1004, 1369–72 (see also Income tax, federal); and estate taxes, 1068–71, 1075; how to fight, 1369–72; and pension plans, 1400; taxpayers' rights and, 1369–72, 1403
International Monetary Market (IMM), 1248
International Social Service, Inc., 853
Interstate Commerce Commission (ICC), 1388; and moving, 303–4, 305
Interstate Land Sales Full Disclosure Act, 1062–63, 1273, 1275
Interviews, job hunting and, 672–74, 708–9
Intestate (dying without leaving a will), 1067–68, 1088
Investigative reports, credit and, 916–17; consumer rights and, 1355–58
Investing (investments), 1103ff.; antiques, 1289–92; art, 1302–10; bibliography on, 1148–50; bonds and money market instruments, 1194–1227; books, 1313–15; borrowing and credit and, 910; "business opportunities" swindles, 738–53; choosing an appraiser, 1319–21; coins, 1280, 1287, 1294–96; collectables, 1287–89; commodity futures, 1246–66; diamonds, 1297–1302; diversification and, 1108; financial futures, 1218–20, 1222–23; financial "supermarkets" and planners, 1126–28; gold, 1279–88; home ownership as, 205; land (real estate), 1267–75; life insurance as, 1030, 1033ff.; mutual funds, 1168–91; Oriental rugs, 1292–94; prints, 1306–10; professional counseling and management firms, 1123–26; small businesses and franchises, 717–53; stamps, 1310–13; stocks, 1101–65; terminology, 1150–65, 1187–91, 1221–27; vintage cars, 1315–19
Investment bankers (syndicates, underwriters), 1157, 1200, 1203, 1224
Investment clubs, stocks and, 1112, 1120–22, 1157; starting, 1120–22
Investment companies (investment trusts), 1168, 1189
Investment counseling and management companies, 1123–28, 1157, 1194; choosing, 1125–26; and commodity futures, 1256–57; financial planning organizations, 1126–28
Investment managers, 1168, 1189, 1194
Investment plans, employees and, 702

Invoice gyps, 729–30
Ionization smoke detector, 256–57
Ironing clothes, 318, 774
"Isolated eating," 83
IUD (intrauterine device), 833–34, 841

Jelly, vaginal, 834–35, 836
Jewelry, 780–85; care of, 784; costume, 57, 782, 783–84, 1286; diamonds, 1296–1302; engagement and wedding rings, 821–22; gold, 781–83, 1285–88; gold-filled, 1286; insuring, 821; karats and alloys, 1285–86; tips for buying, 781–83; watches, 784–85
Jiler, William L., 1254
"Job banks," computerized, 707
Job Corps, 678
Job discrimination, 714–15, 1373–75, 1390. See also specific agencies, groups
Job hunting, 661–74, 708ff.; employment agencies, 667–71, 707; executives and, 708–15ff.; help sources, 665–67; interviews, 672–74, 708–9; quitting or layoffs and, 698, 705–15ff.; résumés, 664–65, 669–70, 672; self-inventory and, 662–64, 708–9; tips for those over forty-five, 714–15
Job Information Centers, 715
Jobs (see also Careers; Employment): career choosing, 631ff.; changing, 698, 706–15; dressing for work, 768–69; education and, 642–47, 679–80; growth areas, 636–42; how to look for and get, 661–74; job satisfaction, 708ff.; key trends, 634ff.; layoffs, 708ff.; occupation and career guide, 647–49; promotion and success guide, 694–95ff.; quitting and, 705ff.; training programs, 675ff.; women and, 634, 680–93
Johnson, Beverly, 688
Joint checking accounts, 35–36
Joint ownership (co-ownership), 1081–84; divorce and, 858; forms of, 1081–83; husbands and wives, 858, 1083–84; prior to 1977, 1084; wills and taxes and, 1071–72, 1081–85
Joint savings account, 888
Joint tenancy, 1082
Jumping juvenile life insurance, 1045
Jung, Carl Gustav, 542
Junior colleges, 679
Junior GI Bill, 595
Junk (lower-quality) bonds, 1217; funds, 1174

Kansas City Board of Trade, 1248, 1258
Katona, Dr. George, 11–12
"Keeping Records, What to Discard," 985
Kelly Auto Market Report (*Blue Book*), 429–30
Kennedy, John F.: and consumer rights, 1326–27; 50-cent coin, 1294–95; Memorial medal, 1287
Keogh Plan, 1008–10, 1189; defined benefit, 1179; and mutual funds, 1180, 1181
Kidney disease, 528; Medicare and, 500
Kinsey, Dr. Alfred, 1060
Kitchen(s), 282–83; check list for home buying and, 175; energy-saving guide,

INDEX 1433

312–15; food storage, 95–97; remodeling, 282–83
Kits: sound equipment, 249; vacation homes, 264
Krugerrand, 1280

Labels (and standards), 54, 108, 324; care instructions, 760–61, 762, 774; clothing, 759–62, 774; complaints, 1393; drugs, 538–39; food, 52, 81, 83, 96, 97–102, 108, 124, 125, 128, 129, 130; wine, 139
Laboratory medical tests, 516, 523; PAT, 531–32
Labor Department, 632, 636, 642, 643, 648, 665, 675, 681, 685, 687, 707, 1004, 1005, 1374, 1390; Bureau of Labor Statistics, 632, 642, 647; and job-training programs, 675, 678; and pension plans, 1004, 1005, 1400; and workers' rights, 1373, 1374, 1376, 1390, 1398
Lamb, 107, 108, 112; bulk buying, 113; grades, 112
Land buying, 1267–75 (*see also* Homesites; Real estate); bargains, 1269–71; gyps aimed at the elderly, 1062–64; hustles, 1274–75; property report and, 1273–74; pros and cons, 1271ff.
Landlords: leases, 266–67; tenants' rights, 1403
Language skills, foreign, jobs and, 640–42
Laparoscopy, 842
Laundry: appliances, when to buy, 58 (*see also* specific kinds); energy-saving guide, 318–19
Lawns, 292–94; gyps, 291; power mowers, 293–94; sprinklers, 293
Laws (legislation), 1326–29 (*see also* specific agencies, aspects, kinds, legislation); anti-discrimination, 1352–55; burial and, 1097–98; consumer rights and, 1326–29, 1335, 1337–38, 1347–62; credit, 1347–62; economic illiteracy and, 1409; land buying and, 1273, 1275; mutual funds and, 1170; stock market and, 1113–14, 1125, 1145–47; warranties, 1338; wills, estates, and trusts, 1067–68; workers' rights and, 1372–78
Lawyers, 1342–47; ads, 1342–43; and auto accidents, 408; choosing, 1343–44; and divorce, 855, 856–57, 859; fees and services, 856, 1344–46; home improvement contracts, 279; jobs for, 638, 640, 645, 656; leases and, 266–69; legal referral services and, 856, 1343; and marriage, 818; and wills and estates, 1070–71, 1074, 1075, 1076, 1077–78, 1080, 1081, 1084
Layettes, 847
League of United Latin Citizens, 594
Leaks, 315; basement gyps, 286–87; in used cars, 433
Leased revenue bonds, 1207
Leaseholds, condominium, 180–81
Lease-rental companies, car, 448–52 (*see also* Renting or leasing cars); buying used cars from, 428–29
Leases (leasing), 266–70, 1350–51; autos (*see* Renting or leasing cars); check list for apartments, 269–70; companies, 448–52, 1351; condominiums, 180–81; consumer rights and, 1350–51; open-end, 1351; second homes and, 266ff.
Leftovers, food, use of, 85–86, 108
Legacies, 1073, 1085–86; general, 1073, 1085; specific, 1073, 1085
Legal Aid Society, 1343, 1399
Legal services, 1342–47, 1384, 1398–99, 1400 (*see also* Lawyers; specific kinds); legal clinics, 1342, 1344, 1398–99; referral services, 856, 1343, 1399, 1400
Leisure time: job market and, 635, 643; and recreation (*see* Recreation); retirement, 995
Letter of intent, 1178, 1189
Letter stock, 1157; funds, 1174
Level term insurance, 1032, 1053
Leverage: futures and, 1219; land buying and, 1272
Liability insurance, 224, 376; home, 220; motor vehicles, 376, 450–52 (*see also* Automobile insurance and liability)
Liability limits insurance, 376
Library, as source of job information, 647, 666
Lien, defined, 217
"Lien wavers," 279
Life expectancy: appliances, 238, 274; retirement and, 991–92, 994; widows and, 1056
Life Extension Institute, 522, 523, 524
Life insurance, 536, 1028–54; amount and affordability, 1031–32; annuities, 1045–46, 1179, 1191; companies, 205, 211, 364, 932, 1037, 1049; contestability clause, 1043; divorce and, 858; finding a "strong" company, 1037, 1048; information sources, 1397–98; kinds, 1032–35ff.; lapsed, 1050–52; "living values," 1029; loans, 932, 1046–47; mail-order, 1047ff.; mutual fund plans, 1180, 1191; need for, 1028–29ff.; retirement and, 1039–45; saving on, 1037–41; switching, 1042–43; widows and, 1028ff., 1059; wills and trusts, 1071, 1079, 1086–87, 1088
"Life insurance exams," 523
Life style (living standards), 1407; credit and debts and, 910, 969; health and, 557; inflation and, 4, 9 (*see also* Inflation); life insurance and, 1031, 1041; retirement income and, 995, 998, 1032
Life tenant marital deduction, 1088–89
Lifetime health monitoring program, 521–22
Lightning and fire protection, 254–55
Lights (lighting): energy-saving guide, 252–53, 309, 317; home buying and, 173; kitchen remodeling and, 283
"Limited edition" collectables, 1287–88
Limited-payment life insurance, 1034, 1053
Limited tax (special tax) bonds, 1207
"Liquidation" ads, 66
Liquid protein supplements, 559
Liquor, cutting costs of, 134–35, 136–42
Listed stock, 1110, 1157–58
Listing, property, defined, 217
Liver, buying, 100, 107, 111, 127

INDEX

Living room, check list for home buying and, 176
Load and no-load mutual funds, 1168–69, 1177–78, 1181, 1189
Loan companies, 916, 929–30. *See also* specific kinds
Loans, 918–25ff.; auto, 339–42, 362–65, 393; basic types and maturities, 917ff.; borrowing and credit and, 906–79 (*see also* Borrowing); charge acounts, 951; consumer rights and complaints, 1347–62, 1386–88; credit cards, 941–50; education (*see* Loans, education); holding down costs, 959–61; home (*see* Home mortgages); interest rate charges, 952–59ff. (*see also* specific kinds); life insurance, 932, 1046–47; sources, 918–25ff.
Loans, education, 588, 590–91, 599–600, 602–12; defaults, 591; deferred tuition payment plan, 600; GSLP, 591, 602, 606–9; interest rates, 924, 931–32; list of available loans, 602–3; NDSL, 591, 602; private lenders, 604–5; shopping for, 602–12; United Student Aid Funds, 603
Loan sharks, 913, 939–40
Local governments (cities): consumer rights and protection and, 1329, 1384, 1389; and information sources, 1395–97; and municipal bonds (*see* Municipal bonds)
Locks, 260–61; bicycle, 458; burglaries and, 260
Long-distance phone calls, 250–52
Long-term certificate accounts, 871
Long-term loan, 918
"Loose money" savings, 889
Loss and Damage of Household Goods—Prevention and Recovery, 301
"Loss off premises," home insurance and, 224
"Lost-opportunity costs," motherhood and, 854
Lots. *See* Homesites; Land buying; Real estate
Lovejoy's College Guide, 613
Low-calorie foods, 81–82, 87, 130; definitions, 81–82
LP (liquefied petroleum) gas, 202
Luggage: auto, gas mileage and, 397; when to buy, 58
Lumber, 273; when to buy, 57

"Macing," used car buying and, 439
Magnuson-Moss Warranty Act, 913
Mail-order buying: auto insurance, 371; consumer rights and, 1336, 1399; contact lenses, 574, 575; credit card sales, 945; distributorship gyps, 748–49; health insurance, 504ff.; home study gyps, 622–23; life insurance, 1047–49; self-improvement books, 63–65; shopping rules, 1335–36
Maintenance and care, auto, 380–91. *See also* Automobile repairs
Maintenance car lease, 444, 445–46
Major medical expense insurance, 483, 484–85, 488, 514, 545; co-insurance, 484–85, 487; "corridor" deductibles, 485;

deductibles, 485
Managed accounts, futures and, 1256–57
Management consultants, 711–15
"Manual of Death Education and Simple Burial" (Morgan), 1093, 1095, 1097
Manual shift transmission, auto, 352, 397
"Manufactured" house, 199
Manufacturers (*see also* specific items, kinds): buying (shopping and saving) and, 52–69; and sales ads, 59–68
Manuscripts and books, investing in, 1313–15
Maps, land buying and, 1269
Margin buying, 1135–37, 1158, 1265; futures, 1219, 1247, 1249; stock, 1135–37; undermargined accounts, 1136
Margin calls, 1136, 1158, 1265
Marina costs, 475
Marital deduction trust, 1089
Marital status, credit rights and, 1353–54
Marriage, 818–54; common-law, 818; corporate success and, 697–98; divorce and, 855–63; family planning and, 830–54; guide to credit and, 828–30; honeymoons, 826–28; life insurance and, 1028–54; and pension plans, 1003–4; property ownership and, 818, 1089; retirement and, 991ff.; Social Security benefits, 1015–17, 1023–28; weddings, 819–28; widows (*see* Widows)
Masonry, house buying and, 172
Mass Consumption Society, The (Katona), 11–12
Master Charge, 942–43, 944
Maternity (motherhood), family planning and, 830–54 (*see also* Family planning); cutting costs, 848–52; and divorce, 855–63; and "lost-opportunity" costs, 854; soaring costs of, 848–52
Maternity benefits, health insurance and, 486–87
Mattresses, buying, 228, 232
Maturities, typical interest rates and, 924ff.
"Meals on Wheels," 551
Meat, buying, 74–76, 87, 88, 106–17; bulk buying, 113–17ff.; grades, 111–12, 115, 116; home freezers and storage, 96, 97, 117–23; labels, 97, 98, 100–1; nutrition, 100; organic, 125–30; savings, 106–17; substitutions, 52, 75, 106, 108; wholesale units, 93
Mechanics, auto, 382–84ff.
Mechanics, jobs for, 639–40, 650, 651, 654, 656
Medals (medallions), "limited edition," 1287–88
Medicaid, 546, 549, 551, 552–56, 844
Medical care and services. *See* Health care
Medic Alert emblem, 569–70, 793
Medical insurance. *See* Health insurance
Medical payments insurance, 224, 376
Medical records, patient's right to, 1364, 1365–66
Medical schools, donating body to, 1092, 1093, 1094, 1096
Medicare, 499–504, 548, 549–50, 551, 552–56, 995, 997, 1023, 1059; assignment payment, 502, 504; co-payments and deductibles, 500; direct payment, 502–3;

INDEX

doctor bills, 502–4; home visits, 501; Hospital Insurance, 499–502; psychiatric care, 545–46; request for payment, 504; Supplementary Medical Insurance, 499, 502–4; what is not covered, 500–1
Medications (drugs), 484, 537–40; caution for travelers, 793; consumer problems, 1392–93; cutting costs, 537–40; HMOs and, 490, 491; reading labels, 98, 538–39; special tips for the elderly, 539–40
Memorial (funeral) services, 1094, 1095
Memorial societies, 1097
Men: marriage and weddings, 818–28; and sterilization, 839–40, 841, 845, 846
Men's and boys' clothing, 759, 765, 768ff. *See also* Clothes
Mental illness (mental health problems), 540–47; choosing treatment, 541–43; clinics and institutes, 544–47; health care and insurance, 486, 492, 493, 510, 545–47; money and time in treatment, 543–47; practitioners, licenses, and titles, 540–41; psychoquacks and, 563–64
Mentally retarded, the, psychoquacks and, 563–64
Meters, utility, how to read, 252–53
MHMA-TCA seals, mobile homes and, 190
Microwave (electronic) ovens, 132–33, 314–15, 320
Midwives, 849
Mileage (*see also* Gasoline): leasing cars and, 445–47, 449; used car buying and (*see* Odometers, auto)
Military service. *See* Veterans
Milk (milk products), 80, 88, 100, 111
Mineral water, bottled, 135–36
"Mingling singles" (unmarried singles), 818, 855, 861 (*see also* Singles); and budgets and money management, 43–46
Minimum wage protection, 1373
Minorities (*see also* specific groups, problems): credit rights, 1354–55; discrimination (*see* Discrimination); employment, 634, 1373–74; and private scholarships, 593–94; and small businesses and franchises, 717–36
Mobile homes, 184–91; costs and prices, 184–86, 189–90; insurance, 221; key disadvantages, 186–87; loans, 185–86; park living, 187–89; shopping for, 189–91
"Modalities" (psychotherapy techniques), 542, 545
Model clearance sales, 237
Model homes, buying on the basis of, 183
Modular housing units, 182, 199, 201
MO (M1, M1+, M2, M3) money supply, 1200–2
Money (*see also* Economics; Money management; specific aspects, problems): budgets and meaning and use of, 21–22; and economic illiteracy, 1406–13; inflation and debasement of, 7, 13; M measures of supply, 1200–2; and monetary policy (*see under* Federal Reserve System)
"Money back guarantee" ads, 64, 65
Money management, 19–49 (*see also* specific aspects, items, kinds, problems); budget keeping and, 19–49; buying and, 52–69; clothing and, 763–68; food costs and, 74ff.; reasons for, 19
Money market funds (liquid asset funds, cash reserve funds), 876, 1172, 1174, 1181
Money market securities, 1199ff.; (*see also* Bonds and money market instruments; specific kinds); defined, 1191, 1224
"Money-matic" machines, 880
Money orders, 875–76
Monthly calendar for bargains, 53, 56–58
Monthly memo savings accounts, 887
Mopeds, 460–61
Morgan, Ernest, 1093, 1095, 1097
Mortgage bonds, 1203–4, 1223; mortgage-pool pass through certificates and mortgage-backed bonds, 1204–6, 1224
Mortgage companies, home mortgage loans, and, 205
Mortgage foreclosures, home buying and, 167
Mortgages, 205–6ff. (*see also* Financing; Home mortgages; Loans; specific aspects, kinds); alternative instruments, 6, 212–15; banks and, 205–6ff. (*see also* specific kinds); refinancing, 936–38, 973
Motels, 824; air travel and, 468, 469–70
Mothers (*see also* Families; Maternity): working, 680–83, 690–92 (*see also* Working women)
Motorcycles, 455–56
Motor homes, 454
Motor-sailer boat, 472, 473–75
Motor Vehicle Information and Cost Savings Act, 440
Moving, 298–305; choosing a mover, 300–2, 303–4; complaints, 1399; cutting costs, 299ff.; damage claims, 305; do-it-yourself, 301–2; employers and, 298, 299, 702; money-saving pointers, 303–5; packing and, 302–3; payment on arrival, 304; preventing and insuring losses, 302–3; receipt ("freight bill"), 305; scheduling, 299–300; types of household moves, 298
MSWs, psychiatric care and, 541, 542, 544, 546
Municipal bonds, tax-exempt, 1103, 1175, 1199, 1202, 1206–9; moratoriums on, 1208; munifunds, 1175, 1180; mutual funds, 1175, 1180; types and yields, 1207–9
Music: teaching jobs, 657; wedding costs and, 824
Mutual funds, 1168–91; choosing and buying, 1182–85; commodity, 1173, 1256–57; families of, 1181, 1189; information services, 1186–87; investment record, 1171–72, 1184–85; load and no-load, 1168–69, 1177–78; munifunds, 1175, 1180; open-end vs. closed-end, 1185–86; ways to buy and use, 1178–81
Mutual savings banks, 867, 871; checking accounts, 872–80; home mortgage loans, 205–6, 210, 264; insurance and "safety," 896–99; loans and, 922, 923–24, 928; savings accounts, 875–93; treasury rate certificates, 888; what they are and do, 871
Mutual wills, 1089

Nader, Ralph, 1006, 1366, 1382, 1384
NASD (National Association of Securities Dealers), 1158–59, 1224; NASDAQ composite index, 1110
National Association for the Advancement of Colored People (NAACP), 594, 1390
National Association of Furniture Manufacturers, 1393
National Association of Home-builders (NAHB) Research Foundation, Inc., 324; Warranty, 183, 198
National Association of Investment Clubs, 1112, 1120
National Association of Realtors, 164, 169, 307
National Association of Trade and Technical Schools, 614, 617
National Automobile Dealers Association, 355, 429, 1385–86
National Automobile Theft Bureau, 416
National Bureau of Standards, 257; Office of Weights and Measures of, 1393
National Center for Educational Brokering, "Directory" of, 684
National Council on Alcoholism, 548
National Credit Union Administration (NCUA), 868, 871, 897, 1355, 1388
National Direct Students Loans (NDSL), 590, 602
National Fire Protection Association (NFPA), 187
National Foundation for Consumer Credit, Inc., 972, 1389
National Hearing Aid Society, 568
National Institute for Occupational Safety and Health, 1377
National Institute for the Psychotherapies, 541, 544
National Labor Relations Act (1934), 1373
National Legal Aid and Defender Association, 1398
National Merit Scholarship Corporation, 593
National Organization for Women (NOW), 691, 844, 1390
National organizations: consumer help and, 1382–84; scholarships and, 593–94
National parks: bike trails, 808–9; camping trips, 809–11; jobs, 657
National Resource Center for Consumers of Legal Services, 1344
National Runaway Hotline, 1389
National Safety Council, 370
National Senior Citizens Law Center, 1400
National Tenants Organization, 1403
National Urban League, 594
National Wildlife Federation, 1391
Natural disasters, home damage and, 259–60
Natural foods, 126–27. *See also* Organic foods
Natural gas home heating, 202, 203; energy-saving guide, 310–28
Natural Resources Defense Council, 1391
Neck breathers, medical emblem and, 569
Necklaces, jewelry, 781
Need analysis, student aid and, 585, 587, 593
"Negative option" selling, 1337

Negotiable Order of Withdrawal (NOW) accounts, 867, 868, 871, 874–75, 922
Neighborhoods. *See* Community, buying or renting a home and
Net asset value (NAV), 1159, 1187
Net worth, 46
New issues, investing and, 1128–29; bonds (underwriters), 1200; mutual funds, 1190; stocks, 1128–29, 1159, 1161; Treasury, 1210
Newspaper reporters, jobs for, 646, 655–56, 750
Newspapers (periodicals): economic illiteracy and, 1412; job information, 666–67; sales ads, 59–68; stock market information, 1110, 1111, 1150
New towns, 184
New versus old house buying, 157–58, 168–69
New York Coffee and Sugar Exchange, 1248, 1258
New York Stock Exchange, 1103, 1104, 1105, 1106, 1107, 1110–11, 1112, 1113–14, 1159, 1247; Bond Trading Room, 1200; brokers and, 1115–16, 1118; "Investors' Information Kit," 1112; margin buying and, 1135–36; what it is, 1113–14
New York Times' Guide to Continuing Education in America, 679
No-fault auto insurance, 365, 366–67, 376–77
No-fault divorce, 860
"No-frills" foods, 86, 91–92
No-load and load mutual funds, 1168–69, 1177–78, 1181, 1189
"No money down" ads, 62
Non-maintenance car lease, 444, 445–46
Non-marketable bonds, 1231, 1243
Non-ownership auto liability, 377
"Nostalgia" collectables, 1288–89
"Notice of deficiency," 1370–71
Nuclear power plants, electric rates and, 203
Nursery equipment, maternity costs and, 846–47, 848, 849, 850, 851, 852
Nursing care: costs, 481; elderly people and (*see* Nursing homes); jobs, 637, 646, 657; Medicare and, 500, 550
Nursing homes, 481, 549–50, 551–52, 553–56; checking and shopping for, 552–56; complaints, 556
Nutrition, food buying and, 80–89 *passim,* 97–102, 106–7; best buys, 99–100, 108–11; daily needs, 88; diet foods, 81–82, 87; fast foods, 142; labels, 81–82, 97–102; organic foods, 125–30
Nutrition Plan for the Elderly, 551–52

Obstetricians' fees, 846–47, 848
Occupational information systems (OIS), 648
Occupational Outlook Handbook, 617, 643–44, 647
Occupational Safety and Health Act and Administration, 1377–78
Occupational training, jobs and, 675ff. *See also* specific kinds, programs, schools
Occupations, 631–43 (*see also* Careers;

Employment; Jobs); college grads and, 643–47; education and, 642–47; growth opportunity areas, 636–42; guides to careers and, 647–48; information sources listed by jobs, 650–61; key trends, 634ff.; self-employment and, 717–53; training programs, 675ff.; working at home, 749–53
Odometers, auto, 419–20, 421; law, 440–41ff.; rollback (tampering with), 378, 419–20, 424, 439, 440ff.; used car buying and, 424, 430, 438, 440–41ff.
Office of Consumer Affairs, 1383–84
Office of Minority Business Enterprises, 728
Office of Veterans' Reemployment Rights, 1363
Office supply fraud, 733
Official Hotel and Resort Guide, 792
Official Mobile Market Report, 190
Official Used Car Guide, 429
Often Asked Questions About the Employee Retirement Security Act of 1974, 1006
Oil changes, auto, 384, 388
Oil heating (*see also* Furnaces; Heating systems): energy-saving guide, 310–28 *passim;* house building and, 202–3
Old Car Value Guide, 1318
Older Americans Act (1973), 551
Old masters, buying art of, 1305, 1306, 1309–10
Old versus new house buying, 157–58, 168
On-the-job training programs, 675–78
Open (thirty-day) charge accounts, 951, 960–61
"Open dating" foods, 101–2
Open-end auto leases, 62, 443, 444–45
Open end credit disclosures, 1348, 1349
Open-end funds, 1190; closed-end funds versus, 1185–86
Open-end leasing, 62, 443, 444–45, 1350–51
Operation Identification, 263
Ophthalmologists, 570, 576, 577
Opticians, 571
Option and option income funds, 1175–76
Options, stock, 1142–45, 1163; call and put, 1142–45; mutual funds, 1175; naked, 1144; straddles, 1144–45
Optometrists, 570–71, 576, 577; jobs as, 658
Oral contraceptives, 832–33, 841, 846
Oral wills, 1077
Order for service, moving and, 303–4
Ordinary life insurance, 1034, 1039, 1044–45, 1053
Organic foods, 83, 125–30
Organization account, 888
Oriental rugs, 1292–94
"Originally" ("original price") ads, 67
Ornaments, jewelry, 780–88
Otologists, 567
Ounces and pounds, unit pricing and, 103–4
Outgo, money management and, 20–49 (*see also* Expenses; Money management; specific items); three classes of, 23–26
Ovens (ranges): common problems, 241; energy-saving guide, 313–15; kitchen remodeling and, 282–83; life expectancy of, 238; microwave, 132–33, 314–15, 320
Overdraft (ready credit) accounts, 874, 925–26
Over-forty-five age bracket, job hunting and, 714–15
Over-the-counter market, 1114, 1159; bonds, 1200
Overweight (obesity), 80–82, 83, 108; diet and low-calorie foods, 81–82; dieting ads and hoaxes, 63, 64, 558–60; self-help books, 81; USDA bulletins and guides, 81
Owner's manuals, use of, 240, 245; appliances, 240, 245; auto gas savings and, 396; lawn mowers, 294

Package vacation tours, 796–97, 797–801; air travel, 791–92, 796–801
"Packaging to price," 7
Packing, moving and, 303
"Packing," used car buying and, 438
Paid-up insurance, 1053
Pain and suffering, auto insurance claim and, 377
Paint, auto, checking, 432, 434
Painting, 272, 280–82; do-it-yourself, 280–82; guidelines, 280; when to buy paints, 58
Paintings (art), investing in, 1302–5; prints, 1306–10
"Palimony," 861
Panel vans, 454
"Panic buttons" (burglary devices), 262
Paraprofessional legal help, 1345
Paraprofessionals, education and, 613ff., 642
Parent Locator Service, 862
Parents (*see also* Children; Families; specific members, problems): cash loans from, 919–20; and children's choice of career, 648–49
Parking, auto, 415, 418–19; costs and savings, 341, 418–19
Parks, mobile, 187–89
Parks, national. *See* National parks
"Par selling," home improvements and, 278
Participating insurance, 1053–54
Participative management, 705
Parties, 140–42; items, when to buy, 58; liquor savings, 134–35, 140–42; wedding receptions, 825–26, 827
Part-time jobs, 684–85, 688, 690
Par value, stock, 1159–60
Passbook loans, 923, 924, 928
Passbook savings accounts, 885–86
Passports, 802
Pass-through issues, 1205
PAT (Pre-admission Testing), 531–32
Patient advocates, 1366–67
"Patient's Bill of Rights," 1364–66
Pattern recognition jobs, 633–34
Pawnbroker, as cash loan source, 938–39
Pay (*see also* Earnings; Income; Wages): fringe benefits, 700–4; inflation and, 10–11 (*see also* Inflation); job success and, 698–99, 700; money management and budgets and, 19–49; salary advances, 921–22; tailored paychecks, 698–99; taxes and, 10–11, 12–15
PAYE ("pay as you earn") plan, 599, 603
"Paying more for less," food costs and, 80–83

INDEX

Payor benefit life insurance, 1045
Payroll deduction plans: mutual funds, 1178–79, 1180, 1187, 1189; savings and, 27, 1119–20; savings bonds, 1230–31, 1236; stock purchases and, 1119–20, 1178–79, 1180, 1187, 1189
Payroll service, automatic, 895
Peanut butter, 97, 111
Pearls, 781, 784
Peepholes, door, 262
Penicillin allergy, 569
Pension Benefits Guarantee Corporation (PBGC), 1001, 1007–8
Pension Rights Center, 1005–6, 1400
Pensions (pension plans and benefits), 1000–8ff. (*see also* specific aspects, kinds, people, plans); consumer rights and protection, 1400; home mortgage loans and, 205; insurance, 1007–8; mutual funds, 1179, 1180; planning for, 1000–1; retirement and, 1000–8, 1009ff.; rights and qualification, 1001–2, 1004–5; safety net for, 1007–8; Simplified Plans, 1006–8; size of, 1002–3; Social Security (*see* Social Security); surviving spouse and, 1003–4; understanding, 1005–6; and veterans, 1054–56; widows and (*see* Widows)
Periodic purchase investment plans, 1119–20, 1178–79, 1187, 1189
Permanent life insurance, 1054
Personal identification numbers (PINs), 896
Personal liability insurance, 224
Personal loans, 922–23, 924, 929
Personal property sales, government, 68–69
Pesticides, organic foods and, 126, 127, 129
Pets, 188, 268
Petty cash fund, 37
Pharmacopoeia, 538
Phone-order credit card sales, 945–46
Phonographs: records, 78; when to buy, 58
Photoelectric smoke detector, 256–57
Photographs, wedding, 823–24
Physical exams (checkups), 518–25
Physicians (doctors), 516–19, 529, 536–37, 559–60, 951; abortions, 843–44; checkups, 518–25; childbirth, 846–47, 848; choosing, 516–17; costs and fees, 481, 483, 496, 525; cutting drug costs, 537–38; eye care, 570–77; family doctors, 517–18; health insurance, 481–87; hearing loss, 567, 568; HMOs, 488–94; jobs for, 634, 646, 658, 750; Medicare and, 502–4; mental health care, 540–48, 563–64; and patient's rights, 1364–67; quacks, 561–66; and second opinions, 534–35; vacation travel and, 793
Physicians' Expense Insurance, 483
Picasso, Pablo, 1303, 1306, 1315
Pickup covers, 454
Pills, birth control, 832–33, 841, 846
Pins, jewelry, 781
PIO Directory, 1118
Pizza, 79, 111
Plan completion insurance, mutual fund, 1180
"Planned debt," 907
Planned Parenthood, 830–31, 841, 844

Planning and zoning. *See* Zoning
Plants: buying 292; energy savings, 317, 319; gardening, 131–32
Plasterboard and plaster, home buying and condition of, 172
Plastering, painting and, 281
Plumbing: fraudulent "repairmen," 287–88; home improvements, 271–72; house building, 201; house buying and, 170; jobs, 659
Pocket calculators, use of: food buying, 85; loan interest, 953
"Pocket Guide to Choosing a Vocational School," 680
Point(s): bond prices, 1224–25; mortgage charges, 209, 218; stock prices, 1160
Point-of-sale terminal (POS), 896
Police: auto accidents and, 406, 407; jobs, 659
"Police" ad gyps, 732
Police cars, used, buying, 424–25, 441
Pollution: complaints, 1391–92, 1400; food costs and, 82–83; home buying and, 162; job market and, 634, 644
Pomander ball, as closet freshener, 774
Ponzi scheme, 742–43
Pooling (car or van pools), 418, 453
Pools, money market, 1199–1200, 1204–5
Population changes (migrations): home buying and, 154, 162, 167; and moving, 298–99
Pork, 108, 109, 111, 112
Portfolios, 1189; balanced, 1194; mutual funds, 1182, 1184–85, 1189; securities, 1160, 1189, 1194; turnover, 1189, 1190
Postage stamps, inflation and, 6
Postal (mail) frauds, 730, 734, 753
Postal Service, United States, 6, 730, 734, 1336; Consumer Advocate, 1399
Potatoes, 79–80, 83, 93
Poultry, 108, 109, 123–24
Pounds and ounces, unit pricing and, 103–6
Power lawn mowers, 293–94
Power steering and brakes, auto, 352–53
Power tools, energy savings and, 319. *See also* specific kinds
Power windows, auto, 354
Precious gems (*see also* Jewelry): characteristics, 822, 1299; engagement and wedding rings, 821–22
Precious metals, 780–88. *See also* Gold buying; Jewelry
Prefab housing, 199, 201; vacation homes, 264
Preferred: bonds, 1160; stocks, 1160
Pregnancies, family planning and, 830–54; abortions and, 842–46; birth-control methods and costs, 831–46; tax tips, 846
Pregnancy, women workers' rights and, 1373–74
Premium, 1225; selling at, 1225
Prenuptial agreement, 1089
Prepaid dental insurance, 497–98
Prepaid legal services, 1344
Prepayment, health plan, 494
Prepayment, home mortgage loans, and, 210
Preservatives, food, 83, 126, 127; labels, 98; organic foods, 126, 127, 128

INDEX

Pressure cooker, use of, 314
Price-earnings (P/E) ratios, stocks and, 1140–42, 1160; annual reports and, 1131; calculating, 1140; meaning of, 1140, 1141
Primal therapy, 542
Prime rate, 1406, 1408
Primitive art, 1305
Print Council of America, 1307
Prints, investing in, 1306–10; seven categories, 1308; value determinants, 1309–10
Privacy, as home buying factor, 152, 166, 188
Privacy, consumer credit rights and, 1355–58, 1366
Privacy and Freedom of Information Acts, 1366
Private brands (private labels), saving on, 53, 86–87
Private disability insurance, 513–14
Private mortgage insurance, 212
Probate of wills, 1076, 1083, 1089
Proctosigmoidoscopy, 524
Productivity, worker, 1407, 1408
Product safety complaints, 1392–93, 1400–3
Professionals, jobs for, 634, 637–38, 642, 643, 666, 667; women and, 684, 685
Professions, college education and, 581
Profit-sharing plans, employees and, 702
Progesterone, 833
Progestin pill, 832–33
Programmer, computer, 646, 652, 750
Project Ezra, 550
Promotions, job, 694–98
Property (property ownership), 818 (*see also* specific aspects, kinds); abandoned or unclaimed, 901–2, 1049–52; chattel mortgage, 974–75; community and "separate," 1083; home insurance and, 219ff.; jointly owned (*see* Joint ownership); land buying, 1261–75 (*see also* Real estate); marriage and divorce and, 818–19, 857–59, 860–61; pawnbroker loans and, 938–39; repossession, 364, 965, 972–73; wills, estates, and trusts and, 1067–68
Property damage liability insurance, auto, 377
Property insurance, 225
Property report, land buying and, 1273–74
Property sales, government, 68–69
Property taxes, 159–60, 180, 186, 623
Proprietary residences, the elderly and, 550. See also Nursing homes
Proprietary schools, 613–22. See also specific kinds
Prospectuses, 1161, 1189–90, 1257
Protein, food buying and, 88, 98, 109–11, 124–25; labels and, 98
Proxy statement, 1190
Prudent-man rule, 1225
PSAT/NMSQT, 593
Psychiatrists, 541–47, 563; fees, 543–47; job market, 659, 750
Psychoanalysts, 541, 542–43, 563; fees, 543–47
Psychologists, 541, 563–64; fees, 543–44; jobs, 659
Psychoquacks, 563–64

Psychotherapy, 541–47; fees, 543–47; quacks, 563–64
Public auctions, 69
"Public charters" air travel, 791–92
Public Citizen Litigation Group, 1384
Public Citizen's Action Manual, A (Ross), 1397
Public Defenders, 1343
Public health jobs, 655
Public Interest Research Group, 1384
Publicly traded investment funds (closed-end funds), 1152–53, 1176; open-end versus, 1185–86
Public Service Commission, 251
Public transportation, 52, 161; buses, 461–63; commuting and (*see* Commuting); home buying and, 161; trains, 463–65; and vacations (*see* Vacations)
Purchase agreement, home buying and, 191–92
Purchase money mortgages, 212, 218
Purchasing power: discretionary, 11, 47–48; guarantees, savings bonds and, 1236
Purified bottled waters, 136
Push-button telephone banking, 896
Put and call options, 1142–45
Pyramid selling swindle, 741–46

Quacks and quack medical devices, 561–66
Qualified retirement plan, defined, 1190
Quitclaim deed, 218
Quoted prices (quotes): bonds, 1198; mutual funds, 1168–69; stocks, 1161

"Rack route" swindle, 738–40
Radial ply tires, 401, 403; and gas mileage, 397, 401
Radiators, energy savings and, 312
Radio(s), 58, 247; AM, 247; auto, 353; broadcasting complaints, 1389; CB, 353; energy savings and, 316, 320; FM, 247; when to buy, 58
Radio and television jobs, 660, 661, 750
Railroads (rail travel), 463–64, 801, 812; Amtrak, 463–64; commuting and, 464–65; handicapped persons and, 794; reservations, 801
Railroad workers, and retirement pensions, 1019, 1058
Ranges (ovens). See Ovens
Rare books, investing in, 1313–15
Ratings, bond, 1204, 1206, 1207, 1209, 1225; lower-quality, 1217
Ready credit (automatic line of credit), 829, 868, 874, 894–95, 925–26
Real estate (real property), 1267–75; appraisals, 169–73; condominiums, 181; contract for sale, 191–92; defined, 218; house buying, 159–60, 161, 164–65, 166, 168; investing in, 1267–75; jobs in, 660; land buying, 1267–75; retirement homesite gyps, 1062–64; terminology, 216–18; title search, 192–93; wills, estates, and trusts, 1067ff.
Real estate agents and brokers: house buying and, 164–65, 167, 168–69, 170,

173; house selling and, 294–98; jobs as, 660
Realtors, 295–98; choosing, 164; house buying and, 164–65, 167, 168–69, 170, 173, 218; house selling and, 295–98
Realtron, 165
Recalls, auto, 393–94, 405, 1341
Record-keeping, 982–86 (*see also* specific items, kinds); budgets and money management and, 22, 31; discarding, 982ff.; safe deposit boxes and, 899–900
Record players, 247, 248, 249
Recreation (*see also* Vacations): land buying and, 1270, 1271, 1272–73; money management and, 29, 48; worker and therapist jobs, 660
Recreational vehicles, 453–55, 809–11; kinds, 454
Recycling, energy savings and, 314
Redemption (or bid) price, 1187, 1190
Refinancing mortgages, 935–38, 973
Refrigerators, 96–97, 237, 238, 283 (*see also* Home freezers); common problems, 242; energy savings and, 313, 320; when to buy, 58
Regional stocks, 1129–30; exchanges, 1113–15
Registered bonds, 1225, 1243
Registration, new securities and, 1161–62
Regular checking accounts, 873–74
Regulations (*see also* Laws; specific kinds, problems): food labels, 86; food prices and, 82–83, 102–4; home buying and zoning and, 162–63, 182, 189; mobile homes and, 186–87, 188–89; unit pricing and, 102–4
Rehabilitation Act, 1367–68
Relatives, cash loans from, 919–21
Remodeling (home improvements), 270–94; choosing a contractor, 277–79; contracts, 277–78, 279; costs and cutting, 271–72, 277–78, 292–94; do-it-yourself, 273–74, 280ff.; gyps and traps to avoid, 283–92; painting, 280–82; repairs (*see* Home repairs); selling your house and, 294–98; warranties, 274–76
Renewable term insurance, 1054
Renting (rents for shelter), 151, 155–57, 177–79; apartments, 151; garages, 266; houses, 155ff., 265; housing for elderly persons and, 307; income and, 266; leases, 266–69; mobile homes, 184–86; second homes, 263–64; versus buying, 155–57
Renting or leasing cars, 62–63, 442–53, 468 (*see also* Leases); choosing companies, 450–52 (*see also* Lease-rental companies); cost vs. ownership, 445ff.; mileage factor, 446, 447, 448–49; moving trailer or van, 301–2
Repairs (*see also* specific items): auto (*see* Automobile repairs); common problems, 240–42; consumer rights and complaints, 1337–42, 1361–62, 1385; cutting costs, 239–42, 245–47; home (*see* Home repairs)
Repossession, debts and, 364, 965, 972
Representatives (Congress), writing to, 1335
Re-siding job swindles, 285

Restaurants, 142–43; eating out, 142–43; tipping, 804
Résumés, job hunting and, 664–65, 669–70, 672, 712, 714
Retailers (retail stores), 52–69 (*see also* specific aspects, items, kinds); "business opportunities" swindles, 738–53; buying and saving and, 52–69; charge accounts, 951; clothing, 766–67, 768; credit and, 912, 951–52 (*see also* Credit); sales ads, 59–68; small businesses and franchises, 717–53; stealing from the boss, 737–40
Retail installment credit, 951–52
Retained-earnings statement, corporate, 1131–32
Retainers, legal, 1346
Retirement, 991–1064; annuities, 1045–46; complaints and help, 1402; expenses and financial needs (*see* Income, retirement); homesite warnings, 958–60; key federal agencies, 1402; legal age changes, 992–95; and life insurance, 1028–54; and pensions, 1000–8; planning for, 991ff.; programs for, 994–95; "shock," 993–95; and Social Security (*see under* Social Security)
Retirement test, 1021–23, 1027
Retreads, tire, 403–4
"Return on investment," 1407, 1408
"Returns," purchases and, 54; furniture, 229
Reupholstering furniture, 229–30
Revenue bonds, 1207, 1225
Reverse annuity mortgage (RAM), 213–14
Revocable living trust, 1090
"Revocation of acceptance," auto, 393
Revolving charge account, 951, 959, 969
Rhythm (calendar) birth-control method, 837–38, 841
Right of curtesy, 1081
Right of dower, 1081
Right of rescission ("cooling-off period"), contracts and, 278, 979, 1349–50
Rights, stock, 1138–39, 1162; pre-emptive, 1138
Rings, engagement and wedding, 821–22
Risk auto insurance, 377
Road tax assessment, 159–60
Roasts, meat, 106–12 *passim*
Robbery (*see also* Burglary; Theft); home insurance and, 223, 224
Rolled gold plate jewelry, 1286
Rollover, defined, 1225
Rollover (renegotiable) mortgage, 215
Roof(s): fire protection, 255; house building, 203–4; house buying and condition of, 172; repair gyps, 284–85; repairs, 273, 284–85
Room service, hotel, 803; tipping, 805
ROTC scholarships, 594
Rugs and carpets, 233–36; avoiding "sharks," 235–36; cleaning, 235; Oriental, investing in, 1292–94; quality, 234–35; wall-to-wall, 233–34, 235; when to buy, 58, 234
Rule of 78s, interest formula and, 953–54
Rural and small town mortgages, 212
Rural family loan, 938
Rust, car, 390–91
R-values, insulation and, 324–25, 326

INDEX

Safe deposit boxes, 887, 899–900
Safe driver auto plan, 377
Safety: appliances, 254–58; auto, 393–94, 404–12, 1386; banking, 896–99; bicycles, 459–60; boats, 472–73; burglary, 260–63; fire, 253–58; flammable products, 1392; food and drugs, 539–40, 1392–93 insulation, 327; jewelry, 784; job and workers' rights, 1376–78; kitchen repairs, 282–83; medical emblems, 569–70; mobile homes, 186, 190; mopeds and motorcycles, 455–56; 461; natural disasters, 259–60; product complaints, 1392–93. 1400–2; retirement pensions, 1007–8; stolen credit cards, 948–50
Sailboats, 472–75
Salary (*see also* Earnings; Pay; Wages): advances, 921–22; career success and, 698–99; fringe benefits, 700–4; job interviews and, 673–74; raises, 674–75; women and, 692–93
"Sale," use in ads of, 67
Sales, 59ff. (*see also* Bargains; Salesmen; specific items, problems); ads, 59–67; advertising terms, 65–68; appliances, 237–38; beauty care, 785–88; calendar for, 56–58; clothing, 765, 766, 768–776; contracts (*see* Contracts; specific items); liquor, 134; rugs and carpets, 234; seasonal, 56–58 (*see also* Seasonal buying)
Sales finance companies, 951
Sales jobs, 637, 639, 645, 653, 656; women and, 685–86
Salesmen (*see also* Sales; specific items, kinds, problems): ads (*see* Advertisements); appliances, 237; bonds, 1220; "business opportunities," 738–53; commodity futures, 1261–64; diamonds, 1299–1302; door-to-door and complaints, 1391; franchises, 721–28; gold, 1281–85; home improvement gyps, 283–92; land, 1274–75; life insurance, 1037ff.; mail-order (*see* Mail-order buying); mutual funds, 1168, 1182, 1185; rugs and carpets, 234, 235–36; small businesses, 719–53
Same-day surgery, 532–33
Sapphires, 783
Savings, 26–27 (*see also* specific aspects, kinds, purposes); banks and (*see* Banks; Savings accounts); bonds and, 1218, 1230ff.; dividend reinvestment, 1117; emergency reserve, 26, 27, 885; "forced," 889–90 (*see also* specific kinds); and investing (*see* Investing; specific kinds); life insurance as, 1029, 1034, 1036; money management and budgets and, 23–27, 33, 34–40, 889; retirement income and, 1008; teenagers and, 32, 33, 34; where to keep, 34–40
Savings accounts, 868, 869, 884–93; assorted interest, 887; certificates of deposit, 886–87; checking account transfers, 873, 874–75; 895; combination checking and, 35, 38, 41; computers and, 893–96; credit and, 829; how much to keep in, 884; insurance and "safety," 896–99; interest on, 867, 890–93; key

forms of, 885; loans and, 923, 924, 928; money management and, 35, 37–39, 41; monthly memo savings, 887; passbook, 885–86; "special purpose," 37–38; time deposit open account, 886; type for you, 888–89; unclaimed money, 901–2
Savings and loan associations (S&Ls), 867, 868, 870–71; checking accounts, 872–79; computer technology, 893–96; home mortgage loans, 205, 210, 212, 264; insurance, 896–99; loans, 928; and savings accounts (*see* Savings accounts); what they are and do, 870–71
Savings banks. *See* Mutual savings banks
Savings bonds, United States, 1230–43; changes and new features, 1236ff.; characteristics of, 1231–36; denominations, 1231, 1237, 1238, 1239; interest rates, 1231–33, 1237–39; lost or stolen, 1234; redeeming, 1233, 1237, 1240; savings and, 1218, 1230ff.; taxes and, 1234–35, 1239–42; terminology, 1242–43
Savings stamps, 1243
Scam, the (small business swindle), 735–36
Scholarships, college education and, 588, 592ff.
Schools (*see also* College and university education; Education; specific kinds): employment in (*see* Teaching jobs); home location and, 153–54; 160–61; taxes and, 160, 161
School savings account, 888–89
Sculpture, investing in, 1304, 1305, 1306, 1309
Seafood. *See* Fish, buying
Seasonal buying, 56–58; autos, 350; calendar for, 53, 56–58; clothing, 764–65, 776; food, 77, 87; homes, 168; moving, 299–300; shoes, 776; travel, 795–96
Seat belts, auto, 391
Second careers, 635, 648; job hunt and, 709–15
Second (vacation) homes, 263–70
Second medical opinions, 495, 534–35, 1394
Second mortgages, 935–36, 1349; companies, 935–36
Secured loans, 923, 924
Securities and Exchange Commission (SEC), 743, 1125, 1131, 1161–62, 1178, 1189, 1403
Securities Investor Protection Corporation (SIPC), 1145–47
Security deposits, renting and, 267
Seeds: buying, 292; lawns, 293
"Seeing eyes" device, 262
Sehnert, Dr. Keith W., 520–21
Selected List of Postsecondary Education Opportunities for Minorities and Women, 594, 685
Self-employment, 717–53 (*see also* Small business, going into); mutual funds and, 1180, 1181; and private pension plans, 1009 (*see also* specific plans); and Social Security, 1019; working at home, 749ff.
Self-improvement (self-help) books, 63–65
Separation agreements, 857, 858–59
Serial bonds, 1207–8, 1225–26

Service, purchases and, 54
Service agencies, consumer rights and complaints and, 1330ff., 1385, 1386–88; warranties and guarantees, 1337–42
Service credit, 951
Service repair stations, auto, 382–84ff.
Services and goods. See Goods and services; specific items, kinds
Sewage disposal: house building and, 204; house buying and, 170–71
"Sewer service" (default judgment), 962–63
Sewing machines, buying, 769–72; brands and models, 769–71; life expectancy of, 238; traps to beware, 771–72
Sex: abortions and, 842–46; birth-control methods, 831–46; as exercise, 557; vigor restorer gyps, 1060
Shade, trees for, 319
Shampoos, 786, 787
Share draft accounts, 867, 868, 871, 874
Shingles, home buying and condition of, 171
Shoes, buying and care of, 774–76; when to buy, 58
Shop manuals (see also Owner's manuals): auto gas savings and, 396
Shopper's Guide to IRAs and Keogh Plans ..., A, 1010
Shopping, buying and, 52–69. See also Buying; specific items, kinds, problems.
Short circuits, 259
Short selling of stocks, 1137–38, 1163; "up-tick rule," 1137
Short-term loan, 918
Showering, energy savings and, 315, 316
Siding swindles, 285–86
Sierra Club, 812–13, 1392
Signatures (signing), checks and, 876, 877, 880
Silver "collectables," 1287–88
Silver futures, 1250
Silverware, when to buy, 58
Simplified employee pension plan, 1006–7, 1179
Single-payment loan, 917
Single-plan major medical insurance plan, 485
Single premium—deferred annuity, 1046
Single-purpose credit cards, 942, 943
Singles (see also "Mingling singles"): and co-ops and condominiums, 177–82; working women, 680–93
SIPC, 1145–47
Sites (lots). See Homesites
Skates, when to buy, 58
Skiing: equipment, when to buy, 58; vacations, 795
Skilled Nursing Facility, Medicare and, 501, 503
Skin care. See Beauty care
Sleeping equipment, buying beds and mattresses, 56–57, 227–28, 232
Slippery surfaces, auto driving and, 413–14
Small business, going into, 717–53; "business opportunities" swindles, 738–53; failure or success factors, 717–19; franchising, 721–28ff.; fundamental rules, 721; gyps, 728–36; record-keeping and, 983–85; survival timetable, 719–20; women and, 685
Small Business Administration (SBA), 719, 728
Small loan ("consumer finance") companies, 929–30
"Small Marketeers Aid #71—Check List for Going into Business," 685
"Small Marketeers Aid #150—Business Plan for Retailers," 685
Small Tax Case procedure, 1369–72
Smoke detectors and alarms, 186, 256–57
Smoking, 519–20, 521–22, 557; quitting, 52, 560–61
Snacks: food bill savings and, 77, 83, 84, 85; nutrition and, 100
Snow tires, 402, 412
Social Security (Administration, benefits, law), 10–11, 549, 556, 1011–28, 1098–99; amendments, 1013, 1016–17, 1021–23; complaints, 1402; deficit problems and solutions, 1011–13; disabilities and 509–11, 513; elderly people and retirement and, 549, 553–56, 991, 992, 995, 997, 999, 1000–1, 1002–3, 1005, 1011–28; eligibility and work credits, 1018–20; inequities and reforms, 1025–27; and Medicare, 499–504, 549–50, 556; Primary Insurance Amount, 1098; private plans and integration with, 1002–3; retirement benefit chart, 1015; scholarships, 594; and SSI, 1018, 1402; survivors' benefits (widows and children), 1003–4, 1015–18, 1023, 1026–27, 1057–58; terminology, 1027–28; women's rights, 1223–27; working in retirement and exempt amounts, 1020–23
Social Security trust funds, 1028
Social worker jobs, 652, 660
Society of Patient Representatives, 1367
Society of Real Estate Appraisers, 170
Soil (see also Gardening and landscaping; Lawns): fertilizers, 126, 127, 129, 293; home buying and, 171, 182; topsoil rackets, 291
Solar energy (solar heating), 202, 327–28; information sources, 328, 1392; pitfalls, 327–28
"Solar Energy and Your Home," 327
Solar Energy Institute of America, 328
"Solar Industry Index," 328
Solar Information Center, 327, 328
"Solar Source Book," 328
"Sold nationally" ads, 67
Solid-state appliances, 316
Somers, Anne, 521–22
Sotheby Parke Bernet, 1289, 1290, 1291, 1302, 1303, 1305
Sound equipment (home listening equipment), 247–50; energy-saving guide, 316, 320; when to buy, 58
Soups, 87, 99; "drained weight," 100
Soybean futures, 1248, 1250
"Space broker" gyps, 734–35
Spaghetti with meatballs label, 97
Spanish language skill, jobs and, 641
Spanish wine, 137, 140
Spark plugs, auto, 397
"Special," use in ads of, 67
Special assessment, home buying and, 159

INDEX

Special checking ("economy") accounts, 872–73, 874, 895
Specialists, stock exchange, 1163
"Special purpose" accounts, 37, 38
Special-purpose (specialty) funds, 1176, 1190
Special savings withdrawal, 887
"Special situation" stocks, 1134–35; dangers, 1134–35
Speculating, 1103ff. (*see also* Investing; specific aspects, kinds); art, 1302–10; commodity futures, 1246–66; diamonds, 1296–1302; gold, 1279–88; interest rate futures, 1218–19; land (real estate), 1268; off-beat and on-target, 1277–1321 (*see also* specific kinds); vintage cars, 1315–19
Speedometers. *See* Odometers, auto
Splits, stock, 1139, 1163
Sportswear, when to buy, 58
Spread, defined, 1226
Spring bottled waters, 135–36
Sprinkler systems, garden, 293
Squatter's rights, title insurance and, 193
SSI, 1018, 1402
Stamps, investing in, 1310–13; do's and don'ts, 1312–13
Standard & Poor's Business Directory, 666
Standard & Poor's indexes, 1110; 500 Stock Index, mutual funds and, 1174, 1181
"Standards of identity," food labels and, 98
"Starter" drug supply, 537
Starting problems, auto, 414
State agricultural experiment stations, 132
State colleges and universities, 597
State employment service offices, 647–48, 707, 715; apprenticeship programs, and, 676
State Farm Mutual, 369
State governments: agencies for vocational schools listed, 618–22; and consumer rights and protection, 391–94, 440, 1329, 1336, 1340, 1384, 1388, 1394; and estate taxes, 1068–71, 1074, 1083–85; information sources, 1395–97; information sources on GSLP listed by state, 606–9; and student aid, 582, 591–92, 606–9; and workers' compensation, 1375–76
Statement of policy, securities, 1190
State Student Incentive Grant program (SSIG), 591–92
Stationery, wedding, 822
Statistics, jobs in, 646, 660
Steaks, buying, 106–16 *passim*
Stealing from the boss, 737–40
Steamer, food, use of, 314
Steering alignment, auto, 413; checking in used car, 436
Stereophonic sound equipment, 58, 248–50, 316, 320
Sterilization, birth-control and, 839–40, 841–42, 845–46; female, 838–39, 841–42; male, 839–40, 841
Stew meat, 107, 110, 113, 114, 115
Stock market letters, 1128
Stocks (stock and securities investments), 1101–65; bibliography, 1147–50; "blue chips," 1132; bonds and, 1194, 1195; borrowing on, 933–34; brokers and commissions, 1115ff.; corporate annual reports and, 1130–32; corporate bankruptcy and, 1407, 1408; dividend reinvestment, 1117–18; dividends, 1109, 1117–18; dollar cost averaging, 1122–23; employee savings plans, 1119–20; financial "supermarkets" and planners, 1126–28; "garbage stocks," 1128–29, 1134; inflation and economy and, 1105; information sources, 1106; investment clubs, 1112, 1120–22; investment goals and, 1106, 1107–8, 1125–26; margin buying, 1135–37; market analysis, 1251–54; market letters, 1128; mutual funds, 1168–91; options, 1142–45; price fluctuations, 1108–9; price indexes, 1110; professional advice and management, 1123ff.; rights and warrants, 1138–39; risks, 1104, 1105–6; selling short, 1137–38; SIPC, 1145–47; "special situations," 1134–35; splits, 1139, 1163; stock exchanges, 1113–14; swindles, 1060, 1118–19; terminology, 1150–65; tips, 1106, 1164
Stolen cars, 415–17; identification forms, 416–17
Stop-loss orders, 1164, 1255, 1266
Stopping payment on checks, 878–79
"Stop Smoking Industry," 560
Storing food (kitchen), 95–97
Stores (*see also* specific aspects, items, kinds): buying and (*see* Buying); consumer credit rights and, 1329–31, 1385, 1386–88; consumer rights and complaints and, 1326ff., 1336, 1359–61, 1386–88; organic foods and, 128–29
Storewide clearance sales, 56–58
Storm-damaged homes, 259–60
Storm windows and doors, 60–61, 172, 311, 322, 323; energy savings and, 311, 322, 323
Straight life insurance, 1034, 1036, 1044–45, 1054
Strawberries, when to buy, 56
Stretch stitch and attachments, 770
Strokes (stroke death rate), 519
"Student Expenses at Postsecondary Institutions," 583
Students (*see also* Youth): and auto insurance, 370–71; education and financing (*see* College and university education)
Subordinated debentures, 1203
Substandard health insurance, 441
Substitutions (switching), saving by, 52, 75, 86, 88, 106, 108, 141
Suburbs: home buying and, 167; land buying and, 1270
Sugar, 81, 82, 83, 87, 99–100; -free foods, 81, 82
Sugar bowl saving method, 35, 40
Suits, men's and boys', when to buy, 58
Summary of Information for Shippers of Household Goods, 301
Summer clothes and fabrics, when to buy, 58
Sunglasses, 571–72, 576–77
Sun screens, 319
Superintendent of Documents, 307
Supermarket food costs, cutting, 741–43. *See also* Food

INDEX

"Supermarkets," investing, 1126–28
Supplemental Educational Opportunity Grant (SEOG), 589–90
Supplemental Security Income (SSI), 1018, 1402
Suppositories, vaginal, 836
Surgery, 531–33; abortions, 842–45; HMOs, 489–94; insurance, 481–87, 488; Medicare and, 499–504; PAT and, 531–32; releases, patient's rights and, 1366; same-day, 532–33; second opinions, 534–35, 1394; "Shopper's Guides" to, 1394–95; sterilization and, 838–39, 841–42, 845–46; walk-in, 532–33
Survey, property, 218
Survivors (survivors' benefits): civil service and railroad workers, 1058; insurance, 1017–18, 1022, 1028; private pensions and, 1003–4; Social Security and (*see* Social Security); veterans and, 1055–56, 1363–64; widows and (*see* Widows)
"Survivor's option," pensions and, 1003
Suspension system, checking in used cars, 433
Swann Galleries, 1313
Sweaters, buying, 767
Swimming pools: energy savings and, 319; gyps, 289–90
Syndicates (investment bankers), 1157, 1200, 1203, 1224
Systems analysts, jobs for, 646–47, 652

Tablecloths, when to buy, 58
Tables, buying, 231
Tailored paychecks, 698–99
"Take Care of Yourself: A Consumer's Guide to Medical Care," 521
Take-home meals, 80
"Take me along" vacations, 811
Tape cartridges, 247, 248
Tape cassettes, 248, 249
Tax Benefits for Older Americans, 997
Tax Court, U. S., 1403; Small Tax Case procedure of, 1369–72
Tax deferment, savings bonds and, 1243
Taxes, 10–11, 12–15 (*see also* specific aspects, items, kinds); alimony and lump sum payments, 857; birth-control expenses, 846; Bite in the Eight-Hour Day (chart), 13; budgets and money management and, 12, 23–26; capital gains (losses), 1104, 1152, 1175, 1187–88; government spending and, 13–15; home buying and, 155–57, 159, 180, 181, 186; inflation and, 10–11, 12–15; record-keeping and, 983, 984; taxpayers' rights and, 1369–72, 1403; wills, estates, and trusts, 1068–71, 1075, 1083–86
Tax-exempt municipal bonds. *See* Municipal bonds, tax-exempt
Tax Foundation, 12–13
Tax-Free Education Plan, 1235–36
Tax-free exchange funds, 1176
Taxis: tipping, 804; used, buying, 424–25, 441
Tax Reform Act (1976), 1069
Tax Reform Research Group, 1403
Tax shelters (*see also* specific kinds, plans): brokers and, 1127; education and, 1235–36; retirement and, 996, 997, 1007, 1008–10
Teaching jobs, 638, 640, 644, 645, 646, 653; at-home, 750; information sources, 661
Technical Analysis of Stock Market Trends (Edwards and Magee), 1253
Technical jobs (technicians), 634, 637, 638, 642, 643, 656, 657, 750; job information, 661; training programs, 675–76
Technical schools, proprietary, 613–22, 680
Technicians (chartists), futures and, 1251, 1252–54
Technology (techniques): high medical costs and, 527–28; medical hoaxes and, 561–66
Teenagers (*see also* Children; Students; Youth): money management and, 31–34
Tele-Care, 551
Telephone redemption, 1190
Telephones, 250–52; consulting doctors by, 525; saving costs, 250–52
Telephone sales calls: diamonds, 1299–1302; gold, 1281–84; land, 1274–75
Telephone transfer banking, 875, 895
Television and radio jobs, 660, 661, 750
Television sets, buying, 58, 242–47; AGC factor, 243; color, guidelines for, 244–45; energy savings and, 316; repairs and repairmen, 245–47; warranties, 1337–38
Tenancy by the entirety, 1082–83
Tenancy in common, 1082
Tenants' rights, 1403
Term insurance, 1032–34, 1036, 1050, 1054; savings account, 887
Termites (termite control), 170, 288–89; swindles, 288–89
"Terrible Williamses," 284–85
Textile Fiber Products Identification Act, 760
Thank-you-notes, wedding, 823, 828
Theft (*see also* Burglary): auto, 415–17; bicycle, 458; credit cards, 948–50; insurance, 218, 223, 224; stealing from the boss, 737–40
Thermostat settings, energy savings and, 311, 312, 316, 321, 323–24
Thirty-day (open) charge account, 951, 960
Three-year college degree programs, 597–98
Thrift shops, clothes buying and, 766
Throttle sticking, auto, 412
Tight money, 1226
Tile setter jobs, 661
Time deposit open accounts, 886
Tips (inside information), investing and, 1106–7, 1164
Tips (tipping), 266, 804–6; guide, 804–6; hotels, 805–6; movers, 303; taxis, 804; winter cruises, 806
"Tips on Home Study Schools," 623
Tires, auto, 58, 388, 389, 398–404; balding, 404; shopping and saving, 398–404; types, 400–1; uniform grading, 401–2; used cars, 430, 433; warranties, 399, 403
Title insurance, 192–93
Title search (abstract of title), 192–93, 194, 216, 218
Toasters, automatic, 238; common problems, 241
Toiletries, 58, 786, 787; organic, 129
Toll-free hotel reservations, 804
Tolls, auto, 341

INDEX

Tomato gardening, 131, 132
Tool and die maker jobs, 661
Tools, power, energy savings and, 319. *See also* specific kinds
Toothpastes, 786–87
Toulouse-Lautrec, art of, 1306, 1308
Tour guides, tipping, 806
Touring bicycles ("English racers"), 457
Tourism (*see also* Vacations): energy shortages and, 811–13
Tour packages, vacation, 796, 797–801; air travel, 791–92, 797–801
Towels, when to buy, 58
Townhouses, 265
Toys, when to buy, 58
Tract houses, 182
Traction, tire, 402
Trade Adjustment program, 1377
Trade apprenticeship programs, 675–76, 1390
Trade association scholarships, 593
Traders, commodity futures and, 1246–66
Trade schools, 581, 597, 614–22, 680; avoiding rip-offs, 617; choosing, 614; and jobs, 613ff.; state agencies listed by state, 618–22; student aid, 582, 591, 593
"Trading down," food savings and, 74, 89–91
Trading your car, 338–40, 377–80, 419–23; and buying a new car, 423–42
Trailers, camping, 454, 809–11
Trails, bike, 807–9
Training, occupational, sources of, 675ff.
Trains. *See* Railroads
Transactional analysis, 543
Transaction card, EFTS and, 895–96; lost, 882
Transfer tax, 1084
Transmission, auto, 352, 397, 436; overhaul, 382, 386
Transportation (travel), 329–475; auto, 334–53; commuting and (*see* Commuting); costs and savings, 29, 161, 458; guides and books, 802–3; home buying and, 161; public (*see* Public transportation); vacation (*see* Vacations)
Transportation Department (DOT), 367, 1386
Travel agents, 470, 797–801
Travel and entertainment (T&E) credit cards, 943, 944
Travel trailers, 454
Treasury bills, bonds, and notes, 1209–15 1217, 1219 (*see also* United States government [Treasury] market securities); savings bonds, 1230–43
Treasury rate certificates, 888
Trees, 292–93; landscaping and gardening traps, 290–91; shade, 319
"Tree surgeons," 291
Trifocals, 572
Triglycerides, 557
Truck-mounted campers, 454
Trucks (vans), 334, 336, 345, 365, 391, 420 (*see also* Automobile buying and ownership); accidents, cost of, 404–12; consumer complaints, 1386, 1388; insurance, 365–66; leasing or renting, 442–53; mileage and trade-in, 419–20; recreational vehicles, 453; renting for moving, 301
Trunkback autos, 359, 362
Trust account, voluntary, 888
Trust companies, 870. *See also* Commercial banks
Trust departments, 869
Trustee(s), estate, 1073, 1075, 1077, 1090; naming, 1073
Trust funds, unit (UITs), 1176
Trusts, 1073, 1084, 1086–87, 1087–90; defined, purpose of, 1086–87; life insurance, 1087; wills and, 1073
Truth in Lending Act. *See* Consumer Credit Protection Act
"Truth in Meat" labeling, 100–1
Tubal sterilization, 838, 842
Tub baths, energy savings and, 315, 316
Tuition financing. *See* Financial aid programs, education
Tuition loan companies, 930–31
Tuition Plan, Inc., 605
Tuna fish, 111, 125
Tune-up, auto, 385, 413
Turkey, 107, 108, 109, 123
"Two-for-one," use in ads of, 67
Two-year colleges, 597, 642, 643

UCR basis, rental prepayment plans and, 498
Ultramodern art, investing in, 1309
Umbrella liability insurance, 225
Unclaimed or abandoned property: forgotten money, 901–2; life insurance, 1050–52
Undercoatings, auto, 391
Understanding Your Utility Bill, 253
Underwriters, 1157; bonds and syndicates, 1200, 1203, 1226; mutual funds, 1190
Underwriters Laboratory (UL) safety seal of approval, 190, 237–38, 254, 255, 262
Unemployment insurance protection, 1375, 1377, 1403
Uniform Simultaneous Death Act, 1075
Uninsured (family protection) motorist insurance, 377
Union membership, 1407, 1408; right to, 1373; scholarships, 593
United Hospital Fund, 550
United States government (*see also* Federal government): (Treasury) market securities, 1194, 1198, 1199, 1202, 1204, 1206, 1207, 1209–15, 1226; buying, 1210–15, 1217; futures, 1219; marketable types, 1209–10; mutual funds, 1175, 1181; savings bonds (*see* Savings bonds, United States)
United Student Aid Funds, 603
Unit pricing, 103–4
Unit trusts (UITs), 1176
Universal joints, dropped drive shaft, auto breakdowns and, 412
Unordered merchandise, 1336–37
Unsatisfied judgment fund, 377
Unwed mothers, and tracing absentee fathers, 862–63
Upholstered furniture, 229, 230
"Up to——% off" ads, 67–68
Urban League LEAP, 676
Urinalysis, 523, 524
Used boat buying, 473–75

INDEX

Used car buying, 423–42, 454; accident wrecks, 425–26; checking, 430, 432–38; clues to age, 430–31; constructive rules for, 427–32; "fleet cars," 428–29; prices, 429; selling price, 442; taxis and police cars, 424–25, 430; traps to avoid, 438–40; warranties, 1342

Used car selling, 377–79

Utility bills, 250–53, 309–28; energy-saving guide, 309–28; home buying and, 168, 171, 172; house building and, 195, 202–3; meter reading, 252–53; problems and complaints, 1403; service credit, 951

Vacation colleges, 612–13
Vacation (second) homes, 263–70
Vacations (vacation travel), 790–813; air travel (see Air travel); bike trails, 807–9; buses, 794, 801, 807–8; camping trips, 809–11; caution on medications, 793; charters, 791–92; cutting costs, 790–813; cutting hotel bills, 803–6; do-it-yourself planning, 801–13 ; duty-free shopping, 796–97; eye care and glasses, 577; handicapped persons and, 793–94; hosteling, 807; hotels (see Hotels); package tours, 791–92, 796, 797–801; paid, 701; tipping, 804–6; travel agents, 470, 797–801
Vacuum cleaners, 238, 241
Vacuum gauge, and auto gasoline savings, 396
Vaginal douche, 840
Vaginal foam, cream or jelly, 834, 835–36, 841
Vaginal suppositories, 836–37
Valets, hotel, tipping, 805
Valuables, safe deposit boxes and, 899–901
"Value," use in ads of, 59, 66, 68
Valve job, auto, 382, 386
Vans (see also Trucks): car pools, 418, 453; panel, 454
"Vapor barrier," basement, 171
Variable annuity, 1191
Variable annuity separate account, 1179, 1191
Variable rate (floating rate), 1227
Variable-rate mortgage, 214–15
Vasectomy, 839–40, 841
Veal, 108, 112, 113
Vegetables, 80, 82, 83, 85, 87, 88, 93; gardening, 131–32; labels, 98; nutrition, 99–100; organic, 125–30
Vending machine swindles, 746–48
Venereal disease, 520, 524, 1394
Venture capital funds, 1176–77
Veterans, Veterans Administration (VA) and, 1055–56, 1362–64; and apprenticeship programs, 676; and condominiums, 179; "death pension," 1364; education benefits, 595; employment rights, 1362–63; and funeral expenses, 1098–99; GI term insurance, 1038–39; and home mortgages, 209, 211–12, 1399; and mobile homes, 185–86, 189, 190; pensions, 1054–55; and Social Security, 1019; and student aid, 595; and trade schools, 615
Veterans Readjustment Benefits Act (1966), 595

Veterinarian jobs, 637, 640, 661
Vickery, Donald M., 521
Victorian International antiques, 1289–90
Vintage cars, 1315–19
Vintage wines, 140
Vinyl roof, auto, 353, 355
Visa credit card, 942–43, 944
Visual problems. See Blind, the; Eye care
Vitamins and minerals, 788, 793, 1060; food buys and, 98, 99–100; organic, 126, 127; 128–29, 130
Vocational rehabilitation jobs, 661
Vocational schools, 581, 597, 613–22; avoiding rip-offs, 617; choosing, 614–17; costs, 581–82; and jobs, 613ff.; state agencies for, 618–22; student aid, 582, 591; students' rights, 1378
Voluntary bankruptcy, 974
Voluntary trust account, 888
Volunteers: and college credit, 685; and the elderly, 550–51
Voting, workers' time off for, 702

Wage assignment, 979
Wage earner plan, Chapter XIII bankruptcy, 973–74
Wage garnishment ("income execution"), 979; consumer rights and, 1358–59, 1389
Wages (see also Earnings; Pay; Salary): fringe benefits, 700–4; housewives' value and, 688–90; inflation and, 5–6, 10–11, 12–15; minimum, 1373; money management and, 19–49; rights and protection, 1382, 1389; taxes and, 10–11, 12–15
"Waiver of premium," insurance clause, 1040
Walk-in surgery, 532–33
Wallich, Dr. Henry, 7–8
Walls and ceilings: home buying and, 171, 172; house building and, 204
Wall Street Journal, The, 723, 1259
Wall-to-wall carpeting, 233–34; cleaning, 235
War bonds, 1243
Wardrobe planning, 763
Warranties, 274–75, 1337–42; appliances, 237–38, 243; auto, 355–56, 357, 381–82, 399–400, 403, 1340–42; consumer rights and complaints, 1337–42, 1403; "express" and "implied," 1338, 1340; guarantees and, 1338; hearing aids, 568; home building, buying, and repairs, 183, 188, 190–91, 198, 232, 274–76, 326; legislation, 1338; making them work, 1339–40; traps and cautions, 1338–40; TV, 243; value of, 1337–38
Warrants, stock, 1138–39, 1165
Washing machines, 240, 318–19. See also specific kinds.
Waste disposal appliances, 237; common problems, 242
Watches, buying, 784–85; care of, 784–85
Water (water heating, water supply), 58, 170–71, 194–95 (see also Plumbing); energy savings and, 310, 311, 312–15, 316–17, 320, 327–28; flow restrictors, 315; solar heating, 327–28
Water damage, home insurance and, 224
Waterproofing basement gyp, 286–87

INDEX

"Wedding palace" catering, 827
Weddings, 819–28; catering, 820ff.; cost of, 819ff.; planning, 821; specific expenses, 820–21; who pays for what, 819, 820–21
Weight, food: drained, 100; unit pricing and, 103–4
Weight loss (*see also* Overweight); ads and hoaxes, 63, 64, 558–60; diet foods and dieting, 80–82
Welfare programs: taxes and, 14–15; tracing absentee fathers and, 862–63
Wheelchairs, vacation travel and, 794
Wheeler, Harvey, 990
Wheels (*see also* Tires): checking in used cars, 437
When You Return to a Storm Damaged Home, 260
Whiskey expenses, 134–35, 136–42; eating out and, 143
White collar crime, 737–38ff.
Whole life insurance, 1034, 1036, 1044–45, 1054
"Wholesale" ("below wholesale") ads, 68
Wholesale units, food, 93
Whole take-home meals, 80
Wider Opportunities for Women (WOW), 684
Widows (widowers), 1056–59; basic facts for, 1056–59; and funeral and burial benefits, 1098–1100; and life insurance, 1028ff., 1059; and pensions, 1003–4, 1054–56, 1364; and Social Security, 1016–17, 1018, 1023, 1026–27, 1057–58; and wills, estates, and trusts, 1067–90
Wilderness Society, 812
Wills, 1067–90; assets not disposable by, 1071–72; changing, 1071; check list for personal affairs, 1078–80; contest, 1076, 1081; disinheriting and, 1080–81; do-it-yourself, 1076–77; estate taxes, 1068–71, 1075, 1084–85; legal help, 1070–71, 1075, 1076; probate, 1076, 1083, 1089; safekeeping, 900, 1078–80; simultaneous deaths and, 1074; terminology, 1087–90; witnesses, 1074, 1076–77
Windows, 60–61, 203; auto, power, 354; insulating and energy savings, 310, 311, 312, 321, 322, 323
Windshield wipers and blades, 412, 413, 414, 432
Wind storms and damages, 186–87, 259–60
Wine, 134–35, 136–42; guides for buying, 139–40
Winter cruises, tipping on, 806
Winter driving, 412–14
Withdrawal (coitus interruptus), 840, 841
Withdrawal plan, mutual funds, 1178, 1181, 1191
Witnesses: auto accidents, 407; wills, 1074, 1076–77
Wives (*see also* Marriage; Women): and cash value of housework, 688–90; and divorce, 855–63; house buying and, 153, 165; life insurance on, 1043; making own will, 1077–78; and Social Security, 509–11, 1015ff., 1023–27; widowed (*see* Widows); wills, 1067–90; working, 9, 680–82 (*see also* Working women)
Women (*see also* Widows; Wives; specific aspects, problems): and beauty care, 785–88; and clothes, 756–78; credit rights, 1352–54; discrimination complaints, 1390–91; employment and wage rights, 675–76, 1373–75; and "empty nest," 682–83; and family planning, 830–31; and jobs, 680ff. (*see also* Working women); and "lost opportunity costs," 854; marriage and divorce, 818–63; and scholarships, 594; and veterans' rights, 1362–64
Wooden furniture, guides for, 231
Wool: carpets, 234; clothing, 760
Work (labor force, workers), 631ff. (*see also* Careers; Employment; Jobs; Workers' rights); alcohol problem, 547–48; job dissatisfaction, 704–6; productivity and living standards, 1407, 1408; women in, 680–93 (*see also* Working women)
Work credits ("quarters of coverage"), Social Security and, 1019–20, 1028
Workers' compensation, 511–13, 1375–76
Workers' rights, 1372–77 (*see also* specific kinds, programs); age and, 1373; complaints, 1390; death expense benefits, 1098–99; equal opportunity, 1373–74, 1390; loss of job and imports competition, 1376–77; minimum wages, 1372; safety and health and, 1377–78; unemployment insurance, 1375, 1403; unions, 1373, 1407, 1408
Working at home, 728–53
Working women, 594, 680–93, 708, 1374 (*see also* Careers; Employment); basic career guides, 683–85; and day-care centers, 690ff.; and family income, 681–82; goals, 684; house buying and, 154, 165; information sources, 684; job success and, 694–98; marriage and credit rating, 828–30; office attire, 768–69; Social Security rights, 1023ff.; working at home, 749–53
Work-study program, college, 589–90
Workweek changes, 634–36
Worm farming gyps, 751–52
Worth, net, 46
"Would you take," used car buying and, 439
Wrinkles, gyps aimed at the elderly and, 1060–61

X-rays, 521, 523, 524, 528, 531–32; dental, 495

Yachting, 472
Yale (deferred tuition) plan, 599, 602
Yankelovich, Daniel, 44
Yard space, zero lot-line homes and, 166–67
Yarns, clothing, 761
Yassky, Al, 543
Yellow Pages, job hunting and, 666
Yield (return), 1191, 1198–99, 1222, 1225; basis, 1221; current, 1154, 1198–99, 1222; stock dividend, 1109–10, 1165; to maturity, 1198–99, 1220, 1227
Yield grades: buying beef in bulk and, 115, 116; fish, 124
You and Your Pension, 1006
Your Clothing Dollar, 758

Youth (*see also* Children; Students): and auto insurance, 370–71; and careers (see Careers); hostels, 807

Zero lot-line homes, 166–67
Zero Population Growth (ZPG), 844

Zigzag stitch and attachments, 770
Zoning (and planning): buying a home and, 162–63, 170–71, 189; home improvements and, 271; house building and, 194; zero lot-line homes, 166–67